W.4

D0320841

LETTERS OF
HUMFREY WANLEY

Humfrey Wanley, by Thomas Hill, 1711. Presented to the Society of Antiquaries by George Vertue in 1755. Reproduced by courtesy of the Society.

The manuscript Wanley holds has not been identified. The text is a version of Matthew 6:19–21, in Greek. The hand is probably of the tenth century.

LETTERS OF
Humfrey Wanley

Palaeographer, Anglo-Saxonist,
Librarian
1672–1726

With an
Appendix of Documents

EDITED BY
P. L. HEYWORTH

CLARENDON PRESS · OXFORD
1989

Oxford University Press, Walton Street, Oxford OX2 6DP

Oxford New York Toronto
Delhi Bombay Calcutta Madras Karachi
Petaling Jaya Singapore Hong Kong Tokyo
Nairobi Dar es Salaam Cape Town
Melbourne Auckland

and associated companies in
Berlin Ibadan

Oxford is a trade mark of Oxford University Press

Published in the United States
by Oxford University Press, New York

British Library Cataloguing in Publication Data

The letters of Humfrey Wanley: palaeographer, Anglo-
Saxonist, librarian, 1672–1726: with an appendix of
documents.
1. Palaeography. Wanley, Humfrey, 1672–1726
I. Heyworth, Peter, 1931–   II. Wanley, Humfrey, 1672–1726
417´.7´0924
ISBN 0-19-812477-5

Set by Joshua Associates Ltd, Oxford
Printed and bound in Great Britain by
Biddles Ltd, Guildford and King's Lynn

TO
HAROLD MOULTON

ACKNOWLEDGEMENTS

I am grateful especially to the staffs of the Bodleian Library and of the British Museum (later the British Library), who shovelled quantities of books and manuscripts across my desk, off and on over a period of nearly twenty years.

Other librarians and archivists to whom I am indebted, as I am to the institutions they serve—or served at the time of their kindness to me—are Mr D. Pepys-Whiteley, Magdalene College, Cambridge; Mr A. Halcrow, Trinity College, Cambridge; Mr H. J. R. Wing, Christ Church, Oxford; Mrs J. S. Cook, Cambridge University Library; Mr A. I. Doyle, University of Durham; Mr A. S. Bell, National Library of Scotland; Mr A. R. B. Fuller, St Paul's Cathedral; Mr Kenneth Smith, Carlisle City Library; Miss Amy G. Foster, Yorkshire Archaeological Society; Miss J. M. Owen, Sion College; the Revd N. S. Moon, Bristol Baptist College; the Revd Wilfred Bradnock, the British and Foreign Bible Society; Mr N. H. Robinson, the Royal Society; Mr A. E. Barker of the SPCK; Mr Anthony Wood, Warwickshire County Record Office; Mr A. A. Dibben and Mr D. J. Rimmer, Coventry City Record Office; Mr Anthony Davis of Coventry Libraries and Museums; and Mr K. C. Newton, Essex Record Office.

No one working on material in the Portland deposit in the British Library can exaggerate the debt he owes to Mr R. W. Goulding, sometime librarian to the Duke of Portland, who organized the archive of the Harley family at Welbeck Abbey, and to Mr Francis Needham, his successor, who supervised its transfer to the British Museum nearly forty years ago.

Help on particular matters was supplied by Mr Harold W. Jones, Mr Charles P. Finlayson, Dr Robert Woof, Mr Philip Styles, Mr S. G. Gillam, Dr J. J. G. Alexander, Mr J. P. Jackson, Mr C. C. Harley, Miss E. M. Walker, Dr M. Steinmann, Sir John Summerson, Mr R. C. Trebilcock, Mr Malcom Parkes, Mr J. S. G. Simmons (on many occasions), Professor Claude Rawson, Dr R. W. Hunt, Mrs P. E. Easterling, Mr David McKitterick, Mr T. D. Rogers, Mr N. H. MacMichael, Miss Annetta Bynum, Professor Deborah Hobson, and my colleagues Ann Dooley, Desmond Neill, George Rigg, Kenneth

Quinn, Douglas Thomson, and Leonard Woodbury. Dr C. E. Wright generously put his immense knowledge of Wanley and things Wanleian at my disposal for more than a dozen years. To my father-in-law, the Revd H. K. Moulton, I owe a special debt.

The late Kenneth Sisam and the late J. A. W. Bennett are the begetters of this volume. Professor Bennett, at Mr Sisam's suggestion, began an edition of Wanley's letters just before the Second World War, abandoned it some years later, and subsequently encouraged me to take it on. It was Mr Sisam who in 1962 drew the attention of my work to the Oxford University Press. At the press Dan Davin, John Bell, and Kim Scott Walwyn have been helpful and understanding; it was at John Bell's request that Neil Ker read the completed manuscript, to the great benefit of the edition in its final form.

I am grateful to the Curators of the Bodleian Library and the Trustees of the British Library for permission to print Wanley's letters and other material in their custody, and similarly to the governing bodies of Cambridge University Library; the Bibliothèque Nationale; the Academy of Sciences, Leningrad; Trinity College, Cambridge; Magdalene College, Cambridge; and the Royal Society, as well as to Essex County Record Office, the Trustees of the Will of the late J. H. C. Evelyn, Mr Arthur A. Houghton Jun., and above all, to His Grace the Duke of Portland, KG.

My work has been supported at various times by the Canada Council and its successor the Social Sciences and Humanities Research Council, and by research funds from the University of Toronto. For their material generosity they have my thanks.

University College   P. L. HEYWORTH
Toronto

CONTENTS

ABBREVIATIONS

BMC	*Catalogue of Books Printed in the XVth Century now in the British Museum*, 9 pts. (1908–62).
Bodleian Letters	*Letters Written by Eminent Persons in the Seventeenth and Eighteenth Centuries . . . from Originals in the Bodleian Library and Ashmolean Museum* [by J. Walker], 2 vols. (Oxford, 1813).
CLA	*Codices Latini Antiquiores*, by E. A. Lowe, 11 vols. and Supplement (Oxford, 1934–71); 2nd edn. of vol. ii (1972).
CMA	*Catalogi Manuscriptorum Angliae et Hiberniae*, by E. Bernard (Oxford, 1697).
Darlow and Moule	T. H. Darlow and H. F. Moule, *Historical Catalogue of the Printed Editions of Holy Scripture in the Library of the British and Foreign Bible Society*, 2 vols. (1968); 2nd edn. rev. A. S. Herbert (1911).
Davis	G. R. C. Davis, *Medieval Cartularies of Great Britain* (1958).
DNB	*Dictionary of National Biography*.
Ellis, *Original Letters*	H. Ellis, *Original Letters of Eminent Literary Men of the Sixteenth, Seventeenth, and Eighteenth Centuries* (Camden Society xxiii, 1843).
GW	*Gesamtkatalog der Wiegendrucke* (Leipzig, 1925–).
Hain	L. Hain, *Repertorium Bibliographicum*, 2 vols. (Stuttgart, 1826–38).
Hain–Copinger	W. A. Copinger, *Supplement to Hain's Repertorium Bibliographicum*, 2 pts. (1895–1902).
Hearne, *Collections*	T. Hearne, *Remarks and Collections of Thomas Hearne*, ed. C. E. Doble *et al.*, 11 vols. (Oxford, 1885–1921).
Hickes, *Thesaurus*	G. Hickes, *Linguarum Veterum Septentrionalium Thesaurus*, 3 vols. (Oxford, 1703–5).
HMC	Reports of the Royal Commission on Historical Manuscripts.
Ker	N. R. Ker, *Catalogue of Manuscripts Containing Anglo-Saxon* (Oxford, 1957).

Macray	W. D. Macray, *Annals of the Bodleian Library*, 2nd edn. (Oxford, 1890).
McClure, *Minutes of the SPCK*	E. McClure, *A Chapter in English Church History: being the Minutes of the Society for Promoting Christian Knowledge for the years 1698–1704, together with abstracts of correspondents' letters during part of the same period* (1888).
Nichols, *Literary Anecdotes*	J. Nichols, *Literary Anecdotes of the Eighteenth Century*, 9 vols. (1812–15).
Nichols, *Illustrations*	J. Nichols, *Illustrations of the Literary History of the Eighteenth Century*, 8 vols. (1817–58).
OED	*The Oxford English Dictionary*.
PBA	*Proceedings of the British Academy*.
Proctor	R. Proctor, *An Index to the Early Printed Books in the British Museum: from the Invention of Printing to the Year MD. With notes of those in the Bodleian Library* (1898).
Sawyer	P. H. Sawyer, *Anglo-Saxon Charters: An Annotated List and Bibliography* (1968).
SC	*A Summary Catalogue of Western Manuscripts in the Bodleian Library at Oxford*, by F. Madan *et al.*, 7 vols. (Oxford, 1895–1953).
STC	*A Short-Title Catalogue of Books Printed in England, Scotland & Ireland and of English Books Printed Abroad 1475–1640*, by A. W. Pollard and G. R. Redgrave (Bibliographical Society, 1926); rev. W. A. Jackson, F. S. Ferguson, and K. F. Pantzer, vol. ii, I–Z (1976).
TLS	*Times Literary Supplement*.
VCH	*Victoria County History*.
Wanley, or *Catalogus*	H. Wanley, *Librorum Veterum Septentrionalium, qui in Angliae Bibliothecis extant . . . Catalogus Historico-Criticus*, vol. ii of Hickes, *Thesaurus* (Oxford, 1705).
Wanley, *Diary*	H. Wanley, *The Diary of Humfrey Wanley 1715–1726*, ed. C. E Wright and Ruth C. Wright, 2 vols. (Bibliographical Society, 1966).
Welbeck Wanleyana	Wanley material preserved among the Harley Papers at Welbeck Abbey.
Wing	D. Wing, *Short-Title Catalogue of Books Printed in England, Scotland, Ireland, Wales, and British*

America and of English Books Printed in other Countries, 1641–1700, 3 vols. (Index Society, New York, 1945–51); 2nd edn. of vol. i (1972).

Wright, *Fontes* C. E. Wright, *Fontes Harleiani. A Study of the Sources of the Harleian Collection of Manuscripts Preserved in the Department of Manuscripts in the British Museum* (1972).

INTRODUCTION

Humfrey Wanley's letters are here collected in print for the first time. My original commission was to prepare for publication an edition of all surviving Wanley letters, but this book has been a long time in the making and prudence now encourages certain economies. As a result only a selection—243 out of nearly 450 letters still extant—is printed. I have tried to ensure that no letter which bears in any important way on Wanley's professional life as scholar and librarian, or on the history of the institutions he served so faithfully, has been left out. The chief omissions are: (i) letters, wholly domestic in nature, written to his wife Ann Wanley during his occasional absences from London; (ii) letters to John Chamberlayne, Secretary of the SPCK whose assistant Wanley was before succeeding him as Secretary in 1702; (iii) letters written by Wanley in the course of his duties as an officer of the SPCK; (iv) those letters, inconsequential in their subject-matter, from among the large numbers written by Wanley to Arthur Charlett, John Bagford, Hans Sloane, and Edward Harley.

A few notes and memoranda not strictly letters have been included in the chronological sequence. A selection of more formal documents, most of them illustrating schemes or proposals touched on in the letters, is printed in the Appendix.

A Handlist of Letters Not Printed records those letters which are omitted from this edition, and annotated typescript copies of these have been deposited in the Bodleian and in the British Library. The letters reproduced in the present volume and those described in the Handlist together represent all the letters of Humfrey Wanley known to me.

This edition follows at a respectful distance the publication of Wanley's *Diary*—the day-to-day account of his professional life as Library-Keeper to Robert Harley, 1st Earl of Oxford, and to Edward Harley, his son, the 2nd Earl—in the splendid edition of C. E. Wright and Ruth C. Wright.[1] The letters cover a period of more than thirty years, from 1694, when Wanley, just out of his apprenticeship to a Coventry draper, was about to remove to Oxford, to his death in 1726,

[1] *The Diary of Humfrey Wanley 1715–1726* (1966).

and they add very considerably to our knowledge of him. They are particularly valuable for the account they give of Wanley's career before he entered the service of the Harleys in 1708—the frustrating years in Oxford and in London when academic indifference and social privilege combined to deny Wanley the settled station in life that he looked for, and obliged him instead to squander his energies on developing the talents that made him the greatest Anglo-Saxonist of his generation, and one of the greatest palaeographers and librarians of his age.

For there is no doubt that Wanley's career can be seen as a happy variation of Stubbs's principle that if you put the worst man in the best place you have all the good ones trying to show how much better they are, and so benefiting the world. He had hopes, more or less well founded, of success in becoming, at different times, Bodley's Librarian, a Fellow of Worcester College, Oxford, Keeper of the Cotton Library, Commissioner of Hackney Coaches, and Historiographer Royal; and he had thoughts, not nearly so well founded (though he prosecuted his candidacy no less vigorously for that), of becoming Library-Keeper to the Lord Chancellor, and of succeeding Richard Bentley as Keeper of the Royal Libraries, William Petyt as Keeper of the Records in the Tower, and John Chamberlayne in his post at the State Paper Office. In all these he failed. Of all he might justifiably have said, as he did on the occasion of one of his disappointments, his being denied admission as a Gentleman Commoner at University College, Oxford, that though people think him a vain, proud fool without common sense, 'But still, I am not such a fool as to desire it, did I not know my self in a capacity, (thanks be to God) to bear it.'[2]

The traditional account, which there seems no reason to disbelieve—despite Thomas Tanner's claim, made after Wanley's death, that Wanley's 'coming out of the Draper's Shop and Settling in a Gown at Oxford was almost entirely owing to me'[3]—is that Wanley came to Oxford in 1695 under the patronage of William Lloyd, Bishop of Coventry and Lichfield. He matriculated at St Edmund Hall, 7 May 1695, and moved to University College later in the year at the invitation of the Master, Arthur Charlett.

He arrived in Oxford with the interests that were the foundation of his later achievements, interests which must have made him cut a rather eccentric figure in the world of a provincial draper, already well

[2] No. 54.   [3] *HMC Portland Papers*, vi, p. 27.

established.[4] Oxford was to transform a young man's appetite for copying old manuscripts and for Northern languages into the mature scholar's mastery of palaeography and of Anglo-Saxon, and the letters of these years present a striking picture of Wanley's rapidly developing and formidable talents—the growth of his knowledge, the refining of his skills, and the maturity of his judgement.

The evidence for Anglo-Saxon is to be found chiefly in Wanley's great catalogue for Anglo-Saxon manuscripts[5] and only incidentally does it find its way into the letters. With palaeography the reverse is the case. His catalogue of Anglo-Saxon manuscripts apart, Wanley's only published work that touches on palaeography is his dissertation in the form of a letter to Narcissus Marsh, 11 July 1701, 'Part of a Letter, written to a Most Reverend Prelate, in answer to one written by his Grace, judging of the Age of MSS. the Style of Learned Authors, Painters, Musicians, &c.'[6] It is in his letters to George Hickes, Thomas Smith, and others that we can see the discipline of palaeography being formulated for English scholarship and from English materials.[7] Wanley's appointment as Assistant at the Bodleian Library in November 1695, within six months of his arrival in Oxford, had given him the freedom of the greatest treasure-house of manuscripts in public or private hands in England, and he lost no time in making himself the master of them. As his experience is enriched by daily contact with the Bodleian collections, we can see him defining for himself the whole range of questions that exercise palaeographers, and turning his powerful mind and his methodical genius to their explanation and, as often as not, to their solution. Hickes was his only competitor, and Hickes, as the letters show and as his own confession makes clear, was his pupil.[8]

Throughout the Oxford years we can see Wanley growing increasingly confident of his own powers and imaginative in his exercise of

---

[4] See his account of a visit to the Cotton Library three weeks before he went into residence at Oxford (no. 6) for evidence of his interest in Anglo-Saxon MSS and of his shrewdness in palaeographical matters.

[5] *Librorum Veterum Septentrionalium . . . Catalogus Historico-Criticus* (Oxford, 1705).

[6] *Philosophical Transactions*, no. 300 (June 1705), pp. 1993–2008. Printed below, no. 79.

[7] See in particular Wanley to Hickes, nos. 26, 27, 31, 32, 45, 54; to T. Smith, nos. 30, 33, 34, 35, 36; to Tanner, no. 6; to Charlett, no. 37; to Gibson, no. 40; to Bagford, no. 42; to Robert Harley, no. 100; to J. Smith, no. 101.

[8] Cf. 'I have learnt more from you, than ever I did from any other man, and living or dying I will make my acknowlegement more wayes than one' (Hickes to Wanley, 14 Mar. 1698, BL Harley MS 3779, fo. 65). At the time of writing Hickes was fifty-five, Wanley twenty-five—and not four years out of the draper's shop.

them. The letters are full of plans for great enterprises. As early as 1695 he had proposed a collection of all the fragments of scripture remaining in Anglo-Saxon—though he thought it fitter for Edward Thwaites of Queen's than for himself.[9] With the encouragement of William Elstob, another of the Oxford Saxonists, early in 1697 he drafted a plan for an 'Alphabetarium', in which specimens of the alphabets of all languages and all ages, taken wherever possible from manuscripts, were to be engraved and printed.[10] In May 1697 Wanley wrote to Thomas Smith, Keeper of the Cotton Library, begging the loan of Cotton Augustus II, 'that Noble book of Saxon charters', adding that he will also attempt to borrow those charters in the Royal Library, those at Lambeth, and also those at Worcester, and that when he has thus 'gotten the whole strength of the Kingdom (of this kind)' into his hands, he proposed to undertake what is in effect a comprehensive work on English diplomatic.[11] He submitted to the Curators of the Bodleian a request to be allowed to remove all manuscript leaves used as pastedowns in printed books in the Library so that they could be arranged to illustrate the development of handwriting.[12] In the summer of 1700 he put forward the grandest scheme of all, proposing to visit the libraries of France, Germany, and Italy to examine their manuscripts, collate important texts, take specimens of handwriting, and search for works—particularly cartularies and other monastic records—bearing on English history; he solicited and got the approval of nearly a dozen influential people, including the Vice-Chancellor of the University, Bodley's Librarian, four Heads of Houses, Samuel Pepys, and Hans Sloane.[13] And throughout the letters of the period

[9] See no. 5. This was, in fact, before he had come into residence at Oxford. The idea surfaced again, briefly, ten years later: see no. 107 and n. 5.

[10] BL Harley MS 6466, fo. 87, d. 17 Jan. 1697. Bodl. MS Eng. bib. c. 3 (*SC* 33184), a manuscript presented by Wanley to Elstob, contains a collection of ancient and modern alphabets in Wanley's hand, together with copies of the Lord's Prayer in forty-nine languages, including Basque, Coptic, and Sardinian.

[11] No. 33. Cf. Edmund Gibson's remarks in a letter to Ralph Thoresby in the same year: 'A young gentleman in Oxford, Mr. (Humphrey) Wanley, is laying the foundation of a Res Diplomatica, for England particularly. He designs and draws admirably well; having, besides, an unaccountable skill in imitating any hand whatsoever.' (*Letters of Eminent Men Addressed to Ralph Thoresby, F.R.S.* [ed. J. Hunter] (1832), i, p. 305).

[12] Memorandum ptd. below, Appendix I.

[13] Memorandum ptd. below, Appendix II. Kenneth Sisam, *Studies in the History of Old English Literature* (Oxford, 1953), p. 265, points out that he no doubt had in mind such works as Mabillon's *Iter Germanicum* and *Iter Italicum* (1695, 1697), with which he was certainly familiar, although his memorandum shows that, as one might expect, Wanley had something much more ambitious in mind.

there are constant references to Wanley's 'Book of Hands'—famous among his contemporaries—a collection of dated or dateable specimens of handwriting, which he intended as the basis of a palaeographical manual tracing the history of writing in the West from the earliest times.[14] These are ambitiously conceived schemes and they are a young man's schemes; most were never begun, none was completed. There is no doubt he would have been wiser to attempt something more manageable. But for Wanley modest ambitions held only moderate attractions.

We do well to remind ourselves how far ahead of their time were the schemes generated by Wanley's exuberant imagination. Of these proposals, the Anglo-Saxon biblical pieces were first collected by A. S. Cook in 1898; the comprehensive study of early English charters had to wait for Kemble and Earle in the nineteenth century and Sawyer and others in the twentieth; Bodleian pastedowns remained unlisted until N. R. Ker's *Pastedowns in Oxford Bindings* was published in 1954. Of the schemes referred to below, put forward by Wanley during his early years in Harley's service, the publication of the Acts of the Privy Council was undertaken by Sir Nicholas Harris Nicholas between 1834 and 1837, while the plan to publish the original sources of English history, begun by Hearne, is really the forerunner of that monumental Victorian enterprise, the Rolls Series. Wanley was one of the first to recognize the importance of *dated* manuscripts for palaeography, and systematic collections of facsimiles of dated manuscripts are only now being made.[15] The only major work he carried through to completion, his catalogue of Anglo-Saxon manuscripts, held the field until N. R. Ker published his *Catalogue of Manuscripts Containing Anglo-Saxon* in 1957.

In December 1700, amidst much rancour and bitterness, Wanley left Oxford for good and settled in London. The precise occasion of his departure is not known, but the letters leave no doubt that he had come to realize that advancement at Oxford was blocked and he saw that his future lay elsewhere. There followed the years of drudgery as Assistant Secretary (later Secretary) of the recently founded SPCK

---

[14] See no. 37 and n. 1, and the memorandum ptd. below, Appendix I.

[15] 'Wanley's great distinction was to formulate and bring into practical use, independently of Montfaucon, a method of dating which to the modern scholar seems too fundamental ever to have needed invention, but whose absence from earlier scholarship is precisely what makes that seem so arbitrary.' (Patricia Easterling, pp. 186–7. See Select List of Printed Books Used for details.)

and as assistant to Hans Sloane, Secretary of the Royal Society. They
are the years which saw the publication of his catalogue of Anglo-
Saxon manuscripts—Wanley seems to have finished all work on it,
except for reading proof and the ordering of plates and indexes, by
1703. They are also years of ill health and unhappiness, and of desper-
ate attempts to find a post more congenial to his interests and his
talents than the SPCK or the Royal Society afforded.

The formal introduction to Robert Harley, the encounter that
decided the course of Wanley's subsequent career, took place in April
1701.[16] There are very few letters from Wanley to Harley still extant,
but a number of those that have survived were written in the year or
two after that first meeting. They suggest a developing relationship
between the two men based on a recognition of the mutual benefits
they offered each other—Harley seeing in Wanley, with his bibliographical expertise and his indefatigable energy, the ideal servant of
his own growing appetite for accumulating books and manuscripts;
Wanley seeing in Harley a patron who might liberate him from the
tedium of merely secretarial employment. In late September 1703
Wanley examined the manuscripts of Sir Simonds D'Ewes at
Stowlangtoft, Suffolk, and if there is no certain evidence that he was
acting as Harley's agent, it was to Harley he reported what he found
there and it was through Wanley, two years later, that Harley
purchased them;[17] in August 1704 Wanley signed the Preface to his
catalogue of Anglo-Saxon manuscripts—published the next year—and
in it extols Harley as his Maecenas; in January 1706 Wanley was busy
'digesting' the D'Ewes manuscripts for Harley;[18] a letter to John
Strype, early in 1707, makes it clear that Wanley is the intermediary
through whom Harley is to be approached by those wishing to gain
access to his library;[19] in April of the same year Wanley made a beginning on the catalogue of Harley's manuscript collections;[20] on 3 June
1708 Wanley submitted, and had accepted, his resignation as Secretary of the SPCK.[21] The long courtship was over; Wanley's future
lay in the service of the Harleys, father and son.

---

[16] Hickes to Robert Harley, 23 Apr. 1701 (*HMC Portland Papers*, iv, p. 16). Wanley may
have made Harley's acquaintance three years earlier: see Charlett's letters to him d. 3,
6 June 1698, Welbeck Wanleyana = BL Loan MS 29/253. [17] No. 103 and n. 3.
[18] Charlett to Wanley, 14 Jan. 1706, Welbeck Wanleyana = BL Loan MS 29/253.
[19] No. 109. [20] Now BL Add. MSS 45701-7.
[21] Wanley attended his last meeting of the SPCK as Secretary on 24 June 1708 (SPCK
Archives, Minutes 1706-9).

The letters suggest that, relieved as Wanley must have been at his
change of station, he did not, at least in his early years as Library-
Keeper to Robert Harley, see himself as remaining in the position for
ever. There is, for example, Wanley's long and unexplained visit to
Longleat in the autumn of 1709, just above a year after entering
Harley's service. He presumably went at the invitation of Lord
Weymouth since he was treated as a guest, but why he was invited and
what he did while he was there is not known; his letters offer no hint of
his business. But it entailed more than three months' absence from
Harley's library, and that is hard to reconcile with the idea of an absolutely fixed and secure post.[22] Four years later the death of Thomas
Rymer, the Historiographer Royal, drew from Wanley an impassioned
plea directed to Harley, by now Lord Treasurer, on behalf of his
claims to succeed to Rymer's office.[23] And at about the same time he
had hopes of a government appointment as Commissioner of the
Hackney Coach Office.

To these years belong the last of Wanley's boldly conceived but
unconsummated historical enterprises. Shortly after coming to the
library in 1708, Wanley had set about a new 'Life' of Cardinal Wolsey,
and though his work on it seems not to have gone beyond collating the
1667 edition of Cavendish's *Life and Death of Cardinal Wolsey* with the
late sixteenth-century manuscript Harley 428, it is clear that he
envisaged a work on a scale which went far beyond that entertained in
biography of the period, a scale not attempted in England until the
publication of the majestic biographies of the second half of the nineteenth century.[24] Five years later in his letters to Harley begging for
Rymer's place, Wanley draws attention to the advanced state of his
edition of three English chronicles of the Middle Ages, undertaken
with the material encouragement of Viscount Weymouth and prosecuted by Wanley quite independently of his official work as Library-
Keeper;[25] to the same time belongs his draft warrant (to be signed by
the Queen) to allow him free access to all libraries in the Kingdom, for

---

[22] Between 1 Aug. and 29 Oct. 1709 all Wanley's letters are written from Longleat: see
Handlist of Letters Not Printed *under* Wanley, Ann. Cf. Charlett's remark, 'I hope Mr
Harly will now be able . . . to find some Post of Settlement for you' (Charlett to Wanley,
10 Dec. 1710, Welbeck Wanleyana = BL Loan MS 29/253).

[23] Nos. 136, 137.

[24] See J. A. W. Bennett, 'Wanley's *Life of Wolsey*', *Bodleian Library Record*, vii (1962–7),
pp. 50–2, and nos. 115, 214.

[25] For a full account, see no. 136 n. 2.

the purpose of examining and transcribing historical materials, and probably also his memorandum on publishing the Acts of the Privy Council.[26]

No doubt this characteristically ambitious agenda represents Wanley's response to the rich collections of historical manuscripts in Harley's library—especially those recently bought from John Strype, the ecclesiastical historian. But it is also evidence of his anxiety to show his engagement in and to demonstrate his capacity for historical studies, and it is presumably also intended to establish his fitness for employment other than that of professional librarian. All came to nothing. The post of Historiographer Royal went to Madox; it may be that Robert Harley had too keen a sense of what he stood to lose if he had acceded to Wanley's request. Weymouth died and the printed volumes of historians died with him. Completion of Wolsey's 'Life' was still being urged on Wanley as late as 1720,[27] but he showed no interest in taking it up again. Of the rest we hear nothing more. Harley's fall from power in 1715 effectively put an end to Wanley's hopes of official preferment, and for the last ten years of his life all of his time and energy was devoted to the great library which is his monument.

From 1713 the tale of Wanley's letters is largely the story of the Harleian Library.[28] For the period before Wanley begins his record in the *Diary*, they provide—especially in the voluminous correspondence with Edward Harley which starts as early as 1711—invaluable evidence for the growth of the collection. For the years in which *Diary* and letters overlap, the letters complement the *Diary*. They augment our knowledge of Wanley's daily business as Library-Keeper and provide considerable amplification of detail. Neither the *Diary*, which is very much an 'official' record, nor the letters bear much witness to Wanley's life independent of the interests which exercised him and the responsibilities which claimed his energies as librarian. But taken with the evidence provided by the Harleian Catalogue—which Wanley had completed as far as Harley 2408 at the time of his death—they may be said to establish his claims to be accounted the greatest librarian of his age. 'Your Lordship must never', remarked Thomas Bacon, MP for Cambridgeshire, writing to Edward Harley after

---

[26] Both ptd. below, Appendix III, IV.
[27] G. Clarke to Charlett, 7 Apr. 1720, Bodl. MS Ballard 20, fo. 145.
[28] For an exhaustive account of the library see Wanley, *Diary*, Introduction.

Wanley's death to recommend a successor, 'expect to find one equal to Wanley.'[29]

EDITORIAL PROCEDURE

Wanley wrote a good, clear, and—when he had reason to take special pains—elegant, italic hand; his letters display the fastidiousness which marks every scribal, secretarial, or bibliographic task that he undertook. He was methodical and consistent in his epistolary habits and he presents very few of the difficulties so familiar to the editor of seventeenth- and early eighteenth-century correspondence. To be random or wayward was not in his character and it is not easy to imagine him writing a careless letter. Wanley often composed preliminary drafts of letters before sending them (they are the authority for many of the texts printed in this edition), and such drafts display nothing of the disorder one might expect to find in a busy man's 'foul papers': it is sometimes difficult to decide whether what survives is a draft or a fair copy.

THE LETTERS

Text. Letters and drafts of letters are largely free from difficult or problematical readings, except in a few cases where the fabric of the letter is damaged, or where the manuscript in which it is found has been carelessly bound and words or parts of words are concealed in the gutter or lost at the edge of the page. Where text has been lost through damage or in binding, square brackets mark the lacuna; where the missing or damaged words or letters can be restored with a fair degree of certainty, they are supplied; in other places an estimate of the amount of text lost is printed between the brackets. No attempt is made to identify or to mark possible losses or omissions in the case of letters the texts of which are derived from printed copies.

Words apparently left out unintentionally by Wanley are supplied; words obviously miswritten are corrected, and attention is drawn to the fact in a note.[30] Deleted words or passages, false starts, etc. are passed over silently except in special cases. Where a word is written

---

[29] Letter to Edward Harley, 22 July 1726; quoted by C. E. Wright, p. 129 of *PBA* xlvi. See Select List of Printed Books Used for details.

[30] Such a remarkably 'clean' text has encouraged simplification of the apparatus by integrating the textual notes, which are few, with the explanatory footnotes.

twice, one is omitted. Interlined words (with the exception of English glosses to non-English texts) are inserted at the appropriate place in the line. Capital letters are, with one or two exceptions, supplied when omitted at the beginning of a sentence.

Punctuation. Punctuation is that of the manuscript (or print where no manuscript exists) with some minor relaxations. Wanley was fastidious in punctuation as in other things and his practice is systematic and methodical. Some of his conventions are eccentric to the modern eye, in particular the use of an apostrophe in third person singular indicative forms ('ha's', 'doe's', 'happen's'), in the occasional use of a semicolon where modern practice would favour a comma, and in combining round brackets used to enclose a parenthesis with other marks of punctuation—comma, semicolon, colon. The last of these conventions is generally modified by removing or reducing the additional punctuation.[31] A full stop is supplied where clearly required at the end of sentences, except in transcripts from texts or in lists, notes, subscriptions, signatures, and other less formal circumstances.

Abbreviations. Although open to the charge that it gives too much weight to mere survival as against Wanley's own (and in many cases early eighteenth-century) practice, only modern conventions in such abbreviations as 'Mr', 'Dr', 'Revd' are retained. Wanley regularly wrote 'S^r' for 'Sir' and 'L^d' for 'Lord', as well as 'M^r', and 'D^r'; 'Hon^d', and 'Honble', as well as 'Rev^d'; 'B^p' for 'Bishop', as well as 'S^t' for 'Saint', and these are expanded without notice and printed on the line. The forms 'y^e', 'y^t' are printed as 'the', 'that', and the occasional forms 'w^t' as 'with' or 'what', and 'w^c' as 'which'; 'ult^o', '4to', etc. as 'ultimo', '4to'; ampersand is retained: '&', '&c'. Where a line above a vowel is used to represent a following *m*, the *m* is supplied; a line through the ascender of some letters—*d, l, b*—is not reproduced. Initials are printed as written: 'A.B.Laud', 'K. Edward', 'Sir J.C.'; 'ff' is printed 'F.'[32] All other suspended forms are expanded without notice.

Transcripts. Four of the letters printed are written in Latin, many more contain words or passages—extracts from printed books, manuscripts,

---

[31] Wanley's practice is not itself consistent and there is evidence to suggest that he was not clear in his own mind what punctuation was appropriate.

[32] Except for bringing superscript letters into line, citations in the footnotes are not subject to any editorial modification.

charters, inscriptions, etc.—in Latin, Greek, French, Welsh, Irish, Anglo-Saxon, and Middle English. One letter[33] reproduces the Runic futhorc, another[34] the Latin, Greek, and Gothic alphabets; a third reproduces *literatim* the first and last words—many of them printers' abbreviations—of both columns of text on every tenth page of an early printed book, together with the colophon.[35] It has been impossible to devise any means of treating such diverse originals consistently. I have taken them individually and attempted to arrive at a sensible and defensible method for reproducing the manuscript in each case.

One general principle I have adopted. Where Wanley explicitly states that he is providing an exact transcript, a 'diplomatic' transcript (or 'specimen' as he would have called it), or where, though he does not say so explicitly, he is clearly providing such a transcript, I attempt to reproduce Wanley's version of the original as nearly as print will allow. I can see no alternative to this. In 1714 Wanley tried to obtain from Arsenius and Gennadius, leaders of a mission to England to enlist help for the Orthodox Church against the Turks, a written confession or 'Certificate' in Greek of their faith; he sent to John Covell, Master of Christ's, a copy 'which is a faithful Copie of the badly-spelt & badly-accented Original, which I keep by me'.[36] To edit such transcripts would be to falsify Wanley's intention and to defeat his purpose; the only modifications I have made are those demanded by the need to accommodate the written copy to modern conventions of typography. Neither have I seen it as proper to correct errors in the originals Wanley was copying, or in the copies Wanley made. Thus, when he writes to ask Edward Lhwyd for help in discovering the contents of an Irish manuscript for the Royal Society, he confesses his ignorance of the language,[37] and his careful transcript displays many errors.

The policy of rendering 'diplomatic' transcripts as Wanley wrote them has not, with very occasional and obvious exceptions, led to any attempt to reproduce letter-forms. In transcripts Wanley followed his

[33] No. 45.
[34] No. 32.
[35] Fust and Schöffer's edn. of Guillaume Durand's *Rationale diuinorum officiorum* (1459); no. 224. Only the colophon is printed.
[36] Wanley to Covell, 21 Dec. 1714, BL Add. MS 22911, fo. 163; ptd. G. Williams, *The Orthodox Church of the East in the Eighteenth Century* (1868), p. lxi.
[37] 'I do not (as I said before) understand the Language, nor do I know any English man besides your self that doe's' (no. 92). The manuscript is now BL Harley MS 5280.

copy in distinguishing such letter-forms as short and long *i*, long *r* and two-shaped *r*, and in writing, where they occurred in his original, such letter-forms as long *s* and flat-topped *g*; as printed such letters follow the form of their modern equivalents.[38] Letters which appear in conjunction with signs as abbreviations, such as ꝑ 'pro', ʮ 'autem', or special signs such as ⁊ 'et', ꝫ 'eius', ꜿ 'con' are printed as written. Superscript signs and letters are retained. Superscript *a* representing omission of preceding *r*, usually in the manuscripts written in a conventional form not recognizable as *a*,[39] is printed as *a* in the few places it appears in the transcripts. There are in practice, and for special reasons, occasional inconsistencies within a particular transcript, most notably in Wanley's transcripts from the Lichfield Gospels, the eighth-century Gospels of St Chad.[40] No attempt is made to identify the places where such inconsistencies occur.

Accents. In the Latin letters they are omitted. In the case of accents and breathings in reproducing Greek, practice is divided. 'Diplomatic' transcripts are covered by the rule described above and they are reproduced as nearly as possible as written; in single words or short phrases (often employed as technical terms) accents and breathings are corrected when wrong and supplied when omitted. In other languages they are reproduced as written. It is often difficult to be confident in identifying the letter over which an accent is written; no doubt Wanley's intention has sometimes been misrepresented.

Typography. Underlining in the letters for which the source of the text is a manuscript is reproduced as italic. In letters for which the source is a printed copy, the heavy use of italic represents eighteenth-century printing house practice rather than Wanley's own and it is not followed. But italics have been kept, and in one or two places added, where experience suggests that Wanley himself would have used them. Bold type is used occasionally in places where it is clear that Wanley intended to 'set off' a word or passage from its context.

---

[38] Exceptions are the runic symbols æ, þ, ð, p, and ʒ.

[39] See N. Denholm-Young, *Handwriting in England and Wales* (Cardiff, 1954), p. 67.

[40] No. 88. A special difficulty arises from Wanley's attempt to reproduce the punctuation of the MS. Since he also uses points and dashes to indicate missing text it is often impossible to decide what are punctuation marks and what are not.

HEAD-NOTES

The identity of the person to whom a letter is directed is in most cases clear, and usually appears in the unambiguous evidence of an address on the letter itself, occasionally in the use of the name in Wanley's opening salutation or elsewhere in the text. In all other cases identification of the correspondent depends upon circumstantial evidence—endorsements, the existence of letters to which the letter in question is a reply, or of a letter which is an answer to it, allusions which associate the letter with a particular person, a reference to the letter in Wanley's *Diary*, etc.—and supplied names are enclosed in square brackets. A question mark following the name indicates that identification falls short of certainty; a rule instead of a name, that the correspondent has not been identified. Correspondents are identified by forename (where known) and surname, occasionally by office, as the Curators of the Bodleian, the Mayor of Leicester—or by title, as the Earl of Denbigh; dignities and honorifics are omitted.[41]

Where a letter or draft is not dated by Wanley, or is incompletely dated, or where the date is missing as a result of damage, an attempt is made to date it as accurately as possible on such other evidence as is available. Postmarks, endorsements by the person to whom the letter is directed, and association with completely dated or reliably datable letters provide the most useful evidence for this purpose.[42] Dates, or parts of dates supplied are enclosed in square brackets.[43] Letters reproduced from a manuscript copy or from a printed text are dated on the authority of the copy or the print. A question mark before a conjectural date indicates a greater, a question mark after it a lesser, degree of doubt.

Dates are those of the Old Style or Julian calendar, but the new year is taken as beginning on 1 January rather than 25 March. Wanley regularly dates letters written between 1 January and 25 March with

[41] Letters directed by Wanley to himself at his London address are taken to be to Ann Wanley his wife. Letters directed to 'Mr Wood' or 'Mr Potter' at various addresses are identifiable as intended for George Hickes. Hickes, Dean of Worcester from 1683, was deprived in 1690 for refusing to take the oath of allegiance to William III, and for nine years was harassed by the civil authorities and lived in constant fear of prosecution. In order to conceal his whereabouts he changed addresses frequently and lived under assumed names.

[42] Postmarks are reported only when they bear on the dating of a letter or for special reasons.

[43] Square brackets used for supplied dates are normally omitted (as are those used for supplied names) in citing letters in the footnotes.

both years, as '29 January 1702/3';[44] this appears in the head-note and elsewhere as '29 January 1703'. The full date as Wanley wrote it is given in the end-note.

END-NOTES

The end-note supplies relevant information under a number of heads.

Manuscript. When the text is printed from Wanley's holograph, this stands first in the entry; where the manuscript is not the letter sent it is identified as a draft, copy, or fair copy, and if it is unsigned that is stated; apparently unfinished, incomplete, or fragmentary texts are so described. Copies in other hands are also noted,[45] and where Wanley's holograph has not been traced, the text is reproduced from such a copy, or from the earliest or most authoritative of the printed texts listed later in the end-note. Only the folio reference of the leaf on which a letter or draft begins is given; where the leaves of a manuscript are numbered by page, or where letters in a manuscript are numbered independently of foliation, by article, this is made clear.

Date. The place at which and the date on which the letter was written.

Address. The name and address of the person to whom the letter is directed or for whom it is intended.[46]

Printed. Earlier printings of the text, with notice given where only part of the letter is reproduced.

Endorsed. Endorsements are printed when they contain evidence necessary for dating a letter, identifying a correspondent, etc., otherwise only selectively.

FOOTNOTES

Wanley's passionate regard for manuscripts extended to the letters of his correspondents, which he seems never to have thrown away. Great

[44] Sometimes he uses only the old year, which can be misleading; thus a letter to Charlett written on 2 Jan. 1703 is dated by Wanley '2 Jan. 1702'.

[45] Wanley had, occasionally at least, while in Edward Harley's service secretarial help with his correspondence. Two letters written from Wimpole on consecutive days (nos. 208, 209) are copies in a hand not Wanley's, but they are endorsed by Wanley as authentic copies of letters sent.

[46] Polite superscriptions such as 'Present', or 'These humbly present' are not reproduced; superscriptions which refer to the contents of the letter—as 'With a parcel of books'—are. Addresses, and subscriptions at the close of letters, are often displayed over three or four lines in manuscript; this has not been followed in printing.

numbers have survived and are preserved together, chiefly and conveniently in two collections—BL Harley MSS 3777–3782, and in Welbeck Wanleyana in a series of boxes numbered BL Loan MSS 29/248–258.[47] Quotations from correspondents' letters is used only sparingly; simple references to letters without quotation of text is more frequent, but even this is introduced only when the matter of the letter referred to bears in a direct way on what Wanley himself writes. The existence of a correspondent's letter related to that of Wanley's printed is not in itself grounds for recording that the letter is extant; by the same token the absence of reference cannot be taken to imply that a related letter has not survived. The very bulk of the associated correspondence[48] makes some such limitation necessary, and similar considerations govern economies practised elsewhere.

Correspondents and other persons are identified at their first appearance, although relevant supplementary information may be given on subsequent occasions. The biographical information provided varies, but information which bears on a person's known relationship to, or interest for, Wanley is preferred to a formal recitation of biographical facts, and in all cases the account given is summary.

Manuscripts are identified as precisely as Wanley's references to them—often vague[49]—allow, by collection and press-mark. References to authoritative scholarly reference works are supplied where relevant: Lowe, *Codices Latini Antiquiores* (*CLA*) for early Latin manuscripts; Ker, *Catalogue of Manuscripts Containing Anglo-Saxon* and Wanley's own *Catalogus Historico-Criticus* for Anglo-Saxon literary material; Sawyer, *Anglo-Saxon Charters*, Davis, *Medieval Cartularies of Great Britain*, etc.; Bernard's *Catalogi Manuscriptorum Angliae et Hiberniae* (*CMA*) is cited for late seventeenth-century private collections, and where otherwise useful; the *Summary Catalogue* number

---

[47] 'Welbeck Wanleyana' is the designation used by C. E. Wright and Ruth C. Wright, the editors of Wanley's *Diary*, to identify the Wanley material found among the miscellaneous Harley papers from Welbeck Abbey deposited on temporary—later indefinite—loan in the British Museum by His Grace the Duke of Portland in 1949; following their practice I use it throughout, in every case in conjunction with the British Museum (now British Library) press-mark. The letters to Wanley in Harley 3777–82 are arranged alphabetically by correspondent, and include, in the appropriate place, letters *from* Wanley to Thomas Tudway. Loan 29/248, 249, and 250 contain letters from Edward Harley to Wanley; Loan 29/251–258 are arranged alphabetically by correspondent.

[48] There are, for example, more than 200 letters from Arthur Charlett and more than 250 from Edward Harley.   [49] See, for example, no. 49.

(*SC*) is provided for Bodleian manuscripts, and where they are available the catalogues of M. R. James are used to identify manuscripts in Cambridge college libraries.[50] Little attempt is made, here or elsewhere, to pursue any matter into the specialist scholarly literature of its subject.[51]

Printed books are identified where Wanley supplies enough information to allow this, and occasionally when he does not; not all the identifications are as confident as the absence of any expression of doubt may suggest. Where, as is usually the case, no indication of edition is given, the first is usually cited. The appropriate vernacular form of an author's name is substituted for the Latin forms commonly used, as modern and English forms of place-names are substituted where the place of publication is printed in Latin. For books printed before 1500 supplementary references to standard scholarly works— *Gesamtkatalog der Wiegendrucke* (*GW*), Hain, *Repertorium Bibliographicum* and Copinger's supplements, Proctor, *Index to the Early Printed Books in the British Museum*[52]—are supplied; for books of later date reference to bibliographical authorities is not systematically provided.

For the years it covers C. E. Wright's and Ruth C. Wright's edition of Wanley's *Diary* has been invaluable; the very great debt I owe it will be clear from the frequency with which it is quoted (usually by page and article rather than by date) in the footnotes.

---

[50] This list is not exhaustive.

[51] Where Wanley passes judgement on the age of a manuscript in the course of referring to it, I make a point of supplying in the identifying footnote the date assigned by modern scholarship, where this can be ascertained. Wanley's reputation as a palaeographer is decisively authenticated by this test, which covers a wide range of material— biblical, classical, historical—in Latin, Greek, and Old English.

[52] Proctor is usually cited in preference to the British Museum *Catalogue of Books Printed in the XVth Century* because of the convenience of the references Proctor supplies to Bodleian copies.

HANDLIST OF LETTERS FROM WANLEY NOT PRINTED IN THE PRESENT EDITION

A date within round brackets means that the identification of the correspondent is conjectural, within square brackets that the date itself is conjectural. Letters misdated by Wanley are corrected and dates omitted are supplied; the evidence for these changes will be found in the notes to the typescript copies of these letters deposited in the Bodleian and the British Library.

ANONYMOUS: [Jan. 1698], BL Harley 4966, art. 32 (fragment), ptd. Nichols, *Literary Anecdotes*, i, p. 94; [Aug. 1702], Welbeck Wanleyana = BL Loan 29/257 (draft); 4 Jan. 1709, ptd. *Bibliotheca Literaria*, iv (1723), p. 3 n^i (MS not traced); 14 Aug. 1711, Welbeck Wanleyana = BL Loan 29/258; 30 Oct. 1713, Welbeck Wanleyana = BL Loan 29/258 (draft); [before 1715], Welbeck Wanleyana = BL Loan 29/258, folder 7 art. 13 (draft); [after 1713], Welbeck Wanleyana = BL Loan 29/258, folder 7 art. 14 (draft).

ANSTIS, John: (19 Sept. 1720), BL Stowe 749, fo. 130.

BAGFORD, John: 12 Apr. 1696, BL Harley 4966, art. 27; 19 Apr. 1696, BL Harley 4966, art. 29; (12 May 1696), BL Harley 4966, art. 30; 17 June 1696, BL Harley 4966, fo. 20; (7 Sept. 1696), BL Harley 4966, art. 35; 27 Sept. 1696, BL Harley 4966, art. 36; (15 Nov. 1696), BL Harley 4966, art. 39; (2 Feb. 1698), BL Harley 4966, art. 33; (6 Mar. 1698), BL Harley 4966, art. 40; 12 July 1698, BL Harley 4966, art. 62; 20 July 1698, BL Harley 4966, art. 63 (fragment); (20 Oct. 1698), BL Harley 4966, art. 64; [(9 Nov. 1698)], BL Harley 4966, art. 66; 19 Jan. 1699, BL Harley 4966, art. 58; 4 May 1699, BL Harley 4966, art. 68; 25 May 1699, BL Harley 4966, art. 69; 15 Aug. 1699, BL Harley 4966, art. 71 (addressed to 'Mr Bagford or Mr Sare'); [(22 Aug.)], BL Harley 4966, art. 70; (25 Aug. 1699), BL Harley 4966, art. 126; 19 Oct. 1699, BL Harley 4966, art. 75; 29 Dec. 1700, BL Harley 4966, art. 76; 25 June 1701, BL Harley 4966, art. 127; [July 1703], BL Harley 4966, art. 38; 7 Mar. 1704, BL Harley 4966, art. 37; 12 Jan. 1705, BL Harley, 4966, art. 65; 28 July 1708, BL Harley 4966, art. 46; [(1709)], BL Harley 4966, art. 156; 16 July 1709, BL Harley 4966, art. 47; 18 Nov. 1709, BL Harley 4966, art. 48; 28 Nov. 1709, BL Harley 4966, art. 28.

BARNES, Joshua: 21 Sept. 1699, Bodleian, Rawl. lett. 40, art. 32.

BATTELEY, John: [(September 1701)], Welbeck, Wanleyana = BL Loan 29/258 (draft).

BEDFORD, Hilkiah: (25 Jan. 1724), Bodleian, Rawl. lett. 42, fo. 195.

BERENCLOW, Bernard: 5 July 1701, Welbeck Wanleyana = BL Loan 29/258.

BOWCHER, Thomas: 3 Mar. 1707, Welbeck Wanleyana = BL Loan 29/251.

CHAMBERLAYNE, John: [18 Dec. 1700], Welbeck Wanleyana = BL Loan 29/252 (draft); 10 January 1701, Welbeck Wanleyana = BL Loan 29/252 (draft); [(Mar. 1701)], Welbeck Wanleyana = BL Loan 29/252; 13 May 1701, Welbeck Wanleyana = BL Loan 29/252 (draft); (16 May 1701), Welbeck Wanleyana = BL Loan 29/252 (draft); 26 July 1701, Welbeck Wanleyana = BL Loan 29/252 (draft); 22 Aug. 1701, Welbeck Wanleyana = BL Loan 29/252 (draft); [(Sept. 1701)], Welbeck Wanleyana = BL Loan 29/252 (draft).

CHARLETT, Arthur: (30 Apr. 1698), Bodleian, Ballard 13, fo. 61; 3 May 1698, Bodleian, Ballard 13, fo. 62; 14 May 1698, Bodleian, Ballard 13, fo. 66; (13 June 1698), Bodleian, Ballard 13, fo. 71, ptd. Ellis, *Original Letters*, pp. 262–4, Nichols, *Literary Anecdotes*, viii, p. 360; J. Hawkins, *A General History of the Science and Practice of Music* (1776), i, p. 392 (incomplete); (24 June 1698), Bodleian, Ballard 13, fo. 72; (1 Jan. 1699), BL Egerton 2260, fo. 222 (draft in Harley 6466, fo. 84); (21 Sept. 1699), ptd. *Letters . . . to and from William Nicolson*, ed. J. Nichols (1809), i, no. 137, p. 340 (MS not traced); [24 July 1700], Welbeck Wanleyana = BL Loan 29/253; [12 Oct. 1700], Bodleian, Ballard 13, fo. 98; [5 Dec. 1700], Bodleian, Ballard 13, fo. 87; 9 Dec. 1700, Bodleian, Ballard 13, fo. 90; 19 Dec. 1700, Bodleian, Ballard 13, fo. 91; 8 Mar. 1701, Bodleian, Ballard 13, fo. 96, extract ptd. Richard, Lord Braybrooke, *Memoirs of Samuel Pepys*, 4th edn. (1854), iv, pp. 303–4; 5 Apr. 1701, Bodleian, Ballard 13, fo. 99; 24 Apr. 1701, Bodleian, Ballard 13, fo. 101; 21 May 1701, Bodleian, Ballard 13, fo. 103 (copy in Bodleian, Rawl. D. 742, fo. 53), extract ptd. *Bodleian Letters*, i, pp. 119–27; 14 June 1701, Welbeck Wanleyana = BL Loan 29/258; (3 Oct. 1704), Bodleian, Ballard 13, fo. 114; [July 1705], ptd. Hearne, *Collections*, i, p. 20 (MS not traced, extracts in Bodleian, Hearne's Diaries 2, pp. 55, 52); 1 Aug. 1705, Bodleian, Ballard 13, fo. 116, extracts ptd. Hearne, *Collections*, i, pp. 23–4; (22 Apr. 1707), Bodleian, Ballard 13, fo. 118; (15 Jan. 1711), Bodleian, Ballard 13, fo. 121; ([(1 Feb. 1711)], Bodleian, Ballard 13, fo. 154; [(June 1711)], Welbeck Wanleyana = BL Loan 29/253 (draft); 19 Nov. 1713, Bodleian, Ballard 13, fo. 122; 28 Nov. 1713, Bodleian, Ballard 13, fo. 124; (18 Feb. 1714), Bodleian, Ballard 13, fo. 128; (5 Jan. 1716), Bodleian, Ballard 13, fo. 133ᵛ; (28 Jan. 1716), Bodleian, Ballard 13, fo. 134; (1 Oct. 1719), Bodleian, Ballard 13, fo. 141; (14 Apr. 1720), Bodleian, Ballard 13, fo. 148; (21 Apr. 1720), Bodleian, Ballard 13, fo. 149; (17 July 1720), Bodleian, Ballard 13, fo. 150.

COVELL, John: 29 Sept. 1699, BL Add. 22910, fo. 488 (copy in Cambridge, University Library Mm.vi.50, fo. 216); 30 Aug. 1701, BL Add. 22911, fo. 2 (copy in Cambridge, University Library Mm.vi.50, fo. 254); 21 Dec. 1714, BL Add.

22911, fo. 163, ptd. G. Williams, *The Orthodox Church of the East in the Eighteenth Century* (1868), pp. lx–lxi.

DU SOUL, Moses: 24 Aug. 1701, BL Harley 4966, art. 125.

GAGNIER, John: 20 Oct. 1724, Welbeck Wanleyana = BL Loan 29/260 misc. 88; 17 November 1724, Welbeck Wanleyana = BL Loan 29/260 misc. 88.

GIBSON, Edmund: 5 July 1696, BL Harley 6430, p. 79 (draft, incomplete).

HARLEY, Edward: 19 May 1716, Welbeck Wanleyana = BL Loan 29/258; 4 Nov. 1716, Welbeck Wanleyana = BL Loan 29/258, extract ptd. A. S. Turberville, *A History of Welbeck Abbey and its Owners* (1938), i, p. 322; 8 Nov. 1716, Welbeck Wanleyana = BL Loan 29/258; 13 Nov. 1716, Welbeck Wanleyana = BL Loan 29/258; 25 Dec. 1716, Welbeck Wanleyana = BL Loan 29/258; 30 Dec. 1716, Welbeck Wanleyana = BL Loan 29/204 fo. 528, summary ptd. *HMC Portland Papers*, v, p. 523; [19 June 1717], Welbeck Wanleyana = BL Loan 29/258; (4 Mar. 1721), Welbeck Wanleyana = BL Loan 29/258; 2 Jan. 1722, Welbeck Wanleyana = BL Loan 29/258.

HICKES, George: (14 Feb. 1699), Bodleian, Eng. hist. c. 6, fo. 33; (18 Mar. 1699), Bodleian, Eng. hist. c. 6, fo. 37; (28 Mar. 1699), Bodleian, Tanner 21, fo. 22; 8 Mar. 1704, Bodleian, Eng. hist. c. 6, fo. 42^b; 11 Mar. 1704, Bodleian, Eng. hist. c. 6, fo. 42^d.

HORSEMAN, H.: 24 Oct. 1723, Welbeck Wanleyana = BL Loan 29/255 (draft).

LAUGHTON, John: 24 Aug. 1701, BL Harley 4966, art. 124.

LE NEVE, Peter: 9 Apr. 1725, BL Harley 4713, fo. 229.

MICKLETON, James: [8 June 1717], Durham University Library, Mickleton and Spearman 13.

MILWARD, John: 29 Mar. 1695, Welbeck Wanleyana = BL Loan 29/256.

MORLEY, John: 21 Mar. 1718, Welbeck Wanleyana = BL Loan 29/255.

NICOLSON, William: 23 June 1702, Welbeck Wanleyana = BL Loan 29/258 (draft).

PATRICK, Simon: [Mar. 1703], Welbeck Wanleyana = BL Loan 29/258 (draft).

PAYNTER, William: [Apr.–May 1700], BL Harley 3779, fo. 19^v.

PEMBROKE, Earl of: (22 Jan. 1702), Welbeck Wanleyana = BL Loan 29/258 (draft).

PEPYS, Samuel: 15 Apr. 1701, ptd. Richard, Lord Braybrooke, *Memoirs of Samuel Pepys* (1825), ii, p. 261 (MS not traced); 12 Oct. 1702, Magdalene College, Cambridge, Pepys 1299 (2) (copy in BL Lansdowne 814, fo. 58).

PRICE, Lady: 11 May 1702, Welbeck Wanleyana = BL Loan 29/258 (draft).

SARE, Richard: see BAGFORD, John, under 15 August 1699.

SLOANE, Hans: 25 June 1700, BL Sloane 4038, fo. 24; 2 Apr. 1701, BL Sloane 4038, fo. 151; 14 Apr. 1701, BL Sloane 4038, fo. 158; 31 July 1701, BL Sloane 4038, fo. 203; 2 Sept. 1701, BL Sloane 4038, fo. 226; [22 Nov. 1701], BL Sloane 4061, fo. 274; [1702], BL Sloane 4061, fo. 266; [1702], BL Sloane 4061, fo. 275; (9 Mar. 1702), BL Sloane 4038, fo. 314; (1 May 1702), BL Sloane 4038, fo. 335; 12 June 1702, BL Sloane 4038, fo. 351; 2 Feb. 1703, BL Sloane 4039, fo. 80; 10 Mar. 1703, BL Sloane 4039, fo. 98; 30 Mar. 1703, BL Sloane 4039, fo. 106; 5 Apr. 1703, BL Sloane 4039, fo. 114; 18 Sept. 1703, BL Sloane 4039, fo. 186; [Oct. 1703], BL Sloane 4061, fo. 264; 19 Oct. 1703, BL Sloane 4039, fo. 202; [Jan. 1704], BL Sloane 4061, fo. 272; ([Jan. 1704]), BL Sloane 4061, fo. 271; 19 Jan. 1704, BL Sloane 4039, fo. 237; (16 Feb. 1704), BL Sloane 4039, fo. 247; 8 Jan. 1705, BL Sloane 4039, fo. 414; [Mar. 1708], BL Sloane 4061 fo. 277; 23 June 1716, BL Sloane 4044, fo. 178; 17 Mar. 1724, BL Sloane 4047, fo. 153.

SMITH, John: (11 Jan. 1709), Bodleian, Eng. hist. c. 6, fo. 43.

SPCK Correspondence: [Apr. 1702], Welbeck Wanleyana = BL Loan 29/258 (draft); [June 1705], Welbeck Wanleyana = BL Loan 29/260 misc. 59 (draft); (23 June 1705), BL Add. 22911, fo. 18 (copy), ptd. Nichols, *Illustrations*, i, pp. 816–18; [Jan. 1707], ptd. Nichols, *Illustrations*, i, p. 818 (MS not traced); 8 Feb. 1707, BL Stowe 748, fo. 56; 22 Oct. 1707, Welbeck Wanleyana = BL Loan 29/258; 15 Apr. 1708, National Library of Scotland 821, fo. 169 (copy); 16 Apr. 1708, ptd. Nichols, *Illustrations*, i, pp. 818–19 (MS not traced).

STRYPE, John: 26 May 1707, Cambridge, University Library Additional 6, fo. 506 (copy in BL Add. 5853, fo. 76); 18 Sept. 1708, Cambridge, University Library Additional 4, fo. 171 (copy in BL Add. 5853, fo. 63ᵛ); 14 Jan. 1710, Cambridge, University Library Additional 6, fo. 594; 20 Aug. 1711, Cambridge, University Library Additional 7, fo. 28 (copy in BL Add. 5853, fo. 98); 5 Sept. 1711, Cambridge, University Library Additional 7, fo. 50.

STUBBS, Philip: (20 Sept. 1712), Welbeck Wanleyana = BL Loan 29/259 misc. 37 (draft); (25 Sept. 1712), Welbeck Wanleyana = BL Loan 29/259 misc. 37 (draft); (11 Oct. 1712), Welbeck Wanleyana = BL Loan 29/259 misc. 37 (draft).

SUTTON, William: 3 Oct. 1723, Welbeck Wanleyana = BL Loan 29/257 (draft).

TANNER, Thomas: 6 July 1698, Bodleian, Tanner 22, fo. 34; 9 Aug.1698, Bodleian, Tanner 22, fo. 98.

THORESBY, Ralph: 25 Jan. 1709, Yorkshire Archaeological Society, Thoresby Correspondence, ptd. J. Hunter, *Letters of Eminent Men Addressed to Ralph Thoresby, F.R.S.*, ii (1832), p. 141; D. H. Atkinson, *Ralph Thoresby, the Topographer: His Town and Times*, ii (Leeds, 1887), pp. 135–6.

THWAITES, Edward: 13 July 1702, Bodleian, Rawl. D. 377, fo. 35.

TUDWAY, Thomas: 24 Dec. 1715, BL Harley 3782, fo. 165, extract ptd. G. Williams, *The Orthodox Church of the East in the Eighteenth Century* (1868), p. xxix.

VAILLANT, Paul: 18 Sept. 1719, Welbeck Wanleyana = BL Loan 29/258.

WANLEY, Ann: 1 Aug. 1709, Welbeck Wanleyana = BL Loan 29/258; 6 Aug. 1709, Welbeck Wanleyana = BL Loan 29/258; 8 Aug. 1709, Welbeck Wanleyana = BL Loan 29/258; 15 Aug. 1709, Welbeck Wanleyana = BL Loan 29/258; [22 Aug. 1709], Welbeck Wanleyana = BL Loan 29/258; 23 Aug. 1709, Welbeck Wanleyana = BL Loan 29/258; [Aug. 1709], Welbeck Wanleyana = BL Loan 29/258; 5 Sept. 1709, Welbeck Wanleyana = BL Loan 29/258; 12 Sept. 1709, Welbeck Wanleyana = BL Loan 29/258; 19 Sept. 1709, Welbeck Wanleyana = BL Loan 29/258; 3 Oct. 1709, Welbeck Wanleyana = BL Loan 29/258; 5 Oct. 1709, Welbeck Wanleyana = BL Loan 29/258; 17 Oct. 1709, Welbeck Wanleyana = BL Loan 29/258; [Oct. 1709], Welbeck Wanleyana = BL Loan 29/258; 29 Oct. 1709, Welbeck Wanleyana = BL Loan 29/258; 31 Oct. 1709, Welbeck Wanleyana = BL Loan 29/258; 10 Feb. 1716, Welbeck Wanleyana = BL Loan 29/258; 12 Feb. 1716, Welbeck Wanleyana = BL Loan 29/258; 19 Feb. 1716, Welbeck Wanleyana = BL Loan 29/258; 4 Mar. 1716, Welbeck Wanleyana = BL Loan 29/258; 6 Mar. 1716, Welbeck Wanleyana = BL Loan 29/258; 11 Mar. 1716, Welbeck Wanleyana = BL Loan 29/258; 13 Mar. 1715, Welbeck Wanleyana = BL Loan 29/258; 14 Mar. 1715, Welbeck Wanleyana = BL Loan 29/258; 18 Mar. 1716, Welbeck Wanleyana = BL Loan 29/258; 21 Mar. 1716, Welbeck Wanleyana = BL Loan 29/258; 25 Mar. 1716, Welbeck Wanleyana = BL Loan 29/258; 8 Apr. 1716, Welbeck Wanleyana = BL Loan 29/258; 12 Apr. 1716, Welbeck Wanleyana = BL Loan 29/258, extract ptd. A. S. Turberville, *A History of Welbeck Abbey and its Owners* (1938), i, p. 370 n. 4; 15 Apr. 1716, Welbeck Wanleyana = BL Loan 29/258; 4 Nov. 1716, Welbeck Wanleyana = BL Loan 29/258; 11 Oct. 1719, Welbeck Wanleyana = BL Loan 29/258; 18 Oct. 1719, Welbeck Wanleyana = BL Loan 29/258; 22 Oct. 1719, Welbeck Wanleyana = BL Loan 29/258; 1 Nov. 1719, Welbeck Wanleyana = BL Loan 29/258; 8 Nov. 1719, Welbeck Wanleyana = BL Loan 29/258; 1 Dec. 1719, Welbeck Wanleyana = BL Loan 29/258; 31 Dec. 1719, Welbeck Wanleyana = BL Loan 29/258.

WANLEY, Samuel: [Aug. 1704], BL Lansdowne 841, fo. 68 (draft) ptd. J. Nichols, *History and Antiquities of Leicester*, iv (1807–11), p. 1048, Nichols, *Literary Anecdotes*, i (1812), pp. 530–2.

ZAMBONI, Giovanni: 14 Oct. 1725, Bodleian, Rawl. lett. 124, fo. 132.

BIBLIOGRAPHY

MANUSCRIPTS

Manuscripts containing copies of letters for which Wanley's originals (sent, fair copies, drafts) survive are not noticed. Letters from Wanley printed in the present edition are referred to by number (No. 11, Nos. 225, 227, etc.); for letters not printed see Handlist of Letters Not Printed.

(i) *Manuscripts containing letters from Wanley*

Cambridge, Magdalene College, Pepys Library 992. No. 96.

Cambridge, Trinity College, O.5.10. No. 11.

Cambridge, University Library, Additional 4. Strype Correspondence. No. 116.

—— Additional 6. Strype Correspondence. Nos. 109, 111, 112, 113, 114.

Chelmsford, Essex Record Office, D/Y 1/1. Holman Correspondence. Nos. 197, 198, 229.

Leningrad, Archive of the Academy of Sciences, Fond 121. Schumacher Papers. Nos. 225, 227, 228.

Linköping, Public Library, Benzelius Correspondence. Rotographs in Uppsala University Library MS G.19. Nos. 70, 106.

London, British Library, Additional 22911. Covell Correspondence. Nos. 122, 125, 127, 131, 138, 142, 152, 153, 156, 157, 162, 166, 167, 169, 170, 172, 173, 174.

—— Additional 28167. No. 193.

—— Additional 42711. No. 89.

—— Additional 44879. Nos. 117, 118.

—— Additional 58079. No. 75.

—— Harley 3782. Nos. 158, 159, 160, 161, 164. (Harley 3777–82 contain letters to Wanley, 1692–1726, arranged alphabetically by correspondent.)

—— Harley 4713. No. 232.

—— Harley 4966. Bagford Correspondence. Nos. 9, 10, 12, 15, 22, 39, 40, 41, 42, 43, 56, 58, 60.

—— Harley 5911. No. 37.

—— Harley 6430. Letter-book of Nathaniel Wanley, 1657–74, and H.W., 1695–6. Nos. 13, 16, 17, 19, 20, 21, 23, 24.

—— Harley 7055. Miscellaneous papers of H.W., 1690–1720. Nos. 97, 120, 121, 126.

—— Harley 7526. Nos. 100, 143.

—— Lansdowne 841. Nos. 103, 104, 108.

—— Sloane 3984. No. 85.

—— Sloane 4037. Sloane Correspondence. No. 51.

—— Sloane 4038. Soane Correspondence. Nos. 71, 82.

—— Sloane 4040. Sloane Correspondence. No. 110.

—— Sloane 4047. Sloane Correspondence. No. 234.

—— Stowe 749. Nos. 168, 212, 223, 239, 240.

—— *Miscellaneous Harley Papers (= Loan 29) from Welbeck Abbey, deposited in the British Library by His Grace the Duke of Portland on indefinite loan (including Welbeck Wanleyana).*

—— Loan 29/204. Nos. 154, 190, 191, 192.

—— Loan 29/205. No. 199.

—— Loan 29/252. Nos. 130, 141. (Loan 29/251-8 contains, with the exceptions listed here and in the next entry, letters to Wanley, 1694–1726, arranged alphabetically by correspondent.)

—— Loan 29/258. Includes Letters from H.W. to Edward Harley, 1712–26, Ann Wanley etc. Nos. 84, 86, 87, 94, 119, 124, 134, 135, 136, 137, 139, 151, 163, 165, 176, 177, 178, 179, 180, 181, 182, 183, 184, 185, 186, 187, 188, 189, 202, 206, 208, 209, 210, 211, 224, 226, 230, 231, 233, 242. (Letters to Wanley from Edward Harley, 1711–24, are in Loan 29/248–50.)

—— Loan 29/259. Miscellaneous papers of H.W. Nos. 123, 128, 129, 133.

—— Loan 29/260. Miscellaneous papers of H.W. Nos. 132, 195, 196, 235, 236.

London, Royal Society, Sh. 648. No. 204.

—— Sh. 649. No. 216.

—— Sh. 650. No. 219.

New York, Collection of Arthur A. Houghton jun., Pepys Correspondence. No. 76.

Oxford, Bodleian Library, Additional C.78 (*SC* 30248). Nos. 221, 222.

—— Ashmole 1817[B] (*SC* 25188). Nos. 78, 88, 92, 95.

—— Autographs d. 21. No. 50.

—— Ballard 1 (*SC* 10787). No. 63.

—— Ballard 8 (*SC* 10794). No. 69.

—— Ballard 13 (*SC* 10799). Charlett Correspondence. Nos. 1, 38, 46, 47, 48, 49, 52, 53, 64, 65, 66, 67, 72, 73, 77, 80, 93, 98, 99, 107, 115, 140, 144, 150, 155, 171, 175, 194, 200, 201, 203, 205, 207, 213, 214, 217, 220.

—— English history c. 6 (*SC* 29726). Hickes Correspondence. Nos. 26, 27, 28, 31, 32, 44, 45, 54, 55, 57, 59, 61, 62, 68, 74, 101, 102, 105.

—— English letters c. 291. Nos. 18, 25.

—— Rawlinson D. 377 (*SC* 15317). Nos. 81, 83.

—— Rawlinson letters 17 (*SC* 15579). Nos. 146, 147, 148, 149.

—— Rawlinson letters 124 (*SC* 15012). Nos. 237, 238, 241, 243.

—— Smith 54 (*SC* 15661). Nos. 14, 29, 30, 33, 34, 35, 36.

—— Tanner 24 (*SC* 9844). Nos. 4, 5, 6, 7, 8.

—— Tanner 25 (*SC* 9845). Nos. 2, 3.

Oxford, Christ Church, Evelyn Collection. Upcott's Autographs. Nos. 90, 91.

Paris, Bibliothèque Nationale, fonds français 17711. No. 218.

(ii) *Select list of manuscripts written, copied, or compiled by Wanley*
(Some MSS in this section which contain letters are also listed in (i)).

Cambridge, Trinity College, O.5.10. Copy of Bodl. MS Auct. F.3.23 (*SC* 2533) (Proclus), transcribed by H.W. for Thomas Gale, 1695.

London, British Library, Additional 6052. H.W.'s catalogue of heraldic MSS in the Harleian Library.

—— Additional 45699, 45700. 'Catalogus Maior' of the Harleian MSS by H.W.

—— Additional 45701-7. 'Catalogus Brevior' of the Harleian MSS by H.W., 1708-26. (The copy from which the first ptd. catalogue of the Harleian collection (1759) was set up.)

—— Additional 45711. H.W.'s index to the Harleian Charters.

—— Harley 3317. Includes a catalogue by H.W. of Anglo-Saxon MSS in the Bodleian, d. 11 Nov. 1691.

—— Harley 3666. Copy of BL Cotton Julius A.xi, art. 4 and Vitellius E.xvii, art. 3 (Benedict of Peterborough) transcribed by H.W., 1713.

—— Harley 3886. Catalogue by H.W. of early editions of printed books owned by Edward Harley, 1722.

—— Harley 4886. Copy of Cotton Tiberius A.x (Dunstable Chronicle) transcribed by H.W., 1713.

—— Harley 4964. H.W.'s Anglo-Saxon Scriptural collection.

—— Harley 6030. H.W.'s Commonplace book, d. 6 Aug. 1687.

—— Harley 6388, 6402, 6863. Miscellaneous collections by H.W. relating to Coventry.

—— Harley 6466. Miscellaneous papers (extracts, memoranda, etc.) by H.W., 1691-1700.

—— Harley 6532. Miscellaneous papers by H.W., 1683-93.

—— Harley 6941. Miscellaneous papers of H.W., 1695-*c*.1700.

—— Harley 7055. Miscellaneous papers of H.W., 1690-1720.

—— Harley 7505. Facsimile copies by H.W. of Warwick deeds, 1690-2.

—— Harley 7514. H.W.'s collection of signs and abbreviations used in Greek MSS.

—— Harley 7578. Includes miscellaneous papers of H.W.

—— Harley 7579. Includes H.W.'s catalogue of 'Libri praestantiores' in the Bodleian Library, 1695.

—— Harley 7627a,b. Catalogue by H.W. of Edward Harley's early Latin printed books, 1721.

—— Lansdowne 677. H.W.'s Memorandum Book, 1721–2.

—— Lansdowne 771, 772. H.W.'s *Diary*, 1715–26.

—— Lansdowne 814. Includes miscellaneous papers of H.W.

—— Lansdowne 815. Subject index by H.W. of Harleian MSS, 1723.

—— Lansdowne 816. Catalogue by H.W. of Edward Harley's printed books at Wimpole Hall, 1716–17.

—— Lansdowne 846. Includes miscellaneous papers of H.W.

—— Sloane 526. Specimens of paper compiled by H.W.

—— Sloane 781. Copy of Theophilus Monachus transcribed by H.W., 1699.

—— Loan 29/259 (Welbeck Wanleyana). Miscellaneous papers of H.W.

—— Loan 29/260 (Welbeck Wanleyana). Miscellaneous papers of H.W.

—— Loan 29/261 (Welbeck Wanleyana). Miscellaneous fragments in H.W.'s hand.

—— Loan 29/270 (Welbeck Wanleyana). H.W.'s catalogue of English coins.

—— Loan 29/271 (Welbeck Wanleyana). H.W.'s collection of signs and abbreviations used in Greek MSS.

—— SPCK Archives, MSS Wanley = CS.3/01.

—— St. Paul's Cathedral, B.13. H.W.'s catalogue of his collection of bibles, prayer-books, etc. sold to the Dean and Chapter, 1707.

Oxford, Bodleian Library, English bibles c. 3 (*SC* 33184). Old English and other linguistic papers by H.W.

—— Savile 53 (*SC* 26121). Copy of part of Magdalen College, Oxford, MS gr. 13 (Porphyrius) transcribed by H.W. for John Wallis, 1695.

—— Library Records. Draft in English of H.W.'s Preface to E. Bernard's *Catalogi Manuscriptorum Angliae et Hiberniae* (1697).

SELECT LIST OF PRINTED BOOKS USED

Printed books and articles about Wanley and his career as scholar and librarian are listed, with an explanatory note where one is needed. Also included are titles which preserve the texts of Wanley letters the originals of which have not been traced, and titles in which letters of Wanley excluded from this edition can be found printed, with a cross-reference to the Handlist of Letters Not Printed. Works cited in the annotation are not listed here, but bibliographical details are supplied in the notes in which they occur; for titles frequently referred to a summary form is used in the annotation, and full details are

supplied in the list of Abbreviations. Standard works of reference are omitted.
All books are published in London unless otherwise stated.

ATKINSON, D. H., *Ralph Thoresby, the Topographer: His Town and Times*, 2 vols. (Leeds, 1885–7). *See* Handlist of Letters Not Printed *under* Thoresby.

BARWICK, G. F., 'Humfrey Wanley and the Harleian Library', *The Library: A Quarterly Review of Bibliography and Library Lore*, NS iii (1902), pp. 24–35, 243–55.

—— 'The Formation of the Harleian Library: Further Notes', *The Library: A Quarterly Review of Bibliography and Library Lore*, 3rd ser. i (1910), pp. 166–71. Extracts from Nathaniel Noel's account book: *see* C. E. Wright, *below*.

BENNETT, J. A. W., 'Bernard's Catalogue', *TLS*, 31 October 1936, p. 887. H.W.'s Preface to *CMA* (Bernard's Catalogue) (1697).

—— 'A Note on the Bodleian', *Oxford Magazine*, 16 June 1938. H.W.'s proposals for improving the Bodleian (extract from Harley MS 7055 fos. 42–4).

—— 'Hickes's "Thesaurus": A Study in Oxford Book-Production', *Essays and Studies*, NS i (1948), pp. 28–45. Includes H.W.'s *Catalogus*.

—— 'Wanley's *Life of Wolsey*', *Bodleian Library Record*, vii (1962–7), pp. 50–2.

BERNARD, E., *Catalogi librorum manuscriptorum Angliae et Hiberniae* (Oxford, 1697). H.W. was the author of four catalogues, compiled the index, and wrote the Preface.

Bibliotheca Literaria. 'An Essay upon the English Translation of the Bible', *Bibliotheca Literaria*, iv (1723), pp. 3–4. *See* Handlist of Letters Not Printed *under* Anonymous.

BRAYBROOKE, Richard, Lord. *Memoirs of Samuel Pepys. Comprising his Diary from 1659 to 1669 . . . and a Selection of his Private Correspondence*, 2 vols. (1825); 4th edn. 4 vols. (1854). *See* Handlist of Letters Not Printed *under* Charlett, Pepys.

BRITISH MUSEUM. *A Catalogue of the Harleian Collection of Manuscripts . . . preserved in the British Museum*, 2 vols. (1759); rev. edn. 4 vols. (1808–12). Descriptions of Harleian MSS 1–2408 by H.W. Source of No. 215.

CHAMBERLAYNE, E., *Angliae Notitiae, or the Present State of England* (1669 f.). The 1702 edn. has an account of the Bodleian, probably by H.W.

COURTNEY, W. P., 'Humfrey Wanley', *Dictionary of National Biography*.

CROSSLEY, J., 'Humphrey Wanley: Autograph Notes of his Family', *Notes and Queries*, 4th ser. v (1870), pp. 142–3. Biographical notes from H.W.'s family bible (BL Loan MS 29/272).

DOUGLAS, David C., 'Humphrey Wanley', *English Scholars 1660–1730*, 2nd edn. (1951), pp. 98–118. H.W. as historical scholar.

DOUTHWAITE, W. R., 'Humfrey Wanley and his Diary', *The Library Chronicle*, i (1884), pp. 87–94, 110–13. On BL Lansdowne MSS 771, 772.

EASTERLING, Patricia, 'Before Palaeography: Notes on Early Descriptions and

Datings of Greek Manuscripts', *Studia Codicologica* (= Festschrift Marcel Richard), *Texte und Untersuchungen zur Geschichte der altchristlichen Literatur*, 124 (1977), pp. 179–87. H.W. as pioneer in the dating of Greek MSS.

ELLIS, H., *Original Letters of Eminent Literary Men of the Sixteenth, Seventeenth, and Eighteenth Centuries* (Camden Society xxiii, 1843). *See* Handlist of Letters Not Printed *under* Charlett.

European Magazine. 'Extract of a Letter from Mr Humfrey Wanley to the Right Honourable Edward Lord Harley, giving some account of the Bishop of Ely's MSS. dated 30th August 1714', *European Magazine*, xxxix (1801), pp. 407–8. Source of No. 145.

EVANS, Joan, *A History of the Society of Antiquaries* (Oxford, 1956). H.W.'s part in refounding the Society of Antiquaries (ch. iii and iv).

GILLAM, S. G., 'The Thomason Tracts', *Bodleian Library Record*, ii (1941–9), pp. 221–5. H.W.'s and the Bodleian's interest in acquiring the collection, 1707–20.

—— and R. W. Hunt, 'The Curators of the Library and Humphrey Wanley', *Bodleian Library Record*, v (1954–6), pp. 85–98. H.W.'s proposals for improving the Bodleian, June 1697 (Harley MS 7055, fos. 42–4).

GIBSON, Strickland, 'Humphrey Wanley and the Bodleian in 1697', *with* 'Bodley's Library in 1697', *Bodleian Quarterly Record*, i (1914–16), pp. 106–12, 136–40. H.W.'s proposals for improving the library, Nov. 1697 (BL Lansdowne MS 814, fos. 86–94).

[HANSON, L.], 'Some Observations Concerning the Invention and Progress of Printing, to the Year 1465', *Bodleian Library Record*, vi (1957–61), pp. 634–5. Establishes H.W.'s authorship.

[HARTLEY, J.], *Catalogus Universalis Librorum in Omni Facultate*, 3 vols. (1699–1709). H.W. may have supplied details about books in the Bodleian. (*See* no. 10 n. 3.)

HAWKINS, J., *A General History of the Science and Practice of Music*, 5 vols. (1776). *See* Handlist of Letters Not Printed *under* Charlett.

HEARNE, Thomas, *Remarks and Collections of Thomas Hearne*, ed. C. E. Doble *et al.* 11 vols. (Oxford Historical Society, 1885–1921). *See* Handlist of Letters Not Printed *under* Charlett.

HEYWORTH, P. L., 'Thomas Smith, Humfrey Wanley and the Cottonian Library', *TLS*, 31 August 1962, p. 660. H.W.'s attempt to supplant Smith as Keeper of the Cotton Library.

—— 'The Old English "Seasons of Fasting"', *Mediaeval Studies*, xxvi (1964), pp. 358–9. The authority of H.W.'s *incipit*, *Catalogus*, p. 219.

—— 'Alfred's "Pastoral Care": MS Cotton Tiberius B.xi', *Notes and Queries*, 216 (1971), pp. 3–4. H.W. and BL MS Cotton Tiberius B.xi.

—— 'A Betty of Claret', *Notes and Queries*, 216 (1971), pp. 51–2.

HEYWORTH, P. L.,'Humfrey Wanley and "Friends" of the Bodleian, 1695–98', *Bodleian Library Record*, ix (1973–8), pp. 219–30.

HICKES, G., *Linguarum Veterum Septentrionalium Thesaurus*, 3 vols. (Oxford, 1703–5). Vol. ii is H.W.'s Catalogue of Anglo-Saxon MSS.

HISTORICAL MANUSCRIPTS COMMISSION. *Manuscripts of the Duke of Portland at Welbeck Abbey*, 10 vols. (1891–1931). *See* Handlist of Letters Not Printed *under* Harley.

HOWARTH, R. G., *Letters and the Second Diary of Samuel Pepys* (1932).

HUSSEY, C., 'Wimpole Hall, Cambridgeshire', *Country Life*, 21, 28 May 1927. Edward Harley's country seat; he transferred his printed books there, catalogue by H.W. 1716–17, BL Lansdowne MS 816.

JAMES, M. R., and JENKINS, C., *Descriptive Catalogue of the Manuscripts in the Library of Lambeth palace* (Cambridge, 1930–2).

McCLURE, E., *A Chapter in English Church History: being the Minutes of the Society for Promoting Christian Knowledge for the years 1698–1704, together with abstracts of correspondents' letters during part of the same period* (1888). H.W. was Assistant to the Secretary from Dec. 1700, Secretary from 1702.

McGATCH, Milton C., 'Humphrey Wanley's Proposal to the Curators of the Bodleian Library on the Usefulness of Manuscript Fragments from Bindings', *Bodleian Library Record*, xi (1982–5), pp. 94–8. Prints H.W.'s memorandum. BL Loan MS 29/259 misc. 29.

NICHOLS, J., *The History and Antiquities of the County of Leicester*, 4 vols. in 8 (1795–1815). *See* Handlist of Letters Not Printed *under* Wanley, Samuel.

—— *Letters on Various Subjects, Literary, Political and Ecclesiastical, to and from William Nicolson, D.D.*, 2 vols. (1809). *See* Handlist of Letters Not Printed *under* Charlett.

—— *Literary Anecdotes of the Eighteenth Century*, 9 vols. (1812–16). *See* Handlist of Letters Not Printed *under* Anonymous, Charlett, Wanley (Samuel).

—— *Illustrations of the Literary History of the Eighteenth Century*, 8 vols. (1817–58). *See* Handlist of Letters Not Printed *under* SPCK.

NIXON, H., 'Harleian bindings', *Studies in the Book Trade in Honour of Graham Pollard*, ed. R. W. Hunt *et al.* (Oxford Bibliographical Society, 1975), pp. 153–94. H.W.'s dealings with Harley's binders.

OSBORNE, T., *Catalogus Bibliothecae Harleianae*, 5 vols. (1743–5). The sale catalogue of the printed books in the Harleian Collection.

PLOMER, H. R, *A Dictionary of the Printers and Booksellers . . . in England Scotland and Ireland from 1668 to 1725* (Bibliographical Society, 1922).

SISAM, K., 'MSS. Bodley 340 and 342: Aelfric's *Catholic Homilies*', *Studies in the History of Old English Literature* (Oxford, 1953), pp. 148–98. This and the next provide the best account of H.W. as Anglo-Saxon scholar.

—— 'Humfrey Wanley', *Studies in the History of Old English Literature*, pp. 259–77.

TANNER, J. R., *Private Correspondence and Miscellaneous Papers of Samuel Pepys, 1679–1703*, 2 vols. (1926).

THORESBY, R., *Letters of Eminent Men Addressed to Ralph Thoresby* [ed. J. Hunter], 2 vols. (1832). *See* Handlist of Letters Not Printed *under* Thoresby.

TURBERVILLE, A. S., *A History of Welbeck Abbey and its Owners*, 2 vols. (1938). *See* Handlist of Letters Not Printed *under* Harley, Wanley (Ann).

VINCENT, J. A. C., 'Wanley's Harleian Journal', *The Genealogist*, NS i (1884), pp. 114–17, 178–82, 256–61. On BL Lansdowne MSS 771, 772.

WAKEMAN, G., 'Humfrey Wanley on Erecting a Library', *The Private Library*, vi (1965), pp. 80–4. H.W.'s proposals for a design for a new library building for Robert Harley (BL Harley MS 7055, fo. 16).

[WALKER, J.], *Letters Written by Eminent Persons in the Seventeenth and Eighteenth Centuries . . . from Originals in the Bodleian Library and Ashmolean Museum*, 2 vols. (Oxford, 1813). *See* Handlist of Letters Not Printed *under* Charlett.

WANLEY, Humfrey, 'Some Observations concerning the Invention and Progress of Printing, to the Year 1465', *Philosophical Transactions*, no. 288 (Nov. and Dec. 1703), pp. 1507–16. H.W.'s history of early printing *see* Hanson, *above*.

—— 'Part of a Letter, written to a Most Reverend Prelate, in answer to one written by his Grace, judging of the Age of MSS. the Style of Learned Authors, Painters, Musicians, &c.', *Philosophical Transactions*, no. 300 (June, 1705), pp. 1993–2008. Source of No. 79.

—— 'An Essay on the Invention of Printing, by Mr. John Bagford; with an Account of his Collections for the same, by Mr. Humfrey Wanley, F.R.S. Communicated in two Letters to Dr. Hans Sloane, R.S. Secr.', *Philosophical Transactions*, no. 310 (Apr.–June 1707), pp. 2397–410.

—— *The Grounds and Principles of the Christian Religion, Explain'd in a Catechetical Discourse, for the Instruction of Young People. Written in French by J. F. Ostervald . . . Rendred into English by Mr. Hum. Wanley: And Revis'd by Geo. Stanhope, D.D.* (1704).

—— *Librorum Veterum Septentrionalium, qui in Angliae Bibliothecis extant . . . Catalogus Historico-Criticus*, vol. ii of Hickes, *Thesaurus* (Oxford, 1705). H.W.'s Catalogue of Anglo-Saxon MSS.

WILLIAMS, G., *The Orthodox Church of the East in the Eighteenth Century, being the Correspondence between the Eastern Patriarchs and the Nonjuring Bishops* (1868). *See* Handlist of Letters Not Printed *under* Covell, Tudway.

WRIGHT, C. E., 'Humfrey Wanley: Saxonist and Library Keeper', *Proceedings of the British Academy*, xlvi (1961), pp. 99–129.

—— 'Edward Harley, 2nd Earl of Oxford, 1689–1741', *The Book Collector*, xi (1962), pp. 158–74.

—— 'A "Lost" Account-Book and the Harleian Library', *British Museum Quarterly*, xxxi (1967), pp. 19–24. Records E. Harley's dealings with Nathaniel Noel, his chief London bookseller.

WRIGHT, C. E., *Fontes Harleiani. A Study of the Sources of the Harleian Collection of Manuscripts Preserved in the Department of Manuscripts in the British Museum* (1972).

—— 'Manuscripts of Italian Provenance in the Harleian Collection in the British Museum: their sources, associations and channels of acquisition', *Cultural Aspects of the Italian Renaissance: Essays in Honour of Paul Oskar Kristeller*, ed. Cecil H. Clough (Manchester and New York, 1976), pp. 462–84. On H.W.'s agents—John Gibson, Andrew Hay, Conyers Middleton, John Wright, and Nathaniel Noel.

—— and Ruth C., *The Diary of Humfrey Wanley 1715–1726*, 2 vols. (Bibliographical Society, 1966).

WRIGHT, Ruth C., 'Letters from Humfrey Wanley to Eric Benzelius and Peter the Great's Librarian', *Durham University Journal*, NS i (1940), pp. 185–97.

THE LETTERS

1. *To* [Arthur Charlett][1] *15 October 1694*

Honored Sir

Since my departure from Oxford,[2] I have been at Warwick, & talked with Mr Fish;[3] who says that Mr Rogers[4] has no antient writings, but some late accounts concerning the fair Chappel in their Collegiate Church,[5] are in his custody. And Mr Bolton[6] ha's nothing but some Writings relating to the Mannor of Warwick, whereof he is the Lord. And as to his own, he has none burnt but the long Roll of the Souldiers under the command of Richard Beauchamp at Calais; & the Account of Thomas Hall for the Bishopric of Lincoln, of which last, I have a Copie, which I think is exact, for I wrote it in the very same hand with

[1] Arthur Charlett (1655–1722), Master of University College, Oxford 1692–1722. Wanley's patron and promoter of young scholars, he was also a gossip and a meddler. Hearne says he was 'commonly called the Gazzeteer or Oxford Intelligencer', and Wanley was for his part described by Hearne as 'the master's Pimp' (Hearne, *Collections*, i, pp. 214, 212). For a satirical portrait of Charlett's gossipy and inconsequential epistolary style, see *Spectator*, no. 43, 19 April 1711.

[2] Wanley seems to have been in Oxford earlier in the month: a Latin manuscript bible (Bodl. MS Auct. D.5.18, *SC* 27664) was presented by him to the Bodleian Library on 10 Oct. 1694.

[3] James Fish the elder († 1702), parish clerk of St Mary's, Warwick. Keeper of the Beauchamp Chapel in the church and 'transcriber of records' (*The Restoration of the Beauchamp Chapel at St Mary's Collegiate Church, Warwick, 1674–1742*, ed. W. Dugdale (Roxburghe Club, 1956), p. 13 n. 1).

Wanley's enquiries were directed towards discovering collections of manuscripts worthy of inclusion in the *Catalogi Librorum Manuscriptorum Angliae* (*CMA*) then being compiled at Oxford. Doubtless he was acting on the instructions of Charlett, who seems to have been in large part responsible for organizing the gathering of material for it (see W. Hopkins to Charlett, 3 Mar. 1694, Bodl. MS Ballard 13, fo. 17; H. Worsley to T. Tanner, 19 Feb. 1695, Bodl. MS Tanner 25, fo. 301; Charlett to T. Smith, 30 July 1695, Bodl. MS Smith 48, fo. 123). Although finally pbd. in 1697 under the name of Edward Bernard (1638–97), Savilian Professor of Astronomy at Oxford, it was very much a collaborative work: see R. W. Hunt, *A Summary Catalogue of Western Manuscripts in the Bodleian Library at Oxford*, i (Oxford, 1953), pp. xxxi–xxxv. Wanley was the author of four catalogues found in it: (1) the Free School at Coventry (*CMA* II. i, nos. 1446–62); (2) Basil Feilding, 4th Earl of Denbigh (*CMA* II. i, nos. 1463–1552); (3) St Mary's Church, Warwick (*CMA* II. i, nos. 6683–715); (4) John Ayres (*CMA* II. i, nos. 7132–45); he also compiled the index, wrote the Preface, and corrected some of the proofs: see Percy Simpson, *Proof-Reading in the Sixteenth, Seventeenth, and Eighteenth Centuries* (Oxford, 1935), pp. 193–4.

[4] Aaron Rogers, Mayor of Warwick 1683–4, 1688–9.

[5] The Beauchamp Chapel in St Mary's.

[6] William Bolton, one of the Commissioners appointed to supervise the rebuilding of Warwick after the disastrous fire of 5 Sept. 1694 (*Warwick County Records*, viii (1953), p. 15; ix (1964), p. xxix), which Wanley alludes to in the next sentence.

the Original.[7] Our Bishop[8] was here saterday was a sennight (going for London) & commanded me to transcribe it, & he would present it to the Bishop of Lincoln in my name, which I have done, & this is the reason why I did not send before now the summ of 4 writings, I found among Mr Fishes things, when I was at Warwick, of which you have as yet had no account.[9] I could wish that I had perused them all together, that so you might have had them ranked in order of time, which would have prevented their being printed so confusedly as they are like to be.

Sir Your book is much talked off, but every body not onely desires but expects an acurate Catalogue of Sir John Cottons MSS, which would at the same time satisfie the world what the Treasure is, that is contained in his Library, & much raise the value of the book it self, which wil be as frequently bought by the French, Italians & others (amongst whom Sir Johns Library is famous) as by Englishmen.[10]

---

[7] Fish's losses in the great fire amounted to £108 (Dugdale, *Beauchamp Chapel*, p. 57). In his Preface to *CMA*, Wanley declares that all the charters which are said in the catalogue to belong to St Mary's, Warwick, belong to James Fish. After his death in 1702 they seem to have passed to his son. In 1721 Wanley was interested in them for the Harleian Library (*Diary*, p. 83 and n. 3). Some years later they were still in the possession of James Fish the younger: Hearne notes that he was said to own 'several valuable Papers', including Wanley's transcript of Richard Beauchamp's will (Hearne, *Collections*, x, pp. 257–8)—presumably made from the copy listed in a volume of transcripts in St Mary's, *CMA* II. i, no. 6712.

The 'long Roll' is *CMA* II. i, no. 6702; according to Wanley (who prints extracts in *CMA*, but see W. Dugdale, *Antiquities of Warwickshire*, ed. W. Thomas (1730), i, p. 406, for fuller extracts), it was about 18 yards long and a quarter of a yard wide. There seems to have been another copy in the Cotton Library: Bodl. MS Add. D.82 (*SC* 30308), an official copy of the report of the Commissioners appointed to examine the Cotton Library in 1702, contains at the end (fo. 185ᵛ) in Wanley's hand (he was one of the Commissioners) a list of charters etc. not found in Thomas Smith's catalogue of the library (*Catalogus Librorum Manuscriptorum Bibliothecae Cottonianae* (Oxford, 1696); under Augustus *capsa* xviii is mentioned 'Retinue of Ric. Earl of Warwick, at Callie'. It is not found in Planta's early nineteenth-century catalogue of the Cotton collection (1802); it may have perished in the fire of 1731. The 'Account of Thomas Hall' is that compiled by John Chedworth, Bishop of Lincoln 1452–71, *CMA* II. i, no. 6710. The ascription in *CMA* of Hall's roll to 32–3 Henry VIII is presumably an error. See further n. 9 below.

[8] William Lloyd (1627–1717), Bishop of Coventry and Lichfield 1692–9, of Worcester 1699–1717, Wanley's patron. It was to him that Wanley was indebted for his removal in May 1695 from a draper's shop in Coventry to St Edmund Hall in Oxford.

[9] Probably the pieces found in BL Harley MS 7505 copied by Wanley from originals in Fish's possession, between June and Oct. 1691. They are: (1) Inventory of Goods of the Collegiate Church of Warwick (fos. 3–8), *CMA* II. i, no. 6706; (2) Valor Terrarum of Warwick Church (fo. 10), *CMA* II. i, no. 6705; (3) Inspeximus of Henry VI (fos. 13–14ᵛ); (4) the Rent Roll of Thomas Hall referred to in n. 7 above (fos. 15–19), *CMA* II. i, no. 6710.

[10] Presumably *CMA*. Bernard's Catalogue contains no account of the Cotton manuscripts, no doubt because Smith's work on the official catalogue was so far advanced.

I think I have some where read, that the Earl of Exeter has some MSS, & particularly some pieces of Gower, (Chaucers Contemporary) which are not yet printed. If I mistake not, he lives near Stamford in Northamptonshire.[11]

Sir Tho: Price at Park-hal in Warwickshire has some MSS.[12] And Madam Gregory of Stivichal a mile hence, ha's some MSS & writings;[13] & as I am inform'd Madam Oxfrige at Whaburley a mile off, ha's some more.[14] But if Mr Kimberley should send his letters to the two last, I believe it would be very difficult to persuade them that they have any, & much more so, to get an account of them.[15]

Sir, I return you my humble thanks, for your extream courtesie & civility to My sister[16] & my self at Oxford; & particularly for the book you gave me, which wil make me renew my acquaintance with the Saxon Tongue, as soon as I can get some more books which I want: for out of Mr Kings book[17] I only transcribed the Saxon Grammar & the Catalogue of the Saxon books, without medling with any thing of Gothic, Runic, Islandic, &c of al which, with the Scotch I can out of yours pretty well furnish my self 'til I buy more.

I think next week to set forward for Lancashire,[18] & when I am there, I wil if possible see Manchester, & send you an account of what I see or hear of there or elsewhere; & if you have any other service to command me, you shal find that I wil supply the weakness of my performance, by my ready obedience, & the sincerity of my intention;

[11] John Cecil (*c.*1648–1700), 5th Earl. His seat was at Burghley House, Stamford.

[12] (1642–?1689), 2nd Baronet.

[13] Probably Catherine, wife of Love-is-God Gregory of Stivichall, Warwickshire. Arthur Gregory, great-grandfather of Love-is-God, was, the late Mr Philip Styles informed me, known to Dugdale and to Sir Simon Archer, to whom he was related by marriage (W. Hamper, *The Life, Diary and Correspondence of Sir William Dugdale* (1827), pp. 171–2). The Gregorys owned the cartulary of Coventry Cathedral priory (= Davis, no. 275).

[14] Not identified.

[15] Jonathan Kimberley, Wanley's father's successor as Vicar of Holy Trinity, Coventry 1681–1713. Wanley was employed by him to examine manuscripts. See Bodl. MS Ballard 30, fo. 50.

[16] Ellen Wright, Wanley's elder sister, born 1663.

[17] Charles King, Vicar of Deddington, Oxford 1697, early friend and correspondent of Wanley, who here probably refers to G. Hickes's *Institutiones Grammaticae Anglo-Saxonicae* (Oxford, 1689). Wanley transcribed from this the Anglo-Saxon Grammar, 15 Oct. 1691, and the Catalogue of Anglo-Saxon manuscripts in the Bodleian, 11 Nov. 1691, now both part of BL Harley MS 3317.

[18] He was certainly there early in the New Year (see Kimberley to Charlett d. 8 Jan. 1695, Bodl. MS Ballard 30, fo. 52) and had returned by mid-Mar. 1695 (see Wanley to Milward, 20 Mar. 1695, Welbeck Wanleyana = BL Loan 29/256).

which doubtless wil prevail with you to believe that your favors are not bestowed on one forgetful or ungrateful, but on the contrary on him, who is cordially devoted to your service, & wil always approve himself
  Sir
     Your most humble most obedient and faithful servant
                                                    Humfrey Wanley

If you please, Sir, to honor me with any of your commands, be pleased to direct yours for me, to be left at Mrs Ellen Wanley[19] at her house in Bishop street in Coventry, & it wil come safe.

Sir, My sister gives her humble service to you, & desired me to certifie you, that she ha's reprimanded my Cozen Green for his neglect, who own's himself in a fault, for receiving one letter from you by Mr Hopkins,[20] & not answering it, but wil quickly make an attonement for it (if he doe's not forget).

MS: Bodleian, Ballard 13, fo. 56. *Date*: 'Coventry October 15th 1694.'

2. *To* Thomas Tanner[1] *15 October 1694*

Sir
     I have sent you, as you see, the inclosed paper,[2] which I wrote presently after my departure from Oxford; & had I not been hindred by some other business, which fell out unexpectedly, you should have received it before now. Sir I do not think that there is any thing in it, of which you were before ignorant, but I thought you might by it, see, that I would be ready to serve you when it lay in my Power. I must needs say, Sir, that I am very proud of the Honor of your Acquaintance, & when we know one another better, I should reckon on Your Friendship, as one of the greatest Happinesses that Fortune could

---

[19] His mother.
[20] William Hopkins (1647–1700), Canon of Worcester.

---

[1] Thomas Tanner (1674–1735), The Queen's College, Oxford 1689, Fellow of All Souls College, Oxford 1697; Chancellor of Norwich 1701, Bishop of St Asaph 1732–5. His manuscript collections came to the Bodleian at his death (now *SC* 9821–10446). After Wanley's death he claimed that his 'coming out of the draper's shop and settling in a gown at Oxford was almost entirely owing to me' (Tanner to Edward Harley, 21 Mar. 1730; *HMC Portland Papers*, vi, p. 27).
[2] Now missing.

bestow on me. In the mean time my Interest (which as I am a Tradesman I ought not to neglect) prompts me to beg a continuance of that
Correspondence, which your goodness caused you to promise me; for
by it, I am assured that my Gain wil be no less great by your letters,
than it was by your Conversation; which I hope I shal enjoy again
about the latter end of January. I am going into Lancashire, & if I
chance t[o] see any thing which may be useful to you, I wil give you
notice of it.

Dr Hicks in his Catalogue of the Saxon MSS in the Bodleyan
Library,[3] [t]ells us, that there is a MS containing the Pentateuch with
Joshua & Judges.[4] I [w]ould desire you if it woud not be too much
trouble, to transcribe the Decalogue [f]rom the 20th Chapter of
Exodus, & send it me at your leisure, with Wickliffes Preface to the
new Testament which you told me off,[5] & I promise you to return [the]
Wicklif safe again & give you as many thanks as you please.

[I] remember you told me that Mr Somners life, first brought yo[u
six letters lost] with these Studies,[6] perhaps so, Peireskius his life did the
same to me [*five letters lost*] Latin by the famous Gassendus, &
Englished by Dr Rand, & in my o[pinion] would be worth your
perusal.[7]

You would much oblige me, Sir, if you would send me word how
you proceed in your studies, what particular passage pleases you, what
is more remarkable than ordinary, what Inscriptions are more rare
than other &c & as this instructs me, you know it likewise fixes them
surer in your mem[ory.]

Sir I beg your Pardon for my freedome with you, who (I belie[ve)]
have not your equal for knowledge, among all the young men in
Engla[nd] of your age; I speak not this to flatter you, for that is a
baseness I am not muc[h] used to, but from the very bottome of my
heart, which sorrows for our separation, as much as it rejoyces that

[3] *Catalogus Librorum Septentrionalium*, appended to his *Institutiones* (Oxford, 1689); the
Bodleian manuscripts are listed between pp. 135 and 147. The Pentateuch here
mentioned stands first in the catalogue.

[4] Bodl. MS Laud misc. 509 (*SC* 942); Ker no. 344, Wanley p. 67.

[5] Probably the so-called *Wyclif's Wicket*, a popular Wycliffite tract: see no. 5 n. 7.

[6] By White Kennett, prefacing Somner's *Treatise of the Roman Ports and Forts in Kent*
(Oxford, 1693).

[7] *The Mirrour of True Nobility and Gentility. Being the Life of the Renowned Nicolaus Claudius
Fabricius Lord of Peiresk* (1657).

I am no stranger to your notice, which good fortune is & shal be highly prized, by

    Sir

        Your most humble servan[t] to command

                                  Humfrey Wanley

Be pleased to direct yours to me to be left with Mrs Ellen Wanley at her house in Bishop street in Coventry.

MS: Bodleian, Tanner 25, fo. 243. *Date*: 'Coventry Octob. 15. 1694' *Address*: 'For Mr Thomas Tanner at his Chamber in Queens Colledge In Oxford.'

3. *To* Thomas Tanner *28 February 1695*

Sir

    I must humbly beg your Pardon for not Answering your obliging & kind Letter before now. God is my witness that my silence proceeded not from Inconstancy or Neglect, but from other Considerations; I am sensible of the Distance of place that is between us, so that I cannot send you a letter but it must cost you 6d, which I think is too much for a how de ye. I sent to Coventry betimes for a Copie of the following service,[1] but my correspondent could not find the MS I di[rect]ed him to, but as soon as he did, he transcribed it & sent it, but thro' his Ignorance of Latin, he made more than 150 errors, which I have mended except 3 or 4. My Tarrying for this, was one hindrance. I thought I should have went to Wiggan, where Lives one Dr Cu[e]rton, who by Report is one of the most Learned & Industrious Antiquaries in England, he ha's Collected many curious Remarks of all the Counties of England, & especially ha's perfected an History of Lancashire.[2] Here I thought I should find somewhat of Wiltshire which might be useful to you.[3] But now I can only tell you, that I have talked with many

[1] Wanley's transcript of the order of service for the burial of Richard Beauchamp (1382–1439), 13th Earl of Warwick, now Bodl. MS Tanner 25, fo. 309. The original is listed *CMA* II. i, no. 6703, in the catalogue of St Mary's, Warwick.

[2] Richard Kuerdon (1623–?1695), born Jackson. A friend of Dugdale, he practised at Preston as a physician, but neglected his practice in favour of antiquities. He issued proposals for a history of Lancashire 'Brigantia Lancastriensis Restaurata' in five vols. folio in 1688, but it came to nothing. His collections for the work are now preserved in the College of Heralds (8 vols.), Chetham Library, Manchester (2 vols.), and the British Library (1 vol.).

[3] Tanner, a native of the county, was engaged in a history of it: see also no. 4.

Gentlemen about the Dr, & they all say, that it is very great Pitty, but his MSS were gotten out of his hands, for he is very poor, & they are likely to be lost, when he dies. My Expectation of sending you something from Wiggan was another Obstacle, I could fil the Page with more, but I hope you wil think I have said enough.

Dear Mr Tanner, give my humble service to Dr Charlote, & ask him if he received a letter from me lately, if he tells you he ha's, desire to know whether he wrote to the Bishop of Lichfield & Coventry, about me or not? if he ha's not, beseech him to tell the Bishop, that he thinks me an honest well-meaning fellow, & one that could be industrious had I encouragement, that I have relied on a man, I thought I might confide in, but am Egregiously fooled, & forced to throw [my][4] self at his Lordships feet, who was pleased to tell me in Coventry, immediately after my return from Oxford, that he would take care of me &c. As soon as I hear from the Bishop, I wil go for London, but I wil take Oxford in my way, on purpose that I may Thank the Dr & you for all your Civilities & favors to me.[5]

I have in my Custody now, a MS which is the History of the Isle of Man which is designed to be printed short[ly], it is at present ver[y] Imperfect & Imethodical, & unfit to be made Public, I am ce[r]tain that when I am at Oxford [I] can augment what is already begun.[6] If you write to me in this Countrey, let it be immediately after the Reception of this, for I hope to be coming to see you within a fortnight, who shal always acknowledge my self

Dear Sir

Your most humble & obliged servant

H. Wanley

Direct yours For the Reverend Mr Wilson at the Earl of Derbies at Knowesley in Lancashire by Warrington bag. & it wil come safe to me[7]

---

[4] MS omits 'my'.

[5] Charlett's letter to Lloyd pressing Wanley's offer of service in the matter of books and manuscripts, d. 7 Apr. 1695, is in Welbeck Wanleyana = BL Loan MS 29/260 misc. 64.

[6] Probably the collections of William Blundell of Crosby, compiled while a resident of Man 1648–c.1656. What may be the original manuscript (intended for the press, but not at that time printed) was in the library of the Earls of Derby at Knowsley at the end of the seventeenth century. There are a number of transcripts extant, one of which Wanley may have carried off. See *Pbns. of the Manx Society*, xxv (1876), pp. xv–xvii.

[7] Thomas Wilson (1663–1755), domestic chaplain to the Earl of Derby 1692–8, Bishop of Sodor and Man (of which the Derbys were Lords) 1698–1755.

MS: Bodleian, Tanner 25, fo. 308. *Date*: 'Liverpoole Feb. 28. 1694/5.' *Address*: 'For Mr Thomas Tanner at his Chamber in Queens Colledge In Oxford.'

4. *To* [Thomas Tanner] *25 March 1695*

Sir

I hope you have received a Letter which I sent you from Liverpool. I remember that I gave you no direction how to send to me again, as indeed I could not, for the Incertainty of my abode would not suffer it, so that I don't wonder that I have not been informed of its safe coming to your hands.

I am, thanks be to God, come safe to Coventry, & thought to have set out for Oxford as to day, but my Journey is now deferred to this day Sennight. As I came from Lancashire, I stepped aside into the Library at Lichfield, which is the only one, I have seen, since I saw you. There are many MSS of value in it, particularly the Gos[p]ells written (as some say) by St Chad;[1] it is a folio a little imperfect at the beginning, & wanting all at the End, from Luke 16th. I am not a competent Judge of its antiquity, having never seen any MSS exceeding antient, tho' I believe that is so. It is in Latin, & the Letters seem large enough to be called Capitalls: In the margent there now & then some notes in Saxon, by not so neat, but evidently a newer hand. There is another folio containing the value of all Bishopricks Archdeaconries, Monasteries, Chantries, &c within the Province of Canterbury: wherein if Wiltshire be included, you may undoubtedly meet with many things, useful to its History. Time would not permit me to tarry there above half an houre, but if I could possibly have tarried the[re] a day or two, I would willingly have transcribed what would have been in my opinion acceptable to you; I made no Remarks as to the Age of the MS, at that time, but now I reflect on it, I suppose it to have been written in or about the time of Hen: 6.[2]

---

[1] Lichfield Cathedral Library, MS 1, the famous eighth-century manuscript of the Gospels, probably written in Wales. Connected with Lichfield Cathedral from the tenth century, it is still in the possession of the Dean and Chapter. *CLA* ii, no. 159, Ker no. 123, Wanley p. 289. See further nos. 83, 88, 92.

[2] Described *CMA* II. i, no. 1413 as 'Taxatio Spiritualium in omni Diocesi totius Angliae' (and as 'Taxatio Papae Nicolae IV', in *Catalogue of the Printed Books and Manuscripts in the Library of the Cathedral Church of Lichfield* (1888), p. [119]), the taxation of a tenth on all ecclesiastical benefices granted to Edward I by Pope Nicholas IV *c*.1291.

I must beg your Pardon, for sending you the Inscription,[3] for I saw it last Saturday in this new & most accurate Edition of Camden, by your friend Mr Gibson: I wish to God that I might be thought worthy the Honor of his Acquaintance when I come to Oxford. His Industry amazes me. For tho' I long since knew of the designed new Edition of Camden, yet I never had the least thought of his being the Editor. I suppos'd he must have some time to rest him, since the finishing of the Saxon Chronicle, a work in my Judgement of more pains, than bulk. Dr Charlote told me, that he was gone to London about the Preface he had written for Camdens Britannia, which joynd to other Circumstances, made me conclude that there were more undertakers of it than one.[4] I beg of God almighty to bless & prosper his Studies, & as he ha's set him before us, as a pattern of Industry & diligence: so he would stir up the Minds of all the Ingenious & Public-spirited to imitate him. 'Tis certain the Effects of it, would be visible in the easie access to knowledge, which would be to those who woud be desirous of it, to say nothing of the Profit as well as Honor it would bring to Church & State.[5]

Dear Sir, give my most Humble service to Dr Charlote, & tell him, that God willing, I will wait on him, the beginning of the n[e]xt week: For then, I hope to kiss both your hands & tell you viva voce, how much, I am

Sir
   Your most humble & obedient servant
         Humfrey Wanley

[3] Now missing.

[4] Edmund Gibson (1669–1748), Fellow of The Queen's College, Oxford 1694; later Lambeth Librarian, Bishop of Lincoln 1716, Bishop of London 1720. He edited and translated into Latin the Anglo-Saxon Chronicle (*Chronicon Saxonicum* (Oxford, 1692))—see further nos. 117, 118—and edited and translated into English Camden's *Britannia* (1695). See his Preface to Camden for an account of the help he had received.

[5] To say nothing of Edmund Gibson, whose industry was no doubt related to his ambition. He had already pbd., in addition to the works mentioned here: (1) *Polemo-Middinia* (1691), a poem ascribed to William Drummond; (2) an account of the manuscripts in the library made by Thomas Tenison (Bishop of Lincoln 1692–5, then Archbishop of Canterbury) when rector of St Martin-in-the-Fields, and of the manuscripts in the collection bequeathed by Dugdale to the Ashmolean Museum, Oxford (1692); (3) an edition of Quintilian (1693)—dedicated to Henry Worsley (see no. 5 n. 7); (4) notes to Brome's edn. of Somner's *Roman Ports and Forts in Kent* (1693); (5) a Latin translation of Somner's *Julii Caesaris Portus Iccius* (1694). The account of the library of St Martin-in-the-Fields was dedicated to Tenison and it successfully procured his patronage.

If you please to return me a letter by this bearer, Direct for me at My mothers house in Bishops street in Coventry, & it wil come safe

MS: Bodleian, Tanner 24, fo. 12. *Date*: 'Coventry March 25. 1695.'

5. *To* Thomas Tanner *16 April 1695*

Dear Mr Tanner.

You see by this that I am a man of my word in writing to you as I promised, tho' I can send you nothing worth the Postage of this, because I have seen nothing since I saw you. Dr Charlote was so kind as to recommend me Esqr Pepys for a sight of Sir John Cottons Library, Esqr Pepys recommended me to Dr Smith, with whom I have been this morning. He tell's me that he wil procure me a sight of it, for half an hour, next Friday in the afternoon;[1] now if you have any service to command me there, for so long time as I shal be in the Library, pray, Sir, send me word by the next Post, & I believe your letter wil come time enough. Give my humble service to Mr Gibson, & ask him where I may buy the Saxon Gospells so cheap as he talks off, or at all. For I have enquired at above 20 Booksellers shops, & could meet but with one, who knew there was any such book, & that was of Foxes Edition.[2] Give my service too, to Mr Thwaites, & tell him I hope one day, to be settled, & send for his Transcript of the Saxon Pentateuch.[3] Dr Smith was so kind as to shew me the latter part of his accurate Catalogue of the Cotton MSS,[4] (which I wish with all my soul that Dr Charlote

[1] Pepys's letter d. 15 Apr. 1695 recommending Wanley to Thomas Smith is ptd. by Howarth, *Letters*, no. 239. Smith (1638–1710) nonjuror and classical scholar, had principal charge of the Cotton Library for some years up to the death of Sir John Cotton in Sept. 1701. Wanley's relations with Smith were troubled from the first: see nos. 32, 33, 34. For Wanley's hopes of supplanting him in 1701 as Keeper of the Library, see 'Thomas Smith, Humfrey Wanley and the Cottonian Library', *TLS*, 31 Aug. 1962, p. 660.

[2] Wanley refers to the Anglo-Saxon and Gothic versions of the gospels ptd. by Junius, Dordrecht 1664–5, reissued Amsterdam 1684. He had to wait a year for a copy, presented to him by Fitzherbert Adams, Rector of Lincoln College, Oxford, and Vice-Chancellor of the University (see no. 15). The edn. of John Foxe the martyrologist was pbd. in 1571.

[3] Edward Thwaites (1667–1711), Fellow of The Queen's College, Oxford 1698, Anglo-Saxonist. Wanley probably refers to Bodl. MS Laud misc. 509 (*SC* 942) (see no. 2, n. 4) used by Thwaites in his *Heptateuchus Anglo-Saxonice* (Oxford, 1698).

[4] Pbd. as *Catalogus Librorum Manuscriptorum Bibliothecae Cottonianae* (Oxford, 1696). Charlett failed to persuade Smith to allow him to make use of his material for *CMA*.

cou'd procure of him) & I found in that leaf I read over, mention made of a book of the Proverbs of Salomon, Lat. in Saxon Characters, with an interlineary Saxon version. This book unless my memory fails me, is not mentioned in the Catalogue at the End of Dr Hickses Saxon Grammar.[5] Perhaps there may be other parts of Scripture besides, in this famous Library, not yet discovered, I wish Mr Thwaites, or some other Lover of the copious & elegant Language of our Fore-fathers, would gather all the Bible together, I mean those parts that are yet remaining in the Saxon Tongue, & where that fails to fill up the breaches with the antienest English Copies which can be found.[6]

As this would be an august monument of that veneration our ancestors had for the sacred volumes, so, I fancy, it would be very serviseable to our present Church. Now I talk of the Bible, I must beg of you, to send me in your next, a Letter to the Gentleman who ha's Wicklefs Preface to the New Testament & to desire him to permit me to copie it:[7] Pray, Sir, do so quickly because I don't know how short my stay may be in Town, & I would willingly have that with me. Direct yours to me at Mrs Watses a Wine-cooper near the Pump in Crutched-Friers & it wil come safe to

Sir

   Your most humble servant

           Humfrey Wanley

MS: Bodleian, Tanner 24, fo. 4. *Date*: 'London Ap. 16.95' *Address*: 'For Mr Tanner at his Chamber in All-Souls Colledge in Oxford.'

[5] Probably Cotton Vespasian D.vi (Ker no. 207 art. a, Wanley p. 243) misdescribed by Hickes *Institutiones* (1689), p. 175, as 'Homiliae quaedam'.

[6] Ten years later Wanley was considering doing this himself: see no. 107.

[7] Henry Worsley (1675–1741), St Edmund Hall, Oxford 1690, Lincoln's Inn 1690, MP for Newton, IOW 1705–14, Ambassador to Portugal 1714, Governor of Barbados 1721. See Worsley to Tanner d. 25 Apr. 1695 (Bodl. MS Tanner 24, fo. 10) for evidence that Wanley designed a life of Wyclif. Worsley lent him a copy of *Wyclif's Wicket* (now BL Harley MS 1666) on this occasion: see no. 7. Worsley was a man of scholarly tastes, generous in lending manuscripts (see Bodl. MSS Tanner 25, fo. 310, Smith 47, fo. 152) and Hearne thought well of him: 'Mr Worsely of Edmund Hall had a design to publish Sr John Fortescue's *Dominium Politicum & Regale*, and several other Pieces of yt Great Man. But this Design vanish't.' 'Twas Mr Worsely the Gentleman Commoner, to whom Dr Gibson dedicated Quintilian, a truly ingenious Gentleman & of eminent Virtues whilst he was of the Hall' (25 Sept. 1710, Hearne, *Collections*, iii, p. 56). His collection of manuscripts is described in *CMA* (II. i, nos. 6849–945); he presented it to Robert Harley at some date before 13 Dec. 1712 (see Wanley, *Diary*, p. xix); now BL Harley MSS 1585–747, with two outliers—Harley 1811, 1812.

6. *To* Thomas Tanner *19 April 1695*

Dear Sir

I am now just come home from Westminster & Sir John Cottons
Library, Mrs Watts gave me yours with other Letters. I humbly thank
you for your readiness in writing to Mr Worsley, tho' I am at present in
a mind not to shew him your Letter; I suppose that it was only [y]our
Love to me that made you write so large an Encomium of me, which
[I] shall never answer if I shou'd live 100 years, & particularly that I am
a perfect Master in the Saxon Tongue, God knows, that I have but a
very little knowledge in it at present, tho' if he continue my Life,
Health & [Le]isure, I wil bestow some oil & pains in the attainment of
it. If I should [st]rike it out of the letter perhaps he would suspect some
foul play, knowing [t]hat Mr Tanner seldome makes blotts; if I stay til
you write another of [a] lower & truer strain, I shall lose much time, &
I know not how long I [sh]all stay here. As to my proceedings with my
Lord Almoner,[1] I refer you to [a] Letter which (God willing) I shall
write to the Master[2] to morrow, for then [I] shall as you wil see, know
more than I do at present. Mr Pepys lives [a]lmost in the way between
Westminster & my lodgings, & as I came home I went to thank him for
his favor to me,[3] I never heard him mention [y]our name, but when I
go to see his Library which he promises to shew [m]e (it wil be either
Monday or Tuesday) I wil make mention of you by the by, as you
desire, & send you word by the next post what he says.

I would willingly have seen in the Cotton Library the MS I told you
off, vizt Ludus Coventriae, vel ludus Corporis Christi,[4] but it is
removed from [i]ts old Station, neither did Dr Smith bring his Catalogue along with him: the [f]irst Book he shewed me was the Famous
Book of Durham, containing the Gospells in Latin written above a
thousand years ago, with a Saxon interlineary version, not much

[1] William Lloyd, Wanley's patron.

[2] Charlett.

[3] Pepys had lived since 1679 in a house in York Buildings, built on the site of York
House on the Westminster waterfront. His 'favor' was the letter of introduction which
gained Wanley admittance to the Cotton Library: see no. 5 n. 1.

[4] Cotton Vespasian D.viii. The attribution of this Corpus Christi play to Coventry
derives from an inscription on the flyleaf, apparently in the hand of Richard James, Sir
Robert Cotton's librarian, and is erroneous. Lincoln has been suggested as the original
place of performance (*The Corpus Christi Play of the English Middle Ages*, ed. R. T. Davies
(1972), pp. 55–6, but on linguistic grounds the hypothesis of Lincoln origin is held to be
untenable (*Medium Ævum*, ix (1940), p. 153).

newer, it is a large folio, incomparably well written (I mean the Latin, & very well & cleanly kept).[5] The hand is the same with St Chads Gospells at Lichfield,[6] & here Dr Bernards Alphabets did me a kindness.[7] He shewed me likewise an interlineary Psalter, written in Latin Capitalls as the other, with a saxon version, with the Songs of the old & new Test:[8] & this MS is almost as ancient as the former, which I forgot to tell you ha's the Canons of Eusebius praefixed. I saw several other Saxon MSS, b[ut] had no time to dwell long on them. I mentioned the Dano-Saxon Gospell[s] to him, the Dr said he knew the book, & would shew it me, but he thoht it to be rather Francic than Danish. But we both forgot it, so I saw it not.[9] Ælfrics Homilies is a very fair book.[10] I would fain have seen the books of Genesis & would have satisfied my self whether either of them were Cædmon or not, but Sir John ha's taken them with him out of the Library.[11] I saw the Samaritan Pentateuch which Bishop Usher gave Sir Robert it is a large folio, & well written.[12] I saw too, the most antie[nt] & incomparable Copy of Genesis,[13] which the Dr said, he thought was older than the Alexandrian MS,[14] it is a large folio, well written, with [a] Picture in almost every page; it is in Capitals without accents & in mo[st] places without any distinction of words, I remembered the Letters of Dr Bernards Greek Alphabets, so I could read it, after my fashion. I tried the Drs Patience a little, for I copied almost a leaf & a half of the fragment of Judith, which is said to be written stylo Cædmoniano:[15]

[5] Cotton Nero D.iv, the Lindisfarne Gospels, the magnificent early eighth-century codex with interlinear Anglo-Saxon gloss of the tenth century. Ker no. 165, Wanley p. 250, *CLA* ii, no. 187.

[6] See no. 4.

[7] Edward Bernard, *Orbis eruditi literatura a charactere Samaritico deducta* (Oxford, 1689), a collection of alphabets engraved on one side of a large sheet of paper. See Wanley's memorandum (d. 17 Jan. 1697) in BL Harley MS 6466, fo. 87 for his suggestions for improving Bernard's collection, and no. 37 for an account of his progress.

[8] Cotton Vespasian A.i, the Vespasian Psalter, Ker no. 203, Wanley p. 221.

[9] Probably Cotton Caligula A.vii, the Heliand in Low German, described as 'Francic' by Wanley in his *Catalogus*, p. 225.

[10] Perhaps Cotton Vitellius C.v. Ker no. 220, Wanley p. 208.

[11] Cotton Claudius B.iv (Ker no. 142, Wanley p. 253) and Cotton Otho B.x, which contains a fragment of Genesis (37: 2 to 50: 25) (Ker no. 177A, art. 19, Wanley p. 190), a volume badly damaged in the fire of 1731, but some fragments of the Genesis remain.

[12] Cotton Claudius B.viii.

[13] Cotton Otho B.vi, the famous 'Cotton Genesis', almost completely destroyed in the fire of 1731. See no. 47 n. 3.

[14] Codex Alexandrinus, BL Royal MS 1.D. v–viii, the great fifth-century codex of the Greek Bible.

[15] Cotton Vitellius A.xv, the 'Beowulf' MS, Ker no. 216, Wanley p. 218. I have not

I know no[t] when I shal copie the rest, for Sir John is not expected
here till Michaelmass. Dr Smith shewed me a note or two concerning
the Etymology of the word Coventre,[16] which I copied out, tho' I was
not a stranger to it before. This is all I have done in an hour & an half
which I spent in the Library, which is not so spatious & well adorn'd
as your Colledge Libraries much less as the Bodleyan. It is a very little
Room, not above half so big as The Masters Study, neither are the
Books many in number, perhaps four or five hundred, tho' in one
Book 3 or 4 mens works may be bound up together. Pray Sir, be so
kind as to send mr Gibsons direction where I may buy the Saxon
Gospells,[17] & you will much add to the Obligations you have allready
conferred on

    Dear Sir
      Your most humble ser[vant]

                        H Wanley

MS: Bodleian, Tanner 24, fo. 1. *Date*: 'London Ap.19. 1695.' *Address*: 'For Mr Tanner at
his Chamber in All-Souls Colledge In Oxford.'

7. *To* [Thomas Tanner] *23 April 1695*

Dear Sir
    To day I waited again on Mr Worsley who ha's received the box of
MSS he lent you.[1] He ha's been so kind as to lend me his Wicklef,
which I wil, God willing transcribe, tho' that which I believe was the
Preface to the New Test: is half wanting.[2] He says he wil lend me his
Postils too.[3] I have seen some more of his sermons in Mr Pepyses
noble Library,[4] he ha's received your book,[5] & speaks extreamly kindly

traced this transcript which would be of interest in view of the damage suffered by the
manuscript in the fire of 1731, nor do I know whether Wanley ever completed it as he
clearly intended.

[16] Not identified.
[17] See no. 5 n. 2.

[1] See Worsley to Tanner d. 25 Apr. 1695, Bodl. MS Tanner 24, fo. 10.
[2] BL Harley MS 1666. See no. 5 n. 7.
[3] *CMA* II. i, no. 6908, now BL Harley MS 1730; described by Wanley in the Harleian
Catalogue as 'really a Collection of Sermons de Tempore, for the whole Year'.
[4] Probably Magdalene College, Cambridge, Pepys MS 2498, entitled 'Wickleefs Sermons' but not in fact sermons—see *Review of English Studies*, xv (1939), pp. 1–15, 129–45.
[5] Probably Tanner's *Notitia Monastica* (Oxford, 1695).

of you, he says, that he wil write to you the next post, & desire you to Continue Dr Heylyns Catalogue of the Nobility down to these times, in truth, it would be a work that would be very beneficial to all that are desirous to know any thing of our English History, & I could heartily wish that you would set upon it. For to speak sincerely, I know none more fit than Mr Tanner, to do his country this piece of service.[6] Mr Pepys do's not in the least imagine that I did talk of you premeditately. My Lord Bishop,[7] thinks to send me to Oxford this term,[8] I hope then I shal have the happiness to see you, & embrace you, for whom I have a true & cordial respect, not to be expressed by words. Pray Sir, give my humble service to the Master,[9] Mr Gibson, & Mr Thwaites, & always reckon me

Dear Sir
>Your most humble servant

>>H Wanley

MS: Bodleian, Tanner 24, fo. 24. *Date*: 'London April 23. 1695.'

8. *To* Thomas Tanner *3 May 1695*

Dear Sir
I now can tell you for certain that I shal be settled in Edmond-hall with Dr Mills, for whom I have already a great respect & honor.[1] I am glad that Oxford must be[2] the place of my Education, for several

[6] P. Heylyn, Ἡρωολογια *Anglorum: or an Help to English History Containing a Succession of All the Kings of England &c.* (1641). Four revisions had appeared by 1680. For an earlier suggestion that it should be revised by Robert Plot, see Ellis, *Original Letters*, pp. 221–2.

[7] Lloyd.

[8] See no. 8 and n. 1.

[9] Charlett.

[1] John Mill (1645–1707), New Testament scholar, Principal of St Edmund Hall, Oxford 1685–1707. If we are to believe Hearne, Wanley's respect was not reciprocated: 'Dr Mill used to say [of Wanley] that he wanted both probity and learning, and that he was sure he would never have either' (Hearne, *Collections*, vi, p. 64).

Wanley's subscription and oath taken on admission to the University d. 9 May 1695, is in Welbeck Wanleyana = BL Loan MS 29/260 misc. 57. Richard Rawlinson notes that the entry of his matriculation in the Bedell's book is in a different hand from the rest and adds: 'Q whether not inserted by himself' (Bodl. MS Rawl. J. 4° 1, fo. 272ᵛ). While at Oxford Wanley was supported by an exhibition, the cost of which was borne by Coventry Council.

[2] me MS.

Reasons, & for this especially, because I can have conversation with you & my other friends. I have had no time til now to tell you that I have received your last weeks letter, tho I transcribed Wicklef[3] thro' last Saterday. For this week I have waited on my Lord[4] often (whose kindness to me encreases) & some of my friends, & have copied many Tunes for the Flute,[5] which I wil bring with me to Oxon. Pray give my most humble service to the Master, & tel him that I take Coach next monday, & on Tuesday (God willing) you shal see

    Dear Sir

        Your most humble & faithful servant

                              H. Wanley

MS: Bodleian, Tanner 24, fo. 41. *Date*: 'London May 3. 1695.' *Address*: 'For Mr Tanner at his Chamber in All Souls Colledge In Oxford.'

9. *To* [John Bagford][1] *15 September 1695*

Sir

    I hope you got safe up to London, tho' I thought you would have sent me word, so before now. I delivered your Catalogues to Mr Tanner & Mr Floyd,[2] with whom I am by this means become acquainted, & hope to be much obliged to him.

    I would beg of you, when next you See Major Ayres,[3] to give my

---

[3] See no. 7.

[4] Lloyd.

[5] In which Wanley was skilled. Thomas Astle also declares that he was 'a very able Composer' (*Catalogue of the Harleian Collection*, i (1808), p. 26). Cf. Charlett's report of the singing of an Italian lady in Oxford: 'What Credit she has among the Masters of Music, you are the best Judge' (Charlett to Wanley d. 27 June 1705, Welbeck Wanleyana = BL Loan MS 29/253).

---

[1] John Bagford (1650–1716), shoemaker, professional collector of, and amateur dealer in, books. Amassed a huge collection of material to do with the history of printing and issued in 1707 *Proposals for an Historical Account of Typography*, which Wanley seems to have drafted, but which came to nothing: see no. 110 and n. 3. His collections were acquired by Harley after his death (much to Hearne's chagrin—see *Collections*, vii, p. 287, under the date 20 Oct. 1721) and are now BL Harley MSS 5892–5998; strays are BL Lansdowne MS 808, Bodl. MSS Tanner 453 and Rawl. D. 396, and probably BL Harley MS 7580. Bagford also owned Harley 5414, 5419.

[2] Apparently William Lloyd (*c*.1674–1718), Chancellor of Worcester 1706–18. But see no. 13.

[3] John Ayres (*fl.* 1680–1700), calligrapher and writing-master of the Hand-and-Pen, St Paul's Churchyard. The rank of major (he is also spoken of as 'Colonel') refers to his position in the city bands.

humble service to him, and[4] ask him if he will part with his Raphael,[5] for Dr Charlet ha's since you went, spoken to me severall times about it. I am in great hast

Sir

Your obliged humble servant

Humfrey Wanley

MS: British Library, Harley 4966, art. 23. *Date*: 'Edmund hall. Sept. 15. 1695.'

10. *To* [John Bagford] *31 October 1695*

Sir

I have been at the Blew Boar & made a strict Enquiry after your things, & at last with much ado, I understoo[d] that one Mathews a Carrier received them about a month since. I went to Mathews his lodgings, but he is at London & nothing can be done til he come's home. In your next, you must send your Friends direction or else it wil be impossible to find it out. I went to Mr Lloyd,[1] but he is gone to Bristoll, when he come's home, which will be some time the next week, I will not fail to tell him what you desire. The Master of University Colledge is likewise gone out of Town, but at his Return I wil acquaint him with what you say of Raphaels Prints of the Bible[2] & the other book you mention, & send you his Answer. I shal have a Grant of that place in the Bodleyan Library I told you off, the 8th day of the next Month; so that I shal be enabled to serve you & the Bookseller according to my Promise.[3] As for the Medals If you cant agree for them 'tis no

---

[4] as MS.

[5] See no. 10 n. 2.

---

[1] See no. 9 and n. 2.

[2] *Imagines Veteris ac Novi Testamenti* (Rome, 1674). Ayres had already parted with his copy but Bagford reports that two further copies were soon to be sold at auction (Bagford to Wanley d. 29 Oct. [1695], Harley 3777, fo. 146).

[3] Wanley had been given notice that at the annual meeting of the Curators of the Bodleian on 8 Nov. he was to be appointed Assistant in the Library at a salary of £12 a year. The bookseller was John Hartley of Holborn (*fl.* 1697–1709), and the service preferred by Wanley presumably had to do with the catalogue of books being compiled by Hartley (see no. 12) from the Bodleian and other libraries, pbd. in 1699 as *Catalogus Universalis Librorum in Omni Facultate* (reissued in 1701 with an index of authors). It may be that Wanley undertook to provide details of books present in the Bodleian but not in the ptd. library catalogue of 1674. In his Preface to vol. i, Hartley makes a point of declaring that many books listed in his catalogue are not in the Oxford catalogue. The

great matter, for I had rather stay til I can better spare money to buy them. Notwithstanding I hope to pay you what I ow you within a fortnight at furthest, for I have been put to many unexpected charges, else I would not have trespassed so much on your Patience who am

Sir

   Your faithful servant

Humfrey Wanley.

MS: British Library, Harley 4966, art. 24. *Date*: 'Edmund-hall Octob. 31. 1695.'

11. *To* [Thomas Gale][1] *7 November 1695*

Honored Sir

I have now, as you see, finished, collated & sent you Proclus, which ha's been a work of much more tediousness than I expected. When I began it I purposed to send it you by last Lammas day at farthest; & seeing it was the first Greek MS I ever copied, I was prevailed upon by our Principal to take 4£ for the Copie. But now since it ha's cost me as much more time as I thought it would, I must needs say that if I have not 40s more, I am & shall be a great loser by it.[2]

You may be pleased to return the money by this bearer, as much in Gold & as little in Half Crowns as you think fit, I know I need not caution you to send what is good, because you must needs be sensible that Bad money will create You & I much trouble. I have put the number of the leaves of the Original MS all along on the extremities of the Margent, because if you should chance to doubt of any thing & to require farther satisfaction, you might be enabled to give the surer

two men remained on good terms and Wanley lodged with Hartley when he finally quit Oxford for London in Dec. 1700. Perhaps Wanley had a hand in Hartley's pbn. of Sir Thomas Bodley's *Reliquiae Bodleianae* in 1703.

---

[1] Thomas Gale (*c*.1635–1702), Regius Professor of Greek at Cambridge 1666–72, High Master of St Paul's 1672–97, Dean of York 1697.

[2] The commentary of Proclus (AD 410–85) on Plato's *Parmenides*, copied from Bodl. MS Auct. F.3.23 (*SC* 2533). The transcript is Trinity College, Cambridge MS 0.5.10, to which this letter and a receipt for £4 are prefixed.

directions for consulting the Original, which if you shal be so minded,
I wil do at any time for yóu, who am
    Honored Sir
        Your most faithful & humble servant

                                 Humfrey Wanley.

MS: Trinity College, Cambridge, 0.5.10; inserted at beginning of Wanley's transcript.
Date: 'Edmund-hall. Nov. 7. 1695.'

12. *To* John Bagford *21 November 1695*

Mr Bagford
    I am heartily sorry that I have kept you so long without your money,
but I wil now pay it here, or send it to London, where or how you
please, with ten thousand thanks.
    The University have given me a new Station in the Bodlejan
Library, & if you send me the Booksellers Direction (I mean that
young man who was here with you & is making that Catalogue of
Books you talked of)[1] I will write to him & proffer him what Assistance
lie's in my Power, & this is meerly for your sake, whom (without
flattery be it spoken) I sincerely respect.
    Mr Lloyd[2] is come home, & when I delivered your Message to him,
he sayd he ha's forgot your Promise. In Expectation of your Answer as
to the payment of the money I remain
    Sir
        Your most humble servant

                                 Humfrey Wanley

MS: British Library, Harley 4966, art. 25. *Date*: 'Edmund-hall. Nov. 21th. 1695.'

13. *To* [William Lloyd] *30 January 1696*

May it please your Lordship,
    I must humbly crave your Lordships pardon for my assertion that
the Acta St Ignatij was not in our Library. Dr Mill told me it was not in

        [1] See no. 10 n. 3.   [2] See no. 9 n. 2.

England, tho' now he is glad he was overseen, & yet I looked over our
Catalogue of MSS to be sure. Had your Lordship sent word where
Arch Bishop Usher said we had it, I should have found it before, tho' I
think now 'tis not too late.[1] By our Catalogue I found the Acta in
Latine amongst Bishop Lauds books, which is at least 400 years old,[2] I
shewed it to Mr Lloyd a master of Arts of Jesus Coll, & a man most
admirably wel versed in our Greek MSS,[3] he told me that Bishop
Usher had printed the same as he remembered in his Appendix to his
Ignatius,[4] I fetched the book & we found that our Copie agreed
verbatim (except now & then a various reading) with the Cottonian
MS,[5] only ours went farther than it, & of the [two] seemed the best
Copie. We likewise [fou]nd the place where he positively said the
Greek was in our Library, & gave us 3 or 4 lines of the Beginning; I was
then resolved to find it if possible. But before I looked for it we took
our Latine Copie I mean that Copie which begins p.29 to Bollandus,[6]
& found them to agree very well together, only at the latter end the
Burgundian MS had these words more than ours *Sed translatio corporis
ejus non minori obsequio 16to Cal. Ian recolitur: praestante Domino nostro Iesu
Christo, qui vivit & regnat in secula seculorum. Amen*.[7] We then viewed all
the Greek MSS we could think on, & at last when we dispaired of finding it, we lighted on it by chance amongst Bishop Lauds books in a
Greek MS which goes under Simeon Metaphrastes his name, but I
question whether he is the author of it,[8] for we compared these Acta

---

[1] See no. 14.

[2] Bodl. MS Laud lat. 31 (*SC* 1549) fos. 118 f., a twelfth-/thirteenth-century copy.

[3] Certain identification of Lloyds at Jesus is difficult in this period (as in most others)
but the most likely candidate is William Lloyd (*c.*1674–1718), Chancellor of Worcester
1714–18. A very considerable objection to this is that he is the son of Bishop Lloyd,
Wanley's patron, to whom the present letter is addressed, and it is hard to believe that
Wanley would be unaware of the relationship, as what follows implies. The younger
Lloyd seems to have helped Gibson in revising his English translation of Camden's
Britannia in 1695, and was author of a work on Greek chronology—which would sort
very well with Wanley's description of him as one 'admirably wel versed in our Greek
MSS' (although the book was said to be chiefly the work of his father).

[4] *Appendix Ignatiana* (1647).

[5] Of the *Acta* ptd. by Usher in the Appendix: Otho D.viii 'burnt to a crust' in the fire
of 1731.

[6] *Acta Sanctorum*, February, i, pp. 13 f.

[7] As cited in *Acta Sanctorum*, February, i, p. 33, par. 21 (n^m).

[8] Bodl. MS Laud Gr. 69 (*SC* 735) fos. 245^v f., an eleventh-century copy. Wanley
seems to have changed his mind about the attribution: under *Simeon* in the index to the
catalogue of Bodleian manuscripts in *CMA* (which is by Wanley), it is assigned to
Simeon Metaphrastes, the principal compiler of the legends of the saints in the Meno-
logia of the Byzantine Church.

with Cortelerius his Metaphrastes, & find them to be vastly different,[9] & yet we have an Anonimous author amongst the Baroccian MSS, which agrees with Cortelerius.[10] Upon the whole, we found that this MS of Bishop Lauds, which the Library keeper (not the book it self, for it is trun[cated)] calls Metaphrastes, is the original of [the] other; & this Copie (to speak modestly) between 7 & 800 years old. There is no Iota subscriptum but τῆι & τῶι, as your Lordship wil see by the following specimen. The Accents are all after the old fashion, & the pointing & hand likewise. Now this being translated into Latin after ages made some interpolations, especially towards the beginning, this is seen in the Cottonian, Bollandus, & our own Latin Copie. But afterwards others added yet much more to make the story more diverting, as we took notice in Cortelerius, & the Baroccian MS which is not above 300 years old. Our antient Acta[11] begins thus

Ἐν ἔτει ἐννάτωι τῆσ βασιλείασ τραιανοῦ καίσαρος δευτέρωι μηνὶ. ἐν ὑπατίαι ἀττικοῦ καὶ σουρβανοῦ καὶ μαρκέλλου. ἰγνάτιοσ ἐπίσκοποσ τῆσ ἐν ἀντιοχείαι ἁγίασ τοῦ Θεοῦ ἐκκλησίασ. δεύτεροσ μετὰ τοὺσ ἀποστό- λους γενόμενοσ. εὐώδιον γὰρ διεδέξατο. μετὰ ἐπιμελεσάτησ φρουρῶν φυλακῆσ. ἀπὸ συρίασ ἐπὶ τὴν ῥώμην παρεπέμφθη τῆσ εἰς χριστὸν ἕνεκα μαρτυρίασ.

I do not doubt but 'tis the same book which Bishop Usher means notwithstanding the little difference there seems to be between them [for] I suppose he never saw it himself [or at] least could not find it again, none of [Lau]ds MSS being then placed, in those shelves where they now stand. For if he could have got the Original which was genuine, 'tis not likely he would have printed Copies, with many Interpolations, & but Translations.

Afterwards we searched into 5 several Latin MSS, containing[12] the lives of Saints, whereof the newest was as old as Bishop Lauds Latin Acta, & the oldest 700 years old, if perchance we might find a just Latin of our oldest Greek; but our labor was in vain. I am heartily glad our Library can afford your Lordship this glorious Monument of Antiquity, which tho' it is very difficult for a beginner, the MS having taken wet in many places, & the letters almost worn out; yet by Mr

[9] Jean-Baptiste Cotelier, *SS Patrum qui temporibus apostolicis floruerunt . . . cum Clementis, Ignatii, Polycarpi Actis atque Martyriis* (Paris, 1672).
[10] Bodl. MS Barocci 192 (*SC* 192) fos. 62ᵛ f.
[11] i.e. Laud Gr. 69.
[12] containg MS.

Lloyds assistance, I hope to have taken a true & fair Copie of it sometime next week, & wil send it your Lordship by the first opportunity.[13]

Our Treasure of Greek MS, is not well known, & I my self since I
have been in this station have found some others, not yet taken notice
of in any of our Catalogues.

I am &c.

MS: British Library, Harley 6430, p. 57; draft, unsigned. *Date*: 'Jan. 30. 1695/6. Univ.
College.'

14. *To* [Thomas Smith] *8 February 1696*

Honored Sir,

I am very sensible of the Favors I have received from you, particularly in shewing me Sir John Cottons Library, which if I had been able,
I should have made requital for, before now.

I know very well too, how unworthy I am of being known to you, Sir;
yet, seeing I am in a new Post in the Bodlejan Library, I presume I may
not be altogether useless. 'Tis Gratitude, Sir, as well as Inclination,
that causes me to proffer you my most humble service; And as an
earnest of it, I thought fit to take this Opportunity of informing you,
that to morrow, I shall (God willing) send up to the Bishop of Cov. &
Lichfield, the Acta S. Ignatij in Greek, which I have copied from an
antient MS in this Library.[1] I know my Lord will lend it you, as soon as
he ha's read it over. It is not altogether free from interpolations; but yet
ha's fewer than the Latin Cottonian Acta, printed by Bishop Usher; of
which likewise we have a Copie between 4 & 500 years old.[2] And it is
different from Cottelerius his Metaphrastes, & Ruinhartus;[3] being
also more noble & genuine. I wish it may prove any ways serviceable to
you in your intended Edition of Ignatius,[4] who am

Honored Sir,

Your most humble servant

Humfrey Wanley.

[13] Sent 9 Feb. 1696: see no. 14.

---

[1] Bodl. MS Laud Gr. 69. See no. 13.
[2] Bodl. MS Laud lat. 31. See no. 13.
[3] Thierri Ruinart, *Acta Primorum Martyrum Sincera et Selecta* (Paris, 1689).
[4] In collaboration with J. Pearson. A specimen was pbd. as early as 1696 (Bodl. MS
Smith 133) but the edn. did not appear until 1709.

I am removed from Edmund-hall to this College, having by the Masters liberality a Chamber in his own lodgings[5]

MS: Bodleian, Smith 54, fo. 73. *Date*: 'University-College. Feb. 8th 1695/6.'

15. *To* [John Bagford] *15 March 1696*

Dear Sir

I had informed you long before now, of my removal from Edmund-hall to this College (where our Master ha's received me into his own Lodgings, & shew's me all the Kindness in the world) had I not sent 3 letters to you before to tell you that the 10s was ready; & hearing nothing from you, I concluded you was dead, sick, or gone a Journey. But being by chance in Edmund hall yesterday morning, your letter came to me & the Parcel directed to me both together. I saw nothing for Mr Lloyd, because the Carter was gone before I read yours, & I think Mr Loyd is out of town.[1] I have not seen Mr Gibson yet, but when I do, I wil tell him. I heartily thank you, for your kindness as to the Sax. & Goth. Gospells, but I shall have no occasion now for one, The Vice-chancellor having already presented me with one in Royall Paper.[2] You forgot to seal up the Parcel, & I think it was opened, because you said there were some prepared Quills, but I saw none besides one prepared Quil entire, & another already made into a Pen. I heartily thank you for 'em & value the book of Painting particularly,[3] with the Stile, which its pitty should be broken at the point. I should be very glad to see any pieces of Antiquity or other Curiosities, as a Chinesse pen, you mentioned, or any of the Brass Pens; for I by a mischance spoiled mine, which I much lamented it having done me much service. If you can procure any, I wil honestly pay & with thanks what you shal think them worth, with these I have now received from you. But I can't now tell what to do as to the 10s, for I hav[e] but one penny in sillver in the world. I have lost by Guineas very much & in a suit of clothes I have lately bought & other things, I lost 3s by every Guinea.

[5] Wanley lodged with Charlett until he left Oxford for good in Dec. 1700.

[1] Bagford's letter d. 12 Mar. 1696, BL Harley MS 3777, fo. 129.
[2] See no. 5 n. 2.
[3] The contents of the parcel are listed by Bagford in his letter, but there is no mention of a 'book of Painting'.

And I have now by me 3 Guineas more which I took at 30s a piece, &
no[w] I cannot let[4] them go for 24s. If you can get them off at 30s or at
28s apiece, which you may perhaps have an opportunity of doing in
London; I wil send them to you & take it as an exceeding kindness to
    Dear Sir
        Your most humble & obliged servant

                                                    H. Wanley.

direct for me at Univ. College.

MS: British Library, Harley 4966, art. 21. *Date*: 'University College March. 15. 1695/6.'

16. *To* [William Lloyd] *2 April 1696*

May &c.

Since the Principal[1] went to London, I have lighted upon another
copie of the Acta Ignatij in Latine,[2] which is the same with one which I
shewed him, & of which I have formerly given your Lordship an
account; both these agree with the Cottonian MSS so far as that goes.[3]

Bishop Usher in his Dissertation on that version of the Septuagint
informes me of the Book of Job which we have of St. Hierom's Translation with Origens Asterisks & Obelisks. When I knew that, I was on
fire till I could see the book, & for the sake of this, I have looked into
every Latine Bible we have, which are between 40 & 50 in number, &
have found it at last.[4] The Title of the book declares it to be translated
by St Hierome out of the Septuagint, & before it is St Hieromes
preface, declaring his great pains & exactness in this Translation &
the use of the Asterisks ✳ & obelisks ÷ vizt to shew where the Hebrew
ha's more than the Greek, or the Greek more than the Hebrew. The
Book it self is quite different from the Vulgar Latine Job which likewise follows in the same book.

This Bible is excellently well written painted & Gilded, about 600
years ago, in 2 huge Volumes, so heavy that a man cannot well carry
them both together, in this order. The first Voll. contains the Penta-

----

[4] get MS.

----

[1] Mill.
[2] Perhaps Bodl. MS Laud misc. 114 (*SC* 1547) fos. 61ᵛ f.
[3] See no. 13.
[4] Bodl. MSS Auct. E. inf. 1–2 (*SC* 2426–7) of the twelfth century.

teuch &c. to the end of the 4 books of Kings, then the Prophets & lastly the 2 abovementioned versions of Job. The second voll. begins with the Psalter in 2 versions likewise, the Vulgate & the Gallic, then Prov. Eccles. Cant. Wisdom. Ecclus. Chronicles, Ezra Ester with the Aporypha. Tobit, then Judith in 2 versions likewise, then Machabees. The New Test. begins with the Acts, then the 7 Catholic Epistles, then the Revel. then Pauls Epistles & last of all the Gospells. The Books are divided into chapters after the old manner (not after Stephen Langtons way)[5] with the number of the chapters & Arguments of them at the beginning of each book (or division) & of verses at the end.

We have 3 Bibles more (about 400 years old apiece) which have the said 2 versions of the Psalms.[6] But another book about 700 years old, or more: has all the 3 versions of the Psalter translated by St Hierome, that after the Hebrew, the Roman & the Gallic,[7] which last book I have shewed the Principal, who can tell your Lordship more of it. The Principal told me we had an Arabic Pentateuch translated from the Septuagint, with Origens Asterisks &c. I found that out too, tho' with some trouble, & shewed it likewise to the Principal. Bishop Usher makes mention of it at the same time as he does of our Job. And some of the Readings are to be found in the Polyglott Bibles. The Preface is not entire nor yet extant.[8] Tho' the Preface of another Arabick Pentateuch we have (which ha's likewise the Asterisks &c) is translated by Dr Pocock when he was very young & first began to study the Language therefore without mention of his name, & printed in Dr Bernard's Aristaeas.[9]

These 2 Pentateuchs are very old, & yet are both written upon Paper, for the Eastern Nations have used Paper longer than we, I can't

---

[5] † 1228. His division of the books of the Bible into chapters has been generally accepted ever since.

[6] Bodl. MSS Auct. D.1.18 (*SC* 2056) of the thirteenth century, Auct. D.3.2 (*SC* 2032) of the early fourteenth century, and Auct. D.3.5 (*SC* 4100) of the thirteenth century.

[7] Bodl. MS Laud lat. 35 (*SC* 1153) written *c*.832–42. I owe the identification to the late Dr R. W. Hunt.

[8] Probably Bodl. MS Laud Or. 258 (*SC* 446) described by Uri (*Bibliothecae Bodleianae codicum manuscriptorum Orientalium . . . Catalogus* (Oxford, 1787), as 'cum praefatione in initio mutila'; the first leaves are now mounted; a modern note says that only one leaf seems to be missing at the beginning.

[9] Probably Bodl. MS Laud Or. 243 (*SC* 445). Both this manuscript and Laud Or. 258 contain the piece ptd. by Bernard 'Ex praefatione in Pentateuchi Arabici bina exemplaria inter MSS Laudina' (*Aristeae Historia LXXII Interpretum* (Oxford, 1692), p. 131).

determine when they first invented it, but I know we have Oriental books upon paper about, if not above 600 years old, & Greek MSS upon paper are common between 3 & 400 years old. Who knows but that the Greeks after the destruction of their Countrey by the Turks, might not bring some of their Manual Arts into these parts of Europe, as well as they did their learning? Indeed their paper (being made of Cotton) is different from that of the first printed books; but yet I fancy ours, tho' made of Raggs, might be but an improvement of theirs. Can it be thought the Author of so useful a Commodity would have concealed his Name, if the Invention was the product of his own Ingenuity, & not learnt from another? or that he would have failed of his due praises amongst so many learned & grateful men as flourished soon after? The use of paper was long before so universal over all the East, that among some thousands of their MSS, I have never yet seen but 2 books in Syriack, one in Coptic, one in Arabic, one in Samaritan, & none in Turkish, Persian &c. Three or 4 in Æthiopic, & but one in Russian in Parchment. The Jews indeed have long used it, & stil do so to this day, & of their writings we have great numbers in Parchment, & some vast Rolls of Leather, which are thought to be very antient, tho' the characters upon them seem very fresh & new to me.

The paper used by the Arabians &c. may be an Improvement of the Chinese which is made (as some say) of silk, they have had books & printing time out of mind; if so, 'tis no wonder we know not who it was that first invented it. The Chinese an delicate but ingenious people might first invent their fine Paper, this might from them be learnt by the Arabs, or Saracens very easily, who might be glad of the invention, but because the matter of it not being so common in their parts of the world; & the paper it self so thin that the Chinese books are mostly printed but on one side of the Paper (their leaves being doubled in their books, are but as ours single) and not so apt to bear writing Ink; I say, the Arabs might from this hint, make their Paper of Cotton, which might be cheaper, more substantial, smooth, & fitter to bear Ink. From them it might as easily come to the Greeks, who having store of Cotton, presently lay aside Parchment & write upon the new Paper, and at last as I said before, bring it into the more Northern Parts of the world, even to Basil, if they wil have it so. Here Cotton being scarce, Necessity the Mother of Inventions, forces them to make use of Raggs, which every Countrey produces, & which being cheap & most convenient for us, ha's continued ever since. I am very sensible, that

Parchment continued long after printing was here used, many books being printed upon it in Greek as well as Latin which have their dates; as well as many others which being without date, go for MSS, as in English one vice versa, being certainly written, pretends to be printed by Wynkin de Word, a noted London Printer.[10] Neither was writing confined to Parchment or Paper alone, for we have an Armenian Book written upon Palm leaves with Ink,[11] not to mention many other such books written (or engraven) with a stile. The Japan Kalendar[12] is upon a particular sort of Paper, it seems to be made of Cotton, but is much thinner & more transparent than the ordinary Cotton paper. And an Alcoran we have in Arabic, written upon Linnen cloth with Pen & Ink, which cloth is yet in the shape of a Cross.[13] My mentioning the Alcoran puts me in mind of a little Arab. MS. containing some Suratas of it, neatly written, & adorned, which book is perfumed, & in my search into the Latin Bibles, I found one about 400 years old, in an old fashioned Velvet cover, perfumed likewise.[14] Quare, whether they were so perfumed out of reverence to the books, or by their sweet smell to incite people to take them up the oftner? However I was well pleas'd that us Christians in this point were not outdone by the Infidels. I have presumed to send your Lordship this account of some of our Books, because I perceive your Lordship was not displeased with the notice I gave, of those Greek MSS, being written upon one another,[15] who am

MS: British Library, Harley 6430, p. 61; draft, unsigned. *Date*: 'April. 2. 96.' *Address*: 'To the same.'

[10] Probably Bodl. MS Arch. Selden B.10 (*SC* 3356) fos. 200–9, a collection of excerpts from Lydgate entitled 'The Proverbs upon the Fall of Princes', copied (in the first quarter of the sixteenth century) as the colophon states, from one of the ptd. edns. of Wynkyn de Worde, *STC* 17026 [1515?] or 17027 [1520?]. I am indebted for this information to Mr Malcolm Parkes.

[11] No Armenian manuscript acquired in the seventeenth century is described by Baronian and Conybeare (*Catalogue of the Armenian Manuscripts in the Bodleian Library* (Oxford, 1918)) as written on palm leaves.

[12] Probably the almanac for the year 1614, now Vet. Or. d. Jap. 1 (R).

[13] Bodl. MS Or. 162ª (*SC* 3626) 'given by Richard Davydge, London merchant, 1653'.

[14] Neither now identifiable, by smell or otherwise.

[15] No. 13.

17. *To* Francis Bugg[1] *6 April 1696*

You must needs think it strange to receive a letter from a man utterly unknown to you. Yet the same motive which make you to publish your useful books, I mean the public good, causes me to become a Petitioner to you, in the behalf of the Public Library of Oxford, in which place I have the Honor of being a Servant to our University.[2] I have seen your Book called The Quakers set in their true Light[3] at the End of which is a Catalogue of 15 books more all written by you. The Quakers have allready presented us with Foxes Journal Barclays works &c.[4] [well?] bound in the best Paper; I'me certain it would be extreamly well taken, if you would be pleased to send us your own Works, which are so capable of Instructing those who are desirous of hearing what can be said on both sides. Here they wil be for ever preserved, & your Donation shal be particularly registred among the other Benefactions, by
  Sir &c.

MS: British Library, Harley 6430, p. 67; draft, unsigned. *Date*: 'April. 6. 1696.' *Address*: 'Mr Bugg.' *Printed*: P. L. Heyworth, 'Humfrey Wanley and "Friends" of the Bodleian, 1695–98', *Bodleian Library Record*, ix (1973–8), p. 220.

18. *To* Edward Owen[1] *16 April 1696*

Honored Sir,
  Yesterday I had the Happiness to see your Son Mr Abraham Owen here. After I had shewn him the Gallery of Pictures adjoyning to our Public Library, I would have begged one of him, to encrease our now

---

[1] Francis Bugg senior, wool-comber, of Mildenhall, Suffolk.
[2] This is the first of a number of begging letters on behalf of the Bodleian: see also nos. 18, 19, 20, 21, 23. See further 'Humfrey Wanley and "Friends" of the Bodleian, 1695–98', *Bodleian Library Record*, ix (1973–8), pp. 219–30.
[3] Pbd. 1696.
[4] Fox's *Journal* (1694), Bodl. press-mark S.1.8.Th., a copy of the first edn., first issue of the work, and Robert Barclay's *Theologiae vere Christianae Apologia* (Amsterdam, 1676), Bodl. press-mark 4° B.41.Th., inscribed 'Donum Authoris', are presumably the works Wanley refers to.

---

[1] Edward Owen († 1705), Mayor of Coventry 1680–1, 1696–7. See *The Letters of Daniel Defoe*, ed. G. H. Healey (Oxford, 1955), p. 105 n. 1.

small number, which does not fill half the Gallery. Mr Owen excused himself by telling me, I had better write to you, Sir, who are so well furnished with some Rarities we want; & would, he thought, be willing to part with them for the public Good.

The things we want in our said Library are such as these, Books, Prints, Medals & Pictures. I am very sensible of the great Collection you have of most of these. We are ready to receive any thing, nothing comes amiss, tho' some things may be more acceptable than others. As for Books, some modern ones in French or Italian; or rather, any thing that is curious, let it be of what Age, Countrey or Language soever. For Prints, Mr Evelyn ha's given us an exceeding great Paper-book, with some Prints in it,[2] but we have room enough in it for Thousands more, let them be either Histories, Postures or Heads. I know, Sir, you have great numbers of them, besides your Mapps, Prospects & Draughts of Fortifications, which if you please to send, we will willingly place in their Order & keep 'em so. Of Medalls, we have already a great Collection, but yet it is capable of receiving large Additions, we have room for Coins of any sort, either old or new, of any Mettal, Size, Prince or Place. Then for Pictures, we have no Histories or Landskips, &c, but all Pourtraits of our Founders on the one side, & of some other eminent Persons on the other. If you please to send any, you need not fear sending a Duplicate, for our Stock is but small, & some of them done by pittiful Masters.[3]

Sir, whatever you send, will be more useful in this University than in Coventry, your Collections will be for ever kept entire, & with care, your name shall be written upon each of them. But if your Donation is worth 40s your Memory shall be preserved in our Book of Benefactions, & the particular things you give, registred in it: and with your Coat of Arms too, painted in their proper Colors, if your Benefaction does reasonably exceed 40s.

By this you may see, Sir, how grateful we are, & shall prove to all our Patrons, & indeed to their own great Honor whenever our Catalogue of them shall be made Public. Altho' at present every body ha's free liberty to peruse it, it lying always ready in a certain place fo[r] that purpose. I shall write this Journey to Major Beak to beg something of

---

[2] See no. 23 n. 2.
[3] 'We have a great Gallery which goes round 3 sides of the Schools, yet we have not above ten or a dozen good Pictures in it, tho' 'twould contain some thousands' (no. 23). The Gallery was the present Upper Reading Room in the Old Bodleian.

him likewise, & shall give him some little account of our Public Joy on this day,[4] who am

Honored Sir

Your most obliged & humble servant

Humfrey Wanley.

MS: Bodleian, Eng. lett. c. 291, fo. 218. Draft in British Library Harley MS 6430, p. 68. *Date*: 'University College April. 16. 1696.' *Printed*: Sotheby's sale cat., 24 June 1975, lot 217 (extracts); P. L. Heyworth, 'Humfrey Wanley and "Friends" of the Bodleian, 1695–98', *Bodleian Library Record*, ix (1973–8), pp. 220–1.

19.   *To* Robert Beake[1]   [*17 April 1696*]

Mr Wakelin informed me in a Letter of his from Coventry, that you would be pleased to write a Line or two to me, by him.[2] But that being too great an Honor, & as I well know you being too ful of business, I could not expect it. However this does not hinder but that I may acquaint you after some sort with those demonstrations of Joy which have been made by our University upon the Thanksgiving.

Our University assembled in Convocation agreed to put their Common Seal to an humble Address to his Majesty, to congratulate his safe tho' wonderful deliverance from the late Barbarous & villanous contrivances form'd against his Sacred Person, & us all. That they could not so much as think upon it without horror & detestation. They acknowleged his Majesty to be invested with a Legal & Rightful Title to the Crown of these Realms, & would to the uttermost of their Power support & defend him in the Possession of it, against the late King James & all his Adherents, according to the late Act made in the first year of K.W. & Q. Mary, & would constantly instill the same Principles of Loyalty & Obedience in to all committed to their Care.

This Address was carried up to London by our Vice-Chancellor, & was received so kindly by his Majesty, that it ha's effectually removed

---

[4] See no. 19 n. 3.

[1] Robert Beake, Mayor of Coventry 1655–6.

[2] Apothecary of Coventry; it is not clear whether this is the same man (then known as 'Colonel Wakelin') who succeeded Wanley as occupant of 3 Duke St., Westminster—Wanley's house in London from 1704–11—and who lived there 1711–15 (*Survey of London xviii: The Strand* (1937), Appendix B, p. 133).

all prejudices (if there were any such) that he could have conceived against us. Yesterday was the Thanksgiving-day, & after prayers in every particular Colledge, as usual; all went to Church where the Vice-Chancellor read Prayers, & a Dr preached a Sermon suitable to the occasion, every thing looked splendid & noble, & the Anthems were sung & played with all cheerfulness. After Dinner the Whole University & all the Town besides almost were gathered together, in the Theater, where was heavenly Consorts of Vocal & Instrumental Music, all composed for the purpose, with Speeches, Declamations & verses spoken by Young Noblemen & Gentlemen, who all came off with applause. For my part, what with their Shouts & Acclamations, so much Music I heard, the Bells continually ringing, Guns at the Bone-fires &c. I am almost deaf, the Noise sounds in my head still.[3]

I have sent you a Paper which gives the names of those who behaved themselves so well in the Theater, with the subject of their several discourses. And a Slavonian or Russian Alphabet, here being Mr Ludolphus who now prints his Russian Grammar, the first of the Kind which has ever yet been made public, & the first Russian that ha's been printed in England.[4]

But Sir, tho' I send these things which are of no value, I am yet Tradesman enough to desire of you things of any value in return; only there is this Difference that I am your humble Petitioner in behalf of the Public, not of my self. And besides my own long knowledge of your Goodness & Public Temper, Mr Abraham Owen ha's encouraged me to beg something or other of you, as I have this Journey too, of his Father. Sir, 'tis not for me to appoint you what or where to give, yet you cannot part with your Rarities to a place where they can be so use-ful, as this, or where they, or your own Memory will be more carefully preserved, as I have sent Alderman Owen word. Your Manuscript set of Mapps, your Weevers funeral Monuments, Mr Gibsons new Camden, your Manuscripts relating to Coventry, would each or all of them be highly acceptable & serviceable to us, or indeed a Thousand other things you have & we want, which wants of ours I hope, Sir, you wil take into your Consideration & supply us as you shal think fit; we

---

[3] The occasion was the University's official celebration of the failure of a plot to assassinate William III, disclosed in the middle of February 1696, which caused great agitation in the country.

[4] The *Grammatica Russica* of Heinrich Wilhelm Ludolf. On the history of the book and its importance, see J. S. G. Simmons, 'H. W. Ludolf and the Printing of his Grammatica Russica at Oxford in 1696', *Oxford Slavonic Papers*, i (1950), pp. 104–29.

will be very Thankful for any thing, even for the old Popish Legend
Mr Ebral ha's of yours; for even that can do us service here, when we
have a mind to convince the Papists, of their Sottish Ignorance &
Superstition.[5]

I am &c.

MS: British Library, Harley 6430, p. 70; draft, unsigned. *Address*: 'To Major Beak.'
Printed: P. L. Heyworth, 'Humfrey Wanley and "Friends" of the Bodleian, 1695–98',
Bodleian Library Record, ix (1973–8), pp. 221–2 (extract).

20. *To* George Keith[1] *9 May 1696*

Sir,

A Letter I received from Mr Crispe inform's me that you have
written lately with much Learning & Judgement against the Quakers,
of whose persuasion, he says, you have been in your younger years,
tho' a Graduate in some University. I wrote a letter to Mr Bugg to beg
his printed works against these Quakers who have presented the
Bodlejan Library here, with G. Foxes Journal, Barclays works &c. My
letter came in to Mr Crisp's[2] hands who sent to me at the said Library
(in which place the University have been pleased to give me a Station)
three books of his own composure, 2 of each with a promise of procuring more from Mr Bugg & others. When he informed me so particularly of your Character, I was resolved to become one of your
Petitioners, for our Library, tho' I am sensible that my Confidence in
writing to a person I never saw may be liable to Censure: Yet a Con-

---

[5] Beake replied: 'I am Sorry yor request cannot prevaile wth me, my stock is soe
smale that the absence of a Gazet would lessen it, nor (in truth) are the things yow
mention fitt to appear in a Bodlejan Library, being at best but refuse, & not worthy of
yor acceptance, yet stuff, meete for my owne Raffling' (d. 21 May 1696, BL Harley MS
3777, fo. 167).

---

[1] George Keith (1639?–1716), MA Marischal College, Aberdeen; after becoming a
Quaker he travelled as an evangelist in Holland and Germany with George Fox and
William Penn before emigrating to America (1684), where he was Surveyor-General in
East New Jersey and then a schoolmaster in Philadelphia. He fell out with his own folk
and attempted to establish a sect called 'Christian Quakers' or 'Keithians', but was
unsuccessful both in America and on his return to England. He conformed to the
Anglican Church in 1700, was an agent of the SPG in America from 1702–4, and died as
rector of Edburton, Sussex.
[2] Thomas Crispe, by whose agency Francis Bugg's donation came to the library: see
no. 17 n. 2. Only Crispe's *Animadversions on Innocency Triumphant* (1694), is present still
in two copies in the Bodleian.

sideration of the public good ha's enabled me to overcome these & some other little difficulties, & even to assure my self of success. The end of your writing is certainly, to inform any who are desirous to inform themselfes of the Tenets of the Quakers, or of the Nature of the Controversy between them & us, to caution those who may be likely to be perverted, or to bring back those [who]³ may have gone over to 'em. Supposing this, your books cannot be placed any where more advantagiously than in our public Library; where students may see the answers to those writings the Quakers think unanswerable. Besides, there they may be all preserved together for posterity; & it shall as long be known who was the Donor, as well as who was the Author. I'me certain the greatest men of our University wil look upon them as a very acceptable present.⁴ *The Snake in the Grass* is famous here, Dr Charlett the Master of our Colledge (who ha's been pleased to give me a Chamber in his own Lodgings) shewed it me in his Study where he has a Collection all books of that sort & expressed a great esteem of it, & wished we had it in the Bodlejan Library;⁵ which I wish too, & hope for from your Generosity, which shall meet with ten thousand Thanks in the Name of the public from

Sir &c.

MS: British Library, Harley 6430, p. 73; draft, unsigned. *Date*: 'May. 9. 96.' *Address*: 'To Mr Keith.' *Printed*: P. L. Heyworth, 'Humfrey Wanley and "Friends" of the Bodleian, 1695–98', *Bodleian Library Record*, ix (1973–8), pp. 222–3.

21. *To* George Keith *15 May 1696*

I promised you the public Thanks if you would be pleased to send us your works at all, which I do sincerely & from my heart, yet, I think I ought to thank you again for your speed; you know the old Adage, qui cito dat, bis dat, at least the Obligation is much greater in giving quickly & cheerfully as you have done. I wil take care to have all the

---

³ MS omits 'who'.

⁴ Keith dispatched to Wanley within a week copies of all his books still in print. On the flyleaf of one of them, *Truth Advanced in the Correction of Many Gross & hurtful Errors* ([New York], 1694), Bodl. press-mark 4° U.73 Th., is the inscription of the donation by Keith, together with the titles of eleven other works by him presented at the same time. See Wanley's letter of acknowledgment, no. 21.

⁵ *The Snake in the Grass: or, Satan Transform'd into An Angel of Light* (1696) is, in fact, by Charles Leslie and was pbd. anonymously.

unbound books bound up decently together, & your name shall be written upon each of them.[1] You are pleased to entertain some thoughts of a Correspondence with me, I could wish I was worthy the favour of a letter from any man of Learning & Integrity, & from you [s]ooner than another. And although my youth (I being not 2 months above 24 years old) might justly hinder you from writing to me, yet the Harmony of our Tempers, & the Respect you shall always find from me, may at least plead, if not prevail in my behalf. I guess at your Disposition by these things. The Character Mr Crispe gave you; Your sending more than I asked you for: vizt your Neighbours book; & I make no question but you will look out for some more books of your own & other mens works too, for us in time.[2] Then the serious mind you desire should go along with the Readers of what you have sent; which disposition, I wish were to be truly found in every Reader & Hearer. And lastly, your profession of being one with all that sincerly believe & love the Lord Jesus Christ, which I hope every true Son of the Church of England does, which Church you know is very Charitable in her Opinions of others, & I trust you wil be no less to

    Sir &c.

MS: British Library, Harley 6430, p. 75; draft, unsigned. *Date*: 'May. 15. 1696.' *Address*: 'To Mr Keith.' *Printed*: P. L. Heyworth, 'Humfrey Wanley and "Friends" of the Bodleian, 1695–98', *Bodleian Library Record*, ix (1973–8), p. 223 (extract).

22. *To* [John Bagford] *24 May 1696*

Sir

    I have received the Books & your Letter for which I return you hearty Thanks.[1] I will give Mr Harding his to morrow. Mr Tanner is out of town, he sent for Nicander for Mr Potter a Fellow of Lincoln College, who is about a new Edition of him, I spake to Mr Potter about

  [1] See no. 20 n. 4.
  [2] Keith sent more books and papers, his own and others, 18 Feb. 1697, and a treatise on geometry by him on 19 Apr. 1697 (BL Harley MS 3780, fos. 20, 22). The treatise was hastily followed a week later by a request that it should neither be sent abroad nor put in the Bodleian, he having been persuaded by a fellow mathematician that it was defective (Keith to Wanley d. 24 Apr. 1697, Harley 3780, fo. 24).

  [1] d. 18 May 1696, BL Harley MS 3777, fo. 126.

it, but he ha's Gorraeus his Edition already.[2] So that you may very well, Pleasure your Friend in London with it. I humbly thank Mr Brand for his present of Trithemius his Polygraphia,[3] which book I know well, but can receive no information from him as to Alphabets, having besides him, seen Wormius, Vulcanius, Palatinus, Gramay, Duretus, Inghiramius,[4] & very many others in print, besides Manuscripts, from whence if I was at leasure, I could collect many hundreds were it worth while. Be pleased to give my most humble service to Mr Brand & tell him I know not how to acquit my self as to his Complements, which are of such a Nature, that I conceive one of them to be due to none but God alone. I know not how to return 'em, but this I say, that I think my self very much obliged to him for his present, & good wishes, & am & shal be willing to serve him or any of his friends in what lies within the compass of my little Sphere, whenever he thinks fit to employ me. One thing I have to desire of you, to send me word of any noble spirited and Worthy Gentlemen, who are Masters of any Curiosities which we want, and are or may be willing to part with them to our Library. The things we want are these, Books, either MSS or Printed. Medalls & Coins, Antient or Modern. Pictures & Prints or Maps &c. Of all these I would that the Bodlejan Library should be the Repository of a good Collection & would think it no trouble to write Letters, if I thought I could speed.[5] Those fragments of Saxon were part of an old MS in the Bodl. Library which contains Ælfric's preface to the following book, which is Genesis translated almost verbatim, & the rest of the Pentateuch, Joshuah & Judges abridged, With the same Ælfric's treatises of the Old & New Testament.[6] I know not what you would have me do with the piece of painting which was at the end of Stair. Don't neglect making enquiry after

[2] John Potter (*c*.1674–1747), Fellow of Lincoln College, Oxford, 1694–1706; later Regius Professor of Hebrew 1707–37, Bishop of Oxford 1715–37, Archbishop of Canterbury 1737–47. The edn. of Nicander is probably one of the sixteenth-century edns. of Joannes Gorraeus the Elder. Potter seems not to have completed his edition.

[3] Johann Tritheim, *Polygraphiae libri sex* ([Oppenheim], 1518).

[4] Perhaps the following: Ole Worm, *Monumenta Danica* (Copenhagen, 1643); Bonaventura Vulcanius, *De literis et lingua Getarum, sive Gothorum* (Leyden, 1597); Jean Baptiste Gramaye, *Specimen litterarum et linguarum universi Orbis* (Ath, [1622]); Giovanni Battista Palatino, *Libro nuovo d'imparare a scrivere tutte sorte lettere antiche et moderne di tutte nationi* (Rome, 1543); Claude Duret, *Thresor de l'Histoire des Langues de cet univers* (Cologny, 1613); Curzio Inghirami, *Ethruscarum Antiquitatum fragmenta* (Frankfurt, 1637)—all treatises on language and writing.

[5] See no. 17 n. 2.

[6] Bodl. MS Laud misc. 509 (*SC* 942). Ker no. 344, Wanley p. 67.

the Curious men, & send me word in your next what may be done with Mr Pepys or Mr Charlton, or any others whom you know better than I,[7] who am

    Sir

      Your most obliged servant

                              Humfrey Wanley

MS: British Library, Harley 4966 art. 31. *Date*: 'Univ. Coll. May 24. 1696.' *Printed*: P. L. Heyworth, 'Humfrey Wanley and "Friends" of the Bodleian, 1695–98', *Bodleian Library Record*, ix (1973–8), p. 220 (extract).

23. *To* Henry Puckering[1] [*? June 1696*]

The fame of your great Liberality to Trinity College in Cambridge ha's long since reached me, who have the Honor to serve this University in the Bodlejan Library. Where tho' we have a good Quantity of books both MSS & printed, yet we want, & have room for Myriads. We have a good foundation for a great Collection of Medalls of all Sorts, vizt. Orientall, Greek, Roman, British, Saxon, English, & modern ones of other Countreys, yet we cannot at present, make a perfect & entire series of any of these. We have a Roman Ring or two, & some few of the Roman gravings upon several stones, yet not so many as to be seen by Strangers. We have a vast large paper book given us by Mr Evelyn with some good Prints in it, as 2 or 3 of Titian, Michael Angelo, Raphael, Alb. Durer, Bassan. Hub. Golkius &c., & about half a score of Reubens, in this book is room for above 30 times more Prints than we have.[2] We have a great Gallery which goes round 3 sides of the Schools, yet we have not above ten or a dozen good Pictures in it, tho' 'twould contain some thousands.[3] This, Sir, is our present State, &

---

[7] In the matter of soliciting gifts for the Bodleian. For Charlton, see no. 24 n. 1.

---

[1] Sir Henry Puckering (1618–1701). In 1691 he gave the bulk of his library to Trinity College, Cambridge, and was afterwards some time in residence there. His gift may have included the Milton manuscripts which found their way to Trinity at about this time.

[2] Bodl. MS Auct. V.3.1. (*SC* 3933). The original donation of prints seems to have been that of Edward Scroop in 1659 (see Macray, p. 428), the donation of the *book* by Evelyn before 1685. 'Bassan.' is presumably an abbreviation of Jacopo Bassano (*c.*1515–92), the Venetian mannerist painter, and no doubt 'Hub. Golkius' conceals the name of Hendrik Goltzius (1558–1617), Dutch engraver and painter.

[3] See no. 18 and n. 3.

tho' we do not expect a Donation as large that Cambridge has received; it being the great Happiness of that University to be the Place of your Education: yet we hope that we shal have sufficient Reason to Register your Name in our Book of Benefactors.[4] Sir, we tell you our Wants, but leave it wholly to you to supply any of them in such measure, as you shall think fit; 'tis our parts to be thankful, not to prescribe to our Patrons.

Tis a Great Credit to oblige 2 Universities, one lies under everlasting engagements to you already, & we would willingly put on the same Chains too & be bound in Gratitude to pray to God Almighty publickly for your Health & prosperity while you live, & give him Thanks for you, when dead.

I am &c.

MS: British Library, Harley 6430, p. 77; draft, unsigned. *Address*: 'To Sir Henry Puckering.' *Printed*: P. L. Heyworth, 'Humfrey Wanley and "Friends" of the Bodleian, 1695–98', *Bodleian Library Record*, ix (1973–8), p. 226.

24. *To* —— [? *July 1696*]

[Em]perors, and the Roman (for I suppose them to be all antient) prove to be those small things of the Low-Empire, they would be worth little or nothing. I my self have now in my Eye above three hundred Coins, which will come for less than a penny apiece, and I am told that there is a Pertinax in Great Brass among them, which alone is worth more than what I can buy them all for. The intrinsic value of the Gold and silver should be looked after, for that may perhaps make 'em worth the money, not to mention the Beauty & Rarity of them.

But, Sir, I fancy you will rather chuse to provide Cabinets for medalls, & leave others to fill them: if so, surely Mr Charleton might be sollicited to bestow his Collection on our University, I understand from several that he is inclinable enough to do it, but that he's not willing that his Rarities should be an accession to anothers Donation, & called by another mans name, as there's no Reason it should.

Could not some such Proposals as these be made to him, that if he pleased the Anatomy school shall be adorned and new wainscoted, &

[4] Puckering seems not to have replied. His name is not found in the Benefactors' Register.

if it will not be large enough to hold all, that it shall either be made bigger, or a part of the Galleries shall be taken in and be made fit for this Purpose. That all the Curiosities now in the said Anatomy School or in the Studies belonging to the Library, and all the Coins given by Arch Bishop Laud & other Benefactors, being some thousands in number, and among which are many every way valuable, shall be brought & placed amongst his, and the whole for ever to be called *Musaeum Charltonianum*? Sir with submission I speak it, why should we lose the most considerable Study in England for want of asking, and especially when there may be some hopes of success? If it should be objected that they cost him a great deal of money, it may be said, that then he will ha[ve] the Honor of being the more noble Benefactor and wil doubtless reap more solid pleasure, in seeing those Curiosities of Art & Nature preserv'd together, in his own Countrey, with daily Additions, to have his Name for ever beloved & honored, Orations & set speeches & praiers made for him alive, that Statues & Inscriptions will be erected to his Memory when dead, rather than to sell them to another Nation, or be torn in pieces by a greedy Executor.[1]

I am &c.

MS: British Library, Harley 6430, p. 81; draft, incomplete. *Printed*: P. L. Heyworth, 'Humfrey Wanley and "Friends" of the Bodleian, 1695–98', *Bodleian Library Record*, ix (1973–8), p. 225 (extract).

25. *To* Edward Owen *17 October 1696*

Honored Sir,

I must humbly beg your Pardon for my Rudeness of not acknowledg[ing] the Honor I have received by your Letter, Sir, the only excuse is, that had I answered it sooner, I should have been dunn'd by the Printers, who are as busy as my self, about a little thing our Master

---

[1] William Charleton, a name assumed by William Courten (1642–1702), friend of John Locke, while living abroad between 1670 and 1684. He owned a much admired collection of coins and medals and of natural history specimens, and on his return to England he established a private museum in his chambers in the Temple. Wanley had already mentioned to Bagford (no. 22) the desirability of acquiring his collection for the Bodleian; see also no. 38. At Charleton's death it went to Hans Sloane: see Wanley to Sloane, 2 Feb. 1703, BL Sloane MS 4039, fo. 80.

(who is now at London) put me upon.[1] As for Sir William Dugdales Warwickshire, tis certainly the most compleat book in it's kind, the world ha's yet seen, and methinks 'tis for the Credit of it, and of our Native Countrey, that such works since undertaken, have fallen far short of [it]s excellencies. But this may be said (without any Reflections on the Memory of that great man) that after all his Harvest, there may be yet some Gleanings, which tho' not so Considerable as what he had the good Fortune to light upon may yet conduce in some measure to satisfie the Curiositie of some, & perchance make a figure in the History it self. You know Sir William was here in Oxford 4 years, & constantly made use of our Manuscripts in the Public Library, yet, it seems, that the Recantation I send herewith, escaped his notice, although the book was in the Library when he studied there.[2] And I know that several Gentlemen whose Writings he quote's, had many others Relating to Warwick-shire which he never saw, and that he perused (or at least quotes) no other MSS of the Cities, than the book of the Gilds & Chantries, nor any belonging to Trinity Church & other places. This Considered, with the want of Prospects in his book, and the dearness of it, it being now out of Print, may cause, that a second Edition of it, with Additions, might not be thought altogether impertinent, and I heartily wish that any body would undertake & go through with it;[3] as for my self I know my self every way unqualified, as well in respect of my want of years and judgement, as of time, which now is so instant upon me, that I cant afford a word or two to some of my best Friends, whose good will I value infinitely, as Mr Greenway & Mr Tipper.[4] I would intreat you, Sir, to give my humble service to them (if you should chance to see them) & tell them that about 3 weeks hence they shall be sure of a Letter, for about that time or somewhat over, I will have 2 or 3 days to my self. This Recantation was written as I think, in the Reign of King Hen. 6. when the Parliament was holden

[1] Perhaps the index to *CMA*.

[2] I have managed to trace neither Wanley's transcript nor the original in the Bodleian from which it was taken.

[3] The 2nd edn. appeared in 1730. But see no. 200 and n. 8.

[4] George Greenway, an old boy of Coventry Free School, matriculated at St John's College, Oxford 1692, aged 17; BA 1696, MA 1703; Vicar of Cubbington, Warwickshire 1699. He was assistant master at the Free School under Samuel Carte, succeeding him as headmaster in 1701, resigning in 1717 on becoming rector of Kympton. John Tipper of Coventry († 1713) was the original projector and first publisher of *The Ladies' Diary* (1704), 'designed for the sole use of the Female Sex', continuously pubd. for more than 150 years.

at the Priory at Coventre, and the Lord Prior being a Peer of the Realm, might easily put to silence a poor Frier, tho' he asserted nothing contrary to the common sense of mankind. Sir I should count it a great Favor if you would be pleased to send me word that this came safe to your hands, for I don't always express my thoughts so freely, and that you would tear off the Recantation when you have done with it, & put it in one of the Manuscripts I gave to Coventre Library,[5] for the[r]e it may be ready for any that may have occasion for it, & indeed ours is written so badly, that 'twould be some Labor to transcribe it again. [T]he [w]ords in the margent are my own, which may somewhat illustrate the Text truely copied by Sir

Your most humble Servant

H. Wanley.

MS: Bodleian, Eng. lett. c. 291, fo. 219. *Date*: 'University College Octob. 17. 1696.' *Address*: 'For The Worshipfull Mr Alderman Owen at his House in Coventre.' *Printed*: Sotheby's sale cat., 24 June 1975, Lot 217 (extracts).

26. *To* George Hickes[1] *29 November 1696*

Viro Reverendo G. H. Humfredus Wanley S.P.D.

Iam nequeo diutus mihi temperare, vir dignissime, quin ad pedes tuas memet abjiciam, delicto veniam deprecans: cujus vel ipsa memoria adeo nos torsit, ut misereret te mei, si modo pars curarum & dolorum tibi fuisset nota. Me criminis ingrati conscium esse fateor; sin vere paenitentis suspiria, suppliciaque diu passa, immitissimi Iudicis gratiam conciliarent, nullus dubito quin te, summi candoris & benignitatis virum, habuero mitiorem.

Scias enim, vir egregie, quod tuae 5to Octobris conscriptiae,[2] in

---

[5] The Donors' Book of Coventry Free School (CUL Add. MS 4467) has (at fo. 32ᵛ) a list of more than two dozen books and manuscripts given by Wanley. In the library *catalogue* (CUL Add. MS 4468) a list—differing slightly—appears at fo. 17ᵛ.

---

[1] George Hickes (1642–1715), Fellow of Lincoln College, Oxford 1664, Chaplain to Charles II 1681, Dean of Worcester 1683. Deprived for refusing to take the oath (1690) and for nine years harassed by the civil authorities, threatened with prosecution, and obliged to keep moving from place to place. Hence the pseudonym 'Mr Wood' used in the address here. See no. 44 n. 8. There is a partial draft (in English) of this letter in BL Harley MS 6430, p. 84.

[2] BL Harley MS 3779, fo. 49.

manus nostras pervenere, in quibus pro humanitate tua me tot laudibus onerasti, ut me tenuitatis meae haud ignarum, ne ad te iterum conscriberem aliquid, prae pudore pene deterruerint. Paucis post diebus, Bromius ille tuus litteras ad seipsum mihi ostendebat, per quas, potestas a me accipiendi Grammaticam Francicam ei data fuit, quam quidem ex praescripto tradidi.[3] Ex altera vero accepi, te velle librum charta emporetica involutum, tibique inscriptum mitti, quam sero attulit Tabellarius piger. Crede mihi, Domine, me graviter commotum fuisse, quod id non facere potuerim; sed consummatam viri fidelitatem expendens, suamque Linguis Septentrionalibus propensiorem, non facti paenitet. Haud ita pridem, Bromius Gram. tuam per plaustrum tibi misisse, me certiorem fecit, speroque illaesam redidisse. Haec tibi scriptis litteris significaveram, si cum meis copia fuisset simul mittendi Cl. Wormij litteras, a te exoptatas, & quas mihi indies expectare jussit. Tandem, quum diem de die distulisset, calamo manum adjungere dignatus est. Tunc vero multis negotiis pene obrutus, non mihi tantum fuit temporis ut ad te scriberem. Et quidem jam nunc necessaria praetermitto, ne nimia procrastinatio te merito iratum redderet. Ecce summam excusationis nostrae, quam ut aequi bonique consulas, enixe rogo, quae siquid apud te valeat, remissionis tuae litterae dolore tabescentem, ad summum felicitatis fastigium promovebunt.

Ignoscas, quaeso, meae temeritati, qui dum tuam vivendi rationem non satis animadverterem, specimina Codd. Saxonicorum ausus sum efflagitare. Qui tamen nihil amplius velim, quam ut Anglo-Saxonicorum nostrorum MSS Catalogus, in manus tuas acuratus perveniret: cui multum conferret notitia quaedam librorum MSS. in aliis Bibliothecis delitescentium. Nec ulla ratione obstabit Speciminum penuria, quo minus Catalogus noster, ante impressam Grammaticam, pro viribus perficiatur. Circa enim initium aestatis proximae (si annuerit Magister) omnes Codices Saxonicos Londini saltem, si non Cantabrigiae me posse videre spero: quae binae Civitates, una cum Oxonia nostra, fere omnia id genus monumenta suis in Bibliothecis continent. Certoque certius est, me cum tot libros propriis oculis spectaverim, in Catalogo ex nostris texendo, multo

---

[3] William Brome (1664–1745), of Ewithington, Hereford. Hickes had lent Worm his manuscript 'Francick' (i.e. Old High German) grammar—ptd. as pt. ii of the *Thesaurus*—instead of the printed 'Islandick' one, and requested Wanley to reclaim it (Hickes to Wanley d. 20 Sept. 1696, BL Harley MS 3779, fo. 48).

fore peritiorem; et fortassis (dicto absit invidia) observationes in eos quasdam subnectendo. Interea loci, maximas haberem gratias si litteris mandares, num Chartae Saxonicae in Bibl. Cottoniana, in Turre Londinensi, & in Archivis Vigorniensibus[4] αὐτόγραφα sint, an ἀπό-γραφα?[5]

Clarissimi Iunij Francicum MS.[6] inspexi, sed in eo non mihi occurrebat littera **b**. Sin dicere fas sit, quid mihi in mentem venerit; Nonne fuerit haec littera **b** in Cottoniano Codice[7] (in quo solo eam reperire tibi licuit) tantum abbreviatae vocis nota, pro **ber**, sicuti **p** in aliis pro **per**? Verbi gratia, **scriban** pro **scriberan**. **haban** pro **haberan**, &c? Aliqui enim ex vetustioribus nostris Codd. MSS. in Germania scriptis, & forsan circiter idem tempus in quo Cod. Cottonianus, cum hoc, aliqua ex parte, quadrare vidérentur. Unius enim aut alterius fronte, haec sunt verba, *Liber Sĉe Marię de Eƀbach*, pro *Eberbach* ut in aliis.[8] Sed de hoc satis superque, viro praesertim, si quis alius, in his versatissimo.

Verba quaedam, uti videas, ex antiquo Canonum Codice, e Collectione Crisconiana descripsi,[9] qui (ut indiciis satis certis appareat) saeculo 9no aut saltem ineunte 10mo calamo exaratus fuit. In hoc,

---

[4] i.e. Worcester Cathedral Library.

[5] This passage is Wanley's first reference to his ambitious plan to examine and describe all extant Anglo-Saxon manuscripts, fulfilled in his *Catalogus* of 1705. He did not manage to visit London to catalogue the material in the Cotton Library until the summer of 1700—and then only through Hickes's intercession with the Curators of the Bodleian and others (see Hickes to Wanley d. 27, 30 Apr., 7 May 1700, BL Harley MS 3779, fos. 127, 129, 131). He had spent some weeks in Cambridge in the late summer and autumn of 1699.

[6] Bodl. MS Junius 25 (*SC* 5137), of the eighth and ninth century, the 'Murbach hymnal' containing Old High German hymns and glossaries; *CLA* ii, no. 242. Hickes's *Thesaurus*, pt. ii, p. 3, has a table of 'Francic' alphabets including one from Junius 25 and one from Cotton Caligula A.vii, mentioned below. Francis Junius (1589–1677), Anglo-Saxonist and philologist, born in Heidelberg, came to England in 1621 as librarian to Thomas Howard, Earl of Arundel. Lived in Oxford 1676–7, to be near his old pupil Thomas Marshall, Rector of Lincoln College. Presented his Anglo-Saxon manuscripts and his philological collections to the Bodleian before his death.

[7] BL Cotton Caligula A.vii, an Old High German Harmony of the Gospels, described by Hickes, *Thesaurus*, pt. ii, p. 6.

[8] A good many of the Laudian manuscripts were from the library of St Mary's, Eberbach.

[9] Bodl. MS Laud misc. 436 (*SC* 882), a collection of apostolic canons, together with those of the early church Councils and decretals of the Popes, compiled by Cresconius, an African bishop of the late sixth century. The manuscript was written *c*.832–42 and has Germanic glosses of the tenth century cited by Wanley in the margins of this letter but not here printed. The omitted glosses are commented on by Hickes in his letter d. 22 Dec. 1696, BL Harley MS 3779, fo. 46.

verba quaedam tanquam obscura, aut per alia Synonyma Latine exponuntur, aut (quod frequentius est) in eorum Lingua vernacula, quam puto Franco-Theotiscam fuisse, a te vero rectius edoceri valde cupio: de lingua etiam horum verborum e Codice paullo minus antiquo, pariterque interlineato, collectorum: de quo, necesse est ut paucula in Catalogo (ob quasdam res Saxonicas) diceremus. Vale vir doctissime, fac ut valetudinem adeo erudito orbi necessariam, diligenter cures. Diu vivas litterarum Septentrionalium ingens instaurator, decus & ornamentum: ne silentium nostrum animo iracundo feas; ab imo enim corde te colo & diligo, in rebus gerendis tua causa, mirum in modum oblector, omnibusque tuis mandatis sedulo & fideliter obtemperabo.

MS: Bodleian, Eng. hist. c. 6, fo. 9. *Date*: 'Oxoniae dabam, e Coll. Univ. 3° Cal. Decemb. 1696.' *Address*: 'For Mr Wood. To be left at Mr Potters a Booksellers Shop at the Sign of the Gun near the West End of St Pauls Church in Ludgate-Street, London.'

27. *To* George Hickes *20 December 1696*

Viro Reverendo G.H. Humfredus Wanley S.P.D.[1]

Gratissimae tuae litterae per quas, me vel culpae cujusvis suspicione apud te laborasse negas, in manus nostras pervenere. Summoque cum gaudio legerim, imo et relegerim cum ex iis intellexerim Te nostrum Amorem et Studium habere satis exploratum: et quas a me rogasti Homilias,[2] si C. Wormio tradendi fuisset copia, crede mihi Domine, nullo modo impediverint aut tempestatis rigor, aut temporis angustiae, aut valetudinis curandae necessitas, quin eas (quam cito fieri poterit) tua causa descripserim. Sed ut ad rem properemus, quid in animo fuit per Septimanam unam et alteram, paucis explicabo.

Memini, cum pro humanitate tua, mecum sermones miscere non dedignareris, te de virorum quorundam doctissimorum erroribus

[1] Draft in English d. 14 Dec. 1696 in BL Harley MS 6430, p. 86.
[2] The vernacular homilies of Wulfstan († 1023, Bishop of Worcester, Archbishop of York). Hickes had asked Wanley for a transcript of Wulfstan material at Oxford on behalf of Christian Worm (1672–1737), Danish theologian, who was in London at the time. Bodley manuscripts containing Wulfstan's sermons are MSS Hatton 113 (formerly Junius 99) (*SC* 5210), Hatton 114 (*SC* 5134), Bodley 343 (*SC* 2406), Junius 121 (*SC* 5232). Worm's interest may have derived from the presence in Copenhagen of a Latin manuscript of Wulfstan (Gl. Kgl. Sam. 1595 in the Kongelige Bibliotek) apparently written by Wulfstan himself.

disserentem, quos ob solam litterarum Septentrionalium ignorantiam contraxerant, et quorum aliqui, dicebas, in nova Grammaticarum tuarum Editione,[3] indigitandi essent. Si fas sit, cogitatiunculam hujusmodi quandam tibi suppeditabo. Nequaquam ac si me Oedipum putarem, sed ut glaciem diffringam, unde Tu, si libet, veram verbi explicationem, quae vel eruditissimos per tota secula confuderit, erueres.

Cum Romanorum arma adeo fuerint invalida, ut Barbaros non poterint diutius cohibere, quin timendae eorum Inundationi cedere cogerentur: miseriae victos persecutae sunt innumerae. Romani enim blandiente Fortuna, diu mundum deterruissent, & ad libitum civitates regionesque devastati essent: Gothi igitur et Vandali aliaeque Gentes, nisi in Romani Nominis ruina, seipsos haud satis incolumes duxerunt, hostesque infensissimos pro viribus spoliati sunt et praedati. Has cum aliis, calamitates Pagani Christianae Religioni acceptas referebant: cum Paulus Orosius, hortante S. Augustino, librum scripserit, a Latinis Auctoribus extractum; in quo, tot et tantas dum vigeret Paganorum Superstitio, miserias orbi inflictas, plane demonstraverit. Hic liber ab eo apellatus est *Ormesta mundi*, vel (ut unus a nostris exemplaribus) *Ormesta, id est, de miseriis mundi*.[4] Quaestio vero fit, quid velit Ormesta? Sane Orosii Editores rari circa illam sese cruciantur, sed Critici nos Etymologiarum alte repetitarum turba pene obruti sunt; inter quos omnium facile Princeps, vir longe doctissimus Ioh. Ger. Vossius; qui cum verbis Ormesta, Hormesta, Orchestra, Hormefta,

---

[3] Hickes had been revising and enlarging the grammars in his *Institutiones* ever since they were first pubd. in 1689; the revised edn. appeared in vol. i of his *Linguarum Veterum Septentrionalium Thesaurus* (1703), of which Wanley's *Catalogus* (1705) comprised vol. ii.

[4] The Bodleian manuscript from which Wanley quotes the title must be Junius 15 (*SC* 5127), Junius's transcript of Cotton Tiberius B.i. Wanley cites the title here given in his description of it in the *Catalogus* (p. 85), but it is not found in the manuscript. It may have been an inscription on a flyleaf, now lost: the manuscript was rebound in the nineteenth century.

Wanley's interest probably derives from that of his friend William Elstob (1673–1715), Anglo-Saxonist and antiquary, Fellow of University College, Oxford 1696. Elstob was engaged in an edn. of Orosius based on Junius 15 at this time. There exists a specimen of the projected edn. (a title-page and two leaves of text), *Hormesta Pauli Orosii quam olim patrio sermone donavit Aelfredus Magnus . . . Ad exemplar Junianum edidit Wilhelmus Elstob* (Oxford, 1699), in BL Lansdowne MS 373, fo. 86, but it was never published. Elstob's transcript came into the hands of Daines Barrington (1727–1800), lawyer and antiquary, and in 1773 he ptd. the text with a translation of his own, 'chiefly', he says in his preface, 'for my own amusement and that of a few antiquarian friends'. It is to be trusted neither for text nor translation (*DNB*). Later the transcript turned up in the library of Trinity College, Oxford, but cannot now be found.

Hormeuta, Hormathus & Hormisda luserit, nihil exinde certi statuere poterit.

Nos haud adeo inanes ac tumidi sumus, ut nostras doctorum sententiis anteponeremus: sin unicuique liceat suam opinionem in medium proferre, cur non mihi? Quid dedecoris est aut cum Hercule, aut ab eo vinci? Dimisso igitur pudore, quid sentiam, libere dicam. Orosius quidem scripsit Latine, sed in animo fuit Titulum alia lingua petitum libro praeponere. Binae tantum aliae tunc temporis, praeter Latinam, ceteris maxime praelucerent; Graeca nempe, et Gothica. Graecarum litterarum, fatente Vossio, penitus expers fuerit, Gothicam quidem callere poterit, quae ut eorum Victoriae indies numero augerent, invaluit: et quae non multo post, ipsam Latinitatem, in Dialectos, Gallicam, Italicam et Hispanicam commutavit. Per Gentes, inquam, Septentrionales fuerunt hae clades, desolationes, &c. comissae, Orosio scribendi ansam praebentes. Nonne ergo ipsi liceret verbum Septentrionale libro praefigere? Quandoquidem vero fragmentum Codicis Argentei quicquid exstat ex veteri Gothorum lingua,[5] in se contineat, nil mirum videtur, si non ipsum verbum invenire in eo poterimus, cujus tamen vestigia fortasse deprehendemus in 𐌀𐍂𐌼𐌀𐌽 *misereri*. In Dictionariolo quoque tuo Islandico **hormunga** significat *aerumna*.[6] Magis vero mihi arridet Saxonica vox **earme**, *miser, inops, desolatus*, &c. quam si licet per tuas Regulas comparare, ex **earme** fit **earmer**, unde in Superlativo gradu **earmest**, haud ita discrepans ab Orosii *Ormesta*. Ejusmodi verbum Gothicum significans *desolationes, calamitates et miseriae maximae*, in mea quidem sententia, Orosij tum libro tum occasioni scribendi valde appositum fuisset. Sed Tu, vir egregie, qui omnes Linguas Septentrionales animo vere Critico coluisti, genuinam verbi significationem facile expiscaberis, et tam parvo negotio, quam verba illa ad te nuperrime a me transmissa, ab Orco revocasti.[7]

Quod attinet ad Chartas Saxonicas, magno gauderem gaudio, si

[5] Codex Argenteus, Uppsala University Library MS DG.I. The magnificent fifth-/ sixth-century copy of the Gospels in Gothic translated from Greek in the fourth century by Ulfilas (*c.*311–83), Apostle of the Goths. It is written on purple vellum in large letters of silver ink; the initial lines of the gospels and the first line of every section of text are in gold letters.

[6] In Hickes's *Institutiones* (1689), the word appears as *hormung*; it is glossed *aerumna* in *Dictionariolum Islandicum* (*Institutiones*, p. 111).

[7] Wanley's conjecture was warmly received by Hickes: 'Conjectura tua de Orosij Ormesta, quae sane acumine tuo haud indigna est, mihi valde placet' (Hickes to Wanley d. 7 Jan. 1696, BL Harley MS 3779, fo. 53ᵛ).

sincera id genus Majorum nostrorum monumenta inspicerem. Tu primus omnium me certiorem fecisti, ex iis aliquas adhuc exstare in Bibliotheca Regia;[8] sed saepenumero legi, ubi Chartae Saxonicae in Turre Londinensi fuerint citatae, et unam legas in Clariss. Somneri Lexico, sub voce **unnan**.[9] Haud ita pridem Apographum Chartae Latino-Saxonicae in Cod. Evangeliorum antiquo Bibliothecae Coll D. Iohan. vidi scriptum. Donationem continet Regis Ægelredi Ecclesiae Dorobernensi, anno (ni male memini) 976.[10] Haec donatio primo Latine scripta fuit, paucissimis verbis, ut mos fuerit istius saeculi. Sin Saxonicam versionem spectes, misere interpolatam judicabis, et cujus ipsa locutio et characterum ductus, manum Semi-Saxonicam plane agnoscant.

Vale.

MS: Bodleian, Eng. hist. c. 6, fo. 11. *Date*: 'e coll. Univ. Oxon. 13. Cal. Ianuarij 1696.' *Address*: 'For Mr Wood at the Sign of the Gun near the West end of St Pauls Church in Ludgate-street London.'

28. *To* George Hickes *18 March 1697*

Reverendo viro G. H. Humfredus Wanley S.P.D.[1]

Per hasce tres praesertim septimanas, in multas de te cogitationes, vir doctissime, diductus fui: nunc in alterius cujusdam manus pervenisse Lupum verebar, nunc me, culpati caussa Wormij, te iratum habuisse.[2] Et sane apud me pene valuisset haec opinio, cum significarent perhumanae tuae litterae,[3] te aegra oppressum valetudine diu decubuisse.

Ni certum recuperatae sanitatis indicium fuissent tuae, propria, nec parca, manu conscriptae: vix credas, quantum in me dolorem injecerit

---

[8] Only one of them authentic—that in BL Royal MS 1.D.ix (Ker no. 247, Wanley p. 181, Sawyer no. 985). Another group, probably all of which are spurious, is found in Royal 13.D.ii.

[9] W. Somner, *Dictionarivm Saxonico-Latino-Anglicum* (Oxford, 1659), citing in full under *unnan* the Patent Roll of 43 Hen. 3.

[10] Listed by Wanley, *Catalogus*, p. 105, from St John's College, Oxford, MS Arch. 3.N.41 (H. O. Coxe, *Catalogus Codicum MSS qui in Collegiis Aulisque Oxoniensibus Hodie Adservantur*, ii (1852), no. cxciv in the catalogue of St John's manuscripts), Sawyer no. 1636.

[1] Draft in English in BL Harley MS 6430, p. 90.

[2] See no. 27 and n. 2.

[3] Hickes to Wanley d. 15 March 1697, BL Harley MS 3779, fo. 55.

ista narratio. Iam vero te sospitem curare laetus jubeo, omnes quoniam boni, praecipuaeque Philo-Saxones, et patriae antiquitatis indagatores, etiam ipse ego, partem nobis in te haud exiguam vendicamus.

Quod meum erga te studium & amorem grato animo accipis, id totum humanitati debetur tuae. Quod etiam pro candore tuo me tantis laudibus ornare pergis, id fateor mihi prae pudore creare molestiam; et si nihil habeam antiquius, nec opto magis, quam ut indies certior fias de diligentia et animo erga te, meo.

Loca in Ælfrico et Iunio a te desiderata, ut videas, transmisi;[4] de quibus, inter alia, Londini viva voce, liberrime tecum sermones miscere velim. Interea valetudinem, quaeso, diligenter curas, et de tuo ad urbem reditu me certiorem facias.

Vale.

MS: Bodleian, Eng. hist. c. 6, fo. 13. *Date*: '15 Kal. Apr. 1696/7.'

29. *To* [Thomas Smith] *6 May 1697*

Reverend Sir,

Hearing that this worthy Gentleman Mr Elstob designed for London speedily, I was bold to return you by him my hearty thanks for all your favors to me. I farther desired him to give himself the trouble of carrying this little MS, which would make me proud, if it might find any place in the Cottonian Library.[1] I procured it in the Countrey not a month since, and know well that it is not much worth (yet it is the best I have) & contains sundry prayers translated out of some religious & ortho[d]ox French mans works. At pag. 89 b. begins Rich. Hampoles Meditation on our Saviors Passion, with some Collections towards the end from St Augustine & St Isidore, all as you see in English, & in my poor opinion, in no despicable

---

[4] Transcribed at the foot of this letter are passages: (i) [Gen. 35: 17 and Exod. 1: 15, 17, 18, 19] from Aelfric's 'Excerpta' from the Pentateuch as found in Bodl. MS Laud misc. 509 (*SC* 942), Ker no. 344, Wanley p. 67; (ii) from Francis Junius's *Etymologicon Linguae Anglicanae*, the autograph of which is Bodl. MSS Junius 4 and 5 (*SC* 5116–17)—and from which the work was ptd. with additions by Edward Lye at Oxford in 1743—the article on *midwife* (Junius 5, fo. 37ᵛ).

---

[1] BL Cotton Titus C.xix. Not listed by H. E. Allen, *Writings Ascribed to Richard Rolle* (1927), pp. 278–9; but see *Medium Ævum*, xxii (1953), p. 95.

character. If I [c]an get up any choiser & more valuable Monuments relating to our England, I [s]hall never think 'em better bestowed, than in the place to which I humbly offer this, [a]s a small token of my profound respect to the Illustrious Family whose name it [be]ars, & a grateful acknowledgement of the great satisfaction I took, when I had the [h]onor to be admitted into it.

I know this Gentleman (one of our Fellows) being, amongst others his Accomplishments, a Lover of, & great proficient in our English History, &c: would think all the Actions of his life scarcely sufficient to recompense the favor of an hours view of this most noble Library; but for that, I am sensible his own Merit, will quickly supersede all I can say.

I had almost forgot to acquaint you of a Note written at the end of one of our Samaritan Pentateuchs,[2] which gives us the Age of yours;[3] it runs thus, Folia postrema haec sex jussu Reverendissimi Praesulis *Gulielmi Laud* Archiepiscopi Cantuariensis descripta sunt ex vetusto, eo que integro, *Bibliothecae Cottonianae* exemplari; quod Anno *Ismaelitarum* seu *Hegirae Malmmedanae* DCCLXIV, i.e. Salutis reparatae MCCCLXII. junctis operis, in Oriente exararunt *Ithamar Ben Aharon* atque *Abraham Ben Abi Nitzaion*, nomine seu auspicijs *Semoki Tobi Isaak Ben Semoki Selomo*[h] *Ben Jacob*, ex Familia *Isburiana*, summo, in agro *Damasceno*, principatu insign[i] Sic *Abraham* ille ad Numerorum calcem, in memorato exemplari subnotavit. I a[m]

    Reverend Sir,
      Your most faithful & obliged servant
                          Humfrey Wanley.

MS: Bodleian, Smith 54, fo. 75. *Date*: 'From the Masters Lodgings in Univ. Coll. May 6. 97.'

30. *To* [Thomas Smith] *17 May 1697*

Reverend Sir,

    I return you my hearty thanks for your kind letter,[1] which certifies me of your receipt of my poor present, already by you placed in the Cottonian Library,[2] which I cordially wish may for ever encrease &

[2] Bodl. MS Laud Or. 270 (*SC* 624). See also no. 30.
[3] BL Cotton Claudius B.viii.

[1] d. 15 May 1697, ptd. Ellis, *Original Letters*, pp. 240–2.
[2] See no. 29.

preserve its own. I sent that MS. only as an earnest of what I hope to procure [f]or it hereafter, knowing that singly, it is not worth the room it takes up. I dispair of ever being able [t]o compass a Saxon MS. in parchment, because they are almost all in publick Libraries: but if we [h]ave any Saxon book here in Oxford, (or indeed, in any other Language) which you want in the Cottoni[a]n Library; be pleased but to say so, and I will copie it as fairly & correctly as I can, & send it thither.

I have notice of some good books up & down, relating to the History of England, with some Re[g]ister books of Religious Houses (these last, as yet, untouch'd by learned men) which, if their owners [w]ill part with them, I will certainly send, to attend their betters there also. I have for these last twelve [m]onths much desired to spend some time in it, but my business will not permitt me a journey to [L]ondon 'till the next year at least.

As to the Samaritan Pentateuch of Arch-Bishop Laud,[3] (one of five, in our publick Library) [it w]as given him by Arch-Bishop Usher, as I learn by this note at the beginning of the book,

Pentateuchum hoc Samaritanum est (in principio & fine mutilatum) antiquissimis Phœnicum litteris descriptum. Ab Ecclesiasticis script-oribus Eusebio, Diodoro Tarsensi, Hieronymo, Cyrillo, Procopio Gazaeo, Anespero, Georgio Syncello et aliis sæpius est citatum. A Cuthæis vero hodiernis una cum aliis aliquot eorum monumentis, redemit

Iacobus Usserius Armachanus
Hiberniae Primas
Qui librum hunc mihi dono dedit
W: Cant:

The words Qui Librum &c. are written by him who wrote the note at the end, I sent you in [m]y last, & who perhaps might be one of Arch-Bishop Lauds Secretaries, who with his own hand wrote the W. Cant.[4] as Arch-Bishop Usher all the rest.

The Catalogue[5] goes on very slowly, by reason of some slackness in

[3] The manuscript referred to is Bodl. MS Laud Or. 270 (*SC* 624). The others are: (1) Bodl. MSS Or. 138, 139, 140 (*SC* 3127–9), which with the Laud manuscript were formerly in the library of James Ussher (1581–1656), historian of Ireland, oriental scholar, chronologist, Archbishop of Armagh 1625, and were bought by the university from his son-in-law, Sir Timothy Tyrrell, of Shotover Lodge, Oxon, in 1683 for £50; (2) MS Pococke 5 (*SC* 5328), which came to the library in 1692.

[4] i.e. the signature is Laud's autograph.   [5] *CMA*.

my Lord of Norwich;[6] else, it might have been published before now. I think the Arch-Bishop of Dublins Catalogue is wholly printed off, if not, the verses shall be inserted.[7] When I see Mr Parker & Mr Wallis, both whom I know; I will perform your Commands to 'em.[8] The news you were pleased to send me of Mr Pepys, affecte[d] me very much. He is a Gentleman whom I sincerely respect and honour, & can't but be concern'd in his welfare, which I beg of God to preserve.[9]

I have found 3 MSS. amongst Arch-Bishop Lauds, whereof one was written at the Command of Huunbertus Bishop of Wirtzburg or Herbipolis in Germany, about 700 years ago, or somewhat more, as I guess by the hand:[10] the other two were give to St Kilian, which I take to be his Monastery; by on[e] Gozbaldus, who is stiled Præsul optimus, perhaps Bishop of Kilia in Holsatia; these two seem to be between 8 & 900 years old each, & the notes signifying the gift of 'em, seem to be written about that time.[11] Now if I knew for certain who these men were, & the time when they were made Bishop and when they died, I should be apt to think these books might be written within that time an[d] consequently, that these would give me a great insight into the age of some scores of MSS we have in the same Library. I know at present of no Author who ha's published Catalogues of the Bishops of those Sees; if you could inform me, or give me the account I desire of this Huunbertus & Gozbaldus, I shall look on it as a great favor to
Reverend Sir,
    Your most faithful & obliged servant
                                        Humfrey Wanley.

The Notes are these, MS.E.78 Laud,[12] containing the books of Deuteron. Josue. Jud. & Ruth imperfect. Incipit liber helle addabari

---

[6] John Moore (1646–1714), book collector, Bishop of Norwich 1691. The 'slackness' may account for Moore's manuscripts (and some printed books) appearing in *CMA* in three parts: *CMA* II. i, pp. 361–84, 390–1, 393–9, with addenda and corrigenda on pp. 399–403.
[7] Narcissus Marsh (1638–1713), orientalist, Archbishop of Dublin 1694–1703. The verses referred to (see Smith to Wanley d. 15 May 1697; Ellis, *Original Letters*, p. 241) were to be inserted after those quoted in the catalogue of Marsh's library, *CMA* II. ii, no. 1937, but this was never done.
[8] Richard Parker († 1726), Fellow of Merton College, Oxford 1693, and John Wallis (1674–1738), orientalist, Laudian Professor of Arabic 1703, to both of whom Smith sent his 'service'.
[9] Pepys had been very ill.   [10] Bodl. MS Laud lat. 92 (*SC* 1601), written 832–42.
[11] Bodl. MS Laud misc. 124, 120 (*SC* 1563, 1358) of the ninth-/tenth-century and the ninth century respectively.
[12] i.e. Laud lat. 92.

quod Græci dicunt Deuteronomium Quem dominus Huunbertus uuirzi-burgagensium episcopus fieri jussit. this book has several Francic words interlin'd & in the margent; and, upon a second view, will (I suppose) be found to be 800 years old.

Cod. MS.L.37. Laud.[13] S. Augustinus in Joannem. Hunc sancto codicem Kyliano praesul opimus Gozbaldus scriptum proprio de jure tradebat. This book seems to be somewhat older than the other, tho' not very much. and this Distich is in so old a hand, that I think Gozbaldus gave them a new book. at the end of the same book Gozbaldus sancto me donavit Kiliano.

Ut dominum pro se cum devoto roget ore.

Cod. MS.I.18. Laud.[14] an imperfect copy of S. Aug. de Civitate Dei, where I find GOSBALDVS ME without any more words, which perhaps if continued, would have told us that he caused the book to be written, or gave it to St Kilian, &c. these two last books are writen in the same hand, perhaps by the same scribe, tho' in different Ink, and as I said before between 800 & 900 years ago, as I suppose upon this 2d review.

MS: Bodleian, Smith 54, fo. 77. *Date*: 'From the Lodgings in Univ. Coll. May 17. 1697.'

31. *To* [George Hickes] *about 2*[*3*] *May 1697*[1]

Reverend Sir,

I yesterday received your kind Letter[2] by Mr Brome, and as you see, have sent you the place you wanted from our Saxon Gospells, with

---

[13] i.e. Laud misc. 124.

[14] i.e. Laud misc. 120.

[1] Wanley seems to have misdated this letter. It is a reply to that of Hickes d. 20 May (BL Harley MS 3779, fo. 59), Hickes's of 26 May (Harley 3779, fo. 61), largely given over to advice on the wisdom of Wanley's approaching Smith directly over the matter of Cotton Augustus ii (with reflections on Smith's difficult character, and a request to Wanley to burn the letter after reading it), is clearly a reply to the present letter. The pattern of the subsequent correspondence between Wanley, Hickes, and Smith makes it very unlikely that it is Hickes's letter that is misdated.

[2] d. 20 May 1697, BL Harley MS 3779, fo. 59. Hickes had requested a copy of an extract from the Rushworth Gospels, an eighth-/ninth-century Irish manuscript of the Gospels (the so-called Gospels of Mac Regol) with interlinear Anglo-Saxon gloss, Bodl. MS Auc. D.2.19 (*SC* 3946); Ker no. 292, Wanley p. 81, *CLA* ii, no. 231. Wanley had earlier given Hickes, and Hickes had subsequently lost, a copy of the interlinear Anglo-Saxon version of Mark 2: 15, 16, together with copies of Runic alphabets, and it is these which Wanley now replaces.

those Alphabets you saw. I had not time to copie them again, so that you have the very paper it self; tho' I have added to them 2 Alphabets more, which are on the back side of the paper. The first of them may be of some use, and appears plainly to be Runic, tho' it's called Alphabetum Anglicum. The other I copied from a MS. that goes under the name of Æthicus,[3] (tho' 'tis none of his) which is so old, that it can't want much of a thousand years, this Alphabet is a part of the work it self, and written in the same hand; and tho' it agree's with the first, on the other page, yet I thought fit to copy it, because some of the Characters are more elegantly made, and perhaps truer: Not to mention the other differences.

I know not whether you have received the Testimonies concerning the Saxon Grammar, which I sent you on Sunday last; or if you have, whether you read my humble petition at the end of them; vizt. Seeing I cannot possibly see London this year, that you would be pleased to borrow the book of Saxon Charters from Sir John Cottons Library Augustus. II.[4] for me. I will willingly submitt to any conditions, or oblige my self in any reasonable bond, so I might but have it here: which if I could obtain, I would use my utmost Interest to get hither likewise, those in Worcester, the Kings & Lambeth Libraries;[5] and then, when I have the whole Treasure of England in that kind, by me, to be seen at one view, I would endeavor to see if one would prove another to be true or false, and how the Hands of England (Latin & Saxon) have gradually altered from the time of Æthelbert King of Kent, to that of King Stephen; and take Specimens of them accordingly. I know you can sooner prevail with Dr Smith than any other, but if you do not think it convenient, that a Collection of so great value should be entrusted with so mean & young a man as I am: I must humbly beg your pardon for this trouble, and desire you not to impute it to any thing else than the ardent desire I had to satisfie my self in that point. I am

---

[3] Bodl. MS Junius 25 (*SC* 5137), *CLA* ii, no. 242, the 'Murbach hymnal', a composite manuscript important for its Old High German hymns and glossaries. It contains (beginning at fo. 2) the Cosmography of Aethicus written in two late eighth-century hands.

[4] Cotton Augustus ii; Wanley p. 258. It contains a great series of early charters and bulls, no fewer than eleven before the ninth century: see A. Bruckner and R. Marichal, *Chartae Latinae Antiquiores*, iii (1963), nos. 182–92.

[5] See no. 33 nn. 14, 15, 16.

Honored Sir
    Your most faithful & obedient Servant

                                                    Humfrey Wanley

MS: Bodleian, Eng. hist. c. 6, fo. 16. *Date*: 'From the Bodlejan Library May 28. 1697.'

32. *To* [George Hickes] *30 May 1697*

Reverend Sir,

I return you my hearty thanks for your trouble in desiring the book of the Dr for me:[1] I knew somewhat of his temper before I wrote, but could not persuade my self that a single Letter of mine could have the desired effect, and therefore thought one word from you would do more than a quire of paper from me. But if he's not inexorable, I'le have it yet. As you say, he took not one syllable of notice of it in his letter,[2] which was in answer to a brace of Questions I sent him, but neither of us can fully resolve 'em as yet, tho' I know somewhat more of the matter now (upon farther examination) than I did when I wrote to him.[3] I hope the Method you put me in will prove the true one,[4] I will follow it exactly, and if he answers my expectation, I shall indeed look upon it as an extraordinary favor.

As to the M. Gothick letters, I will here send you what I find of them;[5] I think I cannot do better than lay down the 2 Alphabets from Arch-Bishop Lauds Acts of the Apostles (which stands thus amongst his Books in our Library F.82.)[6] and afterwards the Gothick, as Mr Junius ha's printed it,[7] for I have some reason to think that the MS. it self at Upsal,[8] is somwhat different from his representation of it, tho' not much.

[1] Presumably BL Cotton Augustus ii: see no. 31.
[2] Smith to Wanley, d. 27 May 1697; ptd. Ellis, *Original Letters*, pp. 242–5.
[3] No. 30.
[4] Set out at length in Hickes to Wanley, d. 26 May 1697, BL Harley MS 3779, fo. 61.
[5] 'glad should I be to see the deduction of the whole [Gothic] Alphabet' (Hickes to Wanley, d. 26 May 1697).
[6] Bodl. MS Laud Gr. 35 (*SC* 1119), Acts of the Apostles in Greek and Latin, a sixth-/ seventh-century codex (Codex E of Acts) written perhaps in Italy and apparently used by Bede, *CLA* ii, no. 251.
[7] *Quatuor D.N. Jesu Christi Euangeliorum Versiones perantiquae duae, Gothica et Anglo-Saxonica*, ed. T. Marshall and F. Junius (Dordrecht, 1664–5).
[8] Codex Argenteus, the unique manuscript copy of the Gothic Gospels, in Uppsala University Library. Ptd. by Junius in his edn. of 1664–5.

Latin. ᴀ bᴄ δᴇ ꝼ ᴄʜɪʟ ᴄᴏɴᴏᴘꝗᴋꜱᴛ ᴜᴠхꝩyᴢ

Greek. ᴀʙᴦᴧᴇᴢʜᴇɪïᴋᴧᴍɪɴᴢᴏᴨᴘᴄᴛꝩÿ ꝼ ᴏᴄхꝓᴄᴏ

Gothick. ᴀ ʙᴦᴧ ᴇ ꝼ ᴄʜɪïᴋᴧᴍɴᴙᴨᴏᴋꜱᴛꝓɴᴀꝩхᴢ

Of which Gothick letters, ꝼᴄʜᴋꜱꜱ seem plainly to come from the Latin Alphabet.

As ᴋᴦïᴋᴧᴍᴨхᴢ from the Greek.

As for ᴇɪɴᴛꝩ (from the last of which, the Saxons seem to have derived their **p**) I think they may be derived from either or both Alphabets; so that all the difficulty lies in the remaining letters.

ᴀ is corrupted from **A** as you may soon perceive.

ᴧ seems to be taken from the above-written Latin δ, only the Diagonal Line is brought down lower; perhaps, for the same Reason for which the Greeks from Δ formed their α which somewhat resembles this.

ᴙ may be a Corruption of **o**, which the Antients constantly made by two strokes. Now thro' carelessness they might make it thus ᴙ, and so the superfluous dashes in time come to be accounted an essential part of the Letter.

ɴ I take to be the above written **u** upside down.

ᴀ may be the Latin **u** as it is every where almost, in old Latin MSS. or else, the above written Latin **q** but shortned in the Perpendicular line.

ꝓ may be derived from **TH** joyned together, but not after the laborious way, vizt. ᴴᴴ, but after an easier manner, such as would represent a sufficient part of 'em both, look as well, and suit with it's fellows better; from this ꝓ I persuade my self that the Saxons borrowed their **þ** to express the sound of ᴇ, which **þ** still suits with Saxon letters better than ꝓ For the other **th**, to wit **Ð** or δ, they are plainly derived from **D** & δ, the diagonal only shewing it to have a different sound from **D**. This makes me be of a contrary opinion to Sir Henry Spelman as to these letters; and indeed his† account of the rest seem's liable to exception. Might not your Francick **b** have the parallel line added, to shew that it differ's in sound from the Common **b**, perhaps approaching to **v** consonant.

o I take to be a plain **o**, and the point in the Center to signifie an

Asper Spirit; the **o** to be pronounced as our **w** but short, and **o** as **hoo**, or **hp** in Saxon. I think I need produce no examples to convince you that this may be as true a Sound of the Letter, as **qu**; for (unless I am too partial to my own fancies) the Gothick Glossary of Mr Junius sufficiently evinces it.[9]

These, Sir, are my thoughts of the Gothick Letters, which if they were invented (as they call it) by Wlfilas in this very form,[10] he seems by it to have been a cunning fellow to make one Alphabet from two; and tis certain his Countrey men were well enough acquainted with Romans & Greeks to know their Letters without any difficulty; and writers of each nation seeing many Characters unknown to them, might well cry out WLFILAS LITERARVM GOTHICARVM INVENTOR, unless they mean, that he was the first who applyed them to the Gothick Language. I should be glad to know your Opinion of what I have written,[11] which I made as short as I could, and whether you have received the Alphabets I sent in my last. The first which you see only prolongs that of Æthicus, is printed with some others gathered by HRabanus Maurus, in Goldastus Tom.II, where you may see, how each copy differs one from another.[12]

   I am Reverend Sir,
      Your most humble & obliged servant

                                          Humfrey Wanley.

† Spelm. Conc. Tom.i. Alphabetum
   Anglo-Saxonicum hic apponimus:
   non integrum illud vetus, cujus
   multi desiderantur characteres, sed quo
   Latinis intermixto literis,
   ipsi Saxones nostri recentiores,
   et nos plerunque in hoc opere retinuimus.[13]

MS: Bodleian, Eng. hist. c. 6, fo. 17. *Date*: 'From the Lodgings in Univ. Coll. May 30. 1697.' *Address*: 'For Mr Wood at Mrs Lees Coffee-house in Pickadilly, near the Corner of St James street, London.'

[9] i.e. the glossary to the edn. of 1664–5.
[10] Ulfilas (*c.*311–*c.*382), Bishop of the Goths and translator of the Gothic New Testament found in Codex Argenteus.
[11] 'I am extreamly pleased wth your derivation of the Gothic Alphabet, and subscribe to it in every thing. you could have sent no treasure more acceptable' (Hickes to Wanley, d. 5 June 1697, BL Harley MS 3779, fo. 63).
[12] Melchior Goldast, *Alamannicarum rerum scriptores* (Frankfurt, 1606), II pt. i, pp. 91–3.
[13] Cited from H. Spelman's *Concilia, decreta, leges, &c.*, i (1639), sig. [[*]3]ᵛ, where Spelman's chart showing the derivation of the alphabet is to be found.

33. *To* Thomas Smith *30 May 1697*

Reverend Sir,

I return you my humble and hearty thanks for you[r] last kind letter,[1] from which [I l]earnt some more particulars relating to the two Bishops, than I knew before.[2] Tho' I was not ab[so]lutely a Stranger to St Kilian, as having before I wrote to you perused Bishop Usher,[3] Sir James Ware,[4] [T]rithemius, Browerus and others as to what they relate concerning him: And also the Rerum Germanicarum Scriptores printed by Reuberus, Pistorius, Goldastus, Meibomius, & Marq. Freherus,[5] from [t]he last of which I find that Gozbaldus Bishop of Wirtzburg died anno 855. 12 kal. Oct. this is [i]n the Annales Fuldenses.[6] But Demochares[7] to whom you refer me to from Baronius[8] gives [m]e this account of them both viz. Huumbertus seu Hubertus, eligitur pridie cal. Ian. 831. Praefuit annis 9. tribus mens. octo diebus. Obijt anno 841. mense Martio.

Godebaldus seu Hubertus[9] Abbas inferioris Altachij perveteris coenobij apud Bavaros, vocatur [p]rimo Aprilis, anno 841. Praefuit 11. annis. Obijt in vigilia S. Matthæi anno 852.

He makes S. Burchardus the first Bishop of Herbipolis, who (he saies) Praefuit annis 40. Obijt [a]nno 791. (2) Mayngudus who died 794. (3) Bernuuolphus who died 800. (4) Luderius who died 804. (5) Aygeluuardus who died 810. (6) Wolfgerus who died 831. and (7) Huumbertus 841. and (8) Godebaldus 852. this account is all along so

---

[1] d. 27 May 1697, ptd. Ellis, *Original Letters*, pp. 242–5.

[2] See no. 30.

[3] *Britannicarum Ecclesiarum Antiquitates* (Dublin, 1639). Smith cites the London edn. of 1687, p. 383.

[4] *De Scriptoribus Hiberniae* (Dublin, 1639). Smith cites pp. 31–2.

[5] Tentative identifications for which works follow: Johann Tritheim, *De Viris Illustribus Ordinis Sancti Benedicti* (Cologne, 1575); Christopher Brouwer, *Fuldensium Antiquitates* (Antwerp, 1612); Justus Reuber, *Veteres Scriptores Germanicorum* (Frankfurt, 1584); Johann Pistorius, *Rerum Germanicarum Veteres Scriptores* (Frankfurt, 1607); Melchior Goldast, *Alamannicarum Rerum Scriptores* (Frankfurt, 1606); Heinrich Meibom, *Rerum Germanicarum* (Helmstadt, 1688); Marquard Freher, *Germanicarum Rerum Scriptores* (Frankfurt, 1600).

[6] *Annales Francorum Fuldenses* ptd. by Freher in *Germanicarum Rerum Scriptores* (1600).

[7] Antoine de Mouchy (called Demochares), *Christianae Religionis, Institutionisque Christi &c.* (Paris, 1562), ii, pp. 68–9.

[8] Cesare Baronius, *Martyrologium Romanum* (Rome, 1586), p. 304.

[9] Wanley is in error: Demochares ii, p. 69 reads 'Godeboldus vulgo Gosuualdus'; Wanley's eye was caught by the previous entry, 'Humbertus seu Hubertus'.

circumstantiated that any body would be apt [t]o believe him; but I cannot reconcile it to what you have been pleased to direct me to elsewhere. For in the Acta Benedictinorum[10] in the life of Eigil I find that he (Eigil) was made Abbas Fuldensis anno 818, died anno 822. in whose time our Humbertus at that time Bishop of Herbipolis, at the command of his Metropolitan Heistolfus Arch-Bishop of Mentz, consecrates two vaults in the Church of Fulda. Haystolphus was (according to Demochares) made Arch. Mogunt. anno 813 and dies anno 825. And the Annales Boiorum[11] in the place you referred me to say Gotsbaldus was Abbat anno 7. Lu[d]ovici Pijssimi Regis, that is, anno 820. that he was Bishop of Wirtzburg anno 15 Ludovici Regis, Indict. 9. that is, anno 828 indict. *8.* or 9 from September as may well be. All this hangs [s]o well together that I can't but credit them sooner than Demochares, whose catalogue is full of Errors in Judgement, as well as Typographical, and perhaps the Annales Fuldenses may be in the right on't when they say Gozbaldus died anno 855. If they are true, Demochares can't be so, and we must be forced to put them both up higher, that is Huumbertus must begin his 9 years in the time of Eigil & Haystolphul, so that Gotsbaldus may succeed him by the year 828 at least.

I suppose by this, it would be a troublesome and knotty piece of work to make a Catalogue of the German Prelates, and for this Intelligence you were pleased to give me, again give you ten thousand thanks.

But I have s[t]ill one more humble Request to you, Sir, which tho' I might get answered another way; yet I am not willing to be obliged to any besides your self for so great a favor. It is that you would be pleased to lend me that Noble book of Saxon Charters (Augustus II.) from the Cottonian Library. I know that for a words speaking I could procure the Vice-Chancellor and ou[r] Master[12] to borrow it of Sir John,[13] who has promised to lend them any book he ha's: but since Sir John reposes such a trust in you, to lend what and where you please, I think there is no occasion for i[t.]

Perhaps, Sir, you may object the unfitness of entrusting so great and

---

[10] Jean Mabillon, *Acta Sanctorum Ordinis S. Benedicti* (Paris, 1668–1701).

[11] Johann Turmair (called Aventinus), *Annales Boiorum* (Basel, 1615).

[12] Charlett.

[13] Sir John Cotton (1621–1702), 3rd Baronet, in whom the ownership of the library was vested.

invaluable a Tre[a]sure in the hands of so young a man as my self: yet
if modesty would permitt me, I might u[rge] in answer, that the University have granted me free ingress & egress to and from all the books
[*word lost*] in the Bodlejan Library, the Keys of which, I have at this
present, in my Pocket. It may be, you may say, what would you do with
it, if you had it by you? If I had that book, I would do my utmost
endeavour to borrow those that lie in the Kings[14] and Lambeth Libraries,[15] and those fiftee[n] at Worcester;[16] which last, I can easily
compass. When thus I have gotten the whole strength of the Kingdom
(of this kind) into my hands, I will endeavor to find out whether there
be any co[un]terfeits among them, or if they be all genuine; since as
you know, the old monks have been severely taxed in this point, but
how undeservedly, I shall then see. This I would prove from the
Wording and Form of the Charters, from the Accounts of Time, and
from the Hand-Writing.

As to the last of these, I should fully satisfie my self of the English
manner of writing from the time of Æthelbert King of Kent, to
K. Stephen, how the hands & Language gradually altered in ages so
remote from us. And to fix these the better in my memory, I would
copie Specimens & Alphabets of each into a book I have for that
purpose, which already ha's some thin[gs] in it of good value.[17] But if
this should not be the best way of using them, I will alter my method to
any other which you shall please to prescribe me. And if ever my
Collections be made publick, the world shal certainly be informed
from whom I received so great a favor as I will take care to let it know
to whom our Library is beholding for the *Shaster* in Mal[a]barick,[18]
the Russian Psalter in Parchment,[19] &c and this as we are bound in

---

[14] See no. 27 n. 8.

[15] Probably those of Henry I and Henry II containing royal grants to Christ Church,
Canterbury, in Latin and English, Lambeth Palace, Cart. misc. x. 109, xi. 1, xi. 2, xi. 3,
etc. (T. A. M. Bishop, *Scriptores Regis* (Oxford, 1961), nos. 399, 400, 401, 402). Hickes,
Thesaurus, p. xvi prints the English version of Cart. misc. xi. 1 (= Bishop no. 400) from a
Cotton charter—Cotton Ch. vii. 1.

[16] Wanley refers to the fifteen listed by Hickes (p. 171 of 'Catalogus Librorum
Septentrionalium' in Hickes's *Institutiones* (1689)) which were omitted by Dugdale from
a catalogue compiled by him in 1643. A copy of both series is in BL Harley MS 4660.
They are calendared by Wanley, *Catalogus*, pp. 299–301.

[17] See no. 37 n. 1.

[18] Bodl. MS Tam. e. 11 (*SC* 2861), a very free translation of the Mānava Dharma
Sāster, according to the Bodleian Catalogue probably the most ancient specimen of
continuous Tamil prose composition in existence, presented by Smith in 1668.

[19] Bodl. MS e Mus. 184 (*SC* 3732), presented by Smith in 1683.

Honor & Gratitude. And indeed, Sir, the great benefit I should have in the loan of this book, will never depart out of my memory, and that you shall find, if we have any thing here that you like; or if I travel, and you have any service to command me abroad; or would desire a transcript of any thing in any forreign Library, as I told you in my last, be pleased Sir, but to say wherein I can serve you, and I will most willingly do it, and living or dying shall always acknowledge this great and extraordinary kindness.

If you please to send it me, I think it will do best in a box, which I will freely pay for; and your kindness would yet be greater, if you could put into it, what Saxon Charters (or Latin made in the time of the Saxons) which are in the boxes you mention in the Preface to your excellent & most exact Catalogue,[20] if there be any, I would willingly have come up to London this Summer, but could not possibly obtain leave, else I would not have given you this trouble who am

Reverend Sir,

Your most obliged & most humble servant

Humfrey Wanley.

MS: Bodleian, Smith 54, fo. 79. *Date*: 'Univ. Coll. May 30. 1697' *Address*: 'For the Reverend Dr Smith, next door to the white Swan, in Dean street near So ho Westminster.'

34. *To* Thomas Smith *20 June 1697*

Reverend Sir,

I received the honour of yours of the 8th instant[1] but have had so much unlook'd for business on my hands, that I could not tell you so before now. I humbly thank you, Sir, for the notice you gave me of the new authors, which I shall think richly worth my while to consult, since 'tis plain the Demochares account of the Bishops of Herbipolis cannot be true. As I told you in my last, I had consulted the Rerum Germanicarum scriptores, and some of Browerus his books,[2] yet not

---

[20] Listed by Wanley at the end of Robert Harley's copy of Smith's official catalogue, pbd. Oxford 1696 (now Bodl. MS Add. D.82), pp. 185-8, presented to Harley as a trustee of the Cotton Library by the Commissioners (of whom Wanley was one) appointed to survey the library in 1703.

---

[1] Ptd. Ellis, *Original Letters*, pp. 245-8.
[2] For the works mentioned here, see Wanley to Smith, 30 May 1697.

finding any thing sufficient to give me satisfaction, I (after much fruit-less enquiry from other learned men) made my application to you, with success. As soon as my business will permit me, I will consult both Bruschius[3] and Bucelinus,[4] and search this matter to the bottom, for two such dates are not to be neglected, as those of our two books.

Sir, I am very sorry I should mention the borrowing that book of the Saxon Charters to you, seeing it can't be lent out, and humbly crave your pardon for my rashness;[5] and tho' there are many other books in that noble Library which would be useful to me in my present design, (which is more relating to the nature of Letters, than to the Diplomata or Charters themselv[es]) yet I shall not for the future, make use any of my friends to get them hither, but content my self 'till I can go to London. To unfold my meaning a little further, my intent is, to trace the Greek and Latine letters from the oldest Monuments of antiquity now extant, as the Marbles and Medals to the MSS. and so down to the present age. When any other Language derives it Character from these as the Coptic or Russian from the Greek, the Francic, Irish, Saxon, &c from the Latin, I shall consider them in their Several times, but the Saxo[n] I would especially bring down from the oldest Charters to the present English hands. The Charters I believe may be older than the books and may determine the age of all the Saxon MSS, with the assista[nce] of some other Remarks, but one cannot rely upon them, till we kn[ow] for certain which be genuine and which not; and to find this, a m[an] had need of the help of all together, this made me so bold, as to desi[re] the book. I am not in hast with my design, which I know will co[st] many years time, and the trouble of a personal view of every bo[ok] in Capital letters in Europe, &c. yet after all, if nobody shal in that time have prevented me, I may have a second vol. de re Anglorum diplomatica,[6] which I pray God grant you health & oppor-tunity to give the world, since undoubtedly you are the most capable of any man now living to do.

As to our publick Library we have not many curious dates, those we have are mostly within 500 years, one or two we have in Greek & Latin of 700 & 800 years a piece, but Sir J. Cotton ha's great store of noble ones, much older, as appears by your excellent Catalogue, which often

---

[3] Caspar Brusch, *Chronologia Monasteriorum Germaniae* (Sulzbach, 1682).
[4] Gabriel Bucelin, *Menologium Benedictinum* (Feldkirch, 1655).
[5] See nos. 31, 33.
[6] i.e. a work to be set against Mabillon's *De Re Diplomatica*.

sets my mouth watring, tho' I know not when I shall be so happy as
to see the books, having no prospect of a Journey upwards. However,
Sir, I give you again my humble and sincere thanks for all your
Favors to me, and shall whenever it lies in my power endeavor to
shew you that I am

 Reverend Sir,

  Your most faithful & obedient servant,

         Humfrey Wanley.

If you please to send me
word what books you want from
hence, I will try to give you some
satisfactory account of them.

MS: Bodleian, Smith 54, fo. 83. *Date*: 'Univ. Coll. June 20. 1697.' *Address*: 'For The
Reverend Dr Smith next door to the Swan in Dean street near So ho square Westminster.' *Printed*: *Bodleian Letters*, i, pp. 80–2 (extract).

35. *To* [Thomas Smith] *5 July 1697*

Reverend & Honored Sir,

 The great kindness you are pleased to shew me in a correspondence
so highly [b]eneficial and useful to me, affect's me so sensibly, that I
can't but return you ten thousand [t]hanks, and earnestly beg of God
almighty to grant you health and will to continue it. [I] know well that
your ordinary occasions must needs find you employment, and when I
[c]onsider the trouble you give your self upon the account of so many
Learned men both in [E]ngland and beyond the Seas, which alone
were sufficient to take up your whole time: I can't but be filled (as it
were) with the warmest and most cordial sense of Gratitude, for those
many and great favors I have all along received from you, tho' without
the least pretence of right, since it could never be in my power to do
you any service. But as I have told you already, did I but know wherein
I might be serviceable to you, I should not be backward.

 I am sorry to hear that so many of the Saxon Charters in the
Cottonian Library are spurious, but still 'tis a comfort that a good
number are remaining there and elsewhere of undoubted authority.
As to the Lombardic Character, we have not a book that I know of,
written in it, I mean agreable to the Specimens of it in Mabillon de

re diplomatica, nor did I ever see any in any other place. In Sir
J. Cottons (I perceive by your Catalogue) there be several,[1] and should
be very happy in a sight of them, but when that will be, I can't tell.
Several of our MSS. are said by Dr Langbain to be written in Lombardic Letters, but they are in the common text or square hand about
[]oo years old, vastly different from Mabillon, as I suppose yours are
also.[2] I suppose your books as the Gospels of St Matt. & St Mark,[3] the
2d Councill of Constantinople[4] &c to be in capital Letters by your
account of them, and by them I could see what the difference is
between this sort of Character and others. Besides what I could lear[n]
from so noble a Date as that of the said Synodical book. Neither are
these with th[e] other books you mention all, whereby I might be
furthered in my design by the use of the Cottonian Library. For to deal
freely with you, Sir, ſho' perhaps I may tell you nothing but what you
know already; the Cottonian Library ha's more choice and valuable
monuments of Antiquity, and greater store of them, than the Bodlejan.
I mean Latin, Saxon & Englis[h.] So that when I had copied
specimens from our chiefest books, I thought I could not do better
than make my Applications to you, for the favor of a date or two from
yours. The only Saxon Date we have is the Saxon Chronicle,[5] tho' we
have 3 or 4 Saxon books besides, at whose age we may give a good

---

[1] In an unsystematic examination of Smith's Cotton catalogue I have found only one
'Langobardic' manuscript—Otho A.i (*CLA* ii, no. 188)—but in his own copy of that
work (now Bodl. Gough London 54) Wanley in a marginal note describes Cotton Nero
A.ii. art. 6 (*CLA* ii, no. 186) as 'litteris Langobardicis'. Mabillon's 'specimens' are
Tabella V, p. 353 of *De Re Diplomatica*, pt. i (Paris, 1681). No Cotton manuscripts are
listed by E. A. Lowe in his 'Hand List of Beneventan MSS', *The Beneventan Script*
(Oxford, 1914), p. 340. On the confusions caused by the use of the term 'Lombardic' or
'Langobardic' to describe the South Italian minuscule script most notably associated
with Monte Cassino, for the traditional name 'Beneventan', see Lowe p. 22 f.

[2] Gerard Langbaine the elder (1609–58), Provost of The Queen's College, Oxford
1646, compiled many catalogues, lists, volumes of excerpts, from and relating to
Bodleian and Oxford manuscripts; twenty-one of these came to Bodley in 1658 and nine
more volumes of Langbaine's adversaria were given by Anthony Wood in 1695 (*SC*
5232ᵃ⁻ᵘ and 8614–22). The fullest description is that by Tanner in *CMA* I. i, pp. 268–71. I
imagine that these collections provide the evidence for Wanley's statement, but I have
not been able to track it to its source.

[3] Cotton Otho C.v, Gospels of St Matthew and St Mark, of the seventh-/eighth-
century, *CLA* ii, no. 125. Badly damaged in the fire of 1731, from which only fragments
of sixty-four leaves survive.

[4] Presumably Cotton Claudius B.v, a ninth-century chronicle of the third (not
second) Council of Constantinople, the Sixth General Council of the Church.

[5] Bodl. MS Laud misc. 636 (*SC* 1003), the Peterborough Chronicle, of the early
twelfth century.

guess at. We have no English date above 300 years old, and but a few Latin ones. We have antient Latin MSS indeed, but they give not the year when they were written, sometimes they tell who they were written by, but then I can't find who Wlricus Raegenbaldus[6] &c should be: So that the oldest Latin Date we have is in the year 818[7] and presently after we have some others, then we want for the 10th & 11th Centuries, but from those we can make a pretty good shift. But 'tis far otherwise with you, who have numbers of them of the best sort.

If the Foundation Charter of Croyland should be the Original,[8] I should be very glad to put it into my book, and would thankfully and safely return it. But if the Gentleman will not be willing to part with it out of his own Custody, I shall not expect it. I forgot [to] mention that the date of our Greek MSS. begin at the 9th Century and hold on to this presen[t.] 'Tis impossible for one Library to Monopolize all things, so that if I finish what I intend, I must travel over Europe, which will be a very pleasing journey to

Honored Sir,

Your most humble & obliged serva[nt]

Humfrey Wanley

MS: Bodleian, Smith 54, fo. 87. *Date*: 'Univ. Coll. July 5. 1697.' *Printed*: *Bodleian Letters*, i, pp. 83–7.

36. *To* [Thomas Smith] *25 July 1697*

Reverend Sir,

I received the favor of yours of the 15th instant,[1] in which you was pleas'd to give me so ample an account of the pretended original

[6] The English scribe (named in the colophon, fo. 71) of Bodl. MS Digby 63 (*SC* 1664), a collection of computistical texts written probably between 867 and 892 in the north of England, Ker no. 319.

[7] Bodl. MS Bodley 849 (*SC* 2602), Bede on the Canonical Epistles: see Wanley to Pepys, 25 June 1699.

[8] The spurious charter of Aethelbald, King of Mercia († 716) purporting to be the foundation charter of Crowland Abbey, Lincs. Sawyer no. 82. There is a partial facsimile in Hickes's *Dissertatio Epistolaris* (pt. iv of the *Thesaurus*) tabula D, p. 71. According to Smith (letter to Wanley d. 3 July 1697, BL Harley MS 3781, fo. 82), it was owned by 'a certain Gentleman of quality in this place' but had not been seen by him. He saw it shortly thereafter and gave an account of it in a letter to Wanley d. 15 July 1697 (Harley 3781, fo. 84). See also no. 100.

[1] Smith to Wanley, d. 15 July 1697, BL Harley MS 3781, fo. 84.

Foundation Charter of Croyland Abbey. The Remarks you make of it & divers others are very curious and instructive, and I heartily pray God to grant you time and opportunity to do our whole Nation the honor you intend it. I am bold upon a passage in yours to crave your Opinion at large, Whether in the Original Saxon Charters the Witnesses always set their names to them in their own hands, or not?[2] I know in Mabillon there are many such, but for many reasons of my own, besides the hints you have given me, I cannot swear to his whole book.[3] I never yet saw a Saxon Charter, but those old Charters I have seen made in the time of K. Henry. 1. and so downwards, tho' they are originals, yet are all in one hand: I mean the scribe after the *Hiis testibus* puts their names down himself, and that stands for good in law, and is so in all that I have seen, as wel before date, as after.

As to the Lombardic Letters, I never (as I said before) saw a book written in them but we[4] have several books resembling that Character which Mabillon (from what authority, I know not) calls Scriptura Saxonica. Which books when you come hither I will shew you.

Sir, you have been pleased to be particularly kind to me ever since I had the good fortune to be recommended to you by Mr Pepys,[5] an acquaintance of whom brings you this. He is a Gentleman (his name Bagford) who is extreamly curious in the several sorts of ink, Parchment, Paper, Binding &[c] used in the old Manuscripts, and would think it a lasting obligation to you if he could compass a sight of the Fragmen[t] of the Gospells in Capitals written on the Ægyptian Papyrus, [ex]stant in the Cottonian Library.[6] I have shewed him many of our Curiosities here, thinking I did the University particular se[r]vice in bringing them out, to a man so intimately known to a[ll]

[2] Given by Smith in a letter d. 24 Aug. 1697, BL Harley MS 3781, fo. 86, with the hope that it will put a stop to all further enquiries about such matters unless Wanley has something new to propose, and the suggestion that 'wee must bee content to let our correspondence drop for the present, til there shall happen a just and gud occasion of keeping it up again.'

[3] Smith suggests that Mabillon is not to be trusted upon his bare word wherever he deals with documents touching the interests of his own order.

[4] be MS.

[5] See R. G. Howarth, *Letters and the Second Diary of Samuel Pepys* (1932), no. 239.

[6] Presumably the sixth-/seventh-century fragment (*CLA* ii, no. 192) mounted by Sir Robert Cotton and prefixed to Cotton Titus C.xv. Described by Lowe as 'Fragmentum operis incerti'. Wanley's belief that it was a fragment of the Gospels perhaps results from confusing the fragment with the manuscript in which it is inserted—Titus C.xv is a Greek uncial manuscript of the Gospels, the so-called Codex Purpureus Petropolitanus.

the curious in London: and should take it as a signal favor if my recommendation could prevail with you (at your leisure) [to] take this pains for the friend of

Reverend & Honored Sir,

Your most humble & faithful servant

Humfrey Wanley

MS: Bodleian, Smith 54, fo. 89. *Date*: 'Univ. Coll. July 25. 1697.'

37. *To* [Arthur Charlett] *11 August 1697*

Honored Sir,

Since you have been pleased to order me to send my book of Specimens up to London: I thought it not amiss to send some account of it too.[1] I think (God willing) to fill it with such like things as I have

[1] The 'book of Specimens' (elsewhere referred to as his 'Book of Hands') was a collection of dated documents and of alphabets derived from them, designed to show the development of writing and to serve as a palaeographical aid in the dating of manuscripts. It had originated some months earlier in a series of conversations between Wanley and William Elstob, and in particular with Wanley's dissatisfaction with the standard work on the subject, E. Bernard's *Orbis eruditi literatura a charactere Samaritico deducta* ([Oxford], 1689), the so-called *Tabula literaria*, an engraved comparative table of twenty-nine alphabets intended to demonstrate the Samaritan origin of writing. This is clear from Wanley's memorandum d. 17 Jan. 1697: 'Mr Elstob & I have been talking about Alphabets several times, & when he has put me to it, I have owned that I could not altogether approve of Dr Bernard's sheet for divers Reasons. He then tells me that I ought not to find fault with what ha's been done already unless I intend to do better my self, and if other mens faults are so material, I ought to rectifie them to the best of my power, &c. I will now take it into consideration and endeavour to find out a Method that may be suitable to the matter' (BL Harley MS 6466, fo. 87)—and an outline of his proposed method followed. Bodl. MS Eng. bib.c.3 (*SC* 33184), a manuscript presented by Wanley to Elstob, contains a collection of ancient and modern alphabets in Wanley's hand, together with copies of the Lord's Prayer in forty-nine languages. An early collection of Alphabets by Wanley is in Harley 6030, fos. 15–18, 20. BL Sloane MS 4061, fos. 268–9 contains a proposal for a palaeographical work taking English hands down to 1700, ptd. below, Appendix I.

On his annual August excursion to London, Charlett had written for Wanley's collection in order to show it to the Lord Chancellor, but it arrived too late. It was instead shown to the Archbishop of Canterbury who was greatly impressed—as he seems to have been on an earlier occasion (Charlett to Wanley d. 17 Aug., 20 Oct. 1697, Welbeck Wanleyana = BL Loan MS 29/253; Gibson to Charlett d. 22 Apr. 1697, Bodl. MS Ballard 5, fo. 114). See also nos. 33, 40.

But by 1701 a grander design than that described in this letter seems to have emerged, as appears from a letter to John Jackson, Pepys's nephew, who was about to set out for England from Spain at the end of a continental tour. Should Jackson come across ancient Greek or Latin manuscripts, Wanley wrote— specifically 'any Greek MS,

already put there. The Languages will be chiefly Greek, Latin, & Saxon. I put each Language by it self, but the Capital Letters I place promiscuously at the beginning. I durst not presume at first to begin with the MSS. themselves, but chose rather to take the 4 specimens from Mabillon[2] which you find pag. 3. I thought that practising upon the foreign books would gain me some experience, and better my hand, and those little specimens might serve pretty well till I could see the Originalls. I afterward ventured upon some specimens that Dr Mill had procured Mr Newton & Burghers[3] to copy from some MSS. abroad, which are in pag. 2. and pag. 14. except the last of that page.

certainly appearing by the Date, or any other Authentic Mark to have been written before the year (from the beginning of the World) 6300, or any Latin MS, appearing by the like certainty to have been written before the year of Christ 700'—he asked him to 'cause 4 or 5 Lines with the Alphabet & the Date to be Copied for me'. He continued: 'Perhaps, Sir, you will think this an odd sort of a Request, but that which I'me now going to make may increase your wonder, 'tis that you would be pleas'd, all along, to buy up as many old pieces of Parchment, written upon, as you can get. By some years pains, I have now purchas'd and receiv'd from my Friends several Thousands of such pieces and fragments, which when I have distributed according to their several Ages & Countreys, I hope to make very useful to some Sorts of Students, upon divers Accounts. Those sorts of Characters which I beg you to be most inquisitive after, are the Capitals; the Gothic, Lombardic or Toletan Letters, call 'em by what name you please, and the Large Spanish Letter of an Inch long, the Minuscules. These you will find common in their old books of Offices' (no. 75).

The collection seems not to have survived. Twenty years later Hearne reports a conversation with Wanley in which Wanley told him that what he did formerly by way of 'Specimens of Hands in all Ages' Lord Weymouth had from him, and that he had no design of doing more that way (26 Aug. 1721, Hearne, *Collections*, vii, p. 272). Ten years later still (7 May 1731, *Collections*, x, p. 413), Hearne writes that he had often heard of this work of Wanley's and he points out that Hickes in *Thesaurus*, p. xxvii, promises tables of Wanley's specimens of old hands in chronological order, but he (Hearne) had seen none in any copy of the book—only Dodwell, he says, was eager to have it printed. Most of Wanley's material, set out in letters to Hickes (e.g. nos. 32, 45) was, in fact, taken over by Hickes and used at appropriate places in his *Thesaurus*—as 'De Literis & Literarum Regulis', (pt. i, cap. i). Cf. no. 32 n. 11.

Hearne goes on to say that Wanley at their last meeting said that Edward Harley had the 'Specimens' from him. While this may be Hearne's inaccurate memory of the conversation of 26 Aug. 1721, there is some evidence to support the statement: BL Harley MS 6991, art. 41 and Harley 6992, art. 41 are autograph letters d. 1574, 1577, which endorsements suggest belonged to the 'Book of Hands', but which were sold by Wanley to Harley. 'Collection of the Different Letters and Hands used in Britain, with Explications of the most common and material Abbreviations' is the first in a list of 'Good Books Wanted' in a draft by Wanley in BL Harley MS 7055 of a constitution for a Society of Antiquaries under a charter of incorporation from Queen Anne. The draft is undated, but probably belongs to early 1708: see Joan Evans, *A History of the Society of Antiquaries* (Oxford, 1956), p. 42.

[2] i.e. *De Re Diplomatica*.
[3] Michael Burghers (1653?–1727), engraver of Oxford. He engraved most of the plates for Hickes's *Thesaurus*. Newton I cannot identify.

Then I copied that in pag. 4. from Lambecius, which is the oldest of all the set. This done, I thought my self tolerably fit to copie from an original, which was of my Lord of Norwich's Gospels,[4] pag. 15. at the end of which I found some secret writing but could make nothing of it, I knew we had books in the publick Library[5] which had such writing, I have since taken specimens of them which you may find pag. 15. spec. 3. & pag. 16. spec. 2. and by chance found the key. I have explained our two books as you may see, and my Lords is Μιχαὴλ ὁ Μαντυλίδης who (I believe) wrote his book. I dare not be so bold, or else I would send his Lordship the Key, which might be useful if his Lordship ha's any more such writing. After my Lords book I copied the Last in pag. 14, and have copied all the rest from books in the publick Library except one from our own College Library,[6] pag. 16. and one from Christ-church, pag. 81. I shall for the future take specimens from no books but what have dates, as most of those in small letters have; or other certain marks whereby we may know the true age of the book, as the last in pag. 14. the 1. 3 & 4. in pag. 80. unless the book be in Capital letters, or in some other particular hand, as Bede's Gospells[7] pag. 120. Caedmon[8] pag. 122. In all the specimens I copie from the Originals, I constantly copie the Alphabets and some time the Great Unciall Letters as that of Bedes book aforesaid; without which, 'tis not easy to read some whole pages written in them, that of the Rule of St Benedict[9] pag. 6. some of which are not common. I always copie the date if there be one, because it is my authority. Sometimes I am curious what place in the book to make choise of, as in our old Gospels[10] pag. 6. you see these words quia deus spiritus est, & ex deo

[4] Probably Cambridge University Library MS Dd. viii. 49 (*CMA* II. i, no. 9220), an early eleventh-century evangelistarium lent by Moore to Mill; an imperfect collation of it appears in the Appendix to Mill's edn. of the Greek New Testament, 1707.

[5] i.e. the Bodleian. One of the MSS in question may be Bodleian MS Laud Gr. 85, according to E. Lobel's note in the Bodleian copy of M. Vogel–V. Gardthausen, *Die Griechischen Schreiber des Mittelalters und der Renaissance* (Leipzig, 1909), p. 315.

[6] University College, of which Wanley was a member.

[7] Bodl. MS Auct. D.2.19 (*SC* 3946), Ker no. 292, Wanley p. 81, *CLA* ii, no. 231. The Rushworth Gospels, an eighth-/ninth-century codex, thought to have belonged to Bede.

[8] Bodl. MS Junius 11 (*SC* 5123), Ker no. 334, Wanley p. 77, of the tenth-/eleventh-century. Old English poetical codex, the so-called Caedmon manuscript.

[9] Probably Bodl. MS Hatton 48 (*SC* 4118), *CLA* ii, no. 240. A seventh-/eighth-century codex, the earliest extant manuscript of the Benedictine Rule.

[10] Probably Bodl. MS Auct. D.2.14 (*SC* 2698), *CLA* ii, no. 230, a seventh-century codex of the Gospels, the so-called St Augustine's Gospels.

natus est. which are not to be seen in any other copie Greek nor Latin, tho' Tertullian, St Hilary, & Fulbertus Carnotensis quote it. So I chose that page of our Acts[11] pag. 5. where besides the στίχοι, you may see that the Latin was written before the Greek (as 'tis certain all such books of scripture were written by Latins not Greeks) and that the copie was revised and corrected, princeps being made out of principes. I once thought to write what remarks I made on any specimen over against it on the blank page, as my deduction of the Maeso-Gothic Letters from both alphabets of these Acts of the Apostles.[12] The deduction of most of the Letters of the Sclavonian Character of Cyrill from the Baroccian Evangelistary,[13] pag. 8. Remarks on the Antiquitie of the MSS. on the Author, the book, Parchment, Paper, hand, how such a letter was brought into fashion or wrote so or so, in that time, &c. but on second thoughts I chose rather to omitt them.

Perhaps you may say, Sir, what do you intend by giving your self this trouble? What use will your book be fit for, when all is done? In answer to these two questions, I humbly beg leave to acquaint you, that I intend to consider the original and progress of writing and Letters, and deduce the severall hands especially Greek & Latin from the oldest monuments to this age.[14] As to the alterations of hands, I must begin with the Marbles & Medals as being older than any books now exstant. These Inscriptions & Coins as well as MSS. I must view with my own eyes, for I will rely on no mans judgement whatsoever, nor will I obtrude any thing on the world, but I will name the place where the original is to be seen. I will give a specimen of the Character with the Alphabet of every Gr. & Lat. book in Capital Letters that I know to be in Europe, with many hundreds of others with dates. By travelling I shall get a vast collection, and shall be able to fix the state of Letters to such & such times. So I will adjust the age of every book in Capital Letters. And I think it will be pleasant if not useful, to see a good portion of the most considerable MSS. in the same character, with the alphabets, and know how old that book or character is. It will, I hope, be thought useful to the publick, in making an end of so many quarels as have arisen, or preventing others that may arise about the antiquity of a book or charter. And many times these are of great importance.

---

[11] Bodl. MS Laud Gr. 35 (*SC* 1119).
[12] i.e. Laud Gr. 35: see no. 32.
[13] Probably Bodl. MS Barocci 202 (*SC* 202), a tenth-century codex.
[14] See no. 92 and no. 84 n. 4.

Besides, with such a Collection a man may soon learn to read the MSS, which would have been well, if many who have published old authors, could have done. There are many others things, such a collection may be serviceable to, in my opinion; but if that will not be granted; 'tis past contradiction, that it is an innocent recreation to mind these things; and I seldom employ my self in it, when I have other business. I am

    Reverend & Honored Sir,

        Your most humble & obedient servant

                                   Humfrey Wanley.

MS: British Library, Harley 5911, fo. 1. *Date*: 'At the Lodgings Aug. 11. 1697.'

38. *To* Arthur Charlett *22 August 1697*

Honored Sir,

    Methinks my case is not much unlike that of some, who having long endured the rigors, hardships & fears of a sudden & violent Tempest; yet at last come safe to their desired haven without loss: the very memory of their past Sufferings is sweet to them, and the safety they enjoy makes ample satisfaction for the dangers they underwent. 'Tis now the same thing with me, the unspeakable grief I endured from the apprehensions I had of your displeasure, is quite vanished as a dream, and your last kind & dear Letter remains as a certain and convincing Testimony of your reconciliation to me. Sir I heartily thank you for your Love to & Care of me, which I desire may be recalled when ever I prove f[a]lse to you.

    As to the Catalogue you send,[1] The Titles are imperfect, & had I not

---

[1] Charlett's catalogue (d. Aug. 1697, in a modern hand) is in Welbeck Wanley-ana = BL Loan MS 29/253. Tentative identifications follow: Jean Foy Vaillant, *Numis-mata aerea imperatorum Augustarum, et Caesarum in coloniis, municipiis et urbibus jure Latio donatis* (Paris, 1688); Charles de Croy, *Regum et imperatorum Romanorum numismata aurea, argentea, aerea &c.* (Antwerp, 1654); Hubert Goltz, *Opera Omnia* (Antwerp, 1645), the 'old Edition' is *Sicilia et magna Graecia, sive historiae urbium et populorum Graeciae ex antiquis numismatibus restitutae* (Bruges, 1576); Giovanni Ciampini, *De sacris aedificiis a Constantino Magno constructis* (Rome, 1693), and *Sacro-historica disquisitio de duobus emblematibus, quae in cimelio Gasparis Cardinalis Carpinei asseruantur* (Rome, 1691); 'Prosper Falusius', presum-ably erroneously for Prospero Parisius (= Parisio), *Rariora Magnae Graeciae Numismata* (Nuremberg, 1683); Jean Foy Vaillant, *Selectiora numismata in aere maximi moduli, e museo Franc de Camps* (Paris, 1694); Jean Harduin, *Antirrheticus de nummis antiquis coloniarum et municipiorum ad J.F. Vaillant* (Paris, 1689); Jacob Oisel, *Thesaurus selectorum numismatum*

known most of them already, I could not understand what they mean; but of all in their order,

* Vaillant numismata. fol. 1£. 15s. 0d. I suppose he means the book de municipijs & Colonijs, if so 'tis a rare book, but too dear, Mr Clement selling the Library one at the same rate.

Ducis Croyaci Numismata fol. 1£. 15. a good book, but I believe dear.

Goltzij Sicilia—& Magna Graecia. These are but 2 volumes of 5. NB the old Edition is best.

* Both Ciampini's books are rare & cheap at 1. 5. 0. a piece. Clements making the Library pay 40s a piece.[2]

* Magnae Graeciæ Numismata fol. this is Prosper Falusius, not dear at 6s

Vaillant Selectiora Numismata 4to you have already.

Harduini Anthirreticus 40 you had better have all his works together.

* Oyselij Numismata 40 1. 5. 0. a very good book, but very dear at this rate.

* Vaillant Numismata Regum Syriæ. 18s a rare book, but methinks dear.

De Wilde Numismata 40 14s a good book, the common rate.

Historia de re nummaria 40 2 voll. 18s I know not this book unless he had named the Author.

Dissertation sur les deux medailles des jeux seculaires 40 2s 6d this can't be dear.

antiquorum (Amsterdam, 1677); Jean Foy Vaillant, *Seleucidarum imperium: sive historia regum Syriae, ad fidem numismatum accommodata* (Paris, 1681); Jacob de Wilde, *Selecta numismata antiqua* (Amsterdam, 1692); Matthew Hostus, *De re nummaria veteri epitome* (Frankfurt, 1570); properly, *Dissertation sur douze Médailles des Jeux séculaires de l'Empereur Domitien* (Versailles, 1684); Jacob Gronovius, *Thesaurus Graecarum Antiquitatum* (Leiden, 1697–1702); Lorenz Beger, *Thesaurus Brandenburgicus selectus: sive gemmarum et numismatum Graecorum et Romanorum in cimeliarchio electorali elegantiorum series* (Coln, 1696–1701), and his *Thesaurus ex thesauro Palatino selectus: sive gemmarum et numismatum quae in electorali cimeliarchio continentur* (Heidelberg, 1685); Johann George Graevius, *Thesaurus antiquitatum Romanorum* (Leyden, 1694–9); Charles Patin, *Familiae Romanae in antiquis numismatibus* (Paris, 1663); Adolph Occo, *Imperatorum Romanorum numismata . . . cura et studio Franciscus Mediobarbi* (Milan, 1683); Abaham van Goorle, *Dactyliotheca, seu annulorum sigillarium, quorum apud priscos tam Graecos quam Romanos usus* (n.p., 1601); Leonardo Agostini, *Gemmae et sculpturae antiquae depictae . . . in Lat. versa ab Jac. Gronovio* (Amsterdam, 1685); Filippo Paruta, *La Sicilia descritta con medaglie, e ristampata con aggiunta da Leonardo Agostini* (Rome, 1649).

  [2] Henry Clements, bookseller of Oxford 1684–1721.

Thesaurus Graecarum Antiquitatum foll. 2£. I know not the book for want of the Authors name.

* Thesaurus Brandenburgicus fol. 2£. This is Begers & is cheap & the rate, you should have all his works, perhaps the last may be the Thesaurus Palatinus, which is also a noble book.

Sick's Infantia Salvatoris 80 3s I know not the book.

* Thesaurus Antiquitatum Romanarum fol. 6. vol. 8£. 10s. od in quires. I take these to be Graevius's they are noble books, & can't be dear.

* Patini Numismata fol. 1£. 15s. od in quires, I believe this may be his Roman families, if so it is not very dear. tho' you should have all his works.

This List is not at all perfect, for you ought to buy Mediobarbus his Roman Coins, a folio of about 40s price in the first place. And Gorlaeus his Dactyliotheca, with Leonardo Augustino, 2, 4tos of Gronovius Edition should be had. Paruta's Sicilian coins printed at Rome with the Additions of Leonardo Augustino, is a very rare & scarce book. And, Sir, if you please to think upon the *Columna Trajana*, the *Columna Antonina*, the *Capita Illustrium*, the *Triumphal Arches of Titus Vespasian & Severus*, or any thing else of that admirable Author,[3] you will find the Prints, &c carry their own recommendation along with them.

I remember, Sir, the last year you wrote to me about the Collection of Mr Seller which you said consisted of 1000 Coins,[4] whereof one third part were Greek, & the whole valued at 300£. 'Tis a great rate, & the coins had need be good, but Mr Charlton ha's the most noble Collection in England, for a private Gentleman, & 'tis worth while even to look upon them.

As for Madam Bernards books, I believe unless you please to interpose the very next Post, we shall go without them. Lately by Mr Vice-Chancellors order I have viewed the MSS, & compared them with what we have already, I gave him a true account of them in writing, confirmed with the suffrages of Mr Tanner, Dr Mill, Mr Thwaites, &c, who all pray that we may not be deprived of so great a Treasure as

---

[3] i.e. Giovanni Pietro Bellori, who provided notes for the splendid engravings of Pietro Sante Bartoli in such works as *Colonna Traiana* (Rome, n.d.), *Columna Antoniona* (Rome, n.d.), and pbd. *Imagines Veterum Illustrium Philosophorum &c.* (Rome, 1685).

[4] *DNB* says only that he possessed 'nearly two hundred coins'. Charlett's letter referred to here is d. 23 Sept. 1696 (Welbeck Wanleyana = BL Loan MS 29/253).

there is, and which we cannot come at any other way, unless by the
Death of Dr Gale, which is a great uncertainty.[5] Yet I find the Curators
are very cold, & Mr Millington[6] begins to grow hot; so that I fear the
books (unless you prevent it) will be speedily transported to London,
to the disgrace & lasting reproach of the University.[7] I am

Honored Sir,

Your most faithful and obedient servant

Humfrey Wanley.

[5] Gale's library was bequeathed to Trinity College, Cambridge by his eldest son,
Roger, in 1738. For his manuscript collections, see *CMA* II. i, p. 185.

[6] Edward Millington († 1703), book-auctioneer of London and Cambridge 1670–
1703.

[7] The affair of Bernard's books was to be a source of trouble to Wanley for the next
five years. Edward Bernard, Savilian Professor of Astronomy at Oxford 1763–91, died in
Jan. 1697 and his wife wished to dispose of his considerable library (see *CMA* II. i,
pp. 226–8), rich in classical and oriental works and including many manuscripts from
the sale of Nicholas Heinsius's library in 1683. The Bodleian was interested in the
library, but indecisive and, as always, chronically short of money. Wanley's 'Catalogus
Librorum (e Bibliotheca D. Ed. Bernardi) in Bodlejana desideratorum' is amongst the
Library Records. Two parcels of books were eventually bought: (1) printed books,
chiefly edns. of the classics not in Bodley; these were purchased directly from Bernard's
widow in Sept. 1697 for £140; (2) manuscripts, oriental and classical, books collated with
manuscripts, Bernard's own working papers and adversaria; these were also purchased
directly from Mrs Bernard for £200. Wanley's account of them for the Vice-Chancellor,
Fitzherbert Adams, is in the Bodleian Archives (Bodl. Archives A.1. formerly Arch. C.8)
together with the catalogues he drew up, and Millington's valuations; this is pbd. with
slight variations, but with the lists of ptd. books and manuscripts much curtailed, by
P. Bliss in his edn. of Wood's *Athenae Oxonienses*, iv (1820), pp. 707–10. There is a
version of Wanley's account of the manuscript portion of Bernard's library in BL
Harley MS 5911, fo. 8, and a catalogue of the ptd. books in BL Sloane MS 825. A complete list of Bernard's books that came to the Bodleian is in the *Summary Catalogue*, iii,
pp. 1–24.

The balance of the library was auctioned by Millington in Oxford on 25 Oct. 1697 and
Wanley was subsequently taken to task by Thomas Hyde, Bodley's Librarian, for allowing certain books to go to auction which should have been purchased for the Bodleian.
A list of these with Wanley's remarks appended is in Bodl. MS Rawl. D.742, fos. 19–20;
Wanley's defence is unimpeachable—of the thirteen works cited by Hyde one was
imperfect, two Wanley had been expressly instructed not to buy, and no fewer than ten
were already in the Bodleian. Five years later Hyde's successor, John Hudson,
advertised his ignorance in two letters complaining that he could not lay his hands on
Bernard's books and asking whether Wanley was able to help him. Wanley did not
conceal his contempt: 'Why should he apprehend them to be out of the Library, before
he had throughly searched it. And why should he desire to be Library-keeper so long, &
yet suffer such a parcel to lie all the while almost under his Nose, & yet know nothing of
them. However, upon this Letter, I directed him how to find them' (BL Harley MS
3779, fo. 302ᵛ). For Wanley's account to a third person of the disposition of Bernard's
books, see no. 86; for evidence that he antagonized Bernard's wife over the business, see
no. 46; for his purchase at Bernard's auction of some books for his own account, see the
lists in Bodl. MS Rawl. D.742, fos. 19–20, arts. 1 and 4, and in his letter to Bagford,
no. 42, arts. 23 and 29.

MS: Bodleian, Ballard 13, fo. 58. *Date*: 'From the Lodgings, Aug. 22. 1697.' *Address*: 'For the Reverend Dr Charlett, To be left with Mr Sare a Bookseller near Graies-Inn gate. London.'

39. *To* John Bagford *21 September 1697*

Mr Bagford,

I sent you word some time since that I received the parcel you sent me within a fortnight after you went hence: I expected the age of each Specimen of Paper, but I believe you forgot it. If you give me Orders I will send you as good an account of the age of your Shreds of Parchment as I can, with another Shred or 2 along with them.[1] The Shred of Greek is not in Capital Letters as you thought, but only some late writing in a big hand.

Our Master desires you to remember the Seal.[2]

I have run over Boxhornius, and there I find he stands stifly for Harlaem against Bernardus Mallincrotius who is for Mentz,[3] he quotes many authors, especially Hadrianus Junius, and tell's you that the book of Laurence Coster's in wooden Types now to be seen at Harlaem is called *Speculum Salutis*.[4] One notable thing in this book is an epistle which you may find before the 5th part of Nic. de Lyra's Bibles printed at Rome 1472, directed to Pope Xystus the 4th which gives an account of the bringing of Printing into Italy by Conrade Sweynhem & Arnold Pannarts, with a Catalogue of what books they Printed, & how many copies at each Impression.[5]

Not long after the French practised the art at Parma in Italy, as you may see by this date I copied at Christ-church Library. Q.2.11.

---

[1] See no. 42.

[2] An engraved monogram for Charlett (Wanley to Bagford, 20 July 1698; BL Harley MS 4966 art. 63) perhaps for use as a bookstamp.

[3] Marcus Zuerius Boxhorn, *De Typographicae Artis Inventione et Inventoribus Dissertatio* (Leyden, 1640); Bernard Mallinckrot, *De Ortu ac Progressu Artis Typographicae Dissertatio Historica, in qua . . . pro Moguntinis contra Harlemensis Concluditur* (Cologne, 1640).

This is the first of a number of letters to Bagford in which Wanley discusses the early history of printing: see also nos. 42, 56, 58, 60. The material in them he later brought together in 'Some Observations Concerning the Invention and Progress of Printing, to the Year 1465', originally read as a paper at a meeting of the Royal Society, 27 Oct. 1703, ptd. in *Philosophical Transactions*, no. 288 (Nov. and Dec. 1703), pp. 1507–16. See *Bodleian Library Record*, vi (1957–61), pp. 634–5.

[4] In fact, *Speculum Humanae Salvationis*.

[5] Hain 10363(5), Proctor 3323. See *GW* 4210 n.

Caij Plynij secundi naturalis historiae libri tricesimi septimi et ultimi finis, impressi Parmae ductu et impensis mei Stephani Coralli Lugdunensis M.CCCC.LXXVI. Regnante invictissimo Principe Galeaceo Maria Mediolani Duce quinto.[6]

As for old books, besides the Bishop of Norwich's Januensis, printed anno. 1460. you may find in Patins Travels, Durandi Rationale printed an 1459, which he says is now in the Public Library of Basil in Switzerland.[7] And if you read Lambecius his Catalogue of the Emperor of Germanies MSS. Lib. II. pag, 989 he will tell you of a Psalter which he found at Inspruck in the Archiducal Library there, the Date whereof is, he says, in these words,

Presens Psalmorum codex venustate capitalium, decoratus, Rubicationibus3 sufficienter distinctus ad inventione artificiosa imprimendi ac characterizandi absque calami ulla exaratione sic effigiatus, et ad eusebiam Dei industrie est consummatus per Ioannem Fust Civem Maguntinum, et Petrum Schoffer de Gernszheim anno Domini millesimo. CCCC. LVII. in Vigilia Assumptionis.[8]

In another place of the same book (I forgot the page, but can find it again, if there be occasion) he gives you this title to one of the MSS.

Apocalypsis S. Ioannis Apostoli & Evangelistae Latino-Germanica chartacea in folio, una cum vita ipsius, & multis figuris *ligno incisis*, quae propter vetustatem suam spectatu sunt dignissima.[9]

I know not what he means by this last book, unless it be such as ours, with 2 leaves pasted together.[10]

I have received a Letter from Major Beake about the printing of Martin-mar-prelate, but it lies among many others, yet you shall be sure of it, one day.

[6] Ed. Philip Beroald. Hain 13091, Proctor 6842; press-mark now e.i.31.

[7] John Moore, Bishop of Norwich: his 'Januensis', i.e. the *Catholicon* of Joannes Balbus (Mainz: [J. Gutenberg ?], 1460) (*GW* 3182, Hain 2254, Proctor 146) is described at length in *CMA* II. i, no. 379. For the *Rationale diuinorum officiorum* ([Mainz:] J. Fust and P. [Schöffer], 1459) (*GW* 9101, Hain 6471, Proctor 66), see Charles Patin, *Travels thro' Germany, Bohemia, Swisserland etc.* (English translation, 1696), p. 166.

[8] Peter Lambeck, *Commentariorum de Augustissima Bibliotheca Caesarea Vindobonensi* (Vienna, 1669). Fust and Schöffer's Latin Psalter of 1457 (Hain 13479, Proctor 64).

[9] Lambeck, *Commentariorum*, ii, p. 772. Probably an edn. of the blockbook described in *Catalogue of Books Printed in the XVth Century now in the British Museum* (1963), i, p. 3, Proctor 38, 39.

[10] Bodl. Auct. M.3.15 (*SC* 988), Proctor 41, is a copy of this xylographic Apocalypse given by Laud; pp. 36 and 37 and pp. 38 and 39 are pasted together. See Wanley, 'Observations', *Philosophical Transactions*, no. 288, p. 1509.

I know not whether any thing that I write be material or not, yet by this you may see I would willingly serve you, If I could. Pray my humble Service to Mr Hartley, Mr Brand, & my friend Mr Wakelin; tell him, tho' I have not much time to write, yet I could spare while to read a Letter of his to

Sir,

Your most obliged Servant

Humfrey Wanley.

Remember the Masters Seal

MS: British Library, Harley 4966, art. 41. *Date*: 'Univ. College Sept. 21. 1697.' *Printed*: Nichols, *Literary Anecdotes*, i, pp. 95–6.

40. *To* [Edmund Gibson] *1 November 1697*

Reverend Sir,

Notwithstanding your many favors you have hitherto heaped on me, I am forced to importune you for one more, in which yet quickness of dispatch (if consistent with your other affairs) will equal the obligation. I extreamly want *the true Saxon Character of King Alfred's time*; we have in the Publick Library (from Hattons) Pope Gregories Pastoral Care in Saxon,[1] which for several reasons, I take to be as old as K. Alfred who translated it, or near upon it; but I cannot be positive in this, and I love 2 strings to my bow. Now Dr Smith says that in the Cottonian Library Tiberius B.XI. (as I remember, for I have not his Cat. by me) there is another Copie of the same book, which formerly belonged to Plegmund Archbishop of Canterbury;[2] if this be so, my curiosity may be easily satisfied, if you get Mr Sturt (by Mr Bagford's means) copie me 10 or a dozen lines exactly from the book, with the Alphabets of the great & small Letters, & Points.[3] Be pleased to take

---

[1] Bodl. MS Hatton 20 (*SC* 4113), formerly Hatton 88; Ker no. 324, Wanley p. 70. The copy of the Alfredian translation of Gregory's Regula Pastoralis sent to Bishop Werfrith of Worcester.

[2] Ker no. 195, Wanley p. 217. Damaged in the Cotton fire of 1731, and again in a fire at the binders in 1864. Eight charred fragments of five leaves have survived; they are reproduced in *Early English Manuscripts in Facsimile*, vol. vi, ed. N. R. Ker (Copenhagen, 1956). The ascription to Plegmund 'antiqua manu' was on the first leaf of the manuscript, whence it was copied by Wanley.

[3] John Sturt (1658–1730), engraver, associate of John Ayres, and engraver of most of his important books on calligraphy.

notice of such a ẏ as this (ȝ) if you find it,[4] for tis in none but old books, and send me a line or two at the end, if the book be perfect. I will take care to gratify Mr Sturt for his pains, and desire you to consider, that if I have it not in 10. days, it will not be so useful to

Dear Sir,

Your most obliged & humble servant

Humfrey Wanley.

MS: British Library, Harley 4966, art. 42. *Date*: 'Univ. Coll. Nov. 1. 1697.' *Printed*: Nichols, *Literary Anecdotes*, i, pp. 96–7.

41. *To* [John Bagford] *2 November 1697*

Dear Sir,

I would beg the favor of you, immediately upon the Receit of this, to go to Mr Gibson, and know of him when he can let Mr Sturt into the Cottonian Library; and to take care to meet him at the time. The business is this: I very much want the true Saxon Character of King Alfreds time, and altho' in the Bodlejan Library there is a Saxon book which I believe may be sufficient to satisfie me,[1] and another Latin book or two which may do pretty well; yet in Sir J. Cotton's there is a Saxon book of undoubted authority,[2] and will surely confirm what we have here. I desire you to procure Mr Sturt to copie me exactly 10 or 12. lines with the Alphabets & Points, where Mr Gibson will direct him; and in the Alphabets not to forget the Letter ẏ if you find it thus (ȝ) nor the (ſ) if you find it thus (þ) but to put them amongst other Letters in the Alphabet. I am very willing to satisfie Mr Sturt to the full for his pains, and therefore you may give him what he asks; or if it will not stand so well with your convenience, I will send the money with the pieces of parchment, and your book, with money for a flute that I shall hereafter direct you to buy. Good Sir, don't neglect this business, & you will much oblige

Your real friend & most humble servant

H Wanley.

---

[4] For Wanley's confusion about the shape of *y* (here written like *yogh*), see no. 41.

[1] i.e. Hatton 20. See no. 40.

[2] i.e. Tiberius B xi. See no. 40. Cf. *Notes and Queries*, 216 (1971), pp. 3–4.

Pardon my hast,
When I wrote to Mr Gibson yesterday,
I was amongst much company in another Gentlemans
Chamber, they disturbed me, & my mind gives me I
made some Mistake about the ẏ (ꝯ) take
care of it; I had no time to read over what
I wrote to him, & have no more no[w.]

MS: British Library, Harley 4966, art. 43. *Date*: 'Univ. Coll. Nov. 2. 1697.' *Printed*: *Notes and Queries*, 216 (1971), pp. 3–4 (extract).

42. *To* John Bagford *27 November 1697*

Dear Sir,

I return you my hearty thanks for all your favors to me, which are & have been so many, that I am almost asham'd to write to you. I received the Specimen which pleas'd me very well, tho' I was sorry you forgot the Alphabets & Points, Pray give my humble service & thanks to Mr Sturt since he will take no money. Our Master desires you not to forget his Cipher[1] & ha's sent you 18s or 18s 6d I know not which, which I included *in the first Printed Page of the old book*, which I shall send next Tuesday by Matthews. I return you likewise the Seals, as thinking them not worth 10s but the stones I keep at 5s and therefore desire you to reckon the odd 12d or 18d to me, & to pay for the book you sent 1s for all which I will repay you at Christmas, when I hope to see you here.

As to my opinion of the old book, I think it could not be printed at Leyden in the year 1443, since it was first composed at Vienna 1444.[2] Yet 'tis not easy to say how the mistake should be rectified. I could wish you would give it to the Publick Library however, for William de Mechlinias sake.[3]

[1] i.e the 'seal' of Wanley's letter of 21 Sept. 1697, no. 39.
[2] *Opusculum Enee Sylvii de duobus amantibus* (Leiden: [Heynricus Heynrici], 14[8]3, but erroneously dated in the colophon 'Anno domini Millesimo CCCC° quadragesimotercio') (Hain 232, Proctor 9160, *BMC* ix, p. 96). It had been sent by Bagford for Wanley's opinion in a letter postmarked 14 Oct. It apparently went to Wanley rather than to the Bodleian; in *Philosophical Transactions*, no. 288 (1703), p. 1514, he describes the book as in his possession.
[3] Presumably because William de Machlinia, English printer (*fl.* 1482–90), was a native of the Low Countries.

Among some other little specimens I shall send you your pieces of Parchment back again,[4] I have numbred them with my black lead pencil, & give you this little account of their age, which I desire you to keep secret, for I may hereafter, when I have seen more such things, & have had a longer conversation with them, be able to judge more nicely.

No 1. In the Irish Character & Language, but not (I believe) very antient.

2. Greek in small Letters, tho' in a large hand, about 200 years old.

3. This is certainly Printed, not Written.

4. About Edward the 4ths time.

5. 2. of them) Which I present you with.) about the beginning of K. Henry. 6.

6. I believe much about the same time.

7. About 300 years old, but scarcely written by an English man.

8. About the same age written by an English man.

9. Perhaps 320 years old.

10. It may be 340 years old.

11. 350 years old.

12. Likely to be above 360 years old. and with no. 7. perhaps written by Flemings.

13. Towards 400 years old, but written in Italy. I present you with it.

14. About 400 years old, rather under. Written by an English Monk, as the last was by a Scribe.

15. 400 years old. Written by a Monk (I believe in Germany, by the form of the Notes.) 2 of these

16. 4 of these, I present you with. Above 400 years old.

17. Above 400 years old towards 500, but scarcely written in England.

18. Above 500 years old.

19. 500 years old.

20. above 500 years old.

21. So this.

22. Towards 600.

23. I bought the book, for this cover to present you with, at Dr Bernards Auction.[5] I take it to be about 600 years old.

---

[4] See no. 39.   [5] See no. 38.

no 24. About the same time with the others.

    25. This may be about the same age, or somewhat older, but Written in Germany.

    26. About the same time.

    27. Between 700 & 800 years old. Written in Germany.

    28. 2 of these I present you with. About 800 years old, or somewhat above, I suppose them written in France, or Flanders.

    29. I bought the book at the Auction, to secure you this cover written in France, between 800 & 900 years ago.

    30. I present you with this, written in some of those countries near 900 years since.

I make this Judgement of these things ex tempore, with[out][6] any recourse to any of the MSS. in the Publick Library, & therefore may be easily mistaken; tho' I hope not many Centuries of years, in any.

I have been bold to send you 2 more dates, which tho' you may have them already, yet it shews how ready I am to serve you, when I think it is in my power. In the publick Library B. 7. 14. *Jur.* is a small Fol. containing these Tracts, *Salus corporis*, *Salus anime*, *Pius contra Venereos* & *Yliada Homeri*,[7] at the end whereof you may find this Distich & Note,

> Hos eme Richardus quos Fax impressit ad unguem
> Calcographus summa sedulitate libros.

Impressum est presens opusculum Londoniis in Divi Pauli semiterio, sub virginei capitis signo. Anno salutis Milesimo quingentesimo nono. Mensis vero Decembris die. xij

Richard Faques.

Another book in our said Library *Barl.* A.1.7.[8] ends with this Note. Igitur Aurelij Augustini ciuitatis orthodoxe sideris prefulgidi de ciuitate Dei opus preclarissimum binis sacre pagine professoribus eximiis id commentantibus rubricis tabulaque discretum precelsa in urbe Moguntina partium Alemanie. non calami per frasim caracterum autem apicibus artificiose elementatum ad laudem trinitatis indiuidue ciuitatis Dei presidis operose est consummatum per Petrum Schoiffer de Gernseheim. Anno domini M.cccc. lxxiij. die. v. mensis Septembris. Presidibus ecclesie katholice Sixto tercio Pontifice summo. sedi autem Moguntine Adolfo secundo presule magnifico. Tenente autem

---

[6] MS omits 'out'.   [7] By William de Saliceto. *STC* 12512.

[8] Augustine, *De Ciuitate Dei, cum commentariis Thomae Valois et Nicolai Trivet* (Mainz: P. Schöffer, 1473) (*GW* 2884, Hain 2057, Proctor 102). Now Bodl. Auct. 7.Q.1.13.

ac gubernante christianismi monarchiam Imperatore serenissimo Frederico tercio Cesare semper Augusto.

I thought to suggest one thing, tho' I know not whether it be material or not, which is that you may easily secure your self from one argument often brought to prove that the Tullies Offices of 1465.[9] was the first book Printed; becaus it has these words *non atramento, plumali canna neque aerea*, &c. since words to that effect were constantly used in the Dates, as well after as before that time, for instance in this book of Schoiffers, & that other in Queens, another copie of which is now in the Bodleyan Library.

Pray give my humble service to Mr Brand, Mr Hartley, Mr Leigh,[10] & Mr Waklin, and send me word at what time I may expect you here in company of Mr Ayres & Mr Sturt, for I would by no means be out of the way.

When you deliver Mr Gibson a small parcell you will find enclosed in yours (which I would have done as soon as possible) Refresh his memory about a Specimen from Dr Stanley[11] which he promised me.

I am loth to trouble you any more at this time, knowing the urgency of your own affairs as well as my own. I pray God bless & reward you for all your kindness to me, which tho' I shall never be able to requite, I shall never forget.

Dear Sir,

    Your faithful friend & most humble servan[t]

                              Humfrey Wanley.

MS: British Library, Harley 4966, art. 44. *Date*: 'Univ. Coll. Nov. 27. 1697.' *Address*: 'For Mr Bagford To be left at Tom's Coffee-house near Ludgate, London.'

43. *To* John Bagford [*January 1698?*][1]

Mr Bagford,

I thank you for the things which you sent me last. I have some prospect of getting all the old shreds of Parchment in the Bodleian

---

[9] Cicero, *De Officiis et Paradoxa* ([Mainz:] J. Fust and P. [Schöffer], 1465) (*GW* 6921, Hain 5238, Proctor 80).

[10] A letter from one Thomas Leigh d. 21 Oct. 1697 (BL Harley MS 3780, fo. 89) shows that he had just visited Wanley in Oxford.   [11] So I read it. See no. 64 n. 24.

---

[1] After 19 Apr. 1696, when Wanley introduced Wakelin to Bagford (Wanley to

Library; and shall Move the Vice-Chancellor & the Curators in it[2] next Thursday. Against which time, I desire you to send me the best way of taking them off, from the book to which they are now annexed. And whether a wet Spunge will weaken the Past which binds some to the Covers of the books, or not. If I can get my request granted, you may conceive what a stock I shall bring up with me to London about May-day. I further desire you to acquaint Mr Wakelin with my coming; and to see for some handsome Chamber for me about Manchester Court, where I was last, that I may not spend time in looking out for one at my coming up. My Service to Major Ayres, Mr Postlethwait,[3] Mr Brand Mr Bullord,[4] &c concludes me

Your friend & servant

Humfrey Wanley.

The Glass you sent does not fit my Eyes, so that
Mr Mareschall[5] must

MS: British Library, Harley 4966, art. 55. *Date*: 'Sunday.'

44. *To* [George Hickes] *18 February 1698*

Reverend & Honored Sir,

Since my last to you, I have been long busied in necessary Business, so that I was forced to put a stop to all my Correspondence, and then being conscious to my self, that my Silence to you might very reasonably be construed as Ingratitude for so many favors; I was much disturb'd, and whilst I argued with my self whether there might be any

Bagford of that date, BL Harley MS 4966, art. 29); probably not 1697 or 1699, when Wanley seems to have spent the spring in Oxford. 1698 is perhaps the most likely year: Wanley was in London from mid-Mar. to early July. Probably before 18 Feb., when he wrote to Hickes that he hoped to be in London a fortnight hence.

[2] i.e. extracting from ptd. books pastedowns derived from old manuscripts. An undated memorandum on the subject directed to the Curators is in Welbeck Wanleyana = BL Loan 29/259 misc. 29, with the approval of Henry Aldrich, Dean of Christ Church, and John Wallis, subscribed; this is ptd. below, Appendix V. A copy in another hand is in BL Harley MS 5911, fo. 10.

[3] Perhaps John Postlethwayte (1650–1713), High Master of St Paul's 1697. A letter from Postlethwayte to Charlett d. 31 May 1698 (Bodl. MS Ballard 34, fo. 88) reports that he met Wanley at Lambeth after Wanley missed him at his house.

[4] John Bullord, bookseller and book-auctioneer of St Paul's Churchyard, London, 1689–1701.

[5] Not identified. All after 'must' lost in trimming.

hopes of Pardon or not, or whether I might not break thro' all my Apprehensions of your Displeasure, and venture to send you a Testimony of my Repentance & Amendment; I was all on a sudden seized with a violent pain in my Teeth, which immediately took away the very capacity of holding a Pen in my Hand; and handled me so rudely, that I have but now recovered it.

But now, Sir, I make hast to throw my self at your feet, I sincerely confess my Offence, and heartily desire you to forgive & forget it. And so much the rather, in that I'me affraid some talk about the Masters being Instrumentall in delaying the Publication of the Saxon Hepta-teuch,[1] might by misrepresentation to you, occasion you to think hardly of him, & of me for his Sake. The Matter of Fact, so as I learn it of the Master, is thus: He always encouraged our friend Mr Thwaites in the undertaking, and promised to take off 20 Copies, as he ha's done. He saw the Dedication[2] & liked it; and upon New-years day Mr Thwaites presented him with one, & he in looking over the book, perceived there was little or nothing which he could understandingly read but the Dedication & the Preface; which last he found to be but about 16 lines, whereas he could have wished it lengthened in to a Dissertation of as many Leaves. And he intimated so much to our said friend, telling him that he had a good occasion to give the World Satis-faction about the Author, the Version, its Nature, Authority, Use, &c. and that for want of this, the Reader had nothing to do but fix his Eyes upon your Name; and that he thought the bringing you out of a Retire-ment, which you had voluntarily chosen, into the World again, was quite contrary to your Inclination;[3] and for that Reason he told Mr Thwaites that he was not willing to send the book with the Dedication, to some great men, who are fast in with the Government. The next day being Sunday, in the Morning before Sermon, in Adam Bromes Chappel at St Maries,[4] the Vice-Chancellor[5] told the Master, that he had stop'd the Publishing the Æsops fables,[6] & the Saxon Hept.

[1] *Heptateuchus, Liber Job et Evangelium Nicodemi Anglo-Saxonice. Historiae Judith Frag-mentum, Dano-Saxonice*, ed. E. Thwaites (Oxford, 1698), from Bodl. MS Laud misc. 509 (*SC* 942).

[2] To Hickes.

[3] Hickes, as a nonjuror, had been ejected from his post as Dean of Worcester at the accession of William III.

[4] The University Church.

[5] John Meare (1649–1710), Principal of Brasenose 1681–1710, Vice-Chancellor 1697–8.

[6] *Fabularum Æsopicarum Delectus*, ed. A. Alsop (Oxford, 1698). Anthony Alsop, 'one of

because that Reflected on Dr Bentley, & this was dedicated to a man who was known to bear no good will to the Government, & the Master said again what he told Mr Thwaites; that [Dr Hickes][7] was as honest a Gentleman as lived; that he was the fittest person to have such a book Dedicated unto; but since he had taken a Resolution to live in private, &c. & there was little else a man could read besides the dedication; he thought he could not do his Friend [Dr Hickes][7] a greater kindness, than to cut it out of that book which he intended to send the Lord Chancellor.[8] And before this time vizt. Sunday Jan. 2. he had not seen Mr Vice-Chancellor, not sent to him, nor received any Message from him in 3 weekes. On Munday Jan. 3. Mr Thwaites waited on Mr Vice-Chancellor, who e'en fairly told him every word the Master said to him the day before, and insisted on them as an Argument for stopping the book. Upon which, our Friend, and many others will not be persuaded but that the Master caused the Vice-Chancellor to stop it, as they broadly say, on purpose to curry favor with the Court. Nor will they be convinced, tho' Mr Hall[9] can shew the Vice-Chancellors hand to stop it, dated Jan. 1st a day before the Master saw him. Sir, I need not tell you that I think the Master wronged, since the matter it self is so plain, and if this be not, there is no such thing as Demonstration in the world. And this I am equally assured of, that he ha's as tender a Love and as true a Respect for you, as one man can have for another or as any friend whose fidelity we find recorded in History.

But enough of that. The Saxon we see flourishes here, more than in all the World besides; we expect K. Ælfreds Boethius by Easter,[10] after which Mr Thwaites will put P. Gregories Pastoral into the Press;[11] and

the lowest and meanest of Aldrich's operators' (*Gentleman's Magazine*, xlix (1779), p. 547), i.e. of the Christ Church men who opposed Bentley in the Phalaris controversy. Besides the harsh words about Bentley in the Preface, Alsop apparently intended the last fable in his edition to be applicable to Bentley (*Gentleman's Magazine*, 1 (1780), p. 221). On Alsop, see further J. Nichols, *Biographical and Literary Anecdotes of William Bowyer* (1782), p. 578. It is curious in view of Wanley's account here that one of the Bodleian copies of Thwaites's *Heptateuch* (press-mark O.T. Anglo-Sax. d.1/1.) has the Imprimatur of the Vice-Chancellor, d. 27 Dec. 1697.

[7] 'Dr Hickes' scratched out, written in margin in another hand.

[8] John, Lord Somers (1651–1716), Lord Chancellor 1693–1700. A friend of Hickes, he was instrumental in procuring on 18 May 1699 an Act of Council ordering the Attorney General to cause a *Noli prosequi* to be entered to all proceedings against Hickes. For Wanley's interest in Somers's library after his death, see no. 178 n. 3.

[9] John Hall, printer at Oxford *c.*1670–1707, in his later years printer-warehouseman to the University.

[10] *Consolationis Philosophiae Libri V*, ed. C. Rawlinson (Oxford, 1698). Meare's Imprimatur is d. 2 Apr. 1698.

[See p. 86 for n. 11]

for ought I know, when that comes out, an honest Gentleman of this
College, may publish Orosius,[12] and so compleat our Royal Founders
works. I know not whether I told you that Bedes Eccles. Hist. a Parchment MS. in Saxon, is in C.C.C. Libra[ry] Mr Wheeloc ha's not used
in his Edition.[13]

I shall (God willing) be in London about a fortnight hence, my
business is to view all the old MSS. I can find there, and to take
Specimens of such as I shall have occasion for; and perhaps publish
from them, & those I have already, the chief Alterations in the Greek &
Latin Character (as used in Books) for near 1300 years; with the
derivations of the Coptic, Russian, Gothic, Runic, Francic, Saxon &
Irish Letters from them, in a Dissertation in the Catalogue of MSS.[14] I
think to lodge in some Inn at Westminster, to be near the Abby,
Cottonian & St James's Libraries, & as soon as I'me arrived I will go to
the sign of the Gun in —— and to Mrs Lee's & leave word there, *that if
any body enquires for one Wanley, he lodges in such a place*, to which, if you
happen to be in London, I pray & hope you will be pleased to send to
me by the Penny-post, or any other way, & this will be the greatest
Satisfaction that can be to

    Reverend Sir,
       Your most humble & most faithful servant

                          Humfrey Wanley.

I took the Boldness to acquaint
the Master with this Letter,
and he gives his humble service
to you, & expresses the greatest
love for you imaginable, & says he is
obliged to no man whatsoever,
so much as he is to you, &c.

MS: Bodleian, Eng. hist. c. 6, fo. 19. *Date*: 'From the Lodgings, Feb. 18. 1697/8.' *Address*:
'For Mr Potter at Mr Bromes House at Ewillington near Hereford. Leave this with
Thomas Dubbirlow a Shoemaker in By-street in Hereford. Herefordshire by way of
London.'

[11] Apparently never completed, although two specimen leaves of an edn. designed by
Thwaites are to be found in Bodl. MS Rawl. D.377, fos. 86–7.

[12] William Elstob. A specimen (title-page and two leaves) d. 1699 of an edn. of
Orosius are extant, but the edn. was never completed. See no. 27 n. 4. Alfred the Great
was the supposed founder of University College.

[13] Probably Corpus Christi College, Oxford, MS 279, pt. 2. Ker no. 354, Wanley
p. 105. Abraham Wheloc pbd. his edn. of Bede at Cambridge in 1643–4.

[14] See no. 37 n. 1.

45. *To* [George Hickes] *6 March 1698*

Reverend & Honored Sir,

   Your kind Letter of Feb. 24. came safe, and delayed my going for London for a fortnight longer, because I might be sure to meet you ther[e]. I will take care of the Runic Alphabets in Stephanius,[1] Mr Seller[2] was so kind as to proffer me the use of the book, and I declined it, as having no occasion for it; but I borrowed Bernardo Aldrete of the Original of the Castilian tongue, in Spanish, of him.[3] In it there are 2 Specimens of the Wisi-Gothic Character, and agree very well with what Mabillon calls the Langobardic. When I go to London, I will carry the book along with me and would by all means that you should read it, if you have not already. I intend this week to write to Dr Sherard (who is Governor to the Marquess of Tavistock)[4] to procure me a Transcript of that book in the Lombardick Language, which is in the Library of Bononia;[5] what the subject-matter of it is, I know not, but I think it must needs be worth procuring & reading.

   I here take the boldness to send you a quarter of an hours thought concerning the Derivation of the Runic Letters; which is absolutely different from the account given of them by Mr Junius & Olaus Wormius,[6] and for that reason you may well blame my rashness, which though I can't but expect, yet I will freely submitt to your censure.

   ᛀ seems to be taken from the Λ (or **A**) very frequent in MSS.
   B is the Roman or Greek B.
   ᛏ from the **C** or Greek *T*.

   [1] Stephan Johannis Stephanius in his *Notae Vberiores in Historiam Danicam Saxonis Grammatici*, pbd. together with his *Saxonis Grammatici Historiae Danicae Libri XVI* (Soroe, 1645). Stephanius discusses runes on p. 14 f. of the *Notae* (note to Preface, p. 2, l. 9). 'Taking care' presumably means procuring copies of the alphabets for Hickes's use in his elaborate discussion of them in pt. iii of the *Thesaurus*.
   [2] Abednego Seller (1646?–1705), non-juring divine. He possessed a good library (twenty-two manuscripts are described in *CMA* II. i, p. 96), but it perished in a fire in Jan. 1700.
   [3] *L'Origen y Institution de la lengua Española* (Rome, 1606).
   [4] William Sherard (1659–1728), botanist and antiquary, Fellow of St John's College, Oxford 1683, Consul to the Turkey Company of Smyrna 1703–17. He bequeathed money to found the Sherardian Chair of Botany at Oxford. Tutor to the Marquess of Tavistock, he was abroad with him in France and Italy from 1695–9. Twenty years later he acted for Wanley in acquiring ptd. books and manuscripts in Europe and the East: see nos. 204, 209, 216, 219, and Wanley, *Diary*, pp. 19(4), 106(11), 124(12) and (1), etc.
   [5] i.e. Bologna.
   [6] Junius in his *Gothicum Glossarium* (Dordrecht, 1665), pp. 1–29; Worm presumably in one of the works in his collected *Antiquitates Danicae* (Copenhagen, 1643–51).

þ is derived from the D only the perpendicular Line is longer. ꓶ is the same with the ꓶ, only the parallel line shews that there is a difference in the sound, ꓶ being as a *T* or *θ*, ꓶ and þ as D or the Saxon þ.

ꝥ from the *Ɛ* which is frequently so made in old MSS.

Ᵽ the Gothic ꟻ distorted.

Ᵽ the point shews a difference in the Sound from the Ᵽ.

ꝉ shews a great variety in the sound of this Letter.

I is an abbreviation of the Latin H, and the semi-circles may shew that sometimes the letter may be pronounced as an H, and sometimes as a *χ*, or *Π*, unless it be an H transvers'd ꭙ.

I the Latin or Greek I.

Ᵽ the Latin or Greek K abbreviated.

Γ from the Greek *Λ*.

Ⴑ from an M turn'd upside down, as it seems.

ⱶ the Lat. N abbreviated.

ꓮ I know not what to make of it, unless this stroke l in it, is so for to be more uniform with the rest of the vowels and the 2 diagonal Lines to shew that it was a different Letter, & perhaps differently pronounced, as o & as w.

Ƀ the point shews it differs in sound from B.

R the Roman R. ꭆ I take to be a quick way of making it.

Ꞃ the Roman S as thus made in MSS Ꞅ, only put on one side, for easiness.

↑ from the Lat. or Gr. *T*. from the Lat Ⴀ(or T) often seen in MSS.

∩ from the Gothic **n**. if not from the Roman V, turn'd upside down.

Ᵽ the point to distinguish it from Ᵽ.

∏ | are likewise by their respective points distinguished from ∩
Ꝧ |

& þ.

'Tis so much the harder to guess at the originall of these Letters, in that we (in England) have no book written in them, whereby we might see in what manner the hand directed the Pen in forming them; and by the variety, seeing the same letter very often, know which is the Essential part of it, and which stroke is left to chance.

I acquainted the master with what you bad me; he said he could not remember that he said so to you: if he did, it might be occasion'd by his grief for Mr Graham,[7] or by his making Sermons at that time, or both. That he never wrote since, was, because he knew not your direction, & constantly heard of you, by Mr Thwaites or me, and will in a good long letter tell you more himself.

Really, Sir, he talks of you with all the Love & Tenderness in the world, and tho' he is troubled that matters should be misrepresented to you,[8] he often says, that your Friendship is too well linked together, & the ties thereof too sacred to be broke thro' upon any mans endeavors: and that if you were never so prejudiced by other peoples contrivance, yet one conference would infallibly undeceive you. I am, with all respect

Honored Sir,

Your most humble and obedient Servant

Humfrey Wanley

MS: Bodleian, Eng. hist. c. 6, fo. 21. *Date*: 'From the Masters Lodgings March 6. 1697/8.' *Address*: 'For Mr Brome at his house at E-Willington near Hereford. Leave this with Tho. Dubbirlow a Shoemaker in By-street in Hereford. Herefordshire. by way of London.'

46. *To* Arthur Charlett *30 April 1698*

Honored Sir,

I just now received your very kind Letter, having dined with Madam Isted[1] to day, where your health went over & over. I will wait on the Dr,[2] and if you had been pleas'd to have given me orders, I would have

---

[7] Richard Graham (or Grahme), of University College, son of James Grahme of Levens, Westmoreland, Keeper of the Privy Purse to James II. He died in 1697. A series of letters from him and his tutor Hugh Todd, describing his college life and last illness, was (with names of persons and places altered) pbd. by F. E. Paget under the title *A Student Penitent of 1695* (1875).

[8] Presumably the business of the dedication of Thwaite's *Heptateuch* to Hickes: see no. 44.

[1] Of Clerkenwell, mother of Thomas Isted who matriculated at University College in 1695. Cf. Charlett's reply: 'Your Letter last night very much disappointed me, who was prepared to receave Mrs Isteds Sentiments of her Son, *where he was, and when expected home*, instead of an Idle Account of drinking Healths, which is never proper to be sayd to Superiors' (1 May 1698, Welbeck Wanleyana = BL Loan MS 29/253). Charlett's letter is full of gratuitous advice: see the quotations below.

[2] Posnicof, Peter the Great's interpreter. Cf. Charlett's remark: 'The Muscovite Doctor talks much of presents for our Library, but Travellers have often not good

been at Oxford before now, for his sake, & return'd hither with him again. His Master (the Czar) gave the Kings servants, at his departure 120 Guineas, which was more than they deserved, they being very rude to him: but to the King, he presented a rough Ruby, which the greatest Jewellers of Amsterdam (as well Jews as Christians) valued at 10000£ sterling; 'tis bored thro' and when it's cut & polished, it must be set upon the top of the Imperial Crown of England.

Yesterday (at the Cotton Library) I met with Mr Chamberlain[3] (son to the Dr) a courteous, modest & learned Gentleman, with Mr Holms[4] Clerk to Mr Petit,[5] we never saw one another before, and yet he was pleas'd to entertain so good an opinion of me at first sight, that he would needs have me dine with him, which I did: his lodgings being not 200 yards from mine: there he ente[r]tain'd me very kindly, &c. From thence we went to the Exchequer, where I was introduced to mr Le Neve,[6] who readily shewed me Doomsday book, the Continuation of it in a lesser volume;[7] the antient Copy of them: the Pipe Roll,[8] with the black & red books of the Exchequer:[9] and we promised to meet all together this night, which I have not been able to do (Company coming to see me) but wrote a note to excuse my self.[10]

Memorys' (Charlett to Wanley d. 1 May 1698, Welbeck Wanleyana = BL Loan MS 29/253).

[3] John Chamberlayne (1666–1723), first Secretary of the SPCK, in which post Wanley succeeded him. He was the son of Edward Chamberlayne (1616–1703), author of *Angliae Notitiae, or the Present State of England* (1669), a handbook of social and political conditions in England, with lists of offices etc., which went through twenty edns. in his own lifetime. For Wanley's later embittered relations with John Chamberlayne, see his letter of 13 May 1701, Welbeck Wanleyana = BL Loan 29/252.

[4] George Holmes (1662–1749), Deputy-Keeper of Records at the Tower 1707–49; later, with Wanley, an early member of the Society of Antiquaries.

[5] William Petyt (1636–1707), of the Inner Temple, Keeper of Records in the Tower 1689. He compiled the very brief account of the Tower rolls in *CMA* II. ii, p. 183.

[6] Peter Le Neve (1661–1729), Norfolk antiquary, Rouge Croix Pursuivant 1690, Norroy King-of-Arms 1704, first President of the Society of Antiquaries 1717–24. For some years before 1706 he was Deputy Chamberlain of the Exchequer.

[7] i.e. vols. i and ii of 'Doomsday Book', sometimes known as Great (vol. i) and Little (vol. ii) Doomsday; they differ in contents, shape, size, script, and scale.

[8] The so-called Great Roll of the Exchequer, comprising the enrolled annual accounts, county by county, of sheriffs and others.

[9] Liber Niger Scaccarii and Liber Rubeus, two copies (compiled in the reign of Henry III) of the returns of the tenants *in capite* in 1166. For a full account of the Liber Rubeus and a notice of the Liber Niger, see J. Hunter, *Three Catalogues Describing the Red Book of the Exchequer &c.* (1838).

[10] Which excuse brought the following reprimand from Charlett: 'Mr Le Neve &c. ought not to be disappointed, such Gentlemen are to be treated with great Exactnesse and Deference, if you put yourself on equal Terms with them, you will find theyr Company very expensive. Remember the advice I gave You of keeping only such

When I return'd to Sir John's,[11] in the afternoon; the Maid told me that Dr Smith had been there since I went (I had met him a little before in Westminster hall, & saluted him, which he returned very coldly) that the Dr was in a great rage at my being there, that he had look'd into my books, and was then more angry than before: that he chid her severely for letting me into the Library, & making it Common; and vowed to write Sir John about it that night, with much more to that purpose. The maid (being my friend) advised me to go to Dr Smith and talk with him, which I did: and as I went, I considered that the Dr had three occasions to think hardly of me: one from Madam Bernards good word of me, who is angry that I did all in my power (one way or other) to help her off with above 400 £ worth of her books.[12] Another, that the Dr is Jealous of my Copying Letters from MSS. and the third, is that I did not apply my self to him in the first place, which was the greatest provocation. When I came to his lodgings nere So ho; he was gone out;[13] I thought I must needs prevent his writing to Sir John: and therefore summoning up all the powers of Rhetorick I was Master of, I wrote him an humble & very submissive Letter; all in his own Stile, that is, I call'd the Library a Venerable place; the Books, sacred reliques of Antiquity, &c. with half a dozen Tautologies: which had so good effect on him, that he came to my Lodgings to day (when I was at Mrs Isteds) and left word, that I had free admittance to the Place; that he desired me to come & see him any day at 11, a clock;[14] and seem'd extreamly pleas'd with

Reverend & Honored Sir,

Your most faithful & humble servant

Humfrey Wanley

Company, as will pay your Reckoning. You must Learn the Act of complaining of Want' (Charlett to Wanley d. 1 May 1698, Welbeck Wanleyana = BL Loan MS 29/253).

[11] i.e. the Cotton Library which was housed at Sir John Cotton's.

[12] Smith was a friend of Edward Bernard who had died in the previous year. For Wanley's involvement in purchasing books from his library for the Bodleian, see no. 38 n. 7. The present remark is presumably ironical—cf. Charlett's comment: 'Mrs Bernard I presume has been as good to You as she promised in representing You Vain Proud & Prodigal' (Charlett to Wanley d. 1 May 1698, Welbeck Wanleyana = BL Loan MS 29/253).

[13] Charlett again: 'Unlesse you can learn to rise early in the Morning, you will do but little businesse' (Charlett to Wanley d. 1 May 1698, Welbeck Wanleyana = BL Loan MS 29/253).

[14] 'I am very glad your affair ended so well with Dr Smith, who most certainly neither admires nor loves You. You see the good Effects of Humility and Submission. Be sure you are very strictly watcht, and must expect to answer very severely for any words or Actions, that advantage may be taken of, to expose You' (Charlett to Wanley d. 1 May 1698, Welbeck Wanleyana = BL Loan MS 29/253).

MS: Bodleian, Ballard 13, fo. 59. *Date*: 'London, April the 30th 1698.' *Address*: 'For the Reverend Dr Charlett Master of University College in Oxford.' *Printed*: Ellis, *Original Letters*, pp. 257–9.

47. *To* Arthur Charlett *13 May 1698*

Honored Sir,

I most humbly thank you for your last kind letter, by which I understand that I used the word *Feasible* to the Vice-Chancellor. I have no Copy of what I wrote: but so far as I remember, I meant no more, than that such a thing is *Feasible*, or *Possible to be done*, *or brought to pass*.[1]

What Informations I have had of Sir John's Love to the University, I had from his own Servant, who told me (under the Rose)[2] of the Writings to Settle the Library upon the Heir; and that Sir John talked of giving the *Greek Genesis*[3] to the University. If it be possible, for Love or Money, or both, I will see these Writings before I come away.

I am sensible, Sir, the University is low; but yet, with submission, if the University have a mind to get that *Invaluable* Collection to Oxford, money must not be wanting. Mr Pepys says, he looks upon that Library as one of the Jewels of the Crown of England; and declared to me, that tho' he is a Cambridge man, yet he had much rather the Library was carried to Oxford. And I don't question but the University might be reimbursed, of all expenses, by some worthy Gentlemen, who have been formerly members of her.[4]

[1] Charlett had written 'We do not know what you meane by the word *Feasible* and wish you be not deceaved as to Sr J. Cottons Inclinations' (Charlett to Wanley d. 10 May 1698; Welbeck Wanleyana = BL Loan MS 29/253). Although Wanley's letter to Meare, the Vice-Chancellor is not extant, it is clear from what follows that Wanley had written enthusiastically about the possibility of obtaining the Cotton Library for the Bodleian. The 'Writings' referred to may be a draft of the terms by which Sir John Cotton, 3rd Baronet (1621–1702), made over the Cotton Library to the nation (not to his heir) two years later; they were incorporated in an Act (12 and 13 William III c. 7) which came into effect on his death in Sept. 1702: see no. 89.   [2] i.e. *sub rosa*.

[3] Cotton Otho B.vi. This famous fifth-century uncial manuscript was largely destroyed in the fire of 1731. Twenty fragments were engraved by Vertue for the Society of Antiquaries in 1744 and inserted in their *Vetusta Monumenta*, i (1747), pls. 67, 68 (really 70, 71). In 1796, when Planta was compiling his Catalogue of the Cottonian manuscripts, only eighteen fragments remained, none of them among the fragments engraved in *VM*. Four fragments had found their way into the possession of the Baptist College at Bristol by 1784; they were bought back by the Museum in 1962.

[4] Cf. Charlett: 'you know the Poverty of the University, and must always talk of that, not of Plenty, as ye way of some is' (Charlett to Wanley d. 10 May 1698; Welbeck Wanleyana = BL Loan MS 29/253).

I call God to witness, Sir, that if I my self had wherewithals I would be at the charge. And I think I cannot better discharge my Conscience & Duty to my Countrey, than by doing all in the Compass of my narrow Sphere, to bring it to a happy Issue. I must humbly beseech you, Sir, to excuse my Zeal in this matter; I have no Interest in it, sep[e]ratly to my self; nor would I have been so forward now, but that I fear Sir Johns Sealing. I am Honored Sir,

Your most faithful servant

Humfrey Wanley.

be pleased to turn over.

I have been at Gresham College Library,[5] where the books in the Picts Language, prove to be Irish:[6] and the books *in Litteris Majusculis*,[7] are only in a good big hand, not in Capital Letters.

MS: Bodleian, Ballard 13, fo. 64. *Date*: 'London, May the 13. 1698.' *Address*: 'For the Reverend Dr Charlett Master of University College in Oxford.' *Printed*: Ellis, *Original Letters*, pp. 259–61; P. L. Heyworth, 'Humfrey Wanley and "Friends" of the Bodleian, 1695–98', *Bodleian Library Record*, ix (1973–8), pp. 229–30.

48. *To* [Arthur Charlett] *26 May 1698*

Honored Sir,

Your last most welcome & kind Letter[1] came safe; bringing along with it the pleasing assurance of my continuance in your grace & favor: a happiness, of which I am truly sensible, & know how to value accordingly. Dr Bentley gives me many fine words, and I hope some time the next week, to take him without an excuse: as for Domesday-book, 'tis a most noble Record, as also the Pipe-Roll of the i year of

---

[5] i.e. the library of the Royal Society.

[6] Probably BL Arundel MSS 313 (*CMA* II. i, no. 3202, descr. as 'Libellus de Arte Medicinali in Lingua Pictica conscriptus'), and 333 (*CMA* II. i, no. 3222, descr. as 'Historia de Terra Pictica, in Lingua Pictica exarata'—which title may derive from Camden: a note on fo. 1, perhaps in his hand, declares 'Historia de terra Pictica in lingua Pictica conscripta'). The Arundel manuscripts came in 1831 to the British Museum from the Royal Society, to which body they had been given by Henry Howard, grandson of Thomas, 2nd Earl of Arundel (1585–1646), who originally brought them together: see further, no. 102.

[7] Presumably such as those so described in Bernard's catalogue, e.g. *CMA* II. i, nos. 3004, 3180.

[1] d. 23 May 1698 (Welbeck Wanleyana = BL Loan MS 29/253).

King John; they are both kept in the Exchequer, and I may use them about 3 hours in a day, but the noise & hurry is such, that I shall find more disturbance there than any where else; my business being not so much to transcribe a few lines from them, as to copy their several Hands exactly.

On Saturday, I must wait on Sir John Chardin, at his house in Tottenham-green, by his appointment:[2] I expect to find there the true Iberian, Gaurian & Kuphic Letters, which I never yet saw: We have indeed some little things printed in the Iberian (or Gjorgian) Character, but I always love to have recourse to the Fountain-head, the well-written Manuscripts.

I am much troubled at my Tutors death, who always carried it like a Gentleman to me. Sir, I never yet offered to intermeddle with the College-affairs, but that Love and Respect I have for my worthy Friend Mr Denison, a good Scholar, and otherwise a person of great merit, I humbly conceive may obtain my Pardon, if I should only presume to put you in mind that he is a Yorkshire man, qualified (or may soon be so) to succeed Mr Siser, and in all probability, likely to become an Ornament to our College, University & Nation.[3]

I saw Dr Bray to day (who sends you his humble service) he tells me that my Lord of Cov. & Lichfield is at Eccleshall in Staffordshire:[4]

---

[2] Sir John Chardin (1643–1713), merchant and jeweller. The remains of his library were sold by James Levy in 1713.

[3] Charlett had reported John Sizer (Fellow of University College, Oxford 1688), Wanley's tutor, seriously ill on 18 May and dead on 23 May. The election of Charles Usher in his place was the occasion of much bitterness. Usher was elected on 16 Dec. 1698 in defiance of Charlett's wishes. It is clear that Usher had no good opinion of the Master and had not concealed his disaffection in the past, and Charlett immediately appealed the election before the Vice-Chancellor and Doctors on 17 and 18 Dec., using Usher's injudicious remarks as evidence. The election was quashed and Usher was censured. William Denison (later Principal of Magdalen Hall 1745–55) was elected to succeed him, but not without strong opposition. Wanley and Prickett the butler organized a party in support of Denison; another group of Fellows were opposed and appealed Usher's ejection to Convocation; and on the Vice-Chancellor refusing the appeal, Usher successfully moved for a mandamus against him in the King's Bench. He also attacked Wanley and the others in a pamphlet, *A Letter to a Member of the Convocation of the University of Oxford, containing the Case of a late Fellow-elect of University College in that University* (1699). The College was split and there was talk of dissolving the common-room and not coming to Hall (W. Carr, *University College* (1902), pp. 163–5). Many years later Wanley was said to have regretted helping Denison supplant Usher (Hearne, *Collections*, viii, p. 304).

[4] Thomas Bray (1656–1730), founder of the scheme to provide for isolated and backward parishes the libraries which bear his name. William Lloyd, Bishop of Lichfield, was his early patron as he was Wanley's.

I will write to my Lord this Post, to recommend me to the Bishop of
Salisbury (a Lover of Antiquities)[5] and will endeavor to get this
Recommendation back'd by my Lord Arch-bishop and the Bishop of
Norwich:[6] this can do me no harm, and may perchance one way or
other prove beneficial to
    Honored Sir,
        Your ever-dutiful & most faithful servant
                                            Humfrey Wanley.

MS: Bodleian , Ballard 13, fo. 68. *Date*: 'London May 26, 1698.' *Printed*: Ellis, *Original
Letters*, pp. 261–2.

49. *To* Arthur Charlett *30 May 1698*

Honored Sir,
    I have at length got the Dr[1] in a perfect good humor, and this day
began to take a Specimen of the Alexandrian MS.[2] the Dr made me
dine with him and treated me with great kindness; after diner, I again
mov'd to see the Library, having been put by 3 or 4 times before; which
he now readily granted. The books lie in unexpressible disorder and
confusion, and have done so, as I have been told, ever since K. Charles
his time. I ghess by the view of them, that there are very many more
Manuscripts than are express'd in Dr Maurice's Catalogue.[3] The
Greek Manuscripts are but few, and those mostly upon paper: there

---

[5] Gilbert Burnet (1643–1715), Bishop of Salisbury 1689, is not famous as a 'Lover of
Antiquities'.
[6] i.e. Tenison and Moore.

[1] Bentley, Keeper of the Royal Library.
[2] Codex Alexandrinus, BL Royal MS 1.D.v–viii, the early fifth-century manuscript
of the Greek bible presented by Cyril Lucar, then Patriarch of Constantinople, to
James I.
[3] I know of no catalogue of the Royal manuscripts of this date except that in *CMA* II.
i, pp. 239–48. Henry Maurice (1648–91), Fellow of Jesus College, Oxford 1668, DD 1683,
Lady Margaret Professor of Divinity at Oxford 1691, is the most likely candidate for
Wanley's 'Dr Maurice'. He was a good scholar, chaplain to Archbishop Sancroft 1680–
91, and hence resident in London for much of that time. But it is unlikely that he was the
author of the catalogue in *CMA*: he died in Oct. 1691, while a preliminary list of collections to be included in *CMA*, pbd. by Bernard in *Philosophical Transactions*, no. 211 (June
1694), pp. 160–1, does not mention the Royal Library. There is evidence to suggest that
Maurice made catalogues for his own use, though none has been identified: see R. W.
Hunt, *A Summary Catalogue of Western Manuscripts in the Bodleian Library at Oxford*, i
(Oxford, 1953), p. xxvii.

are about 3 upon Parchment, whereof I saw 2, they are both of them
pieces of the Septuagint, one of them seem's about 600 years old, of
which I had but a glance:[4] the other (but more valuable book) is about
400 years old, in this the book of Esther is distinguish'd with the Asterisks & Obelisks of St Origen.[5] I remember the Dr told me at Oxford, that
this book was 800 years old; to day, he said it was at least 600 years old; to
which I seem'd to acquiesce, tho' I remember that we have a book or two
in the same hand in the Bodlejan Library which appear by the date
thereof to have been written about 400 years ago; and indeed, considering the nature of the Character, with the older & more recent MSS, it
must needs be about that time. I employed about 5 hours in turning over
a vast heap of Manuscripts, wherein were many very good books,
amongst some indiferent ones. There are some scarce copies of some
Latin Fathers, and many good English Historians, among which, I took
notice of Mathew Paris's history, said to be written with his own hand;
in it, are painted the Pictures of the Kings of England whose acts he
treats of, vizt from William the Conq. to K. Henry the 3d[6] but no mention of King John's being poisoned by a monk, as I have seen represented in Picture & expressed in plain words in a MS as old as K. Edw. 1.
in the Cotton Library.[7] This book of Matthew Paris is likewise considerable for the Coats of Arms of most of the great persons mentioned
in his History, drawn upon the margent of the book, with his own
Picture prostrate at the feet of a Madonna. This Picture is printed in Dr
Watts's Edition, but set upright: Dr Watts's cut resembles the Original
more than, I believe, that did the man.

The second copie formerly belong'd to St Austins at Canterbury,

I found likewise 3 noble Latin copies of the Evangelists, one of them
ha's had its cover which was of Plate (I presume, either massy Gold or
Silver) impiously stole and torn from it. It seem's to have been King
Æthelstans book, for here is a sort of a Pardon of his (in Saxon) to
another man entred therein, and so worded as if it was the Kings
book; but the Text it self is much older.[8]

The second copie formerly belong'd to St Austins at Canterbury,

---

[4] Perhaps BL Royal MS 1.B.ii, an early twelfth-century codex of the major and minor
prophets.

[5] Probably BL Royal MS 1.D.iii of the thirteenth century.

[6] BL Royal MS 14.C.vii, ptd. by William Wats in 1684 as *Historia Major*, the book
referred to below.

[7] Probably Cotton Titus A.xv, the Chronicle of Thomas Wykes, which extends from
the Conquest to 18 Edward I (1289). The account of the poisoning is on fo. 13[r].

[8] BL Royal MS 1.A.xviii of the early tenth century.

and is near a thousand years old, written in the English hand: 'tis ill used, but notwithstanding there remains many Letters which I must needs copie:[9]

The 3d is about 900 years old, in the same English hand, but somewhat newer: in this, besides some variety of Letters, are many considerable Readings, which make this book as choi[c]e as either of the two former, tho' it bee not so gloriously written: I ought to have a specimen of this too.[10]

My paper, Sir, will not permitt me to enlarge any farther on the books I saw, which I humbly beg you Sir, to dispence a little withall, tho' I do stay here beyond my time.[11] I conceive it, Sir, a part of a Library-keepers business to know what books are exstant in other Libraries besides his own; and as this qualifies him the better for his place, so by that means he may prove the more serviceable knowing what Copies of such an Author is in his own Library, and where they may be found elsewhere. I have ee'n finished at Sir John Cottons for this time; and will dispatch at St James's & the Exchequer as fast as possible; and having shewed my book to half a dosen of my Superiors will take my Leave, & return forthwith and, Sir, I will (God willing) take care that my time I spent here shall not be miss'd by the 8th of November.[12] I am

Honored Sir,

Your most faithful & humble servant

Humfrey Wanley

MS: Bodleian, Ballard 13, fo. 69. *Date*: 'London May 30. 1698.' *Address*: 'For the Reverend Dr Charlett Master of University College in Oxford.' *Printed*: *Bodleian Letters*, i, pp. 89–92.

50. *To* Edmund Gibson *9 August 1698*

Reverend Sir,

I have now at length sent you the 3 books I spake of before, which you might have received long since, with many others you wrote for,

[9] Perhaps BL Royal MS 1.D.ix of the early eleventh century.
[10] Perhaps BL Royal MS 1.D.iii of the eleventh century.
[11] Charlett had written on 18 May, 'Your Month is expired'; on 2 June he wrote 'On Munday the VC seemd to ask with some concerne after you, intimating some had been complaining at yr long Absence' (Welbeck Wanleyana = BL Loan MS 29/253).
[12] i.e. for the annual Visitation of the Curators of the Bodleian.

had not your letter miscarried, and the auction proved generally dear. If you please to send the 3s.8d to Mr Sare he will pay it to Mr Millington.[1]

The Septentrional Grammars are put into the press, and in all likelyhood will make a very noble book.[2]

As to the Catalogue of MSS.[3] 'tis e'en finished, they are hard at work upon my lord of Norwiches Appendix, and there is not above 2 sheets of Index[4] with the Preface to print, after which if the Delegates so please, the book may be published.

Honored Sir,
    I am
        Your most faithful & humble servant
                          Humfrey Wanley

	£. s. d.
Orpheus	0. 2. 2.
Symmachus	0. 0. 6
Osorius—	0. 1. 0
	0. 3. 8

To mr Gibson at Lambeth

MS: Bodleian, Autographs d. 21, fo. 152. *Date*: 'From the Lodgings, Aug. 9. 1698.' *Address*: 'To mr Gibson at Lambeth.'

51. *To* Hans Sloane[1] *9 August 1698*

Honored Sir,

    I delivered the brass coin to Dr Hyde, and told him it came from you, to whom he will send the explication of it, if any thing can be

---

[1] Perhaps the following books from Levinz's sale: *Orphei Argonautica, Hymni, et De Lapidibus*, ed. A. C. Eschenbach (Utrecht, 1689), Quintus Aurelius Symmachus, *Epistolarum ad diversos libri X, ex nova recensione J. P. Parei* (Neustadt, 1617), Jeronimo Osorio da Fonseca, *De rebus Emmanuelis, Lusitaniae Regis* (Cologne, 1681); respectively lots 131, 184, and 305 of Libri Miscellanei in Octavo.
[2] i.e. the first three parts of Hickes's *Thesaurus*, containing his Anglo-Saxon and Gothic grammars, a 'Francic' grammar, and the reprint of Jonsson's Icelandic grammar, all pbd. 1703.   [3] *CMA*.   [4] Compiled by Wanley.

---

[1] Hans Sloane (1660–1753), physician, natural historian, and collector. Secretary of

picked out. He is trying what he can do with a coin of Tangrolipix, the first Sultan of the Turks in Persia, which ha's an ill fashion'd Head, & on the reverse a plain Inscription, which the Dr says is in Syriak letters, but I am affraid there will be no great discoveries.

I humbly thank you, Sir, for your many & great favors to me, which I shall never forget, nor refuse to serve you in any thing that lies in my power. Accordingly, I have bought you the following books in the late Auction, which come to 14s which Mr Sare at Graies Inn Gate,[2] to whom I have sent them, will receive.[3] Had not the Auction been generally very dear, you might have expected more, from

Honored Sir,

Your most obliged servant

Humfrey Wanley.

	£ s d
Agliambe.	0. 9. 6.
Fulgosus.	0. 2. 0
Poterius.	0. 2. 6.
	0.14. 0

MS: British Library, Sloane 4037, fo. 106. *Date*: 'From the Masters Lodgings at University Coll. August 9. 1698.' *Address*: 'For the Honred Dr Hans Sloane Secretary to the Royal Society, at his house in Southampton street in Holbourn London.'

52. *To* Arthur Charlett *10 October 1698*

Honored Sir,

Tho' I am not certain whether this will find you in London I can't forbear to acquaint you with the Substance of Dr Hydes discourse with me the last night. He says, that he is heartily weary of the place of

the Royal Society 1693–1712, Baronet 1716. Physician to Queen Anne and George II. His collection, together with the Cotton Library and the Harleian manuscripts, is one of the foundation collections of the British Museum.

[2] Richard Sare († 1724), bookseller of Gray's Inn Gate, Holborn, 1684–1724.

[3] Perhaps the following books from Levinz's sale: Philippus Alegambe, *Bibliotheca Scriptorum Societatis Jesu* (Antwerp, 1643), Battista Fregoso, *De dictis et factis memorabilibus* (Basle, 1541), Pierre Potier, *Opera omnia medica, et chymica* (Leyden, 1645); respectively lot 64 of Libri Miscellanei in Folio, lot 38 of Libri Classici in Quarto, and lot 640 of Libri Miscellanei in Octavo.

Library-keeper; that he must use more exercise in riding out &c. if he intends to preserve his health; which will of necessity hinder his attendance there. He had rather I succeed him than any body else, which I cannot do untill I am a Graduate; that if I have any friends amongst the heads of houses, they cann't do better for me than in procuring for me the degree of Batchellor of Law, that I may be in a Condition to stand for his Place with others, which he will resign as soon as I have obtain'd the said Degree, and (for my sake) will communicate his Intentions to no body else in the mean time. He presses me to get this Degree as soon as possible; urging, that he does not care how soon he is rid of his Place.[1] Altho', Sir, I have as much business on my hands as I can menage, and am now troubled with the old pains in my head, yet I will at all vacant times set my self seriously to the Study of the Civil Law, that I may be in some measure capable of performing the Exercise requisite, and I will take care not to want money for it. I would humbly crave your advise, Sir, upon the premises, which I will exactly follow, as being

> Honored Sir,
>
> Your most obliged & humble servant
>
>   H.W.

MS: Bodleian, Ballard 13, fo. 75. *Date*: 'From the Lodgings Octob. 10. 1698.' *Address*: 'For the Reverend Dr Charlett, To be left with Mr Sare, a Bookseller near Grayes Inn Gate London.' *Printed*: Macray, p. 167 (extract).

53. *To* —— *15 October 1698*

Honored Sir,

Your most welcom & very kind letter found me striving against a painful fit of Sickness, which still get's the Mastery of me to my no small Trouble. Tis all I can do to hold a pen in my hand, nor can I stir out of my Chamber; so that I can't answer yours, nor inform you of our wants so accurately as you may expect, and (perhaps) I might have done, had I been in health.

---

[1] Hyde resigned as Bodley's Librarian in Apr. 1701 on the grounds that he was tired of the drudgery of daily attendance and was anxious to complete his work upon the 'hard places' in Scripture. See his letter ptd. Macray, pp. 170-1. For Wanley's hopes with respect to this degree and his succeeding Hyde, see further his letters to Hickes, nos. 54, 55, 57, 59, 61, 62; but see also no. 66 n. 2, no. 67.

For *Venice* then; Be pleas'd to procure a Specimen of those Gospels, which they say were written by St John Chrysostome, or at least belong'd to him, and not to forget the Gospel of St Mark.[1] We have already a blind Catalogue or two of Cardinal Bessarions MSS,[2] which I trust will be corrected in infinite places, by that which you will transcribe, especially if it gives the year when such a book was written, &c. I have seen Thomasins Bibliothecae Patavinæ, but never could see the Bibliothecae Venetae, which I presume to be as jejune as the other.[3]

For *Rome*. We want an accurate Catalogue of the Manuscripts in the Vatican Library, as it is encreas'd by the Libraries of Heidelberg & Urbin; Catalogues of the MSS in the Archives of the Vatican Church, in the Libraries of Queen Christina, Barbarini, Altieri, Chigi & others. In the Vatican, I wish for a Specimen of their Septuagint in Greek,[4] & of their Virgil & Terence,[5] and by all means a set of the Sculptures taken from the Virgil, which I am heartily glad to hear are printing.[6]

For *Florence*. Be pleas'd to procure a Cat. of the MSS. in the Dominicans Library, which you told me were seldom or never seen by

[1] Wanley probably refers to the twelfth-century cursive manuscript of the Gospels (Venice, S. Marco MS Nanian I.xiv) which once belonged to Chrysostom's *monastery* by the Jordan, according to a note of the original scribe. The 'Gospel of St Mark' (Venice, S. Marco MS S.N., *CLA* x, no. **285 (p. 35)) is part of the early sixth-century uncial of the Gospels now divided between Cividale (Museo Archeologico S.N.), Prague (Knihovna Metropolitaní Kapitoly CIM.1), and St Mark's, Venice; the Gospel of St Mark (wanting the last two quires now at Prague) has been at Venice since 1420. Traditionally shown as St Mark's autograph and kept in the cathedral treasury, it was already by the end of the seventeenth century ruined by damp. For a contemporary description by Bernard Montfaucon see his *Diarium Italicum* (Paris, 1702), pp. 55 f.

[2] i.e. of the manuscripts given to the Cathedral of St Mark's by Bessarion in 1468. Two catalogues of these are to be found in Bodl. MS Auct. F. inf. 1.13 (*SC* 2955); Bodl. MS D'Orville 399 (*SC* 17277) is a copy of a transcript (made in 1606 at Augsburg) of Daniel Hoeschel's Index of Bessarion's Greek manuscripts.

[3] Giacomo Filippo Tomasini, *Bibliothecæ Patavinae Manuscriptae* (Udine, 1639), *Bibliothecae Venetae Manuscriptae* (Udine, 1650).

[4] Codex Vaticanus (MS Vat. gr. 1209) the great fourth-century codex of the Bible in Greek.

[5] The Vergil with 'sculptures' is probably the Vergilius Vaticanus (MS Vat. lat. 3225, *CLA* i, no. 11), a fourth-century manuscript containing fifty-five miniatures. See n. 6. But there are two other early manuscripts of Vergil in the Vatican: Codex Romanus (MS Vat. lat. 3867, *CLA* i, no. 19) of the fifth century, and Codex Palatinus (MS Vatic. Palat. lat. 1631, *CLA* i, no. 99) of the fourth century, the former with nineteen large miniatures. The Terence is Codex Bembinus (MS Vat. lat. 3226, *CLA* i, no. 12), a fourth-/fifth-century manuscript of Terence's *Fabulae*.

[6] The miniatures of the Vergilius Vaticanus had been engraved by Pietro Santi Bartoli in 1677; they were not *printed* until 1725–at the expense of Cardinal Camillo Massimi (J. de Wit, *Die Miniaturen des Vergilius Vaticanus* (Amsterdam, 1959) p. 11).

strangers; and from the Great Dukes Library, a Specimen of the Virgil, & the Pandects in Latin,[7] & some others in Greek I will acquaint you with presently. I have met with a Cat. of the Oriental & Greek MSS in this Library taken by one Langius a Dane in the year 1652, which is as much better than that of Ernstius, as Ernstius is better than none at all.[8] In this of Langius I meet with books that set me almost on fire to go into Italy, only to see them.[9]

He says that (Plut.I. parte posteriori, no. 40.) there is a Copie of the Gospels in Syriac anno Alexandri 1038. i.e. anno Christi 727. that (in eod. Pluteo. no. 56) there is another most antient Copie of the Syriac Gospells, written An. Alexandri 807, i.e. anno Christi, 586. with the Harmonies of Ammonius & Eusebius, &c. That in Plut. III, no. 3 is the Pentateuch in Hebrew with the Targum, Megilloth & Haphtharoth written anno Judaico 4057, i.e. anno Christi 291. which, with some others, [a]re the most antient Oriental MSS. that I ever heard of, whose age are fixed to a certain year, without conjecture. Nor are the Greek MSS much short of them, since in Pluteo IV, no. 1. is the Acts & the Epistles, cum Scholijs & Proemijs optimis & antiquissimis ineditis, script. anno Christi 399. and several MSS, are said to be in muchwhat the same Character with this Noble book, particularly the two Copies of Josephus in Pluteo LXIX, no. 17 & 19. I pass over many other most excellent books for fear of being tedious, begging leave only to mention one more, in Pluteo LXXIV, no. 7. where are the works of 14 of the old Greek Chyrurgions Oribasius, Heliodorus, Asclepiades, &c illustrated with Pictures, and with the Draughts of their Instruments, the book it self, says Langius is plane insignis &

---

[7] Codex Mediceus (MS Laurenziana XXXIX.1, *CLA* iii, no. 296), a fifth-century manuscript of Vergil, and the so-called 'Florentine Pandects' (MS Laurenziana S.N., *CLA* iii, no. 259), a sixth-century codex of the Justinian Digest of Roman Law, both in the Laurentian Library at Florence.

[8] Wanley probably refers to Bodl. MS e. Mus. 162 (*SC* 3622), a catalogue of the Medicean manuscripts at Florence compiled by Wilhelm Lange in 1652; a copy of this made *c.*1700 is Bodl. MS D'Orville 398 (*SC* 17276). It seems first to have been ptd. by Peter Lambeck in his *Prodromus Historiae Literariae* (Frankfurt, 1710). The work of Ernstius referred to is Heinrich Ernst, *Catalogus librorum ... Bibliothecae Mediceae* (Amsterdam, 1641).

[9] Respectively Florence, Laurenziana I.40, descr. A. M. Biscioni, *Bibliothecae Mediceo-Laurentianae Catalogus*, i (Florence, 1752), pp. 33–5; I.56 (descr. Biscioni, pp. 44–57); III.3 (descr. Biscioni, pp. 109–10); IV.1, descr. A. M. Bandini, *Catalogus Codicum Manuscriptorum Bibliothecae Mediceae Laurentianae* (Florence, 1764–70), i, cols. 515–19; LXIX.17, 19 (descr. Bandini, ii, cols. 639–40); LXXIV.7 (descr. Bandini, iii, cols. 53–93).

eximius, in folio magno, litteris majusculis. I would willingly have specimens of these 4 last mentioned.

At *Milan*, I wish you could procure a Catalogue of the MSS in the Ambrosian Library, with specimens of their Latin Josephus, and antient Catullus.[10]

At *Naples*, I hear there is a good Library of MSS. in the possession of the Augustin Friers, if it be so, I must still insist upon the Catalogue; for if they have the best books in the world, & we not know it, 'tis the same to us, as if they were not in being.[11]

I forgot to desire you to enquire at Rome, what Chartularies & Registers of our English Monastaries may be found there.[12]

And now to the Catalogue of books you sent, as I said before, I am imprisoned in my Chamber, and as I have done already I must relate our wants by heart.[13]

---

[10] Josephus is Biblioteca Ambrosiana, Cimelio MS 1 of the sixth-/seventh-century (*CLA* iii, no. 304). There are five manuscripts of Catullus in the Ambrosian Library, none ancient, all of the fifteenth century—the earliest of them, in the opinion of my colleague Professor D. F. S. Thomson, MS M.38 *supra* (*c.*1430).

[11] Wanley's interest in this library is no doubt explained as Wright (*Diary*, p. 372 n. 1) suggests, by the presence there of numbers of manuscripts from the renowned monastery of Bobbio in Northern Italy: see *CLA* iii, nos. 388–403. They had been removed from Bobbio probably by Aulo Giano Parrasio (1470–1522) and found their way into the hands of Cardinal Girolamo Seripando, who at his death (1563) left his library to the Augustinian house of S. Giovanni a Carbonara at Naples. Mabillon and Germain had visited the library in Oct. 1685 and left an account in their *Museum Italicum*, i (1687), pp. 110–11, to which Wanley presumably owed his knowledge of the collection. P. O. Kristeller, *Latin Manuscript Books before 1600*, 3rd edn. (New York, 1960), lists no catalogues of the collection of the Augustinians at Naples. Wanley probably had in mind a written handlist. For Wanley's continuing interest in the library, see no. 215 and his *Diary*, 16 Aug. 1725 (p. 372).

[12] None listed by Davis.

[13] For books listed below, except those to which nn. 14 and 15 refer, tentative identifications follow: Lorenzo Alessandro Zaccagni, *Collectanea monumentorum veterum ecclesiae Graecae ac Latinae* (Rome, 1698); Filippo Buonarroti, *Osservazioni Istoriche sopra alcuni medaglioni antichi* (Rome, 1698); Emmanuel Schelstrate, *Antiquitas Ecclesiae* (Rome, 1697); Joseph Saenz de Aguirre, *Collectio maxima conciliorum omnium Hispaniae et Novi Orbis* (Rome, 1694), *S. Anselmi Theologia* (Rome, 1688–90); Filippo Buonanni, *Numismata summorum pontificum Templi Vaticani fabricam indicantia* (Rome, 1696), *Observationes circa viventia quae in rebus non viventibus reperiuntur, cum micrographia curiosa* (Rome, 1691); Antonio Constantino a Castrovillare, *De Canonibus Apostolorum dissertatio unica* (Rome, 1697); Michel-Ange de la Chausse (= Causeus), *Romanum Museum, sive Thesaurus eruditae antiquitatis* (Rome, 1690); Raffaello Fabretti, *De Columna Trajani Syntagma* (Rome, 1690); Giuseppe Maria Tommasi, *Psalterium juxta duplicem editionem quam romanam dicunt et gallicam* (Rome, 1683); Giovanni Ciampini, *De cruce stationali investigatio historica* (Rome, 1694), *Sacro-historica disquisitio de duobus emblematibus quae in cimelio . . . Gasparis cardinalis Carpinei asservantur* (Rome, 1691), *Examen Libri pontificalis* (Rome, 1688), *De abbreviatorum de parco majori . . . dissertatio historica* (Rome, 1691), *Abbreviatoris de*

* Jacagnij Collectanea Monumentorum Gr. Lat. *Rom.* 1698.40.

* Osservationi Historiche sopra alcuni Medaglioni dell' Abb. Filip. Buonarotti. R. 1698.

Eman. Schelstrati Antiquitas Ecclesiae. Tom. II. the 3d Printing.

Jos. Suent. Card. d'Aguire Concilia Hisp. 4. voll.—Bibliotheca Hisp. 2. voll—Theologia S. Anselmi. 3. voll. fol.

* Bonanni Numismata summorum Pontificum.—Observationes circa viventia quæ in rebus non viventibus reperiuntur.

Ant. Constantini Dissertatio de Canonibus Apostolorum, &c.

* Mich. Ang. Causei Musaeum Romanum.

* Fab[r]ettus de Columna Trajana.

* Jos. Mar. Thomasij Psalterium.

* Ciampinus de Cruce Stationali investig.—*Disquisit. de 2. emblematibus Card. Carpinei.—Exame[n] libri Pontificalis.— De Abbreviatoribus de Parco majori.—De Abbreviatore curiæ compendiariæ.

* Explicatio duorum Sarcophagorum—de S.R.E. Vice-Cancellario.

* Il Tempio Vaticano dal Caval. Carlo Fontana.

* L'Historia Universale dal Franc. Bianchini.

* Prospettiva del P. And. Pozzi.

Syria sacra del Biaggio Tersi

Hieronymi Vitalis Lexicon Mathematicum.

J[oan]. Fr. Vannij Investig. Momentorum, quibus gravia tendunt deorsum.

    * Everything of Pietro Santi Bartoli, & Bellorio except the Columna Trajana & the Capita illustrium.[14]

Ant. Malegonelli Orationes.

---

curia compendiaria (Rome, 1690), *Explicatio duorum sarcophagum, sacrum baptismatis ritum indicantium* (Rome, 1697); Carlo Fontana, *Il Tempio vaticano e sua origine* (Rome, 1694); Francesco Bianchini, *La Istoria universale provata con monumenti* (Rome, 1697); Andrea Pozzo, *Perspectiva pictorum et architectorum* (Rome, 1693); Biagio Terzi, *Siria sacra, descrittione istorico-geograficale* (Rome, 1695); Girolamo Vitale, *Lexicon mathematicum* (Rome, 1690); Giovanni Francesco Vanni, *Investigatio momentorum quibus gravia tendunt deorsum* (Rome, 1693); Antonio de Malegonnelle, *Casus principis, sive de Laudibus Innocenti XII . . . oratio* (Venice, 1692); Giovanni Vincento Gravina, *Opuscula* (Rome, 1696); Giorgio Baglivi, *De Praxi medica* (Rome, 1696); Carlo Giuseppe Imbonati, *Chronicon tragicum* (Rome, 1696); Benedetto Bacchini, *Dell' Istoria del Monastero di S. Benedetto di Polirone* (Modena, 1696); Carlo Bartolemeo Piazza, *Eusevologio Romano, overo delle Opere pie di Roma . . . Con due trattati delle accademie e librerie di Roma* (Rome, 1698); Francisco de Brito Freire, *Nova Lusitania, Historia da Guerra Brasilica* (Lisbon, 1675); Apollonius of Perga, *Conicorum libri quatuor* (Pistoia, 1696); Raffaello Fabretti, *Inscriptionum antiquarum* (Rome, 1699); Alessandro Tassoni, *Annotazioni sopra il 'Vocabolario degli Accademici della Crusca'* (Venice, 1698).

[14] See no. 38 n. 3.

Jani Gravinæ Opuscula
Georg. Baglini Praxis Medica
Car. Jos. Imbonati Chronichon Tragicum.
Historia del Monastero di Pelirone dal R.P.D. Bened. Bacchino.
* Eu[ce]logio Romano, con due trattati delle Accademia [&] Librarie celebri di Roma
Historia dell[a] Guerre di Brasile—
Apoll. Pergei Conica. Pistoij—1696.
* Icones ex antiquiss. Cod. Virgilij in Bibl. Vat.[15]
* Inscriptiones antiquae per Fabrettum.
* The Book of the Masnadi, &c. print. at Ven.
* Observatt. on the Dict. Della Crusca by Alessandro Tassoni.

You will know these books tho' I abbreviate their Titles, which I do, because I write in Pain.

For the books printed by the Congregation de propaganda fide, I suppose you have more of the papers, and therefore may easily find the numbers.[16]

I suppose, we want in the Æthiopici
numb.2.

* Albanenses
no.1.
  Anglici
no.1, & 2.
  * Angollenses
no.1.
  Arabici
no.1,2,3,4,5, & so on except
  the Gospels & Psalter.
  Graeci
all except no. 12, 13, 14, 17 & 18.
  Græco-Lat.
no.5, & ult. i.e. Gram.Gr.Lat.
  Hebraici.
no.1.
  Hibernici.
no.1 & *2.

Armeni
all except no. 5, 6, & 7.
* Bulgari
no.1.
* Congenses
no.1 & 2.
* Giorgiani
no.4.

Latini
no.4,9. *all Bartoloeius in 5
  voll./no. 16, 17, 18, 22, 23,
  25, 27, 28 & 29
Malaici.
no.1.
Persici
no.1.

---

[15] See n. 5 above.
[16] In listing headings and numbers Wanley is presumably referring to a catalogue, but I have not succeeded in identifying it.

    * Japonici.   Valachici
all.   no.1.
    * Illyrici.
all except no.7.
    Italici
all.

I must humbly intreat you, sir, to accept of my hearty thanks for all your favors to me, & to excuse the present abrup[t]ness of
    Your most humble & obedient servant

                                 Humfrey Wanley.

The Master having viewed this List, judge's it too large; 'tis desired therefore that only those books may be bought, which are mark'd with an Asterisk (*) to which may be Added[17]
  * Onuph. Panvinij Antiquitates Veronenses.
  * Paruta's Sicilian Coins, of the Palermo Editi[on]
  * the Capita Illustrium, of Fulv. Ursinus's Edition
  * Han. Caraccio's Prints of the Paintings in the Palazzo Farnese.
  * A compleat sett of the Draughts of the old R[o]man Buildings, in the largest size.

MS: Bodleian, Ballard 13, fo. 77. *Date*: 'From the Masters Lodgings in University College, Oxon, Octob. 15. 1698.'

54. *To* [George Hickes] *9 November 1698*

Honored Sir,
    Your last letter lay long at Edmund Hall, by reason of my Friends absence: and had I not undergone 2 fits of sickness, and been forced to do a twelve-months work, in three months; I would have often written before now. But as the Case stood, I could not answer one letter of all that number that I have received.
    The Visitation of the Library is now over,[1] and I promise, Sir, to

---

[17] Tentative identifications follow: Onofrio Panvinio, *Antiquitatum Veronensium libri VIII* (Padua, 1647); Filippo Paruta, *La Sicilia, descritta con medaglie* (Palermo, 1612); Fulvio Orsini, *Imagines et elogia virorum illustrium et eruditor* (Rome, 1570); Annibale Carracci, *Imagines farnesiani cubiculi* (Rome, [1690?]); Jean-Jacques Boissard, *Topographia Romanae* (Frankfurt, 1597–1602), with maps, plans, views, antiquities, monuments, inscriptions, etc. engraved by J. T. de Bry, pbd. in 6 parts, seldom found complete.

[1] 8 Nov.

make amends for my seeming Neglect: and to send you the Francic Letters,[2] as soon as I know that this came safe to your hand.

Mr Burghers[3] ha's engraven the Saxon Alphabets which I drew, but so rudely, that I think the Prints will not be fit to appear, unless I may have the Liberty to correct the faulty places. In that Plate, you seem to hint as if the Saxon 7 might be taken from one of Tyros Characters, which is like it. I am apt to think that the Saxons never made use of those Abbreviations of Tyro, Seneca, &c. and I would therefore propose another way for the derivation of the 7. I am sensible that the Romans, from whom the Saxons seem to have borrowed their Letters used antiently to write the word Et, either thus **ET** or **ꝫT.** the latter of which in Manuscripts written about a thousand years ago is abbreviated thus **ꝫ**, and the former thus **ꝗ** both which Abbreviations have been varied infinitely, according to the mode of a Countrey, the fancy of the Writer, and the Genius of the age; some of which Variations I here put down.

ET. ꝫ .ꝫ. ꝫ. ꝫ, ꝫ, ꝫ, ꝫ, ꝫ, ꝫ, ꝫ, ꝫ, ꝫ, ꝫ, ꝫ, ꝫ, ꝫ, ꝫ.

this is not Mr Dobbins.

ET, ꝗ, 7, 7, ꝡ, ꝡ, 7, ꝫ, ꝫ, ꝫ, ꝫ, ꝫ, ꝫ, ꝫ, ꝫ, ꝫ,

and a great many more.

By this Derivation, I am almost willing to think that the Saxon 7, might be deduced from the **ꝗ**, as containing a sufficient part of that Abbreviation, as that does of **ET**; but I dare not be positive in this and many more such Deductions, till I have seen the Foreign Libraries, which too, I believe, I scarcely ever shall.[4]

I am still reflecting, day & night, on what you was pl[ea]sed to say to me, Sir, the Truth of which every day confirm's afresh. I have taken pains enough about Dr Bernards Catalogue,[5] but there's no talk about my going to London, nor do I believe I shall be permitted to set a foot therein, in some years: unless ——

---

[2] See no. 57.

[3] Michael Burghers (1653?–1727), Oxford engraver, successor to David Loggan; engraved for the University Press 1676–1720. The alphabet is ptd. *Thesaurus*, I, pt. i, p. 3.

[4] 'Your opinion is more probable that it came from **Eᴛ** and in the additionall table of Alphabets, wch I intend, I will wth your consent thankfully put down your opinion, wth the abbreviations' (Hickes to Wanley d. 15 Nov. 1698, BL Harley MS 3779, fo. 77). This seems not to have been done, but see *Thesaurus*, I, pt. i, p. viii, Specimen IV.

[5] Cf. Wanley's account in the Bodleian Library records of his work on *CMA*: 'As to the Indexes, the making them was as a piece of drudgery imposed upon me by my Superiors in the first year after my matriculation into this University', and see Macray, p. 164.

I am fed with fresh hopes of having the Degree of Batchellor of Law confer'd upon me: and yet but the last Saturday, I was again denied that ordinary & common favor (denied to none but me) of entring Commoner in the house: which tho' it would require some little more Charge than Ordinary: yet I know I should save 10£ a year by it. I am only told that I am a vain, proud fool, without common sense, &c. But still, I am not such a fool as to desire it, did I not know my self in a capacity, (thanks be to God) to bear it.[6]

If this, Sir, comes safe to your hands I would desire the favor of you, as to Direct for *Mr Edward Hayward*[7] in this College, with this Mark upon the Superscription #, and it will certainly find

Honored Sir,

Your most humble and obliged servant

Humfrey Wanley.

MS: Bodleian, Eng. hist. c. 6, fo. 24. *Date*: 'Univ. Coll. Nov. 9. 1698.' *Address*: 'For Mr Potter. To be left at Mr Keebles shop, a Bookseller, at the Turks head in Fleet-street. London.'

55. *To* [George Hickes] *16 December 1698*

Honored Sir,

I thought to have sent you what I intended, before now, and that is the reason why I so long delayed the informing you, that your last kind letter[1] came safe. But now, I find I cannot be so good as my word, till January, being so continually taken up, that I have not any day-light to my self: and I cannot delineate those letters by Candle-light.[2] I lead a sort of an ill life here, not being able to give the Master Content, by my earnest & utmost endeavors. As for the Bachelor of Laws degree, tho' the obtaining it would turn to my great advantage, yet I suppose,

[6] 'I argued the point about your degree yesterday morn a good while, but find that the Master is of two opinions 1. yt it would not now be convenient for you, and 2ly yt it will never be granted you, but in the ordinary method, as it is to all others, that are full standing, and perform exercise' (Hickes to Wanley d. '1698', BL Harley MS 3779, fo. 71). See also no. 52 and n. 1.

[7] Edward Hayward, also of Coventry, matriculated at University College in Feb. 1696.

[1] Probably that of 15 Nov. 1698, BL Harley MS 3779, fo. 77.

[2] The 'Francic' alphabet mentioned in no. 54, it was copied by Wanley before 4 Jan. 1699 (see no. 57) from Bodl. MS Junius 25 (*SC* 5137), the 'Murbach Hymnal'. See *Thesaurus*, I, pt. iii, p. 3.

I shall never have it, till I am standing. I am 4 years standing the next Term, & then I believe I may be permitted to sit among the Servitor Bachelors, below the Junior Commoners; which I will never do, happen what will. In order to prevent it, I will make the master a present of an Epistolar Newyears gift, as other young men do:[3] and if I happen to please him, I will make one more effort towards my entring Commoner, which shall be my last. I am half affraid, that the better my performance, the worse my success may prove. But if I fail, I shall be very willing to accept of any Station in London, that I can menage, and will prove a comfortable subsistence for me. I could wish, indeed, that I was Library keeper to my Lord Chancellor,[4] but how to come in there I know not. Nor have I any friends that can mention such a thing to his Lordship; but what may be easily kept back from doing me any good there, if my departure from hence (with all my faults) be not approv'd of. The thoughts of these things make me melancholly: and you, Sir, are the only person unto whom I ever communicated them. I should be very glad to know that this comes safe to your hands, from

Honored Sir,

Your very humble & most obliged servant

Humfrey Wanley.

Mr Hayward being gone into
the Countrey, I must desire
you to direct for Mr Ryley
at his Chamber in University
College

Oxon[5]

MS: Bodleian, Eng. hist. c. 6, fo. 26. *Date*: 'Univ. Coll. Decb. 16. 1698.' *Address*: 'For Mr Potter at Mr Boyers house, the second door on the left hand in Dover street London.'

56. *To* [John Bagford] *1 January 1699*

Dear Sir,

I received the Parcell which I guessed came from you, tho' there was no letter. As for the little Box with the Ring, it shall be deliver'd to Mr

---

[3] See no. 57, and Wanley to Charlett, 1 Jan. 1699, BL Egerton MS 2260, fo. 22.

[4] John Somers (1651–1716), Lord Chancellor 1697–1700. He possessed a large and valuable library, for the later history of which, see no. 178 n. 3.

[5] John Ryley, matriculated at University College in 1694, BA 1698.

Complin to morrow. For the books, tho' I have no occasion for most of them, yet I will send you the 10s with the money I shall send Mr Bullord for the books he has bought for me. I shall be glad to receive, when you think convenient, the other Catalogues you mention, having many of these already.[1] I thank you heartily for the old pieces of Parchment, amongst which, two pleased me most, vizt that in Greek, which seems to be a fragment of *Ptolemies* works, and the folio leaf, which I believe you may remember, it being hard to read. It is in Lombardic letters, and is a fragment of some old Glossary; perhaps that of *Hrabanus Maurus*. If you have any more of it, I must entreat you to send it to me: as also all the Greek Fragments you can meet with.

I have taken notice of some Dates of the Printed books, which perhaps may please you. But one thing I can't forbear taking notice of, which is this: That I can shew you an Engraven Print, work'd in the Rolling-press, in the year 1481, or before:[2] and so well done, as to shame many of your London Workmen. I thought the Invention of the Rolling-press had not been so antient by some years: and that at first, the Performances in that kind were but mean; whereas this Plate is not ill drawn (especially considering the Time) but graven with a good stroke, & fairly printed, at Wirtzburg in Germany. I would desire you not to fail me of your Opinion of it, by the very first Opportunity:[3] and if you could take occasion to mention it handsomly to Mr Pepys (whom you know to be a great Judge in these matters) to send me word what he says to it. I had some thoughts of writing to him about it, but was not certain whether it would be taken well.

Give my hearty service to my kind friend Mr Brand, and bid him not to buy any of the Jews Almanacks, for I design (as soon as I can get one) to send him one, & you another. In expectation of your answer, I remain Sir,

Your most humble servant

Humfrey Wanley

MS: British Library, Harley 4966, art. 56. *Date*: 'Univ. Coll. Jan 1. 1698.'

[1] A parcel of 'saxon' catalogues sent by Bagford within the week.

[2] The print is that at the end of *Missale secundum usum Ecclesiae Herbipolensis* [G. Reyser: Wurzburg, 1481], Bodl. press-mark Auct.i.Q.i.7; Hain 11309, Proctor 2669. See Macray, pp. 87–8.

[3] Bagford's opinion is given in a letter postmarked 5 Jan. 1699 (BL Harley MS 3777, fo. 156), and see further nos. 58, 60. Wanley wrote to Pepys giving a full account of the book, 25 June 1699 (no. 63). See also no. 39 n. 3.

57. *To* [George Hickes] *4 January 1699*

Honored Sir,

Since I wrote last, the Scales have been turned, and the Master demean's himself towards me, as formerly. I doubt not but that you have heard of frequent Visitations of our College, lately:[1] upon which accounts, I have been somewhat useful in Transcribing Papers, &c. relating thereunto: and my diligence therein ha's (I think) reconciled the Master to me: at least he is grown milder. Notwithstanding this hindrance, I made a shift to finish my designed New-years-gift, & to present it the first of any in the College, but as yet he ha's said nothing to me, either how he like's it, or any thing else about it: It was an Epistle with the Titles & Beginnings of about 114 Homilies of St Chrysostome which we have in this Place in Greek, that were never yet Printed, so far as I know: to find out which, I was forced to compare all our MSS. of Chrysostome with the Printed books, leaf by leaf, and to go over what I had done, more than once, for sureties sake: which took me up almost 3 weeks, though that little Index comes into a Small compass.[2]

I since copied the Francic Alphabets for you, Sir, and he asking me for your[3] Direction, yesterday; I gave it him, and desired him to enclose my Paper in his letter, which I hope you will have received before this comes to your hands.

There is some hopes of my coming in Fellow of Worcester-College, the Mast[er] having commanded me to write a letter to the Arch-Bishop of Canterbury to desire him to engage the Bishop of Worcester in my behalf: and I am told that his Grace ha's express'd himself about it in terms, to my advantage.[4] But for all this, If I could get a good Station in London, I would willingly bid Adieu to Oxford for some time. As for the Degree of Bachelor of Law, I shall have it when I am standing, & not before: tho' at this Juncture, it would be of great advantage to me.[5]

Be pleas'd, Sir, to excuse this hasty Scribble, and always to believe me most honored Sir

Your most humble faithful and obedient servant

Humfrey Wanley.

[1] On the occasion of these Visitations see no. 48 n. 3.
[2] See Wanley to Charlett, 1 Jan. 1699, BL Egerton MS 2260, fo. 22.   [3] you MS.
[4] See no. 61 n. 2. Thomas Tenison (1636–1715) was Archbishop of Canterbury (1694–1715); Edward Stillingfleet (1635–99), Bishop of Worcester (1689–99).
[5] See no. 52 n. 1.

MS: Bodleian, Eng. hist. c. 6, fo. 27. *Date*: 'From the Bodleian Library. Jan. 4. 1698/9.'
Address: 'For Mr Potter, at Mrs Merrys house in King-street, Bloomsbury next door to a
Lamp overagainst the end of Great Russel street London.'

58. *To* John Bagford *11 January 1699*

Mr Bagford.

I received the parcell which you sent me the last week which
pleased me very well, as did the 2d piece of Parchment in Longobardic
letters that came with it: and you must not be angry if I again desire
you to send me another piece or two if you have any. I have received
one Guinea of Mr Complin for you,[1] which I had sent up yesterday
with the Jews Almanacks,[2] had but the Rascal of a Bookbinder got
them ready but you shal be sure of all next week.

I am still in the same mind about the Print, as I was before, vizt that
it was engraven on Copper or Brass in the year 1481, or before.[3] And
my Reasons are these.

Rodolphus Bishop of Wirtzburg ordered the old Missals of his
Church to be inspected, & amended, and a certain number of them to
be compleatly printed by Jorius Ryser the Printer by the 8th of
November anno Domini 1481. which is the date likewise of this decree
of his: and that this Missal should be used in all the Churches of his
Diocess. And at the End of this his Decree is this Print I talk of, being
his own Arms with as fine a Mantling as ever I saw: as also the Arms of
the Diocess suported by 2 Angels the Drapery of whose Robes are good
and with the Picture of St Kilian the Protector of the See. One may
easily see the marks of the Edges of the Plate how deep it is pressed
into the Parchment, &c.

Perhaps you wil say, there might be such an order for Printing the
book in 1481. but how does it appear that it was then Printed?

I suppose that this Jorius Ryser had printed the book before, and
that when the book was finished the Bishop made this Decree by way
of License for its publication. For at the latter end, the Printer has
written his name with the date 1481. in red letters.

And further one Kewsth has testified that the same year, 1481, he

[1] The cost of a seal-ring.
[2] Presumably the Oxford almanacs of Isaac Abendana, pbd. annually, with a Jewish
calendar, 1692–9. See no. 93 n. 5.
[3] See no. 56 and n. 2.

bought the book and for the Parchment, Printing, Rubrication, Illumination & Binding paid 18 Florins. And in another place, he makes a deed of Gift of it for ever to the Parish Church of St Bartholomew in Wirtzburg whereof he was Vicar. And here are the hands of every Vicar of that Church into whose Possession it came, till this Age wherein it was taken away. And I can't believe that the book was carried out of the Church, to have a new Stamp put to it, in order to corroborate an old Decree. Pray do not fail me of your thoughts upon this by your first, and you'l much oblige

Sir,

Your real friend & Servant

Humfrey Wanley.

MS: British Library, Harley 4966, art. 60. *Date*: 'Univ. Coll. Jan. 11. 1698/9.'

59. *To* [George Hickes] *12 January 1699*

Honored Sir,

The Master received your Answer to his Letter,[1] but ha's as yet taken no notice of it to me: but he shewed it to one that acquainted me, in secret, with what related to me, therein.[2] As for my New-years-gift,[3] he told me he had sent it, as it was, to the Arch-Bishop[4] since when, I have never heard a word of it.

As to the Degree of Bachelor of Law, which I have been bidden to hope for any time these two years: I think I am as far from it as ever, excepting the Terms I have kept in the University.[5] Nor do I expect any Preferment here. Dr Hyde ha's long since told me, that he keeps his Station in this place, for my sake alone, and that when I have attained the said Degree, he will resign; and in the mean time conceals his Intentions from the world. This the Master has known this quarter of a year, & promis'd me the Degree; but I never expect it till I am full Standing. The Under-Library-keeper is about to resign, and I find the Master would willingly have me succeed him: but I suppose he would now rather wish another in Dr Hydes place: tho' he was the very first person that put me in hopes of it. And because the abovesaid Degree

[1] Hickes to Charlett, 5 Jan. 1699; Bodl. MS Ballard 12, fo. 134.
[2] The possibility of a Fellowship for Wanley at Worcester College: see no. 61.
[3] See no. 57.   [4] Tenison.   [5] See no. 52.

would qualifie me for it, therefore, I ghess, it has been & is denied me: tho' he ha's been very warm in that too.

As to the Fellowship in Worcester College, I hear no more of it; nor do I expect it, because, one way or other, I believe I shall never have it.

It makes me some times a little Melancholy when I consider that all my greatest Companions are preferr'd & got into Fellowships, except one who in all probability, will be Elected Fellow of Merton the next Term:[6] and I, must still live a servile, sneaking, precarious life: but however, I contentedly submit to Gods will.

In short, Sir, I can not be disappointed of Preferment here: because I have no reason to hope for any.

This next Week I am 4 years Standing; and I expect to have the Priviledges of a Bachelor of Arts in the College denied me, by some of the Fellows, for being Faithful to the Master in the late business:[7] notwithstanding which, besides the Consideration of his sacrificing me to some others, contrary to my repeated desires; I see my self outed of his Favor, and very seldom have any thing but cross Language from him.

These things & many more, make me almost mad; & some blunders of mine which they have occasion'd, make him esteem of & use me as an egregious fool, that cannot speak 3 words of sense together.

I am however, still fully employed, and have much ado to get this little Opportunity of communicating my tormenting thoughts to you, Sir.

I would desire you, Sir, not to write to him any farther, for the present, about my degree; till I inform you how things go: and least he suspect we keep a secret Correspondence together.

I waited on Mr Thwaites not long since, where we talked[8] about several things which might adorn your Book, had I but time to do them as I desire & hope I shall have.[9]

I give you, Sir, my humble & hearty thanks for all your favors to me, and more particularly,[10] for the honor of these your Letters, which alone keep off an oppressing Dispair from

Honored Sir,

Your most faithful & most obliged Servant

Humfrey Wanley.

---

[6] Merton elected no Fellows in 1699, but elected six in 1700.

[7] Presumably the election of Denison as a Fellow of University College: see no. 48.

[8] MS has 'taked'.

[9] Hickes's *Thesaurus*. Thwaites was responsible for seeing the book through the press.   [10] MS has 'particulary'.

MS: Bodleian, Eng. hist. c. 6, fo. 29. *Date*: 'From the Bodleian Library, Jan. 12, 98/9.'
Address: 'For Mr Potter at Mrs Merrys house in Kings-street Bloomsbury, next door to
a Lamp overagainst the end of Great Russel street London.'

60. *To* [John Bagford] *30 January 1699*

Dear Sir,

I expected you would have told me that you received the little Parcel
which I sent you last Tuesday by Matthews the Carrier; and which, I
told you, you might expect without further Order: and that you had
presented one of the Jews Alamanacks to Mr Brand, to whom I wrote
last Wednesday about it: and if you have not already received it, I must
desire you to go forthwith & demand it: because there is all your
money: and I desire you to send me a speedy answer, and rid me of the
fear I am in that the money should miscarry.

As for the Print I told you of, the stroke of the Graver is much finer
than this I send you back, and the Draperies conducted better: but I
think all parts are not so proportionable as this, tho' this may have its
faults too. As for that graving upon Brass, and adjusting it with ordinary
Printing Letter, I have long since take notice of it: and I suppose I can
distinguish it from Wood: for instance I take Georgio Varsaries lives of
the Painters, &c. in Italian to be so engraven upon Brass. But the Print I
mean is certainly Engraven upon a Brass or Copper or Silver Plate, and
certainly wrought off at the Rolling-press, and the marks of the Edges
of the Plate are still very visible, with some touches of the Ink here &
there, as we find at the Edges of our Plates now. And for fear I might be
deceived, I have shewed it to several knowing persons since I wrote to
you, two of whom are Mr Burghers the Graver & Mr John Hall the
Printer, who all do say that that Print was certainly wrought off at the
Rolling Press, or some such like Engine equivalent to it: and did you see
it, you will say the same. And that it was done in the year 1481 or before,
I think I have already satisfied you.

When you send word what you can say more to it, I would desire
you to tell me what people say to the English Account of the
Catalogue of MSS. which was printed in the Philosophical Transactions of the last month.[1] Thus expecting your answer as soon as

[1] 'A Letter wherein is given an Account of the Catalogues of Manuscripts lately
Printed at Oxford', *Philosophical Transactions*, no. 247 (Dec. 1698), pp. 442–60.

possible, & the books from Mr Bullord (to whom my humble service) I remain

    Dear Sir,

       Your most humble servt

                                 H Wanley.

MS: British Library, Harley 4966, art. 67. *Date*: 'Univ. Coll. Janry 30, 1698/9.'

61. *To* [George Hickes] *5 February 1699*

Honored Sir,

    Your very kind Letter of the 28th past,[1] came to my hands the last night, wherein I rejoice to find a full assurance of your hearty good will & affection to me, which I wish I could any ways deserve: and as it lies in my Power, I hope to make it appear, that I shall observe my word inviolably.

    As to my affairs, since my last; the Master ha's never told me of the letter you sent him: but say's that when Worcester College is establish'd my Lord Arch Bishop will secure me a Fellowship there:[2] and carries it very lovingly to me, in respect of what he did some time ago. I acquainted him before the beginning of this Term, which was Jan. 14. that I should be Bachelors standing, and I gave him notice since the Term came in, that I now was so; and ask[ed] him, whether it was too late to enter Commoner? He still dissuaded me from it, and I still continue in the State I was before, that is of an Undergraduate, tho' I conceive the Privileges of a Bachelor of Arts, in this College, to be my

---

[1] BL Harley MS 3779, fo. 82.

[2] The founding of Worcester College, Oxford, was largely the work of Benjamin Woodruffe (1638–1711), Canon of Christ Church 1672, who in 1692 was elected Principal of Gloucester Hall, originally a Benedictine foundation which had in the latter part of the seventeenth century fallen on bad times. When his first scheme for restoring the foundation's fortunes by turning it into a college for visiting Greek clerics fell through, he got hold of a benefaction of £10,000 offered in July 1697 to the University by Sir Thomas Cookes, a Worcestershire man, for the endowment of a college. By 1698 plans for the new college were far advanced, but difficulties over both money and site delayed its establishment until 1714. Hickes had already written to Charlett urging him to support Wanley's claims for a Fellowship at the new college (Hickes to Wanley d. 10 Jan. 1699; BL Harley MS 3779, fo. 80) and Charlett wrote encouragingly to Wanley: 'Whenever Worcester College is established, the Arbp will take care to secure you a Fellowship, but of this take no public notice till You heare farther' (25 Jan. 1699, Welbeck Wanleyana = BL Loan MS 29/253), and so again nearly two years later: see Charlett to Wanley d. 10 Oct. 1700 (Welbeck Wanleyana = BL Loan MS 29/253).

due and no more than what a Gentleman of this College (being a Civilian) had conferr'd upon him, within this twelvemonth, as soon as he was 4 years Standing; tho' he had not been Entred upon the Law-Line in the University two years, as I have been.[3]

As for any thing here, besides necessaries; which I thank God for; I never expect; nay, am almost assured I shall never obtain: and this notion is so well setled in me; that I am now grown very easy & contented with it: and having no reason [to] expect any long settlement here, I begin to look out elsewhere; and am therefore resolved (God willing) to go to Coventry (my native Countrey) about the sixth of March next, and I hope to wait on you at London before my return to Oxon. I have a Cousin at Coventre, who by the late death of her Brother is now worth 2000£ at least: and at the decease of her mother, my Aunt: she will be worth above 1000£ more: She ha's invited me over to Coventry to see her, & so ha's my Mother, at whose house she & my Aunt boards: and I believe things may go so, if they are (as to my Cousin) in the State wherein they were this time 2 years; and if she have not setled her affections upon some other person; as I hear she ha's not: that I may be a married man before I see Oxford again. And as her estate will be sufficient to maintain us comfortably, till the decease of our Parents, whose days I pray God lengthen: so I shall then have my time to my self, and be at leisure to serve you more effectually than I have ever yet done.[4]

I hope 'tis no light, giddy-brain'd Project this, about marrying: I am 27 years old, the 21st day of March next; I do not see that, that Condition of Life, will take me off my Studies, but rather promote them: since my business in the Library will never make me a Scholar, but on the contrary, unfit me for every thing else besides Cataloging of books. I have reason to believe that not only my Cousin & my Aunt her Mother, but all our other Near Relations will be willing to this Match. And if I tarry here longer, and enjoy a Fellowship in Worcester College, till the time be expired for the quitting it, which[5] is ten years; I then may, perhaps, be qualified for a woman with half her Fortune, & p[erhaps] not. In the mean time, my Cousin, is young, well-bred, vertuous, honest, good-humor'd, & not very ugly.

---

[3] See no. 54.
[4] The cousin was Elizabeth Phillipps, daughter of a confectioner of Newgate Street, London. Wanley's hopes were frustrated.
[5] whic MS.

I write these things, to you, Sir, as to my Father, who knowing the world better than I, must consequently see farther, and make a truer judgement of things, than I can: and I hope, Sir, you will be pleas'd to lett me know your opinion, of this (to me) important matter; since I have not desired the favor of any other person whatsoever.[6]

The Alphabets of Domes-day-book, you shall have in my next.[7] As for the Red book of the Exchequer, I have no Specimens of it: and if it be Gervase of Tillebury I do not take it to be the Original, but a later Copie.[8]

Be pleased to direct for Mr Wood, at his Chamber in Univ. Coll.

    #   and your letters will find,

Reverend & Honored Sir,

    Your most humble servant

H. Wanle[y.]

MS: Bodleian, Eng. hist. c. 6, fo. 31. *Date*: 'From the Lodgings Feb. 5. 1698/9.' *Address*: 'For Mr Potter at Mr Merry's house, Bloomsbury, next door to a Lamp overagainst the end of Great Russel street London.'

62. *To* [George Hickes] *28 February 1699*

Reverend & Honored Sir,

I received yesterday your very kind Letter,[1] whereby I am assured that my Unkle Philipps died worth what I was certified of before; within 500£. I heard likewise that my Cosin Eliz: had her fortune set her by her Father, as well as her Brother, and that it was equal to his: but your letter seeming to hint the contrary; or rather, that she had nothing till her Brothers death: I would humbly intreat you, Sir, to send me a word or two more upon that article; as also, whether it was

---

[6] Hickes agrees that the married state 'doth not hinder, but promote studies', and goes on to advise Wanley at great length on the subject (Hickes to Wanley d. 11 Feb. 1699, BL Harley MS 3779, fo. 84).

[7] A facsimile from Domesday is ptd. *Thesaurus*, I, pt. i, fig. II (after p. 144), together with Wanley's 'alphabets' from it.

[8] Wanley refers to the Dialogus de Scaccario, a twelfth-century treatise on the ancient constitution and practice of the Exchequer, found in the so-called Red Book of the Exchequer (PRO, Exchequer, King's Remembrancer, Miscellaneous Books, [E.163/2] no. 2, fos. 31–46) and three other thirteenth-century manuscripts. The work of Richard of Ely, Treasurer of England under Henry II, it was for long attributed to Gervase of Tilbury.

---

[1] d. 24 Feb. 1699, BL Harley MS 3779, fo. 86.

the *Mine* or the *Land* Lottery that my deceased Cousin ventured 60£ upon; for, at present, I suppose them to be two.[2]

I now believe I shall not set forward for Coventre, till Saturday the 11th of March next, and before I go, I shall take care of the sheet of Alphabets: and if you want any thing else in my book, I will cut it out & send it you.

If things fall out so, that I do marry my Cousin, as I do believe I shall; provided what I hear from her at Coventre prove true: I doubt not but I shall have leisure to do what I long since promised; i.e. present you a Catalogue of the Saxon MSS. now remaining in our English Libraries, with some Specimens taken from the Chiefest of them.[3]

I have already been so careful (unless my best friends have been false) that my Cousin ha's as good an opinion of me, as I desire she should have, till I see her my self: and I believe my Aunt will be made more my Friend than ever, before I see her: so that I am apt to fancy 'twill be but a short business, and that my Wife-Elect & I may soon wait on you, Sir, at London, & there pay you our humble respects.

I continue still in the College in the State of an Undergraduate, as I believe I shall always; or, it may be, till within a day or two before I go to Coventre. For two days ago the Master asked me whether I would have my Grace in the House? Which I had long since requested with all humility & submission 3 times over being full standing. And I answer'd yes, if he was pleas'd to think it convenient. And he seem'd to let me know that I might have it in Time.[4]

The Master shewed me at the same time, your last Letter to him, about the Benefactors to your Book: but your former Letter about Emancipating me, he never permitted me to look upon, or ever spake to me about it.[5]

---

[2] See no. 61.

[3] It is interesting that as late as this Wanley had no immediate intention to proceed with the catalogue which forms vol. II of Hickes's *Thesaurus*; indeed, on the evidence of his letter to Charlett of 19 Oct. 1699 (no. 67) it was another six months before his ideas on the matter began to clarify.

[4] See no. 52.

[5] Hickes's account of those who had taken out subscriptions for his *Thesaurus* is in a letter to Charlett d. 27 Jan. 1699, Bodl. MS Ballard 12, fo. 136; Hickes's 'former' letter to Charlett (see also Hickes to Wanley d. 10 Jan. 1699, BL Harley MS 3779, fo. 80) is that of 5 Jan. 1699; 'I hope you will think fit to reward mr Wanley for this publick service wth emancipation, and a degree' (Bodl. MS Ballard 12, fo. 134).

Wishing you, Sir, all health and happiness, and with my humble duty to your good Lady, I remain, with profound respect

Most honored Sir

   Your most faithful most obedient and most dutiful servant

           Humfrey Wanley.

I fear Mr Chamberlain is fallen out with me of late: I not hearing any thing from him, in answer to more letters than one.

Be pleas'd, Sir, to direct your next letter to me, *For Mr Hayward* at his Chamber in this College, with the mark ☊ near the Seal, on the bak side of the Letter. For in a secret Correspondence I think it best to change Names & Marks pretty often.

MS: Bodleian, Eng. hist. c. 6, fo. 34. *Date*: 'Univ. Coll. Feb. 28. 1698.' *Address*: 'For Mr Potter at Mr Mrs Merrys house in Kings-street, Bloomsbury, next door to a Lamp over-against the end of Great Russel-street London.'

63. *To* Samuel Pepys *25 June 1699*

Honorable Sir,

 The Master acquainted me on Thursday last, that he had received a Letter from you, wherein you was pleas'd to signifie a desire of knowing the event of our comparison of the two Greek Manuscript books of Anthems, and *Dr Covells*[1] performance therein: as also my opinion of the Age of those pieces of Parchment you sent with the Letter.

 As to the former; *The Cambridge MS.*[2] is much of the same nature

[1] John Covell (1638–1722), oriental scholar, Fellow of Christ's College, Cambridge 1661, Chaplain to the Levant Company at Constantinople 1670–6, Master of Christ's 1688. For Wanley's later dealings with him, while negotiating the purchase of his manuscript collections for Harley's library, see no. 152 n. 2.

[2] That Wanley refers to a manuscript owned by Thomas Gale, Regius Professor of Greek at Cambridge, seems clear from the following: 'Upon Mr Wanly's shewing his Greek MS. of Anthems, Mr Gale assures us that he gave a letter of the same nature to his own Library at Trinity, and accordingly has sent to borrow it for Dr Wallis, as also in his name we have sent to Dr Covel, who can sing them, to turne some one tune into our modern notes upon five lines' (Charlett to Pepys d. 17 May 1699, ptd. Tanner, *Private Correspondence*, i, p. 173). This must be Trinity College, Cambridge MS O.2.61, a music book for the greater church festivals, probably of the fifteenth century but with some late additional matter, no. 1165 in M. R. James's catalogue of Trinity manuscripts, *CMA* II. i, nos. 6041–3. But according to James, this manuscript was part of the donation of Thomas Gale's manuscripts given by his son Roger Gale (1672–1744) in 1738. It may be that it was part of Thomas Gale's donation of his oriental manuscripts in 1697,

with mine,[3] but much less, & newer. The Compositions are likewise different, as being of other Masters than those who are exstant in my Book, to the number of Threescore. The Tunes are express'd in the same sort of Notes as mine, which *Dr Covell* is so far from being a Master in, that he sent word hither, by *Mr Talbot*, that he thought the Reducing any Tune in that book, to our way of Pricking on five lines, to be impracticable. But that the *Doctor* express'd himself, on this occasion, a little too large, appears by this, that such a thing has been done already, & you may find it in Athanasius Kircher's *Musurgia*,[4] Vol. 1. after pag. 72. and this Author says he was enabled to make such a Reduction, by reading the Manuscript works of *Joannes Kukuzela*, *Chrysaphes*, *Naziz* &c. which, as I take it, yet remain in the *Vatican Library*.

I know, Sir, that this *Kircher* is to be read with much Caution, and that his Credit runs low with many learned men: yet, if he did consider the *antient Greek Musitians*, as he says he did (I mean those since published by *Meibomius* & *Dr Wallis*)[5] and if he did consult the Authors abovementioned that wrote of the *Church-Music of the Greeks*; with a moderate skill in our Music, he or any body else might give us what he has done of the said Church-Music, or as much more as they should think convenient. And this might be done more easily, if they should have the assistance of a Greek vers'd in the Music of his Nation. And the help of many such at *Rome* (being *Latiniz'd*) Father *Kircher* could not want, if he was minded to serve himself of them.

That the Notes we see in these books are expressive of Sounds and are really Tunes to be Sung, I believe, no body will doubt, tho they dont understand them: because the books themselves expressly say so: and in the *Cambridge MS.* I took notice of one Tune which *Andreas Spata* (who compos'd most of the said Book) says he prick'd down ἐξ ἀκοῆς and *Dr Savage* in his *Balliofergus*[6] pag. 121. says of *Nathaniell Conopius a Cretan* who resided at Balliol College here, for some time,

borrowed by him in 1699 as stated in Charlett's letter, and never returned to the library but kept by him, eventually finding its way back with the rest of his collection in 1738.

[3] Now MS 48 in the library of the Society of Antiquaries: on this see Wanley to Charlett, 13 June 1698, ptd. Ellis, *Original Letters*, pp. 262–4.

[4] *Musurgia Universalis* (Rome, 1650).

[5] Presumably Marcus Meibom, *Antiquae musicae auctores septum Graece et Latine* (Amsterdam, 1652), and John Wallis's edn. of Claudius Ptolemaeus's *Harmonica* (Oxford, 1682).

[6] Henry Savage, *Balliofergus: or, a Commentary upon the Foundation . . . of Balliol Colledge* (Oxford, 1668).

that *he had a great book of Music of his own composing; for his skill wherein, his Countrey-men in their Letters to him stiled him* μουσικώτατον: *but that the Notes were such as are not in use with, or understood by any of the Western Churches:* (being I suppose, the same with those in our MSs.) and the Doctor adds, that *he has often heard him sing these words after this manner.*

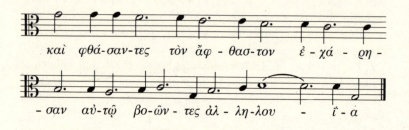

καὶ φθά-σαν-τες τὸν ἄφ - θασ-τον ἐ - χά - ϱη -
- σαν αὐ-τῷ βο-ῶν - τες ἀλ - λη-λου - ἵ - α

I suspecting some faults in this Tune, especially at the beginning; consulted the Doctors own Originall Manuscript, which we have in the Bodleian Library[7] and therein found it expressed as follows.

καὶ φθά-σαν - τες τὸν ἄφ - θασ-τον ἐ - χά - ϱη -
- σαν αὐ-τῷ βο - ῶν - τες ἀλ - λη - λου - ἵ - α

The Doctor does not inform us whether this was a tune of *Conopius's* own making or not: but, methinks, 'tis very like such a common Ground-Bass as this,

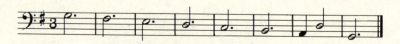

I could heartily wish, Sir, that we had as much of the *Antient Greek-Music*, as we have of their *Modern*; but, to my sorrow, I could never

---

[7] Bodl. MS Barlow 2 (*SC* 6431).

meet with above four Tunes in it. Three of them are Hymns of one Dionysius, inscribed εἰς Μοῦσαν, εἰς Ἀπόλλωνα, & εἰς Νέμεσιν, which *Vincentio Galilei* in his *Dialogo della Musica*[8] pag. 96. says were found at Rome by a Florentine Gentleman in the Library of *Cardinal St Angelo*, and that in a very antient MS. of *Aristides Quintilianus & Bryennius*. The 4th Tune Father *Kircher, Musurg.*, Tom. 1. pag. 541 says he found in the Library of *Messana in Sicily*; and it is a fragment of *Pindar*.

Whether these Tunes were made by good Masters, or were of any value when they were composed, I know not: but this I am sure of, that Mr *Laws* (who was a competent Judge) affirms, that *by composing some of Anacreon's Odes, he found the Greek Tongue full as good as any for Music, and in some particulars sweeter than the Latin, or those Modern ones that descended from the Latin.*[9]

These 4 Tunes last mentioned, are turn'd into our common Notes; the 3 former (as I have reason to think) by *Dr Benjamin Rogers* of *Oxford*,[10] at the instance of *Arch-bishop Usher*: The last was done by *Kircher* in the place above cited. I dont pretend to Judge of the performances of these persons. The truth is, if we may relie on their Representations of them; the Tunes are vile enough. As for *Dr Rogers*, he was well known to be a very able Musitian, but I doubt whether he had much studied the Antient Greek Music; for Father *Kircher* the world is sufficiently informed of his Character & Abilities by Meibomius, one of whose small Complements upon him, I here recite in his own words. *Musicam* (says he) *Graecam disciplinam, quam hactenus Graece doctissimorum virorum vix ullus attrectare ausus fuit, sine ulla fere Graeca litteratura, nullo Graecorum Musicorum lecto, tradere adgressus est Vir Cl. Athanasius Kircherus.* I will say no more upon this subject, but that you have these four songs at the End of the *Oxford* Edition of *Aratus*, printed at the Theater anno 1672.[11]

As to the pieces of *Parchment*, I suppose, Sir, you had them of *Mr Bagford*; from whom likewise, I have reciev'd some hundreds of such pieces & leaves, written att different Times & in different places; which

---

[8] *Dialogo . . . della musica antica e della moderna* (Florence, 1581).

[9] Quoted from Henry Lawes's preface to his first book of *Ayres and Dialogues* (1653).

[10] Organist of Christ Church, Dublin, till 1641, of Magdalen College, Oxford 1665–85, † Oxford 1698.

[11] Ἀράτου Σολέωσ Φαινόμενα καὶ Διοσημεία (Oxford, 1672). Pbd. by Dr John Fell, Dean of Christ Church, Oxford, though his name nowhere occurs. The 'four songs' are the odes of Dionysius set to music (F. Madan, *Oxford Books vol. 3: Oxford Literature 1651–1680* (Oxford, 1931), pp. 264–5.

I intend (when I have gotten some more) to place in a book according to their Age, and the Countrey wherein they were written. The use that I shall make of this Collection, is, that wheresoever I happen to be (having my book with me) I may at any time satisfie my self of the Age & Countrey of any (Latin) MSs. I shall light upon: or if I desire to know what was the usuall Hand of such a Time and Place, my Book may readily inform me.

This Collection of shreads and scraps of old *Parchment* makes me bold to mention to you, Sir, another like Collection of *Paper* that I have made (chiefly, by the help of the same Mr Bagford) when I was last at *London*. This I have put together in 2 Volumes,[12] of which I will venture to give you some account.

The first Volume contains

1 Some of our own Countrey common brown, grey, blew, red & black Paper.

2 Some Eastern Paper written upon in the *East-Indies, Persia, Turkey, & China*, & some ordinary *Chinese* Paper printed upon.

3 Divers sorts of *Chinese* paper as white, green, blew, red, yellow, brown, &c. differing in colour & finess &c.

4 3 Specimens of *Chinese* Paper gilt on the Surface (not on the Edge) and one silver'd. With one specimen of Paper colored & gilded lately in *London*, in imitation of the painting and gilding of our old Manuscripts.

5 Sixteen Sheets of fine *Chinese* paper, gilt silver'd and painted with different fancies. The last is painted in immitation of *Cloth*.

6 Two Pictures (done, perhaps in *China*) after the *Persian* manner. 3 lesser *Chinese* Pictures, printed with Colors. 2 larger *Chinese* pictures, done by hand. The one seems to be of a *Soldier* the other a Mandarine.

7 3 large Sheets of *Chinese* paper two red & one white.

8 A Scroll of *Russian* Writing, being the same that *Mr Ludolph* selected those Letters from, which are engraven in his *Russian* Grammar.

9 Specimens of *Turkish* Paper, painted; in order to be written upon, painted over again, and made up into a book, or books.

10 Common *marbled* Paper; with one Sheet *marbled* on both sides.

11 10 Sheets of the finer *Turkish Marbled* Paper.

---

[12] Now bound as one—BL Sloane MS 526.

12 11 half sheets *Marbled* (like smoke) after a different manner but with great curiosity and Tenderness.

13 6 Sheets of a differing *Marble* (with oil) said to be done in Germany.

14 18 Sheets of Paper colored and flowered coursly, they say, in Holland.

15 3 others done better but of an odder manner.

16 16 Sheets of several colors and Flowers, which look better than those in no. 14.

17 10 Sheets done more Richly than all the rest.

The other Volume is a Collection of sheets & pieces of white *European* Paper, which are plac'd according to their several Marks & Stamps. The Reason why I gathered them together (tho' every sort is still incomplete) was not only to satisfie my Curiosity, in knowing what sort of Paper is in use among so many Nations, or to please my self or friends with looking on the fine Colors, Marbles, &c. but to know whether they would confirm a Notion I have of the Originall of our Paper; which (to me) they do. And farther, I thought that some Time or other, the *History of Paper* might be attempted, and with so much the more hopes of success, when the Author (whoever he may be) has before his Eyes, most of the sorts of that subject that he is to treat about.

Sir, if you have a mind to see either of these books of Paper, or the Pieces of Parchment, or all of them; I will soon send them to you, with some *Original Drawings* that I have,[13] and You may return them when you shall think fit.

But to return to your old Parchments, which you was pleas'd to send hither by *Mr Prickett*, and to ask my opinion of their Age: Sir, I take it as an honour to be consulted by You in this case; especially, since there are many in *London* much better able to inform you, in this matter, than my self; who for these twelve Months, that is, since I came last from *London*, have been forced to mind other business, than Manuscripts. Nor, as I remember, have I since then, lookt into any MS. with intention to observe the handwriting of it, but once, with your worthy, learned and ingenious Relation Mr *Gale*,[14] for about the space of an hour. By such a long disuse, I have lost (I fear) a great deal

---

[13] Perhaps the 'fine drawings' from Holland referred to in Wanley to Bagford, 4 May 1699, BL Harley MS 4966, art. 68.

[14] Thomas Gale m. Barbara, daughter of Thomas Pepys of Impington, Cambridge.

of that niceness in discerning, which the dayly use of so many
thousands of MSs. as are in the *Bodleian Library*, had, at length, given
me: & with that, the benefit of many Observations, which cost me
much Time to make. I must needs say too, Sir, that I think it requires a
man of great experience, to give Judgment on the Age of an entire
book, from the Hand-writing of it: & much more so, when instead of a
whole book, he has only a leaf, or a piece of a leaf to Judge by. Sir, I
dont say this as if I was unwilling to answer your Demands, but that
these Considerations may prevail with you to pardon me & the Errors
I may commit in the following account. I have taken the boldness to
number them; because you should be sure to know which parchment I
mean.[15]

1 Being a fragment of the *Origines* or *Etymologiae* of *St Isidore* Bishop
of *Sevil*, seems by the Hand to be written in *France*, & that about
the time of *Charles the Great*, but rather before than after. It seems
more antient than a Copie of *Bede* on the *Canonical Epistles*, in the
Bodleian Library, which book was written anno 818, or before.[16] If
you please to give your self the trouble of looking into *Mabillon de re
Diplomatica*, I believe, Sir, You will find this piece of Parchment, to
agree pretty well with the last Specimen of the 361st page.[17]

2 Is a leaf of the Gospells, written, as I take it, in *England*, about the
middle or towards the latter end of the 8th Century. I have seen
several Books written in *England* (as I may call it) in this Hand: as
St Chad's Gospells in *Lichfield Library*;[18] *St Eadfrid's* in the Cotton,[19]
& *Venerable Bedes* in the Bodleian;[20] which books being certainly
written in *England*, (by the way) make me ghess, that the Gospells
of *St Matthew* & *St Mark* in the Cotton Library, commonly said to
have been *St Augustine's*, of Canterbury:[21] & *St Salaberga's* Psalter,

[15] These manuscript fragments together with others not mentioned here were
mounted by Pepys in a large folio volume in 1700, now Magdalene College, Cambridge,
Pepys MS 2981. Wanley's remarks in this letter are inserted by another hand adjacent to
the pieces to which they refer. An abbreviated copy (of only ten items) by Philip
Sproson in BL Harley MS 7026, art. 3.

[16] Bodl. MS Bodley 849 (*SC* 2602), so dated on fo. 168ʳ.

[17] Of the 1681 folio edn.

[18] The eighth-century codex at Lichfield, where Wanley had seen it four years
earlier: see no. 4.

[19] Cotton Nero D.iv, the Lindisfarne Gospels (*CLA* ii, no. 187), apparently written by
Eadfrith, Bishop of Lindisfarne in the late seventh or early eighth century.

[20] Bodl. MS Auct. D.2.19 (*SC* 3946), the Rushworth Gospels, an eighth-/ninth-
century codex, thought to be Bede's own.

[21] Cotton Otho C.v., gospels of St Matthew and St Mark (*CLA* ii, no. 125) severely

mentioned by *Mabillon*, *Diplomat* p. 359 were both written in England likewise.[22] Nor did I ever see any book written in this hand in a Forreign Countrey.

3 Is a fragment of the 38th Psalm, & seems, to me, to have been written in *England*, soon after the leaf no. 2. and perhaps, about the end of the 8th Century.

4 Is a fragment of the 8th Chapter of *Daniel*, written also in *England*, the hand approaching nearer to that we call the *Saxon*. To the best of my remembrance, there is in *Sir John Cottons* book of *Saxon Charters*,[23] one in, or near this hand, which if it have a Date, would easily determine the Age of this. And the Register of the Benefactors to *Durham Abbey* or *Cathedral Church*, written with Letters of Gold & Silver; which is in the *Cotton Library*, under the Head of *Domitian*; is, as I remember, in a hand very like this.[24] And, if I'me not mistaken, *King Egbert* is the last King Registred therein, before the book was continued by later hands.

5 Is a leaf containing some short Explication of the later end of *Martianus Capella de Nuptijs Philologiae*, & of the beginning of his Tract de *Arte Grammatica*. 'Tis written in Saxon Letters, as I ghess, about the Time of King *Alfred*.

6 Is a fragment of some such Notes as the former, upon some other Author, I doubt whether this was written by an *English* hand, tho there be a mixture of the *English* Letter in it. But it seems to be written about the latter end of the 10th Century.

7 Is a fragment of *Priscians Grammar*, & seems to be written beyond the Seas, not much after no. 6.

8 Is a leaf of an *Antiphonal*, for ought I know, written in *England*, and 'tis likely about the latter end of the 12th Century. This leaf shews that they did lay their Gold indifferently, either upon a Yellow or red Ground. As for the Music, I see 'tis upon 4 lines; but there are MSs. in the *Bodleian Library* where the Music is prick'd but upon

damaged in the fire of 1731. Described by Wanley in a note in his own copy of Smith's *Catalogus* (now Bodl. Gough London 54) as 'Charactere antiquo Saxonico', dated by Lowe to the seventh or eighth century.

[22] Berlin, Deutsche Staatsbibl. MS Hamilton 553 (*CLA* viii, no. 1048), an eighth-century psalter written in Northumbria, it belonged to the monastery of St Jean at Laon and was traditionally associated with St Salaberga († 665), founder and first abbess. J. Mabillon, *De Re Diplomatica* (Paris, 1681), reproduces the hand, Tabella viii, p. 359.

[23] Cotton Augustus ii.

[24] Cotton Domitian vii, the Liber Vitae of Durham.

one line, and many without any lines at all as is the Music of the *Greeks, Russes & Armenians* at this day. But in such Latin MSS. the difference of sound, is to be learn'd from the scituation of the Notes.

9 I fancy might be written in *Italy* about the same Time with or not long after no. 8. It looks like a fragment of some Commentary on Coloss. 1. 16. but whose, is not, I suppose, worth the while to enquire after.

10 Bears it Date along with it, in these words *Anno Regni Regis Edwardi tertij post conquestum septimo*. Give me leave to add, Sir, something about these words *post conquestum*. I have seen several Charters, Deeds &c. bearing Date such a year of King *Henry filij Regis Iohannis*. And some of King Edward the first, who was stiled therein *filius Regis Henrici*.[25] And many of *K. Edward* the Second call'd likewise *filij Regis Edwardi*. After this King Edward the Third came to the Crown, I concieve they would not give him the Title of *Edwardi filij Regis Edwardi*, because his Father was so stil'd before him. Therefore this Title was found out, *Edwardus tertius post conquestum*, which at the same Time, did also distinguish him from *King Edward the Elder, & King Edward the Confessor*, who both reign'd before the Conquest. Now I would humbly crave your opinion, Sir, whether it was very proper for the succeding Kings to make use of the said words in imitation of King Edward the third? as (for instance) *King Richard the second* to be stiled *Richardus post Conquestum secundus*; *Henricus post conquestum quartus*, &c. as if we had had Kings of those names before the Conquest?

11 Seems to be written in *K. Henry* the 6ths Reign &

12 Somewhat before.

13 About *K. Edward* the 4ths Time.

14 Is a part of a *Breviary* written in *France* or *Flanders* about K. Henry the 7ths Time. I was thinking, that the book whereunto this leaf did once belong, might have been written for some of the Heirs or Descendants from the *Beauchamps Earls of Warwick* by the Ragged staffe so often painted therein. And this, Sir, may suffice for the old Parchments, unless you please to start any new Question about them.

I have now, Sir, one request to make you, which is to know *Mr Evelyns* opinion of a print that I am going to give you an account of.

---

[25] Sentence beginning 'And some of King Edward &c.' in Wanley's hand.

I shew'd it to *Mr Gale* and did beg the favour of him to acquaint you with it: but now, having this opportunity I take the boldness to inform you of it myself.

We have in the *Bodleian Library* a *Missale secondum usum Ecclesiae Herbipolensis*, which being a great folio, in parchment, with very fine illuminations, has been all along lookt upon as a Manuscript, tho' any one who has been us'd to such things would see immediately, that 'tis a printed book.[26] The occasion of printing it was this: *Rodulphus Bp of Wirtzberg*, finding many of the *Missals* of his Church, &c. to be imbezeled, or otherwise corrupted, he orders the books that remained, to be examined, and from them a new service book to be composed, which he commands to be printed by Jorius Ryser the Printer, and that the Edition should be compleatly finished by the 8th day of November 1481. All this, and a great deal more, he testifies in an Instrument at the beginning of the book, which bears the same date with the former vizt. the 8th of Nov. 1481. And I believe the book was printed by, or before that day; because at the end of the book is *written* Io.R.1481 being the said Printers name. And at the End of the Instrument aforesaid, is an Engraven Print, being (as I take it) the Arms of the *Bishop*, & the Arms of the *See*, which last is supported by two Angels, with St *Kilian* standing behind it. The former has only a fine Mantling about it. These coats of Arms, I take to be as the *Seal* giving a fuller authority to the Instrument preceding it. This is the *Print* I mean; 'tis engraven, in my opinion, either on Silver or on Brass. Twas evidently wrought off at the Rolling press, for one may plainly see the marks of the Edges of the Plate, and I have been told, by several Engravers & Printers unto whom I have shew'd it, that it was certainly Printed off by a Rolling Press, & that it could be done no other way. That it was not done long afterwards, these are Arguments: first, that the *Compositor* left a Vacancy on purpose to be fill'd up with this Print: & 2dly that this book was bought within less than two months after the Date aforesaid. For one *William Kewsth* Vicar of *St Bartholomews Parish* in *Wirtzburg*, in a written note, testifies, that the same year i.e. 1481 he paid for the printing (of this book) parchment, illumination, & binding, 18 Florins. And afterwards vizt. anno 1486, he gave it to his Church, where it continued (as appears by the succeeding Vicars hands) till the soldiers of *Gustavus Adolphus* sacrilegiously plunderd & rifled that place. As to

---

[26] Bodl. press-mark Auct.i.Q.i.7. See no. 56.

the print it self, 'tis so well engraven, & the Workman had so good a stroke, that I believe half the Workmen in *London*, cannot now do better; and that which makes me admire it, is, that *Mr Evelyn* in his incomparable *History of Chalcography*, p. 35. should be of the opinion that this sort of work is not so antient.[27] His words are these: *The art of Engraving & working off, from Plates of Copper, which we call Prints, was not yet appearing, or born with us, till about the Year 1490*. and this, Sir, which I talk of, shews that the Art was not altogether in its Infancy anno 1481 which was before *Albert Durers* time.

Sir, when you see Mr Evelyn next, if you will give your self the Trouble of consulting him about this affair: 'twill be a great satisfaction, as well as honour to me to know the result.

I have now no more to add to this long Letter: but that as to the *Note* which you are pleas'd to say I sent you, and which you intimate, might be supplied out of our *Statute book*: that I dont (at present) rightly understand you;[28] but when you shall think fit to explain your self more particularly, what note it was I sent, & what you would have transcribed out of our Statute book it shall be done with all readiness, by
    Honorable Sir,
        Your most obliged faithfull & humbly devoted Servant.
                                    Humfrey Wanley.

MS: Bodleian, Ballard 1, fo. 124; fair copy in another hand, corrected by Wanley.[29] *Date*: 'From the Masters Lodgings, at University College; Oxon. June 25. 1699.' *Address*: 'For

[27] John Evelyn, *Sculptura: or, the History and Art of Chalcography and Engraving in Copper* (1662).
[28] The source of Wanley's perplexity may be a question of Pepys's which Charlett seems to be alluding to in a letter to Pepys d. 17 May 1699: 'I have sent you a copy of a letter from Bremen directed to our Vice Chancellor. Mr Wanly is ashamed the other is so short. I think in some of our Public Statutes the prices (?) of those times are most authentically stated' (*Letters and the Second Diary of Samuel Pepys*, ed. R. G. Howarth (1932), no. 260). But this helps hardly at all to make the business clearer.
[29] The version of this letter (d. 25 and 26 June 1699) actually sent to Pepys was lot 246 in Sotheby's sale of 25 Mar. 1974. It went to Quaritch for £1,100 but I have not managed to trace the present owner and have not seen the letter.
Sotheby's catalogue description (pp. 49–50) provides evidence that the letter sent contained material not in the copy printed here, in particular remarks 'on the editing of manuscripts in relation to a proposed edition of Strabo; giving the location of manuscripts of Strabo known to him in England and on the continent', criticisms of librarians for failing to produce catalogues of the collections in their care, and comments on and locations of manuscripts of Catullus, Tibullus, and Propertius. There is good reason to believe that Bodleian MS Ballard 48, fos. 160–1 is a copy (d. 26 June 1699) of that part of the additional material relating to Strabo and the deficiencies of librarians: the passage censuring librarians is quoted by the Sotheby cata-

the Honorable Saml. Pepys Esqr at his House in Buckingham-street in York buildings, in the Strand, London.' *Printed*: Ellis, *Original Letters*, pp. 272–82 (incomplete);
Sotheby's sale cat., 25 Mar. 1974, lot 246 (extracts).

64. *To* Arthur Charlett[1] *2 September 1699*

Reverend & Honored Sir,

In my last I gave you an account of my coming hither on Wednesday night past. On Thursday morning I waited on Mr Laughton[2] at
Trinity College, who was very busie, but however, at last, took me
with all freedom into the College Library, the description of which, I
need not trouble you withall. Some of the books I enquired after,
could not be found on the sudden; but I made a shift to proke out a
few of them myself, being left alone by Mr Laughton, who was sent
for in hast to the Vice-Chancellor.

After I had satisfied my curiositie there for the present; I went to
the Schools, and found Mr Laughton in the publick Library. He was
pleas'd to shew me presently most of the books that I shall have occasion to use, which satisfied me very much. And he came with me
hither & helped me to take the Chamber where I lodge & board at a
private house. I then went to my Inn & discharged it, & received your
very kind letter, in pursuance of which, I have accordingly written to
the two Gentlemen mentioned therein.

I met at Trinity College with Mr Buckeridge, Mr Norgrove, Mr
Allen, & Mr Ellison of C.C.C. Oxon,[3] who engaged me to dine with

loguer and except for unimportant scribal variations is identical with the passage on the
same subject in Ballard 48.

I do not incorporate the extra material from Ballard 48 in the text for the following
reasons: (1) the copy is not in Wanley's hand, and there is neither evidence of authorship, nor evidence to suggest that it is an extract from a letter; (2) the version of the letter
of 25 June printed here is clearly a 'finished' text, and it is not obvious where such a long
passage as that in Ballard 48 could find a place; (3) the Sotheby letter appears to be a
'second edition' which if available in full would properly displace the version printed
here, but there seems to be no case for conflating two distinct versions. In view of its
interest, however, I print the passage from Ballard 48 in Appendix VI.

---

[1] Address taken from Ellis, pasted over in the manuscript. Elsewhere words lost in
the course of repairing a much frayed letter are written in, presumably by the repairer,
and are not distinguished in the ptd. text.

[2] John Laughton (1650–1712), Fellow of Trinity College, Cambridge, University
Librarian 1686–1712. He compiled the account of Trinity manuscripts for *CMA*.

[3] Only Cuthbert Ellison (1678–1719), Fellow of Corpus Christi College, Oxford 1702,
can be identified with certainty.

them, which I did. After dinner, we all went together to visit some of the College Libraries & Chappels, as Gonvile & Caius, where I delivered your letter to Dr Brady, (Dr Rhoderic being gone to Ely)[4] The Dr[5] is extreamly sick, but yet on the mending hand. We saw several other Colleges, as Sydney, Magdalen, St John's &c. At night we were regaled with a very good Consort of Music; where I was much taken with some Italian Songs, which Mr Pate[6] brought from Rome, and a Gentleman here, sang excellently well.

There I met with Mr Annesley,[7] who did me the honor to desire my acquaintance, &c. We came away together, and betimes, in the morning I waited on him at his Chamber (preventing his calling on me at mine, as he purposed.) We went to Bennet College,[8] where I delivered Dr Greens Letter to Mr Kidman,[9] who courteously took us into the Manuscript Library forthwith; and with some difficulty all the books were found that I shall use. Take 'em all together, and they'l appear to be a most noble parcel of books, and one shall seldome meet with so many antient Copies of several Authors, in so small a number of MSS. as are here. In a word this Library answers its Character throughly, except in those MSS. which are said to have once belonged to Theodore Archbishop of Canterbury. Theodore lived (as I remember) in the 7th Century, and I verily think some of these were written 700 years after he was dead. They have MSS. old enough to have been his; but, I know not why, they put his name to more recent books. At the bottom of the first page of Homer, I find the word ΘΕΟΔΩΡΟΣ, but it seems to me to have been the name either of him at whose charge the book was written, or else of the Illuminator.[10] As for the book it self, 'tis a recent paper Copie.[11] It seems that Archbishop Parker was

---

[4] Robert Brady (1628–1700), Master of Caius College, Cambridge 1660, Regius Professor of Physic 1677, physician to Charles II and James II; Charles Roderick († 1712), Fellow of King's College, Cambridge 1671, Provost 1689, Prebend of Ely 1691, Dean 1708.   [5] 'Dr Brady' in margin.

[6] William Pate (1666–1746), 'the learned woollendraper'. See *DNB*.

[7] Arthur Annesley († 1737), Fellow of Magdalene College, Cambridge 1700, succeeded his brother as 5th Earl of Anglesey 1710.

[8] i.e. Corpus Christi College, Cambridge.

[9] Charles Kidman (1663–1740), Fellow of Corpus 1685 and later President.

[10] See the index to M. Vogel–V. Gardthausen, *Die griechischen Schreiber des Mittelalters und der Renaissance* (Leipzig, 1909) for the great number of ancient scribes named Theodore.

[11] M. R. James, *Descriptive Catalogue of Manuscripts in Corpus Christi College, Cambridge* (Cambridge, 1912), no. 81, a fifteenth-century manuscript of Homer. For Wanley's opinion on the identity of this Theodore, given twenty-five years later, see James i, pp. 166–7.

abused in this matter, for these Notes of Theodores owning such & such books, are written in his hand: But when their Catalogue is new printed, I suppose, we shall hear no more of Arch-Bishop Theodore, unless it be in the Penitential.[12] I had the curiosity to enquire for some other books, with the titles of which I was not well satisfied, the Origen on Luke,[13] & Ambrose's Hexa[e]meron which are said to be written *litteris peregrinis*, are in Langobardic letters.[14] I hope to shew you specimens of both of them, with several others. The book which had this Title *Liber valde peregrina lingua, & characteribus plane ignotis exaratus*, is a late Arabic Tract.[15] The book said to be written lingua & litteris Aramicis, is an Armenian Psalter.[16] I don't know but the Arch-bishop might buy these 2 last books soon after the Trade was opened to Turkey: if so, he might have been easily imposed upon.[17] The Saxon books here are many in number, & very fine ones, I began to take an account of them to day, & will finish as soon as I can, but it will be some time first.

From Bennet College Mr Annesley & I went each home; and at one a clock met again and visited some other Libraries, and at Emanuel College we met with Mr Barnes,[18] to whom I presented Mr Dean of Christchurche's Service,[19] & yours, which he kindly returns by me. He took us into the Library, where with much ado we found some of the books I was minded to see. By them & more which I have seen, I perceive one can hardly rely on their descriptions of books; for he that takes the Catalogue of his College MSS. describes them as they appear to him indeed, but having scarcely ever seen any others, he makes but poor work on't. As for the fragment of the Psalms in Greek Capitals which they cried up so; I hope to shew you a Specimen of it, which I shal take for the singularity of its character.[20] I can scarcely

---

[12] James no. 265, an eleventh-century manuscript penitential, laws, etc. See no. 65.

[13] James no. 334, an eighth-century manuscript of Origen on Luke, *CLA* ii, no. 128.

[14] James no. 193, an eighth-century manuscript, *CLA* ii, no. 124. According to James this and the previous manuscript are both in a 'Lombardic' hand.

[15] James no. 401, a theological tract with commentary, of the sixteenth century.

[16] James no. 478, an Armenian psalter of the ? thirteenth century.

[17] i.e. Matthew Parker (1504–75), Archbishop of Canterbury, who left his great collection of manuscripts to Corpus Christi College, Cambridge.

[18] Josuah Barnes (1654–1712), Fellow of Emmanuel College, Cambridge 1678, Professor of Greek at Cambridge 1695. He supplied the account of Emmanuel manuscripts for *CMA*. Bentley said of him that he knew as much Greek as an Athenian cobbler, i.e. he possessed a ready facility but no critical sense.

[19] Aldrich.

[20] M. R. James, *Western Manuscripts in the Library of Emmanuel College* (Cambridge,

think it to have been written by a Greek, but if it was, I believe it was by the hand of some woman. As for that book which in the Catalogue of MSS is called *Efesney* & said to be written *lingua Denvistica*;[21] I find the Title written in the book it self to be thus, *Liber dictus Ejesney, scriptus lingua Ienvista*. The Character is that of the *Gauri*, and the Language I suppose to be the same. I desire you, Sir, to do me the favor as to acquaint Dr Hyde with my finding this book, and that I will copie for him 3 or 4 lines from it: And I will enquire at Clare-hall for another book in the same language that he mention'd to me.

I can't forbear mentioning two books that I light upon in Bennets College Library. The one is the Excerpta *Hogeri Abbatis*, from divers Musical Authors.[22] I don't, at present, know who this Abbat Hogere was; but the Music is upon lines, with Letters instead of Notes; and I expect more from it, than from any antient Musical Author in Latin that I have yet seen. I intend (when I h[ave] pretty well got over my business) to send Mr Dean of Christchurch a Specimen of it;[23] if I like it as well upon the second view, as I did at the first.

In another book in the same place, amongst other valuable things, I met with a most ample account of the Consecration & Coronation of our Antient Kings & Queens: 'tis much larger than any copie of the Liber Regalis I ever saw.[24] I have good reason to think th[e] book wherein this is found, to have been written before the Conquest; and the Catalogues taking no notice of any such matter, I believe it may have been neglected till now: unless Dr Stanley ha's found it. I'me half in a mind to transcribe it, & let it go abroad in the Catalogue: but I'me sensible the warm people of two opposite parties, will be ready to blame my forwardness. I would fain, Sir, know your sentiments of it; but to me it appears an important Piece. I have as much more to say to you, Sir, as what I've written, but I'me really weary with

---

1904), no. 253, *CMA* I. iii, no. 32. A twelfth-century fragment, James declares 'certainly not written by a Greek (or in Greece): and . . . probably written in England' (p. 155). This and the next were later borrowed by Wanley: see Wanley to Barnes, 21 Sept. 1699, Bodl. MS Rawl. lett. 40, art. 32.

[21] *CMA* I. iii, no. 52.

[22] James no. 260, a tenth-century manuscript from Christ Church, Canterbury.

[23] Aldrich was a talented amateur musician.

[24] James no. 146, art. 17, a Winchester benedictional of the tenth-/eleventh-century bound up with a Worcester manuscript of slightly later date. It is described in the catalogue of William Stanley (Master 1693–8) pbd. 1722, where the manuscript appears as D.III. The Coronation service is ptd. by L. G. W. Legg, *English Coronation Records* (1901).

working to day, & I must write two letters more by this Post: but by
the next journey of the Cambridge Carrier, you shall not fail of the
rest, from

Most Honored Sir,
        Your faithful & humbly devoted servant

                                        Humfrey Wanley.

From Mrs Ray's house near Trinity College.

MS: Bodleian, Ballard 13, fo. 79. *Date*: 'Cambridge, Septemb. 2. 1699.' *Address*: 'For The
Reverend Dr Charlett, Master of University College in Oxford by way of London.'
Printed: Ellis, *Original Letters*, pp. 284–8.

65. *To* Arthur Charlett *17 September 1699*

Reverend & Honor'd Sir,

Mr Tanner at the end of your last letter, having given me advise of
your going out of Town, I was loth to write before now, because I
thought my letter would come never the sooner to your hands. I sent
you word, Sir, that in pursuance of your Orders, I had written to the 2
Gentlemen, and I doubt not but they have signified so much to you
before this time.

You may remember, Sir, the talk you was pleas'd to have with me,
about Mr Hartley's late Catalogue of books, wherein he puts down an
English Bible of 1520, & that in Romans 1.1. there are these words *Paul
a knave of Jesus Christ*.[1] When I was at London, I saw the very book he
meant (which was formerly the Duke of Lauderdail's)[2] and any body
may easily see, that it was first printed *Paul an apostle*; but now we read
there, Paul *an kneawe* of Jesus Christ, these letters *apostl* being
scratched out, & *kneaw* being pasted in the book in the place of them.
Besides, the English never wrote *kneawe* for knave, & supposing that
they had, they would not have said *an kneawe*, as they did properly say
an apostle. The book it self was printed since 1520. but some of the

---

[1] For John Hartley's *Catalogus Universalis* (1699), see no. 10 n. 3. The bible (listed by
Hartley vol. ii, p. G1 as a folio, but the date given is 1519) is the first edn. of 'Matthew's
version', 1537, the real primary version of the English Bible, Darlow and Moule no. 34,
STC 2066. It later found its way into the Harleian Library: see Osborne, *Catalogus Bibliothecae Harleianae*, i (1743), no. 154, p. 9.

[2] John Maitland († 1682), Duke of Lauderdale in the peerage of Scotland. His library
was sold at auction in May 1690 after being in pawn for some years.

numeral letters are scratched out, to make it seem the older; as supposing it was MDXXXVII, by rasing the 4 last letters out, it becomes MDXX. but I have taken such notice of the book, that I shall easily, find one of the same impression in the Bodleian Library. I persuade my self, Sir, that that place in Fullers Church History of Brittain, where he (untruly) saies that such words may be seen in 2 MSS in the Bodleyan Library, was the occasion of corrupting this printed book. The place in *Fuller*, may be found by searching the References to *Wiclef* & his Books from the *Index*.[3]

I desire the favor of you, Sir, to give my humble service to Mr Grabe,[4] and to ask him whether he is of the opinion that the Penetential which he copied here at Bennet College, be Theodores?[5] I must needs say, sir, that I begin to doubt it very much, for these Reasons. (1.) The book it self is Anonymous. (2.) the two Titles that have Theodores name to them, can't be much relied on: the newer (which is in Mr Parkers hand, the ArchBishops son)[6] being, in all probability taken from the older. This last neither, is not so antient as the book by some Centuries, & even in the place where we now read *Theodori*, was formerly written ECGBERHTI. (3.) the book quotes *Bedes Eccles. History*, & even Alcuinus, who lived long after Theodorus was dead & rotten. And some other passages in the book may be justly excepted against.

With my service to Mr Tanner, I desire he may know, Sir, that I would willingly serve him in greater matters than those he mentions, but I am not versed in those Authors he writes about, and to compare them all along with the printed books, is out of my power. But notwithstanding, I will give him (when I see him) that account of them, that I shall be able to take.

I thought I should have left Cambridge in a fortnight's time, but tho' I employ my self here 12 hours every day amongst their MSS. I have

---

[3] Wanley's account is independently confirmed by John Strype, who owned a copy: see Strype's letter d. 2 Dec. 1706, BL Harley MS 3781, fo. 121. Wanley may be right in imputing the corruption to Fuller: the 'knave' word is not to be found in the Wyclifite version of the Bible from which Fuller (*Church History* (1655), bk. iv, par. 25 (p. 142)) implies it comes.

[4] Johann Ernst Grabe (1666–1711), Prussian patristic and biblical scholar. He migrated to England from Königsberg and received a pension from William III; he was resident in Oxford from about 1696 and became chaplain of Christ Church in 1700.

[5] M. R. James, *Descriptive Catalogue of Manuscripts in Corpus Christi College, Cambridge* (Cambridge, 1912), no. 265. See no. 64 n. 12.

[6] John Parker († 1618), eldest son of Matthew Parker.

not done half my business: and at my return, I hope to give you, Sir, a very satisfactory account of my spending my time, this Journey.

Here was a great preparation for observing the Ecclipse, a room darkned, Telescopes fixed, & every thing put in order on purpose; & happy that man that could be admitted; but after some hours waiting for black Wednesday, *parturiunt montes* [and] the Gentlemen having dined with Duke Humfrey, came out very gravely into the warm Sun, cursing their Tabl[e]s, &c. & were as well laughed at, as the Sons of Art at London, who hired the Monument for the same purpose.[7] I am
Reverend Sir,
Your most obedient & humbly devoted servant
Humfrey Wanley.

MS: Bodleian, Ballard 13, fo. 81. *Date*: 'From Mrs Ray's house near Trinity College in Cambridge, September 17. 1699.' *Address*: 'For the Reverend Dr Charlett Master of University College in Oxford by way of London.' *Printed*: *Bodleian Letters*, i, pp. 95–7 (extracts).

66. *To* Arthur Charlett *28 September 1699*

Reverend & Honor'd Sir,
You were altogether in the Right when you said that I might read the old Manuscripts during the Ecclipse, as well as if there had been none at all:[1] for I was then reading & writing from them all the while at Bennet College: and I will assure you, Sir, that notwithstanding the obscurity of 10 or 11 digits of the Suns body; the remaining part lighted me so well, that I had no need of Candles.

I am glad to hear that I am likely to be beholden to the Fellows; and am very willing to receive that or any other obligation which they shall think fit to lay upon me.[2] Mr Laughton ha's carried me to Dr Covel, since his return home. The Dr recieved me with all the kindness in the world, & kept me there almost all the day: Shewed me his books, &

[7] The partial eclipse of 13 Sept. 1699 did not live up to the expectations it had aroused: see no. 66. 'Having dined with Duke Humfrey' refers to the saying 'To dine with Duke Humfrey' = to go without dinner.

[1] Charlett to Wanley d. 22 Sept. 1699, Welbeck Wanleyana = BL Loan MS 29/253.
[2] 'I beleive you may depend upon having the Priviledge of a Graduate, allowed You at your Returne, on some Occasion lately the Fellows having expressed theyr willing Inclinations to it' (Charlett to Wanley, 22 Sept. 1699). See Wanley to Charlett, no. 52 n. 1 and no. 67.

proffered me the use of what I pleased. I borrowed his Greek Evangel-istary in Capital Letters; which is by much, the noblest book of the kind that I ever saw.[3] I have just now finished a Specimen that I have taken of it: And I have several books now by me, in my chamber, of that value, that, was the worst of them mine, I would not take 20£ for it. The truth is, the Cambridge Gentlemen, are extreamly courteous & obliging, & excepting those of Bennet College, I can borrow what books I please.

I have by me a great Folio which I borrowed out of Trinity College Library. It contains the 3 Latin Versions of the Psalter made by St Hierome, vizt the Hebrew, Roman & Gallic. The Hebrew is interlined all along with a French Version. The Roman likewise with a Saxon Version, & the Gallic with a Latin Gloss, besides other Marginal Notes. After the Psalter, comes the Cantici sacri, Pater noster, Creeds, &c. in Latin, French & Saxon. Before every Psalm, &c is a large Picture explaining it: which notwithstanding the meanness of the drawing, if they were well considered, may be of good use to an indus-trious Philologer. I trouble you, sir, with this description, the rather, because at the end, there is the Picture of *Eadwin* a Monk that wrote the book, & a large Draught of the Monastery that he lived in: and I wish Mr Tanner were here; for perhaps, he might be able to find out what Monastery it might be. I desire the favor of you, Sir, to ask him if he ha's met with any *Eadwin* about the time of King Stephen (for the book seems to be so old) that was famous for writing & painting, as several others have been noted to be, both before & since this Monks time. My present conjecture is, that the Monastery may be St Augustines in Canterbury; but I have but one reason and that a poor one for it.[4]

I am with much respect Honor'd Sir,
Your most humbly devoted Servant

H. Wanley.

MS: Bodleian, Ballard 13, fo. 83. *Date*: 'Cambridge, Sept. 28. 1699.' *Address*: 'For the Reverend Dr Charlett, Master of University College in Oxford. by way of London.' *Printed*: Ellis, *Original Letters*, pp. 288–90.

[3] 'Evangelistarium splendidissimum' of the tenth century, purchased by Wanley together with Covell's other manuscripts for the Harleian Library in 1716. Now BL Harley MS 5598.
[4] Trinity College, Cambridge MS R.17.1, M. R. James, *Western Manuscripts in the Library of Trinity College, Cambridge* (Cambridge, 1900–4), no. 987 (Ker no. 91, Wanley p. 168)—the so-called 'Canterbury Psalter'. James and Ker date it *c*.1150 and ascribe it to Christ Church, Canterbury.

67. *To* Arthur Charlett *19 October 1699*

Reverend & Honored Sir,

I hope Mr Arch-Deacon of Carlisle's[1] Letter which I sent you, together with my answer to it, came safe; and that you did me the Favor to Seal the last, & send it as directed. If they have miscarried, I'me very sorry, because Mr Arch-deacon may thereupon think himself neglected, and that he ha's Reason to complain of me. I sent them by that Person who came hither with the two Danish Gentlemen; which the Carrier hearing of, grumbled at exceedingly, & vow'd never to bring me any Letters from Oxford: but he was not so good as his Word, for the last night, he brought me a letter from Mr Elstob (tho' a week after it ought to have been delivered to me.) By this letter I am inform['d] that the Society have been pleas'd to conferr upon me all the Privileges of a Commoner Bacchelor of Arts; which I take as a Special Favor, and do accordingly return them my hearty thanks for it; with promise of behaving my self in such a manner, as not to give them just occasion to repent their Kindness; or to deny me the Degree of Bacchelor of Laws, when I am full Standing for it, and shall judge it necessary to desire it. And further, Sir, I do return you my humble & hearty Thanks for this late Favor, and in a more particular manner: becau[se] I'me fully persuaded, that not only I should never have had it without your concurrence with the Society; but that you were pleas'd to be the First-mover in [it] and that my Advancement in the College, is plainly the Effect of your Love to, [and] good Opinion of me.[2]

Curiosity, Sir, is a thing natural to all mankind, and more especially to all Men of Letters: And therefore it will be no wonder, if I take it for granted [that] you desire to know what it is that keeps me here all this while, and when I design to return to Oxford. Of both which particulars, I take the boldness to give you some account.

I assure you, Sir, that it is not young, idle Company that detains me so much longer than I said & expected: but really the business that I came upon, which I have found much more considerable than I could have thought for. Tis 7 weeks since I came hither, and I never wrought harder in my life for 7 weeks together, than I have now done: And yet

[1] William Nicolson (1655–1727), Fellow of The Queen's College, Oxford 1679. Archdeacon of Carlisle 1682, Bishop 1702.   [2] See nos. 54, 59, 61.

I have not finished, nor shall I be able to finish this Journey: for Sir Thomas Bodley's Bell begin's to sound so loudly in my Ears, that I shall not be at quiet, till I'me actually in his Library.

But, Sir, you ought not to think, that there are So many Saxon MSS. in this place, as to keep a man 7 weeks in barely transcribing their Titles. No, Sir, had that been all I had to do, I might have done in 7 hours. But I have look'd over more than 7 score MSS. to see if I could find any Saxon words in them, and all to no purpose: and to take an accurate account of those books wherein I succeeded. I have not contented my self with saying *Liber Homiliarum Saxonicarum*, but noted the *Day* it was proper for, the *Place of Scripture* it treats upon, with some lines of the Beginning & End. By this means I have been able to compare one homilie with another, to find which do agree, which differ, which Copie ha's more on the same Text, & which less, &c. For other Saxon books, I have copied large pieces of them; on purpose to compare them with other books in other Libraries, that I might thereby know how they agree together. For I find we have more Copies of the same book, than I thought of, as I believe I shall make appear. I have further transcribed all manner of Epistles, Wills, Covenants, Notes, Charms, Verses, Catalogues, &c. that I foresee may be of use to the book: this & a great deal more than I say, ha's been one occasion of my tarrying so long. In one word, if Dr Hicks will accept from me a Catalogue of all the Saxon MSS that I know of in England, I will do my endeavor to restore many (hitherto) Anonymous Tracts to their proper Authors; will specifie particularly, whatever has been printed & what not; with a multitude of Remarks & Observations that I have not met with in the former Edition of his book.[3] With this Catalogue, I shall annex the Specimens of the Characters of the most Considerable MSS. of the languages of the Northern Nations, as the Gothic, Francic, Langobardic, & Islandic, besides the Saxon, with Specimens of MSS. in Welsh, Cornish, Scotch & Irish.[4] And by way of Digression, if upon mature deliberation it be thought necessary, I may make Specimens of the four famous Greek MSS of England, vizt Sir J. Cottons Genesis,[5] the Alexandrian MS.[6] Arch. Lauds Acts of the

---

[3] i.e. in the catalogue of Anglo-Saxon manuscripts annexed to Hickes's *Institutiones* (Oxford, 1689), pp. 133 f.

[4] In fact Hickes took over Wanley's collections of northern scripts of various kinds and pbd. them in vol. i. of the *Thesaurus*. Wanley's 'Digression' was accounted unnecessary.

[5] Cotton Otho B vi, largely destroyed in the fire of 1731. See no. 47.

[6] Codex Alexandrinus, BL Royal MS 1. D. v–viii.

Apostles,[7] and Beza's book here,[8] with the fragment of the Greek Gospels in the Cotton Library, which I take to be older than any of them.[9] The taking some of these Specimens will keep me here till the latter end of the next week; and in the beginning of the Week following I will (God willing) wait on you, Sir, and shew you what I have been talking ab[o]ut all this while. And I desire, Sir, that Mr Thwaites may be told (with my humble service) that I shall bring with me a Scotch MS of Receipts, an antient Lat. Eng. Dictionary contain[i]ng the words of the Eastern-English,[10] whereby Mr Benson may secure many old words from being buried in the grave of everlasting Oblivion;[11] with one antient Volume of the Antient Christian Poets, at the end of which, are[12] [man]y L[at]in [*several words lost*] (o[r w]hat h[e] pleases to call [em]) m[ade in] [*some words lost*] & celebrating the praises of Otdo, Heinrich, & Cuonrad the Emperors, Gunnild the Empress & many others, with pieces of the old Teutonic Mythology, and some remains of the Francic Poetry mingled with Latin; two Saxon Peices of which kind I have found here & copied.

Sir, the narrowness of my Time & Paper will not permit me to trouble you much farther for the present, nor indeed, any more till my parting from Cambridge.

Dr Mountague the Master of Trinity College invited me to dine with him Yesterda[y] together with the Vice-Master and Dr Stubbes,[13] where they all remembered your health, with Mr Dean of Christ-Church, Dr Wake, the Rector of Lincoln, &c with much respect. And

[7] Bodl. MS Laud Gr. 35 (*SC* 1119), a seventh-century codex (Codex E of Acts) apparently used by Bede.

[8] Cambridge University Library MS Nn. ii.41, *CLA* ii, no. 140. Greek and Latin manuscript of Gospels and Acts (Codex Bezae) probably of the fifth century, presented to the University by Theodore Beza in 1581.

[9] Cotton Titus C.xv, a sixth-century uncial manuscript (Codex Purpureus), four leaves containing parts of Matt. and John. Other fragments are in the Vatican and in Vienna.

[10] Ellis identifies this as BL Harley MS 221, the so-called 'Promptorium Parvulorum', an English–Latin dictionary compiled in 1440. I have not identified the other two manuscripts mentioned.

[11] Thwaites, Praelector in Anglo-Saxon at The Queen's College, Oxford, had difficulty in procuring sufficient copies of Somner's Anglo-Saxon dictionary (1659) for his pupils, and this led to the issue in 1701 of a 2nd edn. augmented by Thomas Benson. It is presumably to this that Wanley refers.

[12] Ellis, *Original Letters*, here reads 'many Latin Hymns, Odes, or Songs (or what he pleases to call them), made in memory of and celebrating of Otdo' etc. (p. 293).

[13] Wolfran Stubbs († 1719), Fellow of Trinity College, Cambridge 1661, Vice-Master 1703, Regius Professor of Hebrew 1688–99.

Mr Annesley sends you & Mr Dennison his very [hum]ble service, and I with my thanks & service to Mr Denison whom I hear is returned & the whole Society, take leave to subscribe my self,

Most honored Sir,

Your most humble obedient Servant

Humfrey Wanley.

MS: Bodleian, Ballard 13, fo. 85. *Date*: 'Cambridge, Octob 19. 1699.' *Address*: 'For the Reverend Dr Charlett Master of University-College Oxford.' *Printed*: Ellis, *Original Letters*, pp. 290–4.

68. *To* [George Hickes] *26 November 1699*

Most Honor'd Sir

I have received your two last kind letters,[1] with the Parcell from Matthews,[2] and have sent you the Agreement between the Monasteries, which I cut out of the Catalogue, & which I desire you to preserve with the other Leaves.[3]

As for St Chad's book, you may remember *the notes written therein by later hands*, are extreamly hard to be read, the Ink being almost worn out, or otherwise defaced; but however I send you what I can, as follow's.[4]

(1) + her sutelað an þæt godwine earwiges sunu hæfþ gelæd fullelade æt þan unriht wife þe leofgar b*isceop* hyne tihte *ond þæt* wæs[5] æt licitfelda.,

(2) Ostenditur hic quod emit + gelhi + filius arihtiud hoc euangelium de cingal et dedit illi *pro* illo equm optimum et dedit *pro* anima sua istum euangelium de*o* et *san*c*to* teliaui super altare.

+ gel hi + filius arihtiud . ., . ., et + cincenu + filius gripiud . .,

(3) surexit rutbulc filius liuit ha gener tutri dierchm tir telih haioid

---

[1] d. 21, 23 Nov. 1699, BL Harley MS 3779, fos. 111, 113.

[2] Wanley's catalogue of Anglo-Saxon manuscripts taken at Cambridge and left with Hickes on Wanley's return to Oxford via London.

[3] An eleventh-century agreement of confraternity between the Prior of Worcester and the Abbots of Evesham, Chertsey, etc., in Corpus Christi College, Cambridge MS 111. See Ker no. 35, Wanley p. 149.

[4] The marginal notes in the eighth-century gospels at Lichfield, first seen by Wanley in Mar. 1695: see no. 4. Requested by Hickes in his letters of 21, 23 Nov., and ptd. by him *Thesaurus*, I. pt. iv, Dissertatio Epistolaris, p. 11 and in part by Wanley p. 289. See also no. 95.

[5] In an uncharacteristic error of transcription, Wanley omits 'læd' after 'wæs'.

ilau elcu filius geling haluidt iuguret amgucant pel cantanndi hodie et dipro tant gener tutri o guir imguodant irde[*three letters lost*]n guragun tagc rodetit elcu guetig eq*us* tres uache, tres uache nouidligi na*us*ir nibe cas ig ridu dimedichat [gu]etig bit did braut [*five letters lost*]at guetig nis minn tutbulc hai cenca i*n*ois oisou°̀ [*rest of letter lost*]

MS: Bodleian, Eng. hist. c. 6, fo. 38; fragment. *Date*: 'Univ. Coll. Nov. 26. 1699.' *Address*: 'For The Reverend D[*rest of line lost*] in Kingstreet Bloomsb[*rest of line lost*] farthest Lamp towards [*rest of line lost*].'

69. *To* [Narcissus Marsh] *18 January 1700*

May it please your Grace,

The Master telling me that he should have an Opportunity of sending to your Grace to morrow; I desired his leave to answer the latter part of your Graces last Letter to him[1] about St Columb's Gospells,[2] the Specimen whereof he procured from your Grace, upon my account.[3] Mr Dodwell[4] first gave me notice of the book about 3 years since. And supposing it to have been written above 1000 years ago; I thought a Specimen of it might be of good use to me, in fixing the Age of other antient books written in a like Hand. But upon sight of the Specimen, I could easily see, that it does not come up to that Age: but appears rather to have been written about the middle of the 8th Century; suppose, about the year 740.

Had it been written by St Columb, 'tis very likely, the Letters would have been all Capitals, according to the way of writing such books in that Age. And after the Writing in Capitals went out of Fashion, as being too laborious; the Writing of the 7th Century, was (commonly) larger, & nearer to the shape of Capitals, than the Writing in this book appears to be. Your Grace knows well that Mr O Flaherties Note at the beginning of the book (Liber autem hic scriptus est manu ipsius B. Columkille per spatium 12 dierum ann. Dom. 560) is no good Authority in a case of this Nature, unless it be supported by sufficient

---

[1] Marsh to Charlett d. 30 Nov. 1699, Bodl. MS Ballard 8, fo. 6; it includes the specimen referred to.

[2] The 'Book of Durrow', seventh-century codex of the Gospels (Codex Durmachensis), Trinity College, Dublin MS 57 (A.IV.5), *CLA* ii, no. 273.

[3] See Marsh to Charlett d. 31 May 1699, Bodl. MS Ballard 8, fo. 4.

[4] Henry Dodwell (1641–1711), nonjuror and theologian, formerly Fellow of Trinity College, Dublin.

Testimonies from Antien Writers, or Proofs from the book it self. But the Hand Writing of the book (as I said before) shews it to be newer; & I don't see that he quotes any Author that says St Columb wrote it himself. And I am farther apt to believe that the contrary does rather appear to be true, from the silence (in this particular) of Flannius his Inscription upon the Cover; as also of Sir James Ware in his book de Scriptoribus Hiberniae,[5] where he treats largely concerning this Saint, and in all probability would have mentioned this book of St Columbs writing, if he had thought or known that it had been his. Archbishop Usher indeed mentions it, in his Britannicarum Eccles. Antiquit. Edit. Lond.[6] pag. 361 in these words, *In regio Comitatu ea est, Durrogh vulgo appellata: quae Monasterium habuit S. Columbae nomine insigne: inter cujus* κειμήλια, *Evangeliorum codex vetustissimus asservabatur, quem ipsius Columbae fuisse monachi dictitabant: ex quo, & non minoris antiquitatis altero, eidem Columbae assignato (quem in urbe Kelles sive Kenlis dicta, Midenses sacrum habent) diligenti cum editione vulgata Latina collatione facta; in nostros usus variantium Lectionum binos libellos concinnavimus*. By this it may be seen that the Monks only pretended that St Columb was once the owner of it. And I suppose it was at first called St Columbs Gospells, because it appertained to his Church or Monastery, as many such Books here in England, have for the same Reason been called St Augustines St Chads, St Teliau's, &c. because they belonged to their Churches; but in process of time it ha's been said that these Saints wrote them with their own Hands.

As for the Various Readings of this book & the Kenlis Copie;[7] I doubt not but they were considerable; otherwise that most learned & judicious Prelate would not have been at the trouble of collating them. Tho' I can't but take notice, that this Copie (of St Columbs) reads with St Hierome *visum est et mihi adsecuto a principio*, &c. instead of *visum est et mihi* ET SPIRITVI SANCTO *adsecuto*, &c. which I have observed in an antient Copy of the 4 Evangelists in the Bodleian Library, that I take to be one of the 2 Copies of the Gospels which Pope Gregory the Great sent to St Augustine of Canterbury, upon his Conversion of K. Ethelbert.[8] And the same Reading is in the Maeso-Gothic Version of the

---

[5] *De Scriptoribus Hiberniae* (Dublin, 1639).   [6] The edn. of 1687.

[7] i.e. the 'Book of Kells'. Evangelia of the eighth century (Codex Kenanensis), Trinity College, Dublin MS 58 (A.I.6), *CLA* ii, no. 274.

[8] i.e. the so-called 'Gospels of St Augustine', a sixth-/seventh-century codex (Codex Oxoniensis), Bodl. MS Auct. D.2.14 (*SC* 2698), *CLA* ii, no. 230. See no. 37. The other copy referred to is Corpus Christi College, Cambridge MS 286 of the sixth century, *CLA* ii, no. 126.

Gospels, which was translated by Wlfilas immediatly from the Greek,[9] tho' now we don't see it in any Greek MS.

As for the way of Writing observed in this book, without any good distinction of Words, &c. 'tis nothing but what is common with other old MSS. And when our Present Chapters & Verses came up, is not unknown to many. The Capitula in your Graces MS. are absolutely different from our Chapters, but conformable to the Canons at the beginning of the book; which Canons were compiled by Eusebius, after Ammonius, & not by Hierome.

Your Graces high Station, & multiplicity of Affairs both in Church & State keeps me from offending by too long a Letter. Otherwise I would have presumed to enquire of your Grace, whether there be any MSS. in the Irish Language in Dublin, in the same Hand with this of St Columb? for older, I suppose, there is none. As also, what sort of Arabic Character that is which they call Kufic, and was the common Character before Ibn Moclah invented that which is now in use: for, I understand, your Grace ha's some Suratas of the Al Coran in Kufic Letters, which Dr Bernard bought at Golius's Auction.[10] And tho I understand neither Irish nor Arabic, yet I may have occasion to consider the Letters of both Languages. Thus with my hearty Thanks to your Grace, humbly begging your Graces blessing, I remain

   May it please &c.

MS: Bodleian, Ballard 8, fo. 8; draft, unsigned. *Date*: 'From the Masters Lodgings in University College Oxon. Jan. 18. 1699/700.'

70. *To* Erik Benzelius[1] [*?October 1700*]

Worthy Sir,

I am here with a very good Friend who would be proud of the Honor of your Acquaintance. I ghess that by this time your dinner is

---

[9] Codex Argenteus, Uppsala University Library MS DG.1.

[10] Edward Bernard bought oriental manuscripts on Marsh's behalf at the dispersal of the library of Jacob Golius at Leyden in Oct. 1696. He secured 274 out of 407 possessed by Golius. The manuscripts referred to are presumably those listed in *CMA* II. ii, nos. 1281, 1284, 1285.

[1] Erik Benzelius the younger (1675–1743), Swedish scholar and theologian, afterwards Archbishop of Uppsala. He was in London and Cambridge in May, June, and July, and later in the year at Oxford, where he was introduced to Wanley.

over; if it be, I hope one Glass of wine will rather help than hinder its
Digestion. And at Library hours you shall certainly be attended upon
thither, by

    Sir,

        Your most faithful, humble servant

                                       Humfrey Wanley.

MS: Uppsala, University Library G.19:1a, fo. 92b.[2] *Address*: 'For Mr Benzelius, at Mr
Conyon's house near the Theater.' *Printed*: Ruth C. Wright, 'Letters from Humfrey
Wanley to Eric Benzelius and Peter the Great's Librarian', *Durham University Journal*,
NS i (1940), pp. 186–7.

71. *To* Hans Sloane   *12 December 1700*

Most Honored Sir,

    Since you went from hence, I procured a Vulgar-Latin Bible, with
which I compared your MS.[1] thro' the first Chapter to the Romans,
which I thought would be a sufficient Specimen of the whole. They
both agreed together all along, without any material Difference; that
is, there were 3 words in the Chapter, which were not written in your
MS. in the same Order as they are Printed: and two other Words,
which differed from those in the Text of the Printed Bible, but then
these words were put into the Margin, as Various Readings of other
Copies.

    As to the Age of your MS. I am confirm'd in the Opinion I was in
yesternight, when you was pleas'd to bring it (with the other) to me. I
told you then, that I thought the MS. might be written in the Reign of
K. Henry the II. And that I had seen such a book written by the Hand
(or Command) of Alexander Neckham.[2] And, you know Sir, that at the
last, we found in one part of the Book, that that piece was written
whilst Eugenius III was Pope.

    Now, Sir, if you please, we will see how this hangs together.

    King Henry II died in the year of Christ 1189. Alexander Neckham,
as I remember (for I want those books that give an account of him) was

---

[2] A rotograph of the original in the collection of Benzelius letters at Linköping,
Sweden.

---

[1] Perhaps BL Sloane MS 539, a twelfth-century manuscript of the Epistles.
[2] Perhaps MS Jesus College, Oxford 94, glosses on the Psalter, which Dr R. W. Hunt
thought may be in Neckham's hand.

then a young man (the fittest Age for writing books) and flourished in this Kings Days; as afterwards, in those of his Sons, the Kings Richard & John. And as for Pope Eugenius III, he reigned (as Helvicus say's) but 7 years, 4 months, & 12 days: that is, from the year 1183 (which was in the time of K. Henry II) to the year 1191; within which time, I guess your Manuscript to have been written.

I now return them back again, Sir, with many Thanks for the Sight of them. But (as I am bound in the strictest bonds of Honor & Gratitude) I cordially return you ten Thousand Thanks, for those many & great Favors, you have been pleased to confer upon me, ever since I had first the good Fortune to fall under your Notice.[3] And more particularly, for this last great Benefit of saving my Life, by your great Care & Skill. I am heartily sorry, Sir, that it doe's not now lie in my power to shew you by some signal Service or other, the just Sentiments I have of your Favors; what a Value & Honor I have for your Person; and what a Regard I have to your Interests, and to every thing that ha's any Relation to you. And farther I say, Sir, and I willingly give it you under my hand, That I profess my self for ever your Servant; and that nothing will more overjoy me, than an Opportunity of doing you some acceptable piece of Service, whereby I may convince you by my Actions, of the Sincerity of my Words. And it is my very earnest desire, that you will be pleas'd firmly to believe me in a very particular manner, that is, really and without Complement

Most Honored Sir,

Your most faithful & humbly devoted servant,

Humfrey Wanley

MS: British Library, Sloane 4038, fo. 105. *Date*: 'Holbourn, Decemb. 12. 1700.' *Address*: 'For The [Hond Dr Hans Sloane at his house] in great Russel st[re]et n[e]ar Bloomsbury square with 2 parchment books.'

72. *To* Arthur Charlett 2[4] *December 1700*

Honored Sir,

I hope Mr Elstob ha's been so kind (upon my entreaty) as to have put the business of weighing & copying the old Roman Weights into some Forwardness, by this Time. And if I had the Weights of them all,

---

[3] Sloane was Wanley's doctor for some years after his arrival in London.

soon; I could wait on my Lord with that account, which will very much oblige him.

I take the Boldness to acquaint you, Sir, with a piece of News; which is, that Yesterday in the Evening, I was Settled in the Station of *Assistant to the Secretary of the (Honorable) Society for Promoting Christian Knowledge*.[1] You easily perceive that it is a Religious Society: The Members of it, are Lords Temporal & Spiritual, Knights, Eminent Clergy-men & Gentlemen; all of them Men of Probity, Worth and Honor. These by their joynt Contributions in Money, and by their Counsils, make it their Business to stop the Current of Debauchery & Profaneness, & promote the Salvation of Men's Souls; and that by several Prudent Methods; some whereof, are the Printing Good Books, and Founding Charity-Schools, &c. whereof more ample mention is made in a *sheet of Paper* lately Printed;[2] one of which, I will enclose in my Next, if you have it not already, and do desire it. The Secretary is a Gentleman, a Member of the Society, who ha's served them without any Salary or Reward.[3] And as the Business is not great, so I could not expect much. However, they have now actually setled 40£ per annum (the same as Dr Hyde's in the Bodleian Library) as my Present Salary; and I have full Assurances of their adding more to it this first year, and that my Title of *Assistant*, &c. (Tho' I don't insist on it) will be in a few weeks, changed for a more Reputable one. The Considerations which moved me to accept of it, were such as these, My want of Health in Oxford, tho' that I should have dispenced with, if I had had any manner of Prospect of living Comfortably there by my Labors. To this, was added the great Discouragement (to call it by a soft Name) I lately received from Mr Vice-Chancellor;[4] which was spread about London before I came hither; and (so far as I can find) spoken of by none, without Indignation & Resentment. Another motive was my being out of Business. Another, the Consideration of gaining the Favor of so many considerable Persons, which (thanks be to God) I have very fair assurances of already. And I thought it so

---

[1] Wanley had accepted the post by 16 Dec. (*Minutes of the SPCK*, ed. McClure, p. 99); he was then ordered to attend the next meeting of the Society on 23 Dec.

[2] In margin: 'vizt. A Short Account of the Several Kinds of Societies, set up of Late years, for the promoting of God's Worship, for the Reformation of Manners, and *for the Propogation of Christian Knowledge*'.

[3] Chamberlayne.

[4] Roger Mander, Master of Balliol College, Oxford 1687–1705, Vice-Chancellor 1700–2. What the 'great Discouragement' was is not clear.

much my Interest to accept of this Station (offered me in the name of the Society at my Chamber, by a Doctor of Divinity & their Secretary)[5] that I would have served them Gratis, rather than have refused. Nor am I without hopes of coming into other Business in time, according as my Behavior, Industry & Fidelity gives Satisfaction to my Superiors, whose Favor I shall not want, If I deserve it.

But, Sir, this is not all; I think it my Duty as much to obviate any Suspicions of Neglect, or Ingratitude to you, as to avoid those Vices themselves. You may justly say, that it look's but very indifferently on my Side, to be Treated with, to take time to Consider, and to enter upon a new sort of Business, without so much as ever[6] acquainting you it: To which I answer, that before it was first mentioned to me, I was obliged by promise to keep secret what should be said; which I did promise.[7] But afterwards I desired Liberty of Consulting one Friend, but was denied, and Reasons given for that Denial. Besides this Promise, I was doubtful of the Issue; for Time began to run away apace, and I did not see the Business much advanced; so that I was fearful that if I should send you such a sort of a Story, and afterwards be disappointed; it would cause you to withdraw that Esteem, which (at present) you are pleased to give me so many Fresh Tokens of. As to the Relation you desire; I have what follow's from the first Hand; but there being Promises of Secrecy too, I can't send you much Intelligence.

Mr Sare & Mr Hindmarsh another Bookseller, agree upon [print]ing Josephus, if they could have it translated from the Greek by Sir Roger le Strange. Sir R. undertake's it, and in about 8 years finishe's it. Hindmarsh die's, and his Widow marries one Parker a Silkman. The Copie is sent down to Oxford to be compared with the Original; and Afterwards, Mr Sare brings in his bill of extraordinary Charges, which amounted to 160£. As (for example) *So much spent upon Sir R. during so many years — So much for Messages & Portage, during so many years, &c.* without descending to any particular time. He demands half this Bill of Parker, who denie's it; and Prefer's a Bill in Chancery against him. Hereupon some Friends interpose (my Author one) they get both Mr S. & Parker together, & hearing the Cause from the Bottom, they,

⟩

[5] White Kennett and Chamberlayne.   [6] every MS.

[7] But cf. Charlett's reply: 'I had an Intimation of it some weeks before and I find it was no News to other of your Acquaintance' (31 Dec. 1700, Welbeck Wanleyana = BL Loan MS 29/253).

at last, get them into a Bond of 500£ a man, to Stand to the Arbitration of two Indifferent Persons. Upon this Mr Sare has chosen Mr Awnsh. Churchil, and the matter is upon the point of being adjusted.[8]

Dr Chetwood ha's since my last but one, seem'd to change his mind as to the Printing his Sermon. He promised Mr Hartley the Copie more than once, and engaged m[e] to Correct it. But now, he's gone into the Countrey, and, I believe, 'twil slip thro'.[9]

I am Honored Sir,

Your most humble & obedient servant

Humfrey Wanley.

MS: Bodleian, Ballard 13, fo. 92. *Date*: 'London, Dec. 2[4] 1700.' *Address*: 'For the Reverend Dr Charlett Master of University College, Oxford.'

73. *To* Arthur Charlett *28 December 1700*

Honored Sir,

Since I am to be entrusted with the Ordering & Keeping the Papers of a great Society; I thought it would be a shame to have my own lie in Confusion. Therefore I have spent this whole day in Methodizing them, & have not yet much above half done. My Saxon Catalogue shall not suffer by my new Business.

Mr Cook is dead, I send you a Catalogue of his books, many of which (I believe) will go dear. I shall not be at the Auction, it interfering with my Business.[1]

I will write to the President of St Johns some time the next Week, and give you notice thereof, that you may have an Opportunity of reading the best account I shall get of a very Strange matter.[2]

---

[8] This translation of L'Estrange's was finally pbd. by Sare alone in 1702.

[9] Knightly Chetwood (1650–1720), Archdeacon of York 1688, Dean of Gloucester 1707. The sermon, preached at St Paul's Cathedral on 6 Dec., was pbd. by Samuel Carr in 1701.

---

[1] Henry Cook (1642–1700), painter, pupil of Salvator Rosa, much employed by the nobility for house decoration. His large collection of paintings and drawings was sold 26 Mar. 1700, before his death on 18 Nov. His library was sold by John Bullord, 30 Dec. 1700.

[2] Perhaps a reference to 'the great Discouragement . . . lately received from Mr Vice-Chancellor' (no. 72). Cf. Charlett's remark: 'I beleive, you may do well, to remind and thank, the President of St Johns for his Civility to you, and his Promise to represent your Petition to the Vice Chancellor and Delegates of the Library' (Charlett to Wanley d. 15 Dec. 1700, Welbeck Wanleyana = BL Loan MS 29/253).

As to the Alexandrian MS. which is the Book whence the Oxford Edition of the Greek Psalter (which you are pleas'd to write to me about) was Copied: 'Tis an old and very common Observation that the Orthography of the Greek Language is therein often neglected. A[n]d when I used the books some years ago, I found what others said about that matter [*nine letters lost*].[3]

This seeming Negligence may be accounted for two ways. The Tradition is that the Alexandrian book (I call the 4 voll. by the name of MS. or book) was written by one Thecla a devout woman, not long after the first Council of Nice:[4] which (however) is not my Opinion, who from the Uniformity & admirable Elegancy of the Letters, & the Accuracy of the Copie, do judge it rather the Work of a Man, & he a man of Understanding too, as well as of Patience. And 'tis beyond Contradiction, that it must have been written either by a woman or by a man. If by the Pious Theela, she might be godly enough, but not any great Scholar, perhaps she might not have been so used to the Remnants of the Alexandrian Library (which Ammianus Marcellinus says was remaining in his time) and might (like other women) have got an habit of Spelling false. And I know a very antient Greek MS. in the Bodleian Library, which from the Roughness of the Character & the miserable false spelling, pointing & accenting, you would almost swear was the work of one who was more us'd to handle a Needle than a Pen. The likê Roughness may be seen in some Latin Prayers, written in Capital Letters by the Hand of a woman, a thousand years ago, and which are now in the Bodleian Library; another book I know in the same Library, written in Latin by a Nun, about 4 or 5 hundred years ago, fairly enough, but yet faulty.[5] But if this Alex. MS. was written by a man (as I believe it was not only for the Reason above-mentioned,

[3] What follows is Wanley's response to Charlett's request for his 'Opinion of the false Spellings in the Alexandrian MS, represented in the Praeface to the *Psalterium Alexandrinum*, of the Theatre Edition' (Charlett to Wanley d. 27 Dec. 1700, Welbeck Wanleyana = BL Loan MS 29/253). Thomas Gale, the editor of this Oxford edn. (1678) complains in his unsigned preface (sig. A2) of the itacism of the manuscript.

[4] An Arabic note of the thirteenth or fourteenth century in Codex Alexandrinus [= BL Royal MS 1. D. v–viii] fo. 4b states that the manuscript was written by Thecla the Martyr; a Latin note (fo. 2), by Cyril Lucar, Patriarch of Alexandria 1602–21 and the donor of the manuscript to Charles I, repeats the assertion as a tradition, adding that Thecla was a noble lady of Egypt, that the manuscript was written shortly after the Council of Nicaea [AD 325], and that Thecla's name was originally written at the end of the manuscript but was lost before Cyril's time (*British Museum: Catalogue of Western Manuscripts in the Old Royal and King's Collections* (1921), i, p. 17).

[5] The references are too vague to identify the manuscripts mentioned.

but because this very book was the Standard for all the Copies of that Patriarchate, for above a thousand years together, in order to have them brought & Corrected according to it) there is a more probable Reason to be given for the Neglect of the Antient Orthography. The *Antiquarius* (for that is the proper Title of this sort of Book-Writers) wrote amongst others who wrote at the same time, or he wrote in his Cell alone, which is my Opinion in the present Case. If joyntly with others, Then One held the Original dictated, & the Antiquarij wrote after him, not seeing the Original. Now the Greek Pronunciation differing from ours, if the Dictator sai[e]s τίς, τῆς, ταῖς or τοῖς, the Antiquarius who perhaps did not so much regard the Sence or Connexion, presently wrote down τιc for the Greeks pronounce (& have long done so) all these words alike. Besides, in time, the orthography changed in the Greek Tongue, as it hath done in others. And the Greeks did not undervalue their present language, or way of writing; or endeavor to reforme it to the pure Attic of Isocrates or other Antients. Nay they seemed rather in all their MSS. to write many words, not as they were in the original, but according to the more Modern Fashion; Just as the Normanno-Saxons in Transcribing old Copies, corrupted the Orthography, as a late Editor of Chaucer ha's done;[6] all for the best as they thought. So that these very Faults, might be the Effect of the Labor & Study of the Antiquarius, in his own Chamber. And to instance an old MS. wherein there is such Faults; I make bold to cite the Old Fragments of the Greek Gospels in the Cotton Library, written in very large Uncial Letters of Silver & Gold, which I take to be older than the Alexandrian MS.[7] from the form of the Letters &c. (not to mention its exactly answering the Description which St Hierome in his *Prologue to Job*, gives of the *antient books of his Time*). In these fragments are the same Faults, as CΠIPAN for σπεῖραν, ΚΥΡΗΝΕΟΝ for κυρηναῖον, ΕΡΧΟΜΕ ΚΑΙ ΠΑΡΑΛΗΜΨΟΜΕ for ἔρχομαι καὶ παραλήμψομαι, ΕΙΜΕΙ for εἰμί, ΜΙΖΩΝ for μείζων & very many others. And I could bring thousands of Examples from other books Antient & Modern; but I forbear & rather refer to any such book if it be written in the Levant. Be pleased, Sir, to tell me whose Satisfaction this is designed for,[8] & pardon my hast, & want of Books, and spare my

---

[6] Presumably Dryden in his text of the *Knight's Tale*, *Nun's Priest's Tale*, etc. in his *Fables* (1700).

[7] Cotton Titus C.xv. The itacism is noted by Smith in his catalogue of the Cotton manuscripts (1696).

[*See opposite page for n. 8*]

faults for the Post being ready to go, I have not time to read over what I have written; but am

Your humble servt

H.W.

MS: Bodleian, Ballard 13, fo. 95. *Date*: 'London, Decb. 28. 1700.' *Address*: 'For the Reverend Dr Charlett Master of University College Oxford.' *Printed*: *Bodleian Letters*, i, pp. 109–13.

74. *To* [George Hickes] *8 March 1701*

Honor'd Sir

I send this on purpose to prevent any disturbance that may arise in your mind by reason of your not having the Paper about the Crosses Return'd to you, with the Additions before this time.[1]

I have been 3 Times at Sir John Cottons about this Affair. At the First time, I did very diligently & carefully look over all the Charters in the Great book,[2] and in the Drawers. And upon the Whole thought it best to come again with you, to have your particular Directions which Crosses I should draw out. For there are three with different Crosses made since the Conquest. Nor are all those Original Charters which have different Crosses, for I find some in Copies. And there is one *Copie* above 800 years old, which is the Oldest Copie I ever yet saw. There are also not only many particular Charters, but also particular-ities in Charters which deserve your own Consideration & Inspection. As for instance some Charters which you have in the Textus Roffen-sis;[3] and others worthy the taking notice of upon the account of their particular manner of placing the Crosses, &c. Being hindred from

---

[8] 'my own Satisfaction, as I put my Studdy into a New Method, and ranging all the Theater Books together . . . I casually read the Bps Praeface to the Alexandrian Psalter' (Charlett to Wanley d. 31 Dec. 1700; Welbeck Wanleyana = BL Loan MS 29/253).

[1] Wanley presumably refers to the section in Hickes's 'Dissertatio Epistolaris' (*Thesaurus* I, pt. iv, p. 68 f.) where the signing of charters by the witnesses with crosses is discussed. Tabula C (facing p. 71) has facsimiles of crosses taken from a number of Cottonian manuscripts, presumably the result of Wanley 'drawing them out' on a later occasion.

[2] Cotton Augustus ii.

[3] Rochester Cathedral Library MS A.3.5, an early twelfth-century Rochester manu-script in two parts: pt. i, an important collection of Anglo-Saxon legal texts (fos. 1–118); pt. ii, largely a cartulary of Rochester Cathedral Priory (fos. 119–235), Ker no. 373, Wanley p. 273.

waiting on you, I went to Sir John's again, thinking to rely upon my own judgement, but the family being to dine soon after, I went away. This morning again (thinking to be early enough) I went thither at 8 a clock, and lingred thereabouts till past eleven, with out being admitted, Mr Redmans[4] being gone out. I will try my Fortune again on Munday morning, and shall be glad to meet you there, that I may shew you what I have now mention'd. If you think another time may do as well, I will however go thither, and bring or send you back the Paper with such Additions as I shal conceive to be most for your Purpose. I being sincerely and with all Respect

 Honor'd Sir,

  Your very humble servant

              H. Wanley

MS: Bodleian, Eng. hist. c. 6, fo. 39. *Date*: 'Holbo[u]rn, March 8. 1700/1.'

---

75. *To* John Jackson *7 April 1701*[1]

Sir,

 A Letter or Epistle is justly Defin'd *Absentis ad Absentem Colloquium*, since by Writing, one Friend can communicate his Thoughts to another upon any Occasion, tho' the Distance between them be never so great; and I can by this Means acquaint you in Madrid with my present Business, almost as well as if I was actually speaking to you. 'Tis true, the inequality of my Circumstances to yours, and the few Opportunities I have had of being better known to you, do not allow me to call you my Friend: but I can truly say, that you have always had

---

[4] Presumably a Cotton family servant.

---

[1] This letter was begun on 11 Mar., but it comes naturally here with that of Wanley to Pepys of this date. Braybrooke ptd. the present letter from the original in the Pepys–Cockerell collection. By the time Tanner calendared the Pepys–Cockerell letters, it was missing: it does not appear in the chronological list ptd. by Tanner in *Private Correspondence*, ii, p. 333 f. It turned up in Sotheby's sale of 25 Mar. 1974 (lot 247) and went to Quaritch for £550.

John Jackson (1673–1724), the younger of Pepys's two nephews, was his favourite, and subsequently his heir. Jackson was at the end of a two-year tour of Europe wholly financed by Pepys. At the time of writing, he was in Madrid preparing to return to England. He was employed by others to acquire books abroad: see the list of Italian books prepared for him by Capt. Charles Hatton and Thomas Gale (Christ Church, Oxford, MS Evelyn Letters i, art. 25) and the list of books procured for Pepys on the same journey (Evelyn Letters i, art. 20).

more than a common Friends share in my Breast. I have often consider'd with pleasure, the happiness you enjoy, in having the benefit of a gentile and liberal Education joyn'd to those great Gifts which Nature ha's bestowed upon you: and then, that all should be Crown'd by your Relation to such an Unkle, who by allowing you to Travel & see the most considerable things in the World with your own Eyes; doe's take the true way to render you one day as eminent and as useful to it as he ha's been.

That day in which I had first the Honor to wait on him, I look upon as one of the most fortunate ones of my Life; and it was that day too, which gave me the first Opportunity of admiring the natural sweetness of your Temper, and your obliging and instructive Conversation. The Respect that I then conceived for you, ha's all along encreased, and I have often wish'd, that by doing you some acceptable service, I might shew you what a Value I have for you. But there being no Occasion to use me, it ha's not hitherto been in my power to convince you how strong my Inclinations might be. And in stead thereof, I find my self oblig'd to have recourse to you for some Kindnesses, which as I know not well how to ask: so I know not how to procure by any other Means.

Considering then the smallness of our personal Acquaintance, and the Trouble and Charge that may attend the granting my Requests; in good manners, I ought not to disturb you with them. But since the business is not base or dishonest in it self, and that Mr Pepys ha's allow'd me to propose my Wants to you: I will take the boldness to press upon your good Nature with the same freedom, as I would have you draw a like Bill upon me, whenever you shall think fit.

Gentlemen of such Consideration & Judgement as you are, as in the main, they propose a certain & fix'd End of their Travels: so they do commonly put down beforehand that which they hear is worthy their taking notice of in every place they go to. This enable's them oftentimes by asking after particular things, to get a sight of that which might otherwise have escap'd them. I know your short Notes of this kind are very full & exact, and that both your Curiosity & Experience are even what I could wish them. This then shall save you from being pester'd for the present with any Questions relating to the Present State in general of those foreign Countreys which you have surveyd; or to the most remarkable Curiosities either Natural or Artificial, which are to be found therein: because at your Return, I hope I shall have the good Fortune to hear you discourse of such matters at large. Only one thing I would beg of you, that as you happen to see or hear of any Person whatsoever, who from a mean Birth & Education, ha's by his proper Merit, risen to an extraordinary degree of Eminence in his particular Way; that you would take the trouble to inform your self of the strength of that mans Genius, what Improvements he made to his Natural Endowments, what Methods he took in order to gain those Improvements,[2] and what Advantages have accrued to the Public thereby.

Sir, the Countrey you are in, is said to be very fertile in those things which (tho' I have left Oxford, and am fix'd here in Town) may yet serve as an innocent Recreation to amuse my self withal, when I'me wearied with other necessary business. And it may be considered according to those different Nations who have possess'd it, I mean the native Spaniards or Aborigines, the Carthaginians, Romans, Goths, Saracens, & the present People whom I take to be a mixture of all the former, with the Addition of some Jews. Of the two first Nations, I believe you will meet with few Remains that can be of use. However, enquiry may be made whether the Biscainers have any books among them written in their most antient Language Medalls I know there are many, with barbarous Heads of these old Spaniards engraven on them, the Inscriptions being sometimes in Roman, & sometimes in strange Letters which are called Punic, but how truly I know not. One Lastanosa did about 40 or 50 years ago, print at Huesca a Collection of such medals (in 4to) taken from many of the best Cabinets in Spain. The Title of his book begin's thus, *Museo de las Medallas desconnoscidas Españolas*.[3] I desire you, Sir, to buy this book for me if you can get it at a reasonable price, for here in England, I could never hear[4] of any more than two of them. Upon Enquiry, you will easily meet with such Medals; if you do, be pleas'd to confer with any ingenious Spaniar'd, and try to pick out an Alphabet, or even any one word that you can be sure of. If this can be done & improv'd, some Light may be brought to many a dark passage in History. If you meet with any Punic Inscription, be pleas'd to have it copied exactly. We have in Gresham College, Copies of all the Hetruscan Inscriptions that do now remain in Italy,[5] the Letters of some of them are of the same kind with the

---

[2] Improvents MS.

[3] Vincencio Juan de Lastanosa, *Museo de las Medallas desconoscidas Españolas* (Huesca, 1645).   [4] here MS.

[5] Probably contained in the portfolio of inscriptions, drawings, etc., Royal Society

Punic; and when they are brought together, perhaps something may be made out from them.

7. April. 1701.

Dear Sir, a Conjunction of unlucky Accidents have fallen out, as it were on purpose to hinder me from finishing this Letter, which otherwise might have come to your Hands by this Time. But now, having gotten 2 hours to my self, I will take the Boldness to go forwards with it.

I am inform'd that there are many noble Roman Antiquities yet extant in Spain, of which the Spaniards have been such diligent Observers, that I hear they have written the History of all the noted Cities and Towns of that large Countrey, with great Learning, Fidelity & Judgement. Whether they have in these books preserv'd these Curiosities by good Draughts, I very much doubt; and for my own particular, I should be glad to see such Books describing the chiefest and most celebrated places of Spain, as I have seen of Italy, France, &c. Or if they have not been so careful; I could willingly look upon some new delineations of the Roman Buildings near Sevil, and in other places: But the Costs must needs be too great for me to give any Orders in this Matter. But if you meet with any Inscriptions that have not been already Published, and the Subject of them is remarkable: I would beg the Favor to have such Copied truly as to the Lection, and no matter for the Shape of the Letters.

As to the more Modern Antiquities of the Goths in Spain; I have a greater desire to see something relating to them, than I have for the Roman, notwithstanding the Politeness of the one Nation, and the rude Barbarity of the other. And this, because the Remains of the Goths are but few; and also, because they were akin to us. Therefore I do earnestly intreat you, Sir, to enquire after any Books or Inscriptions in their Antient Language. I hear that there are such books in Spain, but I know not whereabouts. They may be found in Countrey Villages or in Libraries. If you find any such antient Gothic Book (the Language being older than the Castilian, and different from it) I desire it may be bought, if it be any part of the Scripture, or a Translation from any Latin Author now extant. If there be such things, but not to be sold, I desire that such a book may be Copied, or part of it, as you

MS 596, listed as no. 143 in J. O. Halliwell's *Catalogue of Miscellaneous Manuscripts of the Royal Society* (1840).

shall think fit. Perhaps, the Character may not be the same with the Maeso-Gothic, but may agree better with some Specimens in a Spanish book thus Entituled, *L'Origen y Institucion de la lengua Española, por Don Bernardo Aldrete, en Roma*, 1606. and with some other Specimens in Father Mabillons Diplomatique: but that need not hinder the buying or Transcribing them.

As to the Moors, I have but little to say. I have been told that in Spain there ha's been lately found a very antient Copie of the Gospells in Arabic, much different from ours. You will be able (at Sevil) to find out what truth there can be in such a Report. I would also know whether the History of the Conquest of Spain by the Moors, said to be compos'd in Arabic by Abentarique (if I remember his Name aright) and Translated into Spanish by Don Miguel de Luna, be Authentic and to be relied on, or not.[6] You know the Story concerning the Opening some Room in the Palace by Roderic the last King of the Goths, before the Coming of the Moors: I would know the Truth of that Story, and whether there are any Remainders of those Buildings still in being. Tis said that there are yet remaining either at Sevil, or at Toledo, many old Inscriptions which none could understand. That King Philip the 3d sent to Erpenius in Holland,[7] to come over and try his Skil in them, which Erpenius durst not venture to do, notwithstanding the Kings Safe-Conduct. If any of these Inscriptions do remain, and the Characters be Gothic, Runic, or any thing else but Arabic, I desire a Copie of one or two of them, as also of that imperfect Hebrew Inscription, which is in the Wall of the Cathedral Church at Sevil, near the great Gate.

I know your own Curiosity will lead you into all the Libraries you come near. I would intreat you, Sir, to take Notice of the Numbers of Books in every Library, and particularly of the MSS. and amongst these, to put down the Names of such books as the Spaniards seem to value most. If you find a good number of Greek MSS in any Library, and an accurate Catalogue of them; I should be glad to see that Catalogue. When in any great Church you are admitted to the Sight of their Reliques, 'tis possible that upon enquiry, you may meet with some very antient Copies of the Psalms, Gospels, or other parts of the Scripture written in Capital Letters, and perhaps they may be gilt with

[6] *Histoire de la Conqueste d'Espagne par les Mores, composée en arabe par Abulcacim Tariff Abentariq . . . traduite en Espagnol par Michel de Luna* (Paris, 1680).
[7] Thomas van Erpe (1584–1624), oriental scholar.

Silver or Gold upon fine purple-colour'd Parchment. If you see any
such, be pleas'd to cause 4 or 5 lines with the Alphabet to be
delineated for me. If these books be in Latin, and differ considerably
from the Vulgate of St Hierom; be pleas'd to get such a book Collated
or Copied, except the Psalms, Job & Judith, for in all probability it may
prove the Italic Version so much wanted. And I would also desire that
if at any time you see any Greek MS, certainly appearing by the Date,
or any other Authentic Mark to have been written before the year
(from the beginning of the World) 6300, or any Latin MS, appearing by
the like certainty to have been written before the year of Christ 700,
that you would from such books, cause 4 or 5 Lines with the Alphabet
& the Date to be Copied for me. Perhaps, Sir, you will think this an
odd sort of a Request, but that which I'me now going to make may
increase your wonder, 'tis that you would be pleas'd, all along, to buy
up as many old pieces of Parchment, written upon, as you can get. By
some years pains, I have now purchas'd and receiv'd from my Friends
several Thousands of such pieces and fragments, which when I have
distributed according to their several Ages & Countreys, I hope to
make very useful to some Sorts of Students, upon divers Accounts.
Those sorts of Characters which I beg you to be most inquisitive after,
are the Capitals; the Gothic, Lombardic or Toletan Letters, call 'em
by what name you please, and the Large Spanish Letter of an Inch
long, the Minuscules. These you will find common in their old books
of Offices.

I desire you likewise to enquire after the Libraries of Antonio
Augustino, Diego Hurtado, Cardinal Ximenes at Complutum, and
that of the Escurial, in what Condition the books are in, what
Numbers, and which are the most curious.[8] If this Letter shall find you
at Madrid, I doubt not but you will of your own accord go to the
Escurial, and if that Library be not burnt (as I hear it is, and most of
the books destroyed or stollen) I desire that you would take good
notice of two books, the one they will tell you is the Gospells, written
by St Augustine of Hippo and the other, the Bible written in Capitals
by the Command of the Emperor Conrad,[9] I would have Specimens of

---

[8] Antonio Augustino (1517–86), Archbishop of Tarragona, and Diego Hurtado de
Mendoza (*c.*1503–75), diplomat and collector, especially of Greek manuscripts,
possessed two of the greatest private libraries of sixteenth-century Spain, both now in
the Escorial. Francisco Ximénez de Cisneros (1436–1517), Cardinal Archbishop of
Toledo, was the designer and executor of the Complutensian Polyglot.
[9] Wanley means Augustine's tract *De Baptismo Parvulorum*, El Escorial, MS Camarín

these, if they will suffer 'em to be taken, which I much doubt, having read the grievous Complaint of Balthasar Corderius and Alexander Barvoëtius against the Friers that kept the Library in their time.[10]

Be pleas'd likewise to inform your self, of the Antiquity of the Castilian Tongue, and procure the Lords prayer therein as old as may be.

I would be glad if you would inform your self of the Rise & Progress of Printing amongst them, and of the Dates of their oldest Printed books.

I forgot to mention to you six books, said to be in the Escurial, containing the true Pictures & Resemblances of all the Birds, Beasts, Fishes, Plants, and other Natural Curiosities found by the Spaniards in America, at their Coming there. Upon sight of them, you will easily satisfie your self of their exactness & worth.

One thing more I have to trouble you with. They Say, the Spaniards are very good Musitians. I desire some of their best Aires, or Solo's, put down upon five Lines, with Bars, and in our modern Notes, together with their Graces. As when they Prick a long Note, and in performing do run a Division upon it, I would have the long Note made big & gross, and the division made[11] above or below it in smaller Notes. I hear the Spanish Musitians have a strange sort of Musical Notes peculiar to themselves; if it be so, I desire a short tune in them Explain'd by the same in those that are more usual to us.

Lastly, dear Sir, I must [b]eg your Pardon for this long Letter, which I would not have troublesome to you, by any means. Perhaps it may come too late, and you may be just upon your Return: and that may be hastned likewise by the bad prospect of Affairs. However it be, Satisfaction in any one of the particulars I have written, is as much as I can expect supposing that your Stay will be yet longer than it is likely to be. I pray God to have you in his Keeping, to conduct and prosper you in all your ways, and at length to bring you back in Safety, where

de las Relíquias S.N., a seventh-century manuscript held to be autograph and treated as a relic, *CLA* xi, no. 1629, and the so-called CodexAureus, El Escorial, MS Vitrinàs 17, an eleventh-century codex of the Gospels written by order of Emperor Conrad II.

[10] Balthasar Cordier, *De bibliotheca regia S. Laurentii Scorialensi in Hispania epistolae duae*, in *De Bibliothecis atque Archivis virorum clarissimorum . . . libelli et commentationes*, ed. Joachim Johann Mader (Helmstadt, 1666); Alexandre Barvoet, *Catalogus praecipuorum auctorum ineditorum Graece MSS. qui in Bibliotheca Scorialensi asservantur* (Antwerp, 1648). Hieronymites, Augustinian hermits, possessed the royal monastery of Escorial and hence were custodians of its library.

[11] mad MS.

none will more heartily rejoice to see you again and embrace you, then

Honor'd Sir,

Your most faithful humble servant

Humfrey Wanley.

MS: British Library, Add. 58079 E. Partial draft in Welbeck Wanleyana = British Library, Loan 29/258. *Date*: 'London, March 11. 1700/1' with continuation dated '7. April. 1701.' *Printed*: Richard, Lord Braybrooke, *Memoirs of Samuel Pepys* (1825), ii, pp. 254–60 (incomplete); J. Smith, *Life, Journals, and Correspondence of Pepys* (1841), ii, pp. 357–8 (extracts); Sotheby's sale cat., 25 Mar. 1974, lot 247 (extracts).

76. *To* Samuel Pepys *7 April 1701*

Honorable Sir,

'Tis mere Shame that make's me not able to appear before You, after I had obtain'd Your permission to write to Your worthy Nephew almost a Month since, and have finish'd my Letter but even now.[1] It look's as if I was one of a light, vain Temper, hot & eager to undertake and begin a thing, without Constancy & Patience enough to bring it to a Conclusion. But as I intimated to Mr Jackson my want of Time: so when I shall have made you acquainted with that multiplicity of business which I labor under, I hope, honorable Sir, I shall not want your Candid Excuse.

I'me affraid that my Letter is of too fresh a Date to be sent; if so, I can blame none but my self, who ought to have made more hast. If it be not yet too late, I continue my humble Request to You, Sir, that you would be Pleas'd to send it, together with a Tender of my best Services; which your Nephew shall always Command, even as the great Favors I have received from You, do well deserve.[2]

If any thing which I have written to him be impertinent, likely to prove troublesome, or doe's otherways deserve Correction: I beseech You, Sir, to dash it out with your Pen, [&] it shall be look'd upon as a sure token of your Love and Affection to

Honorable Sir,

Your most obliged, most faithful & humbly devoted Servant

Humfrey Wanley

[1] See no. 75 n. 1.

[2] It was too late: see Pepys's reply d. 7 Apr., ptd. R. G. Howarth, *Letters and the Second Diary of Samuel Pepys* (1932), no. 298. See also Pepys to Wanley d. 14 Apr. 1701 (Howarth no. 300), 20 May 1701 (Howarth no. 302), 8 Nov. 1701 (no. 306).

MS: Pepys Cockerell iv, fo. 54, now in the collection of Mr Arthur A. Houghton jun., Queenstown, Maryland. Draft in Welbeck Wanleyana = British Library, Loan 29/258. *Date*: 'From Mr Pleahill's at the Chirurgeons Arms, in Castle-yard Holbourn. 7. April 1701.' *Address*: 'For the Honble Samuel Pepys Esq.' *Endorsed*: 'April. 7th 1701. Mr Wanley to S.P. accompanying a Letter of Enquiries for Mr Jackson in Spain', in another hand. *Printed*: Richard, Lord Braybrooke, *Memoirs of Samuel Pepys* (1825), ii, pp. 253–4; J. R. Tanner, *Private Correspondence and Miscellaneous Papers of Samuel Pepys, 1679–1703*, ii (1926), no. 435; R. G. Howarth, *Letters and the Second Diary of Samuel Pepys* (1932), no. 297.

77. *To* Arthur Charlett *11 June 1701*

Honor'd Sir,

I congratulate your safe Return to Oxford,[1] & return you my humble thanks for your last very kind Letter, which I received yesterday.

I have enquired after the Three particulars you mention, and am answer'd thus;

The last large Map of England may be had in 12 single Sheets, and may be bound up in the shape of a Pocket-book.[2] But it must be then carried in a Portmanteau, it being too large for the Pockett. Since this is so, it seem's not very useful for your purpose, who in travelling upon the Road, can't well be suppos'd to be at leasure, at every turn, to undo your Portmanteau in Order to consult it.

The new Description of England,[3] is a large 8vo with 53 Maps of the several Counties; the price is 8s. The Maps may (for ought I know) be well perform'd: but I doubt the Description may not be quite so accurate.

I hear the London Bible, is every way more beautiful than that printed at Oxford.[4]

I accidentally met Dr Hudson at the Bishop of Worcester's Lodgings, with whom I had some business. The Dr appointed me to meet him at the Court of Requests, but I tarried long with my Lord, whom I afterwards waited on to the D. of Devonshire's, and so to the Parliament house. I then sought for Dr Hudson above an hour, but in vain.

---

[1] Charlett had just returned from another 'therapeutic' progress to see Badminton and Longleat, and had taken in Bath and Bristol on his way.

[2] Probably the wall-map in 15 sheets ptd. and sold by Christopher Browne in Ludgate Street, London, 1700, ptd. as *Nova Totius Angliae Tabula* (1735).

[3] Robert Morden's *New Description and State of England* (1701).

[4] Two folio edns. of the Bible were pbd. in 1701, one supervised by William Lloyd, Bishop of Worcester (and Wanley's patron), ptd. at London by Charles Bill (Darlow and Moule no. 868), the other at Oxford (Darlow and Moule no. 867).

However, I don't dispair of seeing him again, and then I can tell him so much by word of mouth, relating to the Library, as will save me the labor of writing many letters to him, which I'me not able to do.[5] I have seen Dr Shadwell,[6] who deserves that great Reputation he ha's. I met also Dr Hicks of Magd.Coll.[7] He asked me about my business in Town: which I was sorry I could not inform him of; Tho' our Society now grow's every day more & more public. The Charter for the new Corporation, is drawn up, ha's actually pass'd the King in Council, and is now passing thro' the Several Offices.[8] Sir, if you had been a Correspondent member of our Society, I could have order'd the matter so, that you should have been mention'd by name in the Charter: but of this, more, when I shall have the Honor to see you in Town.

I'me sorry to hear that Mr Pepys ha's put off his Journey to Oxford. I'le wait on him & talk with him about it. Mr Jackson is in his way home from Lisbon. I had written a long letter to him containing many Queries relating to Spain, considering it, as under the Aborigines, Carthaginians, Romans, Goths, Moors, & their late Kings. But it being written too late, Mr Pepys thought it not advisable to send it, but rather reserve it till Mr Jackson's Return.[9]

I have seen Dr Gregory,[10] and tho' I labor under a hurry of business, yet I hope to be in some measure useful to him.

I must always own my self obliged to the Principal of Brazen-Nose College,[11] and will wait upon him. Be pleas'd, Sir, to let me know wherein you thought I could be useful to him. I'le give him the Warden of A.S.'s direction, whom with the Dean of Xt Church & many others of our University, I have not had time to wait upon.

Sir, You giving me leave to communicate the A.B. of Dublin's

[5] Hudson was seeking ways to make the Bodleian more useful, and in particular planned a new Catalogue to the library and invited Wanley's advice: see Charlett to Wanley d. 9, 23, 27 Apr. 1701, Welbeck Wanleyana = BL Loan MS 29/253.

[6] John Shadwell (1671–1747), matriculated at University College, Oxford 1685; MD 1701, FRS 1701, physician to Queen Anne, George I, and George II; knighted 1715.

[7] John Hickes, Fellow of Magdalen College, Oxford 1682, DD 1701, Canon of Exeter 1706.

[8] The Society for the Propagation of the Gospel in Foreign Parts was incorporated as a distinct body by letters patent d. 16 June 1701. See *Minutes of the SPCK*, ed. McClure, 5 May 1701 (p. 132).

[9] See no. 75.

[10] David Gregory (1661–1708), Savilian Professor of Astronomy at Oxford 1691. His *Astronomiae Elementa* was pbd. at Oxford in 1702.

[11] John Meare, Principal of Brasenose College, Oxford 1681–70.

Paper[12] to whom I pleas'd, I have left it with Mr Gibson. I take it back, and some time the next week, draw up what I have to say to it, and send it you immediatly.

I humbly thank you for the proffer of your Favor (if you had been in Town) as to the Cotton Library.[13] It continues as it is during the Life of Sir John: but at the next Sessions, 'tis highly probable that a bill will be brought in, to unite it with the Kings, to build a Case for both, and to appoint Officers & their Salaries. This will for ever keep it from Oxford, who might have had it, had the University thought fit to have used all their endeavors to procure it; even then when I first wrote to the then V. Chancellor about it.

Mr Cockman came to me this Morning, desiring me to go with him hither, to see the MSS of Tully in this Library, which I readily did, tho' very busy. We have found more tracts of him, than were express'd in the Catalogue, whereof one is antient. He desire's to collate those that he ha's present occasion for; which ca[nnot be] done without a written Order of the Royal Society. They meet just now, and I am again come hither to recommend him to Dr Sloane, to whom Mr Cockman should have brought a Letter Recommendatory from you, upon a triple account, as a Friend to both, as Head of that College whereof Mr Cockman is a Member, and as having engag[ed] Mr Cockman in this design.[14]

Here is little news stirring. The King goes to Holland quickly. If his native Air be not as propitious as it ha's [h]itherto been, some wise & knowing men are of Opinion that he will not be long-liv'd.

The Society are met, and I am always with sincerity & respect Reverend Sir,

[12] A 'Familiar Letter', called by Marsh a 'Winters Evening thought', sent by Marsh to Charlett and forwarded by him to Wanley for answer (Charlett to Wanley d. 27 Apr., 27 May 1701. Welbeck Wanleyana = BL Loan MS 29/253). For Wanley's long and detailed reply, ptd. in *Philosophical Transactions*, no. 300 (June 1705), pp. 1993–2008, see no. 79.

[13] 'Had I been in London, I should have recommended You to some station in the Cotton Bibl.' (Charlett to Wanley d. 25 May 1701, and see no. 80). For Wanley's subsequent hopes for the Cotton Library, see no. 89 and also no. 80 n. 3.

[14] Thomas Cockman, Fellow of University College, Oxford 1697, pbd. edns. of Cicero's *De Officiis* in 1695, and of *De Oratione* in 1696 and 1706. There were numerous manuscripts of Cicero in the library of the Royal Society (all transferred to the British Museum in 1831 as part of the Arundel collection); the 'antient' manuscript may be the twelfth-century copy of his *De Inventione Rhetorica* in BL Arundel MS 348. The catalogue referred to by Wanley is presumably that compiled by William Perry, ptd. *CMA* II. i, pp. 74–84.

Your most obedient humble servant

H. Wanley.

Dr Sloan ha's procur'd Mr Cockman the liberty of studying here. Mr Cockman send's you his humble duty.

MS: Bodleian, Ballard 13, fo. 105. *Date*: 'Gresham College June 11. 1701.' *Address*: 'For The Reverend Dr Charlett Master of University College Oxford.'

78. *To* —— [*?mid-1701*][1]

With my very humble service to Mr Lhwyd, be pleas'd to acquaint him, that there belongs to Lichfield Cathedral a book called *Textus S. Ceaddae*. It formerly contain'd the 4 Evangelists in Latin, [bu]t now goes no farther (as I take it) then to the 10 verse of the 3 Cap. of Luke. This book appears to be a thousand years old; being written in round, gross Saxon letters, such as they used when they came of the Capitals into a Smaller hand. This book one *Cingal* bought, giving *pro eo, equum optimum*, and it was bestowed afterwards (I think, by him) upon the Church of Llandaff, being there called St Teliau's or St Eliud's Gospells. As appear's by several Notes written therein. Amongst other things I remember Some British Proper names, as Owen & Theodore or Tudor, with some Sentences in the same Language. And some of this writing seems to be 900 years old, it agreeing with the Saxon hands of the Time, as all other British MSS. I have yet seen, do. How the book came to Lichfield I know not, but it appears to have been there these 700 years, by a note in the Saxon Language which is written in a Hand so old. I take that antient piece of the Gospels in the Public Library in Cambridge, containing[2] the Latter End of St Luke (I think from the Cap. & vers. mentioned before) with the Gospel of St John to be the Remaining part of this book. But when I saw it, having no occasion to turn over it, I know not whether there be any British

[1] Wanley seems to be reporting from memory (he had first seen St Chad's Gospels at Lichfield in 1695: see no. 4), so this must be dated before 18 Oct. 1701 when he had the manuscript in his possession in London (see no. 83), yet after the autumn of 1699 when he saw in Cambridge the gospel fragment (probably Cambridge University Library MS Kk.i.24) referred to here. Lhwyd, on the other hand, spent much of 1700 in Ireland and Cornwall and was in Brittany for some weeks early in 1701; in neither place was he likely to be easily accessible. I place the letter here arbitrarily.

[2] contining MS.

writing therein or not. As for The Text of both books, they are not exactly that of St Hierom's Version, nor yet that of the old Italic.[3]

MS: Bodleian, Ashmole 1817[B], fo. 196; draft, unsigned. *Endorsed*: 'From Mr Wanley'.

79. *To* [Narcissus Marsh] *11 July 1701*[1]

The substance of what your Grace is pleas'd to say about Manuscripts and Copied Writings (as I apprehend it) is, That 'tis not only possible, but very easie, upon the perusal of a written Book, to pronounce in what Age or Century it was written, supposing a man to be tolerably well vers'd in Books of that Language or Country. And that this judgment may be made, only by observing the Shape and Figure of the Letters of the Book, which (as all other things) have their fix'd Periods for their Duration: as being form'd this way in such a Century, and such a way in the next; Time only (which alters the outward state of other things) working this Change in Letters also, of what Age, Language, or Country soever they be. And then as to Original Compositions, your Grace is of Opinion, That the Style and Diction of any noted Author being well observ'd, 'tis very easie to discover such others of his Works as have gone abroad without his Name; and also the very time when the Author Liv'd.

'Tis evident, my Lord, that a man may judge of some MSS by the Hand; and of the Genuine and Spurious Works of some Authors; and of the time likewise, wherein they liv'd, by the style of them; but whether this be so easie a Work, and that the Rules men generally go by in these cases, are always infallible Guides, is what (I own) I very much doubt of.

Suppose, my Lord, for instance, a man should bring to any Antiquary a good MS. Copy of the Hebrew Bible, Pentateuch, or Psalter, written in a small common Letter, without Points, without fine Knots,

[3] For a fuller account of the manuscript, see no. 88. On St Chad's Gospels and the Cambridge fragment, see no. 83 n. 2.

[1] Ptd. as 'Part of a Letter, written to a Most Reverend Prelate, in answer to one written by his Grace, judging of the Age of MSS. the Style of Learned Authors, Painters, Musicians, &c. By Mr Humfrey Wanley. London, July 11. 1701', which print is followed here. The fragmentary draft in BL Lansdowne MS 814 is, in the catalogue of the Lansdowne collection, erroneously attributed to Wanley's father, Nathaniel. That Marsh is the 'Prelate' is clear from no. 77, but the letter to which this is a reply seems not to have survived.

and Flourishes, without Pictures, and great Letters, or any thing that should look like Pompous: Suppose that the Ink, Parchment, &c. should carry a seeming face of Antiquity with them, and that a man should say his MS. was 1000, 1200, or 1300 years old, when as really, it was written within a very few years: Could he from the Hand alone soon find out the Cheat?

All the Hebrew MSS. that I have as yet seen, are written either with Samaritan or Chaldee Letters. As to the Samaritan, I own they bear a good resemblance one to another, and that they differ very much from those Samaritan Characters, which we find stamped upon divers truly Antient and Genuine Coins. But then there seems to be such a Resemblance (as to the Character) between those Coins struck in Ages far distant from one another, that 'tis hard (from the Consideration of the Metal, its Fabrick, Weight, from the Shapes of the Letters in the Inscription, &c.) to say which Coin was made in the time of David, or Solomon, and which no older than the time of the Machabees; this being rather to be gathered from the Words and Meaning of their Inscriptions, than from the Figure of the Characters which Compose them. The same may be said, in a great measure, of the old Greek, Punic, Roman, Brittish and other Coins.

The Chaldee Character has indeed varied in tract of time, according to the different Fancies and Humours of men. The Even plain Letter, I think, is the most Ancient. This they altered into a more neat way of making it, as your Grace finds in R. Stephens Hebrew Bibles.[2] There is a third fashion, of waving the perpendicular strokes like Rays, as your Grace remembers in some of the Hebrew Coins exhibited in the Prolegomena to the Polyglott Bibles. Then fourthly, there is a large fat Letter in the MS Rituals and Liturgies, besides the Rabbinical Letters of Italy and Germany, with their Offspring; the Litterae Coronatae, and perhaps others that I never saw: (Not to mention here the Jewish Custom of writing the Vulgar Language of the Country wherein they live, with Hebrew Letters). It seems a hard matter, my Lord, to trace the Original and Progress of all these ways of Writing, so, as upon the bare sight of a MS. written in the Hebrew Language or Character, to say, by the shape of the Letters of this Book it appears to be so old: and it seems much more difficult to assign the particular

---

[2] Between 1539 and 1544 Robert Estienne (1503–59), commonly known by the name 'Stephanus', pbd. the whole Hebrew OT in separate parts in 4°, and between 1544 and 1546 another edn. in 16°. See Darlow and Moule no. 589.

Province or Countrey wherein each Hebrew Book was written, as for example, in Italy, France, Spain, Portugal, England, Holland, Germany, Poland, Barbary, Persia, India, in the several Provinces of Turkey, &c.

The same almost may be said of the Greek Manuscripts, in which Language there has been a great diversity of Writing, according to the different humours of the Scribes, the Fashion then in use, or the Manner of that particular Province, in which such a Book was written. Nor is it easie (tho one would be apt to take such Differences for so many Land-marks), to tell the Age of a Greek MS. without the Date; and I never yet saw such a Date so high as the year 6400, according to the Greek Computation. And it is still much harder, from any Remarks about the Character, Illumination, Ink, Parchment, Paper, Binding, &c. to find out what Country [*Wanley's note*: If a man is born in one Country and writes a Book in another, keeping still to the Character and manner of Writing used in his own Country, I look upon it as the same thing as if he wrote it at home. And therefore I look upon the Greek MSS. which Angelus Borgecius wrote at Paris, as if they were written in Candy, where he was Born.[3] And so (amongst many others) to instance in a Latin MS, I look upon a Copy of Pope Gregory's Pastoral Care, (now remaining in the Bodleian Library)[4] as a noble Monument of our Saxon Ancestors: Tho St Willibald wrote it, perhaps, at Mount Cassinum in Italy, and afterwards (as it is probable) carried it with him into Germany, where it remain'd at Wurtzburg till that City was plunder'd by the Swedes about 70 years ago], Province, or Island, such a Greek Book should be written in, or what Country-man the Scribe shou'd be. [*Wanley's note*: Now this may in some measure be done by Latin MSS. because there are greater plenty of them. For even I, by exactly observing the nature of the Characters,

[3] A memorandum from Wanley to Edward Harley in BL Harley MS 7055 (fo. 48) lists books Harley should make a point of seeing in the Bodleian, including Arch. B.89 and 90 = MSS Auct. F.4.15 and 16, *SC* 3078, 3079, 'Two of the books written by Angelus Vergecius [= Borgecius], & painted by his Daughter'. MS Auct. F.4.15, a finely illuminated manuscript of Manuel Philes, was written by Vergecius at Paris in 1564, as was Auct. F.4.16, an illuminated copy of John Camaterus.

Angelos Bergikios, a Cretan scribe, was active in the middle years of the sixteenth century; from about 1540 to the late 1560s he seems to have been working in Paris. M. Vogel and V. Gardthausen, *Die griechischen Schreiber des Mittelalters und der Renaissance* (Leipzig, 1909), list at least 15 manuscripts said to have been copied by him in Paris. I am indebted for this information to Professor Patricia Easterling.

[4] Bodl. MS Laud misc. 263 (*SC* 1000), a ninth-century copy of Gregory's Pastoral Care in Latin.

&c. of those MSS. whose Country I was sure of, have afterwards been enabled to say, that this Book looks as if it had been written in France, Italy, Spain, Germany, the Netherlands, England, Ireland, &c. and, it may be, about such a time.] Nay, and what does farther add to the Difficulty, is, that 'tis known that the shapes of the Majuscule Letters found in Greek MSS, have been retain'd for above 600 years together, with little Variation; and also, that some MSS. written with Minuscules and with Accents, are older than some others which want them. And also, that the present Greek Copistes or Librarij have three or four different Hands commonly used by them, one being their own Common Hand, the others an Imitation of old MSS, which are more beautiful, but troublesome in writing, than their ordinary Running Hands: It being customary, as I have been told, when a man wants a Copy of such a Book to be written, for the Copiste to ask in what Hand it must be written (for one Hand, it may be, is more Costly than another); and according as they agree, the Book is written. And thus I have seen some very new Things written in the same Hand with Books which are certainly 400 years old.

What Methods Learned Men have taken, in order to inform themselves of the different Ages of MSS, I know not, but my own has been this. I have been careful to get all the Dates I could, wherein 'twas said that such an individual MS was written, at such a time, or by such a particular person; every Book with a Date, being as a Standard whereby to know the Age of those Books of the same or a like Hand, and of those that are not very much older or newer. Where Dates have been wanting in some Books, perhaps they have had some Succession of Emperors, Kings, Popes, Bishops, or other Officers; and setting down the continuance of their Predecessors for so many years, months, and days, if there be only the naked Name of him who is the last in order (all other Circumstances concurring), I then judge the Book to have been written during the Life or Reign of such a person. Especially if that Succession be afterwards continu'd by a more recent Hand, or that there be two such Successions, as of Kings and Bishops, and the last of each happen to be Contemporaries. Other Observations I have made from Historical Notes and Ecclesiastical Tables, in some Books. At other times I light upon some Authentic Charter or Original Writing, in the same Hand with such a Book as I have remembered to have formerly seen, but without any guess at the Age of it. The Age of the Charter being known, that of the Book is then known also: for I never entertain'd any Notion, or relied upon any Observation, but as I found it confirm'd by the Suffrage of concurring Circumstances, and sufficient Authority.

But even in Dates, I have found that a man ought to be very Cautious; for some have been altered by later Hands, for corrupt and base Ends. Some are so worded, as when one thinks that the time they mention, is the time when the MS. was finish'd by the Copiste, or Bookwriter; it is meant only as to the time when the Author finish'd his Composition. Other Books are Post-dated that they might be accounted New. Of this last kind, is a Greek MS. I saw in the University Library at Cambridge, which, as appears by a written Annotation therein, was bought such a year at Rome, for so much; and yet the Date pretends that the Book was written at Rome in such a year, which happens to be two years after it was bought and paid for.[5] The Reason of these Post-Dates was, because, before Printing came up, a Book was by how much the Newer, by so much the more Valuable. An old Book might be bought for an old Song (as we say), but he that transcribed a fresh Copy must be paid for his pains. And therefore, I have found in some Catalogues of the MSS. formerly extant in our Abbey-Libraries, that when they said such a Book was *Liber Vetus*, they would often add, *& inutilis*; but *Liber Novus* was *Nitidus*, *eleganter scriptus*, *lectu facilis*, &c. which mean Opinion of the Ancient Copies, by the way, may have been the Occasion of the Loss of many a good Author.

The Librarii or Book-writers were from the time of the Romans a particular company of men, and their Business a Trade: But tho Book-writing was their profession, yet they afterwards had but a third part of the business.

Learning (after the Erection of Monasteries), was chiefly in the hands of the Clergy; and they were for the most part Regulars, and liv'd in Monasteries: Amongst these were always many industrious men, who wrote continually new Copies of old Books, for their own use, or for the Monastery, or for both; which seems to have swallowed up above half the business. Then, if an extraordinary Book was to be written, for the standing, and more particular Use of the Church or Monastery, the Antiquarius must be sent for, to write it in large

---

[5] CUL MS Ii.iv.16, Theodore Gaza's *Greek Grammar*, copied at Rome by Ioannes Rhosos in 1479 as he claims in his subscription on fo. 159^r. But a note by John Shirwood († 1493) on fo. 159^v says it was bought at Rome in 1476. It came to Cambridge from Méric Casaubon's library, bought by Thomas Gale.

Characters, after the old manner, and such a Copy they knew would last for many Ages, without Renovation. Between these two sorts of People, the Writing-Monks and Antiquarii, the poor Librarij or common Scriptores (who had Families to maintain) could hardly earn their Bread. This put them upon a quicker way of dispatch, that so they might undersell one another: And in order to this Dispatch, they would employ several persons, at one time, in writing the same Book (each person, except him who wrote the first Skin, beginning where his Fellow was to leave off): Or else, they would form the Letters smaller and leaner, and make use of more Jugations and Abbreviations than usually others did. And this, my Lord, is the only account that I can give; for that Variety of Hands which in former Ages, being learn'd of, or borrow'd from the Romans, was commonly us'd, and in fashion at the same time, and in the same Country (throughout these Western Parts of Europe) and for their growing less and less for one Age after another. An Instance of this may be given from the Hands of England, which about the year of our Lord 730 was of three sorts.

I. The Roman Capitals, still retain'd, and kept up by the Antiquarij, in some Books and Charters.

II. The more Sett Saxon Letters (which have a near affinity with the more Antient Irish Characters, as being with them derived from the Roman) which were used as the Common Hand of the Age, by the Monks in their Books, and some Charters of their Dictating and Writing.

III. The Running Saxon Letters, fuller of Abbreviations, and something of kin to the Longbardic and Franco-Gallic (both which, with this third sort, were also of Roman Original) and was used by these Librarij in their Books and in the Charters; as also by some Authors who wrote much, as Bede, &c.

There was another sort of Bookwriters still in use, namely, the Notarij, whose business it was to take Tryals and Pleadings at Courts of Judicature; to write as Amanuenses from the mouth of an Author; and to take Homilies and Sermons at Church, from the Mouth of the Preacher. These Notarij made use of Notae or Marks instead of Letters: But when, in Process of Time, Letters were usually written small and quick, and Abbreviations grew Common, the Notarij were turn'd off, unless they would write Books in Long Hand, as other Librarij did, and their Notae grew out of use; and most of their Performances in Notes or Marks have been since destroy'd.

Suppose then, my Lord, that a man had one Latin Book of each of the four sorts above-mentioned laid before him, written all at a time, and without any Date or Note of the Age: Would not he be ready to say that the three first were older than one another? As that that in Capitals was older than that in the Midling Hand; and this again older than that in the Running and smaller Hand? and that such a Book written in the Notae being all full of marks, was not Latin, but of some other unknown Language? But to come down later; Suppose that a person should have some recenter Books or Charters laid before him in the Pipe, Text, Exchequer, Chancery, Court, and Common Hands, all written at the same time, would not he be apt to say, that one seem'd to him to be older than another, and that they were the Hands of several Nations?

If it be difficult for an Inquisitive Person to be a perfect Master in all the Successions of Hands, that have been us'd in his own Country, so far as he may be guided by the Monuments therein extant (and I never heard of any Man that was such a Master) surely, it must be more difficult to pronounce the Age of those Books, from the Hand, which were written in other Countries, in an unknown Language. And what may make a Man yet more liable to mistakes (besides the want of Dates in the most Antient Greek, Latin and other MSS) was the Practice of many Writers, still to Use the very same Hand when in Years, as they learnt when they were Young; like as many Antient People, who do yet continue to write the Roman and Secretary Hands, which were more fashionable 50 or 60 years ago, than now. I forbear to trouble your Grace with any more Words upon this head, or to make mention of the different ways of Writing in any other Language: because I find this Letter will prove larger than I intended. I will therefore (with your Grace's leave) touch upon the next Head in your Graces Learn'd Essay, shewing the great Easiness of finding out an Author, and the Time he liv'd in, by his Style and Phrase.

I wish, my Lord, that it was as easie to discover the Villanous Authors of some Treasonable and Scandalous Libels, by their Style, as it has been to find out the Printers, by the Paper and Letter. Could this be done, it might not be unuseful to the Government. But People have learnt the knack of changing their Style, upon Occasion, so Artificially, as not to be discovered, but when they themselves are willing to be known. Who would have thought that Erasmus wrote the *Epistolae obscurorum Virorum?* Or that some of the Nicer, nay, the most Eminent Modern Criticks could have been impos'd upon by their familiar and near Acquaintance, who trump'd upon them their own recent Performances for invaluable fragments of the Antients, whose other works these very Critics had lying before them? It has been a frequent Practice in all Ages for poor Scribblers to father their wretched Offspring upon Illustrious Persons: and the disparity between the Genuine works of the one, and the Spurious pieces of the other being evident enough, it has been easie to distinguish between the Gold and the Brass. But, my Lord, I would humbly ask this Question, Is all that is even now by learned men ascribed to some Antient Voluminous Greek and Latin Authors, undoubtedly theirs? May not there still some supposititious pieces lurk among them, which have the luck to be receiv'd, only because they have been more ingeniously counterfeited? Nay, may not the same person in the course of his Life, even alter and vary his Style and Phrase unwittingly, and without any design to do so? I think Mr Richardson somewhere in his Answer to Amyntor,[6] upon occasion of the difference in point of Style between the Revelation of St John and his other Works, between the Prophecy of Jeremiah and his Lamentations, does tell us from Dr Cave, that the consideration of the Times when a man writes, or of the Persons to whom, or the Subjects about which, or the Temper of Body, or the Humour he is in when he writes, or the Care and Pains that he takes in Writing, may Occasion such Alterations in his Style, as that no certain Rule can be inferr'd from thence.

And if, my Lord, it was really possible to find out the Time when an Author liv'd, only by diligent Reading his Works, surely the World wou'd have been long since Agreed as to the Time when Homer lived, though they could not tell where he was born. And I believe even in the List of Ecclesiastical Writers there are some, and those not of the least consideration, who (notwithstanding their Works have been read over and over) are still reckon'd to be of incertain Age.

As for Pictures, though I have much less Experience in them, than I had once in MSS. yet I will not deny but that the Works of an hundred Masters (besides those your Grace has been pleas'd to mention) may be known by the Hands, tho they may be almost as different as their

[6] J. Richardson, *The Canon of the New Testament Vindicated; in answer to the Objections of J.T.* [= *John Toland*], *in his Amyntor* (1700). Wing R. 1384.

several Hands in Writing: But that one Painter can't Copy from another, so exactly, as that in tract of time it shall not be known which Picture is the Original, is what I dare not assert.

It has been frequently practis'd by Painters to borrow Pictures of those who are Lovers and Judges of such things, to Copy them, and to return their Copies for the Originals, without any discovery made by the discerning Owners. And I believe it possible (tho exceeding difficult) for a great Master to Copy a Picture so, that when they both stand together, a good Judge shall not dare positively to say which is the Copy and which not: Nor he that drew the Original, dare to own, that he could imitate his own Handywork better than a Stranger has done. There are a great many stories common among Painters, to this purpose. And one wou'd not think it much more difficult, for a Man to imitate a Drawing or Picture, than to counterfeit another Mans Hand-writing, which some People can do most exactly. And others with Pen and Ink will Copy after any thing that is Printed so nicely, as that one would affirm their Writing to be printed off at the Press.

Your Grace's Notions of discerning the Age as well as the Hand of the Painter, by his Picture, is very curious, and altogether new to me: And I doubt not but there is a great deal in it. I only want the whole Works of some great Painter, with an Account of the time when he wrought each Piece, to fit me for the making the Experiment. And why might not this Notion be advanc'd a little farther, and the Painter's Complexion be known by his Pictures, as well as his Age? As supposing that the Sanguine do naturally run upon Pourtraits, Poetical Histories, Nudities, &c. The Cholerick upon Battel-pieces, Sea-fights, Fire-pieces by Land or Sea, Tempests, &c. The Phlegmatick upon the Still-life, Flower-pieces, Birds, Beasts, Fishes, &c. and the Melancholic upon Landskips, Architecture, Pieces of Perspective, &c. Not but that the different Genius of a Country, or the Desires of a good Customer, may oblige a Painter to work upon a subject, which he had no great Fancy for.

As to the difference in the works of Painters grown old, in respect of what they did when young, I doubt no certain Rules can be Establish'd as to their Performances in that kind. I know, my Lord, that Painters do generally live faster than other men, which may at length occasion a failure in their Sight and Memory, a trepidation in their Hands, &c. And yet I never heard that Michael Angelo, Alb. Durer,

Titian, and others, painted worse at the latter end of their long lives, than they did before. Nay, I hear that Signior Verrio, tho grown old, Paints now far better than ever, and is grown almost asham'd of some of his own Works which he Painted at Windsor Castle in the time of K. Charles II.[7] There may be this in it, that Aged Persons having attain'd, thro long Practice, to a greater Experience, to a more Solid and Mature Judgment than they had when younger, are more Cautious of that which they let go out of their Hands; and correct those flashy touches of their Pencil, and other superfluous Irregularities, which they and others were formerly very fond of.

As for the Flame and Motion of the Eyes in a Picture, or the Breath in its Mouth, I can say but little, having as yet never had the happiness to see such Rarities, tho I have been admitted to the sight of some of the best Pieces of the most Celebrated Masters.

As to the Painters Painting a Living or Moving thing, so that one shall almost discern the Motion, and see the Bird Flying, the Horse or Hound Running, &c. that is more easie, especially when assisted with the friendly and pregnant fancy of the Charm'd Spectator. In the Still life indeed, the Eye is quickly deceiv'd, and tho there are, I believe, several Masters now living more Excellent at it than ever Zeuxis and Parrhasius were; yet still, with all their Art, 'tis very difficult to impose upon a man so, as to make him believe 'tis not a Picture, but the very Life that he sees before him.

Musicians seem to be under the same Predicament with Painters, since they are observ'd to live Fast, as also the Poets. 'Tis by the Practice of many years that they attain to a just Knowledge and Mastery in their respective Arts; and as their first Compositions are little and light, suitable to the Mercurial temper of heedless and inconstant Youth; So, in time, this wears off, and as their Experience and Judgment encreases, their Compositions grow more solid and sound. A Young Man may make a better Minuet or Jigg, but the Elder a more sound Service or Anthem. The Music of the former (with other Accomplishments) may go a great way towards the enticing a foolish Girl to Love; but that of the latter Excites the Devotion, moves the Affections, and raises the Passions of those truly Religious Souls, who

---

[7] Antonio Verrio (1639?–1707). Italian painter brought to England by Charles II and subsequently court painter until his death. Employed by Charles II to paint ceilings in Windsor Castle, but little remains of his work there owing to alterations in the nineteenth century.

take pleasure in singing praises to the Honour and Glory of his name, who lives for ever and ever.

If your Grace shall say, that the very best Painters, Musicians and Poets dyed young, or at least before they attain'd to an advanc'd Age, when they would have fail'd or grown dull, as others did: I must beg leave to say that Old Men are of two sorts, either those who are much affected with their Age and weakned, or those who are not.

If a Man be born of unsound Parents, or hath liv'd all along in an Air disagreeable to his Constitution, or has his Constitution always unhealthful, or has liv'd an intemperate or debauch'd Life, or has been crush'd by any heavy Misfortunes, or always liv'd in Poverty or Discontent; 'tis no wonder, if in spight of all this, he attains to old Age: but then he will probably lose the Clearness of his Head, the fix'd Attention of his Mind, the Brightness of his Parts, which he might be formerly noted for. If a Man has never had any of these disadvantages to wrestle with, but has all along been bless'd with the Contrary: then, he being bred up to a profession, and always following it, his judgment therein still encreases, and his Hand (one would think) should be more nimble and ready, and the Man a better Painter, Musician or Orator than ever: And why not a better Poet too? I say, with submission, my Lord, if Mr Dryden (tho he was said to be unhealthy at last) wou'd have taken as much pains, or had been Allowed time to his Mind for revising his later Poems, as in some of his former, they might have been as well, if not better accepted. I don't see that 'tis old Age that does a Man this diskindness, but rather, that 'tis the Accidents that do too often attend it, which yet many are freed from to the very last.

Suppose then, my Lord, if Raphael or Vandike, or the late Mr H. Purcell, or Alessandro Stradella, should have continued their Practice of Painting and Music till they grew old, from the Accidents attending which, suppose them (as a great many other People) to be very free, might we not then have justly expected from them, even greater Wonders than they had ever before perform'd? I won't say that an old General is fitter to be trusted than a young one; or that the late Mareschal Schomberg at his death, was a better Souldier (notwithstanding his Age) than the Present Kings of Sweden and Poland: But rather, that the Study of Divinity, or of the Laws, do seem as nice and large as those of Painting and Music. Now the old and sage Men of those Professions are every where most regarded, they are found to have the ripest Judgments, and they are deservedly employed in the most weighty Affairs appertaining to their Professions. And it has been seen (as was partly said before) that some Painters and Musicians have not at all fail'd as they grew old, but kept that great Reputation to the last, which they had before acquir'd.

My Lord, upon the whole, it seems to me (tho I know my Opinion is of no weight) that there is a gradual and sensible alteration in the appearance of things, and especially in the Scripture or Hand-writing of MSS. Now these ought to be consider'd with respect to the particular places wherein they were written.

Every Country is suppos'd to have remaining in it, the greatest Variety and most considerable Monuments of its own Characters; unless they are known to be carried away to other places. And therefore, if any man be desirous of considering the Letters of any Language that has been confin'd to any one particular Region or Province; 'tis but going thither, and it's ten to one, but (if he be diligent) he may satisfie his Curiosity very well. For Example, Suppose I should be willing to consider the Nature of the Irish Letters, their Original, Progress and Variations, with their Relation to the Roman, Franco & Anglo-Saxon: this might be done by travelling Ireland principally, by taking a trip into the Scotch Highlands, and perhaps into the Isle of Man, and by consulting some English and other Libraries, whither some Irish MSS have been carried.

If I would consider the French, Italian, Spanish, or English Hands, each Country affords sufficient Helps. But if a Man would consider the Letters of a Dead or Living Language, which spread far, and has been, or is us'd in several Countries: he can't be suppos'd a perfect Master in all the ways of writing that Language, till he has consider'd the whole State and Succession of its Letters in each of those Countries: Amongst those Languages I reckon the Hebrew, Arabic, Turkish, Armenian, Persian, Greek, Latin, Teutonic, Sclavonian, &c. And tho Latin is common amongst us, and every body is pronouncing the Age of a Latin MS, yet I think they would do well to enquire where as well as when a Book was written. And if they are certain that such a Latin Book was written in such a particular Country, or Province, 'tis then more easie, by considering the Succession of Letters us'd in that Province, or by comparing it with other Books written therein, to say how old it is. For want of this consideration many Learned Persons have been almost always out in their Calculations, and have pronounc'd at

Random. If then, my Lord, this Method appears Rational, and even Necessary, in order to attain a sufficient Measure of this sort of Knowledge; it follows, that 'tis no easie matter to assign the Age even of a Latin MS, no, not even in England, where yet I suppose there may be as great a Variety of Latin Hands, as in most other Countries.

As for Painting and Music, they are Arts that I have always had a great Love and Affection for. I know very well that each Painters Hand and each Musicians Manner differs from another, but whether there is a gradual and remarkable Variation from themselves in the Course of their Lives, is what I never heard asserted. This is certain, that they can change their way of Painting and Composing at pleasure; and therefore, Mr H. Purcel's Dulcibella is said not to be like his other Music; and Mr Fuller the Painter could put one of his Pieces upon Sir Peter Lely for a most incomparable Picture of Mich. Angelo. But then these Changes and Variations from their usual Manners are very seldom made. And a man generally pursues and practices that which is most agreeable to his own Genius. For this Reason, when a Painters Hand is fixed, his Manner is then limited, and so when a Curious Person comes into a Gallery, he knows that this Picture was done by Ryley, Kneller, Vandyke, Dobson, Tintoret, &c. and that to be a Copy after Reubens, Georgeon, Salv.Rosa, Han. Caraccio, Pietro di Cortona, &c. When he comes to an Opera, to a Consort, or to Church, not knowing before-hand what Music is to be perform'd, yet he may soon discern that it was compos'd by Corelli, Baptist, Bassani, Charissimi, Blow, Purcell, &c. And so upon Reading an Antient Author, a sagacious and learned Person may find, that he writes according to the manner of such an Age, that the Style imitates such another, or that the Book, tho it bears such a Man's Name, yet might, perhaps, be more truly ascribed to another, with whose Style it more exactly agrees: As for Example, that Piece of S. Cyril's publish'd from the Escurial MS. by Barthasar Corderius, is thought (by reason of the Analogy in point of Style) to be Origen's:[8] But then, whether all this can be always done, done easily and without Errors, is the doubt. And it seems yet a greater difficulty, certainly to discover how old the Painter, Musician, Poet, Orator, or other Author was, when he

---

[8] Nineteen Greek homilies of Origen on Jeremiah were first pbd. by Balthasar Corderius in 1648 from a manuscript in the Escorial, where they are attributed to Cyril Alexandrinus: *S.P.N. Cyrilli... Homiliae xix in Ieremiam prophetam... ex antiquissimo codice M.S. Regiae Bibliothecae Scorialensis descriptae* (Antwerp, 1648).

finish'd any one piece of his Works, unless a man is plainly told so:
This being a sort of Knowledge, that those who have been otherwise
sufficiently experienc'd in their several Arts and Professions, have not
as yet pretended to.

MS: British Library, Lansdowne 814, fo. 95; fragmentary draft. *Date*: 'London, July 11.
1701.' *Printed*: *Philosophical Transactions*, no. 300 (June 1705), pp. 1993–2008.

80. *To* [Arthur Charlett] *23 September 1701*

Honor'd Sir,

Since your departure,[1] in obedience to your Commands I waited on
Mr Speaker,[2] who was pleas'd to be extremly kind to me, and tell's me
I shall, in time, be really sensible of his good Opinion of me, &c. As to
the Cotton Library, he is heartily for me, and thinks there is no great
danger of my being put by: and that if I should miss of it, that my
friends would take other measures about me.[3]

I acquainted him, from you, with the Method used in the late
Election of the Astronomy-Professor, which mightily pleas'd him.[4]
He thank's you for the Hint, and say's he will make you a visit when
he comes to Oxford; which will be, as I think, about the beginning of

[1] Charlett was in the habit of spending Aug. in London: see Charlett to Wanley d.
28 July 1702, Welbeck Wanleyana = BL Loan MS 29/253.
[2] Robert Harley (1661–1724), MP 1690, Speaker of the House of Commons 1701–5,
created 1st Earl of Oxford and Mortimer 1711, Lord Treasurer 1711, Wanley's patron.
[3] Almost from the moment he took up the Assistant Secretaryship of the SPCK,
Wanley set about trying to escape from it to something more congenial, and seems to
have been especially interested in a post at the Cotton Library. Towards the end of
his life Sir John Cotton, grandson of the founder of the library, decided to leave it to
the nation at his death, and in June 1701 the statute making it over (12 and 13 William
III c. 7) became law. Dr Thomas Smith, a friend of Sir John Cotton and for many
years the unofficial keeper of the library, thus found himself in a precarious position.
At Sir John's death (which would bring the act into effect) he could, as a nonjuror,
expect little sympathy from the Trustees—three of whom (including Harley) were
government appointees—as he and everyone else realized. From the first Charlett
encouraged Wanley in his hopes to succeed Smith: see no. 77 n. 13. Early in Sept.
1701 Cotton fell seriously ill and there seems to have been a rumour current that he
was dead: see *TLS*, 31 Aug. 1962, p. 660 n. 4. For Wanley's prompt action a year later,
when he heard of Cotton's death on 12 Sept. 1702, see no. 89, for the subsequent
intrigue and Wanley's failure to get the post, see P. L. Heyworth in *TLS*, 31 Aug.
1962, p. 660.
[4] See no. 93 n. 1.

the next Week. This Notice I thought would not be unacceptable from

Most Honor'd Sir,

　　Your very humble and obedient servant

Humfrey Wanley.

MS: Bodleian, Ballard 13, fo. 107. *Date*: 'Sept. 23. 1701.'

81. *To* Edward Thwaites *30 September 1701*

Dear Sir,

Mr Dean[1] is as positive that he gave me back that Leaf of Copy which you want,[2] as Mr Bush[3] is that he took it. I not finding it, was oblig'd to compose it afresh, as well as I could, by memory, not having, as you know, the MS. by me. Bid Mr Bush distribute all that is Set after the Lords Prayer, i.e. *Quis librum scripsit, &c.* and instead thereof, to insert from this Paper *Hunc Librum*, &c.

Bid him to Correct the faults there being great Numbers in the Page you sent,[4] whereof here folow some, lin. 7, lege Æthelstanus; lin. 19, Reliquiae, & Faemnum; lin. 26, *vocant*; lin. 27, instead of *D. Hieronymi*, say *Versionis Vulgatae*; lin. 29. gehalgad; lin. 31. swilce; lin. 32, Panem; lin. 36, patiaris.

I have put into Mr Dean's hands all the Catalogue for Cambridge University, so that you may procede with Printing the Remaining part of the Oxford Catalogue as briskly as you can. You will remember to alter the *Running-Title* as soon as you have done with the Bodleian Library.

I want the Lambeth-book of Normanno-Saxon Homilies[5] which Mr Dean tells me you have; as also St Chads book,[6] in Order to take an account of them. I therefore do earnestly intreat you, Sir, to send

---

[1] i.e. Hickes.

[2] Thwaites was in charge of seeing Hickes's *Thesaurus* and Wanley's *Catalogus* through the press.

[3] Edmund Bush, Oxford printer 1696–1705, the printer of Wanley's *Catalogus*.

[4] *Catalogus*, p. 81; in the Bodleian copy three of the nine errors remain uncorrected.

[5] James and Jenkins, *Descriptive Catalogue*, no. 487. Wanley p. 266; facs. in *Thesaurus*, bk. i, figs. VI, VII (after p. 144).

[6] i.e. the so-called 'St Chad's Gospels' at Lichfield. Wanley acknowledges its receipt in his letter to Thwaites, 18 Oct. 1701 (no. 83), and it is clear from his letter to Lhwyd, 14 Sept. 1702 (no. 88), that at that date he still had it in his possession.

them up, either to Mr Dean or to me; and I will safely re[s]tore them to you again at any time that you shal be pleas'd to appoint, or only St Chads, [&] give the other to Mr Gibson,[7] according as you please to direct

Dear Sir,

    Your most humble servant

                                 Humfrey Wanley.

I pray you don't deny me the Books. I have not heard from Mr Grabe.

MS: Bodleian, Rawl. D. 377, fo. 65. *Date*: 'London. Sept. 30. 1701.' *Address*: 'For The Reverend Mr Thwaites, Fellow of Queens College, in Oxford.'

82. *To* Hans Sloane *12 October 1701*

Most Honor'd Sir,

    I went yesterday morning to the Dean of Worcester's[1] in order to review the remaining part of my Catalogue[2] which I had prepared. We finished, but it was so late in the day before I could take my leave of him that I thought there would be hardly time sufficient to enter upon the Catalogue of your Books at your house.[3] For that Reason I came directly home, & applied my self to those Papers which must be Copied against to morrow Sennight, some of which being very long, and to day being a broken day (since I must attend our S— and dispatch some of their business before I meet 'em) I thought you would be better pleas'd if I should transcribe them as fast as I can.[4] In order to this I find that I want The Translations of two Letters of Mr Leeuwenhoeck to you, dated 5 April, & the 2 of August last, as also the original Dissertation of Mounsier Reneaume which I translated & gave you back the last time that I had the Honor to see you.[5] If you can

---

[7] Lambeth Librarian.

[1] Hickes.   [2] Of Anglo-Saxon manuscripts.

[3] Wanley never completed this catalogue of Sloane's MSS. What he did accomplish is now in BL Sloane MS 3972 B.

[4] Wanley was Assistant Secretary to the Royal Society (a post he owed to Sloane, who was Secretary) from Nov. 1700 to Nov. 1706; the first date is given as 1701 in the printed series, but the original minutes record this as 1700.

[5] There is a paper of Leuwenhoeck's d. 15 (not 5) Apr. 1701 in *Philosophical Transactions*, no. 270 (Mar. and Apr. 1701), pp. 821–4; I can find no communication of his d. 2 Aug. 1701. Reneaume's piece is ptd. *Philosophical Transactions*, no. 273 (Aug. 1701), pp. 908–11.

find these 3 Papers I intreat you, Sir, to send em by this bearer: if not, I
will go forwards with the others. I find some written Accounts of
Printed Books,[6] which I suppose are inserted into the Transactions;
be pleas'd to lett me know whether I should transcribe them into the
Register or not. But above all, Sir, let me beg of you to do me the
Justice to believe that I do not differre the finishing the Catalogue of
those few of your books which I had begun, out of any inconstancy of
Temper, or want of respect for you; but that I only dispatch that
business first, which you said was in most hast, & consequently would
have soonest done by Honor'd Sir

    Your most faithful & obedient servant

Humfrey Wanley.

MS: British Library, Sloane 4038, fo. 252. *Date*: '12 Octob. 1701.' *Address*: 'To The
Honor'd Dr Hans Sloane.'

83. *To* Edward Thwaites *18 October 1701*

Dear Sir,

    To day Mr Dean brought me St Chad's book, which I take exceed-
ing kindly, in your sending it at my request.[1] I will write to Dr Covel to
borrow that MS out of the University Library of Cambridge, which I
take to be the latter part of this, & compare them together.[2]

    I hope you go on with the Catalogue, be pleas'd to send me the
sheets, from pag. 80. I have shew'd the Dean the whole Catalogue for
Cambridge, which he approves of, and especially the Dissert. about
Lupus.[3] I intend another about *Ælfric* in the Cottonian Catalogue,
having one Land-mark for his Works which, I think, [h]a's not yet
been taken notice of. I shall make two *Ælfric's*, but then I shall give

---

[6] Of general scientific interest, often appended to the *Philosophical Transactions*.

[1] See no. 81.

[2] Wanley probably refers to Cambridge University Library MS Kk.i.24, an Evangelia
of the eighth century. Lowe, *CLA* ii, no. 138, describes the manuscript as 'Anglo-Saxon
majuscule saec. VIII' and suggests a Northumbrian centre for writing; he describes St
Chad's Gospels (no. 159) as 'Insular majuscule saec. VIII¹' and suggests a Welsh centre
for writing. The fact that the hands are similar and that the Lichfield manuscript
contains Matt. to Luke 3: 9 while the Cambridge manuscript contains Luke 1: 15 to John
20: 7 probably misled Wanley, writing as he was from memory.

[3] For Wanley's dissertation on 'Lupus' [= Wulfstan], see his account of Corpus
Christi College, Cambridge MS 201, *Catalogus*, p. 140.

the works of both Mr Wharton's Ælfrics to one; and produce another not so commonly known.[4]

I hear Mr Arch-deacon Nicholson is coming; pray tell me where & when I may wait on him.

I'me infinitly concern'd about the Letter I sent Mr Grabe, having heard nothing from him, tho' I wrote since; pray send the reason of his silence, & the Pap[er] I sent him,[5] to

Reverend & dearest friend

    Your eternally devoted servant

                      H. Wanley.

MS: Bodleian, Rawl. D. 377, fo. 57. *Date*: 'London, October 18, 1701.' *Address*: 'For The Reverend Mr Thwaites, Fellow of Queen's College in Oxon.'

84. *To* [Robert Harley ?][1] *7 April 1702*

Since I had the Honor to see you last, I have been inform'd by divers Gentlemen worthy of Credit, that the Reverend Dr Bentley will soon be remov'd from his Place of Keeper of her Majesties Libraries,[2] and many of my Friends say they think me in some Measure qualified to Succeed him therein. Sir, if you shall be pleas'd to have the same favorable Opinion of me, I would most humbly beg to be Honord with your Countenance and Recommendation either to my Lords the Duke of Ormond, the Earl of Rochester, the Earl of Marlborough,[3] or to her Majesty, as you in your great Wisdom shall think fit. I hear that some others are making Interest for it, which make's me take the boldness to write to you, lest an Opportunity should be lost before I shall have the Honor to speak to you in Person. They may deserve her Majesties Grace in this Affair much better than my self: yet, I can assure you, Sir, that if I am put in to this agreable Station, I will (by Gods help) clean

---

[4] Wanley does not seem to have carried out this plan for a dissertation on Aelfric.

[5] Thwaites replied that Grabe is too overwhelmed with business to write (Thwaites to Wanley d. 20 Oct. 1701, BL Harley MS 3781, fo. 202), and adds 'your observations on Ælfric & lupus will lead us thro' two dark mazes'.

---

[1] Wanley uses 'Honorable Sir' as a valedictory only in his letters to Harley.

[2] There seems to be no basis for the rumour Wanley refers to. Bentley held the Keepership until 1725, when he was succeeded by his son, a boy of 16 or 17.

[3] James Butler (1665–1745), 2nd Duke of Ormonde; Laurence Hyde (1641–1711), 1st Earl of Rochester; John Churchill (1650–1722), 1st Earl of Marlborough. All were influential at Court.

all the Books and the Place, and find room therein to set them all
Regularly upon Shelves, and then take an exact Catalogue of them
according to such Letters and Numbers as I shall put upon them
(which also shall be so contriv'd as to fit any other Place, upon occasion) and when the Library shall be brought into a Method, I would
attend & keep it in Order, to the Honor of her Majesty, and the
Benefit of Learned Men.

Sir, if you shall rather be pleas'd to have me employ'd in Collecting
and Publishing the Hands of England, according to the Proposal that I
did my self the Honor to leave with you, or think, that such a work
can't be compatible with that Station; I humbly submit to your Judgement in this all other matters, and shall glory in governing my self
according as you shall think fit to direct[4]

Honorable Sir,

MS: Welbeck Wanleyana = British Library, Loan 29/258; draft, unsigned. *Date*: 'April.
7. 1702.'

85. *To* George Hickes *10 May 1702*

Reverend & Honor'd Sir,

I have received your short, but very kind Letter; and if my Head had
not been distracted with multiplicity of business, I should have sent
you some account of the MS,[1] as I did intend. 'Tis one tract amongst
others that compose's the book. The Author was a Dalmation; and the
Copie was written in Italy upon Paper, about the year 1463. It takes up
but 6 Leaves in 4to, and for that Reason, a Present might be made of it
to Mr Benzelius; for your little Boy can as easily read it as your or my
Hand[2]

MS: British Library, Sloane 3984, fo. 289; fragment. *Date*: 'May. 10. 1702.' *Address*: 'To
the Very Reverend Doctor Hickes at his house next beyond the farthest Lamp towards
the fields in Kingstreet Bloomsbury.'

---

[4] BL Sloane MS 4061, fos. 268–9 contains Wanley's account of a design for a palaeographical work taking English hands down to 1700, ptd. below, Appendix 1. See also no.
92 and no. 37 n. 1.

---

[1] A note in another hand reads 'Iuvenci Crelij vita Attilae Hunnorum regis Cod. 215'.
[2] The rest torn off.

86. *To* [Arthur Charlett?] *10 May 1702*

Reverend & Honor'd Sir,

Wednesdays & Thursdays keeping me always particularly engag'd I could not do my self the honor to wait on you till Friday at 6 a clock in the Morning, when I learn't that you was gone out of Town above an hour before. This make's me very Sorry to be depriv'd of the happiness of your Conversation, and of making you acquainted with some matters that are not so proper to be treated of by Letters. I have received a Letter from Dr Hudson, desiring some Account of the Royal Societies MS Copie of Plinies Epistles;[1] and to know what is become of those books bought by the University out of Dr Bernards Study, which are mention'd in a written account that I took of them, which books he can't find in the Library, and which (he say's) he doe's not believe to be there: for, as he adds, the Curators will expect an Account of them at the Visitation.[2] I don't doubt but the Doctor think's that either Dr Hyde or I have embezled or stollen them, or otherwise he would have made use of Expressions better becoming a Gentleman than those I read in his Letter. But however, I shall be very willing to inform him, in order to prevent any future Clamors.

Doctor Bernards books were either Manuscripts, or Printed books. Of the Latter, those in Folio, I chain'd up amongst others, stopping up the Gaps with them. The Quarto's also & most of the 8vos are placed amongst the others, where there were gaps, or Shelves that were never before fill'd. All these I Letter'd & Number'd, and entred into the Interleaved Catalogue. Some few were not done, I being employed in other business, & sent away before I could finish. These few (perhaps 30 or 40 small books) were in the Study in the Gallery; so that if he ha's not lost any of them himself all the Printed books are certainly in the Library.

The MSS are either those written by himself or by others. The former I placed in those Cupboards Super R &c. Art. where he will find them with the Originals of Sir Henry Savils Chrysostom.[3] The Other MSS. in various Languages, I plac'd amongst others in NE.

---

[1] Probably BL Arundel MS 154, a composite volume in which the epistles begin at fo. 41ᵛ.

[2] On the business of Bernard's books, see no. 38 n. 7.

[3] Pbd. 8 vols. folio (Eton, 1610–13). The original manuscript 'copy' is in Bodl. MSS Auct. E.3. 1–16, 4. 1–6 (*SC* 2774–2783ᵐ).

stopping Gaps & filling Shelves with them as far as they would go. He will easily distinguish them from the rest, from my entring the Names of them in the Curating book belonging to the Greek Professor who always Visits that part.

One would think the Doctor should have [made] pretty sure these books were not in the Library, before he should write in the manner he did. I easily believe he ha's never seen them, because I know a Gentleman who had great Occasion for one of them, but it could not be found. And I humbly conceive that he ha's not yet so fully made himself acquainted with some of the rest, as he may do in time; because A Certain Gentleman went on purpose from hence to Oxford to consult some of Mr Dodworths MS. being 161 in number,[4] and which lie all together, and yet the Doctor, tho' intreated could not find these neither. And so the Gentleman was forc'd to return from Oxford as wise as he went.

MS: Welbeck Wanleyana = British Library, Loan 29/258; draft, unfinished? *Date*: '10. May 1702.'

87. *To* John Smith[1] *23 May 1702*

Reverend Sir,

The now Lord Bishop of Carlile,[2] when last in Town, was pleas'd to tell me that he had written to you about sending up hither (at my humble Request) two very Antient Manuscripts belonging to your Cathedral-Library, whereof you did before send up some Lines of each to the late Dean of Worcester;[3] and farther, that you had return'd

---

[4] At his death Dodsworth's manuscripts passed to his patron, the 3rd Lord Fairfax, with whose own manuscripts they came to the Bodleian in 1673. Now Bodl. MSS Dodsworth 1–161 (*SC* 4143–5101, 27693). MS Dodsworth 161 (*SC* 27693) did not come to the library until 1736, when it was presented by Francis Drake.

[1] John Smith (1659–1715), historian, of St John's College, Cambridge, Treasurer of Durham 1699; his edn. of Bede was completed by his son and pbd. 1722.

[2] Nicolson was nominated 8 May 1702, consecrated 14 June.

[3] The manuscripts are Durham Cathedral Library MSS A.II.17, two fragments of a seventh-/eighth-century Gospel (R. A. B. Mynors, *Durham Cathedral Manuscripts* (Oxford, 1939), nos. 3–4, Ker No. 105, Wanley p. 298, *CLA* ii, nos. 149, 150), and A.IV.19, a tenth-century service book—the Durham Ritual (Mynors no. 14, Ker no. 106, Wanley p. 295). They were sent by Smith 6 June 1702—not the first time that Durham manuscripts had been sent to London for Wanley's use, as is clear from Hickes to Wanley d. Sept. 1700 (BL Harley MS 3779, fo. 149) and Smith to Wanley d. 6 June 1702 (BL Harley

for Answer, that your Reverend Chapter was willing to comply with my Request; but since that the Dean of Durham[4] was in Town, 'twould be but decent to apply to him for his Consent.

This, Sir, at first sight appear'd highly reasonable, & even necessary to be done, in point of good manners; and tho' I was not absolutely a Stranger to him, yet I was willing to tarry till Mr Pickering[5] should come up (to whom I have the honor to be known) and then I thought I should the more easily obtain the Favor I desir'd. Accordingly, Sir, I have waited on Mr Pickering who very kindly took me to Mr Dean, and he presently granted my Request with all the Civility & Readiness in the World.

Sir, I now take the boldness to acquaint you with the very Reverend Deans Consent for me to peruse those two books here: and I humbly intreat you to send them to me with all speed, because a Work I'me engag'd in cannot go forward till I have them here.

My Lord of Carlile shew'd me the Titles of 5 Charters in your Treasury, all dated before the Conquest; and (as I remember) of K. Eadgar. If it would not be inconvenient, I should be extremely glad to peruse them also.[6] And I faithfully promise to restore safe either to Mr Dean of Durham or to You, Sir, the said MSS. or what ever else besides, you shall think fit to entrust me with, within a Month after I receive them.

I have been told that the Registers of your Cathedral are all entire from the Conquest. I would humbly intreat you, Sir, to let me know whether there be any Saxon Wills or other Instruments in that Language Entred into them; as they are in divers other Registers that I have seen.[7] Be pleas'd to believe that tho' I'me a Stranger, I have yet a great Respect & Veneration for your Person & Learning; and

---

MS 3781, fo. 88). Wanley seems still to have had the present manuscripts in his possession as late as Apr. 1704: see Smith to Wanley d. 13 Apr. 1704, Harley 3781, fo. 100.

[4] John Mountague, Dean of Durham 1700, formerly Master of Trinity College, Cambridge 1682.

[5] Theophilus Pickering (1662–1711), Fellow of Sidney Sussex College, Cambridge 1682, Canon of Durham 1692.

[6] Four 'Scotch' charters were sent by Smith with the manuscripts. 'But be not mistaken in their Date, they were none of ym before ye Conquest, for K. Edgar ye oldest of ym, was not till ye latter End of Wm Rufus' (Smith to Wanley d. 6 June 1702).

[7] 'as for Saxon Wills, or any other Instrumts in yt Language I never cd meet with, or hear of any, but yt wch I sent to Dr Hickes' (Smith to Wanley d. 6 June 1702). For the very full records at Durham Cathedral, see Davis, nos. 324, 326–39, 341–6, 348.

that I shall in every thing that I am capable, endeavor to approve my self

&c.

MS: Welbeck Wanleyana = British Library, Loan 29/258; draft, unsigned. *Date*: '23. May. 1702.' *Address*: 'To Doctor Smith at Durham.'

88. *To* Edward Lhwyd *14 September 1702*

Worthy Sir,

'Twould have been the greatest Satisfaction in the world for me to have enjoyed your most instructive Conversation in Oxford when I was there,[1] tho' but for an hour. I should then have return'd you my unfeigned thanks for all your past Favors by word of mouth, as I now do by Letter: and I should have mention'd that MS, now in my Custody,[2] which you sent your Gentleman hither to see. 'Tis a Latin Copie of the Gospells, written in the old round Saxon Character, just the same with that of St Salaberga's Psalter in Mabillon's Diplomatique,[3] and ha's very many British Names of Men, &c. entred on the Margin, &c. of such (as I suppose) who were, one way or other, Benefactors to the Church of *Llandaff*, to which this venerable book did belong, before it was Carried to Lichfield Church, where 'tis now called *Textus Si Ceaddae*. It now want's all beyond the 9th verse of the 3d Chap. of St Luke, and being lately bound, the Bookbinder in making the Edges of the Leaves even, ha's cut away a great part of those Marginal Entries, which I believe you would have put some value upon, if they had been entire. Those that are in continued Sentences, I here send you (except one that I can't pick out) written somewhat like to the Originals, tho' not so painfully as if I intended to give you a compleat Specimen of them; for 'ere it be long, you shall have the book in Oxford. The Proper names here, as in other MSS. begin with a small Letter.[4]

[1] Wanley may have visited Coventry in Aug. and taken in Oxford on the way back.
[2] St Chad's Gospels from Lichfield Cathedral. Wanley had had the manuscript in his possession since Oct. 1701: see no. 83. See further on it nos. 4, 92.
[3] Berlin, Deutsche Staatsbibl. MS Hamilton 553 (*CLA* viii, no. 1048), an eighth-century psalter written in Northumbria and traditionally associated with St Salaberga († 665), founder and first Abbess of the monastery of St Jean at Laon. Hand reproduced by J. Mabillon, *De Re Diplomatica* (Paris, 1681), Tabella viii, p. 359.
[4] Glosses of abbreviations etc. supplied by Wanley in the margin are reproduced

Osdendit ista scriptio ꝑ[1] dedert. ris. et luith grethi. treb guidauo Imal-
itiduch cimarguich. . . . . . . .est h̄[3] ÷ census 3̇[4]. douceint torth. hama-
harum. ī irham. hadouceint torth. ī irgaein. hahuch. ha. . . . .
ucerit manñuclenn. dō 5̄/7 sco eḷiudo. ds̄.[6].ī̇. .saturnnguid. .ī̇. .nobis .ī̇.
guurci. .ī̇. cutulf. .ī̇. . de laicis. qnguernn .ī̇. collbiu .ī̇. coho[ ]ge[ ] .ī̇.
ermm .ī̇. hour°d .ī̇. ꟷ̇cunq custodierit b̄[7]dictus erit. 7 ꟷ̇ franxerit
maladict3[8] erit. a dō. . The Form of this Entry, may serve to explain
the next a little. Osdendit ista ꝯscriptio[9] ꝑ dederunt. ris. hahirm . . .
. . . . .ubracma. behet hirmaī guidauc. ofoid
celli irlath . behet camdubr. isem hichet triuceint torth . h. . . . . .
rum. huguorthoueir emeninn. .ds̄[10] ōī pō .ī̇. saturnguid sacēr[11] .ī̇. nobis
.ī̇. gurci .ī̇. cutulf .ī̇. de laicis. cinguern .ī̇. . . . .ī̇. cohorget .ī̇. . . . .
erinin .ī̇. . . .꞉.dierit. . . . . .dictu. . . . .ꟷ̇ fraɪ. . . .it. m. . . . . .tus er. . . . .

Ostenditur híc quod emit † gelhi † filius. arihtiud. hóc euangelium.
de cingal.[12] et dedit illi[13] ꝑ[14] illo equm optimum. et dedit ꝑ anima sua
istum euangelium dō et sc̄. teliaui. super altare.

    † gelhi † filius. arihtiud . ., . ., et † cincénu †
    filius. gripiud . .,

Surexit tutbulc fili3[15] liuit hagener tutri dierchim tir telih. haioid ilau
elcu fili3 gelhig haluidt iuguret amgucant pel amtanndi hodiịdet
dipro tant gener tutri ó guir imguodant irdegion guragun tagc rodetit
elcu guetig eq3 tres uache, tres uache nouidligi nam[16] ir nibe câs igridu
dimedichat. . guetig ḅit did braut grefiat guetig nisminn tutbulc
haicenctlîois oisou ð[17], towards the bottom of the page follow's in the
same hand † teliau ī gurgint ī cinhilinn ī sps ī, tota familia teliaui. de
laicís numin m̄[18] aidan .ī̇ signou m̄ iacou ī berthutis ī Cinda ī. ꟷ̇c̄q3
custodierit benedict3 ēr, ꟷ̇c̄q3 frangerit maladict3 ēr 3,, —

here using Wanley's numbering. An incomplete interlinear translation by Lhwyd is
omitted.

1 quod. 2 ui. 3 hoc est. 4 ejus. 5 Deo & Sancto. 6 Deus testis. 7 bene. 8 tus. 9 con. 10 deus omnipotens
testis. 11 Sacerdos. 12 ci. 13 et. 14 pro. 15 filius. 16 forte *nam* aut *naum*. 17 Nota sensus imperf.
18 forte *minister*. 19 mi. 20 ni. 21 propter. 22 ber. 23 filius. 24 filius. 25 tur. 26 autem. 27 cujus. 28 pop-
ulus. 29 si. 30 diminih. 31 ꝑ vulgo scribitur pro *per* nonne autem hic legendum *apud*?

Here follow's another, but exceedingly maimed by the ignorant Bookbinder. . . .cceē ÷ . . . .dene lit. . . .iþ iiii. fi. . . .ledni. gu. . . ngirnn. . . . .llch[20]. et. . .ci. . . . . rthiud. . . .aint[21] li. . . .otemi[19] ble^. . . .filio sul. . .etsemini . . . in sempi. . . .num. ꝑp̄. . .to ħ ÷. .e ꝯ dedit. . . lib̄ta[22]. . s q̊tuor. . .os et oc. . . .incias. . . .ā idoneís . .estibꝫ.de. . . . . is. Riguo. . n. filius. . . . .íc. guen. . .filīs[23]. . . . .r. guo. luíc. . .edan. Ov . . . .f.guur[24]. . . . .um. mer. . .an .f. salus. arthan .f. cimulch. iudri .f. iudnerth. De clericís v̊ Nobis episcopus teiliav. . .turnguid sacerdos teîliav. dubrmo. et cuhelin. filiꝫ epīs. Saꝛ̄nbiu[25] cam ibiav. et sulgen. . . . . .asticꝫ q̊ ħ fidelit̄ scripsit. . q̊ custodierit ħ decretv̄ lib̄tatis bleidiud 7ꝑ lis ꝫ sit. . . .ctꝫ. q̊ hr̄[26] n̄ custodierit. sít maledictꝫ á dō et a teiliav In cs̄[27] euangelio scrip̄ ÷ et . . at omnis pls̄[28] fiat fiat. .,

Sir, lest you should be desirous of so much as I can read of that imperfect Entry above mention'd, I will put it down, as I can make it out of the two pages wherein it is written

ostendit ista consripsio[29] nobilitatē mainaur med diminih[30] et mensurā ꝫ aꝑ[31] huerdic̄ guid maunditoldar ī guo . . l. . uit clundirit cellrin dili homour dibir main ī lucaid. on the other page is illius ıı . . . .teii h. .c. . . .tu . . . . . . .ıc g. . . . . . . .i. . c. . .t. . I. . . .n. . . . .ut. . .e. . . .et i. . . . . .cunc i. . . .mu. . . . . .em. . . . .d. . . . . .no. . i. . . .i ma. . . .et lu. . . . . . ono. . . .pinal et cod. . . . . . . .dipulindes. uendi. cimer diap ferrus dipenna. . . . . .ircaru diooit bahne diguo an ben lunndirhitir melin dimaugles dirit bri. . .guidiaꝑ Istil dilicat dipulretino. . . . .I imniddi aꝑ he. . . . .

This lasty Entry seem's to me to be somewhat older than the rest, tho' they are all very antient and if from any of the Records of Llandaff-Church you can find out the certain time of Saturnguid or the other Witnesses, I shall be very glad to know it. As for the Time of Gelhi the Son of Arihtiud, I believe a MS in the Bodleian library viz. NE.D.2.19.[5] will bring some light to it, for to the best of my Memory, this Donation is written in a Hand very like to a great part of that, which seems (by a Paschal Table) to have been written about the year

[5] Bodl. MS Auct. F.4.32 (*SC* 2176), made up of four manuscripts (A–D) written between the ninth and eleventh centuries in Brittany, Wales, and England. See Wanley on B in *Catalogus*, p. 63, and his letter to Lhwyd, no. 95 n. 9.

817. The same MS. may be worth your consulting upon the account of very many antient British words written therein by way of Gloss between the lines, as also in the text about fol. 23. I do also remember another MS, viz. NE.B.5.9.[6] wherein are two of St Augustines Epistles written by the Hand of one *Bledian*, whom, perhaps, you may have read of. In this MS of Bledian's also are many words interlined upon the Text, or mixed with it, part whereof you may find to be British. I forbear to mention the Most Antient Gospels written by the hand of *Mac regol*,[7] because I know you have seen them. There is a Charter in the Cotton Library, of one of the Saxon Kings, concerning some lands in Cornwall,[8] wherein are preserved many of the Antient names of Places in that County. But to return to o[ur] MS. I was saying that there are very many names of particular persons written [here] & there; those which are written with the greatest accuracy, and perhaps as soon [as, or] before any of the rest, are these two; perhaps the oldest Specimen of the British [lan]guage now remaining.

I beseech you, Sir, to take in good part the trouble I give you of this Letter, and to let me know what Sense you pick out of the British words which are faithfully written, notwithstanding any seeming mistakes in the Latin as Osdendit, &c. and to oblige me with your Conjectures of the Persons, for I must mention this book in a Catalogue that I'me composing, of all the Anglo-Saxon MSS, I can find,

---

[6] Bodl. MS Bodley 572 (*SC* 2026), made up of four manuscripts written in the ninth and tenth centuries in England and France. 'Bledian's' manuscript = MS B of the tenth century, written in Cornwall or Wales.

[7] Rushworth Gospels, Bodl. MS Auct. D.2.19 (*SC* 3946).

[8] Perhaps Wanley has in mind the epitome of early grants made to Sherborne Abbey, in Devon and Cornwall, written by a monk of Sherborne in the late fourteenth century, preserved in Cotton Faustina A.ii, ptd. by W. Dugdale, *Monasticon Anglicanum*, i (1817), p. 337. It is not strictly a charter, but it does contain many names. Two other possibilities, an original charter d. 949 in Cotton Augustus ii recording a grant by King Eadred of land in Berkshire in exchange for land in Cornwall (ptd. W. de Gray Birch, *Cartularium Saxonicum*, iii (1893), no. 877), Sawyer no. 552, and a seventeenth-century copy of a charter of Edward the Confessor d. 1050 in Cleopatra E.i. (ptd. Dugdale ii, pp. 536–7 (no. X)), Sawyer no. 1021, contain few names. For a discussion of early charters relating to Cornwall, see *Transactions of the Royal Historical Society*, 5th Series, iii (1953), pp. 101–24.

because there a[re] some Entries made in that language also.[9] With a
particular assurance of my great respect for your Person & Learning,
and a tender of my best services, I remain
> Sir,
>> Your most faithful humble servant

Humfrey Wanley

MS: Bodleian, Ashmole 1817[B], fo. 197. *Date*: 'From Mr Berenclow's in New Street, by
Fetter lane, London. 14 September 1702.' *Address*: 'To Mr Lhwyd Keeper of the Ashmolean Musaeum Oxford.'

89. *To* Samuel Pepys *15 September 1702*

Honorable Sir,
  Some Friends of mine do assure me that Sir John Cotton died at his
Countery-Seat on Saturday last;[1] and do put me upon appearing as
Candidate for the Custody of the Cottonian Library, when the
Trustees in whom it is now invested (who are The Lord Chancellor or
Keeper & the Speaker of the House of Commons for the time being,
Mr Harley the late Speaker, Sir Robert Cotton, Mr Cotton of
Connington, Mr Cotton of Giddin, & Mr Hanbury of the Inner
Temple) shall think fit to chuse a Library keeper.[2]

[9] Wanley p. 289.

---

[1] Cotton had died at Connington Castle, Huntingdon on 12 Sept.

[2] On Cotton's death the Act by which he made over the Library to the nation (12 and
13 William III, c. 7) came into effect and the right and property in the Library descended
to seven trustees—three appointed by the Government and four from the Cotton family.
At this date the official trustees were Sir Nathan Wright (1654–1721), Lord Keeper, Sir
John Holt (1642–1710), Lord Chief Justice, and Robert Harley (1661–1724), Speaker of
the House of Commons. For the family trustees, Sir Robert Cotton, Philip Cotton,
Robert Cotton (later 5th Baronet), and William Hanbury—who eventually managed to
get himself appointed Keeper—see E. Edwards, *Lives of the Founders of the British Museum*
(1870), i, pp. 136–7.
  The original official trustees were Holt, Harley, and Lord Somers (1651–1716), who
was both Lord Chancellor and Lord Keeper. In Apr. 1700 Somers resigned his offices
and a month later Wright succeeded him as Lord Keeper. Wanley seems to have been in
some doubt whether the trusteeship was held in respect of the office of Lord Chancellor
or that of Lord Keeper.
  William III's death in Mar. 1702 resulted in the automatic dissolution of Parliament.
A new one was summoned on 2 July, but did not meet until 20 Oct. There seems to have
been some doubt whether Harley would be Speaker of the new Parliament (see
W. Paterson to Harley d. 6 Aug. 1702, *HMC Portland Papers*, iv, p. 43); but the certainty of
his election seems to have been assured before Wanley wrote this letter (see T. Foley to
Harley d. 1 Sept. 1702, *HMC Portland Papers*, iv, p. 45).

Together with your Favor, upon this Occasion, I would most humbly intreat you, Sir, to learn from Dr Smith (without mentioning me) when the Trustees will meet, whether there will be any Oaths impos'd, whether he himself be resolv'd to Stand, or what else You in your Wisdom shall think fit. As there is no Salary annex'd to this Station, I can safely say that I am not desirous of it for Profits sake; but only, that I might be in a better Capacity of serving my Countrey,[3] which ha's always been the utmost Ambition of

Honorable Sir,
    Your most obliged humble servant
                                        Humfrey Wanley.

MS: British Library, Add. 42711, fo. 46. *Date*: 'London. 15 September 1702.' *Address*: 'To The Honorable Samuel Pepys Esquire, at Clapham.' *Printed*: *A Guide to a Select Exhibition of Cottonian Manuscripts* (Oxford, 1931), pp. 8–9; P. L. Heyworth, 'Thomas Smith, Humfrey Wanley and the Cottonian Library', *TLS*, 31 Aug. 1962, p. 660.

90. *To* Samuel Pepys *25 September 1702*

Honorable Sir,

I have so great and just a Sense of your Favors to me, that I should think my future Life to be wholly spent in your Service, would prove to be too scanty a Recompense. And God know's how sorry I am, that I have no more to Offer you than my bare Thanks, for the continuance your Estimation of me during so many years, and which, upon this Occasion, I find doe's rather Encrease than Decay. I can freely own, Honorable Sir, that Doctor Smith ha's better Pretensions to the Custody of the Cottonian Library than any other Person: and if he would but allow an easy access to it, he should have my Vote, were I any ways concern'd therein. I know, Sir, the long Friendship & Acquaintance that ha's been between you, besides other Considerations, would not decently suffer you to countenance me openly against him, nor can I desire it.[1] 'Tis by the persuasions of my Friends that

[3] For a full account of this affair see P. L. Heyworth in *TLS*, 31 Aug. 1962, p. 660. Pepys's reply is ptd. by Howarth, *Letters*, no. 332; see also Pepys to Wanley d. 24 Sept. 1702, Howarth no. 333, and no. 80 n. 3. For Wanley's earlier hope of procuring the Cotton Library for Oxford, see no. 47.

[1] Pepys wrote back that Smith intended to stand and he felt obliged to support him, but 'Dr. Smith not succeeding, I would neglect noe interest I have in the World to further yours' (Pepys to Wanley d. 24 Sept. 1702, ptd. Howarth, *Letters*, no. 333).

I have went thus far, and I must own that my Inclination to have an uncontrouled Liberty of Searching into the History and Antiquities of our Nation, doe's so far second them; that I could be willing to serve in that place always, without a Salary; and rather, jointly with the Doctor, than not at all.[2]

Had Sir John died the last year, I know I might have relied upon the Favor of Mr Harley, which, If he shall now deny me, I will instantly quit all further Pretensions.[3] But I don't expect to know his Opinion till his Return, which will be in the middle of the next Month. In the mean time, Honorable Sir, be pleas'd to allow me to lay the enclos'd Letter before you and Mr Jackson, since my Acquaintance with Doctor Shadwell is not sufficient to warrant my personal Application to him, in the behalf of Mr Bouchier whose vertues I am not altogether a Stranger to; and whose Fathers (*the Regius Professor of Law*) Kindnesses to me in Oxford, have been many & great. I know that 2 words from You Sir, Madam Skinner, or Mr Jackson (to both whom, I humbly beg my Services may be presented) may induce the Doctor to serve the Young Gentleman, which may prove the best means of spending hereafter a fair Estate, in the course of his Life to [the advantage of] his Country and to the Reputation of his Colledge.[4] And 'tis certain, Sir, that your Endeavors in this Affair will be look'd upon as a particular Act of Kindness by the Master of University College; and more especially by him, who is bound to be, whilst he lives

Honorable Sir,

Your most obliged & devoted humble servant

Humfrey Wanley.

[2] That is, if Smith could be persuaded to resign as Librarian in favour of Wanley, Wanley would undertake to pay him a portion of the salary he would receive. This was Bentley's arrangement when he took over the Royal Libraries in 1694: he agreed to pay James Thynne (who in 1677 had been appointed to the office of Librarian conjointly with his brother Henry Frederick Thynne for the term of their two lives) £100 a year for life out of the salary in exchange for *de facto* control of the libraries, and this reversion was duly sanctioned by Queen Mary.

[3] See no. 80.

[4] In a letter d. 22 Sept. 1702 (ptd. Tanner, *Private Correspondence*, ii, no. 488), William Denison requested Wanley's intercession with Dr John Shadwell (either personally, or via Pepys—who was Shadwell's godfather—or John Jackson, Pepys's nephew) to support James Bouchier of St Alban Hall as a candidate for election to a Fellowship of All Souls in Nov. Shadwell, physician in ordinary to Queen Anne, was also a Fellow of All Souls. Bouchier got his Fellowship and succeeded his father, Thomas Bouchier, both as Regius Professor of Civil Law (1712) and as Principal of St Alban Hall (1723). See no. 91.

MS: Christ Church, Oxford, Evelyn Collection: Original Letters collected by William Upcott. Collectors of Books, I. 1595–1774, art. 53. *Date*: 'New Street. Friday 25. September. 1702.' *Address*: 'To the Honorable Samuel Pepys Esqr at Clapham.'

91. *To* [Samuel Pepys] *30 October 1702*

Honorable Sir,

'Tis with the greatest Shame and Confusion in the World, that I do now appear before you, whom I have so many great Obligations to; whose very kind Letter I have not sooner Answer'd; and whose Letters from Dr Shadwell I have not before Return'd, as I ought to have done. This last failure, I'me so very Conscious of, that I can scarcely have the Face to crave your Pardon for a Fault that I can't, in any wise, forgive in my Self. Yes, Sir, I'me the more Asham'd in regard that tho' I'me no Stranger to that great Exactness of yours (which I have Resolv'd to imitate, for the future, as far as I can) Yet, that even after I might yet have had hopes of obtaining your Pardon, some days have Elapsed before I desir'd it, as I now do, from my very Soul. I need not be told, Honorable Sir, that my Silence for these last days, does seem to Relish of Negligence & Disrespect towards you; for the Atoning for this, (since I know no better way) I will fairly acquaint you how it came to pass, that I have behav'd my self no better.

I did not suppose, Sir, that you would any more want the Doctors Letters, and therefore did take the Liberty (which my late Reflexions have told me I should not have done, with your Leave first Obtain'd) to send them to my worthy Friend,[1] by which He might the better see the Doctors Respect & Value for You & Mr Jackson; as also be convincingly satisfied of the Drs real Intentions to serve his Pupil. I bad him to return them to me, & told him that I thought they ought to acknowledge to You & Mr Jackson, the Favours you have been pleas'd to shew them; as the enclosed Letters from Mr Denison will shew: the First of which desires to Keep Dr Shadwell's (which I, of myself, thought not convenient) and The other Restore's them.

But all this while, Honorable Sir, both before and since, I have been so hurried and fatigued, at home & abroad, that I really have wanted time to write in, (as I have also, for the very taking my Food & Sleep) and thought it not at all decent to send you the Letters, without my

---

[1] Not identified. For the matters referred to see no. 90 n. 4.

Excuses along with them. This my business ha's also prevented me
from sending You & Mr Jackson the humble Services of Mr Keith (a
most worthy friend of Mr Jacksons) & Mr Isted, whom (if you please to
give me leave) I shall wait on to Clapham on Monday next, they
Designing you a Visit, and begging the Opportunity of your Coach at
Lambeth, by 10 a clock that Morning. I will bring your Daille[2] along
with me, and will some time the next Week visit Lambeth Library,
where I shall not forget to compare the Form of Bidding Prayer in
Anthony Harmer with the Original Manuscript.[3]

In the mean time, Be pleas'd, Sir, to accept the Oldest Form of
Bidding Prayer, that I ever met with. 'Tis, as you will see, in Latin, and
I found it in a manuscript in the Bodleian Library (there inscrib'd
Super D. &c. Art. 76).[4] 'Tis one of those very Missals, which Bp
Leofric (who liv'd before & after the Conquest) gave to his new
Cathedral Church of Exeter. 'Tis a thick book, & was written & fill'd
up by a great many different Hands. That part which follow's was
written about 700 years ago (as I judg'd by the Hand) is extant fol. 13
and is in the following words.

Oremus fratres karissimi domini misericordiam pro fratribus ac
sororibus nostris ab oriente usque ad occidentem ut et illi orent pro
nobis unusquisque in diuersis locis per christum dominum nostrum.

Oremus etiam pro unitate aecclesiarum pro infirmis pro debilibus
pro captiuis pro paenitentibus pro laborantibus pro nauigantibus pro
iter agentibus pro elemosinas facientibus pro defunctorum spiritibus et
pro his qui non communicant ut det illis dominus dignam agere
paenitentiam per christum dominum nostrum.

Oremus etiam domini misericordiam pro spiritibus carorum
nostrorum pausantium. ill. ut eis dominus placidum refrigerium tribu-
ere dignetur et in locum quietis ac refrigerii sanctorum suorum inter-
cessione eos transferat per ihesum christum dominum nostrum.

I humbly beg to hear to morrow, whether you will be pleas'd to

---

[2] Perhaps one of the works of Jean Daillé the elder (1594–1670), French Protestant
theologian.

[3] Lambeth MS 216, James and Jenkins, *Descriptive Catalogue*, p. 347; the prayer is at
fo. 111 and was transcribed by Wanley three months later: see no. 96. It is ptd. by
Anthony Harmer [i.e. Henry Wharton] in *A Specimen of Some Errors and Defects in the
History of the Reformation by Gilbert Burnet* (1693), pp. 166–8. Wharton refers to it at p. 68 of
his text.

[4] Bodl. MS Bodley 579 (*SC* 2675), the Leofric Missal, one of three missals known to
have been used in the English church before the Conquest, put together for Leofric,
Bishop of Exeter 1050–72.

forgive the abovemention'd failings, and on Munday to accept of the personal submission of

Honorable Sir,

Your most obliged, & faithful, humble servant

Humfrey Wanley.

MS: Christ Church, Oxford, Evelyn Collection: Original Letters collected by William Upcott. Collectors of Books, I. 1595–1774, art. 54. *Date*: 'London Octob. 30. 1702.'

92. *To* Edward Lhwyd *24 December 1702*

Worthy Sir,

I received your kind Letter, and do give you my very hearty thanks for it, and if there had been any extraordinary occasion, I should have answer'd your Quaeries before this time.

There are no more British Entries *at large* in St Chad's book (as it's call'd) than those I sent you.[1] All the rest are only single Names, of which the most antient are those I sent, and my meaning was, that I did believe those Names to be the most Antient Remains of the British Language *in Writing*, that are now to be found in England.

As for the Gospells written by **Macregol**, the Tradition is, that they did formerly belong to Venerable Bede; they have an interlineary Dano-Saxonic Version, written by two devout Priests the one named **Færmen** who Gloss'd Matthew & part of Mark, the others name was **Owun** who Gloss'd all the Rest.[2] The Book is in the Bodleian Library, kept in a Box, & *Mr Crab*[3] know's it.

I know of a Copie of St Pauls Epistles written in Latin by Venerable Bede himself.[4]

May not Færmen & Owun be British Names?

Sir John Cotton being dead, the Library is Shut up, & as yet no Library-keeper chosen. When one may have access to it, I will copie out that old Charter relating to *Cornwall* for you.[5]

[1] See no. 88.
[2] The Rushworth Gospels, Bodl. MS Auct. D.2.19 (*SC* 3946), *CLA* ii, no. 231, Ker no. 292, Wanley p. 81, written before AD 822.
[3] Joseph Crabb, Under-Keeper of the Bodleian.
[4] Trinity College, Cambridge MS B.10.5, an eighth-century manuscript erroneously ascribed to Bede. M. R. James, *Catalogue of Western Manuscripts at Trinity College, Cambridge*, i (Cambridge, 1900), no. 216, R. A. B. Mynors, *Durham Cathedral Manuscripts* (Oxford, 1939), no. 8, *CLA* ii, no. 133, Ker no. 83, Wanley p. 241. [5] See no. 88 n. 8.

I thank you heartily for your Translation of that Note from St Chads book; and shall be very glad [to][6] have the rest at your leasure.

Altho' I do not understand the Irish or Welsh Languages, yet when I see a book written in either of the[m] I can easily, and at first sight distinguish them: and for the future will not fail to give you notice of such as I shall hereafter light upon.

You know those in both Languages, or Latine scripti litteris Hibernicis, in the Cotton Library.[7]

The 2 MSS. in Gresham Coll. Library, said to be in the Picts Language are both Irish.[8]

At my desire the Arch-bishop of Dublin sent to Dr Charlet a Specimen of *St Columb's Gospels*; by which it appear'd, that that Saint did not write them with his own hand, as was pretended; for it seem'd that the book was not written till about the year 760 or 770.[9]

I have now in my Custody a Psalter belonging to St John's College in Cambridge, written as one said in antient Saxon Letters, with marginal Notes, Glosses, &c. in very small characters by the same hand that wrote the Text. At first sight I found 'em to be Irish Letters; and in one place, 2 or 3 Irish Words. The book seem's to be 800 years old.[10]

I have now also by me 2 Copies of the Gospels each as old as St Chad's; they belong to Durham Church.[11]

I have also other antient MSS. by me older & newer than the above-mention'd; which I take notice of to you, that if your business brings you to Town in any time, you may have a sight & the use of them before I return them.

[6] MS omits 'to'.

[7] Some Cotton manuscripts (or parts of them) in Irish are: Nero A.vii, Titus A.xxv, Vespasian E.ii, Vespasian F.xii, and a fragment of a (late) manuscript burned in 1731—see Cotton Appendix LI. Some in Welsh are: Caligula A.iii, Cleopatra A.xiv, Cleopatra B.v, Domitian viii, Vespasian A.xiv, Vespasian E.xi, Vitellius C.ix.

[8] Probably BL Arundel MSS 313, 333, two medical manuscripts given by Henry Howard, afterwards 12th Duke of Norfolk, to the Royal Society in 1681, purchased by the British Museum in 1831. See no. 47 n. 6.

[9] See no. 69.

[10] St John's College, Cambridge MS C.9, a (?) tenth-century psalter. M. R. James, *Catalogue of Manuscripts in St John's College, Cambridge* (Cambridge, 1913), no. 59.

[11] Durham Cathedral MS. A.II.17. Fos. 2–102, a very incomplete copy of a late seventh- or early eighth-century manuscript of the Gospels (*CLA* ii, no. 149, Mynors, no. 4, Ker no. 105, Wanley p. 298); fos. 103–11, a fragment of Luke from a different manuscript of approximately the same date (*CLA* ii, no. 150, Mynors, no. 3). The two fragments seem to have been bound together since the tenth century or earlier; it is clear from Wanley's catalogue entry that he was aware they came from different manuscripts.

I believe that some time or other I shall be commanded by my Superiors to compose a Compleat Book concerning the Original and Progress of Writing, in divers Countries, particularly in England: and to exhibit Specimens of all the several Hands used in England: at least so far as can be found.[12] This ha's put me upon the Enquiring into the Original of the Saxon Character, and also to look upon what Welsh & Irish Books I could. I can establish nothing certain as yet: but my present Notion (and the more I consider it, the more Reasons I have to confirm it) is, that the English-Saxons, the Welsh & the Irish had their Letters from one Common Fountain, that is from the Romans, or from Rome. I am sensible of the Remains of the Runic Letters amongst the Saxons; and do believe that some knowledge of them might creep in amongst the British; but since it appears that even the Runic Letters are derived from the Roman, That doe's not hinder the Saxon Welsh, & Irish Letters coming from the Roman, as well as the French; German; & Spanish. I would beg the Favor of you to give me your Opinion about this matter, which will be so much the more welcome, in that I am told you have bent your thoughts this way, and I know you have seen more than most men alive.

I have drawn out many Alphabets, Inscriptions & Specimens of the Saxon & Runic hands, which will be publish'd in Dr Hickes's book: and have promised to give him a sort of Series of the Saxon Hands from the 7th to the 11th or 12th Centuries.[13]

I think I have seen in the Phil. Trans. a Letter of Mr Hickes's with some Inscriptions which you found, in Cornwal:[14] Mr Hickes did shew me your Letter about a twelmonth ago, or more: To the best of my Remembrance, one of those Inscriptions was like this **cɪl roron** which you Read *Cil Roron*, and thought it might denote the Flight or Slaughter of the Saxon's there. I did at first read it *Cil Soson*, which may perhaps confirm your Conjecture; and 'tis certain that **r** or ꞃ is a very usual way of writing an S, in the old MSS.

[12] See no. 37 n. 1.
[13] For Wanley's Saxon alphabets, see *Thesaurus*, bk. i, p. 3; for his Saxon hands, see bk. i, plates between pp. 144 and 145, 176 and 177; for runic alphabets and inscriptions see bk. iii, plates between pp. 4 and 5.
[14] The only appropriate letter is 'An Account of some Roman, French, and Irish Inscriptions and Antiquities, lately found in Scotland and Ireland, by Mr Edw. Lluyd, Communicated to the Publisher from Mr John Hicks, of Trewithier in Cornwall', in the *Philosophical Transactions* for Feb. 1700. But there is nothing from Cornwall and the inscription cited by Wanley does not appear. Wanley is clearly speaking from memory and may have in mind something that was in the original letter but was not printed.

Pray, Sir, be pleas'd to excuse this my free way of writing te'e, without any Ceremony or previous Thoughts, since 'tis occasion'd only by the great Regard & Value that I have for you, and that I know you have good Nature enough to excuse a Letter from a man distracted with a great variety & hurry of business, tho' it be not so cautiously or smoothly drawn up.

Yesterday at Gresham College a Gentleman shewed an Irish MS, which the Society refer'd to me to give them some account of next Wednesday.[15] I do not (as I said before) understand the Language, nor do I know any English man besides your self that doe's, and therefore do take the boldness to intreat you to send me (by Mondays post) the English of the following Lines, putting only before them the *no.* of the *fol.* they belong to.[16]

Saturday, 26th. Decb.

I have not had time to finish what I had begun, nor can I put down the first words of the remaining Tracts in this MS. and being unwilling to lose the benefit of a Letter from you by Mondays Post in answer to this;[17] I take my Leave of you for the Present, wishing you a merry Christmass, a happy New Year, continual Health, success in all your learned Studies & other Affairs, & a Long Life, and am sincerely
    Sir
      Your most affectionate faithful humble servant
                           H. Wanley

MS: Bodleian, Ashmole 1817^B, fo. 199. *Date*: 'From Mr Berenclow's in New-Street by Fetter Lane London. 24. Decemb. 1702.' *Address*: 'To Mr Lhwyd Keeper of the Ashmolean Museum in Oxford.'

[15] According to the minutes of the meeting of the Royal Society of 23 Dec. 'an Antient Manuscript formerly Sir Henry Spelmans' introduced by 'Mr Bembde'. Now BL Harley MS 5280, a sixteenth-century manuscript of miscellaneous Irish material, it was still in Bembde's possession nearly twenty years later, according to a note in Wanley's Memorandum Book, 15 May 1721 (ptd. Wanley, *Diary*, p. 432).

[16] Wanley's transcript is omitted.

[17] Lhwyd's reply d. 6 Jan. 1703, ptd. *Life and Letters of Edward Lhwyd*, ed. R. T. Gunther, Early Science in Oxford, XIV (Oxford, 1945), pp. 478–80.

93. *To* Arthur Charlett *2 January 1703*

Honor'd Sir,

I received your kind Letter[1] safe, and should have answer'd it more particularly than I can do now, had the Speaker[2] been in health, to whom I did intend to have taken the Liberty of shewing it, without asking your Previous Consent. I shall suddenly wait on him again, and will not fail to acquaint him with the Respect that you have long had for him, and hope to have a Commission from him to present you with his Services.

I have delayed all this while the giving you an account of the E. of Clarendons Books being in Town;[3] now I can say, that I saw them to

[1] Charlett to Wanley d. 30 Dec. 1702, with Charlett's account of the method of proceeding in the election of David Gregory as Savilian Professor of Astronomy at Oxford in 1691. It is of great interest and worth quoting at length. 'I have not the Honor, to be acquainted with the Speaker, otherwise would relate to him the method, the Rt Honorable Electors chose, at ye Election of Dr Gregory to be Professor of Astronomy. They agreed to send the names of all the Candidates, to all the Eminent Mathematicians of the two Universitys & London viz. Dr Wallis, Sr Charles Scarborough, Mr Newton, Sr Christ. Wren, Mr Flamsted, Dr Bernard. Dr Gregory having the Majority in the Preference was most happily sent to us, at a Time, when the Chief of them was a Present Enemy to Oxford. But the present Master of ye Rolls, being then first Commissioner of the Seals governed that affair, to whom I got Dr Radcliff to offer this Reference as a safe and short Expedient to guide and Determ. theyr Choice'. In such an independent election for the Cotton Librarianship, Wanley's claims might be expected to be recognised, as Charlett goes on to suggest. 'Should any Freind of yours propose among the Governors, to consult the Two Library Keepers of the Two Universitys, the Two Vice Chans the Curators of either Library, the Keeper of the Kings library, or the Possessors of any great or celebrated Studdys, such as Dr Sloane, Bp of Norwich, Mr Pepys, Deane of Cxt Church Dr Wallis &c By any or such like Honest Politick Methods of Tryall and Distinction, Mr Wanly would be most safe in the Opinion of . . .' (Welbeck Wanleyana = BL Loan MS 29/253). But see no. 80; presumably Charlett had forgotten that he had already told Wanley of it.

[2] Robert Harley, one of the official trustees of the Cotton Library.

[3] Presumably those of Henry Hyde (1638–1709), 2nd Earl of Clarendon, who in his own lifetime had to sell off most of his library because of pecuniary difficulties. Clarendon's books are probably those which appear (without attribution) in *Catalogue of the Library of a Person of Honour . . . with near 1000 choice MSS . . . relating to the Estate of England and Ireland . . . among which are about 300 Volumes in Folio of the Rotuli Parliamentorum. To be sold by Christopher Bateman, at the Bible and Crown in Pater-Noster-Row* (n.d., but *List of Catalogues of English Book Sales 1676-1900 now in the British Museum* (1915), p. 23 conjectures [1700?]; A. N. L. Munby and Lenore Coral, *British Book Sale Catalogues 1676-1800: A Union List* (1977), p. 23, Conjecture [1709?]). This appears from a comparison of Wanley's description in this letter with the books listed in the catalogue. In the section *Libri manuscripti* (*Catalogue*, pp. 36–7) only Rotuli Parliamentorum and the journals of the Lords and Commons are listed, but manuscripts are scattered about generously elsewhere—in *Libri in Folio* in particular. Thus, the Persian manuscripts mentioned are probably nos. 584–5 ('Jolestaan, pulcherrime scripta, lingua Persica' and 'Ms. alterum,

day at Mr Bateman's, who will sell the Manuscripts by Auction. They
are not yet put into any Order, but still in Boxes & Bags confus'd with
the Printed Books. However I am of opinion that all the MSS. in
Parchment, and such others as do appertain to *Learning* rather than to
Affairs of *State* or *Business*, might be well secur'd in the Bodleian
Library. I have seen 10 or 12 Arabic & Persian MSS. 3 Greek MSS.
one a very old Book of Homiles of Greg. Nazianzen, Basil, Chrysostom &c. Another, that is a Collection out of Apsyrtus, Hierecles & 9
other authors *de re Veterinaria*, the third a Copie of Thucydides, tis
not old, but however you have nothing of him in the Bodleian, but the
Speeches, in a little Baroc. MS.[4]

I have seen 4 or 5 Registers of Monasteries, &c. they are good &
Valuable.

I have seen some of the Irish MSS. which are still worth the buying:
so far, that if the University do not interpose, I will buy 2 of them for
my own use, let them cost what they will.

lingua Persica'), and the Registers of Monasteries such lots as no. 254 'Antient Charters
and Donations to several Monasteries in England, in English, on Vellum'—all of *Libri in
Folio*; the Thucydides, lot 7 (*Libri in Quarto*). Cf. also lot 252 'Seven Oriental MSS fairly
written ' (*Libri in Quarto*).
      Wanley's account in this letter moved Charlett to consult senior members in
residence, including Hudson, Bodley's Librarian, and all agreed that the manuscripts
should be purchased for the Library by Wanley (Charlett to Wanley d. 4 Jan. 1703; Welbeck Wanleyana = BL Loan MS 29/253). The sale was long delayed—Bagford writing
to Lhwyd on 14 Dec. 1703 reports that Bateman has purchased Clarendon's books and
he will send Lhwyd a catalogue as soon as it is printed (Bodl. MS Ashmole 1814,
fo. 129)—and then the manuscripts were not sold. But a number of the most valuable of
them, the Irish manuscripts mentioned by Wanley here, did finally come to the
Bodleian Library. Originally accumulated by Sir James Ware (1594–1666), Auditor-
General for Ireland 1632, student of Irish history and antiquities, at his death they seem
to have gone to his son Robert, and later (it is not clear how) they found their way into
Hyde's possession, presumably while he was Viceroy of Ireland in 1685–6. In 1692 they
were catalogued by Edmund Gibson as being then in Archbishop Tenison's library at
Westminster (perhaps deposited by Clarendon, who spent much of 1690 and 1691 a
prisoner in the Tower). This catalogue is rptd. in *CMA* II. ii, pp. 3–15. After Clarendon's death in 1709, the manuscripts are found in the possession of James Brydges
(1673–1744), 1st Duke of Chandos. They were dispersed at the Chandos sale in 1747 and
the manuscripts seem to have been shared between Richard Rawlinson, who took most
of the vellum manuscripts, and Robert Pococke, successively Bishop of Ossory and of
Meath, who took chiefly the *collectanea*. Rawlinson's manuscripts came to the Bodleian
at his death in 1755. After Pococke's death in 1765, his share went to the British Museum
in two parts: first, through his cousin Jeremiah Milles, Dean of Exeter, in 1766; second,
in 1767 under Pococke's own bequest (R. Flower, *Catalogue of Irish Manuscripts in the
British Museum*, iii (1953), pp. 11–12). For an earlier attempt by Wanley to get Clarendon's and Ware's manuscripts for the Bodleian, see Charlett to Wanley d. 25 June, 7, 12
July 1700; Welbeck Wanleyana = BL Loan MS 29/253.

      [4] Bodl. MS Barocci 7 (*SC* 7), a fifteenth-century manuscript 'in 4to minimo'.

There are many hundred Volumes of MSS. besides, vizt Treaties, Parliament Rolls, &c. not so proper (as I am of opinion) for the Bodleian Library. If the University give me their Commission (and if my Lords of Clar. & Roch. do not buy them of Mr Bateman, but they be sold by Auction) I will buy for them what they order me to buy; or, if they please, what I, who am upon the spot, shall think worthy to be preserv'd. All this in great hast from

Honor'd Sir,

Your most oblig'd humble servant

H. Wanley

I humbly thank you Sir for Mr Allen, & Mr Readings Almanac.[5] Dr Chamberlayne had no hand in the new [edit]ion. I at first asking wrote something in it, and h[av]e had the Justice done me to have 2 Paragraphs left out in one Place [*five letters lost*] Bodl. Library) & many Erra[ta] printed in others.[6]

---

[5] Thomas Allen (1666–1732), Fellow of University College, Oxford; William Reading (1675–1744), of University College. Charlett had reported that Reading 'having a mind, to imitate Abendana ... has tryd his Skill on an Almanack' (Charlett to Wanley d. 30 Dec. 1702; Welbeck Wanleyana = BL Loan MS 29/253), and later that he had 'taken out all that was curious, whether true or false, of a little Pocket Almanac printed by Bp Fell, in 1673 now very rare to be seen' (Charlett to Wanley d. 11 Jan. 1703; Welbeck Wanleyana = BL Loan MS 29/253).

The first Oxford Almanack, that for 1673, is attributed by F. Madan (*Oxford Books: Oxford Literature 1651–1680*, vol. 3 (Oxford, 1931), no. 2957) to the Revd Maurice Wheeler, a minor Canon of Christ Church and Rector of St Ebbe's. It was too successful for its own good: 20,500 of the bound version (16mo) were ptd., and 15,000 of a folio sheet almanac—which has run in a continuous series to the present day. But the Stationers' Company had a monopoly of almanacs and ptd. twenty or thirty every year. Both the Oxford publications were promptly bought off by the Stationers' Company and presumably destroyed. Madan believes no copy of the sheet almanac for 1673 survives; the bound version is very rare. Isaac Abendana (*c.*1650–1710), the Jewish scholar, pbd. at Oxford 'Jewish Kalendars'—almanacs for the years 1692–9. It intersperses both Jewish material and Oxford University material of the sort today found in the University diary: lists of officers, of colleges and halls, and dates of university terms etc. The almanac for 1703 (here referred to) excludes all the Jewish material and augments the Oxford material with such things as a list of post roads to Oxford from various places in the country, the official tariffs for Oxford carriers and a timetable of departures and arrivals, a list of times at which the various professors read, and much other miscellaneous material, for example the cycle of proctors in the University, lists of benefactors to the University and the Bodleian Library, in addition to such things as a table of regnal years since the Conquest, tables for calculating interest at 6 per cent, and (in the almanac itself) horticultural instructions month by month. At the end of 'A Catalogue of Books printing at the Theater' is 'The Jewish Almanack begun by Abendana, and continued by W. R. U. C. 1703', confirming what Charlett says here.

[6] Wanley refers to the *Angliae Notitiae, or the Present State of England* of Edward Chamberlayne (1663–1703), John Chamberlayne's father. First pbd. in 1669 it had gone

MS: Bodleian, Ballard 13, fo. 111. *Date*: 'London. 2 Jan. 1702.' *Address*: 'To the Reverend Dr Charlett Master of University Colleg[e in] Oxford.'

94. *To* [Robert Harley] [*? January 1703*] [1]

When I ask'd Leave to shew you those Sheets of my Catalogue, that are already Printed, I thought that I should have receiv'd yesterday by the Oxford Coaches some more which are already wrought off; and this is the Reason why I have deferr'd sending till now. I was willing indeed that you should see what is said of the famous Copie of the Gospels in Latin & Saxon, which Mr Selden, Dr Smith & others do speak very largely of;[2] but however, I shall certainly have these Sheets, by that time that you can run over what I now send. Those that are now in the Press, do contain an account of the Saxon Charters extant in that Noble Cartulary of Worcester noted TIB.A.13.[3] (except 3 of them, that I had some doubts about, & would not venture to Print, till I can see the Book again:)[4] and of those Originals, or pretended Originals, that are pasted into the Book AVG.II, or are found in the Drawers,[5] which I have been very free in Censuring, according as I have found occasion. And I do not know, but all these may be actually wrought off, before the Trustees will meet & choose a Keeper for that invaluable Collection.[6]

Sir, By what I now write, it appear's, that I have not described these Saxon MSS. in the Order that they are placed in, for which there was a sufficient Reason; but then, at the End of the Work, I shall bring them & those of other Libraries, into that Order; so that any one may know

through nineteen edns. by 1700. Under the general heading of 'Magnificence of Oxford', the 1700 edn. contains a perfunctory account of the Bodleian (pt. iii, pp. 441-2); the 1702 edn. has a detailed and much expanded version (pt. iii, pp. 449-55), probably Wanley's work.

---

[1] On the verso of p. 1, 'written with Mr Mores Ink. Jan. 26. 1702/3', which approximate date suits the other evidence well enough.

[2] Cotton Nero D.iv, the Lindisfarne Gospels, *CLA* ii, no. 187, Ker no. 165, Wanley p. 250.

[3] Ker no. 190, Wanley p. 254.

[4] No doubt the three left blank (nos. I, III, XVI) in Wanley p. 254.

[5] For Cotton Augustus ii, see Wanley p. 258; for those charters 'In Pixidibus', see p. 263.

[6] See no. 80 n. 3.

where to turn to the account given of any book treated of in the Catalogue.[7]

It happen's that some Latin Treatises are bound up with Saxon Tracts into the same Volume. If so, I think my self at liberty to take notice of it, or to let it alone as I shal think fit. so; pag. 26 I put down a Summons to Convocation, tho' it be all in Latin.[8]

I have never mentioned any of our modern authors to their Disparagement throughout the whole, tho' I have had numberless opportunities of doing so, if I had been willing. For instance, p. 71. I talk of the Saxon Version of Pope Gregories Dialogues.[9] Dr Cave in his Historia Litteraria ascribes this Version to King Ælfred, who only made the Praeface to it. I could have brought very many testimonies to the Contrary, but for brevities sake, content my self with producing only the Authority of Asser, which cannot be question'd, and this without any saucy Reflexion on the Dr on this or any other occasion. So, in the Cotton Library, the first MS. that ha's any thing in the Saxon Language, is IVLIVS.A.2. where Dr Smith shew's us a *Fragmentum Historicum a Creatione Mundi ad tempora Regum Saxonum* & says, In fine agitur de futuro Christi adventu ad Iudicium. This Tract being in Latin, I was thinking to have omitted it, & not to tell all the World that the Dr did not know that it was but a piece of Bede de Temporibus: but at last I thought 'twould to do harm to put down that Title as it is, without mentioning the Doctor.[10] This method I have all along observed, except only in my account of the above-mention'd book of the Gospels.[11] I contradict his and Mabillon's opinion that LVCANVS was *St Lukes* true Name; I thinking that it[12] was only a Latin termination added to LVCA as he is always written in the most Antient Gospels in Bennet College Library, which they enlarged into LVCANVS, as they Made BEDANVS, OFFANVS &c. from Baeda, Offa, &c.

---

[7] Presumably 'Syllabus Bibliothecarum' which stands, in fact, at the end of the Preface.

[8] In Bodl. MS Hatton 113 (*SC* 5210), formerly MS Junius 99. Wanley p. 26.

[9] In his description of Bodl. MS Hatton 76 (*SC* 4125), Wanley p. 71. William Cave's *Scriptorum Ecclesiasticorum Historia Literaria* was pbd. in 2 vols. (1688, 1698).

[10] T. Smith, *Catalogus Librorum Manuscriptorum Bibliothecae Cottonianae* (Oxford, 1696), p. 1. In Wanley's own copy (Bodl. Gough London 54) Smith's entry is deleted and the Bede ascription written in the margin by Wanley. His correction in the *Catalogus* is at p. 183.

[11] i.e. Cotton Nero D.iv. Wanley's dissertation on Luke is in his *Catalogus*, p. 251.

[12] is MS.

I know, Sir, that you will compare this Catalogue, not only with Dr Smiths, but with the Great Cat. Printed at Oxford,[13] & with Dr Hickes's in the first Edition of his Grammars.[14] And do humbly intreat you to believe, that when I am found to differ from them, that I had seen them, but actually having the MS in my hands, I thought it better to put it as it is.

I have putt down the beginning & end of most of the Tracts, especially Homilies, to lett the Reader see which are, and are not the Same, & in order to refer the more certainly to them by Index; a little rough Sketch of which is at the End.

I being Absent from the Press, there are many Typographical Erratas, & other mistakes, some of which I have Corrected, & will endeavor to find out the Rest.

In short, Hon. Sir, I submitt it entirely to your better Judgement: and since you have been pleas'd to allow me to praefix your Name before it,[15] I shall also humbly beg you to give me leave to shew you those particular Sheets, before they go to the Press; It being, as I humbly conceive, very requisite for every Honorable Person to know in what manner his Name is made use of, before it be publish'd to all the World, and an Author's Mistake, tho' well meant, be thereby become unalterable. But this matter is not yet in hast, the Saxon MSS. of the other Public & Private Libraries of England, being first to be described.

Sir, Mr Milward[16] ha's told me of your most kind Reception of him, and that by your Orders he is to attend you on Saturday next. I humbly beg to be admitted likewise with him, not so much for a sight of those Pictures, that you will be pleas'd then to shew him (tho' I am an admirer of Painting) as for the obtaining an Opportunity of half a Quarter of an hour, concerning my other Affairs,[17] which at present do take up all my Thoughts.

I beseech the God of Heaven to reward you for all your great Favors to me, and do assure you, that no man Living can have a juster Sense

---

[13] *CMA*.

[14] 'Catalogus Veterum Librorum Septentrionalium' in Hickes's *Institutiones* (Oxford, 1689), pp. 133–82.

[15] Preface, dedicated to Harley, d. 28 Aug. 1704.

[16] For correspondence between Wanley and Milward, see Welbeck Wanleyana = BL Loan MS 29/256.

[17] Presumably the business of the Keepership of the Cotton Library.

of them than my self, and that I am with all the Sincerity & Respect in the World,

&c.

MS: Welbeck Wanleyana = British Library, Loan 29/258; draft, unsigned.

95. *To* Edward Lhwyd *29 January 1703*

Worthy Sir,

Your last kind Letter not coming by the time that I wish'd it might, about 2 hours before I was to carry the Irish MS to Gresham Coll,[1] I drew up something, to shew them that I was willing to have serv'd them had I been able: which Paper I send you, as you see, & desire you to restore it, the next time that you shall favor me with another of your Learned Letters. I thank you for your Etymologies of the Names of Færmen & Owun, which may also be accounted for by considering them as Saxon. And I doubt not but that several Nations might have Owuns, Owens, or Owins, all mollified from older & Rougher Names. So the Saxon's seem to have taken theirs from *Odin* or *Woden*, and the Irish theirs from *Eugenius*; such sorts of Derivations being usual amongst divers nations.

The Irish MSS. at Gresham Coll.[2] are not very old; written long since the destruction of the Picts, and have many Latin Words in them. I have not yet waited on my Lord of Norwich, but when I do, I will borrow the MS you mention, & send you some of the Irish Notes that are written therein.[3] In the mean time, I send you all the Irish words that are in the old Psalter of St Johns Coll in Cambridge,[4] having strictly turn'd it over for that purpose, & found these that

[1] See no. 92 and n. 15. Lhwyd's reply to the present letter, d. 8 Feb. 1703, is in *Life and Letters of Edward Lhwyd*, ed. R. T. Gunther, Early Science in Oxford, XIV (Oxford, 1945), p. 495.

[2] BL Arundel MSS 313, 333: see no. 47 n. 6.

[3] 'In ye Catalogue of my Ld of Norwich's Manuscripts I find mention of a very ancient Gospel in ye Irish characters which has in the Margin, some Irish Genealogies &c.' (Lhwyd to Wanley d. 21 Sept. 1702, BL Harley MS 3780, fo. 96). Almost certainly Cambridge University Library MS Ii.vi.32, an eighth-/ninth-century (?) manuscript of the Gospels (three of them unfinished). In blank parts of some folios and in some margins is written a small cartulary of Deer, in Gaelic and Latin (twelfth-century). There is a note of Wanley's about it in BL Add. MS 22911, fo. 3.

[4] St John's College, Cambridge MS C.9, M. R. James, *Catalogue of Manuscripts in St John's College, Cambridge* (Cambridge, 1913), no. 59.

follow written by the same hand amongst the Latin explications.[5]
These are all the words that I can find for your turn, tho' I can't
warrant them to be all Irish. The Psalter is about 800 years old, & did
formerly belong to Tho. Wriothesley Earl of Southampton.

I send you also a Note that I transcribed from the End of a MS. in
the Lambeth Library, perhaps the perusal of it may not be ungrateful
to you. I beg you to send it back with the other Paper.

You seem to be of opinion that the Irish had their Letters from the
Britains, & the Saxons from both. My Notion is that all three Nations
had them from the Romans; and the more I consider it, the more
Arguments I find for it: but will not establish any thing as certain, till I
can have as great Demonstration as the Subject is capable of, and that,
at last, I hope to attain to. You are pleas'd to Mention the Monument
of Kadvan K. of North-Wales, this I suppose to be an Epitaph on
Stone, & not to be written in Parchment An. 607. but be it either the
one or the other, a Copie of it will extremely oblige me.[6]

I beg you to send me a Translation of those other Entries into St
Chad's Book, because I would insert them into my Catalogue, with
Honorable mention of your Name.[7] Dr Hickes ha's already printed
them in his Book now in the Press, but (as it seems to me) not without
Typographical Errata, &c.[8]

You was pleas'd to tell me that you had perus'd the Bodleian MS.
mark'd NE. D. 2. 19.[9] I have something to hint to you about it, which

---

[5] The list of Irish words is omitted.

[6] The monument is 'a rude stone above the church door at Lhan Gadwaladr in
Anglesey' p̃td. *Philosophical Transactions*, no. 269 (Feb. 1700), pp. 766 (erroneously 790)–
8. Lhwyd corrects Wanley's belief that the stone is d. 617 (in fact, Wanley writes '607')
and points out that he only said that Cadvan was one of the British commanders at the
Battle of Bangor, which according to the Anglo-Saxon Chronicle was in that year.

[7] See Wanley, *Catalogus*, p. 290.

[8] *Thesaurus*, bk. iv, p. 11: see no. 68.

[9] Bodl. MS Auct. F.4.32 (*SC* 2176), once owned by St Dunstan. It is made up of four
parts, distinct in origin, which come from separate books: (1) a quire of the grammatical
work of Eutyches on the conjugation of the verb (fos. 1–9), of the ninth century; (2) a
homily in OE on the Invention of the Cross (fos. 10–18), second half of the eleventh
century; (3) Wanley's 'Lections of the Scripture', very varied in content, since Henry
Bradshaw (who described it as 'the patriarch of all Welsh Books known') usually
referred to as 'Liber Commonei' or, in the works of Celtic scholars, as 'codex Oxoniensis prior' (fos. 19ʳ–36ᵛ), of the early ninth century; (4) Ovid, *Ars amatoria*, bk. i (fos. 37ʳ–
47ʳ), perhaps of the eighth-/ninth-century. Wanley has from memory inverted arts. 2
and 3. The runic alphabet is on fo. 20ʳ, the paschal table (for 817–32) on fo. 21ʳ. Arts. 3
and 4 contain Welsh glosses. See *Saint Dunstan's Classbook from Glastonbury*, ed. R. W.
Hunt, Umbrae Codicum Occidentalium IV (Amsterdam, 1961). Wanley describes it in
his *Catalogus*, p. 63; Hickes, *Thesaurus*, bk. i, opposite p. 144, has a facsimile of the

perhaps you have not taken notice of. You know that it consist's chiefly
of 4 Tracts, viz. 1. Eutices de discernendis Conjugationibus. 2. the
Lections out of the Scripture, &c. 3 the Saxon Homily. 4 the first Book
of Ovid de arte Amandi. In the 2d & 4th Tracts you find many British
Words Glossing others, & particularly a sort of Runic Alphabet said to
be British, & a Paschal Table from the year 816 (as I remember) which
in all probability was the very year when that Tract was written. Dr
Hickes in the *first* Edition of his Grammars saies that Tract is written
Litteris Hibernicis; in *this*, *Litteris Saxonicis*.[10] But my opinion is that this
whole Tract is *Litteris Cambro-Britannicis*, for these 3 Reasons. I.
because of the Welsh words found therein (and this may countenance
your claim to the Text of the last Tract, since the Saxon & Welsh
Hands differ'd no more from one another, than 2 Copies of the same
Original Picture). II the Alphabet, said to be the Work of a Britain & III
the Hand wherein that part of the Book is written, which appears to be
just like (for I well remember it, tho' I have not seen the book these 3
years) just like, I say, to the Notification that was caused to be Entred
into St Chad's Book, by Gelhi upon his buying it of Cingal, & presenting it to Llandaff church.[11] So that by the former Date, not only the
Natiore of the Hand, but the time of writing it, seems to be pointed at.
But this is not all, I know not but one of the most illustrious Monuments of the old Welsh Church may be extant in that valuable Tract. I
mean those Lections out of the Scriptures in Greek & Latin (the
Greek being in *Latin* as well as in *Latino-Greek* Characters) the Latin
translation of which I take to be part of that antient Version, which the
Western Church us'd before St Hierom corrected it. Of this Old & (I
might say) Primitive Version, all the books are lost, except a Psalter or
two: So that when Flaminius Nobilius took upon him to retrieve it, he
was forced to collect it from the Commentaries of the antient Latin
Fathers, & to supply of himself those Texts which he could not find in
them.[12] You have his Version with the Roman Septuagint, Printed at

portrait of St Dunstan (fo. 1ʳ of the MS), and opposite p. 168 a number of facsimiles
including one of the runic alphabet on fo. 20ʳ.

[10] Hickes, *Institutiones* (1689), p. 149, *Thesaurus*, bk. i, p. 144.

[11] St Chad's Gospels, p. 141 of the manuscript, quoted by Wanley, *Catalogus*, p. 289.
On p. 290 Wanley makes the point he makes here: that the hand of the first 'annotation'
on fol. 71 of the Codex Ceaddae is very like the hand of the notes in Bodl. MS Auct.
F.4.32; but he does not say which bit of Auct. F.4.32.

[12] Wanley refers to *Vetus Testamentum secundum LXX Latine redditum* patched up by
Flaminius Nobilius and others from fragments of the Old Latin version of the Bible.
First ptd. in 1588 at Rome (Darlow and Moule ii,no. 6179) it was rptd. by Johannes

Paris by Morinus, in the Bodl. Libr. with which I intreat you to compare this MS. as also with Hierom, & the Vulgar Latin. I think I need not tell you that the New Testament in this Version is so scarce, that there are no more MSS books of it known, than *Bezas* at Cambrige,[13] containing the Gospels & Acts; *2 MSS of Pauls Epistles* in France (one in the Kings Library, the o[ther] in that of St Germains);[14] and *Lauds Acts of the Apostles*,[15] all which are both in Greek & Latin, as that I recommend You to; and none of them ha's been yet Printed. At the bottom of one of the pages in this same Tract, I found the Note which I then copied & now send you; it being of that Hand that I call the *Running Saxon*, and which w[as] as appears by this Specimen, in use also with the *Britains*, if you will allow that Tract to be written by a *Welsh Hand*, as I do. I beg you to tell me your Thoughts of *Othei Quiri*, which I do not understand.[16] I was thinking of τῷ Θεῷ κυρίῳ corruptly written, but that wont do. It may be they are proper Names, or that *Patre* may be a Proper name (as you know one *Pater* was Bishop of Llandaff) but this you still know best.

The Irish Lexicon printed at Louvain, that you have,[17] I suppose is the same with one that is in *Bibl. Bodl.* You know that there is also a *Catechism* in Irish with an Alphabet, & some directions for Reading that Language.[18] I understand that the Duke of Argyle ha's a MS Grammar & Lexicon for the High-land Irish,[19] and am laying out for the getting you a Sight & the perusal of them: and if the Duke of Gordon[20] ha's any thing that may be serviceable to you, I believe I can procure them.

Morinus in 1628 as part of the authorized reprint of the Sixtine edn. of the Septuagint of 1586 (1587) (Darlow and Moule ii, no. 4674).

[13] Cambridge University Library MS Nn.ii.41, Codex Bezae, fifth-century manuscript of the New Testament in Greek and Latin, *CLA* ii, no. 140. Theodore Beza (1519–1605) acquired it from the loot of the Church of St Irenaeus at Lyons in 1562, and presented it to Cambridge University Library in 1581.

[14] Paris, Bibl. Nat. Grec. MS 107, Codex Claromontanus, fifth-century manuscript of the Epistles in Greek and Latin, *CLA* v, no. 521; Codex Sangermanensis, tenth-century manuscript of the Epistles in Greek and Latin, now at Leningrad, no. XX in [E. Muralt], *Catalogue des Manuscrits Grecs de la Bibliothèque Impériale Publique* (St Petersburg, 1864), where it is ascribed to the seventh century.

[15] Bodl. MS Laud Gr. 35 (*SC* 1119).

[16] i.e. MS Auct. F.4.32. At the foot of fo. 19ᵛ is the inscription: 'Finit opus in domino o thei quiri altisimo meo patre commoneo scriptum simul ac magistro'.

[17] Michael Clergy, *Lexicon Hibernicum* (Louvain, 1643).

[18] Perhaps that of Maelbrighde Hussey ptd. at Louvain, not after 1619. *A Catalogue of the Bradshaw Collection of Irish Books in the University Library Cambridge* (1916), no. 6111.

[19] Not identified. Archibald Campbell († 1703), 1st Duke of Argyll.

[20] George Gordon (1649–1716), 1st Duke of Gordon.

I am acquainted with the Bishop of the Isle of Man;[21] those People speak a sort of Irish, if you have any Queries, &c. I can send them to him, and hope for Answers.

Pray, Sir, let me know how old you take the oldest *Welsh* writing to be that you have seen? You know of the two Latin MSS. in Bibl. Bodl. written in Irish Letters,[22] the reading of which will mightily facilitate the Reading the MSS in the Irish Language. I'me affraid the length of my Letter may displease you, and therefore will at this time only subscribe my Self

Sir

    Your most humble servant

H. Wanley

MS: Bodleian, Ashmole 1817[B], fo. 201. *Date*: 'London 29. January. 1702/3.' *Address*: 'To Mr Lhwyd, Keeper of the Ashmolean Musaeum at Oxford.'

96. *To* Samuel Pepys *3 February 1703*

Honorable Sir,

I return you my humble Thanks for your favors to me since I had the Honor to wait on you last. I have been often ill of late, being troubled with my old Pains in my Head, occasion'd by Colds, but have nevertheless ventur'd to Lambeth, where, in the MS Library, I found the Form of Bidding Prayer Printed by Mr Wharton. I was loth to spoil your Book, and therefore noted down the differences in a piece of Paper, which being about to send you, I thought it might not be so intelligible, as if I transcrib'd the whole, making use of the Corrections in their proper places; which I have accordingly done, and do beg your acceptance of it, with your Pardon for Keeping your Book so long.[1]

In the MS. *Jesus* is always written **Jhu**. I was loth to write it otherwise, as doubting whether our antient English wrote it at length thus *Jhesu*; tho' it may be, that the writing an *h* in that word, might be the occasion of its being pronounced as if written with an J Consonant.

In this MS, as in hundreds of others, two of the Saxon Letters are

---

[21] See no. 3 n. 7.
[22] Probably Bodl. MSS Laud misc. 610 (*SC* 1132), and Laud misc. 615 (*SC* 784).

---

[1] See no. 91 and n. 3. Wanley's transcript is inserted in Pepys's copy of Wharton's book.

retain'd, vizt. ȝ *ge* (written thus ȝ & ᵹ and þ *thorn* (written thus þ). The power of the first was originally as γ of the Greeks, then, as *y* or *ee* pronounced quick, afterwards as *gh* in the middle of words. I thought twas better to retain it in the Enclosed Copie, than[2] to express it by *y* or *g*, as Mr Harmer, or by *z* as many other late Authors led by the authority of the later MSS (where 'tis sometimes put for a *z* or *s*) have done.

As to the þ or *th*, I chose rather to write it as I have done, lest you should think me too superstitious, especially when there could be no mistake in putting it as it is. I only observe, that about the time of the first Printing in England, it was often times made open, thus, ɣ & þ whereby it might either be taken for the *my* **y**, or else (to save charges) they thought it might be well enough signified by the **y**, without making particular Punches & Matrices for it.

Some day the last week, an unknown person left here the Oxford Epinicion[3] with the note that is before the first Page of it. I being acquainted with many Mr Jacksons, & percieving that the backside of the Note did relate to our College, wrote to the Master about it, but receiving no Answer from him, I take the boldness, of my self to present it to Mr Jackson your Nephew, whom I honor much beyond all those of his Name that I know, & do humbly intreat you, Sir, to give it to him.

I remembring your Enquiries after the antient Prizes of things, took notice of two large MSS. in the Lambeth Library being Leiger-books of some Kentish Monastery, & containing only the Accounts of their Expences from the time of K. Henry 3. for some Ages after.[4] I believe many Notices to this Purpose might be Collected from them: tho' as it seem'd to me, that they that gave in the Accounts, did almost in every thing charge the Monastery with more than was really paid; the prices generally running high, considering the time.

The Keeper of the Cotton Library will not be chosen till after the Session is over, by which time, I believe, that my Account of the Saxon MSS. there, will be all printed.[5] I cannot tell where the

---

[2] that MS.

[3] *Epinicion Oxoniense, sive solennis gratulatio ob res feliciter ... gestas a copiis ... reginae Annae* (Oxford, 1702).

[4] Probably Lambeth Palace MSS 1212, 1213, thirteenth-/fourteenth-century manuscripts containing a variety of muniment material relating to Christ Church, Canterbury, including the accounts of various offices. James and Jenkins, *Descriptive Catalogue*, nos. 1212, 1213, Davis nos. 159, 201.   [5] See no. 89.

Choice will fall, but 'tis generally thought, that 'twill not be upon the
Doctor.[6]

Honorable Sir, with my humble services to Madam Skinner & Mr
Jackson,

I remain with all possible respect
Your most humble & dutiful servant

H. Wanley.

Thursday.

MS: Magdalene College, Cambridge, Pepys 992; inserted after p. 166 of A. Harmer
[H. Wharton], *A Specimen of some Errors and Defects in the History of the Reformation of the
Church of England* (1693). *Date*: 'London, Wednesday, Febr. 3. 1702/3.' *Address*: 'To the
Honorable Samuel Pepys Esqr at Clapham.'

97. *To* Robert Harley *29 May 1703*

Honorable Sir,

I presume in Sending this, not only to return you my most hearty
Thanks for all those many & great Favors which you have been pleas'd
to bestow upon me, from time to time; but humbly to present you with
my Thoughts in Writing, concerning the Method to be pursued by the
Inspectors of the Cottonian Library,[1] in Order to their Exhibiting to
Your Honors a Compleat List of all that is contain'd therein.

I am not certain what Method they will go by in this Matter,
whether by one Common Scheme, which seems the best way; or else
every one of them by his own, which may make their Work Irregular,
and not so Useful.

If the Books in the Library were only to have their Leaves
Number'd and to be Compar'd with Dr Smith's Catalogue (as some of
the Inspectors do Apprehend) the work will be at an end, as soon as
they can find all things in their Places, which the Doctor ha's
specified. But I understand your Honors Commands otherwise: it
seem'd to me, as if your Honors could do nothing till you knew justly
the Number & Quality of all that is Vested in You by the Act of

---

[6] T. Smith.

[1] Matthew Hutton (1639–1711), antiquary, Rector of Aynhoe, Northants 1677, John
Anstis, Thomas Smith (the erstwhile Librarian), and Wanley himself. See no. 9

Parliament;[2] and this cann[ot] be known but by correcting the Errors in the Doctors Catalogue (if any such be found) and by supplying all that is *wanting* therein.

Sir, I am fearful that there may arise some difference in Opinion among the Inspectors, as to what is *Wanting* in Dr Smith's Catalogue. The Act of Parliament ha's most judiciously observed one thing vizt *the not Numbering the Leaves of Every Book*: and I shall reckon (till I see Your Honors judge otherwise) the passing over the Particular Charters in the Chartularies, and the particular Letters, Records, &c. in very many other Volumes, to be another great Omission, in that elaborate Work. The Inspectors perhaps may say that twould be intolerable Drudgery to sett down so many Myriads of them as there are but I think this Fatigue is recompensed by the Honor they have to obey your Commands, and by the use this their Labor may be of, to posterity; as long as the Library shall endure; by preventing the *Stealing* of Original Papers, or *Selling* them by a Villanous Library-keeper who might substitute imperfect Copies in place of the Originals deliver'd to him; & by Informing all Parties concern'd, of what is really Contain'd in the Chartularies, who by the Catalogue (if so drawn up & Printed) might easily see, at home, whether they have occasion to Consult them, or not.[3]

But in Order to prevent any disputes upon this Account, & to shew that in Saying what I have now done, and in the enclosed Paper,[4] I do not intend to lay a burden upon the other Gentlemen, & not share in it my self: If your Honors shall think it fit to Order me so to do, I will undertake, and (with Gods Assistance) do my utmost to Compleat Dr Smiths Catalogue.

1. As to those Books which have any thing in them written in
   the Saxon Tongue, or in its Dialects: and these are, about   96.
   A great Number of which, do contain many Tracts that have

---

[2] 'An Act for the better settling and preserving the Library kept in the House at Westminster called Cotton House in the Name and Family of the Cottons for the Benefit of the Publick', 12 and 13 William III c. 7 (1700–1). The Act required the Library-Keeper, within six months of his appointment, to compile a new catalogue of the manuscript collections showing not only titles 'but also the Number of the Pages and Folio's thereunto belonging'.

[3] See the long lists of charters inserted by Wanley at the end of Harley's copy of Smith's catalogue, Bodl. MS Add. D.82.

[4] Wanley's *Proposals* for the Cotton Library, BL Harley MS 7055, fos. 26 (draft), 27 (fair copy).

no relation to these Languages and some of them are *Chartularies*.

2. As to the other Chartularies, which are in number, about   109.
3. As to those Volumes containing the Lives of Saints, which besides those included in the First Article, are in number, about   16
4. As to those Books of Scripture, Rituals, Canons of Councils, &c. not included in the first Article, & are in number, about   23

      ————
      244
      ————

This is above a fourth part of the Library as to the number of Books (which according to Dr Smith, are but about 921 in all) but very much more, if considered by the number of particular Titles to be taken.

Besides this, if the Right Honorable the Trustees do think it fit: I will undertake to sett in Order the *Loose Charters* & *Coins*, according to the enclosed, or any other Method that shall be thought more proper.[5]

MS: British Library, Harley 7055, fo. 25; draft, unfinished? *Date*: '29. May. 1703.' *Address*: 'To Mr Speaker.'

98. *To* Arthur Charlett *1 June 1703*

Honor'd Sir,

This day I saw your Letter to Mr Sare of the 24th of May, wherein you was pleas'd kindly to enquire after my health, which by Dr Sloane's means is so far mended, that I was able to say to the Dr to day, that I feel nothing now, but a little sickness in the Evenings, when my Victuals will rise again in my Stomach; but I was not long since very bad indeed. The Trustees for the Cottonian Library have agreed to meet the 22d Instant, and may then for ought I know, make choise of a Library-keeper; if the Election be then made, the choise, in probability, will fall upon Mr Anstis, who ha's made himself well known to the

---

[5] At the time of the inspection there seems to have been no suggestion of payment, but nine years later Wanley put in a claim for remuneration stating that 'he constantly attended for a month together' at the Library (*Calendar of Treasury Books*, XXVI pt. ii (1954), p. 168). Payment of £60 was authorized 17 Mar. 1712 (*CTB*, XXVI pt. ii, p. 193).

Trustees.[1] Next Saturday Dr Hutton, Dr Smith, Mr Anstis, & my self, in pursuance of a late Order of the Trustees, are to *Inspect the Library, to see what it contain's, and what is Wanting*. Dr Smith is of Opinion that this is only to tell the number of the books: I think that a nice & strict Examination is meant by the Trustees, as it is indeed highly necessary, both in respect of the Publick, & of the Library-keeper, who ever he may be. Accordingly, I have drawn up a Paper for their Lordships perusal,[2] which if it be follow'd, will be sufficient to discover any loss that shall happen, either by Theft, or Change, that is, when an Original is taken, & a Copie put in the room of it: and will be also a Security to the Library-keeper, who otherwise, will be charg'd as having the Custody of Authentic-pieces, & Originals, when many of them are indeed, but Copies or Counterfeits. How this Proposal will be relish'd I do not yet know, but when I do I will take the Liberty of acquainting you, and of assuring you that I am, with due respect

    Honor'd Sir,

      Your most faithful humble servant

                    Humfrey Wanley.

Sir, I humbly beg leave that Mr Denison may send [me] my Tankard, &c.

MS: Bodleian, Ballard 13, fo. 112. *Date*: 'London. 1. June 1703.' *Address*: 'To the Reverend Dr Charlett, Master of University College in Oxford.' *Printed*: P. L. Heyworth, 'Thomas Smith, Humfrey Wanley and the Cottonian Library', *TLS*, 31 August 1962, p. 660 (extract).

99. *To* Arthur Charlett 6[*July*] 1703[1]

Honor'd Sir,

    I humbly thank you for your kind Invitation of me to Oxford,[2] which if my business would permit, I would embrace; but as it is, I cannot

---

[1] The appointment of a Library-Keeper was not finally decided upon until June 1706. William Hanbury, husband of Sir John Cotton's granddaughter by his first marriage and one of the family Trustees of the Library, was the successful candidate. He was thus by a very undesirable plurality both Trustee and Keeper.

[2] i.e. Wanley's proposals in BL Harley MS 7055, fos. 26, 27.

---

[1] That Wanley erroneously wrote 'June' for 'July' is clear from the postmark which is July. This is a reply to Charlett's letter d. 2 July 1703 (Welbeck Wanleyana = BL Loan MS 29/253).   [2] To a College celebration.

now stirr out of Town. I have been 3 times at the Heralds Office,[3] & have been assured by so many Office[r]s there, that there is no such thing as you want: and th[a]t they do believe that the Heralds not assisting at the Sole[m]nity, there could be no such thing entred into their book[s] and Mr Dale[4] said, that he had desired Dr Lloyd[5] to acquaint you from him, that there was no such thing in the Office. Nor can I remember any [such] thing any where else.

I told you, Sir, in my last, that the Trustees would n[ot] come to an Election at their last Meeting, as they did not. They returned us their thanks, and kindly accepte[d] our Report, & the Result of our Inspection, the former of which I drew up, the latter I had transcribed into the Speakers Catalogue. By the Speakers Order I am to Enter the same into two other Catalogues,[6] for my Lord Keeper & my Lord Chief Justice; and am, now, in hopes, that when the Case of the Library is enlarged, & the Keeper Chosen, that 'twill be to my satisfaction. I take the boldness to renew my request that my Tankard may be sent me by the next Waggon, because I have, & have had, very great occasion for it, 'twill be taken as a very great obligation & favor to

Honor'd Sir,

Your most obedient humble Servant

Humfrey Wa[nley.]

MS: Bodleian, Ballard 13, fo. 113. *Date*: '6. June. 1703.' *Address*: 'To the Reverend Dr. Charlett Master of University College Oxford.'

[3] On 13 June Charlett had asked 'whether you have met with any where in any MS any Particular Account of any Royal Procession Thro Oxford, Qu. Eliz. K.J.1st &c?' (Welbeck Wanleyana = BL Loan MS 29/253). On 2 July he asked Wanley 'to examine the Heralds Office in the yeare 1605, when K. James came to Oxford, and the Procession was settled by Garter K of Arms, as Sr W. Wake in his Rex Platonicus tells us, whether the Place of the Mayor and Recorder be there adjusted' (Welbeck Wanleyana = BL Loan MS 29/253). On this dispute between University and City over precedence, see Thwaites to Wanley, 18 Sept. 1702 (BL Harley MS 3781, fo. 216).

[4] Robert Dale (1666–1722), Blanc Lion Pursuivant Extraordinary under Queen Anne (an office extinct since the late eighteenth-century), later (1721) Richmond Herald.

[5] Probably Nathaniel (later Sir Nathaniel) Lloyd (1669–1745), Fellow of All Souls College, Oxford 1689, DCL 1696, Master of Trinity Hall, Cambridge 1710–35, a London advocate, friend and correspondent of Charlett.

[6] i.e. the copies of Smith's official Cotton catalogue (1696), annotated and augmented by Wanley as a result of the inspection of the Library, and presented to the official Trustees. The Lord Keeper's copy is in the library of George III in the British Library (press-mark 125.I.11); the Lord Chief Justice's is BL Add. MS 46911; Harley's own, Bodl. MS Add. D.82.

100. *To* [Robert Harley] *6 July 1703*

Honorable Sir,

I return you all possible Thanks for the great Honor you are pleas'd
to do me, in writing to me with your own hand.[1] I did on Saturday
morning receive 20 Guineas of Mr Bateman[2] for Mr Sturt, and did
immediatly pay him 15 of them, for which I present you with his
receipt herein enclosed, and with his consent, I keep the rest, till the
whole be finished which he promise's to do with all speed. He doe's
desire the use of the Original again,[3] in order to the doing it more
accurately, which I will send for to morrow at noon, and transmit it to
him forthwith.

The greatest Objection to the Charter that I have, is that about the
Character in which it is written; and which (to me) seem's newer than
the Conquest. Those of Dr Hickes are taken from the Expression, and
other such like Circumstances.[4] I am not, Honorable Sir, so pre-
sumptuous as to set up for a Judge, in these nice Matters, wherein
'tis so easy to be mistaken, and do therefore most humbly crave your
Honors pardon, for any forwardness I may have been guilty of, that
may look like a Censure of it. And I shall be most heartily glad, if upon
your examination, who are a most exact Judge in this & all other kinds
of Learning, this Charter shall, at last, be pronounced genuine. Nor
will then, any scruples formerly raised, in the least take away from its
Authority, but rather enhance it & secure it for the future. As to
Ingulfus, I humbly beg leave to observe; that some learned men do not
think the History bearing his Name, or at least a great part of it, to be
his.[5] And many Charters recited in that book are vehemently
suspected as Spurious. One I can mention particularly, viz. the
Foundation Charter of Croyland-Abbey, which was (or seem's to have

---

[1] This is a reply to Harley's letter d. 6 July 1703 (Welbeck Wanleyana = BL Loan
MS 29/255).

[2] Christopher Bateman (*fl.* 1699–1730), bookseller of the Bible and Crown, Pater-
noster Row, the foremost London bookseller of his day.

[3] i.e. the original of the copy of the charter of King Edgar d. 964 (Sawyer no. 731)
owned by Harley and engraved by Sturt for insertion at the end of Hickes's 'Dissertatio
Epistolaris', *Thesaurus*, bk. iv, after p. 159. The charter (d. by Sawyer to the early twelfth
century) is now BL Harley MS 7513.

[4] Hickes's discussion is in *Thesaurus*, bk. iv, pp. 86–7, 152. Expert opinion is almost
unanimous in denouncing it as spurious.

[5] i.e. the spurious Historia Monasteria Croylandensis attributed to the Abbot
Ingulph (1085–1109).

been) taken from a pretended Original now in being, and not much older (if any thing at all) than K. Henry the 2ds time.[6] This joyned to the Errata's observed by you, Honorable Sir, make the inferences gathered from thence, to stand upon a tottering Foundation.

The Letter *K*, I find in the old Saxons Writings of all Ages, and in this Charter, it seem's to me to suit with the rest of the hand. I dare not be positive in my Opinion of its Antiquity, lest I should be mistaken: but, Sir, in the Cottonian Library there are so many Books & Charters, as will very easily determine the Age of it, whatever it be. I shall be proud of the Honor of waiting on you there, at any time, when you shall be pleas'd to make a comparison; and in the mean time, will look out of my old fragments, such pieces of Parchment as will explain my meaning better than I can do by words, and do my self the Honor to shew them to you.

The Gentleman you was pleas'd to order to bring me my Lord Keepers Catalogue, ha's not yet brought it. I humbly thank you, Sir, for your great favor to me therein, and will get it, and my Lord Chief Justices, done with all the Speed I can.[7]

As to the names of the Subscribers,[8] I thought it best, to send you Mr Sturts first Copie, which doe's better represent the Original than any thing that I can do, on a sudden; with the following Transcript of them in common Letters.

Ego Eadgar basileus anglorum & imperator regum gentium cum con[se]nsu principum & archuntorum meorum hanc meam munificentiam signo crucis Christi corroboro.

Ego Ælfthryth regina consensi & signo crucis confirmavi

Ego Dunstan archiepiscopus doruuernensis aecclesiae chri*sti* consensi & subscripsi.

Ego Oscytel archiep*iscopus* eboracensis aecclesiae consensi & subscripsi.

Ego Ælfstan episcopus consensi	Ego Æscwi abbas.
Ego Æthelwold ep*iscopus* cons*ensi*	Ego Osgar abb*as*
Ego Oswald ep*iscopus* c*onsensi*	Ego Ælfstan abb*as*
Ego Osulf ep*iscopus* cons*ensi*	Ego Æthelgar abb*as*
Ego Wynsi ep*iscopus* con*sensi*	Ego Ælfric abb*as*
Ego Wulfric ep*iscopus* con*sensi*	Ego Kineward abb*as*

---

[6] See no. 35 n. 8.   [7] See no. 99 n. 6.
[8] i.e. the witnesses to Edgar's charter.

Ego Ælfere dux.

Ego Brihtnoth dux.

Ego Ordgar dux.

Ego Ælfaeh dux.

Ego Æthelwold dux.

Ego Æthelwine dux.

Ego Brihtferth. minister

Ego Ælfwine. m*inister*

Ego Æthelward. m*inister*

Ego Wulstan. m*inister*

Ego Eanulf. m*inister*

Ego Osulf. m*inister*

Ego Wulstan. m*inister*

Ego Leofwine. m*inister*

Ego Ælfward. m*inister*

Ego Æthelmund m*inister*

Ego Osward. m*inister*

Ego Leofwine. m*inister*

With this, Honorable Sir, I do presume to send you that head of Sir P.P. Reubens drawn with a Pen,[9] which I took the boldness to mention to you, and shall look upon your acceptance of it, as a signal Honor & Favor. It ha's indeed been misused before it came to my hands, but what remains shew's it to have been done by one who was an excellent workman. I beg pardon for the tediousness of this, and with my humble thanks for all the great favors which I have received from you, & with my ardent prayers[10] for the continuance of your Health & Prosperity, I remain with all Submission & Respect

Honorable Sir,

Your most obliged & most dutiful humble servant

Humfrey Wanley.

MS: British Library, Harley 7526, fo. 148. Copy in BL Add. MS 4253, fo. 9. *Date*: '6. July 1703.'

101. *To* John Smith *28 August 1703*

Reverend Sir,

Yesterday in the Evening I received your Commands, which rejoiced me very much, especially when I found my self capable of yielding such Answers to your Queries, as may in some measure prove satisfactory to you.[1] I know not whether you have as yet seen my

---

[9] Not traced.   [10] prays MS.

---

[1] Smith's letter d. 24 Aug. 1703, BL Harley MS 3781, fo. 96.

worthy Friend Mr Elstob, who went hence for the North about 3 weeks ago. I told him that I would do my self the Honor to write to Your self, Sir, and to my Lord of Carlile,[2] by him; but my continual hurry of Business would not permit me to do as I intended. If you have not yet seen him, then this must beg your Pardon for my long silence; if you have, I know he ha's presented my most humble Services te'e, & Thanks for all your great favors, conferr'd on me an utter stranger. But as to your Questions,

1 *Whether I borrowed my Lord of Norwiche's MS of Bede's Ecclesiastical History,*[3] *in order to publish a new Edition of it?* No Sir; I borrowed it, for a week, only to see whether I could find any thing therein which might be proper to be inserted into my Catalogue of Saxon MSS: accordingly I did observe somewhat that I lik'd, and which is printed off, from whence I extract what I here presume to send you.

2. *How I come to know the Age of this book, which Dr Hickes tell's you, from me, is within* TEN *years of Bedes time? and thro' what hands it came to my Lord?* As to the first of these two particulars, I cannot be positive; but yet think there is good reason to conclude that this book was copied (and perhaps, in the Monastery of *Wiremouth*) in the year 737, that is, within *two* years of Bedes time. For it bears that face of Antiquity with it; that at first sight, I judged it to be between 900 & 1000 years old only by the hand: because it agree's, as to the Character (which is, a sort of the *antient, lean, cursory, Sax*[*on*]) with a Copie of Pope Gregories Pastoral, in the Bodlejan Library, which was written by St Willibald whilst he was Deacon (that is, between the years 731 & 740)[4] and it agrees also, with the Hands of divers Original Charters, of that Age, which I have seen. But what I yet more rely on, a short List of the Northumbrian Kings, with some few Chronological Notes, which differ from those at the end of other Copies of this Book, and therefore seem peculiar to this, viz. Anno dxluii. Ida regnare coepit a quo regalis Nordanhymbrorum prosapia originem tenet et xii an*nos* in regno permansit. Post hunc Glappa i an*num*. Adda uiii. Ædilric iiii. Theodric uii. Friduuald ui. Hussa uiii. Ædilfrid xxiiii. Æduini xvii. Osuald uiiii. Osuiu

---

[2] William Nicolson.

[3] Cambridge University Library MS Kk.v.16, early eighth-century manuscript of Bede's Historia Ecclesiastica, the 'Moore Bede'. Formerly owned by John Moore, Bishop of Ely, *CLA* ii, no. 139, Ker no. 25, Wanley p. 287.

[4] Bodl. Laud misc. 263 (*SC* 1000), traditionally ascribed to Willibald and d. to the eighth century, but held by Lowe (*CLA* ii, p. xiii) to be definitely of the ninth century or later.

xxuiii. Ecgfrid xv. Aldfrid xx. Osred xi. Coinred ii. Osric xi. Ceoluulf
uiii. This was the last year of Ceolwlf's reign, and it seems that this
List was drawn up, upon the Resignation of that Prince, & before the
Inauguration of Eadberht his Successor, who is not here named. Bede
could not be the Author of this List, because he died in the year 735,
and the Resignation of Ceolwlf did not destroy the Kingdom, but that
other Princes reigning after him, they would have been mentioned in
this List, if it was written in later times. But the other Chronological
Notes, confirm the time when the above-written List was set down,
they are written in the following words, by the same Antient hand that
wrote the whole book,

Baptizauit Paulinus ante an*nos* cxi. (*vid. Chron. Sax. ad. an.* 626).

Eclipsis an*te* an*nos* lxxiii. (*vid. Chron. Sax. ad an.* 664).

Penda moritur an*te* an*nos* lxxix.

Pugna Ecgfridi an*te* an*nos* lxiii.

Ælfuini ante an*nos* luiii. (vid. Chron. Sax. ad an. 679).

Monasterium aet Uiuraemoda (*i.e. constructum fuit*) an*te* an*nos* lxiiii.
(*vid. Simeon. Dunelm. lib. i. cap. 14*).

Cometae uisae an*te* an*nos* uiii. (*vid. Chron. Sax. ad an.* 729)

Eodem an*te* pat*er* Ecgberct transiuit ad Chr*istu*m (*vid*. Chron. Sax. ad
an. 728).

Angli in Brit*annium* an*te* an*nos* ccxcii. (vid. Bed. Eccles. Hist. lib.
5.cap. 24).

Of these 9 Notes, you see, Sir, that 7 of them are confirmed by the
references adjoined to them. The other two, viz. that of Penda's
Death, & Ecgfrid's Battle, are somewhat obscure. I cannot think this
Penda to be the Mercian King, because the year of his Death doe's not
come right, to this account, but rather some eminent Northumbrian of
the same Name. But the Saxon Chronicle seem's to hint at this Battle
of K. Egfrid (as I remember) at the year 679, if you please to consult the
place. And it seem's unquestionable, that all these concurring in the
year 737, that was the year when these Events were noted down thus at
the End of the Book, in the same manner as at the beginning of our
Almanacs; for otherwise, were they transcribed out of an antienter
book, into this; the whole account must needs be known by the Transcriber to have been false; and tis an hundred to one but he would have
added the Names of the succeeding Kings after Ceolwlf; such annotations I have seen, made by divers hands in other Books, Greek &

Latin, but have no reason to suspect it here, not only because of the
Hand which is as old as the Time pretended to by these Notes: but
because this Book seems to have been, presently after, carried into
France. For the book being (as it seem's) not written by a *Librarius*
for sale, but by a Student for his own use; the Hand is not so elegant,
& plain, as the books written for sale generally were, the Hand is a
kind of Running-hand, with many notes of Abbreviations & Ligatures, the spaces between Word & Word very rare, &c: which when
the book came to be read in France, by some honest man, who was
not used to our English Hand, forced him very often (especially at
the beginning of the book) to supply the Points when wanting, to
divide one Word from another, & to write the Words at length,
where obscured by Contractions & Ligatures. And these Emenda-
tions are in a French Hand[5] of 900 years old; which French hand,
was then (as improved from the Roman) much different from that of
the Saxons, who (as the Irish still do) did then retain what their
Ancestors had learnt from Rome. For a Confirmation of the Antiquity of these Corrections in the French hand; at the end of the
Book (after the notes above said in the Saxon hand and upon the
same leaf) come some imperfect Collections in the French Hand,
some of which begin thus, ITEM EX DECRETIS PAPAE GREGORII IUNIORIS
qui nunc romanam catholicam regit matrem aecclesiam. This
Gregoriu[s] I (who have not the Decretals by me to search) do take
to be Pope Greg. the 2d who was elected A.D. 753. as Greg. the IIId
was Elected A.D. 769. If you will say, Sir, that this *nunc* also, must be
transcribed by a later hand out of an antienter Copie; I should think
it a little strange, to find people in both nations so careless, &c. and
yet this French Hand, compared with other MSS. that have *dates*, &
with Mabillon, is as antient as Carolus Magnus's time. The book
remained in France till after the Peace of Ryswick, when one Mr
Cuningham a Scotch Gentleman (who is about a new Edition of the
Justinian Code, &c.)[6] bought it with many other valuable MSS.
Greek, Latin, &c. at a public Auction, & having brought them all
over, sold them to my Lord of Norwich.

[5] Lowe 'North French'.

[6] Alexander Cunningham (1655?–1730), Professor of Civil Law at Edinburgh from
c.1698 to 1710, and thereafter resident at The Hague. His projected book on the
Pandects was never pbd. Lowe's account of the provenance of this manuscript does not
mention Cunningham; Ker's does.

3. As to your 3d Query, I must confess, Sir, that I have not compared this MS. with those in the Cotton Library, nor indeed could not, the Library being shut up. The oldest of those, is that inscribed TIBERIUS C.3[7] which Mr Whelock used, but whether carefully or not, I cannot tell. I have not his Edition now by me, but do remember, that sometimes he puts down the differing Spelling of a Proper Name, as he found it in this Cotton Book, wherein I think he was not so regular as he might have been. For why should he put down in the Text the Name as corrupted by Posterity, when from this Book, he might have had it as Bede wrote it? Or indeed, why should he make a Modern Copie the Foundation of his Edition, when antienter Copies were to be had, and were even perused by him? This difference in writing Proper Names, between the old & newer Copies, I observed when I had my Lords Book by me: and if I had had time, I would have collected all that were in the book, & have taken a Specimen of the Hand of it, with the Alphabets, &c. You may please, Sir, to observe it a little, by what I have sent you above, as for instance, among the Kings, you find K. *Edwine* written thus in the MS. **Æduini**, and yet this is justified (if I am not much mistaken) by his Coin, in Speed's Chronicle.[8] I have formerly look'd upon the Cotton Book TIB. C. 3. Tis elegantly written by a Book-Writer, and therefore may not possibly be so correct, as my Lords. 'Tis also exceeding antient, & as your Learned Correspondent says, *Bedae fere coœvus*, but if I had both books together, I believe I could tell whether my Lords book[9] is oldest, or about the same age, which otherwise I dare not say; nor whether one Copie be better than the other, since before your kind letter came I had no business to make the comparison.

4. Sir you are pleas'd to ask me whether my Lords book ha's those places in it, which were not translated by K. Ælfred? Yes Sir, they are there, and it ha's likewise the Contents of the Chapters of each book, set down at the beginning of the book, which I do not remember in Whelocks Edition.

---

[7] Presumably in error for Tiberius C.ii, an eighth-century copy of Bede (*CLA* ii, no. 191) used by Wheloc in his edn. of the Historia Ecclesiastica (Cambridge, 1643).

[8] Speed's *History of Great Britaine* (1611), a chronological account of the English kings, displays at the head of each chapter an engraving of the arms and (sometimes) a coin of each monarch. Under Edwin, 'the Great King of Northumberland' (p. 333), no coin is reproduced; but it appears (presumably erroneously) on the facing page under the name of Redwald (p. 332) in the account of whom Edwin figures.

[9] whethe my Lords books MS.

This, Sir, is as plain an Answer as I can give to your Quaeries, which I hope you will be pleased to accept candidly, tho' it is not worded so accuratly as it might be: for my business pressing hard upon me, I cannot have time to read over what I have written. One thing more I take the liberty of acquainting you with; that this Book, confirm's a most ingenious Conjecture of Dr Hickes, who reading over the Saxon Version (or Paraphrase) of Bede, in *Lib*.IV. *Cap*.24. observed the Song of Caedmon, to be in *Verse*, & answering to Bedes *Latin* Words, which made him ghess, that K. Ælfred when he came to that place, did not translate Bede, but put in Caedmons own Words, which were then extant. And from this, he was induced to believe, that the printed book ascribed by Mr Junius, &c. to Caedmon, is not his, but a later composition. So, the Dr ha's printed this Song, in his Grammars now in the Press, mending some faults therein:[10] and I in this MS. upon the same leaf of Parchment with the abovewritten List & Notes, *but before them*, and (I verily think) by the same hand (tho' in lesser characters) was glad to find the same, with Caedmons name to it, in the following words, which being, as the rest, written A.D. 737 I take to be one of the most antient Specimens of our language any where extant. Nu scylun hergan. hefaen ricaes uard. metudaes maecti. end his mod gidanc. uerc uuldur fadur. sue he uundra gihuaes. eci drictin. ora stelidae; He aerist scopa. elda barnum. heben til-hrofe. haleg scepen. tha middun geard. moncynnaes uard. eci dryctin. aefter tiadae. firu[m] foldu. frea allmectig; Primo cantauit Caedmon istud carmen.

These words are thus written in the MS. afte[r] the old Orthography, but I add the distinguishing points which are not in the MS. The Orthography of all living Languages does change in tract of time; and as these said words, would have been differently written 200 years after; so, I have seen some Saxon Homilies of Ælfric as he composed them: and the same transcribed after the Conquest, into the Normanno-Saxon Dialect, the same words written after the then modish manner, & some Phrases changed. I will take care to return you the Books & Charters within a few weeks, and am with all due respect

Reverend Sir,

  Your most obliged humble & obedient servant

              Humfrey Wanley.

MS: Bodleian, Eng. hist. c. 6, fo. 40. *Date*: 'London. 28. August. 1703.' *Address*: 'To the Reverend Dr Smith Prebendary of Durham.'

[10] *Thesaurus*, bk. i, p. 187.

102. *To* [George Hickes?] *7 September 1703*

Honor'd Sir,

I received your kind Letter, and am glad to find that my tarrying in Town till now, is not caus'd by any negligence or failure in me; but that I am obliged to wait for those Recommendations which Mr Speaker was pleas'd to give me hopes of, & Order me to tarry for. I acquainted Mr Nelson with the matter at large, and I doubt not, but he ha's told you, that I had rather have gone than to have continued here so long, as I do. I believe also that such a Journey[1] will contribute towards the establishment of my health which is not so firm as I could wish. I have of late, been grievously afflicted, by turns, with Pains in my left Breast, with Gravel, Giddinesses in my Head, & now for some days with Cholic, which trouble's me at this instant: but all these shall not hinder my Journey, tho' I should fall downright sick, on the way.

As to the Books which you are pleas'd to ask me about, I cannot now tell whence, or from whom, I had it, that A.B. Lauds Acts Apost.[2] came from Germany: but to the best of my remembrance, I read such a thing in one of his Letters to the University, when he borrowed it again of them, after he had given it with many others at the same time. A very great number of the MSS. given by this Prelate, were formerly belonging to the Monasticall & Cathedral Libraries in Germany, & being taken away by the Soldiers of Gustavus Adolphus, were bought up by Thomas Howard Earl of Arundel, who was then in those parts, more of these books are yet in the Arundellian Library at Gresham College;[3] and others at Naworth Castle.[4]

---

[1] Presumably to view D'Ewes's manuscripts: see no. 103.

[2] Bodl. MS Laud Gr. 35 (*SC* 1119), 'Codex Laudianus', sixth-/seventh-century manuscript in Greek and Latin, *CLA* ii, no. 251. Many of the manuscripts from Laud's third donation of 1639 (of which this is one) came from the library of St Kylian's at Würzburg. But H. H. E. Craster (*Bodleian Quarterly Record*, ii (1917–19), pp. 288–90) believes the German provenance unproved and favours an Italian one; Lowe says only 'presumably acquired from the Continent'.

[3] Thomas Howard (1585–1646), 2nd Earl of Arundel, collector and patron of the arts. His printed books were presented by his grandson (at John Evelyn's request) to the Royal Society in 1681 and the manuscripts were divided between the Royal Society and the College of Arms. With one exception, all the manuscripts but the Hebrew and Oriental (which remained with the Royal Society) were transferred to the British Museum in 1831.

Thomas Howard was the only son of Philip, Earl of Arundel, by Anne, daughter of Thomas, Lord Dacre of Gilsland. Naworth in Cumberland came into the Howard family through the marriage of Anne Dacre's youngest sister Elizabeth (whose inherit-

[*See opposite page for n. 3 cont. and n. 4*]

As to Beza's book,[5] it was found at the plundering of the Monastery of St Irenaeus by Lions in France, A.D. 1562 & given by Beza to the Cambridge Library, A.D. 1581. but seems to have been written in a Different Countray from that of Lauds: It seem's also to have been in the hands of some Members of the Greek Church, for a good while after its being written. What I say may seem confused, but may be understood, if you'l suppose it to have been written in some part of Afric, which was in communion with the Latin Church, & where Latin was spoken.[6] These People had need of the Greek Original (like the rest of the Latins): after this, the book seems to have been carried to Egypt or some region thereabouts, where Greek was better understood than Latin. Here the ἀναγνώματα acc[ord]ing to the rites of the Greek Church, seem to have been put down on the Margin, in Letters befitting Coptics writing Greek; with the word Τέλος at the end of the Lections, which at fol. 10,b &c. is written in plain Coptic Letters: and in other parts of the book, there are divers Latin words (particularly at fol. 27) which are written after the same rude manner, as the Latins used to write Greek, & evidently shew that the Scribe was a stranger to the Language. In process of time, the book came to Lions, & divers Leaves being wanting, they seem to have been there restored by a Latin hand, some different from the first. Du Pin & F. Simon[7] say that the Codex Claromontanus in the

---

ance it was) to Lord William Howard. Philip and William Howard were both sons of Thomas, 4th Duke of Norfolk, attainted and executed in 1572; and Anne and Elizabeth Dacre were both stepdaughters of his, by virtue of their mother Elizabeth, widow of Thomas, Lord Dacre of Gilsland, being his third wife.

[4] Wanley's knowledge of Naworth manuscripts presumably derives from the catalogue by Hugh Todd, Canon of Carlisle, in *CMA*, II. i, p. 14, nos. 611–75. It is difficult to know which of these Wanley believes to have derived from 'Monasticall & Cathedral Libraries in Germany'; most have a distinctly English look. Neither is it easy to see how books bought by Thomas Howard got to Naworth. The Naworth library was chiefly accumulated by Lord William Howard (1563–1640)—the 'Belted Will' of Scott's *Lay of the Last Minstrel*—the uncle of Thomas, 2nd Earl of Arundel. It is clear that some of the Naworth manuscripts descended from Lord William Howard to his nephew (e.g. those which are to be found in the Arundel collection in the College of Arms), but there is no evidence of any traffic going the other way. The Naworth manuscripts are now dispersed. Many came into the Harleian Collection on the purchase by Wanley of manuscripts from John Warburton (1689–1759), antiquary and Somerset Herald (1720), on 15 July 1720. See Wanley, *Diary*, under 16 July 1720 (p. 58), where a list is given and the Naworth manuscripts identified where possible.

[5] Cambridge University Library MS Nn.ii.41, 'Codex Bezae', early fifth-century manuscript of the New Testament, *CLA* ii, no. 140.

[6] Lowe (*CLA*): 'a near-East centre most likely'; for Laud Gr. 35, 'probably in Sardinia'.

[7] Louis Ellies Du Pin (1657–1719), French ecclesiastical scholar. 'F. Simon' may be

F.K's Library[8] is the second part of this book, but by what I can gather by a small Specimen I have of it, I cannot be of their mind. I write this to you in some pain, & find my head & Stomack forbids me to write more, but if you shal have any farther Queries, I will willingly do my best to answer them, being most sincerely & with all Respect
Honord Sir,

Your most obliged humble servant

H. Wanley

MS: Bodleian, Eng. hist. c. 6, fo. 42a. *Date*: '7 Sept. 1703.'

103. *To* Robert Harley [*19 October 1703*][1]

[Since][2] you was pleas'd to allow me the Honor of writing to you in Herefordshire, and I have not hitherto done it, Your Honor may very well judge me to be careless, idle, and ingrateful; This, Sir, according to the outward appearance of things. But when I take the Liberty of assuring you that I came up from Suffolk[3] not well; and that I have had a fit of Sickness, & a bruised Leg, by a fall, since then: I hope I shall obtain your Honors pardon; especially, since this is the first day that

Jean-François Simon, the French antiquary, but it seems more likely that Wanley is referring to Richard Simon (1638–1712), a French scholar who wrote extensively about biblical manuscripts: see his *Histoire critique du Vieux Testament* (Rotterdam, 1685).

[8] Paris, Bibl. Nat. Grec. MS 107, fifth century, *CLA* v, no. 521.

<hr>

[1] Postmarked 19 Oct.

[2] A diagonal tear across the folded sheet affects all four pages, removing date, salutation, and much text.

[3] Wanley visited Sir Simonds D'Ewes (*c.*1670–1722), 3rd baronet at Stowlangtoft, Suffolk, between 18 Sept. when he wrote to Sloane in advance of setting out and 13 Oct. when D'Ewes wrote retrospectively of his visit (Welbeck Wanleyana = BL Loan MS 29/254). He must have arrived on 22 Sept., since the great St Matthew's Fair began at Bury St Edmunds on the previous day. The purpose of his journey was to view the library formed by D'Ewes's grandfather (1602–50), 1st baronet and antiquary, described in this letter. Wanley urged Robert Harley to buy it if the money could not be found to purchase it on the nation's behalf (see no. 104), which he did through the agency of Wanley on 4 Oct. 1705 for £450. It is clear from D'Ewes's letters to Wanley that he was throughout kept in ignorance of the identity of the purchaser—Harley is generally referred to as Wanley's 'friend'. D'Ewes's manuscripts now run from Harley 1–600 approximately, with a few exceptions and outliers: see Wright, *Fontes*, under D'Ewes for a full list. On D'Ewes's library see A. G. Watson, *The Library of Sir Simonds D'Ewes* (1966), and for Wanley's negotiations see pp. 56–61, where this letter is in part printed and from which I take most of my identifications of manuscripts.

I set my foot to the Ground, which whilst it lay on a Chair, rendred me incapable of writing.

As bound in Gratitude, I return you, Sir, ten thousand thanks, for the Honor & Favor of your Recommendation to Sir Robert Davers,[4] who is not only a very worthy Gentleman, but (what I especially Love in him) he bears a cordial respect & affection for You. I happen'd to come to Bury at the beginning of the Fair, and He with all his Family being come likewise, I went the next day in his Calash to Stow-hall, having his Letter, & another from my Lady D'ewes[5] (then in Bury) to Sir Symonds. He is a Gentleman very well beloved in his neighbourhood, of great integrity & good humor, 36 years of age, Master of a plentifull Estate, and keep's a very good Table. He knew of my coming before hand, and I having the great Honor to be recommended by Mr Speaker,[6] found an easy admittance into the Library, and had all the Civility in the World shew'd me, during my stay there; which was till the day before I was to take Coach for London; for he would not part with me sooner. [two lines lost] of this Sir Symonds. The [rest of line lost] escaped much better. These compose the Library as 'tis, [rest of line lost] Amongst the Printed books, there is a very good Collection of those that treat of Coins, either Antient or Modern, of the several present Countreys of Europe, as well as of the Greek & Roman. There are also many old English books printed upon, or about the time of the Reformation; many other unlicensed books, or books printed beyond the Seas in English, or Latin, by English men against the Government in those times; Proclamations, &c. And these seem to have been despised by the Plunderers. By what remains of the Prints, they seem to have been once a very valuable Collection, and the same of the Drawings; many very good one's of both sorts still remaining. There are some few more MSS. than are mentioned in the great Catalogue;[7] take them all together, they are of almost all sorts. Here are some in Hebrew, Syriac, Arabic, Persian, &c. with divers Chinese books, all with pompous Titles, and I do believe, were dearly bought of Mr Greaves,[8] who knew how to value the books that he got up, in the East. They are almost all modern, and as I believe not so great rarities, as

---

[4] (1653–1722), 2nd Baronet, of Rougham, Suffolk.
[5] Delarivière D'Ewes. Letters to Wanley from her are in BL Harley MS 3778.
[6] Robert Harley.
[7] CMA. D'Ewes's manuscripts are described in CMA II. i, pp. 385–8.
[8] John Greaves (1602–52), mathematician and orientalist.

when Sir Symonds bought them. There is but one Greek MS, which is modern & imperfect: to the best of my remembrance it contain's a Collection of Passages out of the Fathers, & some Ascetical Writers.[9] Among the other MSS. to my great disappointment, I found that those which were, in particular, magnified by Mr Tyrrel,[10] would not answer. The Latin Bibles are all modern, and of the Vulgate Version, without any curious or different Readings [*four lines lost*] which I trans [*rest of line lost*] Nunnery of Shaftbury, [*rest of line lost* cor]ruptly written) in this I found a [*rest of line lost*] rious one, at the end of his Life; and perhaps, the sa [*rest of line lost*] but whether he lighted upon this, at last, I can't tell. Here are some [*rest of line lost*] story, some old & fair Homily-books, but those that I thought most curious, are [1.A Letter of] the Chapter of Rochester to A.B. Anselm, desiring his Approbation of their Choise of Gundulfus for their Bishop,[11] of whom they give an extraordinary Character. This Letter, tho' not written on a Single page (like that of Waldhere bishop of London in the Cotton-Library)[12] and tho' it want's the Subscriptions mention'd therein; yet I take it to be the Original, & perceive a Leaf to be cut out, wheron they might have been put down. 2. An old Copie of Alcuine's Epistles,[13] wherein A.B. Usher ha's noted that there are almost 80 more than were printed in his time: and I do not know of any newer Edition of Alcuine's Works. 3. A copie of an Astronomical book (I suppose Julius Hyginus, or Aratus) with Cicero's Verses, and some Excerpta out of Felix Capella.[14] There are 2 Copies of this Work in the Cotton-Library,[15] both of 'em antient & beautifull; but in neither respect comparable to this; which seem's to have been written by a French Hand, about 1000 years ago. The Inscriptions in the Constellations are always in Capital Letters, but the V [*four lines lost*] the other 5. [*beg. of line lost*] pose the other 5 are in [*beg. of line lost*] 6 or 700 old writings for them [*beg. of line lost*] mbred & laid in Order, but are now in Confusion. As [*two words lost*], I could find no more books in Parchment, than an imperfect Copie of [Ael]fric's Grammar,[16] and a thin book containing some Medicines against the [D]ead-Palsie, a Narration about St Oswald, &

---

[9] Watson suggests that this is Wanley's (faulty) recollection of BL Harley 263, a sixteenth-century copy of Gregory the Great's Dialogues—one of only two of D'Ewes's Greek manuscripts to be traced.

[10] Presumably James Tyrrel (1642–1718), historical writer.

[11] Not found by Watson.   [12] Cotton Augustus ii, art. 18.

[13] BL Harley MS 208.   [14] BL Harley MS 647.

[15] Cotton Tiberius B.v., arts. 39, 45; Tiberius C.ii.

[16] BL Harley MS 107.

some Laws of the Kings Eadgar & Cnute.[17] He[re] are indeed Transcripts of divers Saxon Charters, from several Chartularies, as of Eynesham, Ramsey,[18] &c. with some Papers of Mr Junius,[19] which he might leave here behind him.

As to the more Modern MSS. here are almost infinite collections, concerning the History, Laws, Customs, &c. of our Nation, about the State of the Abbeys, the Reformation, &c. As well Originals, as Transcripts. Of these, some were written by Sir Symonds, others by his Clerks, who must needs have earn'd vast sums of him.[20] Here are many books and Rolls, about Pedigrees & Matters of Heraldry. Here are bundles of Original Letters of our Kings, Queens, Ministers of State, Nobility, Learned Men, &c. And other bundles [of Le]tters to & from Sir Symonds, relating to Learned Affairs. With a great number of Vo[lumes i]n his own hand, either in Latin, or in Cypher; being, as I suppose, a Diary of his Life.[21]

Here was also a very Numerous Collection of Coins, of all sorts. This ha's been likewise grievously plunder'd. But what it was, appears by a Catalogue of them, which I found by chance in the Library.[22] There are some remaining, but they were lent to Dr Hutchinson[23] when I was there, so that I did not see them.

Among these Books I found a Fragment of John Lydgate's Poems, with Sir Robt Cotton's Name upon it:[24] as also a small Paper-book in Quarto, written by one Malines a Merchant, about Trade & Commerce, with *Robertus Cotton Bruceus*, written upon it.[25] I took (as I thought) a Convenient opportunity, of acquainting Sir Symonds that there were such books in his Library belonging to yours at Westminster, that they were of no value; and that the Honorable Trustees of the Cottonian Library, would take it very kindly of him, and he would make them a very handsome & proper Complement, in presenting them with these two Tracts. He demurr'd upon it, and I would not carry the matter too far, lest he should think I came to be a

[17] BL Harley MS 55.
[18] Eynsham charters in BL Harley MS 258, Ramsey charters in Harley 294, 298, 311, 312.
[19] Not found.
[20] For details of payments see extracts of D'Ewes's accounts ptd. Watson, pp. 249 f. from Harley 7660.
[21] BL Harley MSS 481-4.
[22] BL Harley MSS 254-5.
[23] Francis Hutchinson (1660-1739), perpetual curate of St James's, Bury St Edmunds at this time, Bishop of Down and Connor 1720.
[24] BL Harley MS 525.
[25] BL Harley MS 513.

Spy upon his Library; but I believe, if you are so pleas'd, Sir, they may easily be had, yet; together with another printed book which ha's the same Name upon it. In the Hall, is a great number of Pictures. The Chiefest, is a Whole-Length piece of a Woman, the first of the Family that came over to England.[26] This shew's better to me, than any of Holben's that I ever yet saw. The next is a 3/4 piece of Sir Robert Cotton, very finely done; perhaps by Dobson, for it doe's not seem to be Van-Dyke's.[27] The best of the rest is the old Duke of Buckingham (Villiers) in his Ducal Robes. Some of the rest are good, some indifferent, others not worth Naming; as a Collection of the Heads of the Kings of England, which I suppose to be done from no Originals, and are consequently of no Authority.

I humbly beg your Pardon, Honorable Sir, for the tediousness of this Letter, which that I may not spin out any longer, I will here take my leave, begging of God to prosper you in all your designs, and to send you a good Journey up to Town, when the Public Affairs shall call you hither; and that you would be pleas'd always to Honor me with the continuance of your good Opinion, than which, nothing in this World is so highly priz'd by

Honorable Sir,
> Your most faithful, & most dutiful humble servant
>> Humfrey Wanley.

MS: British Library, Lansdowne 841, fo. 66. *Date*: torn off. *Address*: 'To the Honble Robert Harley Esqr Speaker to the Honble House of Commons, at Brampton-Castle in Hereford-shire.' *Printed*: A. G. Watson, *The Library of Sir Simonds D'Ewes* (1966), pp. 57–8 (extract).

104. *To* [Robert Harley?] *20 November 1703*

Honorable Sir,

I being sensible that the Public Affairs must needs take up the best part of your Time, have thought that 'twould best become me, not to

---

[26] Watson suggests rather Alice Ravenscroft, D'Ewes's great-grandmother.

[27] After the sale of his library, offered by D'Ewes to Wanley (letter d. 12 Nov. 1705, BL Harley MS 3778, fo. 186) and acquired by him in Jan. 1706—see Harley 3778, fo. 188. Wanley still owned it as late as Oct. 1709, when he had hopes of selling it to Lord Weymouth: see Wanley to his wife, 3 Oct. 1709, Welbeck Wanleyana = BL Loan MS 29/258. It seems, in fact, to have passed to Harley rather than to Weymouth—see Watson p. 90 n. 295 for the picture's subsequent and confused history which can be traced down to 1952—but its present whereabouts is unknown.

wait on you so often as I would, but only upon such occasions, as might plead for my boldness. This consideration, Sir, make's me now to acquaint your Honor in writing with what I have particularly to say to you, that I may not take up your time to morrow, when I design to wait on you but may have your opinion in two words.

My chiefest Concern is about the Cottonian Library. I know not what ha's been done by Sir Christopher Wren, since you was pleas'd to shew me the new-made Wooden Case for half the books under *Julius*.[1] I presume now, only to put your Honor in mind (if it be not so order'd already) that since each Shelf is to be as long again as they are now, that it may be convenient to cause a little wooden Block or Stay to be made, which standing upright next after the last book of any shelf not full, will keep them all from falling.

Another thing which I presume to acquaint you with, is, that Sir Symond's D'Ewes being pleas'd to honor me with a particular Kindness & Esteem, I have taken the liberty of enquiring of him whether he will part with his Library.[2] And I find that he is not unwilling to do so, and that at a much easier rate than I could think for. I dare say, that 'twould be a noble addition to the Cottonian Library, perhap's the best that can be had, any where, at present. If your Hono[r] shall judge it impracticable to persuade Her Majesty to buy them for the Cotton Library, in whose Coffers such a Sum as will purchase them, is scarcely perceiveable: Then, Sir, if you shall have a mind of them your self, I will take care that you shall have them cheaper than any other person whatsoever. I know that many have their Eies upon this Collection, but none as yet have ask'd the Price of them: I have ventur'd to do so, and have great Reason to believe, that when ever they are sold, I shall go a good way toward making the bargain. If your Honor shall be willing to buy them (and they will not cost much) 'twil be easy to take such a Catalogue of the whole, as may satisfie you of their worth, tho' you do not see them beforehand, but if you was there your self, you would be much better satisfied. I am desirous of having this Collection in Town, for the Public good, and rather in a Public place than in Private Hands; but of all private Gentlemen's Studies, first yours. I have not spoken to any body, as yet, of this Matter, nor will not, 'till I have your Answer, that you may not

---

[1] An estimate for a room to house the Cottonian collection, laid before Lord Godolphin by Sir Christopher Wren, is in BL Harley MS 6580, art. 77.

[2] See no. 103.

be forestalled. I presume to send the enclosed letter from Dr Osi-ander[3] to (as I am told) one of the K. of Prussia's new Bishops, only as a piece of News, that you may observe the K. of Swedens Inclination as to a toleration of Calvinism, or an union among Protestants. Be pleas'd to pardon my boldness, which only my gratefull Sense of your manifold Favors & Benefits to me ha's caused, and they shall never be forgotten by him who is with all possible respect

Honorable Sir,

Your most dutiful & obedient humble servant

Humfrey Wanley

MS: British Library, Lansdowne 841, fo. 63. *Date*: '20. Nov. 1703.' *Printed*: A. G. Watson, *The Library of Sir Simonds D'Ewes* (1966), p. 56 (extract).

105. *To* George Hickes *10 March 1704*

Honor'd Sir,

I received your kind Letter, and since that, the Papers from Oxford. I am heartily sorry that this book should procure you such uneasiness on all sides, which you shall find entirely taken away on mine.[1] I am upon the finishing the Index (which it seem's is the most wanted) this I will work constantly at, till I have quite done all that they have sent me, & then I shall transcribe it for the Press and you may [here]by rest assured that I will send them the Beginning of it to Print, the very next Post after that which brings up the last Sheets. But I hope they will Print the Index a little faster than they do the Catalogue.

If you will have the Preface done first, it shall be done. But I think the best time for it & the Specimens will be while they print this.

You seem, Sir, not to understand what I wrote te'e about the 5 Guineas. I remember that I told you before, that 'twas Mr Speaker's opinion as well as mine that the Engraver should not have the whole Money till he had wholly finished the Plate. I the[refor]e, when he brought me those Printed Copies which you saw, paid him 15 Guineas (which I received but that very day) & told him that as soon as he had

---

[3] Presumably Johann Osiander (1657–1724), German Protestant theologian and poli-tician.

---

[1] The book is Wanley's *Catalogus*. Hickes's uneasiness at the delay in publication is eloquently expressed in his letter d. 8 Mar. 1704, BL Harley MS 3779, fo. 207.

finished the whole, I would pay him the Rest. His Receipt for the 15 Guineas I gave to the Speaker, who know's all this to be so. I have written to Mr Sturt to engrave the Dedication & amendments according to your last Letter, and did allow him till to morrow-morning to bring home the Plate & Proofs to me. The 5 Guineas have lain by me ever since, untouch'd: if Mr Sturt doe's not do as he ought, I will deliver up the money to you, & speak no more in his behalf.[2] Pray, Sir, be easy and depend upon the dispatch of him who is with all Sincerity & Respect

Reverend Sir,

Your most faithful, humble servant

H. Wanley

MS: Bodleian, Eng. hist. c. 6, fo. 42ᶜ. *Date*: '10. March. 1703/4.' *Address*: 'To the Reverend Dr Hickes. Ormond-street near Red-lion-Fields.'

106. *To* [Erik Benzelius] *28 August 1704*

Honord & Dear Sir, .

When I had the great happiness to enjoy your very instructive Conversation here,[1] you was pleas'd to make me many solemn Promises of a continuance of your Friendship, and that in token thereof you would certainly write to me from Paris whither you was then going, as also from Cologne, before your Return to Upsal. Some years pass'd, before I ever heard of you, from the time of your Departure, and I always heartily lamented your Silence, because I have a real Respect for your Person and all possible Veneration for your Learning & other extraordinary Qualifications. At last Dr Hickes gave me a Letter from you, which mentioned some others which before that you had done me the Honor to write to me, but I received none of those. In this Letter which came to my hands, you was pleas'd to desire me to talk to my good friend Mr Grabe (who will be with me this day) concerning the Greek MS of Philo Judaeus in the Bodleian Library.[2] Mr Grabe & I were both in London at that time, & I have continued here ever since

[2] See no. 100.

[1] See no. 70.

[2] Bodl. MS Selden supra 12 (*SC* 3400). Benzelius had used it at Oxford while working on an edn. of Philo-Judaeus.

your departure from England, being employed in business which requires me to live in Town. Mr Grabe (who is very much your Friend) was extremely sorry that he was not capable of serving you, because of the great hurry which the Publishing of Irenaeus, &c.[3] had brought upon him, but however, he promis'd to write to you about it, which I perceive he ha's not done.

As for my self, I have been all along as busy as Mr Grabe, and have had scarcely time to eat or Sleep, and no time at all, comparatively speaking, for Study.

All that I have been able to do that Way, in so many years Time, ha's been but to finish my Catalogue of Anglo-Saxon MSS, which sometimes my other Affairs would not allow me to take into my hands once in half a year. Some learned men here are pleas'd to like it as it is; but I assure you, Dear Sir, I could have made it much better, if I had had my Time to my self. It will be publish'd the next Term, together with Dr Hickes's larger work, wherein you will find his Dissertatio Epistolaris ad D. Bartholnaeum Shower, to be full of uncommon Learning, relating to the Laws, Customs, &c. of our Saxon Ancestors. In the same book will be likewise Publish'd a Tract of Sir Andrew Fountaine's, concerning the Saxon Coins,[4] and Types of as many could be found in England, being 3 times more in number than those which are already Publish'd, and they will be very well engraven; and perhaps not unacceptable to Mr Elias Brenner & other Learned Gentlemen of your Friends.[5] Dr Hickes send's you his Services, and bad me tell you that he ha's not yet received Stiernhoeck de Iure Suecorum veteri.[6]

Mr Grabe ha's at last undertaken to give us a New Edition of the Septuagint, and labours thereupon, day & night.[7] All his Collations hitherto, he brings to the Standard of the Roman Copie,[8] and I believe that he will, at last, prefer that to the Copie of Aldus Manutius,[9] which

[3] Pbd. 1702.

[4] Sir Andrew Fountaine (1676–1753); of Narford, Norfolk. His 'Numismata Anglo-Saxonica et Danica Illustrata' is ptd. in Hickes, *Thesaurus*, bk. v.

[5] Elias Brenner (1647–1717), author of *Thesaurus Nummorum Sueo-Gothicorum* (Stockholm, 1691). There is an account of his work in Wanley's *Catalogus*, pp. 318–19.

[6] Johan Olofsson Stiernhöök (1596–1675). *De Jure Sveonum et Gothorum Vetusto* (Stockholm, 1672).

[7] Pbd. Oxford, 1707–20. The first part by himself in 1707–9; the rest after his death, from Grabe's transcript.

[8] Codex Vaticanus (MS Vat. gr. 1209), fourth-century manuscript of the Greek Bible.

[9] Pbd. Venice, 1518. Darlow and Moule no. 4594. Apart from the Complutensian Polyglot, this is the *editio princeps* of the complete Bible in Greek, ed. by Andreas Aso-

after many nice observations, seems to be much better than the Roman. The Roman Copie wanting almost the whole book of Genesis, that want Mr Grabe will supply from other most antient Copies. Of all these the chiefest is that which, I believe, you saw in the Cottonian Library;[10] which, if I have any Judgement in such Matters, is older than the Alexandrian MS in her Majesties Royal Library;[11] Older than Vossius's Fragments of the Pentateuch;[12] Older than the Vatican or Roman Copie; and even older than the Emperors Fragments described by Lambecius & Nysselius.[13] If you ask me how old it is? my Answer must be, that I believe it to have been written in the Greater Asia, before the time of Constantine the Great: and as I think I have Reason to say so; so, it seems to me that the Emperors fragments were written since the time of that Christian Emperor, and that the others are not so antient. Among them all, Vossius's MS. is the best Copie as being a part of Origens Version distinguish'd with ✳ & ÷ but this book is exceedingly imperfect, and wants very many Leaves, some few of which are in Thuanus & Colberts Libraries.[14] The Cottonian book of Genesis agrees with Vossius, but now & then give's some Various Lections worthy of Remark. The Alexandrian book is mix'd with other Versions, but still better (in many books of Scripture) than the Roman Copie which Mr Grabe thinks to have been the Κοινή. In short, Dear Sir, Mr Grabe's Design, is truly worthy of himself, which is, to give us the Text after the Κοινή, & also after Origen, together with the ÷ & ∴✳; and as many of the Readings of the Versions of Aquila, Symmachus, & Theodotion,[15] as can be retrieved. For this end he will

---

lanus, Manutius's father-in-law. The Psalter is a reprint of the Aldine Psalter (not later than 1498).

[10] Cotton Otho B.vi, fifth-century manuscript.

[11] Codex Alexandrinus, fifth-century manuscript; BL Royal MS 1.D.v–viii.

[12] Codex Sarravianus, manuscript of the Greek OT probably of the fifth century. There are 130 leaves in the University Library at Leyden (cod. Voss. Graec. Q.8), 22 in the Bibliothèque Nationale at Paris (MS Grec.17), one in the Leningrad Public Library (MS Greek 3 in the Saltykov-Shchedrin Library).

[13] Peter Lambeck (1628–80), the Imperial Librarian, and Daniel von Nessel (1644–1700), his successor in the post. Lambeck's description is in his *Commentariorum de Augustissima Bibliotheca Caesarea Vindobonensi*, 2nd edn. (Vienna, 1766–90), iii, pp. 3–31, Nessel's in his *Catalogus Codicum Manuscriptorum Graecorum Augustissimae Bibliothecae Caesareae Vindobonensis* (Vienna and Nuremberg, 1690), i, pp. 49–102.

[14] The Paris fragment of Codex Sarravianus came to the Royal Library in 1732 with the collection of Jean Baptiste Colbert (1619–83); I am not clear what part of the manuscript was in the library of Jacques Auguste de Thou (1553–1617), dispersed in the eighteenth century.

[See p. 238 for n. 15]

look over all the Fathers Greek & Latine, whose Works can be of use to him, and procure the Readings of most of the best Foreign Copies. In England we have besides the Alexandrian MS. other very antient and good Copies of all parts of the old Testament in Greek, whereof one Copie of the Prophets, about 600 years old, now in the Queens Library,[16] was noted with the ※ & ÷, as you know two Arabick Copies of the Pentateuch, in the Bodleyan Library are.[17] But I tire your patience, Dear Sir, with the recital of these things which you know much better than my self. I will only add this, that out of a very antient Copie of Primasius's Comments on the Apocalypse, which I believe was written 1100 years ago,[18] I have extracted almost all the Old Italic Version of that book, which being compared with the Version of St Hierome publish'd by Martianaeus,[19] shew's as an Original Picture to a Copie.

I have also retrieved a Copie of Ven. Bedae Ecclesiast. Historia Gentis Anglorum, which by many Signs seems to have been written in the year 737, soon after the death of the Author. The Bishop of Norwich ha's bought it, and sent it to Dr John Smith a Praebendary of Durham, who as I did advise will make this antient Copie his Text for a new Edition, which he will give you more correct than any former.[20] There is another Copie of the same work as antient almost as this,[21] but I mention'd this to you, because that in the same hand with that which wrote the Book, is extant that Song of Caedmon in Saxon

---

[15] On these second-century Greek translations of the OT, see F. Kenyon, *Our Bible and the Ancient Manuscripts*, 5th edn. (1958), pp. 103–5.

[16] BL Royal MS 1.B.ii, an early twelfth-century manuscript of the major and minor prophets in Greek.

[17] Probably Bodl. MS Laud Or. 258 (*SC* 446) and Laud Or. 243 (*SC* 445), on which see no. 16.

[18] Bodl. MS Douce 140 (*SC* 21714), a seventh-/eighth-century manuscript, *CLA* ii, no. 237. It was owned in 1697 (*CMA* II. i, no. 7626) by Robert Burscough (1651–1709), Rector of Totnes, Archdeacon of Barnstaple 1703. It was lent by Burscough to Wanley in June 1702; see Burscough to Wanley d. 1, 15 June 1702, BL Harley MS 3778, fos. 1, 3. Burscough's collection of manuscripts was sold to Harley for £40 by Burscough's widow in 1715, but the Primasius was not among them. It had presumably already passed to Walter Clavell of Smedmore, Dorset, and the Middle Temple. The Primasius was acquired by Douce at auction in 1802.

[19] *Sancti Hieronymi Operum*, 5 vols. (Paris, 1693–1706). The Apocalypse appears in vol. i (1693), which is ed. by the Benedictines of St Maur; Martianay edited vols. ii–v (1699 f.).

[20] Cambridge University Library MS Kk.v.16. See no. 101. Smith died in 1715 with less than a quarter of the work through the press; it was completed by his son George Smith, by 1722.

[21] Cotton Tiberius C.ii, an eighth-century copy. *CLA* ii, no. 191.

rendred into Latin by Bede (Lib. IV. Cap. 24.) which I think is the oldest Specimen of our Language that I have yet seen, unless I except some proper names of Persons & Places in some old Diplomata.

The former mention I made of my Catalogue, & this of our Saxon, makes me think of your Runes many specimens of which I have met with in turning over the old MSS. and have accordingly mention'd them in my Catalogue; and some of them will be seen engraven in the Book.[22] Mr Broms the bearer of this Letter, whom I take for an honest, worthy, & a Learned Gentleman,[23] told me the other day, that you have no more books in Sueden, which are written with Runic Letters, than that Fragment publish'd by Mr Perinskiold, and now reprinted by Dr Hickes:[24] I want to know, what that book written with Runick Letters in the Emperors Library does contain; for an English Gentleman who saw it, says there is such a book there.[25] Being upon this Subject, I cannot forbear to acquaint you, that some years ago I found a Tract in the Cottonian Library (omitted in Dr Smiths Catalogue) written in Dano-Saxon Poetry, and describing some Wars between Beowulf a King of the Danes of the Family of the Scyldingi, and some of your Suedish Princes.[26] Pray, Dear Sir, have you any Histories about such a King & such Wars? if you have, be pleas'd to let me have notice of it, for which I will return you hearty Thanks in my next.

You know, Sir, that upon Sir John Cotton's Request, his invaluable Library by a speciall Act of Parliament, was made unalienable, and 7 Trustees appointed to take Care of it for ever, whereof 3 are the Lord High Chancellor or Keeper of the Great Seal; The Lord Chief Justice of the Queens Bench; & the Speaker of the House of Commons; all for the time being: and 4 Gentlemen of the Cotton Family upon any of whose Decease the Heir is to appoint others. But he being displeas'd with the Settling the Library thus on the Publick, ha's hindred matters so, that the Trustees could not yet Elect a Library-keeper, or any ways render it useful to the Public, but by lending out a book now & then, as

[22] For Wanley's references to runes, see *Catalogus*, Index VI, under 'Runicae Litterae' etc.; for engravings, see Hickes, *Thesaurus*, bk. iii, 'Grammaticae Islandicae', plates I–VI, between pp. 4 and 5.
[23] Ingemund Bröms, the author of *Vandalorum in Africa Imperium Graduale Dissertatione Expositum* (Upsala, 1697).
[24] This is the spurious *Historia Hialmari Regis*, actually written by L. Halpap. J. Peringskiold pubd. a facsimile at Stockholm in 1700, and this was rptd. by Hickes, *Thesaurus*, bk. iv, 'Dissertatio Epistolaris', pp. 123–47.
[25] Not identified.
[26] Cotton Vitellius A.xv, fos. 132–201ᵛ Ker no. 216, Wanley, p. 218.

the book of Genesis for Mr Grabe to collate, and the noble book containing the Original Charters of our Saxon Kings which I am now about to borrow of them.[27] Her Majesty ha's offer'd to furnish a Convenient Room about the Parliament house, and at her own Charge to fit up all convenient Apartments for Students, for the Library keeper, &c and to settle an yearly Salary upon the Library-keeper, but this Young Sir John would do nothing, & thus the Library continue's shut up.[28]

I am Dear & Honor'd Sir with all the Respect in the World,

Your most faithfull, & obliged humble servant

Humfrey Wanley.

MS: Uppsala, University Library G:19:1b, fo. 206.[29] *Date*: 'From Mr Berenclow's house, in Duke-street, York-buildings, London. 28.August. 1704.' *Printed*: Ruth C. Wright, 'Letters from Humfrey Wanley to Eric Benzelius and Peter the Great's Librarian', *Durham University Journal*, NS i (1940), pp. 187–92.

107. *To* [Arthur Charlett] *3 July* [*1705*][1]

Reverend & Honor'd Sir,

I return you my hearty Thanks for the Paper you was pleas'd to send me, and for the Notices of books I found therein, amongst which, Mr Tanners, Mr Grabe's and Dr Hudsons Catalogue of the Printed Bodleyan Books,[2] will be very acceptable to me, and I doubt not but[3] he will take care that the Printed Books among *Junius's* & *Lauds* MSS (which are not a few) shall not be forgotten. In reading the Paper, I could not but smile, percieving that my name *Humfrey* which is a Saxon Name, and which I as the Saxons did, do always write with an f, should there be printed with *ph*, as if I knew no better; and yet the

---

[27] Cotton Augustus A.ii.

[28] On the long wrangle over the choice of a new Keeper for the Cotton Library, see *TLS* (1962), p. 660. The Cotton heir was Sir John Cotton (1679–1731), 4th baronet, the donor's grandson.

[29] A rotograph of the original in the collection of Benzelius letters at Linköping, Sweden.

---

[1] See n. 5. below.

[2] The fourth Bodleian Catalogue of ptd. books was pbd. in 1738. Largely the work of Hearne and completed soon after his appointment as Janitor in the Library in 1702, Hudson hoped to pass it off as his own, but was frustrated. On the history of the episode, see Macray, pp. 172, 212–14, and also no. 115.

[3] be MS.

truer & Saxon way should be given to Dr Hody,[4] who never as I know
of, studied the Language. I have some thoughts of collecting all the
pieces & fragments of Scripture which remain in the Saxon Language
into one Volume.[5] Twill be a work of great trouble & pains, and of
some use; but before I go about it, I would willingly know the opinion
of my Friends about it, and of yours Particularly. I have written to Mr
Thwaites for one of his Heptateuchs,[6] for mine never came up hither
from Oxford; bu[t] he not sending it to me, who am (as everybody is in
a new design) in hast, I humbly intreat you, Sir, if you have *two* to let
me have *one*; for which any recompense shall be made. I doubt not but
that the dosen of Mr Whiston's Sermons which I last sent to you, came
safe; and would gladly know what good Effects they have had.[7] I think
to send you a new Account of Charity-Schools in a little time,[8] who am
with all due respect,

    Reverend Sir,
      Your most oblig'd humble servant

                            Humfrey Wanley

The Master

MS: Bodleian, Ballard 13, fo. 115. *Date*: 'Duke-street, 3 July.'

108. *To* [Robert Harley?] *31 October 1706*

In my last I presum'd to acquaint you that I had not, as then, near
finish'd the Reparation of Your Seals, the Multitude of them being

[4] Humphrey Hody (1659–1707), Fellow of Wadham College, Oxford 1685, Regius
Professor of Greek at Oxford 1698.

[5] See Nicolson to Wanley d. 20 Aug. 1705 (ptd. *Letters . . . to and from W. Nicolson*, ed.
J. Nichols (1809), ii, no. 322, pp. 650–2), for comments on Wanley's plan to publish scriptural pieces in OE. See Hearne, *Collections*, i, pp. 43–4, for evidence that in Sept. 1705
Wanley was asking to borrow manuscripts from the Bodleian for an edn. of the Bible in
Saxon he was undertaking. Wanley's collection (never completed) is now BL Harley MS
4964; extracts by Henry Ellis are in Cambridge University Library Addit. MS 4481, fos.
37–48. Wanley had first mooted the idea (as proper for E. Thwaites rather than himself)
ten years earlier: see no. 5.   [6] *Heptateuchus Anglo-Saxonice* (Oxford, 1698).

[7] William Whiston (1667–1752), mathematician and theologian. He succeeded
Newton in the Lucasian Professorship in 1703, but was deprived of it and banished from
the university in 1710 for eccentric theological opinions, which he augmented and continued to propagate until his death.

[8] 'An Account of the Methods whereby the Charity-Schools have been Erected and
Managed. And of the Encouragement given to them' (1704), with (p. 4) a list of places
where schools are already established (Bodl. press-mark R.1.19. Jur. (16)).

very great. I have not protracted or lost any time from them since, and yet I have not done; but by what Remains, I ghess that all the good I can do them, will be at an end by Wednesday next. I am really grieved at the Havock which ha's been made with those which are now Irreparable, and more especially when from those which remain, I am convinced that our Ancestors for many Ages together, were not so rough & unpolish'd as some think, but rather Men of Curiosity, Lovers & Judges, & consequently Encouragers of Good Workmanship. I do not say that the Antient Seal-Cutters could Draw altogether so Correctly, or did so well understand the Symmetry of an Humane Figure, as the Best of our Moderns do; but then their Work is generally Bolder, a greater Relievo, and oftentimes a Better Air.

In this Great Treasure of Seals very many are Particularly Curious, and deserve to [be] exhibited in Print, not only for the goodness of the Workmanship, or because they are *adhuc inedita*, but because the world may from them see the fashions or Habits of Different Ages, the Devises & Arms of Honorable Families, Sees, Monasteries, &c. Not to mention the Commemoration of some Great Actions, whereof your Honor has observed Instances In them. Besides, many of these Seals, are Impressions from Antiquities, some of Grecian, but mostly of Roman Workmanship, which I suppose were found & putt into Rings used by Curious Persons, & are Capable of making a good Addition to the last Edition of Gorlaeus's Dactyliotheca.[1] But above all, I most admire, a large Round Seal Counte[r]sealed with the Proper Inscriptions, and a third Epigraphe upon the Edge, just as on our Crowns or Half-Crown-pieces. I never saw but that one of the kind, and tis several Centuries of years old. We have had much Rain; I pray God send Your Honor Y[our] Lady, & the young Ladies [a] Good Journey up, being,

MS: British Library, Lansdowne 841, fo. 73; draft, unsigned. *Date*: '31 Octob. 1706.'

---

[1] Abraham van Goorle, *Dactyliotheca seu annulorum sigillarium quorum apud priscos tam Graecos quam Romanos usus promptuarium* (Leiden, 1695).

109. *To* John Strype[1] *14 January 1707*

Reverend Sir,

I received your very kind & Instructive Letter[2] concerning the different Editions of our old English Bibles, for which great favor I return you my most hearty Thanks. And so much the rather, because comparing it with divers of the books themselves, I find it, for the most part, agreable to them. I have augmented my Stock, a little farther since you saw it, by the Acquisition of some more Bibles & Testaments, which are Exceedingly scarce, and not mentioned by you in that Ingenious Letter, nor by any other that I know of: And I expect to get more soon.

Mr Secretary[3] is extremely hurried during this Parliament time, so that I have not had an Opportunity of making known your Request[4] to Him as yet. But I will do it, & send you the Result. I Believe, you may promise your self from his Courtesie & Candor, all the Liberty you can desire in perusing & transcribing his old Papers, and you may be sure I shall not forget you.

And I must request the performance of that Favor you was pleas'd to promise me, namely the Loan of your 3 old Bibles, vizt that of 1537, that of Matth. Parker of 1572, & that which you ghess to be of 1549 (but, as I believe, of 1551:)[5] I will willingly pay the Carriage & Portage of them backwards & forwards; and do intreat you not to deny, what will so extremly oblige me to be, Reverend Sir,

Your most humble servant

Humfrey Wanley.

MS: Cambridge University Library, Additional 6, fo. 524. Copy in BL Add. MS 5853, fo. 79. *Date*: 'Duke-street, York-buildings, Westminster, 14 Janry, 1706.' *Address*: 'To

[1] John Strype (1643–1737), ecclesiastical historian and biographer, perpetual curate of Low Leyton, Essex, 1669.

[2] 2 Dec. 1706, BL Harley MS 3781, fo. 121.

[3] Robert Harley: he was Secretary of State for the Northern Department, 18 May 1704–Feb. 1708. Wanley did not resign as Secretary of the SPCK until June 1708, but he was clearly unofficial library-keeper to Harley for some time before that.

[4] To examine the manuscripts of John Stowe (1525?–1605), chronicler and antiquary, whose historical collections had come to Harley with D'Ewes's library. See Wright, *Fontes*, under Stowe for a list.

[5] From the account given by Strype in his letter of 2 Dec. 1706: (1) 1537 = the 1st edn. of 'Matthew's version', Darlow and Moule no. 34, *STC* 2066; (2) 1572 = the 'Bishops' Bible', 2nd folio edn., Darlow and Moule no. 132, *STC* 2107; (3) 1549 = the folio edn. ptd. by John Day, Darlow and Moule no. 74, *STC* 2077. Strype never sent them.

The Reverend Mr Strype Rector of Low-Leyton in Essex.' *Endorsed*: 'Mr Wanley Secretary harlies library' by Strype.

110. *To* Hans Sloane *6 May 1707*

Sir,

I remember that some time ago I have heard You & several other Gentlemen speak of Mr Bagfords Design of giving the World a New History of Printing, vizt of the Original of the Art, & of the Progress of it throughout Europe, &c.[1] Since then I have seen Mr Bagford's Collection,[2] of which I thought an Account would not be unacceptable to you; but since my business will not presently permitt me to wait on you in person, I take the liberty of sending this with my humble Services to you.

His Collection consist's chiefly of *Title-Pages* & other *Fragments* putt together into Books, many of them in some sort of Order & Method, & others not. *Ex. gr.*

In one Volume there are Specimens of *Letters* of all Sorts, as well those used in foreign Countreys, as in England.

In another are Titles and Fragments of Almanacks from A.D. 1537 downwards; with Titles of *Bibles*, Law books &c. Printed by the *Company of Stationers* in *London*.

In Other Volumes are The Titles of Books of all Kinds printed by the *London Printers*, disposed into some sort of Order, vizt as to the Subject of the Book, or dwelling-place of the Printer.

In others, are Title-pages of Books printed in *Oxford* & *Cambridge*.

In others, Title-pages of those printed in *Scotland* & *Ireland*.

Title-pages & Frontispieces, with other Specimens of the Works of our *English Engravers*.

[1] Ptd. with unimportant verbal differences as the first part of a paper, 'An Essay on the Invention of Printing, by Mr John Bagford; with an Account of his Collections for the same, by Mr Humfrey Wanley, F.R.S. Communicated in two Letters to Dr Hans Sloane, R.S. Secr.' in *Philosophical Transactions*, no. 310 (Apr.–June 1707), pp. 2397–410. Wanley may have been responsible for Bagford's 'Essay' as well as his own 'Account': T. F. Dibdin refers to it (*Bibliomania* (1876), p. 326) as 'the slender Memorial of Printing . . . drawn up by Wanley for Bagford'. Dibdin quotes no authority for this statement, but it probably derives from William Oldys in his life of Caxton, *Bibliographica Britannica*, II (1748), p. 1230 n'. Two drafts of the beginning of Bagford's 'Essay' are in Bodl. MS Tanner 453, fos. 1–4, 6–11; they are not in Bagford's hand, but the second is corrected by him.

[2] Now BL Harley MSS 5892–5998, and perhaps Harley 7580; outliers are Bodl. MSS Tanner 453 and Rawl. D.396, fos. 1–83.

Titles of Books Printed by *Roman Catholics*, *Presbyterians*, *Quakers*, by other *Sectaries*, by *Seditious persons* &c.

Cutts of *Monuments*, *Tombs*, *Funeralls*, &c. in *England*.

Cutts of the same in Foreign parts, with Cutts of the Manner of *Executing Criminals*.

Cutts with some Drawings of Habits of diverse Nations, of several Trades, of *Utensils*, *Weapons*, *Fountains*, or *Wells*, with other Prints useful in *Joyners* & *Masons* Work.

Cutts of figures in different Postures as *Writing*, *Reading*, *Meditation*, with all the *Utensils* used in Writing &c. during some Ages. Cutts of *Schools*. The *Heads* of some *Arithmeticians*; *Alphabets*; Specimens of *Knott-work*, & some *Great Text* & other Letters. Specimens of *Letter-Graving*. *Heads* of Writing Masters, *Dutch*, *French*, *English*. Specimens of Letters Engraven in *Small*; as also of *Short-Hand*, &c. Heads of *Shorthand* Writers, & Specimens of their Works, & many other things.

Title-pages of *Books* & *Printers Devices* Printing in the *Spanish Netherlands*, *Spain* & *Portugal*; Titles of Books published by *English Catholics*, Alphabets of *Plantine Letter*, &c.

Title-pages, *Alphabets*, & *Printers Devices* used in *Basil*, *Zurick*, & other places in *Switzerland*.

The like for the *United Netherlands*.

The like for *France*.

The like for *Germany*, with some others of *Poland*, *Switzerland*, *Denmark*, *Bohemia*, & *France*.

The like for *Italy*, with some others of Geneva, Sicily, &c.

Collection of *Acts of Parliament*, *Ordonances*, *Proclamations*, &c. *Regulating Printing*; with many other Papers.

Proposals for Printing particular Books.

Catalogues of Books, relating to Painting, Printing, &c. Specimens of Paper differently Coloured—*Marks* on the Outsides of Reams of Paper; with *Orders*, *Cases*, *Reasons*, &c. relating to the *Manufacture*.

Old *Prints* or *Cutts* from A.D. 1467 with the *Effigies* & *Devices* of many Printers *Foreigners* & *English*, with othe[r] *Cutts* & Speecimens of *Paper*, &c.

Collection of *Epitaphs* of the *Printers* in *Basil*; with the *Life of John Froben*; Catalogues of Books &c.

Collections relating to the Lives of the *Engravers* of divers Countreys.

Titles of Books Printed in most Parts of Europe, before the year 1500.

Collection of *Patents* for Printing *Law-books*, &c.

Some German Cards.

With many other Volumes of Collections of the kinds above-mentioned, tho' not so well sorted.

And these Title-Pages of Books are really useful, upon many Accounts, vizt as being Authentic & exact, when as in most Catalogues, the Titles are abbreviated & otherways imperfect. Besides, these Titles informed me of many Books I had never heard of before; and from them I have been enabled to enquire for several Books, some of which I have since procured to my great Satisfaction. And it is my Opinion, that there are but few Curious men, but upon the View of this Collection, will own they have mett with many *pieces*, in their several ways, which they knew not of Before. And thus we see, that a single Leaf of Paper, tho' not valuable in its self, when come to be part of a Collection may be of good use many ways; as either in respect of the *Matter* it Treat's of, in respect of the *Mark of the Paper, of the Date, Printers Name, Countrey, Title, Faculty, &c.*

Mr Bagford ha's also a very plentiful Collection of the Titles of Books remarkable & Curious, which he ha's taken from the Books themselves. And when they are of such sorts, as now are seldome to be seen compleat, he ha's made such observations, as that the several Editions shall be certainly known, tho' your book be Imperfect at Beginning & End.

Mr Bagford also says, that tho' his Collection is not putt into exact Order, that nevertheless his Book or *History of Printing* shall be drawn up with that Regularity, as shall answer any Gentlemans Desire & Expectation.[3]

I hope you will excuse the Trouble of this, and continue to believe that I am most sincerely

Honor'd Sir,

Your most humble & most obliged Servant

Humfrey Wanley.

---

[3] Bagford went so far as issuing a formal printed prospectus, 'Proposals for Printing an Historical Account, of that most Universally Celebrated, as well as Useful Art of Typography', which exists in two edns. Copies of the first edn. are in Bodl. MSS Tanner 470, fos. 284–5, Rawl. D.399, fos. 1–2 (and in a volume with Bodl. press-mark L.1.16.Jur., pp. 5–6) and there are three copies in BL Harley MS 5995, fos. 250–5; a copy of the second edn. is in Bodl. MS Rawl. D.375, fos. 87a–d. The *History* never appeared although as late as Feb. 1714 Bagford still resolved to go on with it: see Hearne, *Collections*, iv, pp. 307–8.

MS: British Library, Sloane 4040, fo. 355. *Date*: 'Duke-street, York-buildings, 6 May, 1707.' *Address*: 'To The Honor'd Dr Hans Sloane at Gresham College in Bishop-street.' *Printed*: *Philosophical Transactions*, no. 310 (Apr.–June 1707), pp. 2407–10; Nichols, *Literary Anecdotes*, i, pp. 532–6.

III. *To* John Strype *14 May 1707*

Reverend Sir,

I return you my most hearty Thanks for your kind Letter,[1] and Invitation to your house. I have in my Collection (which is encreased since you saw it) three Copies of the New Testament Printed by Jugg and Inscribed to K.E.6.[2] but none of them are perfect; and therefore I desire you would be pleas'd to buy that Book for me, and I will honestly repay you whatever it shall cost. If you're loth to venture your Bibles hither, I will be sure to wait on you some time this Somer at Layton; and when I do, I hope I shall want to buy not above one, or two of them at most. I have got an imperfect one of 1537; with divers others that are not mentioned in your former Letter:[3] and to day (with Marbeck's Concordance)[4] I bought W. Tindals Pentateuch, with large Prefaces to each book, Printed A.D. 1534, in 8vo.

Mr Secretary Harley ha's bought the Manuscripts of the late Bishop Stillingfleet's Library, wherein are divers things, I believe, in your way. When you are desirous of perusing J. Stow's books, &c. upon letting me know, I believe I can easily procure you all the Liberty you can desire; for I am, sincerely,

 Reverend Sir,

  Your most humble servant,

      Humfrey Wanley.

MS: Cambridge University Library, Additional 6, fo. 522. *Date*: 'Duke-street, York buildings 14 May 1707.' *Address*: 'To The Reverend Mr Strype Rector of Low-Layton in Essex.'

[1] 13 May 1707, BL Harley MS 3781, fo. 123.
[2] Jugge's revision of Tyndale's version of the NT, undated but almost certainly 1552 (Darlow and Moule no. 99, *STC* 2867).   [3] 2 Dec. 1706, BL Harley MS 3781, fo. 121.
[4] (1550), *STC* 17300, and the 2nd edn. of Tyndale's Pentateuch, Darlow and Moule no. 8, *STC* 2351.

112. *To* John Strype *10 June 1708*

Reverend Sir,

I perceive by yours that the Letter[1] I wrote to you since Mr Harley's going into the Countrey did not come to your Hands, for which I am very Sorry. I did not write it presently, because I heard it would be a Fortnight before he should arrive at Brampton-Castle,[2] and perhaps there might happen some Occasion of writing to him about your Affair; and then a speedy Answer would be necessary. But the Subject of mine, was to acquaint you, that Mr Harley after having perus'd the Account you have drawn up, as to those Books;[3] and after finding that so great parts of them have been Printed, as there are; is nevertheless willing to give you thirty pounds for them, which is a great sum of money for Ten Books, in this time of Scarcity. You know, Sir, at this Rate you are a very considerable gainer, you have had the use of these Books, and can never hope for a Better Chapman. If you oblige him in this matter, you will find him your Customer for other things, you shall think fit to part to part with. Be pleas'd to let me have your Answer, or rather to bring the books with you, and the Money shall be ready. I am

Reverend Sir,

Your most humble servant

H. Wanley.

MS: Cambridge University Library, Additional 6, fo. 577. *Date*: 'York-buildings, 10. June, 1708.' *Address*: 'To The Reverend Mr Strype Rector of Low-Layton in Essex.'

113. *To* John Strype *8 July 1708*

Reverend Sir,

I received your Letter, and had written a speedy Answer to you, had not I been visited with a great Calamity, at the same time. My poor

---

[1] 7 June 1708, BL Harley MS 3781, fo. 125.

[2] The Harley seat at Brampton-Bryan in Herefordshire, ten miles west of Ludlow. Robert Harley is buried in the parish church there.

[3] Presumably an account of the papers of John Foxe (1516–87), the martyrologist (as appears from Strype to Wanley d. 23 Sept. 1708, BL Harley MS 3781, fo. 137), which were on offer to Harley. Foxe's papers passed to Sir Richard Willis on his marriage in about 1658 to Alice Foxe, only child of Foxe's grandson, Thomas. They were lent to Strype by their son, Sir Thomas Foxe Willys, shortly before he died, a lunatic, in 1701. Eleven manuscripts were finally bought for 40 guineas (Wanley to Strype, 25 July 1708) and these are probably BL Harley MSS 416–26 (Wanley, *Diary*, p. xxi).

Wife[1] ha's had a grievous fitt of Sickness, which ha's almost Distracted me; but, thanks be to God, she is much better, and begin's to recover her Strength. You misunderstood me a little about my Bidding for your Books. We believe they are books of Value, and therefore, by Mr Harleys Order, I Offer'd you 30 pounds for them; which in this time of Scarcity, I think is a good Sum of Money: And the money, as I said before is Ready; and this I did say, without meaning, or believing that Mr Strype wanted, or had Occasion for that or any other Sum. You say, Sir, that you do not think to part with them under fourty Guineas. I have no Orders from Mr Harley to advance above what I bad you before, yet I doubt not but that he might be induced to give you 40£ for them, if that will satisfie. I would advise you to take that price, and to bring them along with you, as soon as conveniently you may. Thirty pounds I can help you to forthwith, and the other ten, I will secure to you, till Mr Harleys pleasure therein be known. I have not written to him about it as yet, but will do so to night, tho' I cannot tell when my Letter may find him, he being not at present, at his own Seat.

I hope you will not stick at the Trifle that is now between us. And indeed in Conscience I can bid you no more, whether you will lett us have them, or no. And whether Mr Harley ha's them or not, at that Rate; you may promise your self all the Assistance his Library can afford you, as likewise those notes Relating to A.Bishop. Parker,[2] or any thing else in the Power of

Reverend Sir,

Your most humble servant

Humfrey Wanley.

My Service to your Lady unknown. And, pray Sir, lett me hear from you speedily, letting me have timely notice of Your coming that I may be sure to be in the Way.

MS: Cambridge University Library, Additional 6, fo. 575. Copy in BL Add. MSS 5853, fo. 82. *Date*: 'York-buildings, July 8. 1708.' *Address*: 'To The Reverend Mr Strype Rector of Low-Leighton in Essex.'

[1] Ann or Anna, daughter of Thomas Bourchier of Newcastle-upon-Tyne, and his wife Dorothy Whitfield of Salop; widow of Bernard Martin Berenclow, by whom she had several children; died 1722. Wanley had three children by her, none surviving infancy.

[2] From Strype's letter (d. 7 June 1708, BL Harley MS 3781, fo. 125) it appears that the 'notes' referred to are in Wanley's account, in his *Catalogus*, of the manuscripts of Corpus Christi College, Cambridge. Strype was collecting material for his *Life* of Parker: see no. 116.

114. *To* John Strype *25 July 1708*

Reverend Sir,

I have not yet had an Opportunity of mentioning to Mr Harley the Sum you insist upon, for your eleven books, being fourty Guineas. I think it a great deal of money for so small a number; but since we have had so much communication about it, and you have taken so much pains about the Catalogue, &c: I will venture to Agree with you for them at that price, tho' it is the dearest bargain I ever bought.

But in Order to shield me from any displeasure which may be conceived against me for my facility; and also for you own Sake, who may oblige a worthy and a powerfull Friend thereby; I would desire you to throw in something farther; any thing that you can spare, be it Manuscript or Printed, or Letters or other loose papers of what kind so ever.[1]

Since then that we are Agreed, I desire you to bring us the books as soon as possible. I have reserved a Shelf for them, where I design to place them all together,[2] as soon as you shall deliver them to

Reverend Sir,

Your most humble servant,

Humfrey Wanley.

MS: Cambridge University Library, Additional 6, fo. 584. Copy in BL Add. MS 5853, fo. 82ᵛ. *Date*: '25th July, 1708. Duke-street, York-buildings, Westmr.' *Address*: 'To the Reverend Mr Strype Rector of Low-Leyton in Essex.'

115. *To* Arthur Charlett *10 November 1708*

Reverend Sir,

I received the favor of your very kind Letter, for which I return you my most hearty Thanks: I am not prepar'd as yet to give a full Answer to all the particulars contain'd therin; but would not delay writing any longer, lest my too long silence should not be taken in good Part. As to your conferring with Mr Dean of Christ-church about my Intention of

[1] Agreed to by Strype: letter d. 31 July [1708], BL Harley MS 3781, fo. 133.
[2] Wright (Wanley, *Diary*, p. xxi) points out that they do indeed begin a new shelf, their original press-marks running from 39.B.1.

Publishing an account of the Life of Cardinal Wolsey,[1] I return you many Thanks: But if my Intentions shall have the Honor of his Approbation, I shall go much farther than the setting of Cavendish in his own true light.[2] For that Author was not made privy to very many important Affairs which concern'd his Master, or pass'd thro' his hands: and which have not been fully set forth (for ought I have yet found) to this day. When the Parliament sitt's, I will not fail to wait on Mr Dean with my Book, and crave the benefit of his Advice thereupon.

As to the 3 Authors treating upon the Vatican-Library, I can say little. You your Self, Sir, can judge best whether your Angelo Roccha be perfect. Dr Sloane (to whom you wrote, upon that Occasion) ha's Mutio Pansa. The other Author I am a Stranger to.[3]

As to the Collection of Pamphlets you was pleas'd to Command me to enquire after, they chiefly relate to the Seditions rais'd, or propagated between the years 1640 & 1660 with the several Loyal Papers publish'd during that Interval;[4] But perhaps, the Collection is not to be confin'd within that Compass of Time, nor to those Subjects alone. There are likewise, the Autographs, from whence some of them were

---

[1] Charlett had taken the opportunity to mention Wanley's plan to edit Cavendish's *Life* of Wolsey, founder of Christ Church, to Henry Aldrich, Dean of the House. Aldrich was 'extremely pleased' and suggested that Wanley meet him in London to discuss it with him (Charlett to Wanley d. 1 Nov. 1708, Welbeck Wanleyana = BL Loan MS 29/253).

[2] Wanley's interleaved and corrected copy of the 1667 edn. of Cavendish, now in the Bodleian (press-mark Gough Oxon. 22). It contains Wanley's collation of the ptd. text with BL Harley MS 428. Wanley never finished his projected Life. See further J. A. W. Bennett, 'Wanley's *Life of Wolsey*', *Bodleian Library Record*, vii (1962–7), pp. 50–2.

[3] Angelo Rocca, *Bibliotheca Apostolica Vaticana* (Rome, 1591). Mutio Pansa, *Della Libraria Vaticana* (Rome, 1590); Wanley's 'other Author' is Antonio Ciccarelli, according to Charlett, 1 Nov. 1708, Welbeck Wanleyana = BL Loan MS 29/253.

[4] The Thomason Tracts, the great collection of more than 22,000 pamphlets, newspapers, and some manuscripts, relating to the period of the Commonwealth, eventually bought by George III for £300 in 1761 and given by him to the British Museum in 1762. Bagford had recently been in Oxford with a proposal for selling them, and Charlett asked for details of price etc. from Wanley. It seems that a catalogue was actually sent to Oxford but, in Charlett's absence, was returned by the Vice-Chancellor on the advice of Hudson, Bodley's Librarian, and Hearne (Charlett to Wanley d. 6 Mar. 1710, Welbeck Wanleyana = BL Loan MS 29/253). But late in 1710 Charlett declared the University to be still interested, while insistent that they would not interfere if Harley intended to buy them (Charlett to Wanley d. 21 Dec. 1710, Welbeck Wanleyana = BL Loan MS 29/253). Charlett enquired again on behalf of the Bodleian ten years later: see nos. 205, 207, 217. On the early history of the collection see the preface to the official *Catalogue* by G. K. Fortescue. For the Bodleian Library's interest in them between 1717 and 1721, see S. G. Gillam, 'The Thomason Tracts', *Bodleian Library Record*, ii (1941–9), pp. 221–5.

printed (which may still be of use) and MSS. of other Authors upon
the said Subj[e]cts, which were never Printed at all. The Books are
well bound, and preserved in Presses; and the Titles of them are
entred into a Catalogue consisting of 12 Volumes in folio.[5] You may
imagine, that they[6] are not closely written, for indeed, fewer Volumes
would contain them. They were collected by the Command of King
Charles II & by the great Charge, & Industry of his Bookbinder, but
not delivered, because there was no money to pay for them. And a considerable parcel of Printed Rabbinical Books, had the same fate; i.e. to
lie hid in the same Bookbinders boxes, ever since. Another Parcel
there is, besides the former, being books which belong to the Royal
Library, Some finely bound in Turkey Leather, & Gilt, & others half
finished, or but begun, but which were Detain'd upon account of
Debts due from the Crown. The Right to the two first Parcels, i.e. to
the Pamphlets (as they are called) and to the said Rabbinical Books, is
(as I am told) in several Persons, claiming from the abovementioned
Person. And they are now (or were not long ago) in the Custody of one
Mr Sissen a Druggist at the Red Cross in Ludgate-street. 'Tis said
they would have taken 1000£ ready money for the said Pamphlets, &
Rabbinical Books; and proportionably cheaper for either Parcel. The
owners have a Respect for Mr Bagford, and as I hear, he ha's a better
Interest with them, than any other Person that I know.

This is all, Sir, that I can acquaint you with touching that Collection, the Owners, or the Price at present. And the time it ha's taken me
in inquiring, ha's hindred my setting Pen to Paper so long, and not
Concluding till now.

We have had the MS. of Josephus up from Dr Hudson,[7] to whom I
beg my humble services may be presented. Mr Bagford at his return
from Oxford, told me that he ha's a MS. relating to Cardinal Wolsey,[8]
but what it was he could not say, only that the Doctor was pleas'd to
shew an Inclination of Lending it to me, if there should be occasion.
I would gladly know what it contains, and then I can easily ghess
whether it will afford any fresh Matter.

[5] Attributed by Bagford to Marmaduke Foster, auctioneer (Fortescue, *Catalogue*, p.
xviii), now BL press-mark C.38.h.21.

[6] these Titles *written above*.

[7] Hudson was editing Josephus; left unfinished at his death, it was pubd. post-
humously by A. Hall—*Flavii Josephi Opera* (Oxford, 1720). The manuscript referred to
may be Harley 5116—but it is not among the list of twenty-two edns. and manuscripts
used by him.   [8] Not identified.

I hear, they are transcribing the Catalogue of the Printed Books in the Bodleyan Library for the Press.[9] I hope in the future Edition two Omissions in Dr Hydes Catalogue will be amply accounted for, i.e. by Inserting the Names of the Printers, to Books of Learning, which have had several Editions: And by putting down precisely the volume of the Book. For its *place* in the Bodleyan Library is no certain Rule to go by; And Dr Hyde own's he looks on all 8vos and Books in *less* Volumes, as 8vos. Which is wrong; and by these Methods a man can never tell (without the Trouble of Inquiry) whether he ha's any book in his Study fit to bestow on the Library or not (if the same book be there before) because the Editions were not fix'd. And for the same Reason, among others, the Printers Name, and the Volume, ought to be added to the Titles of very many others. Another Defect, as I remember, was this. When the book had no Date, the Doctor made this mark ——, which occur's likewise, when the Date was overlook'd: and this ha's made a Confusion in Gentlemens Studies, and multiplied Editions without cause. But, when a book was only *imperfect*, to put the Mark —— still increas'd the Confusion.

Sir, The bell Rings, & now the Postman is at door, I am loth to defer this till another opportunity, and therefore with all due respects remain

Reverend Sir,

Your most obliged & humble Servant

H. Wanley

pardon my scrible I know not what I have written

MS: Bodleian, Ballard 13, fo. 119. *Date*: 'London, 10. November, 1708.' *Address*: 'To The Reverend Dr Charlet Master of University College in Oxford.' *Printed*: S. G. Gillam, 'The Thomason Tracts', *Bodleian Library Record*, ii (1941–9), p. 223 (extract); J. A. W. Bennett, 'Wanley's *Life of Wolsey*', *Bodleian Library Record*, vii (1962–7), pp. 50–2 (extracts).

116. *To* John Strype *25 January 1709*

Reverend Sir,

I must here answer your two last Letters;[1] The former, wherin you thought I tax'd you too hardly, about your Books, and desir'd me to

---

[9] See no. 107 n. 2.

---

[1] 23 Sept. [1708], Jan. [1709], BL Harley MS 3781, fos. 137, 129.

represent you fairly to Mr Harley, &c. I thought needed no Speedy Answer, because you mistook my meaning, which was Jocular, & not Harsh. I intending no more thereby, than that the old Custome observed in buying & Selling old books, should be continued: according to which, 'tis usual to specify what is imperfect, & what not. And I have represented you Honorably to Mr Harley, who is your humble servant as much as you can desire. I shall go to Mr Wyat[2] about his Copie of your Annals, wherein I thank you heartily for the great pains & the many things you have brought to light, which otherwise might long (if not always) have remained in dark Oblivion. My book I subscribed for was for a Friend who is now out of England, but I will take it my self, and pay Mr Wyat for it, as soon as I go that way, which cannot be yet in some days, I having sprained my left Leg in walking thro' the slippery Streets. I know you're about the Life of that Venerable Prelate Matthew Parker,[3] I would hint something to you about him, and have some printed Books relating to him (in my Study) which shall be at your Service, when you shall think fit to call upon me. The History of the Nagshead[4] (which I think you purposely omit in your Annals) must be mentioned therein at large. I think Bishop Bramhall[5] ha's written best upon that Subject. If you have not his book by you, Mr Harley will lend it to you when you please. I am

  Good Sir,

    Your most humble servant

                      Humfrey Wanley.

MS: Cambridge University Library, Additional 4, fo. 172. Copy in BL Add. MS 5853, fo. 64. *Date*: 'Duke-street, York-buildings, 25. Jan. 1708/9.' *Address*: 'To The Reverend Mr Strype Rector of Low Leighton in Essex.'

  [2] John Wyat or Wyatt, bookseller, of the Rose and Crown, St Paul's Churchyard 1690–*c*.1720, publisher for the Nonconformists. Strype's *Annals of the Reformation* was announced by him in his letter to Wanley d. Jan. [1709] as already published.

  [3] *The Life and Acts of Matthew Parker* (1711).

  [4] i.e. Christopher Holywood, *De Investiganda Vera ac Visibili Christi Ecclesia Libellus* (Antwerp, 1604), a Jesuit attempt to discredit the validity of Parker's episcopal consecration.

  [5] John Bramhall, Ῥομφαια διστομος ὀξεια; *or, the Church of England defended . . . Wherein the fable of the Nags-head Ordination is detected* (1659).

117. *To* Edmund Gibson *25 January 1709*

Reverend Sir,

'Tis long since, that, upon your mentioning a design of Reprinting your Chronicon Saxonicum,[1] I promised to collate certain MSS. in the Cottonian Library, which you had not an Opportunity of consulting, when you was a Student in Oxford. That Promise of mine ha's many times since, come into my mind, but I could not perform it without more than ordinary inconvenience to my self, at a time, wherein (as far as I could see) you was in no great hast. But, now, it ha's so happen'd, that at the same time, I have found out a way to come at the Books necessary to be perused, in order to your second Edition, and have also time enough to peruse them. Whereby I can shew that I promised at first no more than I meant to perform; and that I think my self now bound, in honor, to perform (since it lies in my power) what I promised so long ago. In Short, Sir, I have (upon my bond of 100£) borrowed 3 Saxon Chronicles from the Cottonian Library, which are therin inscribed OTHO B. 11.—TIBER. B.I.—& TIBER. B.4. which books are as yet (for ought I know to the contrary) untouched.[2] There are two other Saxon Chronicles in the same Library, viz. TIBER. A.6.[3]—and DOMIT. 8.[4] but I did not borrow them, because you made use of Transcripts from them in your elaborate Edition. For the latter, I take to be the Archetypon to that which you call *Cot.* And the former (the Copie of which you call *Cant.*) to be still remaining, a venerable Book; and, next to that in Bennet College Library,[5] the oldest Exemplar of the Saxon Annals now Remaining. In bringing the 3 MSS. abovesaid home, I chanced to slip, and have sprained thereby my left Leg, which hinders me from attending you, and consequently from talking with you about some other things which might be thought of in your next Edition. One is, that the MS in Bennet College should be collated

[1] Pbd. Oxford, 1692. The second edn. was never completed.

[2] Otho B.xi = Ker no. 180, art. 3, Wanley p. 219; Tiberius B.i = Ker no. 191, art. 4, Wanley p. 219; Tiberius B.iv = Ker no. 192, Wanley p. 220. Otho B.xi was badly damaged in the fire of 1731 and only a fragment of the Chronicle text survives. Unfortunately Wanley did not collate it, since Gibson had used a transcript of it for his edn. See no. 118.

[3] Fos. 1–34 (late tenth century), Ker no. 188, Wanley pp. 219, 199.

[4] Ker no. 148, Wanley p. 130.

[5] The Parker Chronicle, Corpus Christi College, Cambridge MS 173, fos. 1ᵛ–32ᵛ, written from *c.*900 onwards, Ker no. 39, Wanley p. 130.

afresh, and the antient Orthography thereof, preserved; so far as that book goes. Likewise TIB. A.6. being an Old book, since your Transcript *Cant.* was written by one who did not understand the Language.[6] Also, that those Chronological Notes (being in the Saxon Language) and Extant in CALIG. A. 15 about fol. 128, b. should be thrown in, at their severall years.[7] As likewise a Fragment about the time of K. Henry I. in DOMIT. 9.[8]

The book inscribed DOMIT. 8. should be revised, if it were only to shew the places wherin the old writing is rased out, and new Stories putt in about former Synods or Convocations. I would also have inserted into the new Edition (if it be not in this present book) the Account of the Succession of the West-Saxon Kings, which formerly belonged to TIB. A.6. and is now bound up in TIB. A. 3.[9] It begin's **Ða wæs agangen**. There are many Copies of it, at Oxford, &c. And Lastly I would have you look upon the Chorographical Maps (in Saxon) of Laurence Noel, in DOMIT. 18.[10] Some Historical Notes and the Names of Towns, &c. mentioned in the Saxon-Chronicle extant in JVL. C. 6.[11] & some Excerpta from such Chronicles, VITEL. D.7.[12] And if my service herein will be acceptable to you, I will consult these and save you as much Trouble as I can.

But, in the first place, I think the 3 books I have now by me, should be collated. And therefore I would desire you to send me a Chronicle with Paper pasted to all the Margins, that I may have room herin to write what shall be necessary. And this as soon as may be.[13] But in case you have not one of your books by you, I must spoil my own which you gave me almost 13 years ago, and which I have ever since kept for your sake.

If 'twould not be too much trouble, I would intreat you to call on

---

[6] Probably the sixteenth-century copy in Bodl. MS Laud misc. 661, fos. 1–43 (*SC* 1201).

[7] See Ker no. 139, art. r; now at fos. 133–7.

[8] A single leaf (early twelfth century) from a chronicle containing parts of annals for 1113 and 1114; Ker no. 150, Wanley p. 239.

[9] At fo. 178, Ker no. 188, art. 2. Ker lists two other copies, one (Bodl. MS Laud misc. 661, fos. 44–5) at Oxford.

[10] Fos. 99ʳ–123ʳ. Laurence Nowell, the early Anglo-Saxonist and antiquary.

[11] Presumably those in art. 15. The manuscript also contains miscellaneous historical notes.

[12] Cotton Vitellius D.vii was much damaged in the fire of 1731.

[13] Gibson seems to have sent Wanley an interleaved copy of the 1692 edn.—now BL Add. MS 44879. It contains Wanley's collation of Tiberius B.i and Tiberius B.iv; the present letter and no. 118 are inserted.

me, & see these 3 MSS. and in the mean time, to send me your
Commands by the Penny-post, which will be received with all Respect
by him who is,

Reverend Sir,

Your most obliged servant

Humfrey Wanley.

MS: British Library, Add. 44879, fo. iv. *Date*: 'Duke-street, York-buildings, 25. January, 1708/9.' *Address*: 'To the Reverend Dr Gibson, at his house in Lambeth.'

118. *To* [Edmund Gibson] *19 April 1709*

Reverend Sir,

I am heartily sorry that I was not come home by the time that my Lord of Carlile[1] & Yourself were pleas'd to call here. Had I but dream'd of so great a favor, I should not have been absent. You had not been gone a quarter of an hour before I return'd, and then I did not know where to attend you.

Sir, 'tis high time to give you an account of your Saxon Chronicle with which you have been pleased to entrust me. Had not the Collating of the second Volume of Dr Grabes Septuagint very much hindred me,[2] I should have finished with it before this time. For one of the MSS. need's not be Collated, you having used a Transcript of it at Oxford.[3] Of the other two, I have chosen to begin with that which is the larger, and am got (at this time) to A.D. 1012. the book ending (I mean what is therin written in the first Hand) with the year 1075.[4] The other MS. being the Chronicle of Abendon,[5] is shorter than this; and consequently will go off with more ease. Unless you command me to Compare the Poetical Tract De Mensibus, which is Prefix'd to it,[6] & Printed by Dr Hickes; and which I think signifies little to your Annals.

My Method in Collating, is to take Notice of every Reading (which

---

[1] William Nicolson.

[2] In fact, vol. iv of the complete work (4 vols., 1707–20), but the second to be printed. It may be that Wanley contemplated a new edn. of the Septuagint. BL Sloane MS 4061 contains a memorandum in his hand, 'Some Thoughts concerning a New Edn of the Septuagint' (fo. 265), ptd. Nichols, *Literary Anecdotes*, i, pp. 102–3.

[3] Cotton Otho B.xi.

[4] Cotton Tiberius B.iv. But Ker distinguishes five hands up to the annal for 1054.

[5] Cotton Tiberius B.i.

[6] At fos. 112–14ᵛ, ptd. Hickes, *Thesaurus*, bk. i, pp. 203–8.

occurr's in the first Hand; for of those putt down by Josselyne,[7] from books still remaining, I am not mindfull) lett such Readings be never so trivial, as an **a** for **o**; a **y** for **i** or vice versa. Nay, farther, where the MS is manifestly in the fault, & you have Printed the true Reading already. For my design is to present you (as it were) copies of these MSS. And I leave it to your Judgement to alter as you shall find meet. And Alterations will be made, I perceive, by the help of this Book; for sometimes I find what sett's all the other MSS to rights, where they were faulty. Not to mention readings of less note, more accurate, or (if you please) more Saxon, than the Print.[8] As for fresh Matter, you having used almost all the extant Books, do not look for much. But I can assure you I have mett with some already, not only augmenting what is already putt down to such or such years; but filling up some Gaps, where the Year was Blank, & nothing said. And I perceive that I have more fresh matter to come, than ha's occurr'd as yet; such being (as you know Sir) the nature of these books. I have almost finished with Dr Grabe, & shall then soon dispatch this small piece of service; I being most sincerely

Reverend Sir,

Your most humble servant

Humfrey Wanley.

MS: British Library, Add. 44879, fo. vi. *Date*: 'York-buildings, 19. April, 1709.' *Printed*: P. L. Heyworth, 'The Old English "Seasons of Fasting"', *Mediaeval Studies*, xxvi (1964), pp. 358–9 (extract).

119. *To* —— *16 September 1710*

Reverend Sir,

I have not forgott your late Commands, whereby I am required to Sett down in Writing such Hints as I conceive fitt to be putt into Practise for the Preservation & Enlargement of the New Library at St Pauls;[1] and accordingly I do with as much Frankness as Submission,

---

[7] John Joscelyn (1529–1603), antiquary and Anglo-Saxonist, Latin Secretary to Abp. Parker 1558. Tiberius B.iv. contains readings inserted by him from four other copies of the Anglo-Saxon Chronicle, and it probably at one time belonged to him.

[8] See P. L. Heyworth in *Mediaeval Studies*, xxvi (1964), 358–9.

---

[1] The rebuilding of St Paul's to the design of Sir Christopher Wren was completed

communicate to you the following Hasty & Indigested Notes, which shew only my Private & humble Opinion; and which entirely submitt to your Grave Judgement, & Disposal.

I look upon this Library, not only as a Library belonging to the Dean & Chapter of a Cathedral Church, but as the Chiefest Public Library in the Metropolis (If I may say so) of Great Britain. As such I believe both Natives & Foreigners will take it; as Such I would have it Endow'd & Furnish'd; and as Such, I would have its Honor & Reputation Consider'd upon all Occasions.

You was pleas'd to tell me the other Night, that the Library is open'd, & how the books are dispos'd: from which I conclude that the Governors have already made Choice of a Library-Keeper; who, to be sure, is a Man of Eminency, Abilities, Activity, Industry, Candor, & Integrity, because these Qualifications shining in the Chief Officer on the Place, it's Reputation will be best Fix'd, and You the Commissioners will also have the best Hopes of seing it Flourish, and Answer the other parts of your Costly & Unparallel'd Fabrick.

For the Security of the Library, I would have the Keeper, & all Servants employ'd therein, Sworn to be true to their Trust, not to Imbezle or otherwise wilfully Damnifie any of the Books, &c. nor Suffer any wilful Damage to be done to the same without timely discovery of the Offender, and Generally, to observe all the Statutes of the Library.

It will be an Incouragement to your Library-Keeper, if his Deputy or Assistant, be putt in by & depend on him; they will the better agree together, which will be an ease to 'em both in the discharging their Duties.

I would have the Library-Keeper & his Deputy oblig'd to attend every day (except Holidays) from eight of the clock in the Morning till Twelve at Noon. In the Winter time of the Year, for the Afternoon (since the Town is then always full) from one of the Clock 'till four; and in the Somer Season, from two, 'till five or Six.

The Library-Keeper's business may be the Disposing of the Books, & acquainting himself with them, the Care of Entring Benefactions & Solliciting others, Receiving Strangers of the best Quality, compiling the Catalogue, & fixing the same in his Memory. And as the Catalogue is what is contain'd in a Library, So the Library-Keeper should be the Index to the Catalogue; and not only help the Student to the book he

by 1710. For a description of the Library, see Jane Lang, *Rebuilding St. Paul's after the Great Fire of London* (Oxford, 1956), pp. 226–7.

ask's for, but readily direct him to others in the same Way, which might not be thought of without this Assistance.

The Deputy may be always ready to accomodate the Student with the books he want's, every Student putting down the day & year, the Marks of the Book he want's, & his Name (in a Paper Book to be kept for that purpose) which Name & Marks may be cross'd upon the return of the Book. He should also be ready to receive Strangers; to Shew them if they desire it, the Chief Curiosities of the Library; & to have a watchful Eie upon all Comers, least any thing be Stollen.

And since there is most likely to be a great Confluence of all Sorts of People to this Library, which if not prevented will absolutely debarre any mortall from Studying there, by reason of the intolerable Noise & Confusion: I could Wish, that the Governors of the Place would appoint a Person of known Honesty constantly to attend, during Library-hours, att the Bottom of the Stairs, who should be oblig'd to admitt every Gentleman of the Clergy, or other Noted Student, Gratis; and keep out every body else who will not give three pence to be admitted. This Money to be putt into a Box as it is received, to be secur'd by Several Locks, and at Appointed Times to be Open'd by [*blank*] should be deliver'd to the Governors; and if the Library encrease in Reputation & Use it may go a great way in Paying off Salaries, and other incidental Charges of the Library. And for the Justification of this Servant insisting upon the Payment of such money, A Table may be putt up, wherein may be express'd in large Letters, in English, Latin, & French, that all persons who expect to have admittance into the Library, must first give three pence to the Servant there attending. Another Table in the same 3 Languages may be hung up at the Door of the Library, which the Deputy should Shew all persons at their Coming in, whereby they may be warned to forbear making a Noise to the Disturbance of the Students, and refrain from handling or plucking any Book or other thing out of its Place. The Man at the bottom of the Stairs who Collects the Money aforesaid, May be the Porter of the Library, and be oblig'd out of Library-Hours to sweep & Clean the same dayly, or as often as there shall be occasion & to wipe & Clean every Book, once in every Three Months.

I believe it might be for the Convenience & Benefit of the Library, if some Standing Orders or Rules were made for the better government of the Place, among other Things, whereby it might be for ever Provided,

That No Book be ever Lent or Carried out of the Library upon any pretence whatsoever; unless it be to be Bound (if there be no Convenience for a Book-binder in the Appurtenances of the Library), in case of Fire, or such like Emergency. By such an Order, the Library will best keep it's own, answer the Expectation of such Students who shall repair thither on purpose to consult it, & no person can be disoblig'd.

That no Fire, Lighted Candle, or Lighted Tobacco, be ever Suffer'd in the Library.[2]

That no Eating or Drinking be ever permitted there.

That no Student be Suffer'd to Scrible, or write Notes in any Book without the Approbation of the Library keeper.

Since it is found that the Placing of Books according to their Faculties, & Sciences, take's up much more than Sufficient Room; and that by thus placing a Small book next to a Large one, the Beauty of the Library will be destroyed, the Great Books damaged, the Library-keepers Labour doubled, and even this Method, in process of Time, thro' the Accession of New Books, become impracticable: that Books of a Bigness be Sett together, without respect of Faculty, Art, or Language, where being once Entred into the Catalogue they may always remain, and by the same Catalogue be always readily found.

And forasmuch as it is found by Experience, that Chains (with their Loops, Iron Rods, Smith's Work etc.) are a certain Charge & Burthen to a Library; that they are not a Sufficient Security against a Thief; nor even a Direction for the putting a Book into its own Place: 'tis propos'd, that this Expence be sav'd & the Ratling Noise & Intanglement of Chains, together with the Marring of Books be prevented: since the Deputie-Library-keeper's Constant Eie upon all Students & Comers, who are warned by the Table abovementioned not to Medle with the Books will keep them together. And the Letter & Number being written in the Inside of each Book, its proper place after taking out, is known with all Ease & Certainty.

The Catalogue may be made like to that of the Bodleyan Library, which is always known to half the Students of the Kingdom, & is the Easiest, in Practise.[3] The Library-keeper might do well in making a general List of the Books sorted according to the Faculties, Arts, & other Heads, which would be of Singular Use. Besides these, He

---

[2] Libray MS.   [3] But see Wanley's criticisms of it, no. 115.

should make another short List of all the Books, according as they
Stand, expressing the Author only, or Subject of each Book or Tract,
together with its Letter & Number, in several small Books, to be
called *Visitation-Books*.

Since it is not fitting that the Library should be disfurnished by
Lending out the Books, the Students should be Accomodated with
Tables, Desks, Chairs, &c.

Sir I crave your pardon for this long Letter, tho' it contain only what
at present Occur's to my Imagination. If I am obscure and you shall
desire me to explain my Meaning; or if you would know more particularly my Opinion how the Cabinet, Drawers, Large Books, &c. which I
have mentioned, should be contrived, or any thing else wherein I may
be capable of serving the Commissioners, You may depend on the
ready Service of

Sir Your most faithful & obedient Servant

MS: Welbeck Wanleyana = British Library, Loan 29/258; draft, unsigned. *Date*: 'Sept.
16. 1710.'

120. *To* [Robert Harley] [*June 1711?*][1]

I presume humbly to desire your Lordship, to secure Doctor
Huttons Collections relating to the Succession of the Bishops, Deans,
& other Dignitaries of Cathedral Churches, and to the Abbats &
Priors of the old Monasteries. I lately borrowed some of those of the
last kind, & gave him a Note under my Hand for them. These will be
the greatest help towards the intended work with your Lordships
Charters; and without their Assistance, I am bold to say, that work will
never be well done.[2]

MS: British Library, Harley 7055, fo. 14; draft, unsigned.

[1] Harley assumed the office of Lord Treasurer on 29 May 1711, Hutton died on 27
June 1711. This and the following letter stand next to one another in BL Harley 7055.
[2] Hutton presented charters to Harley (Harl. Ch. 83.A.21–83.C.9), see Wanley, *Diary*,
p. 176(14); his manuscript collections came by purchase—'at a very dear Rate' (*Harleian
Catalogue*, under Harley 7520), now BL Harley MSS 6950–85, 7519–21; according to
Hearne (*Collections*, iii, p. 280), Harley paid £150 for them.

121. *To* [Robert Harley] [*June 1711?*]

May it please your Lordship to Pardon the following Advertisement.

Yesterday a Gentleman (a Stranger to me) came to me, and after some ordinary Talk, open'd Himself to this Effect: That there is an Irish Baron, a Churchman, a person of a clear Character, in all Respects, worth in Land & Money Ten Thousand Pounds a Year, who desire's to be made a Viscount of Great Britain. In which matter, if he may have your Lordships Favor; He will Give Five Thousand Pounds to such Uses as your Lordship shall direct. Also, that there is an English Gentleman, of as Good Character & Estate as the other, who desires to be a Baron of Great Britain; who In Consideration of the same Favor, will Sacrifice Five Thousand Pounds as your Lordship shall Appoint.[1] My Answer to this was, that it is not my Business to intermedle with such Matters; And that I did believe my Lord Treasurer would not be concern'd in it, especially as to one part of the Proposal; and so I desir'd to be Excus'd. But afterwards, upon farther Communication with him, finding him Resolute to proceed, & fearing that he might make use of some other person to Hand this Proposal to your Lordship, whereby it might take Air; I told him I would take some Time to Consider of it. But gave him no Sign or Encouragement to Hope that your Lordship would comply with their Desires. Nay I said roundly I durst not, nor ever would be so Mad as to mention any such Matter to your Lordship, and thus sent Him away.[2] I suppose I shall hear of him again in a few days; and if I shall then have any thing to say to Him from your Lordship, so; If not, I will shutt my hands of Him.

My Lord, I humbly crave Pardon, for intermedling with any Affairs so far out of my Sphere, & so nearly relating to your Lordship; but your Lordship will be pleas'd to consider, that He found me out, & not I Him. And that I thought it nearly concern'd your Lordship, notwithstanding the Scorn & Contempt your Lordship should treat this Proposal with, that no more should know such a thing was ever intended.

MS: British Library, Harley 7055, fo. 14; draft, unsigned.

---

[1] 'That these Persons were very tender of their Names, and would never suffer them to be made known to an' cancelled.   [2] 'with an Air of Discouragement' cancelled.

122. *To* John Covell *6 March 1712*

Reverend Sir,

Mr Kemp joyn's with me in hearty Thanks for your kind favors to us in Cambridge; and take's your kind Enquiry after him in very thankful Part. As to his Scipio Africanus, I have seen it this day; upon the Adverse side is a Mans Naked Head, with this Epigraphe P. SCIPIO AFRIC. on the Reverse is a Figure standing in a Triumphal Chariot drawn by Four Horses, & this Inscription CART. SVBAC. If you have any more Quaeries about this or any other of his Coins, I shall be sure to answer them to the best of my Power.

I did not think it necessary to make mention of your South-Sea-Chart[1] to my Lord Treasurer, for two Reasons. First because I perceived you Set a far greater Value upon it, than any body I knew, would give. And Secondly, I did not believe that either His Lordship or the Company are under any want of those kind of Charts.

If it will be in the Compass of either Mr Kemp's Abilities or mine to be Serviceable unto you, You may with all Freedom Command him or

Reverend Sir,
Your most obliged humble servant

Humfrey Wanley.

MS: British Library, Add. 22911, fo. 142. Copy in Cambridge University Library MS Mm.vi.50, fo. 280. *Date*: 'Thursday 6 March, 1711/12.' *Address*: 'To The Reverend Dr Covel Master of Christs College in Cambrige.'

---

[1] A chart 'of all the seas and Ports in the East and West Indyes' (Covell to Wanley d. 2 May 1712; Welbeck Wanleyana = BL Loan 29/254). Apparently finally purchased for twelve guineas—see Wanley to Edward Harley, 4 Dec. 1716. Not identified. Harley MS 3450 includes charts of the East Indies and West Indies by Joan Martines d. 1578, but was acquired from Andrew Hay. Harley MSS 4252–6, John Marshall's Journals and Memoranda relative to the East Indies, did belong to Covell, but they do not contain any maps. Robert Harley had been chosen a governor of the South Sea Company, 15 Aug. 1711.

123. *To* Philip Stubbs[1] *2 July 1712*

Reverend Sir

My Lord Treasurer has been some time since apprized of your Desire to serve him in the Buying of Monsieur Aymon's MSS,[2] about which I did send a Letter to Holland directed for you, which His Lordship hath been informed did not come to your Hands: & that therefore you returned back to England without them. And forasmuch as your other occasions do Require your Presence there at this Time: & your opportunity of serving His Lordship in that affair will be still the same: He is pleased by me to impart his Mind unto you, not doubting but that you will pursue th[e] same with all Fidelity & Diligence, according to the Assurances I have given in your behalf, that He may have an occasion of letting you know in what Thankfull part He receives this Instance of your Respect & Affection for Him.

His Lordship judgith that it will be best to transact nothing with Mr Aymon, but before one or more prudent Friends, who may also assist you in beating down the Extravagant & Exorbitant Price which Mr Aymon hath sett upon them: of which Price, & the Impracticableness of Vending them at, He desireth you to make the Monsieur fully sensible: but always concealing His Lordships Name, from Mr Aymon, & all others.

At your first Coming, you may let him understand, that you have heard He hath more MSS than those He mention'd in his two Catalogues (which will herewith be redelivered unto you, & which you are to bring back); if He hath, be pleased to find me out an accurate List of them, with all Speed.

[1] Philip Stubbs (1665–1738), Rector of St James, Garlickhythe 1708–19, active in the SPCK.
[2] Jean Aymon (1661–1734), French renegade priest and adventurer; he stole manuscripts from the Royal Library in Paris in 1707 and fled to The Hague. The manuscripts in his possession were first brought to Wanley's attention by John Toland, who drew up the catalogue used by Wanley here: see the remarks in Wanley's description of BL Harley MS 1802. For Stubbs's preliminary account of some of the manuscripts listed here, see his letter d. 27–8 Mar. 1712 in Welbeck Wanleyana (= BL Loan MS 29/257); a fuller description ('A Brief Account of the Books, Parchments, & Papers, lately brought from Holland by ye Revd Mr Phil. Stubs') by Wanley d. 10 Jan. 1713 is in Welbeck Wanleyana (= BL Loan MS 29/259 misc. 37) and is cited below. The business dragged on, much to Wanley's annoyance, and was not finally wrapped up until 1721: see Wanley, *Diary*, pp. 107 (14), 124 (12), and further, Wanley, *Diary*, p. xxiii and p. 2 n. 4. Stubbs also negotiated on Harley's behalf for the small collection of Sir Bulstrode Whitelocke (1605–75), the Parliamentarian: see Wanley, *Diary*, p. xxii.

You are desired to compare every Book with the said Catalogues, & to take special regard that each Book do answer the Character which Monsieur Aymon hath given of them.

As to the Method of your proceeding, it is thought adviseable for you (with your Friends) to Beat down the Price of every Book by it self, as low as possibly you can. Then, laying the Books of the first Parcel together, induce him to abate so much more in consideration of your taking off so many of them off his Hands: Then add the second Parcel to the first if they may be had for a reasonable Price: & at the last, Try to persuade him to throw in Richard de Sancto Victore[3] for nothing, or a small matter.

The first Parcel for which my Lord hath occasion,

No. II in the French Catalogue	Quatuor Evangelia Latine, litteris Uncialibus.[4]
	Fragmenta Epistolarum St Pauli, Graece et Latine, litteris Uncialibus.[5]
	Epistolae D. Pauli, cum Canonicis: ubi Ep. 1a B. Johannis, AD PARTHOS, inscribitur.[6]
No. III	Epistolae D. Pauli, Epistolae Canonicae, nec non Liber Apocalypseos.[7]
No. VIII	Registrum Datariae Romanae, 2 Vol.[8]
No. VI	Soliloquia Confucij Sinice: cum alijs, II Vol.[9]
No. IX	Epistolae Cardinalis Viscontij de Concilio Tridentino[10]

---

[3] BL Harley MS 1762 = Brief Account no. 5.

[4] BL Harley MS 1775 = Brief Account no. 13.

[5] Formerly BL Harley MS 1773 = Brief Account no. 14, twelve leaves of the Codex Claromontanus (CLA v, no. 521), stolen by Aymon from the Royal Collection in Paris and restored by Edward Harley in 1729. Aymon apparently demanded one million Guilders for it: see no. 129.

[6] BL Harley MS 7551, art. 6 = Brief Account no. 7.

[7] BL Harley MS 1772 = Brief Account no. 8.

[8] BL Harley MS 1850–2 = Brief Account no. 11.

[9] In fact two ptd. books and so described by Wanley in Brief Account no. 3.

[10] BL Harley MS 3479 = Brief Account, postscript. Acquired through William Sherard, 29 Nov. 1721: see Wanley, Diary, pp. 106(11), 107(14), 124(12).

No. VIII in the Latin Catalogue   Quatuor Evangelia, cum Catena Patrum Latinorum: Litteris, ut opinor, Hybernicis.[11]

No. IV   Epistola prima D. Johannis, unica Membrana.[12]

These Books you are desired to buy: but at as cheap a Rate as you possibly [c]an.

The Second Parcel which my Lord doth not so much want.

No. X in the French Catalogue: Epistolae Cardinalis de Sancta Cruce:[13] nec non Reginae Catharinae de Medicis.[14]

No. V   Epistolae Suleimani Turcarum Sultani.[15]

No. II in the Latin Catalogue: Epistolae Canonicae et Ep: ad Romanos[16] wherein Mr Aymon doth not specify any curious Reading.

If these may be had at such a Rate, as you, in your Discretion may think reasonable, buy them: if not, leave them. As for Theologia Muhammedana,[17] & Richard de Sancto Victore, MSS Copies of them are frequently in England.

When you pay for them (for fear of French After-Claps) take a Receipt of the Monsieur: & cause your Friends to attest it: upon your Return, & Delivery of the Books, My Lord will pay you the Money laid out. Thus wishing you a safe & prosperous Voyage, I take my leave of you this 2d day of July 1712, being

     Reverend Sir

         your most faithfull humble Servant

                          Humfrey Wanley.

---

[11] BL Harley MS 1802 = Brief Account no. 12.
[12] BL Harley MS 7551, art. 7 = Brief Account no. 1.
[13] BL Harley MS 3479 = Brief Account no. 10.
[14] BL Harley MS 7016, fos. 7–10 = Brief Account no. 10.
[15] BL Harley MS 1815 = Brief Account no. 4.
[16] BL Harley MS 7551, art. 8 = Brief Account no. 6.
[17] Brief Account, postscript. Later apparently wanted, but not obtained: see Wanley, *Diary*, p. 107 (14).

Pray buy for me a Spanish Book, thus intituled Museo de las Medallas disconnoscidas Españolas par Bernardo Aldrete,[18] or leave Order for it.

MS: Welbeck Wanleyana = British Library, Loan 29/259 misc. 37; fair copy in another hand, with draft in Wanley's hand. *Endorsed*: 'Instructions for the Revd Mr. Stubs to buy Monsr Aymon's MSS. in Holland.'

124. *To* Edward Harley[1] *31 August 1712*

My Lord,

The next Saturday there will be due to me from my Lord-Treasurer £11:19:0, which I must earnestly beseech you to procure for me by this time to morrow, or else I shall be putt to public Shame, by an old acquaintance who of late hath born too hard upon me; and to whom I ow the greatest part of the money.

I have been so bold as to write about it to my Lord from Chelsea; and if the matter was not really so urgent as it is, I would not now trouble your Lordship with it.

I heartily congratulate your Lordships good State of Recovery. For my own part, I have gotten a violent Cough, & a kind of Dizziness in my Head, which groweth Worse & Worse. I profess I am so ill, that I would stay to morrow at Chelsea to look after my self a little, were it not for Receiving this small Matter, which I cannot possibly do without.

Good my Lord, be pleased to excuse this hasty Scribble of him who is as much as any man alive,

Your Lordships most faithful & sincerely devoted Servant

H. Wanley.

MS: Welbeck Wanleyana = British Library, Loan 29/258. *Date*: 'Thursday 31. Aug. 1712.' *Address*: 'To The Right Honble the Lord Harley.'

---

[18] Wanted by Wanley as a gift for Kemp: see no. 128.

---

[1] Edward Harley (1689–1741), 2nd Earl of Oxford, succeeded to the title on the death of his father in 1724.

125. *To* John Covell *8 September 1712*

Reverend Sir,

   Lest that you should think me too long Silent, I take this Opportunity of letting you know that I have not been unmindful of you, all this
While, although I have not as yet brought the little Affair about the
Sea-Chart to the desired Effect.[1] I was near it this last Week having
gott it before my Lord-Treasurer, in Order to his once Seeing it, &
giving his Commands thereupon: but, at that very Instant, some
Persons of the first Quality coming in upon Publick Business, I was
forced to take away the Chart & my Self too.

   I have caused it to be nicely Inspected by Capt. Dampeir,[2] & divers
other Gentlemen who are the best Judges of this Sort of Things, in
Town. They all agreed (although asked Singly) that there hath been
much Pains Spent thereon, so as that it must have needs Cost a very
great Sum of Money, if the Maker ever Sold it. But, alass Sir, they find
it to be unaccurate, and consequently of little or no Use. For all the
Errors of the Old Charts are retained here; none of the more modern
Improvements are found herein; And lately, Dr Halley[3] having proved
that the Eastern Continent was placed Wrong in the Maps by 300
Leagues, the Sea-Charts are now amended in that Respect. Moreover
there were many Islands & other Places Discovered & known, when
this Chart was made, which are not therein mentioned. Lastly, they
say that they would not expect any Instruction from thence, but only as
to Places in the East Indies, Brazil, &c. in Possession of the Portu-
guese; and even there they desire accuracy, and say the Chart is often
faulty & imperfect.

   This being the true State of the matter, & I being still desirous
of doing you some Service about it; would dispose of it here, in
such Manner as may be to your Satisfaction. But since, upon its
having been inspected, I cannot procure you so much as I before
hoped for, I would desire you to specifie somewhat that will content
you for it, & I will quickly procure it; or else deliver it back to good
Mr Cook. Be pleased to lett me have your Commands directed to

[1] See no. 122.
[2] William Dampier (1652–1715), circumnavigator and hydrographer.
[3] Edmond Halley (1656–1742), astronomer and scientist.

be Left for me, at the Lord Treasurers in York-buildings, & they will find,

    Reverend Sir,

       Your most obliged, & faithful humble servant,

                                   Humfrey Wanley.

MS: British Library, Add. 22911, fo. 144. *Date*: '8 September 1712.' *Address*: 'To The Reverend Dr Covel Master of Christs College in Cambridge.'

126. *To* George Daniel [*28 September 1712*][1]

Sir,

    The Right Honorable the Lord Treasurers Library, as to the Antiquity or Written part of it, having in about 7 Years, encreased to 2000 Manuscript Books, 1000 Rolls, & 13000 Charters or Deeds, among which those in the Greek & Oriental Languages are but few; You, Sir, who are on the Spot, and, as it were, in the Centre of the East, are desired by him to afford your Assistance in procuring for his Lordship such things as are in these parts very rarely or not at all to be found.

    Comparing the Greek with the other Languages of the East; we look upon the Greek as containing the Books of most Solid & useful Learning; and the others more with an Eie of Curiosity.

    In both these Respects, my Lord Treasurer is willing to buy books. And it may happen, that his Lordship may give a greater Price for a Curiosity, than for a Book which a Learned man may think more useful.

    The Materials of Books or Writings are respected as a mere Curiosity, and yet may be very Valuable. On this account it is, that if you can procure any thing, in any Language, antiently written upon Bark (Phillyra) or upon the old Egyptian Papyrus (and such things may be met with) you are desired to secure them.

    Antiquity in Books sometimes cometh also under the same Predicament. For we often see a recent Copie more correct & Complete than an Older Book of the same kind. And yet such is our Veneration for Antiquity, that where ever you can find a Greek Book or part of a Book

---

[1] Wanley endorsed a five-line partial summary of this letter (Welbeck Wanleyana = BL Loan MS 29/259 misc. 49), 'Instructions for George Daniel the Grecian, going for Smyrna. 28 Septr 1712'. Apart from this Commission and Wanley's note d. 30 Sept. 1713 (no. 133), Daniel cannot be further identified.

written in Capital, Uncial, or Majuscule Letters (such as resemble th[ose] Inscriptions on Marble-Stones) you are desired also to secure them, lett the Subject be what it will, or although you may have gott never so many Copies of the same thing before.

As to Greek Books (Manuscripts I always mean, not meaning that you should be troubled about any thing Printed) they are pretty scarce in England, except in our Publick Libraries. For this Reason it is, that you are desired to secure all the Greek MSS you can, when ever you find them Cheap. And such Bargains you may frequently meet with upon the Decease of the Greek Priests or Bishops, when a whole Collection may be had at once (as not long since after the Death of Dositheus the late Patriarch of Jerusalem)[2] and some English Cloth, or other Commodity may be used in way of Truck, instead of Money.

Greek MSS. are (with reference to the matter of them) of two Sorts, Sacred & Prophane, or Christian & Heathen. The Heathen are respected for their Learning, and the Christian have also their Use.

All Greek Historians we Value, whether they be Heathen or Christian, Antient or Modern. So that you can never load us too much with the Works of Thucydides, Polybius, Dion Cassius, Diodorus Siculus, Plutarch, Diogenes Laertius, Photius, Eusebius, and such like Nicephorus Callistus.

The Heathen Poets, & Classicks, are good; as Homer, Menander, Sophocles, Euripides, Aristophanes, &c. and some of their Grammarians & Lexicographers.

The Philosophers as Plato, Aristotle, Orators as Demosthenes, Isocrates, Mathematitians as Euclide, Pappus, Aristarchus.

The Physitians, as Hippocrates, Galen, Nicander, Aëtius (with the Chirurgions) Dioscorides.

The Laws of the Greek Empire, are to be sought after, and the Novell Constitutions of every Emperor (even Christian) if you can get them.

In short, the works of any Greek Heathen will be acceptable here.

As to the Works of Greek Christians, more Caution may be used, least you be Imposed upon. For such Books are more plentiful and yet more Valued by their Clergy, who make more use of them. They are partly of these Kinds,

Books of Scripture. Here I should be very glad if you can procure

---

[2] Patriarch of Jerusalem 1665–1706, aged 107 at his death.

a Complete Bible of the Old & New Testament, in one or more Volumes, written by one Hand, which had long been a Standard in some Old Cathedral or other Church. If such a Bible be not to be had, be pleased to get for my Lord, an Old Copy in Parchment, of the Old Testament or Septuagint, with such Marks as these here & there ※ ÷ ◡ ⁓, or else without those Marks if they cannot be had. Get also the other Books of the New Testament, as Occasions happen, and you will find Psalters & Gospels the most Common.

As for their Lectionaries, Evangelistaries, their Extracts out of the Scripture, Prayers, Troparies, Synaxaries, and in short, all their Liturgical Books, they need not be sought for singly, but only bought as they happen to come in Collections.

My Lord would be glad of a good, old, & fair Copie of their Meneion or Menology, but let it not be that of Symeon Metaphrastes, or other Lying Greeks. And here I may say, by the by, that my Lord doth not regard their Books of Visions, Dreams, Prophecies, Charms, Philosophers Stone, Chimistry, &c.

Get what you Can of the Works of the Fathers of the Three first Centuries, particularly of Origen. As for the others, they are not so rare, and those of Chryostom, Basil, Gregory Nazianzen, Athanasius, Joannes Damascenus, Joannes Philoponus, & such like, they are Common, as you will find, and consequently will come at an easier rate.

My Lord would be glad of an Old Synodicon for the Acts of the Antient Councils, and that you would see to gett the Canons of all the Greek Councils down to the Present Time: as also the Laws & Ordinances of all the Christian Emperors, & their Ministers, with the Byzantine Historians, and Chronicles of particular Churches & Monasteries. Although upon Enquiry you will find the Libraries of Churches & Monasteries to be most miserably Plundered; yet by Diligent & Careful Search, you will find many Things in Private Studies, Cells & Corners, that will turn to good Accompt.

One thing I must, in especial manner recommend to your more particular Care. It is plain that the Cathedral Churches & Monasteries must have had a Legal Foundation there, as well as here; and that the Benefactions in Land, must have been conveyed to them by Deeds there, as well as here. And we know it to be so. Now I would have you to procure as many Original Deeds in Greek, as you possibly can, taking special Care of the Seals, whether they be of Metal or of Wax.

The Old Churches & Monasteries have Offices or Places where these things & their other Books of Entries & Records lie. Buy up all these that you can, they will come Cheap, & will be of Excellent Use. Moreover, I would desire you to save all the Original Letters you can get, with other things of Private use as Books of Expenses & Accompts, if they be in the Greek Language. In their Churches you will also find some long Rolls of Parchment written upon in Greek, save all them, lett their Subject be Prayers, or what it will.

My Lord will be glad, of an Antient Copy of the Old Testament in Syriac, from the Maronites of Mount Libanus, if it be written upon Parchment.

The like of a Bible in the Georgian, Ethiopian or Abyssine and Armenian Languages.

For the Hebrew, my Lord is & will be pretty well furnished; but a Volume of their Law, rolled upon a Stick, & finely written would not be unacceptable.

It is said that the Samaritans at Sichem in Palestine, are almost if not quite Extinct. They had an old Volume of the Law, written in their proper Character, which would be a Rarity here.

My Lord would be glad of the Bible in the Coptic Language, from Cairo. The Coptic Character being large, it will take up divers Volumes. The Books of the Psalter & Gospels, especially with the Arabic Version, are the most Common.

As for Arabic, Turkish, Persian, and other less known languages spoken in the East, my Lord hath not much Opinion of them; and therefore he giveth no particular Commission about them; only this, that a good History, or Book of Travels will be welcome in any Language.

As to a Method to be taken in procuring them, that it may not interfere too much with your other Affairs, my Lord would desire you to employ the Chaplain to the Factory, who is always deemed to be a Man of Letters, and to use his Judgement as to the Matter of a Book, otherwise you may be imposed upon by false Accounts. You would do well to use many Emisaries, especially Jews & Greeks; among the latter their Bishops may be easily retained. These men will Easily furnish you with Rolls, Deeds, & Letters, and from Antioch, Alexandria, Jerusalem, Bethlehem, Nazareth, Ephesus, and other old Churches on Mount Sina, &c you may get the Books wherein they Entered Copies of the Deeds relating to their Foundation & Endowment, which we should much Value.

It would be well, to do all as privatly as may be; for if it should take too much Air, & one Emissary know that any other is employed besides himself, the price of the Commodity will soon be Raised. And therefore upon the bringing in of any Parcel, it may be laid up, & not looked into untill the time cometh for the Return of the Turkey Fleet, when all may be Packed up in such manner as to take no damage by Rats, or Wet, & so sent for England.

MS: British Library, Harley 7055, fo. 17; draft, unsigned. *Endorsed*: 'Instructions for procuring Gr[   ] MSS. George Daniel &c.'

127. *To* John Covell   *30 September 1712*

Reverend Sir,

I received your last kind Letter (for the favour of which I am very thankfull) but have not had an Opportunity of communicating the Contents thereof unto my Lord Treasurer, because of his great Business; nor to my Lord Harley, because he is in the Countrey; but I will take as much Care of it as if it was my own Concern, & hope to give you Satisfaction at the long Run.

Mr Paul of Jesus College[1] hath informed me, that our old Friend Mr Laughton is Deceased; and that His Friends have Advised him to Stand as Candidate for the Office of Keeper of the University-Library; and hearing that I had the happiness to be known to the Eminently Learned Master of Christs-College, he desired me to Recommend him to your Favor, in Order to be Pricked by the Heads of Houses, for One of the Two. My Acquaintance with the Gentleman, is not of very long Standing; but I do believe him to be a person very well qualified for the Place, where the Manuscripts are of very great Value, and require the Constant Residence of an Officer sufficiently Skilled that Way. If you intend not to fill up the Place with some Gentleman of your own College, or be no otherways already Engaged; I shall take your favorable Countenance & Assistance of my Friend Mr Paul, as another great Obligation laid upon me; and always rejoyce that my Recommendation had some Weight with one so much my Superior, & for whom I have so great Respect.

[1] George Paul († 1714), Fellow of Jesus College, Cambridge 1704–14. The successful candidate was Philip Brooke († 1759), Fellow of St John's College, Cambridge 1701–17, who held the post until 1718.

It being now turn'd of a Year since I was at Cambridge; I must Crave leave to putt you in Mind of the promise you was pleased to make unto me, with Regard to your Manuscripts. Namely, that I should be the Purchaser of them all, at a Reasonable Price; and that in Order thereunto, you would send me up a Catalogue of them within twelve Months. The time being expired, I shall be glad to see the Catalogue, and to know your Demand;[2] and so much the rather, as that I am ready as to the Money-Matter. I beg your Answer, which may still be directed to be left for me at my Lord Treasurers, where it will come safe to the Hands of

Reverend Sir,

  Your most obliged, & very humble servant

           Humfrey Wanley.

Mr Kemp is very much your servant.

MS: British Library, Add. 22911, fo. 146. Copy in Cambridge University Library MS Mm. vi. 50, fo. 280. *Date*: 'Chelsea, 30 September 1712.' *Address*: 'To The Reverend Dr Covel Master of Christs College in Cambridge.'

128. *To* [Philip Stubbs] *18 October 1712*

Reverend Sir,

I had not an Opportunity of Returning an Answer to yours of the 14th Instant until now. In my last, before I received yours with that of Mr Johnson[1] therein Enclosed, I gave you an Hint touching the unnecessariness of giving previous Notice to the Market that a Chapman was coming, from such a Distance. And 'tis observed here, that thereupon, those on the other side of the Water, int[end] to hold their Goods to a Price thereupon. My Opinion is (if you go) that you should agree for the Things comprehended in the Article relating to Confucius,[2] mentioned in Mr Johnson's Letter as about to be Printed (inducing them to abate according to the Value of a Squeezed Orange)[3] that you should take a Note for the Delivery of the same to

---

[2] Not sent until Jan. 1716. Now BL Add. MS 22911 fos. 180–3.

[1] Thomas Johnson (*fl.* 1715–26), bookseller at The Hague. Involved in the abortive attempt to print Aymon's manuscripts in 1715: see Wanley, *Diary*, p. 6(4).

[2] See no. 129 n. 1.

[3] Wanley's usual term for a manuscript which has been printed.

you or your Order, at such a time, and at such a Low Price; and as to
the Remainder, to pursue your former Instructions.

I long to have this troublesome Business brought to some good
Issue, and will be responsible for the Museo de las Medallas, which I
design for a Present to your good Friend Mr Kemp; unto whom I am
very much Obliged. We drank to your good Voiage just now; and my
Lord Yarmouth[4] will be willing to see You upon your Return. I am
&c.

MS: Welbeck Wanleyana = British Library, Loan 29/259 misc. 37; draft, unsigned.
Date: '18 October 1712.'

129. *To* Philip Stubbs *20 November 1712*

Reverend Sir,

I have received yours dated the 4th Instant from the Hague, with the
Enclosed Paper, which brought me the First certain News of your
Arrival in Holland. For I did not look upon an[o]ther Letter which I
received from you the 27 of October last, beginning thus, *You find by
this that I am in Holland* to be CERTAIN; because it bare no Date either as
to Time or Place, nor had any Stamp upon it to shew in What Bag it
came up to the Post-Office, where it was, however, Stamp'd with $\left(\frac{OC}{25}\right)$

In my last of the 18 October 1712 (which I perceive came to your
Hands) I thought I had said enough. But since you still Want farther
Advice, in the Absence of my Principals (who are not yet returned
from Windsor) I presume to declare my Private Opinion,

That the Chinese books (of which I always thought the Soliloquies
of Confucius to be part) at 150 Guilders, and Visconti's Epistles at 100
Guilders, are the greatest Rates for Squeezed Oranges that I have yet
heard of; especially adding 50 Guilders more for Confucius.[1]

---

[4] William Paston (1654–1732), 2nd Earl of Yarmouth.

[1] Wanley's 'Brief Account' (see no. 123 n. 2) lists two lots of Chinese books: (1) 'Two
Printed Chinese Books, entituled Soliloquia Confucij' (Brief Account no. 3) and (2)
'The Translation of the Works of Confucius, with Chinese Maps, & other Books relating to the late Conduct of the Jesuits in China' (Brief Account, postscript). Aymon was
unwilling to sell either the Confucius 'Translation' or the Visconti at the time, but
promised to let Wanley have them within two years: see n. 4 below. This perhaps had to
do with a plan to publish them (Wanley, *Diary*, p. 6(4))—hence Wanley's reference to
'Squeezed Oranges' here. Only the Visconti appears to have been pbd. by Aymon (as

That I cannot say much about the History of Paolo IV,[2] because there is no mention of the first & last Words of each of the five Books, which would have enabled me to have compared it with some of the MSS. of that Life, to be found in England. This must therefore be left to your Discretion also.

As to the piece of the Epistles Gr. & Lat. N.6.[3] which You say would be worth, if in[t]ire 1000000 or a Milion of Guilders, I know not after whose Judgement such a Valuation was made. Sure I am no book was ever yet sold at a price comparable to it. King Charles I upon the receipt of the four Volumes of the Alexandrian MS. (being worth more than twenty of this Book of the Epistles supposing it were perfect) as a Present from Cyrillus Lucaris together with many other valuable MSS although he were a Great Monarch, and had a true Notion of their Worth, returned out of his Royal Bounty no more than 500£, which was yet thought a great deal too much.

You will do therefore Well to beat down this Extravagant Price to a much more Moderate Rate; for as the Cast Stands (notwithstanding what he may pretend) there is no fear of Interlopers. Shew the poor Man, that no Seller upon the face of the Earth ever Valued his goods to that height of Exorbitance, as himself: and that if he has A mind of your Ready Money, he must come at it, by Reasonable dealing, & not otherwise.

As to these Chinese things, Visconti, & the Theologia Mohammedana, take a sufficient Note for their Delivery (at the lowest Rate possible) unto You or Your Order, by or upon such particular Day or Days, as you shall Agree.[4]

I know not that Dr Swift[5] hath written such a Book as you mention,

---

Lettres, anecdotes et mémoires historiques du Nonce Visconti) and that not until 1719. As late as 1721 Wanley was still trying to obtain the *manuscripts* of these works (Wanley, *Diary*, p. 107(14)); he was successful only in getting the Visconti (Wanley, *Diary*, p. 124(12)), now BL Harley MS 3479.

[2] BL Harley MS 1763 = Brief Account no. 9.

[3] i.e. the fragment of Codex Claromontanus: see Wanley to Stubbs, no. 123 n. 5.

[4] Cf. Brief Account, postscript: 'Mr Stubs saith, that the Monsieur not being willing (nor indeed able, at this time) to Sell the Letters of Cardinal Visconti disclosing the Intrigues used in the Council of Trent: The Translation of the Works of Confucius, with Chinese Maps, & other Books relating to the late Conduct of the Jesuits in China, being the Authentic Books; And the Persian Author treating of the Mahumetan Theology: He hath taken Security for their being safely Delivered unto Him or His Order, within Two Years next Ensuing, He then Paying for them 200 Gilders more.' But see n. 1 above.

[5] Presumably Jonathan Swift (1667–1745), Dean of St Patrick's.

nor have seen any thing upon the Subject; my Studies, as you know, lying another way.

With hearty Prayers for your safe Return with the Cargo,⁶ I remain.

MS: Welbeck Wanleyana = British Library, Loan 29/259 misc. 37; draft, unsigned. *Date*: '20 Nov. 1712.' *Address*: 'to Mr Stubs at the Hague.'

130. *To* [The Mayor of Leicester]¹ *9 December 1712*

Sir,

With all due Respect I crave Leave to acquaint you, that some time since, the Magistrates of your Corporation were pleas'd to favor me with the Loan of a Greek Manuscript of the New Testament, out of your Leceister-Library.² I borrowed it only to renew my Acquaintance with the Greek Written-Hand, & the Abbreviations used therein; to which my intent, the book prove's of singular Use, being all of as Bad & Difficult Writing, as I could wish. Upon this only Account I am desirous of keeping it always by me. And that I may do so, I am willing to give in Exchange for it, Books of far Greater Use & Value.³ Your Book is Imperfect at both Ends; very Modern, comparitively speaking; and very Erroneously Written. Notwithstanding which, as also that the Readings thereof have been Collected & Published by Dr Mill:⁴ I propose to give for it (besides Dr Gale's Antoninus,⁵ which

---

⁶ The purchase must have been completed by the end of the year: the first draft of Wanley's 'Brief Account' is d. 3 Jan. 1713 (Welbeck Wanleyana = BL Loan MS 29/259 misc. 37).

¹ John Cooper (1669–1740), Mayor of Leicester in 1712. He was courted by Wanley in the spring of 1712 when in London, in the hope that his succession as mayor would improve Wanley's chances of acquiring the manuscript he writes about here, since the incumbent mayor was recalcitrant.
² Carte, Vicar of St Martin, Leicester (of which Cooper was churchwarden), intermediary: he writes (7 Apr. 1712; Welbeck Wanleyana = BL Loan 29/252) that Wanley had permission to borrow the Leicester Codex for three months or more, but the Corporation was unwilling to let it go permanently. Wanley was not easily deterred, as is clear from a note on the back of a letter d. 22 Mar. 1713: 'Sr. George Beaumont, or Mr Winstanley, or both, may be applied unto, in Order to getting the MS. Greek Testament from the Corporation of Leicester, & giving it here' (BL Harley MS 3780, fo. 304ᵛ). Beaumont and Stanley were MPs for Leicester. See also no. 141. Codex Leicestrensis was given to the city by Thomas Hayne of Trussington, Leicestershire, with his other books in 1641. It was collated by Mill at Oxford in 1671.   ³ Wanley valued it at 40s.
⁴ In his edn. of the NT (Oxford, 1707), Darlow and Moule no. 4725.
⁵ *Iter Britanniarum* (1709).

I lately sent to the Library by my worthy friend Mr Carte) the same Dr
Mill's Edition of the Greek Testament, which gives You, Your own
Book again, together with the particular Readings of many Scores of
Greek MSS much more antient and authentic, than this of Yours. I
will also give Dr Grabe's Edition of Irenaeus,[6] one of the first Fathers
of the Church: and do Consent that the Name of the Person who gave
this MS. Testament, be putt upon these Valuable Books of mine, as if
he had given the same; in such Manner as to You shall be found meet,
and without any mention of me. Hereupon, I appeal to all mankind,
whether I do not deal Fairly and Honorably by You. And as to the
Intent of the Donor, I think I answer it better than if the Book were to
be always in your Library. For, to be sure, he put his Book there, that
it might be of some use to the Divines in & about Leicester. How
much Time they have spent upon it, is much better known to themselves, than to me. But this I am sure of, that Dr Mill's Book will
prove of far greater use to them than this; if the Most Correct Text,
the Greatest Variety of the best Readings, and his own most laborious
& Learned Notes & Discourses, be Valued among You, as much they
are in the rest of England, and in all other Parts of Europe. And if a
Book may be supposed to be more useful where it is dayly inspected,
rather than where it may be almost totally neglected & forgotten. You
may also, if you shall Judge it necessary, Cause a Memorandum to be
Entred in some proper place, specifying this Exchange, and the
Terms thereof: to the End that if at any time hereafter, any person
shall Enquire for the Book (which I believe will never happen, after
what Dr Mill hath Written about it) He may be Directed to me, from
whom he will have full Satisfaction. Sir I beg that you will be pleased
to communicate the Contents of this to the other Magistrates of the
Corporation, whom with You I take to be Governors of the Library. I
shall receive their Compliance with me herein as a Favor, and shall be
thereby Encouraged as Occasions may happen, to be a better Benefactor to the same [place],[7] than they may now think of. I desire also
that you would come to a Resolution about it with convenient Speed,
and that I may be apprised of the same, because in all affairs wherein I
happen to be concerned, I love to come to a Point as soon as I may. I
hope, one day, to see Leicester again, which I look upon (in a manner)
as my Native Countrey. When I shall be so happy, I shall be sure to lett

---

[6] *Irenaeus Contra Haereses Libri Quinque* (Oxford, 1702).
[7] Written over original 'Library'?

You and all your Worshipful Bretheren know, with what Zeal &
Sincerity I am,

MS: Welbeck Wanleyana = British Library, Loan 29/252; draft, unsigned. *Date*:
'9 December 1712.'

131. *To* John Covell *19 March 1713*

Reverend Sir,

Your two last Letters came safe to my Hands; the former whereof I
communicated to our worthy friend Mr Cooke, who soon after (thro'
mismenagement of those who attended him in his sickness, as I have
heard) deceased. I shewed him the Sea-Chart again,[1] which hath all
alone been in my custody, in a Closet which I alone keep the Key of;
and shewed him that my Lord could never yet have time to look upon
it. That it had, however, been viewed by some well Skilled in those
Matters; and that although my Lord ha's no great Opinion of it, he had
yet so much Respect for the Learned Master of Christs College, as to
make him an handsome Present, in lieu of it. And therefore I looked
upon it as Sold: it not being for my Lords Honor to Send it back, when
it had been kept so long. So much for that.

As to your MSS. when I was last at Cambridge, I came upon my
own acct and (having a little of the Ready) was willing to buy them at a
reasonable Price: and therefore in my last I did ag[a]in desire a Catalogue of them according to your Promise. But since, in your last but
one, and especially in the last, you seem willing that my Lord should
have them, I durst not Interfere with my Lord, but therefore resign up
to him my Pretensions, and have Communicated yours to him accordingly. I must therefore desire you to send up a short Catalogue
speedily, specifying not only the Contents, but the Bigness of each
book, and a Reasonable Price for the whole: and I will do my endeavor
to serve you in the Affair, to the best of my Power; who am
     Reverend Sir,
          Your most obliged, humble servant

H. Wanley.

MS: British Library, Add. 22911, fo. 156. Copy in Cambridge University Library MS
Mm.vi.50, fo. 282. *Date*: '19 March 1712/3.' *Address*: 'To The Reverend Dr Covell
Master of Christs College in Cambridge.'

[1] See no. 122 n. 1.

132. *To* John Gagnier[1] *26 June 1713*

Reverend Sir,

Although I have not hitherto been able to procure you due Satisfaction for the piece of Service you did my Lord Treasurer, in Translating part of the Hebrew Star I shewed you in His Library; I nevertheless (at the request of a Friend) presume to recommend the Bearer hereof Rabbi Daniel Cohen de Azevedo to Your Favor & Protection, during the short Time of his Stay in Oxford.[2] His Business there is only the Satisfaction of a Travellers Curiosity; and the Sight of 3 or 4 Colleges, the Theater, Musaeum, Scholes, & Bodleyan Library, all that he desire's. He is reported to be a man very well learned in the Hebrew Literature; and therefore if you shew him any Curious Books in the Bodleyan Library his Discourses thereupon may, perhaps, by you be found worthy the Hearing.

In some time to come I hope to be admitted to the Sight of many Original Stars, and authentic Records of the Jews, before they were Banished out of England by K. Edward I. When I have seen them, you shall not fail of an account thereof from him, who is with true Respect
    Reverend Sir,
        Your most humble servant
                                                        Humfrey Wanley.

MS: Welbeck Wanleyana = British Library, Loan 29/260 misc. 88. *Date*: '26 June 1713.' *Address*: 'To The Reverend Mr Garnier Professor of Hebrew in the University of Oxford, at his House in Halliwell.'

133. *To* George Daniel *30 September 1713*

Mr George Daniel, you are desired to bring to me from Smyrna the book in the hand of Papa Seraphim there, being as you say the works of Homer & of Chrysostom, in one thick Volume of Parchment. And

[1] John Gagnier (?1670–1740), Hebrew and Arabic scholar, a Frenchman who settled at Oxford under the patronage of William Lloyd, Bishop of Worcester (Wanley's patron). Professor of Arabic 1724. He supplied Wanley with titles for oriental works purchased for the Library.

[2] Wright suggests (Wanley, *Diary*, Biographical Index, p. 439) that he was a member of the notable Sephardic Jewish family, members of the Bevis Marks Synagogue. In 1721 (*Diary*, p. 106 (6)) Alzevedo offered for sale to Wanley modern Hebrew manuscripts for the Harleian Library.

also two other books in the hands of the Kandelautus of St George's
Church in Smyrna, being the one of Chrysostom's Works, the other
of Andreas Cretensis, for which books I allow you two Guineas.

NB. I have farther in my note delivered to mr Daniel, desired him to
Enquire after all other sorts of Greek Books, Rolls, Deeds, Letters, or
Leaves.

MS: Welbeck Wanleyana = British Library Loan MS 29/259 misc. 40. *Date*: '30 September 1713'. *Endorsed*: 'Sptembr:30:1713 I pormis to bring the sid Books on the rect: of
tow gines George Daniel.'[1]

134. *To* the Earl of Denbigh[1]   *28 November 1713*

May &c.

It is with all possible Submission that I take upon me to appear
before You in this Manner. I am the Person whom Your Lordship,
about twenty years ago, was pleased to Honor with your Permission of
taking a Catalogue of your Old Written Books, which was afterward
Printed at Oxford.[2] At that time You also spake to me concerning my
Father, who was Chaplain to the Noble Earl your Unkle.[3]

Since then, I have often thought of those Books; and now having
(for many Years) had the Care & Custody of My Lord Treasurers
Library, wherein there are two Thousand Books of the like kind (not
to mention 1000 Rolls, & 13000 Deeds) I not only study how to keep
together what is got already but to augment this great Collection as far
as I am able: and, I can truly say, that my Success ha's in the main been
answerable to my Industry.

I hear that there is a great Friendship between my Noble Lord the
Lord Treasurer & Your Illustrious Lordship; which without doubt is
cultivated by both with all that Honor & those mutual good Wishes, as
become such Great Personages, and Sett them forth as shining

---

[1] Daniel's receipt d. 8 Oct. 1713 follows, although the manuscripts seem not to have
found their way into the Harleian Library.

[1] Basil Feilding (1668–1717), 4th Earl of Denbigh.
[2] *CMA* II. i, 35–9.
[3] Nathaniel Wanley (1634–80), Vicar of Holy Trinity, Coventry 1662, and chaplain to
Basil Feilding (*c.*1608–75), 2nd Earl. He compiled in 1670 a history of the Feilding
family (ptd. in J. Nichols, *The History and Antiquities of the County of Leicestershire*, iv (1815),
pp. 273–90) beginning, characteristically, with an account of the Habsburgs.

Examples for meaner Men to imitate. But percieving that notwith-standing the Collection My Lord ha's already made, there is still Room for new Accessions, and not finding that Your Lordship intendeth to Establish any Library of Antiquities at Newenham,[4] I have been thinking that it would be a Generous & a truly Noble Action, if your Lordship should throw those Old Things, into this Library where they will be always preserved to Your Lordships own Honor & Glory & the Public Use; where Your Noble Memory will be always gratefully kept up (my Lords Catalogue always declaring their Names who at any time give him Old Books) and whereby, you may lay my Lord-Treasurer under an indespensible Obligation of Return-ing his Thanks to Your Lordship.

My Lord, what I have above written, is all of mine own Hand, and altogether without my Lord-Treasurer's, or any other Mortals know-ledge. If Your Lordship, shall think it fitting to lay an Obligation on my Lord-Treasurer, in this manner, (for altho' He wanteth not Money to buy Old Books withal, I yet have more Manners, than to talk of Money here) I would humbly desire that it may be done speedily. If your Lordship is not willing to part with anything of that kind, there is no harm done, for My Lord Treasurer nor nobody else, as I said before, know's of this my writyng, nor (in this Case) ever shall.[5] Only, I would humbly beg one line of Answer hereunto, that I may be apprised of Your Lordships noble Pleasure herein, because I am not only by Hereditary Right, but by my own sincere & profound Devo-tion, &c.

MS: Welbeck Wanleyana = British Library, Loan 29/258; draft, unsigned. *Date*: '28 Nov. 1713.' *Address*: 'To the Earl of Denbigh.'

135. *To* —— *28 November 1713*

Reverend Sir,

I suppose the Gentleman whom you sent unto me, hath before this, done me justice in declaring how willing I am to serve him (would it lie

[4] Newnham Paddox, Monks Kirby, Warwickshire, the Feilding family seat since the time of Henry VI.

[5] Wright (*Diary*, p. xxviii n. 2) points out that Wanley's appeal was unsuccessful and the manuscripts remained in the family until at least 1851, when many were acquired by the British Museum (Add. MSS 18629–73).

in my power) for your sake. But that is not[1] the only occasion of this Letter, but rather another matter wherein your Friendly Assistance will be of great service unto me. You remember The Papers I shewed You when we talked upon my Book now on the Stocks,[2] which (together with what I acquainted you that Mr Elphinstone[3] hath written for me) is a sufficient Demonstration that the Work is pretty far advanced, so that it beginneth to be time that I should look about for other Helps which may Illustrate or Confirm the Writings I am about to Sett forth in Print. Among these I account the Chronicle in the Lambeth-Library, entitled Scala Mundi, (FOL. XXII) to be one.[4] Now, honest Mr Williams[5] this Bearer, having kindly promised to give me the Transcription of any Book, &c. during these Winter Months, I should be exceedingly Obliged if you could speedily procure me the loan of the said Book for this Purpose; which I do assure you, shall go into no mans hands but Mr Williams's and my own.

MS: Welbeck Wanleyana = British Library, Loan 29/258; draft, unsigned. *Date*: '28 November 1713.'

136. *To* [Robert Harley] *15 December 1713*

May &c.

I am acquainted that Mr Rymer Her Majesties Historiographer[1] deceased Yesterday, and therefore am an humble Petitioner for Your Lordships High Protection, Countenance, & Favor, that I may be admitted to Succeed him. How I am qualified for the Employment, is much Better known to Your Excellence than to any other. As to my Private Demeanor, so many Years in your House, I think 'tis plain Enough, that No Shadow of an Imputation can be laid upon Me. Your Lordship was pleased, about 15 years ago, to Promise to See me advanced in my Way; and that this is in my Way, is plain enough; since

[1] non MS.

[2] See no. 136.

[3] John Elphinstone, Under-Keeper of the Cotton Library.

[4] James and Jenkins, *Descriptive Catalogue*, no. 22. A composite manuscript of the fifteenth century, three works, from the first of which the manuscript takes its name.

[5] Moses Williams (1686–1742), Welsh antiquary, for some time sub-librarian of the Ashmolean Museum.

[1] Thomas Rymer (1641–1713), Historiographer Royal 1692.

I am now actually engaged in the Publication of some of our English Historians, in Two Volumes in Folio; towards which work I have already gotten near two hundred Sheets of Paper, written mostly by my own Hand and which I hope to see come forth into the World with as much Reputation as any Book of the like Kind hath here mett withal.[2]

I am not how ever, of an over-weening Opinion of my fitness for this Station, above those who may be Candidates on this occasion: but this I may venture to assert, that those who may better Deserve it, are also already better Provided for than I am. I beg to be Admitted to Your Audience on this Occasion, and am with the greatest Reverence,

MS: Welbeck Wanleyana = British Library, Loan 29/258; draft, unsigned. *Date*: '15 Decr. 1713.'

[2] See Wanley's 'Proposal for Printing a Volume of Old English Historians, from my Lords Library' (n.d.) ptd. below, Appendix VII. As early as 1697 he was thinking of collecting manuscripts relating to the history of England (including cartularies of monastic houses) for the Cotton Library (see Wanley to T. Smith, 17 May 1697), and BL Stowe MS 80 is a catalogue compiled by Wanley (but not in his hand) of English historians, printed and unprinted, in the Cotton collection. The prime mover in the present enterprise was Thomas Thynne, 1st Viscount Weymouth. He gave Wanley £100, promised him as much again for a dedication, and agreed to take fifty copies of the work when it was published. It was Wanley's intention to print the Dunstable Chronicle, that of Benedict of Peterborough, and the Lanercost Annals, with copious illustrative material in the way of notes, charters, seals, monuments, epitaphs, a glossary, and an index to the whole; but this characteristically ambitious plan had to be abandoned and it was decided that he should print the text alone. See Wanley's account in BL Harley MS 3777, fo. 218.

Wanley himself transcribed Benedict of Peterborough and the Dunstable Chronicle: the former, from Cotton Julius A.xi, art. 4 (with lacunae and variants supplied from Cotton Vitellius E.xvii, art. 3, a MS severely damaged in the Cotton fire of 1731), is BL Harley MS 3666; the latter, from Cotton Tiberius A.x (also severely damaged in 1731), is BL Harley MS 4886. The Lanercost Annals were transcribed by John Elphinstone, Under-Keeper of the Cotton Library (Elphinstone to Wanley, 4 Dec. 1713, Welbeck Wanleyana = BL Loan MS 29/254) from Cotton Claudius D.vii. Elphinstone's transcript is BL Harley MSS. 3424–5.

The computation of copy for the projected volume by the printer William Bowyer is in BL Harley MS 3777, fo. 218. But the enterprise foundered with the death of Weymouth on 28 July 1714. Charlett urged Wanley to take it up again four years later (Charlett to Wanley d. 9 May 1718, BL Harley MS 3778, fo. 45ᵛ) but nothing came of it. Two of Wanley's transcripts were eventually ptd. by Hearne—the Dunstable Chronicle (1733) and Benedict of Peterborough (1735); of Wanley's transcript of the latter, Stubbs, re-editing the text in 1867, said 'This copy is a miracle of correctness; every variation, every change of hand, the beginning of every folio, every transposition, every lacuna, every occasional gap, is most carefully noted (*Gesta Regis Henrici Secundi Benedicti Abbatis* (Rolls Series, 1867), i, pt. xxxiv).

137. *To* [Robert Harley] *17 December 1713*

May, &c.

After my most humble Thanks for the Honor you was pleased to do
me Yesterday, I crave Leave to renew my Request for this Office of
Historiographer, which I have fixed my Mind upon for many years
past, and have taken much pains to Qualify my Self for, and consequently shall be grieved to see bestowed upon another whose
pretentions may be lighter than Mine. If it be but 100£ per annum[1] I
am content, and can look upon it as a mark of the Public Countenance,
& Encouragement to proceed in my poor Studies. But if it must be
given to a Man of a Great Estate, as a Feather to His Fine Cap; and
poor I who have Laboured above twenty years to fit my self for Service
and have but few things to ask for be rejected & thrust-aside. What
must I say! I must bid adieu to old Books, and try if I can get a Lively-
hood in another Way! I have born up against many heavy Discourage-
ments for a long time, in hopes of obtaining Ease some day or other:
But if I who am actually advanced so far toward the bringing to Light
divers of our Unpublished Historians, shall see my expected Reward
conferred on another who never had an intention of doing the like
service. How can I behave my Self! What will the World think of me?
What Censure may I not apprehend, as if I had deservedly fell under
Your High Displeasure? My Lord, I humbly beg Pardon for this
[Ea]rnestness: I am under an Extreme Concern, lest this Thing,
should be given away from Me. I must therefore shelter my Self under
Your most Powerful Protection. I am told the Duke[2] can only Recommend, & that it is Her Royal Majesty, or Your Lordship under Her,
who may give the Place. And if it is your Noble Intention that I shall
not now be Postponed, Your [Ex]cellence in your Consummate
Wisdom, easily knoweth How to induce His Grace to consent that
You who have been the general Mecænas should Now Encourage an
Old Servant to Serve You for the Future with as much Spirit & Chear-
fulness, as he hath hitherto done with Fidelity & Diligence.[3] I forbear

---

[1] Rymer's salary had been £200.

[2] Perhaps John Sheffield (1647–1721), 1st Duke of Buckingham and Normanby 1703,
Lord Steward of the Household 1710, Lord President of the Council 1711, one of Queen
Anne's favourites.

[3] The post went to Thomas Madox (1666–1727), historian of the Exchequer (1711); he
was admitted to the office on 12 July 1714.

farther to Trouble Your Lordship, but remain with intire Submission to your Lordships Pleasure, in this & all things,
  May, &c.

MS: Welbeck Wanleyana = British Library, Loan 29/258; draft, unsigned. *Date*: '17 Dec. 1713.'

138. *To* John Covell *26 December 1713*

Reverend Sir,

Your last kind Letter of the 10th Instant[1] came safe. I had before that time written to my Lord Harley at Wymple, desiring his Lordship to pay you for the Chart, as reason is.[2] His Lordship was pleased to answer, that He had seen you, and then did think of the Affair, but not judging that a fit Opportunity, he deferred it, to the time that he should make you his Intended Visit in Cambridge. Since then, he is come up to Town, & I have apprised Him, & My Noble Lord Treasurer also, of the Contents of Yours; and You may assure your Self of your being Nobly paid; although my Lord Treasurer never yet had so much time to himself, as to Call for the Chart.

As for your other MSS. my Lord Treasurer all along expected a Catalogue of the whole Cargo, according to the Promise you made me.[3] And when, instead of a Catalogue of the whole, you sent up only an account of those in Hebrew,[4] his Expectation was not answered thereby. For he doth not want Hebrew MSS, having already those which are more Beautiful, more Antient, more Rare, & more Valuable (not to add, more in Number) than those I saw in your Closett: although he be still willing to pay for a Parcel of any Value, wherein such Books may be found.

If I may, therefore, advise in this Matter, it shall be to transmitt unto me a Short Catalogue of the whole, as Sorted into their respective Languages and Sizes. And that You would Sett a Reasonable Price

---

[1] BL Harley MS 3778, fo. 107.

[2] This is the first evidence of Edward Harley's active interest in the Library. Wimpole, near Royston, Cambridge, was Edward Harley's family seat, inherited by his wife Henrietta Cavendish, from her father John Holles, 1st Duke of Newcastle (of the creation of 1694), † 1711; the Harleys were married at Wimpole in Aug. 1713. The estate was sold in 1740 to Lord Chancellor Hardwicke to pay off a debt of £100,000.

[3] See no. 127 and n. 2.

[4] See Covell to Wanley d. 21 Mar. 1713, BL Harley MS 3778, fo. 105.

upon the Whole. Which being done, I believe my Lord will soon send me down to you; and upon a View, the Things being found to answer the Catalogue, the Money shall be paid immediatly, before a Leaf is carried off the Spot. This I take to be the best Method for You. When you have the Money in your Purse you know how to turn it, how to Employ it, how to Give it. If You leave the Things to Your Executors, they will not be able to sell them so well as You your Self may now do. If you leave them to any Library, You lose the Money by the Bargain, & your Benefaction will not be Valued at half the Worth, laid out in Common Printed Books. Be pleased to favor me with an Answer hereunto, and believe that Mr Kemp is as well affected to your Service, as

> Reverend Sir,
>> Your most humble servant,
>>> Humfrey Wanley.

MS: British Library, Add. 22911, fo. 160. Copy in Cambridge University Library MS Mm.vi.50, fo. 283. *Date*: '26 December 1713.' *Address*: 'To The Reverend Dr Covell Master of Christs College in Cambridge.'

139. *To* [Robert Harley] *30 December 1713*

May it please your most Excellent Lordship,

This day my friend Mr Moses Williams presented a MS. to your Library which formerly belonged to Mr Edw. Lhwyd of Oxford, of whom he borrowed it, & since had it given to him by Mr Lhwyd of Gogarthan.[1] Therein is an Interlude in the Cornish tongue, which Mr Edward Lhwyd collated with another Copie of the same at Oxford.[2] There is also an English Translation of the same. There is also Dr Davies's Collection of Welsh Proverbs, written with his own Hand, & an Auctarium to the same. I have placed the book at 94.A.21.[3] This Mr Williams, to my knowledge hath taken pains to serve your Lordship in Library-matters, and will do more the next Somer: & only desire's your Excellence & my Lord Harley to Subscribe to his Book, 12s. each for the first Payment.[4] Thus, now, we know of Five Manuscripts in the

[1] Williams had served as sub-librarian to Lhwyd (✝ 1709) at the Ashmolean Museum. Lhwyd's mother was a native of Gogerddan, Cardiganshire.

[2] Bodl. MS Bodley 219 (*SC* 3020), a transcript d. 1611.

[3] BL Harley MS 1867.

[4] A new edn. of the Welsh grammar (1621) of John Davies and the Welsh dictionary (1632) of John and Thomas Davies. Williams's proposal never came to anything.

Cornish Language; two in Your own Library, as many in the Bodleyan, & one in the Cottonian.[5]

Mr Paul[6] hath received his Things from Cambridge, and shewed me (in the Gross) what Answers to this List,

No.	1.	Letters French	66	No.	2.	Letters French & Italian	26
	3.	Denmark & Sweden (with 8 Copies) in all	46		4	— Mixt Languages	32
	5	— (Most of) Brunswick	29		6.	— Mixt.	23
	7.	— Q. of Bohemia (with 9 Palatines)	41		8	—Mixt.	13
	9	— Mixt	29		10	— Scotch	37
	11	— English	34		12	— English	22
	13(1)	E. of Salisbury & Lord Conway	36		13(2)	English	44
	14(1)	relating to Lady Arabella	50				
	15.	Mislaid; but since found as Mr Paul saith			16.	— To Prince Henry	22
	17.	— of the House of Nassau (taken from no. 7)	6		19	— of the Royal Family	21
		Copies of Letters from Prince Henry	82			— Latin	61
		to the R. Family	27			— Copied (as before) by Sir Adam Newton	16
		Papers relating to Prince Henry	27			Two small Parcels of Petitions to Pr.Henry	
		Warant for the E. of Essex's Commission at Cales				Old Deeds (some few Curious)	34

Mr Paul demandeth 40 Guineas for the Parcel, & is in most mighty hast for the money; always talking of his other Chapmen, &c. He will

[5] All identified and described by Wanley in the entry for Harley 1782 in the *Harleian Catalogue*: BL Harley MSS 1782, 1867; Bodl. MSS Bodley 219 (*SC* 3020), Bodley 791 (*SC* 2639); Cotton Vespasian A.xiv.

[6] Presumably George Paul. Wanley had supported his candidacy for the post of Librarian to the University of Cambridge, left vacant on the death of John Laughton in 1712: see no. 127. Laughton's collections seem to have descended to Paul, who sold part of them to Wanley together with some material of his own. Paul, however, died before the sale was completed. Some of Laughton's papers (letters and single documents) appear to have reached Wanley before Paul's death (no. 142), but the balance of Paul's (and presumably Laughton's) collections passed to Thomas Baker (1656–1740), the Cambridge antiquary who sold 'a small Parcel' to Robert Harley, 14 Mar. 1715 (*Diary*, p. 4 (5)). There is a list by Wanley of the papers acquired from Paul in BL Lansdowne MS 814, fos. 52–4ᵛ; they are now widely scattered throughout the Harleian collection. See Wright, *Fontes*, under Paul, for a full account of the business; Wright has no entry for Laughton in *Fontes*, but the evidence of no. 142 suggests that some at least of the Paul material in fact originally belonged to Laughton.

attend your Lordship to morrow, to know your Pleasure. This is one Parcel taken from a vast Quantity of Papers, & I suppose the remainder will be so parcelled out hereafter.

I make bold to present your Illustrious Lordship with 3 Old Deeds (which Mr Baker sent me the last week from Cambridge) as my poor New-years gift;[7] which I beg may be accepted for my good wills sake, although at this time I have nothing better. Thus heartily praying that Your Lordship may enjoy an happy New Year & very very many, I remain

May it please your Excellency,

Your most dutiful, & most faithful servant

H. Wanley.

MS: Welbeck Wanleyana = British Library, Loan 29/258. *Date*: '30 December 1713.'

140. *To* Arthur Charlett *4 February 1714*

Reverend Sir,

On the other part of this Paper you will find a Series of the Abbats of Hide, which I have faithfully Extracted from my Lords Chartulary.[1] I bought the Book about a year ago of a Broker;[2] and shall be glad to be informed how you came to hear of it; for it may be, by your means, I may know to whom it formerly belonged.

If there be any great Occasion, perhaps I may be able to make this Catalogue of the Abbats of Hide more complete.

I remember not long since, you desired to know how the Precedency was adjusted among the Abbats & Priors, in Parliament.[3] This I could not answer, because hitherto I have not been able to satisfie my self in that point. I think, however, that the Abbat of St Albans

---

[7] Not identified.

[1] BL Harley MS 1761, late fourteenth-century cartulary of the Benedictine Abbey of Hyde (New Minster), Winchester. Davis no. 1048. The 'Series' is omitted here.

[2] Inscribed by Wanley on verso of flyleaf 'Bought of Hancock the Devils Broker'; BL Harley MS 6338 is similarly inscribed. According to Davis, Peter Le Neve had formerly owned it.

[3] Charlett was apparently acting on behalf of Hearne (the publisher) or Browne Willis (the author). Amongst the appendices to Hearne's edn. of Leland's *Collectanea* (Oxford, 1715) is one (vol. vi, pp. 97–264) entitled 'A View of the Mitred Abbeys, with a Catalogue of their Respective Abbats' by Browne Willis. The 'series' of the abbots is found on pp. 232–4.

had the first Place; that there hath been four Houses of Convocation in former times, as there are two now; and that the Common Notion about Mitred Abbats is not adroit; since it may be easily proved, that divers Abbats sat in Parliament who were not Mitred; and that divers others who were Mitred, did not Sit in Parliament.

I would gladly know whether these Enquiries are only for private Satisfaction; or that some Antiquity-book (if I may make use of such a Word) is about to be Printed: and if so; what it is, and by whom.

As you say Sir, my Lords Library goe's on bravely. He ha's laid in some Hundreds of Pounds worth of MSS. this last Quarter; and is not, in the least deterred from buying such others as may be for his Purpose. There are some in Oxford, which formerly did belong to Mr Edward Lhywd, late Keeper of the Ashmolean Musaeum. If they may be had at a Reasonable Market-price, I believe his Lordship might be induced to buy them. I shall be glad to know what may be done therein;[4] and if this Service might be furthered by your Means, I shall not fail of acquainting him with the Obligation that he would thereby have unto You: as I have already apprised him of the Honor & Kindness you intend for Him; I mean the Bible to be Printed on Vellum.[5] I am, at this time in some hast more than Ordinary; but shall always remain with the truest Respect,

Reverend Sir,

Your most obliged, humble Servant

Humfrey Wanley.

MS: Bodleian, Ballard 13, fo. 126. *Date*: '4 Febr. 1713/4.' *Address*: 'To The Reverend Dr Charlett Master of University-College in Oxford.'

[4] Charlett replied that after Lhwyd's death in 1709 his collections had been seques-tered for debt, but that if they escaped the Bodleian Library he would try to get an option for Wanley (19 Feb. 1714; Welbeck Wanleyana = BL Loan MS 29/253). The manuscripts had been offered for sale to Jesus College, Oxford, as well as to the Univer-sity, but owing to a quarrel between Lhwyd and John Wynne (1667–1743) then Fellow, later (1712) Principal, they were declined. They were sold to Sir Thomas Sebright (1692–1736), Bart., of Beechwood, Herts., Jesus College, Oxford 1705, MP for Hertford-shire in four Parliaments from 1715 till his death. See further nos. 144, 168, 171, 175, and Wanley, *Diary*, p. 2(3) and nn. 2, 3 (for full references). For the subsequent history of Lhwyd's manuscripts, see *DNB* under Lhuyd.

[5] The magnificent folio edn. of 1717 ptd. in large type by J. Baskett. Darlow and Moule no. 943. It was unfortunately disfigured by many misprints (one of which, the headline 'The parable of the vinegar' (for 'vineyard') in Luke 20, gives it its name, the 'Vinegar Bible') and earned the nickname 'A Baskett-ful of Errors'. Three vellum copies are known: Bodleian Library, British Library, and one at Blenheim Palace.

141. *To* [Samuel Carte] *9 March 1714*

Reverend Sir,

In pursuance of the Direction Your Son left for me, I can assure you that the Greek Testament is delivered accordingly, and the Note I gave for it taken up. I am very thankful to you all who have been Kind to me with Relation to it; and Especially to the Worthy Mr Cowper, whose Civility I will neither Forget, nor Forbear to Retaliate when it shal be in my Power: and perhaps such a Time may Happen.[1]

And, now my Hand is in, I will beg a little more of Your Patience: this same Book having given me such an Opportunity of Conversing with You, as possibly may not present its self again: or, at least, not quickly.

When the Contest was about Your Vicarage, You know how Zealous I was for Your Interests.[2] During that time a Countrey-man who know's You, in Conversation with me, made this Observation, Mr Carte Love's dearly that Folks should do for Him; but He will do for nobody: Which, when I began to Call into Question, I found Him prepared to Defend.

As to the Success of my Endeavors to Serve You, I can again with truth, assure You that it was Greater than I did expect, or did even Know when I saw You last at Town. For, When ever Your Service required my Attendance, I never Grudged or Spared Money, Time, or Labor.

This same Book ministred unto You a fair Occasi[o]n of being Even with me, in Good Will. By Your Courtesie, indeed, I had the Liberty of looking on it Here. But when I desired to purchase it (not to beg it) Lord! how many Difficulties arose and what an Outcry was Set up! Arch-deacon Rogers[3] proved Treacherous; The Aldermen were grown Obstreperous & some even Outragious; The Schoolmaster was

---

[1] See no. 130.

[2] Wanley's acquaintance with Carte was of long standing. In 1691 Carte, then Head-master of Coventry Free School, supplied Wanley with charters, the property of Sir William Boughton, which Wanley copied in Nov. of that year: see BL Harley MS 7505, fos. 20–21. In July–Oct. 1712 Carte had found himself in a contest for the vicarage of St Martin's, Leicester, which living he had effectively held for twelve years, but his legal claim to which was doubtful. His case is set out at length in letters to Wanley d. 25, 27 Aug., 10, 13 Sept., 8 Oct. 1712 (BL Harley MS 3778, fos. 15 f.). It is not clear what services Wanley was able to afford him.

[3] John Rogers, Archdeacon of Leicester 1703–15.

Angry; Nay, the University of Oxford had bidden no less than An Hundred Pounds for it, not knowing (to be sure) any other way of laying out their Money; with other Excuses of equal Likelyhood & Authority. When I told them to a Clergyman of Learning who both knows You, & hath seen the Book in my Hands, Prithee, said He, lett Him alone & the Book too, for though the Thing is but of small Value in itself, He will Bamboozle thee at last; and so I must needs say, I have found it. For notwithstanding more Cautions about You than I have mentioned, I was resolved to Drive the Nail forward, that I might see how far it would go, where it would stop.

You have therefore, Sir, the Book again, delivered in the same Condition as it came to Me (notwithstanding your friend hath taken it out of the Paper I had carefully wrapped & tied it up in). And although I was, before, willing (for my fancies sake only) to be the purchaser of it, even after I had Spent more upon it than it is worth, my Curiosity is now quite abated. For My Lords Library can hourly supply me with things of the same kind better than that is, and many more are Coming. Had You been but by a Tenth Part so Active & Ready to Oblige me, as I was to Serve You, You had Bound me to do both You & Yours lasting Service, the Means whereof will not long be out of my Hands. But as Things are, the Obligation was not laid upon me; and as my good Luck would have it I am Free.

You See, Sir, I have written Freely unto You; and that I may do, because I can live without any Book in Leicester-Library, to which I give an hearty Farewell, being

    Sir,

       Your humble servant.

MS: Welbeck Wanleyana = British Library, Loan 29/252; draft, unsigned. *Date*: '9 March 1713/4.'

142. *To* John Covell *8 April 1714*

Reverend Sir,

    Those things of Mr John Laughton which I lately bought of Mr Paul for my good Lord, are all single Papers & Parchment Deeds; there not being any one book whatsoever among them. Mr Paul had some of Mr Laughton's Manuscript books up here in Town, I bought none of

them, nor was admitted to see them all; nor did ever hear[1] him
mention any Greek book as being among them. Perhaps Mr Baker of
St John's College may give you some account of it.[2] My Lord hath
(among other his Greek MSS.) two more modern than the rest, One is
a Collection of the Hymns & Anthems used in the Church, sett to
Music by divers Greek Masters; which Notarius then Bishop of
Caesarea, now Patriarch of Jerusalem, gave to Colonel Worseley.[3] The
other (after a Tract de Praeceptorum atque Consiliorum Evangel-
icorum differentia by Maximus Bishop of Cytherea, Printed at Venice,
in Greek & Latin, A.D. 1602:) containeth the Enchiridion of the same
Maximus Margunius, upon the same subject, with two Epistles or
Prefaces, the one written with Red Ink, the other with Black. His
ἀνασκευὴ τῶν κυριωτέρων ἐπιχειρημάτων τῆς γενομένης πρὸς τὸ
αὐτοῦ Ἐγχειρίδιον Ἀπολογίας, written at Venice in March A.D.
1621. Then followeth Μανουήλου τοῦ Μοσχιώτου λόγος ἀπολογη-
τικὸς πρὸς τοὺς λέγοντας μὴ ἔχειν ἀνάγκην τὸν χριστιανὸν καὶ τὰς
βουλὰς τοῦ Σωτῆρος πρὸς Σωτηρίαν φυλάττειν, ἀλλὰ δύνασθαι
σώζεσθαι τούτων μὴ φυλαττομένων. Then follow Old Maximus his
Centuries de Charitate, well known unto You: then Τοῦ Φιλῆ στίχοι
πολιτικοὶ κατανυκτικοί, and τοῦ αὐτοῦ (ὡς φασὶ) τὰ λοίσθια
πνέοντος: and lastly, what I much Value, a Tract in the Vulgar Greek
written against the Jews (in Egypt, ann Dni 1628, or A.M. ζρλς) by the
famous Cyrillus Lucaris; with this Title, Σύντομος πραγματεία κατ᾽
Ἰουδαίων, ἐν ἁπλῇ Διαλέκτῳ παρὰ τοῦ σοφωτάτου Ἀλεξ-
ανδρείας κυρίου Κυρίλλου τοῦ Λουκάρεος συγγραφεῖσα παρα-
κλησίᾳ τινὸς χρησίμου χριστιανοῦ ὀνόματι κὺρ. Γεωργίου
Παργατοῦ Κυπρίου.[4] My Lord hath also an Original Letter of the
above-mentioned Maximus Bishop of Cytherea to David Hoeschel-
ius: and another of Gabriel Metropolite of Philadelphia to Sir Henry
Savile:[5] and some other Original Letters of Greek Bishops are in the
Cottonian Library. My Lord hath also the Book published by the
Sieur Aymon in Holland from the French Kings MS. which, to be
sure, you have an Exemplar of:[6] and I expect a Good Cargo of things

---

[1] here MS.   [2] See no. 139 and n. 6.   [3] BL Harley MS 1613.
[4] BL Harley MS 1803.
[5] The letter to Hoeschel I have not found; the letter to Savile is BL Harley MS 7002,
art. 10.
[6] Jean Aymon's book is *Monumens authentiques de la religion des grecs, et de la fausseté de
plusieurs confessions de foi des chrétiens orientaux* (The Hague, 1708), a printing of a manuscript account of the Synod of Jerusalem held in 1672, stolen from the Royal Library in

from Turkey this Somer. So far for Greek things. As for Hebrew, my Lord hath bought not long since, one of the Volumes of the Law written upon about 40 Skins, with the Rollers, Bandage & Cloak, as I call them; these last of Rich Silk. It is six & twenty Inches Broad, & Thirty Yards or 90 foot long, and formerly stood in the Synagogue at Tunis, and from thence came hither.[7]

Now, Sir, for Your Chart.[8] I protest I am asham'd that you have not been paid all this while, the Price being but a small Sum: and, indeed, I believe nothing but the smalness of the matter hath occasioned this Long delay. I keep it in a Closet adjoyning to the Library, and have several Times putt my Lord in Mind of it, but hitherto he could never have leasure to look thereon. There can be no talk of Returning it again on Your Hands; for that would be not for my Lords Honor: instead of that, I would have him pay you more than the Price agreed on; and this I have directly mentioned both to his Lordship, & also to my Lord Harley. I am sorry such a Trifle should hang so long in arrear, when my Lord hath paid away so many hundreds of Guineas for Books, since that thing came hither. In my last Letter I putt his Lordship in mind of it, and will continue to do the same, as soon as things grow a little more sedate in Parliament. In the mean time, I could wish that you would send me a Catalogue of your other MSS, Greek, Latin, &c. and sett one Reasonable Price upon the whole, according to Your Promise, and I will treat with You thereupon, and pay you the Money too, before I remove a leaf from the Premises.

If the things coming from Turkey, or any of them shall prove to your purpose, I will certainly advertise you thereof; for I am sincerely
  Reverend Sir,
    Your most faithful friend, & most humble servant
                                          Humfrey Wanley.

MS: British Library, Add. 22911, fo. 161. *Date*: '8 April 1714.' *Address*: 'To The Reverend Doctor Covell Master of Christs College in Cambridge.'

Paris, together with letters from Cyril Lucar, Patriarch of Constantinople, and other documents.
  [7] BL Harley MS 7619, a large double roll containing the Pentateuch.
  [8] See Wanley to Covell, no. 122 and n. 1, no. 131.

143. *To* Thomas Harley[1] *27 April 1714*

Honorable Sir,

St Origen the most Learned Father of the Christian Church (as
some have styled him) who flourished A.D. 230. finding the Holy
Scriptures of the Old Testament, as translated into the Greek Tongue,
to be very much Corrupted, or at least one Version or Copie very dis-
crepant from another: took much pains in restoring them to their
primitive purity; and at the same time also did illustrate the same by
Exhibiting the Hebrew Original, & the several Greek Versions, at one
View, all written Columnatim. Which great Work proving too Charge-
able & tedious for common transcription, is now almost utterly lost:
nothing but certain Citations from it being left.

St Origen did moreover abbrige that elaborate work, by bringing
the Sum of all the Translations into ONE TEXT; distinguishing the same
all along with particular Marks; as an ASTERISK * (or ※) where such
Word or Words were extant in the Hebrew, and not found in the
Version of the Septuagint: an OBELISK ÷ (or ÷) when such a Word or
Expression was read in the Septuagint, but not seen in the Hebrew: a
LIMNISK ÷, or HYPO-LIMNISK ~, when any thing was taken from the
other Versions. This work, as the former did, met with the Constant
applause of the Antient Fathers; but now (through the Iniquity of
Time) is, for the much greater part, lost. Which Loss hath not only
been occasioned by the Revolutions & Calamities that have so long
afflicted the Greek Church, but also by the Negligence of their
Scribes: who generally either wholly Neglected the said Marks, or else
inserted but some few of them; as by divers Books yet extant, doth
appear.

Among some very few of the best things which escaped the general
Fate, One was a Book written in the Syriac Language by the Help
whereof Andreas Masius restored the Septuagint Version of Joshua to
that State wherein Origen left it, by his Book Dedicated to the Spanish
King Philip II, printed at Antwerp A.D. 1574.[2] What Opinion he had

---

[1] Cousin to Robert Harley. He was Envoy Extraordinary at Hanover, 24 Apr.–
14 May 1714. For his dispatches see *HMC Portland Papers*, v. It is unlikely that he had
opportunity to fulfil Wanley's commission: see T. Harley to R. Harley d. [1]–11 May
1714, designing to set out from Hanover 'next Tuesday' (*HMC Portland Papers*, v, p. 433).
That Wanley was unsuccessful is clear from Wanley, *Diary*, pp. 139 (7), 174(8). The
manuscript has not been identified.

[*See opposite page for n. 2*]

of this Book, what was its Antiquity & Accuracy, and how much it Contained, may be seen from the following Citations from him.

'Et ne quis me putet augurantem levibus conjecturis, meaeque opinionis commenta sequentem, judicium hoc nunc facere; Habeo aliquot Sacrae Historiae Libros, qui et conversi in Linguam Syricam, et scripti sunt ALEXANDRIAE; anno ab Alexandro Magno [*margin*: Alexander died before Christ, years 321. Since Christs Incarnation, Years 1713. Years since Alexanders death 2034. Year of Alexander when the book was wrote 927. Years since the book was wrote 1107] novies centesimo vicesimo septimo: hoc est, ante hos Nongentos & quinquaginta annos. Su[m] inquam, conversi ad verbum de Graeco Exemplari quod manu Eusebij ad Origenis libros qui in Caesariensis Ecclesiae Bibliotheca asservabantur, fuerat emendatum, cum huic ad eam rem adjutor fuisset suus Pamphilus. In quibus libris meis Syricis, cum omnes ubique Notae, quas dixi, summa Cura atque incredibili Diligentia sint appositae: neque magno labore, neque ullo errore deprehendi a Me judicarique, ea quae modo dicebam potuerunt.'

'tum Interpretem Syrum ubique autorem certissimum habui; qui ea Graeca ad verbum expressit ante annos nongentos, quae in Adamantij Hexaplis ab Eusebio in Nobili illa Caesariensi Bibliotheca fuere collocata'

'Habeo enim ab illo Interprete Syro etiam Judicum Historias, & Regum; praeterea Paralipomena, Ezdram, Esther, Judith: denique Tobiae, et Deuteronomij bonam partem.'

Since this learned-mans time, this inestimable Jewel hath been Praised by nobody that I know of: I am sure the Editor of our Polyglott[3] have nothing of it but from Him. Nor could I ever get any Notice of it (excepting only in Oxford, from a Dutch Gentleman-Traveller, who told me that it was some where in Gelderland) until my late very learned Friend Dr John-Ernest Grabe acquainted me that he had received Notice from Germany, that it was in the Possession of Dr Lent or Dr Lens (or some such Name) Professor of the Arabic or Oriental Languages at the University of Helmstad.[4]

---

[2] *Josuae Imperatoris Historia, Illustrata atque Explicata ab Andrea Masio* (Antwerp, 1574).

[3] Brian Walton (*c.*1600–61), his polyglot Bible pbd. 1655–7 in 6 vols., Darlow and Moule no. 1445.

[4] Johann Lent, author of *De Moderna Theologia Iudaica* (Herborn, 1694).

This Professor had also a Collection of Manuscripts Oriental, and perhaps in Greek & Latin: all which are now said to [be] in the Hands of his Son, who is still a very Young Man, and liveth in the Countrey somewhere near Helmstad.

The book I have been speaking of, being (in this late time of the World) become One of the most Valuable, that by Gods goo[d] Providence is left unto the Christian Church; my Lord-Treasurer is willing to purchase the same, as well to secure it from utter Perishing, as from coming into Popish Hands; and therefore He desireth Your Honor to exert Your usual Diligence and Dexterity, in procuring the same.

That Family offered Dr Grabes Brother (who is Secretary to the King of Prussia) to Lend it, upon a Pledge of about Sixty Poun[ds] Value. They therefore thought such a Sum to be worth more than their Book. You may, perhaps, come the sooner to it by means of Dr Eckhart History-Professor of Helmstad,[5] if he be now at Hanover, as he often is. An Occasion of talking to him about it may be had by Asking him whether he received the last Somer a Letter & a Book from Me? and so, pian piano, enquiring about the Professors of that University, their Learning, Libraries, &c. as you very well know how, untill you are told the Pla[ce] where, and the Person with whom the Book is to be found.

When You have got into the House, be pleased to look over all the Collection of Manuscripts, as if it were only to satisfie Your Curiosity in the Generall, without professed Enquiry after this particular Book, unless it doth not occurr unto you in your Inspection. I am humbly of Opinion that You will find it written upon Parchment, in no big Volume, and in the Estrangel or Nestorian Character (but rather in the former) of both which I have given you the Alphabets in the former Leaf.[6] But that You may be certainly sure, that What You may see & the People may warant for the Book wanted (in Case Massius nor none else hath written an account of it in the Beginning nor End) be pleased to look nicely up and down in the Text for these Marks * or ✲· ⸓ ÷ ~ and ε (which last denotes the End or Conclusion of a distinguished Reading). If you meet them pretty frequent, & the Hand not unconformable from the Alphabet above, You have the Book which my Lord wanteth, and which must be procured although at a great price, and not be left behind You.

[5] Johann Georg von Eckhart (1664–1730), German historian and antiquarian.
[6] Omitted here.

If the whole Collection of Manuscripts shall seem to amount to no extraordinary Sum; I think it would be better to buy them all at a Lump, than to treat Singly upon this Book: but if the whole shall be too great a Purchase, it would do well to gett a Catalogue of what is therein Contained, the Price they demand; and to bring away this Book being borrowed upon Caution given: for they may be farther treated with, from hence for the remainder, as Opportunities may give leave, the main Matter being to secure this Individual Book, which will not only adorn My Lord-Treasurer my Masters Library (which is already very richly furnished) but prove a public & lasting Advantage to Christendome in general, and to this Nation in particular.

Thus with my most hearty Respects, & sincere Wishes for Your Safe Return from so long a Journey, I remain,

Honorable Sir,

Your most humble & obedient Servant

Humfrey Wanley.

MS: British Library, Harley 7526, fo. 150. *Date*: '27 April 1714.' *Address*: 'To The Honorable Thomas Harley Esqr her Majesties Envoy-Extraordinary, at the Court of Hanover.' *Printed*: Nichols, *Literary Anecdotes*, i, pp. 536–40.

144. *To* [Arthur Charlett] *24 August 1714*

Reverend Sir,

You may please to remember that some time since, I took an occasion of writing unto You concerning the MSS left by Mr Lhwyd deceased; as to which, you was pleased to answer, that my Noble Lord should have the next Option of them, in Case the University did not buy them.[1]

Since then, I have been informed, that the very best book of that whole Collection, being a Welsh MS is gotten into Jesus-College-Library;[2] and that my Lord Mansel[3] is about procuring the remainder. I would gladly know what truth there is in these Reports; what Right

[1] See no. 140 n. 4.

[2] 'The Red Book of Hergest' (Llyfr Coch o Hergest), Jesus College, Oxford MS 111. It did not belong to Lhwyd but had been misappropriated by him from Jesus in 1701, shortly after it was given to the college by Thomas Wilkins of Llanblethian, Glamorgan, as appears from Wilkins's inscription in the manuscript d. 26 Mar. 1714.

[3] Thomas Mansell (*c*.1668–1723), first Baron Mansell of Margam, Glamorgan. He matriculated at Jesus in 1685.

Jesus-College hath to that Book; and whether the others are Secured by the University, or designed to be so or not.

Thus forbearing to be farther troublesome, and in hopes of a Line in answer I remain, with great respect,

> Reverend Sir,
>> Your most obliged & most humble servant
>>> Humfrey Wanley.

MS: Bodleian, Ballard 13, fo. 129. *Date*: 'Coach-Office in Surrey-street in the Strand 24 August 1714.'

145. *To* [Edward Harley] *30 August 1714*

1. Whereas my Lord Bishop[1] formerly did cause his MSS. to be numbered successively as they were brought in; that good order was discontinued divers years before his decease; so that those necessary marks are wanting in many of them.

2. Many books which have been so marked do now want the said numbers; either by being newly bound, or by being mangled through negligence or petulancy.

3. Many others which still have their marks cannot easily be found in the printed catalogue,[2] because they were either erroneously marked at first; or else the print is faulty; or both.

---

[1] John Moore, Bishop of Ely, died 31 July 1714. His library of more than 30,000 ptd. books and manuscripts was kept at Ely Place, Holborn, near the Bishop's London residence. Shortly after Wanley's inspection reported here, the books were offered to Harley for not less than £8,000 (BL Harley MS 3778, fo.75), but Harley declined to pay so much, hoping to pick up those he wanted when the library went to auction. In fact, the collection did not go to auction, but was purchased by George I for £6,450 and presented by him to Cambridge University, 20 Sept. 1715.

[2] It is impossible to identify with certainty all manuscripts now in Cambridge University Library which once belonged to Moore. Royal Library book-plates affixed to Moore's books at the time of their presentation by George I were used for general purposes during the eighteenth century and are found in many volumes which were never part of Moore's collection. Moore was also generous with his books; some out on loan at the time of his death were not returned until several years later, and it seems likely that a number were not returned at all: Bodl. MS Add. D.81 (*SC* 3030), a catalogue of Moore's ptd. books d. about 1710–13, contains (on fo. 466ʳᵛ) lists of books and manuscripts lent 1709–14, including some noted by Wanley in this letter as missing. Non-returned books probably account for manuscripts in the catalogues of Moore's library in *CMA* which never seem to have reached Cambridge. CUL MS Oo.vii.50² is a catalogue of accessions (numbered 831–1025) to Moore's library between the time *CMA* was pbd. and Moore's death, compiled by Thomas Tanner, Moore's son-in-law. There

4. Divers MSS. of value mentioned in the said printed Catalogue could not be produced to me, being either lent out, mislaid, or lost. Such are, Two Copies of Suetonius,[3] said to be lent to Dr. Bentley. A fine Register of the See of Hereford,[4] said to be lent to the present Lord Bishop of Hereford. Ovidius de Nuce,[5] an exceeding old copy, lent or mislaid. Tullie's Tusculan Questions, mentioned in the said printed Catalogue. No. 32.[6] Original Epistles of our ancient learned Protestant Divines. No. 125.[7] Statutes of Norwich Cathedral temp. R. Hen. VIII. No. 203.[8] Charters of Westminster Church. No. 223.[9] Old Chartulary of Ely. No. 236.[10] Books of Queen Elizabeth's Jewels. No. 254,255.[11] Pars Γεωπονικῶμ cum aliis Graecis, man vet. No. 87.[12] Index Librorum Graecorum Bibliothecae Palatinae per Dav. Hamaxungum. No. 671.[13] The Original Foundation Charter of the Cathedral Church of Norwich. No. 160.[14] Bedae Histor. Eccles. formerly belonging to the Monastery of Plympton;[15] and many others too tedious here to enumerate.

•

is an eighteenth-century key to this (MS Oo.vii.56) giving the present shelf-marks of the works in Tanner's list. I quote below the evidence from these sources which bears on the manuscripts referred to by Wanley.

[3] Probably (1) Tanner no. 989, 'C. Suetonius de Vita Caesarum, fol. pergam', a very fine twelfth-century MS which, according to the key, is now MS Kk.v.24. (2) MS Dd.x.41, a Suetonius in a fine fifteenth-century humanistic hand, which bears the Moore book-plate. The list of loans in Bodl. MS Add. D.81 records one MS of Suetonius lent to a 'Mr Needham' (presumably Peter Needham, Moore's protege) 17 July 1713, another lent to Bentley, 2 Jan. 1714.

[4] CUL MS Dd.x.18 is a Hereford Register (Davis no. 483) which once belonged to Moore, but neither this nor Bodl. MSS Jones 23 (SC 8930) and Rawl. B.329 (Davis nos. 480, 481, 482), Hereford cartularies of the thirteenth and thirteenth-/fourteenth-centuries, respectively, can be identified with CMA II. i, no. 9327, presumably the MS referred to by Wanley.

[5] Tanner lists an Ovid, no. 1019, but the key gives no Cambridge class-mark for it. It seems never to have been received there.

[6] CMA II. i, no. 9218. Bodl. MS Add. D.81 records a 'Tusc. Quaest. MS.' lent to 'Mr Davis' 29 Aug. 1710. Not identified.   [7] CMA II. i, no. 9311, CUL MS Ee.ii.34.

[8] CMA II. i, no. 9389. Not identified.   [9] CMA II. i, no. 9409. Not identified.

[10] CMA II, i, no. 9422. Possibly BL Egerton MS 3047 (Davis no. 371), the first part of a general cartulary of which Bodl. MS Ashmole 801, fos. 74–143 (Davis no. 372) is a continuation. There is evidence that Egerton 3047 was once in the possession of a bishop (or bishops) of Ely: see British Museum. Catalogue of Additions to the Manuscripts, 1926–1930 (1959), under Egerton 3047 (pp. 228–30). But it is not old: it is of fifteenth-century date.

[11] CMA II. i, nos. 9440–1. Not identified.

[12] CMA II. i, no. 9273. CUL MS Dd.iii.86, no. 11.

[13] CMA II. i, no. 9857. CUL MS Dd.xii.70.   [14] CMA II. i, no. 9346. Not identified.

[15] Probably BL Add. MS 14250 of the twelfth century, the only surviving manuscript from the Augustinian Priory at Plympton, Devon, acquired in 1843 from the library of Jeremiah Milles, Dean of Exeter, † 1784.

5. Through the negligence or petulancy above-mentioned, or else mere stupidity, books which were out of their bindings have been quite disjoined, so that their several parts cannot be found and put together: which is the fault of the Leiger book of Ossulverstone[16] and others. In like sort the modern letters were thrown on the ground and trodden under foot; nay, very lately part of them were burned on purpose, and others industriously mangled with the penknife.

6. This management needed not to have been introduced into that place, where my Lord Bishop bought all manuscripts that offered, good, bad, or indifferent, without making any delectus. This custom hath in process of time raised the vast number of old books of small or no value, which I found there, such as vulgar Latin Bibles, Psalters, Primers, and other Books of Superstitious Devotion, Old Scholemen, Postils, Sermons, and such trash; heaps of common place Books and Notes of Divinity, Law, Physic, Chirurgery, Heraldry, Philosopher's Stone, &c. Rubbish Reports and such trumpery stuff that make one sick to look at them, being really fitter for any other room in the house rather than the library.

7. Another thing hath been omitted that might have advanced the price of the Collection; I mean, the putting down some note of the curiosity and usefulness of such a book or books. My Lord of Ely was certainly apprised of such matters; as that this was the work of such a person; or the handwriting of such another; or fit to be consulted on such an occasion; but this knowledge being now dead with him, the price of those books is lowered thereby.

8. Some manuscripts have been found placed among the printed books of the classical kind: as to this sort of MSS. here I find the Latin Classicks to be almost all of them recent copies. As to the Greek manuscripts (taking them in the whole), there are but two very ancient books among them, both which are imperfect;[17] the rest being, for the far greater part (like the Latin classics), later copies and paper transcripts.

9. As to the parcel of Oriental Manuscripts lately belonging to Dr. Sike, of Cambridge,[18] most of them suffer by being unknown. More-

---

[16] Perhaps CUL MS Dd.iii.87(20), a small fifteenth-century cartulary of Ossulverstone or Owston, Davis no. 738.   [17] Not identified.

[18] Henry Sike or Sykes, Regius Professor of Divinity at Cambridge, 1705–12, oriental scholar of Bremen. The only manuscript in the University Library known to have belonged to him is Dd.ix.49, a treatise on Muhammadan ritual and law in Spanish, given to Sike in 1703. There is no evidence of the 'parcel' referred to by Wanley here.

over, the parcel seems to have been garbled before my Lord of Ely bought it, and wanting the proper titles, the languages being not cultivated, it can now be but of little worth.

These are some of the observations I have made, &c.

MS: Not traced. *Printed*: *European Magazine*, xxxix (1801), pp. 407–8. *Endorsed*: in printed head-note 'Extract of a Letter from Mr. Humfrey Wanley to the Right Honourable Edward Lord Harley, giving some Account of the Bishop of Ely's MSS. dated 30th August 1714. (Now First Published.)'

146. *To* Thomas Hearne *13 October 1714*

Good Sir,

Your Letter to Mr Anstis of the 5th Instant,[1] was Communicated to me just now, upon occasion of my old friend honest Anthony Woods Life; which Letter I promised to Answer; because I found that some part thereof did also relate to your John Leland,[2] with regard to whom I was willing to take this Opportunity of saying somewhat to you.

I believe Mr Anstis did not give his MS. of A. Woods Life to my Lord Oxford, but to my Lord Harley.[3] The book never came into my Custody, nor did I ever see it. Both their Lordships are now at Wymple near Cambridge; but by this Post I shall write to my Lord Harley, and will make mention thereof in my Letter, so as that it may be sent to you as soon as may be. For I well know that his Lordship hath a true Respect for you.

As to John Leland, I know not how much you have published of him, because I have hitherto seen but the two first of your Volumes.[4] But for the sake of our Old Friendship, I use a Friends Liberty in advertising you, that I have seen some fragments of his Itinerary in the Cottonian Library, written by his own Hand,[5] as I sent you word by several of your Friends some Years ago.

[1] Ptd. Hearne, *Collections*, iv, pp. 412–13.
[2] (1506?–1552). Hearne edited his *Itinerary* (Oxford, 1710–12) and his *Collectanea* (Oxford, [1715]).
[3] BL Harley MS 5409. Wanley is right: see Anstis to Hearne d. 15 Sept. 1714, Hearne, *Collections*, iv, p. 405. Anstis had presented the manuscript to Edward Harley in 1712.
[4] Presumably of the 6 vol. *Collectanea*, the last volume of which was printing in Nov. 1714 (Hearne, *Collections*, iv, p. 425), although 1715 is the date on the title-page (but found only in vol. i).
[5] Wanley probably refers to Cotton Julius C.vi, a volume of over 250 leaves containing copies of miscellaneous material from the *Itinerary*. There is a fragment of Leland's

In my Noble Lord Oxford's Library is a modern MS. marked 68.D.24. being a fair Transcript of the Itinerary, which perhaps (if compared) may supply some Defects in the Print. At the End, is an Alphabetical Table of the proper Names, under this Title, *Index hujus Voluminis compositus per me Willielmum Dugdale 15 Julij Ao 1657*; but notwithstanding the word *me*, it seemeth not to be of his handwriting, as perhaps being drawn up by him, but Entred here by another.[6]

There is also another MS. Inscribed 62.A.20 belonging formerly to the great Bishop Stillingfleet, and before his time to Judge Dodderige.[7] It is on the outside Entituled a Geography of some Counties: but I take it to be part of Lelands Itinerary, wherein is a pretty deal, not to be met with in the Volume abovementioned (it may be) copied from the Cottonian Fragments.

In another MS. noted 38.B.7. is a Tract, which I believe to be (for the most part) of Lelands Hand-Writing, with this Title, *Fundationes Ecclesiarum Cathedralium, Monasteriorum, et Collegiorum subscriptorum* (above 50 in number) *sunt registratae in hoc Libro*:[8] and I perceive that Mr Roger Dodsworth was of the same Opinion by the Citation of it, which you may find in the Oxford Catalogue of MSS. pag. 202. Col. 2. no. 4180.[9]

Among some old Papers which I sold to my Lord, and are not as yet Bound up, are some Imperfect Fragments, of his Handwriting (if I mistake not) being part of a First Draught of a Treatise against Polydore Vergil; which I know not whether it hath been ever Printed or not.[10]

These several Things in my Lords Library (since you are enquiring after the man) may perhaps be worthy your Sight. But since your business may not permitt you to come hither to them, if you shall

---

autograph in Cotton Vespasian F.ix, fos. 198–9 (ptd. by Hearne in his 2nd edn. (1744), ix, pp. 133–4), but there is hardly enough of it to support Wanley's suggestion in the next paragraph but one that Harley 842 is copied from it.

[6] BL Harley MS 1346 contains the first seven books of the *Itinerary*, apparently copied from Harley 6266 (which contains nine of the ten books). Neither is Dugdale's autograph, but Harley 6266 may have been copied for him.

[7] BL Harley MS 842. Sir John Doddrige (1555–1628) was a Justice of the King's Bench 1612.　　　　　　　　　　　　　　　　[8] Now BL Harley MS 358, fos. 27–70.

[9] In a volume of extracts by Dodsworth from the collections of D'Ewes, Bodl. MS Dodsworth 38 (*SC* 4180). The 'Oxford Catalogue of MSS' = *CMA*.

[10] 'Codrus, Sive Laus et Defensio Gallofridi Arturii Monumetensis Contra Polydorum Vergilium', ptd. for the first time by Hearne in his edn. of Leland's *Collectanea* (*Ioannis Lelandi Antiquarii de Rebus Britannicis Collectanea*, Oxford [1715]) v, pp. 1–10. I cannot identify the manuscript.

desire it of me, I will speak to my Noble Lord, (who will return up to Town within a few days) that I may be allowed to send you them down to Oxford for a reasonable Time.

I know not whether it will be worth while to inform you that I have found frequent mention of the Man, & many Citations from his Books, in R. Hollinsheads Chronicle.

In the Bodleyan Library NE. F.7.4. are some Verses at the Beginning, written by Leland;[11] and, as I remember, there are some other books in the Royal Library, which have Verses or Inscriptions by his Hand.[12] These I will search after, & send you, if you shall think it worth the while.

Now I am talking of Inscriptions in Books, I will trouble you with one more inserted at the bottom of the first Page of the MS. 63.C.25.[13] The book is antient & fairly written, and was a 4to but upon its Second Binding was pared into an 8vo it was Bishop Stillingfleets book, (for my Lord bought all his MSS.) but seemeth formerly to have been placed in your Bodleyan Library; for the Inscription (which is written within a sort of Altar, like some others I have seen in the same place, given to Sir Tho. Bodley by the same Gentleman) saith thus, GENIO LOCI. BODLEO RESTITV: BONO PVBLICO ROBERT: COTTON CONNINGTON: HIC LL. M.D.D. M.DI.II. It once appertained to some Monastery, as appears by the remains of a more antient Inscription, where the Name of the Place is industriously erased. I had forgotten to say that it containeth two Anonymous Comments on the Song of Salomon; and think this more Modern Note not worthy Remembrance, *Mr Cobs saith that this tractatus erat ad Bodleum Colledge et est in Cantica Canticorum incerti autem authoris est. pretium £1.5s.od.*

Be pleased to give my humble respects to Doctor Hudson, and excuse the Trouble I, unasked, give you of this; and I shall own my self
  Sir,
    Your very humble servant
                                    Humfrey Wanley.

MS: Bodleian, Rawl. lett. 17, fo. 61. *Date*: 'Coach-Office in Surrey-street, in the Strand, London 13 October 1714.' *Address*: 'To Mr Hearne at the Bodleyan Library in Oxford.' *Endorsed*: 'Not recd till Friday Oct. 21st.' *Printed*: Hearne, *Collections*, iv, pp. 415–16 (summary and extracts).

[11] Now Bodl. MS Bodley 354 (*SC* 2432); the verses 'Carmen Joannis Leylandi Londenensis' are on fo. ii.

[12] Latin verses in BL Royal MS 1.A.xviii at fo. 2, and in Royal MS 18.A.lxiv.

[13] BL Harley MS 988.

147. *To* Thomas Hearne *27 October 1714*

Sir,

I received Your Letter in answer to mine, which I sent according to the Date it bare. I have inquired of every-body in my family concerning it, but none can say any thing to the matter: nevertheless I should be glad to know how the date of the Post-mark corresponded to it.[1]

I have made your Request known to my Lord, who like a true Patron & Encourager of Learning, as he is, hath been pleased to give me leave to send you the Books & Papers relating to Leland, you sending me a receipt for the same according to the form which I shall putt down anon, that (in Case of Your, or my Mortality) the things may be regained.

As to the Tract of Leland about the foundations of Churches, you will find it in the book 38.B.7, at fol. 27. I can easily believe it to be of his Hand, according as is noted in the Oxford Catalogue.[2] You will observe the Alteration of the Hand at fol. 54, which yet I will not say can't be Lelands (as that at fol. 56, I take to be Dr John Dee's running-hand, & that at fol. 17b, I well know to be honest John Stowe's, whose Collections are mostly in my Lords Library) nor that the remaining leaves, viz from fol. 61 to fol. 69 inclusive, may not be most probably attributed unto him.[3] Of this matter, you who have so many of that great Mans books in your Custody, will be the best judge.[4] I shall say no more of this book at present (which consists only of a parcel of loose fragments, I putt together) but that the hand of these last leaves from fol. 61, or at least some of them, is the same with that of many of the loose Leaves about to be transmitted to you.

These loose Leaves,[5] I bought in a parcel of old Papers, which I afterwards Sold to my Lord; (whose Commands I have not yet received for the Binding up, of one of the most Valuable parcels of Papers in England) whereby, I shall be able to send them to you, free

---

[1] Wanley's letter of 13 Oct. (postmarked 14 Oct.) was not received by Hearne until 21 Oct. His reply d. 23 Oct. is ptd. Hearne, *Collections*, iv, pp. 423–4.

[2] BL Harley MS 358, fo. 27 f., *CMA* I. i, no. 4180: see no. 146 n. 9.

[3] The three hands (fos. 27–53, 54–5, 61–9) are, I think, all different, and none of them Leland's.

[4] The Bodleian possesses the manuscripts of Leland's *Collectanea* and his *Commentarii de Scriptoribus Britannicis* (Bodl. MSS Top. gen. c. 1–4, *SC* 3117–20), and the *Itinerary* (Bodl. MSS Top. gen. e. 8–15, *SC* 3121–3ᵉ, 6615).

[5] Presumably the tract against Polydore Vergil (see no. 146 and n. 10).

from the encumbrance of other Company. You will find them in two Hands; the one a rough Draught, the other a fair Copie. I think they are not printed in the *Assertio Arthuri*; but whether they are part of the *Codrus* I know not, because I have not yet seen the book.[6]

As for the book 62.A.20.[7] I will take it (before I send it to you) to the Cottonian-Library, and compare it with the fragments of Leland there. If I find that they are contained in it, I will tell you so; if they shall prove still fresh, I will transcribe them for you. I will also be at the pains of rummaging in his Majesties Royal Library; & if I find any of Lelands Verses there, you shall have them.[8]

As for my Lords Manuscript of the Canticles, designed for the Bodleyan Library by Sir Robert Cotton;[9] I know not how you find it to have once belonged to Humfrey Duke of Gloucester. My Lord ha's, indeed, two of his Books which we know to have been His, for certain; because one of them (which was given to his Lordship) hath a Note therein of his Hand-Writing;[10] and the other hath his Armes & Stile on the out-side, as also His Library-mark. This last (which was bought of Sir Simonds D'Ewes)[11] together with the Cotton-MS. of the Canticles, I besought His Lordship to give to the University for your Library; and I hope His Lordship will do so, in a little time.

As for Anthony Woods Diary, I suppose it may be still at New-Castle House among my Lord Harleys books.[12] His Lordship is Expected in Town about Christmass, and then I will speak to him about it, for You.

---

[6] Leland's *Assertio inclytissimi Arturij, regis Britanniae* (1544), trans. Richard Robinson, 1582. An imperfect copy of it was in Harley's library two years later, see Edward Harley to Wanley d. 2 Feb. 1716, Welbeck Wanleyana = BL Loan MS 29/248. For the *Codrus* see no. 146 and nn. 4, 10.

[7] BL Harley MS 842. For the Cotton fragments see no. 146 n. 5.

[8] See no. 146 n. 12. [9] BL Harley MS 988.

[10] BL Harley MS 1705, a Latin version of Plato's *Republic* trans. by Pier Candido Decembrio.

[11] BL Harley MS 33, William Ockham's *Dialogus de heresi*. (See A. G. Watson, *The Library of Sir Simonds D'Ewes* (1966), pp. 121–2. The two labels on which Duke Humfrey's 'Armes & Stile' and his 'Library-mark' appear are illustrated in *Bodleian Library Record*, v (1954–6), plate vi (facing p. 177).

[12] i.e. Wood's autobiography, extant in two drafts. The earlier is BL Harley MS 5409 given to Edward Harley by John Anstis in 1712 (see no. 146 n. 3), who obtained it from Robert Dale the herald; it brings the narrative down to the end of Mar. 1660. Harley lent this to Hearne who collated it with the later version in Bodl. MS Tanner 102 (*SC* 9928). Hearne's transcript of Harley 5409 is now Bodl. MS Rawl. D.97 (*SC* 12915); the Tanner version is ptd. by Hearne at p. 438 f. of his edn. of *Thomae Caii Vindiciae Antiquitatis Academiae Oxon* (Oxford, 1730).

Thus, Sir, You see how willing I am to Serve You: Now, I must desire you to do some-what for Me. My Request is, that you would instantly see the worthy Mr Tickell of Queen's, and ask him if he did lately receive a Letter from me? If he ha's, be pleased to lett me know whether he ha's borrowed the Books from Lincoln College for me, or not? If he ha's; when & how I may expect them?[13]

Now for Sending my Lords Books to you; I would that you should send some friend, in whom you can confide, to me at the Coach-Office any day at two o'clock, and I will deliver them to any body that shall bring me Your receipt. If you have no such Friend here, write your Receipt in your Letter by the Post, & letting me know the Carriers or Coach-mans Name, Inne, & Time of Setting out of Towne, I will accordingly send them to You, who am with Sincerity

 Sir

  Your old Friend & very Humble Servant

        Humfrey Wanley.

I do hereby acknowledge that I have Borrowed & Received of the Right Honorable Robert Earl of Oxford, Three Manuscript books; the One, Marked 38.B.7. consisting of divers Tracts & Fragments, written upon 225 Leaves in fol. The Second, marked 62.A.20. being Collections out of John Lelands Itinerary, in 93 folio-Leaves. The Third, marked 68.D.24; being a fair Transcript of the same Itinerary, with an Index at the End, written on 519 Pages in fol. together with 14 loose folio-Leaves, supposed to be written by the Hand of the said John Leland.[14] All which Books and Leaves, I promise to restore within the space of a Month, as witness my Hand this day of
  &c.

N.B. I specifie a month; but you shall be allowed as much time, as shall be reasonable & convenient.

MS: Bodleian, Rawl. lett. 17, fo. 63. *Date*: '27 October 1714.' *Address*: 'To Mr Hearne at the Bodleyan Library in Oxford.' *Printed*: Hearne, *Collections*, iv, pp. 421–2 (summary); Macray, pp. 9–10 (extract).

[13] See no. 150 and n. 12.
[14] For these manuscripts see no. 146.

148. *To* Thomas Hearne *9 November 1714*

Sir, Your second letter[1] came safe, just as I was going (with one of my Lords MSS) to the Cottonian Library, in order to do you service.[2] But finding so unexpected a return for my good will,[3] I forbare the Journey, and blamed my self for being too forward already.

Tis childish to suppose that what I did for you with my Lord, was done merely on my own head, without his Privity & Consent. And your Letter shew's that You, & not His Lordship is SUSPICIOUS.

Those that borrow books out of Libraries here, are very glad, if they can gett them by their bare Notes. I have been often put to the Charge of Bonds. When Mr Tickel borrowed my Lords Lucan, the Master of University sent up his own Note for it, before the book was moved from its place: and in good will & friendship to You, I left four Notes under mine own Hand [befo]re I brought the books & Papers hither. When I begged the Favor of my [Lord] for you, urging that Your business would not allow you to come to Town, &c. An Oxford friend of Yours said it would be a Kindness to You, if I should send you down a Form of a Receipt, and His Lordship was of the same Opinion. This I did, and nobody thought of breaking any Custome, upon your Accompt. But forasmuchas you suppose to have better measure from my Lord Harley; I have returned the things, taken up my Notes; and refer you to His Lordship; who hath been pleased to send me word that he will look out A. Wood's book[4] for you, upon his coming up.

I never saw any Printed Rolls of the Great Feasts you mention, but those in the Bodleyan Archives;[5] but, perhaps, others may be found in

---

[1] 31 Oct. 1714 (BL Harley MS 3779, fo. 36), summarized and excerpted Hearne, *Collections*, iv, pp. 422–3.

[2] BL Harley MS 842: see no. 147.

[3] Hearne objected to the receipt acknowledging the loan of Leland manuscripts sent by Wanley with his letter of 27 Oct. 1714 for Hearne to sign.

[4] BL Harley MS 5409: see no. 147 n. 12.

[5] Hearne (*Collections*, iv, pp. 422–3) enquires about 'a printed Roll about the Great Feasts of Archbps. Nevill and Warham'. Bodl. MS Bodley Rolls 8(*SC* 2968) contains accounts of the enthronement of George Neville (1433?–1476), Archbishop of York 1465–76, and of William Warham (1450?–1532), Archbishop of Canterbury 1504–32, ptd. as a roll some nine feet long. *STC* 25072 (also at *STC* 5998, which is a ghost) records only the Bodleian copy, but there is also a fragmentary version in Bodl. press-mark Douce W.273. The accounts are ptd. by Hearne in *Ioannis Lelandi Antiquarii de Rebus Britannicis Collectanea* Oxford [1715], vi, pp. 2–14, 16–34.

the Library of Bennet College, among Arch-Bishop Parkers Printed books. Thus, in some hast, I remain,

Sir,

Your most humble servant

Humfrey Wanley.

MS: Bodleian, Rawl. lett. 17, fo. 59. *Date*: 'Coach-Office. Nov. 9. 1714.' *Address*: 'To Mr Hearne at the Bodleyan Library in Oxford.' *Printed*: Hearne, *Collections*, iv, pp. 425–6 (extract and summary).

149. *To* Thomas Hearne *13 November 1714*

Sir

I think your First Inference[1] is not right to the point; because it cannot be Supposed that a faithful Servant will betray his Trust, or a prudent one Act beyond his Commission.

As for the second it is better grounded. Indeed I shewed to my Lord the Letter I had written unto you, before I sealed it; but pointed to the form of the Receipt, desiring that his Lordship would be pleased to look it over. When his Lordship had read the beginning thereof, he returned it unto me, saying that he believed it was rightly done, &c.

Mr Hearne, now you see the Truth of the matter! Don't lett us fall out up[o]n Trifles. We are brother-Library-keepers;[2] and by a friendly Correspondence, may benefit one another (considering the Advantage of our Scituation) much more than we can ever pretend to do by wrangling. I am not at all angry at what ha's happened, and am as willing to serve you now, as I was before. In your Service I desire to be excused only this one Article; which is the borrowing my Lords Books & Papers of Leland, through my means. If you apply to my Noble Lord Harley about them, they may easily be had; but I think it will not *now* be so proper for me to meddle any farther in the Matter. In any other reasonable thing You will find me very much

Sir Your humble servant

Humfrey Wanley.

[1] For Hearne's inferences see his letter d. 11 Nov. 1714 (BL Harley MS 3779, fo. 38), summarized and excerpted in Hearne, *Collections*, iv, pp. 426–7. His rejoinder d. 17 Nov. (a draft of which, apparently not sent, is ptd. *Collections*, iv, p. 434) is in *Collections*, iv, p. 429. On the dispute see also the correspondence between Hearne and Anstis ptd. *Collections*, iv, pp. 425, 426, 430, 434.

[2] Hearne was Second Keeper of the Bodleian.

MS: Bodleian, Rawl. lett. 17, fo. 65. *Date*: 'Coach-Office, 13. Novr 1714.' *Address*: 'To Mr Thomas Hearne at the Bodleyan Library in Oxford. *Printed*: Hearne, *Collections*, iv, p. 427 (extracts).

150. *To* Arthur Charlett *15 November 1714*

Reverend Sir,

Your very kind Letter of the 10th Instant[1] came safe to hand; and I am most heartily thankful for so great a favor.

Mr Theyer's MSS.[2] were bought by the late Bishop of London[3] for King Charles II; His Lordship kept them with him, till within these late years, that he sent them to Doctor Bentley at St James's, and they are now carried to Cotton-house in Westminster. I cannot say positively, that the Greek MS. of Aristotle[4] is among them; but if You or Mr Wilkinson shall desire it, I will go thither; and, if it can be found, will send you some account of it.

I perceive Mr Wilkinson goe's only by Lambinus's Translation; Leonardus Aretinus (who was a Learned man) made one; a Manuscript of which, I gave to the Library at Coventre, when I was an Apprentice;[5] and, perhaps, other versions may be found. As to the Greek, I know of no other written Copies, but those in the Printed Catalogue.[6]

I suppose that Mr Wilkinson in his Account of Aristotle, will take Care to insert the Narration concerning His Works, and the Fate

---

[1] In Welbeck Wanleyana = BL Loan MS 29/253).

[2] The Theyer collection (*CMA* II. i, pp. 198–203) descended to John Theyer (1597–1673) from his grandfather Thomas Theyer who married the sister of Richard Hart, last Prior of Llanthony, and in turn direct to John Theyer's grandson Charles. There is some doubt about the date of the purchase for the Royal Collection. G. E. Warner and J. P. Gilson suggest that the purchase was made *c*.1678 (*Catalogue of Western Manuscripts in the Old Royal and King's Collections* (1921), I, p. xxvi). If they are right, on the evidence of this letter it was not actually incorporated until thirty years later. Now scattered throughout the Royal Collection, see Warner and Gilson, pp. xxxiii–xxxiv.

[3] Henry Compton (1632–1713), Bishop of London 1674.

[4] BL Royal MS 16.C.xxi. William Wilkinson of The Queen's College, Oxford (on whose behalf Charlett is enquiring and whose proposals he encloses) pbd. his edn. of Aristotle's *Ethics* in 1716.

[5] *CMA* II. i, no. 1462, an imperfect fifteenth-century copy of a Latin translation by Leonardo Aretinus. It is listed as 'Aristotelis Ethica Lat MS' under Wanley's name in the Donors' Book of Coventry Free School (now Cambridge University Library Add. MS 4467), but it is not among the 46 lots from the school library auctioned by Hodgson & Co., 11 Nov. 1908, lots 288–333.

[6] i.e. *CMA*.

they met withal; for, notwithstanding the positiveness of some men, Many things may now be found among his Works, which were not written by Him.

I think You want a New Funt of Greek Letter at Your Press; the Specimen shew's that what You use now, is Irregular, & otherwise faulty.

I humbly thank you, Sir, for your Remembrance of me in the College.[7] As I have no Children Living, I hope I shall one day be able to shew a token of my Gratitude for the favors I received therein.

Mr Kemp & I often drink to your good health; and he is ready for you at any time; giving him only previous notice to be at home. I am, with due respect,

Reverend Sir,

Your most obliged, & most humble servant

H. Wanley.

P.S. In Order to refresh my Memory touching Aristotles Ethics, I looked over some loose Notes I took from the late Bishop of Elie's & other Libraries. There I found what I thought I had some Idea of; namely, that the Bishop had a Copie of this Book in Greek, written on Parchment in the Year 6782; that is, A.D. 1274; as appear's by the Date at the End thereof.[8] Perhaps it may be of good Note & Value.

You have not yet been pleased to send me any satisfactory account about the late Mr Edward Lhwyds MSS.[9]

I hear You intend to buy the late Bishop of Elies Library; I wish I may be apprised farther about Your Intentions in that matter; for many buyers have started up.[10]

Before the receipt of your last, I did not know that you was actually resident in Oxford: otherwise I should have been bold in troubling you about borrowing two Greek MSS. from the Library of Lincoln-College.[11] I wrote to Mr Tickell, but understand that he is absent.

---

[7] Charlett wrote that in the event of the Master's Lodgings being rebuilt a room in them would still be known by Wanley's name 'as it is at Present'. It seems that Wanley's room had recently been converted into a bedroom for Charlett. See Charlett to Wanley d. 10 Nov. 1713, Welbeck Wanleyana = BL Loan MS 29/253.

[8] Cambridge University Library MS Ii.v.44.

[9] See no. 140 n. 4.   [10] See no. 145.

[11] Apparently two listed in the catalogue of Sir George Wheeler's manuscripts, *CMA* II. i, pp. 357–8 (Hudson to Wanley d. 13 Nov. 1714, BL Harley MS 3779, fo. 320). One is certainly (on the evidence of no. 155) MS Lincoln College Greek xxxv, a fourteenth-century manuscript of a 'Typicon' or monastic rule (perhaps *CMA* II. i, no. 9118), bought by Wheeler in Constantinople, according to a letter from him in Welbeck

I then applied my self to Dr Hudson, who will be so kind as to serve me. By this post I send him my Note, hoping that the books will be found, & sent to me accordingly. They are for my own use; and shall by no means go out of my hands, till I return them. I should be glad, Sir, if you would be pleased to signifie this to the most worthy Rector of that College.[12] He was formerly pleased (through your recommendation) to be my singular Friend & Patron; and never suffered me to want his Countenance or Protection; which favors I shall never forget, although His Station put's me into a want of Capacity to requite them. Let him know that I will not detain them too long,[13] although they come to me in the darkest time of the year, when my Noble Lords business hold's me play all the morning, till One; and, I now (beginning to step into years) dare no more Read or Write by Candle-light.

MS: Bodleian, Ballard 13, fo. 130. *Date*: 'Coach-Office, 15 Novr. 1714.' *Address*: 'To The Reverend Dr Charlett, Master of University College in Oxford.'

151. *To* [——] Bateman[1] *June 1715*

By the advice & encouragement of my very worthy friend Mr Granger,[2] I presume, Sir, to take the Liberty of a friend with You. To whom, although I am not so happy as to be personally known; yet I have seen, in the hands of your Relations such Specimens of your Ingenuity & Merit, as have created in me a regard capable to induce me (were it in my power) to do you much greater services than I now desire.

Wanleyana = BL Loan MS 29/258; Wanley's transcript made in Apr. 1715 is BL Harley MS 6505. The other manuscript I have not identified.

[12] Fitzherbert Adams, Rector of Lincoln College, Oxford 1685–1719.

[13] Wanley still had the 'Typicon' in his possession on 19 Nov. 1715: see his letter to Hudson of that date (no. 155). Six years later it was suspected that he still had not returned it (Wanley, *Diary*, p. 98(12)); it was found in 'an heap of Rubbish of the late Dr. Adams's things ... he himself having kept it out of the College-Library to his Death ... which was no fault of mine' (Wanley, *Diary*, p. 226(19)).

---

[1] Perhaps the 'Esqr Bateman' who offered Wanley some manuscript fragments in Aug. 1720: see Wanley, *Diary*, p. 65(13) and n. 3.

[2] Presumably Thomas Granger († 1732), Clerk to the Committee of Private Trade, East India Company, 1687–1732, and collector. Bodl. Gough London 54 is Wanley's copy of T. Smith's Catalogue of the Cotton Library (1696) with a presentation inscription to Thomas Granger d. 8 June 1715. Edward Harley bought the Lovel Lectionary (BL Harley MS 7026, fos. 4–20) at the sale of his library in 1733.

Among other your shining qualities, I am not unapprised of your early inclinations to Learning, of the progress you made therein before your departure from England; of the various Languages & Experience in Business which you have since acquired: all which noble qualifications render you still more capable of serving me.

I am a person who have spent some time in poring over Old Books; many sorts of which having come under my Cognisance, in English Libraries, especially those of our Universities, whither my own poor affairs will not suffer me often to resort: I have begun to think of making a little Collection of my own; of which I may be the Master, and which I may consequently consult at my own leasure without controul.

In Order to this, I would desire you would be pleased to buy me a Greek Bible, containing the Books of the Old & New Testament, written upon Velum or Parchment by the same, or a like hand, in one or more Volumes. To be sure such a Book may be met with, in the Patriarchal Library at Antioch, or in the Libraries, or Churches of the Greeks, Metropolitical, Episcopal, or Monastical: of all which as to the parts wherein you have sojourned, you must needs have the most exact knowledge. In case such a book doth not presently occurr, or not soon come into your hands: rather than receive nothing from you by the next return; I would desire the Septuagint, or some part of it; some Greek MSS. books of the Antient Pagan or Christian Authors; or even what you please: as, a Gjorgian Bible; the old Testament in Syriac; or some Book of the Mendaean Christians; as to which I will rely intirely upon your judgement & integrity. I add no more now than this as I doubt not, but that you will procure somewhat for me at as reasonable & moderate price as you can: so, I promise, upon receipt of the goods, to pay the same to worthy Mr Granger, or your other order; being, with a most sincere respect

  Good Sir,
    Your most faithful, humble servant

In case the Psalter come's with other books of the Old Testament, in the same Volumes; I except not against it.

MS: Welbeck Wanleyana = British Library, Loan 29/258; draft. *Date*: 'June 1715.' *Address*: 'To Mr Bateman at Isphâhan.'

152. *To* John Covell *18 September 1715*

Reverend Sir,

I return you my most humble & hearty Thanks for all your great Favors & Civilities, shewn daily unto me during this my last abode at Cambridge.

My Noble Lord is pleased to accept, in good part, that poor List I was enabled to make of your Manuscripts;[1] is willing to purchase them at an honest and reasonable price; and you may take the Money for them as soon as you shall think fitting; for it lie's dead by him, & ready for you.[2]

If you gratifie his Curiosity before the Edge & Appetite are worn off; I believe he may be induced to buy all your other Curiosities, Antient & Modern: but all dependeth upon the manner of your putting this parcel of MSS. into his Hands. You have seen the World, & understand it as well as any man. Suffer me to advise you to sell your things your self, & take the ready money now that you have it in your power.

Be pleased to give my humble service to the Ladies, & lett your Niece know that in London she shall be as welcome to me & my poor Wife as my Sister. My Wife, is fallen Sick; and therefore I go up to London by the next Coach. I shall carry up a piece of Venison (now unkilled) along with me; & can heartily wish that the Ladies, You & Mr Annesley, &c. could be at the eating of it. I send your good servant, some of my Syrupus Altheae, which I hope may do her service, & remain with all gratitude,

    Reverend Doctor,

        Your most faithful, & most obliged servant

                        Humfrey Wanley.

MS: British Library, Add. 22911, fo. 171. Copy in Cambridge University Library MS Mm.vi.50, fo. 290. *Date*: 'Wimple 18 September, 1715.' *Address*: 'To The Reverend Doctor Covell, Master of Christs-College in Cambridge.'

[1] Not traced. A catalogue made in 1715 by Covell himself is BL Add. MS 22911, fos. 180–3.

[2] E. Harley was very keen to get Covell's collection of manuscripts: 'Dr Covels things will be worth all these Heraldical things over & over; I had rather loose all these then the Drs' (Harley to Wanley d. 24 Oct. 1715; Welbeck Wanleyana = BL Loan MS 29/248). For the prolonged and often acrimonious negotiations, see Wanley's letters to Covell (nos. 127, 131, 142, 156, 157, 162, 166, 167, 170), to Tudway (nos. 158, 159, 160, 161, 164, 169), and to E. Harley (no. 163).

153. *To* John Covell *11 October 1715*

Reverend Sir,

After my most hearty Thanks for the many & great Favors which you was pleased to shew unto me at Cambridge, and which I shall never forget: I lay hold upon this Opportunity of acquainting you, that I did hope & expect to have had the honor & happiness of seeing you here, when you accompanied the Cambridge-Address to his Majesty;[1] but my earnest wishes proved all in vain, For you came not to me, and I knew not where to find You.

My intention was to have exhorted you, according to the many promises you made me, to proceed in bringing the Price of Your MSS. to one Sum, reasonable and fitting to be demanded and allowed. This may be easily done, and might have been done whilst I was with you. But, however, since you took time to the end of the first week in November, I hope I shall have your resolution by then, at the farthest. In the mean while, I desire to hear from you by the first Post; that you will remember me respectfully to Doctor Tudway;[2] and that you will always esteem me

Reverend Sir,

Your most faithful, & most obliged servant

Humfrey Wanley.

MS: British Library, Add. 22911, fo. 175. Copy in Cambridge University Library MS Mm.vi.50, fo. 291. *Date*: 'Coach-Office in Surrey street, in the Strand, 11 October, 1715.' *Address*: 'To The Reverend Dr Covel, Master of Christs College in Cambridge.'

[1] An address to George I in thanks for his purchase and presentation to the University of the library of John Moore, Bishop of Ely, 29 Sept. 1715 (pbd. *London Gazette*, no. 5368).

[2] Thomas Tudway (1656–1726), organist of King's and Pembroke Colleges, and Great St Mary's, Cambridge, Professor of Music 1705. He acted for Wanley in the negotiations with Covell, and between 1712 and 1724 compiled for Harley a representative set of musical compositions for the services of the Anglican Church, then quite unobtainable, principally founded on the old choir-books of Ely, finally running to 6 vols. and 3000 pages, now in BL Harley MS 7337–42. Harley 7443 contains music composed by him for the consecration of the Chapel at Wimpole in 1724.

154. *To* [Edward Harley] *12 October 1715*

May it please your Lordship,
  Your Noble & Candid Acceptance of my poor Service, in retrieving
the 2d Vol. of Catalogue[1] is a great Incouragement for me to proceed
in fulfilling your Pleasure on all other Occasions; as also, what I am
particularly bound to you for. I am Sorry that the Greek Psalter
proveth so recent, in your Lordships Opinion; and that the Alcoran
proveth to be but on Paper, when it was waranted to be written upon
Parchment.[2] Arabic books upon Parchment, are most exceedingly
rare; for which reason I wonder'd that my Noble Lord your Father
should reject that which I offered unto Him, at a price beneath it's
Value. However when I shall see these books, I shall be able to say
more. My first Book of Caesars Commentaries translated by the late
French King,[3] was bound in Velum, with his Arms & Orders stamped
on both Sides the Cover. Mr Howel[4] hath not been with me this Week,
being busied with design to get into the Charterhouse. In truth, the
poor man hath formerly been Industrious; but is now superannuated. I
am affraid, that some more Actions have been clap'd on Mr Andrews,[5]
since his first being cast into Prison. I will inquire, and certifie what
shall appear, to your Lordship. The Catalogue above, come's from the
Booksellers at Beaufort-Buildings.[6] They have more, which (with
these) came from the late Auction in Holland. I offer'd my Assistance,
in Cataloguing the smaller books for You because I found them most
curious; but they declined the same. This, they (at my Invitation) have
done; but in their own way. Herein, books are inserted, which I know
you have already; & others are left out, which perhaps you have Not.
  My poor Wife with the utmost sense of Gratitude to my Noble
Lady, *as also my self* concur's with me, as
  Your Lordships most obedient & most humble Servant
                                                    H. Wanley.

MS: Welbeck Wanleyana = British Library, Loan 29/204, fo. 513. *Date*: '12 October
1715.' *Printed*: *HMC Portland Papers*, v, p. 520 (extracts).

[1] Not identified.   [2] Neither MS identified.
[3] *La Guerre des Suisses* (Paris, 1651).
[4] Probably Henry Howell, Arms Painter, Master of the Painter-Stainers Company
1699, one of Wanley's agents: see Wanley, *Diary*, p. 7(5).
[5] Not identified.
[6] Not identified.

155. *To* John Hudson *19 November 1715*

Reverend Sir,

Some days ago I received per penny-post, yours of the 8th Instant.[1] In answer whereunto, I beg leave to acquaint you, that I finished my Transcript of the MS. Typicon which I borrowed (through your favor) from Lincoln-College, a good while since. I cannot yet meet with a proper Workman who will lay Gold on Velum for me at a reasonable price. This must be done, or I cannot have the Pictures faithfully & exactly Copied;[2] as I intend to have done (cost what it will) when the days shall grow longer.

I have no intentions of Printing at this present:[3] and am a pretty good Judge of both Bern. Montfalcon's books by you mentioned; having them both in mine own poor Study.[4] As to his Palaeographia; excepting some few things, I could have made as good a book from our English Libraries & Collections, alone: in lieu whereof, I can assure you, that they can both Correct & Supply him, much farther than any man can imagine, who hath not perused him diligently, & also spent much time in our Public Libraries & Private Studies.

I cannot imagine what you mean, by Casaubon's Remarks upon any Josephus in the *Cotton-Library*.[5] If you will please to explain your self, I will gladly endeavor to serve you, who am already,

    Sir,

        Your most obliged, humble servant

                          Humfrey Wanley.

[1] Welbeck Wanleyana = BL Loan MS 29/255.

[2] See no. 150 and n. 11; the text is prefaced by twelve full-page and one half-page illuminations.

[3] Hudson urged publication of Wanley's 'Book of Specimens', for which see no. 37 n. 1.

[4] Probably Bernard de Montfaucon's *Diarium Italicum* (Paris, 1702) an account of the principal libraries of Italy and their contents, and his *Palaeographia Graeca* (Paris, 1708), a book illustrating the history of Greek writing and letter-forms. It seems likely that Wanley owned a copy of the *Diarium Italicum*—his commission to Andrew Hay five years later (no. 215), directing Hay to buy ancient manuscripts for Edward Harley while travelling through Italy, derives in large part from Montfaucon's work. He certainly owned a copy of Montfaucon's *Palaeographia Graeca*, mentioned here: a copy with Wanley's signature of ownership and annotated in Wanley's hand is in the possession of the editor of the present edition.

[5] Hudson asked Wanley to examine a manuscript of Josephus in the Cotton Library and to report on Casaubon's marginal annotations. There are no manuscripts of Josephus in the Cotton Library.

MS: Bodleian, Ballard 13, fo. 132. *Date*: '19 Novr 1715.' *Address*: 'To The Reverend Dr John Hudson, Principal of St Maries Hall, & Head-Library-keeper to the University of Oxford.'

156. *To* John Covell *19 November 1715*

Reverend Sir,

I must crave your pardon, if I again put you in mind of me. The first week of this Month hath now been expired some time; and the examination of your Manuscripts need not detain you long, in order to the fixing a reasonable price upon them.[1] Pray lett me know your determination with speed, that I may give you my opinion thereupon, & afterward make a Report to my Noble Lord, which may be suitable to the good opinion he is pleased to conceive of both of us.

The sooner we finish this affair of the Manuscripts, the sooner we shall begin with the next parcel; be they, either the Antiquities, or the Printed books, as you shall please to order it. And, indeed, the sooner you may putt a Sum of Money into your Coffers; which is more to your Interest, than the possession of a parcel of old Books.

Reverend Sir,

   I am,

      Your most obliged, humble servant

                                        Humfrey Wanley.

MS: British Library, Add. 22911, fo. 176. Copy in Cambridge University Library MS Mm.vi 50, fo. 292. *Date*: 'Coach-Office in Surrey-street, 19 November 1715.' *Address*: 'To The Reverend Doctor John Covell Master of Christs College in Cambridge.'

157. *To* John Covell *10 December 1715*

Reverend Sir,

Not having had the happiness of hearing from you a very considerable time, I take the boldness of putting you in mind of my Noble Lord; who by keeping a particular Sum of Money by him, upon your occasion, hath (in reality) procured unto himself the Office of your Treasurer.

Now Treasurers, you know, Bankers, and such sort of people,

---

[1] See no. 153.

generally sett to Interest other mens money, which hath lain long in
their Hands uncalled for. Why, therefore, may not You take this
Money out of His Lordships Hands, and dispose of it in your own
Name? Nothing hinder's this, but your long detention of a parcel of
old musty Parchments & Papers; which look not so pleasantly to the
Eie as the ready Aurum obryzum doth to

    Reverend Sir,

        Your most humble servant

                              Humfrey Wanley.

MS: British Library, Add. 22911, fo. 178. Copy in Cambridge University Library MS
Mm.vi.50, fo. 292. *Date*: 'Coach-Office, 10 December 1715.' *Address*: 'To The Reverend
Dr Covel Master of Christs-College in Cambridge.'

158. *To* Thomas Tudway *10 December 1715*

Worthy Doctor,

Some business more than ordinary hath hindred me from answering your two last Letters until now.[1] And even now, my hurry is so
great, that I cannot gain time enough to converse with you in so large a
manner as I would. You may therefore please to excuse me if I tell you
in short, That

My poor Wife will be bold, in presenting your Lady with some Tea
& Coffee, soon.

The next day I received your Letter to Mr Church,[2] I carried it to
his House, & left it for Him; with a direction how to send any parcel
to you, by my means. If you have not heard from him since; you
know how to spur him up, by the Post.

The very thought of Spurring, bring's the Stimulating or Extimulat-
ing Notion or Idea of Goading into my Head. Surely, either one or the
other must be a good Recipe for the Master of Christs. I think
presently to put a Rowell on my Pen to him; and shall confide that you
being nearer, will Act Shamgars part[3] Prudently, in my good Lords
behalf. Indeed the Doctor is to blame, in acting thus by a person of my

---

[1] This is a reply to Tudway's d. 25 Nov. 1715, BL Harley MS 3782, fo. 31.

[2] John Church (1675?–1741), musician and composer, Gentleman of the Chapel
Royal 1697, Master of the Choristers at Westminster Abbey 1704.

[3] Judg. 3: 31: 'Shamgar the son of Anath, which smote of the Philistines six hundred
men with an ox goad'.

Lords Birth, Qualifications, & Estate. And yet, I know my Lord will forgive him, even although it should be Christmass before he come's to his long-expected resolution.

Among the Notes you sent in your last, I observe the Tune of Mr Lamb,[4] in a Key different from that you wrote in the Book you gave me. As to this I would gladly have the other parts in Score, that I may insert the same into the said Book. I am with true respect Sir,

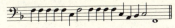

Your much obliged servant
Humfrey Wanley.

MS: British Library, Harley 3782, fo. 161. *Date*: 'Saturday 10 December 1715.' *Address*: 'To Doctor Tudway, at his house over-against Pembroke-Hall in Cambridge.'

159. *To* Thomas Tudway *20 December 1715*

Worthy Doctor,

I beseech you never do Your self & me the Injustice, as to believe that your Letters were ever unwelcome or tedious to me. Although my many avocations do not allow me to be always the most punctual of your Correspondents.

I am glad, that Dr Covel is about bringing this long-winded business to a Period. When I come down to Cambridge (If I cannot do it conveniently before) I will bring with me my Wifes poor present to your Lady.

I delivered your second Letter into Mr Churches own hands. He said he had not finished what you require from him. I desired him to send forthwith what he had done, and putt him into the easiest method. You may therefore expect soon to hear from him, either by the way of Mr Vaillant the Bookseller,[1] or from Wymple.

I have gotten one Volume of Church-Music used at Durham;[2] you shall see't. I wish I had all the Parts; but since that cannot now be obtained, I must be content for the present. I have, however, procured

---

[4] Probably Benjamin Lamb, organist of Eton College Chapel in the early eighteenth century, and verger of St George's Chapel, Windsor.

---

[1] Paul Vaillant (1672–1739), bookseller in the Strand, in partnership with his brother Isaac.

[2] Not identified.

my friend to write thither; and you shall be apprised of the result, in due time.

I heartily thank you for your inclosed paper of Church-Tunes.

Pray keep Dr Covel warm this cold weather; and believe me to be sincerely

    Sir,

        Your most obliged & very humble servant

                              H. Wanley.

MS: British Library, Harley 3782, fo. 163. *Date*: 'Coach-Office, 20 December 1715.' *Address*: 'To Dr Tudway, at his House against Pembroke-hall in Cambridge.'

160. *To* Thomas Tudway *5 January 1716*

Worthy, good Doctor,

I beseech you not to be troubled for me, who am not sorry for my self. As to the Malice of all who have wronged me, I am not sollicitous. I thank God, I can forgive them, and take my Rest in Innocence. And, I had rather have one kind Thought, one good Look, from the Noble Lord & Lady, whose House is now become my Refuge; than receive as much Gold as would fill the large Room I now write in from those Men: And I know most assuredly, I may yet be advanced by their Bretheren, if I would take the pains to Sollicit their favor; which, hitherto, I never yet did, although I have lived long in way of amity with them. For it is not in my Nature to be too morose or churlish to any man; lett his Party, or Religion, be what it will. In such Cases, every man must answer for himself; Candor & Civility being due to all.

Pray lett the Master of Christs know, that really 'tis time for a man of his Years & supposed Gravity, to leave-off trifling with a Personage of my Noble Lords Birth, Quality, & Fortunes. And in short, if he doth not soon Conclude, I will cause his Statue to be Erected (made of Bath-mettal) upon a Leaden Pedestal, & both Sett on a Sandy Soil. There he shall be represented, with the largest Spanish Spectacles, squinnying upon the most worm-eaten of all his Manuscripts, with his old Roman Weights & a Chinese pair of false Scales; as attempting to make every abbreviation, or mis-spelled word, equiponderous, & equivalent in value, to the best Sentence in Ecclesiasticus.

To punne with you a little (not in your politer manner, but in mine own Rougher Way) I must confess, in answer to yours, that I have not been at Church a good while.[1] I mean (and such is the vileness of my Punne, to say nothing of the Clinch,[2] that I must be forced to explain my meaning) I have not seen Mr Church since I told you so in one of my former Letters. He know's how to send to you; and it is not in my power to make him write against his will. When the weather is grown so mild that I dare venture out (for now every little Cold blast seizeth the hinder part of my right Leg) I will endeavor to find him out again, and by a good Glass of Wine, warme both his Inclination to Serve, & his Affection to Love you; which last is best.

But to leave prating, now, in cold weather, when a warm Supper is coming up; believe that I am, with all truth

Sir,

Your much-obliged Servant

Humfrey Wanley.

MS: British Library, Harley 3782, fo. 167. *Date*: 'From my Lord Harley's house in St James's Square, 5 January 1715/6.' *Address*: 'To Doctor Thomas Tudway at his house against Pembroke-hall in Cambridge.'

161. *To* Thomas Tudway *17 January 1716*

Worthy Doctor,

Your kind Letter of the 8th Instant came safe to hand, and I should have acknowledged my receipt thereof (by letting you know that I sent your Letter to Mr Church, forthwith, by the Penny-post) before now; but that I waited for Dr Covel's Letter, according to the Notice you gave me.[1]

As to the Armes you speak of, my Lord hath a stamp of them at

---

[1] Tudway's appetite for punning was notorious. On 28 July 1706 he had been sentenced for offensive punning to be 'degraded from all degrees, taken and to be taken', and was deprived of his Professorship of Music at Cambridge and of his posts as organist at King's, Pembroke, and Great St Mary's. On 10 Mar. 1707 he publicly made submission and retractation in the Regent House. He was then formally absolved and reinstated in all his appointments.

[2] i.e. the word-play.

---

[1] Of Covell's promise to let Wanley have a catalogue of, and a price for, his collection of manuscripts.

Wymple, as I believe.[2] You may borrow it by Mr Jeffreys with ease enough, if it be there.

Since then, I have received the Doctors Estimate;[3] and your last Letter of the 15th instant,[4] for which I most heartily thank you. As to the Estimate, it is so extravagantly wide of all Reason & Equity, that I know not what to say about it. Considering the Masters Learning & Good Sense in other matters, it make's the matter yet more intricate & unaccountable. I am loath to think he had any intention to banter a noble Lord, merely because he is a Lover and a Patron of Learning. As for my self, I care not how I may be jested upon. And yet I know that such a parcel of Books as the Doctors is, never yet produced a third part of the Sum by Him demanded. I am apprehensive that this business may pull down my Lords anger upon me, who promised him much better Quarter from the Doctor; and this makes me keep his Papers still in my Hands. I am Good Sir,

    Your most faithful & very humble Servant

                    Humfrey Wanley.

If the Doctor would moderate his first Demand to £400; I might have more Courage to send his Papers to my Lord. In the mean time I can assure you that His Manuscripts are not worth near that Sum.

MS: British Library, Harley 3782, fo. 169. *Date*: 'St James's Square 17 January 1715/6.' *Address*: 'To Doctor Thomas Tudway, at his house against Pembroke-hall in Cambridge.'

162. *To* John Covell *24 January 1716*

Reverend Sir,

Yours of the 19th Instant[1] came not timely enough to my hands, for me to answer by the same Post: but, I shall do it now, hoping that this will arrive timely, and to your Satisfaction.

I must again crave leave to continue in my former opinion that you would do well to moderate your Sum Total, before I make your

  [2] Tudway had proposed (letter d. 8 Jan. 1716, BL Harley MS 3782, fo. 34) to have Harley's arms stamped on books he intended to present to Harley.

  [3] See no. 162 n. 2.

  [4] BL Harley MS 3782, fo. 35.

———

  [1] BL Harley MS 3778, fo. 115, with marginal glosses by Wanley.

proposal known to my Noble Lord; because almost all your things are by much over-prized, so far as (in my poor judgement) to forbid or fore-close any Treaty.[2] Such like Cases also happen, when any Prince or State layeth an overgreat Duty on the Importation or Exportation of some sorts of goods. It amounteth to a Prohibition, & the goods therefore lie on the hands of the Seller. How much better therefore, & wiselier, might you deal by my Lord, in moderating this so unreasonable total, that (like a Sulphureous Steam) is enough to knock a man backwards; when, by the soon taking of a reasonable Sum, and that sufficiently *round*, you have the opportunity of improveing it daily, untill you add a greater unto it, by what my Lord will give you for your Antiquities, and such of your Printed Books as he may have a liking to?

In order to induce you to this, I am very willing to join issue with you touching the Value of your ἀποστολάριον the book by you most Valued, & insisted upon:[3] although, at present, I do not intirely agree with you touching the reason of that Term. But let that pass! You know, Sir, full well, that the Books of the Acts, St Pauls, & the Catholic Epistles, take not up so much room as the Four Gospels & the Apocalypse: that the whole New Testament taketh not up one Third part of the room of the Canonical Books of the Old Testament: nor is larger than the Apocryphal Books, & Clement to the Corinthians, as they are now extant in the Alexandrian MS: which is thought to be almost as old again as your Apostolarion; was actually the Standard Bible for the whole Patriarchate, during at least One Thousand years; came fresh & untouched to King Charles I (whereas your book hath been deflowered by Dr Mill, &c.) and is now the most valuable Bible in the Christian world, and containeth about Nine parts in Ten more than yours; and those of the scarcer pieces too: Now you valuing this little book at 50 Guineas, would rate the whole Bible written in the same Manner at 500 Guineas; a price which no Prince in Christendome ever did, or, I believe, ever will give. I am sure that King Charles I contented Cyril Lucaris, with a less Sum (yet given as an instance of his Royal Bounty & Munificence) in full payment, not only for the Alexandrian Bible abovementioned, but for about 40 other Greek MSS. still remaining in the Royal Library; not to mention those Lent or

[2] In his letter of 13 Jan. 1716, Covell had set a price of 500 guineas on his manuscripts. This, in Covell's words, put Wanley into a 'cold fit' (BL Harley MS 3778, fo. 15).

[3] BL Harley MS 5537. See no. 164 and n. 2.

Taken away; nor those of Arch-bishop Laude, which I believe were also paid for, with that very Money.[4]

Again: The Baroccian MSS. now at Oxford, being the most valuable parcel that ever came into England, consisteth of 264 Greek books, beside some few others.[5] These (after Notice, in print, was given all over Europe) were bought of the Owners at Venice, by a London-Bookseller; who brought them over, and at length sold them to William Earl of Pembroke for 700 Pounds; and, to be sure, got so well by the bargain, as to make such a Voiage turn to accompt. Now that Sum doth not come to Three Pounds per book, taking one with another; whereas you asking 348 Guineas, for 40 Greek MSS. the demand amounteth to above Eight Guineas & an half per book. A rate never sett, heard, or thought of before; & asked now, at a time, when (by reason of the Importation of so many hundreds, since the Arrival of the Baroccian) this sort of Commodity (for I talk in way of Trade) hath done, doth, & will fall, in the Market.

You esteem your Apostolarion as a jewel, because you never saw another; and therefore compare it to either of the two largest Diamonds in Europe, which you call mere Rarities, and things of no use. Alass Sir, the matter doth not stand there; for Diamonds still take their Value from their Weight by the Carat, from their Shape, & from their Water or Beauty; according to which, they bring their known Value in money, without more ado. Now consider this Book in the same manner; what will, or can it bring? O but (say you Sir) 'tis a jewel in Scarcity, for I never saw but this one any where. I cannot help that. I have seen Six, all better books than yours, at Oxford alone: and I can direct to some Scores more in foreign Libraries. Moreover, I have seen divers single MSS. each containing the Canon of the New Testament (which your Apostolarion cannot pretend to do) and yet scarcely any of them cost Five Pounds per book singly.

[4] The suggestion that Charles I bought the Codex Alexandrinus is a tendentious and unfounded conjecture on Wanley's part, as are the imputations that other manuscripts came with it, and that Laud was involved. Cyril Lucar, Patriarch of Constantinople, first presented Codex Alexandrinus to James I through Sir Thomas Roe, the English Ambassador to Constantinople, but the King died before it reached Roe. Subsequently it was presented to Charles I.

[5] The manuscripts of Giacomo Barocci of Venice were, according to Ussher, 'brought into England by Mr. [Henry] Featherstone the stationer' in 1628 (see Macray, p. 68). They were bought and presented to Oxford by William Herbert, 3rd Earl of Pembroke, Chancellor of the University, at the instigation of Laud. Wanley's figure may be an error for 246, which is the figure mentioned in the title of the Baroccian manuscripts in *CMA* I. i, p. 1, although not all are Greek.

As for the other MSS. by you mentioned, I saw them all; & I marked all, so far as I thought they deserved the Pains. I have a good Liking to *Bobovius's Musical MS.*[6] as a pretty thing; and am a Lover of Music my self. Which Love hath made me observe some Arabian & Turkish Songs that I have seen, with their own Notes, done by themselves. As for your *Arabic Translation of the Greek Euchologion*;[7] I had much rather it had been in the Greek Original, that I & others might have understood it. But in respect of Neatness & Beauty, it will by no means compare with a vast number of Oriental MSS. which I have seen & had in mine hands. The *Poran*, by what I have read of it in English (for either the whole, or greatest part, is in print) I perceive to be full of Dreams & Fables; yet am willing it should come among the Herd.[8] The *Clavicula Salomonis*,[9] is an idle & ridiculous Imposture of the moderns. You are far from having the only book of it. I often see them in Town & Countrey, not only in French, but in Italian, Spanish, Latin, & English. The Copies are numerous, & their owners fall the Price, for that reason. What I have written being matters of Fact, and what you either do know already to be true, or may soon know all to be so; I doubt not but that you will now Moderate your total Price, and descend to one more reasonable, which I may communicate to my Lord. I dare not do it by the present; although I am sincerely, and with grateful respect for your many favors,

Reverend Sir,

Your most humble, & obliged servant

Humfrey Wanley.

P.S. I forgott, in writing, to say somewhat touching that part of your Letter relating to an intire *Menander*.[10] You would give 1000 Pounds for a good, stanch, intire Copie. I believe so, because such a book being intirely fresh; long wished for, but in vain; would, undoubtedly, produce that Sum, from the Booksellers of England, Holland, France, & Germany, by Selling the ἀπόγραφα unto them all, as near to the

---

[6] BL Harley MS 3409, an account of the new Seraglio at Constantinople in 1665 by Alberto Bobovio.

[7] BL Harley MS 5460. A seventeenth-century copy of a horologium (not a euchologion), but that this is the manuscript is clear from Covell to Wanley d. 19 Jan. 1716, Harley 3778, fo. 115 and no. 164.

[8] BL Harley MSS 4252–6: see Covell to Wanley d. 19 Jan. 1716, Harley 3778, fo. 115.

[9] BL Harley MS 3981, a French translation from the Italian version of the original Hebrew.

[10] BL Harley MS 3778, fo. 115.

same time as possible. Perhaps such a book may be found if well looked after. For, I remember, I saw (about 20 years ago) a Printed Catalogue of certain Greek MSS. *then* remaining in certain Libraries in Turkey;[11] viz. about the midst of our Queen Elizabeth's Reign, where a *Menander integer* was enumerated. Who know's but that not only that individual Book, but also many other Exemplars of the same Poet, may be yet remaining?

MS: British Library, Add. 22911, fo. 185. Copy in Cambridge University Library MS Mm.vi.50, fo. 293. *Date*: 'From my Lords house in St James's Square, 24 Jan. 1715/6.' *Address*: 'To The Reverend Dr Covel Master of Christs College in Cambridge.'

163. *To* [Edward Harley] *24 January 1716*

May it please your Noble Lordship,

It was after five, this Evening, before your most kind Letter came into my hands. All your Letters have hitherto come safe, and all those from others come safe also, although they are directed unto me at this very house of your Lordships.

My Lord, the first thing I shall do to morrow-morning, God Willing, will be to take Coach to Mr Noel's,[1] and there putt all your Business into the most easie & proper Method that I can. And I hope to give your Lordship a good account thereof, by the next Post.

I shall write presently to honest Dr Tudway. I believe his whole business in Town, is to gett some fine Pieces of Church Music for your Lordship. I have already drawn up a Letter to Dr Covell, in Answer to that which I shall herein send inclosed.[2] The Doctor play's close & cunning; but I do not fear the Encounter. I think he will be somewhat battered by this. If he will think fitt to stand by his rating most of his other books, he shall be sure to have as much more, in proportion. And upon communication, the Reasons shall be given him, how &

---

[11] The catalogue of Greek manuscripts including a Menander is a well-known forgery: see P. Maas, *Byzantinische Zeitschrift*, 38 (1939), p. 201.

---

[1] Nathaniel Noel (*fl.* 1681–*c.*1753), the bookseller principally used by Harley. His agent George Suttie obtained many manuscripts for Harley from the Continent. See Wanley, *Diary*, Biographical Index, for full references. The business referred to was the selection of books from Hickes's library, part of which he was selling off: see the account in no. 165.

[2] For Wanley's letters to Tudway and Covell, see nos. 162, 164. Covell's letter to Wanley d. 19 Jan. 1716 is in BL Harley MS 3788, fo. 115.

wherein he is mistaken. And yet, after all, he is the craftiest Old Fox that I ever dealt withall; & hath kept me longer in expectation than any other man ever did. As to his yielding to my Valuation now, I think it not yet time for that matter. That must be done in Company, and he must give Security to stand to [*two letters lost*]ne award: otherwise, notwithstanding all such Whim-whams as are expressed in his [& Dr] Tudways Letters, he would Fly-off, if mine Arbitration should not please him. He must there[fore] give me more occasion to lay on a little more. In short, his Defect is this; he ha's consulted & used his own books sufficiently, but either doth not, or will not, know what things are in other places. He may think he gain's much thereby: but, I know, I shall even for that reason gain the better of him.

According to the promise I made in my last, I shall likewise send herewith my Transcript of Dr May of Giessen's Paper to Dr Bray:[3] which perhaps may not be altogether unuseful on another occasion. One thing I beg leave to observe, out of an History of the Bohemian Persecutions, which I have for you, although omitted by him, that FRATRES is not to be understood of *Friers* or Regulars, but of Friends or Lay-BRETHEREN. Thus my book saith pag., 62, 63, (being privatly printed A.1648)[4] "Imperavit igitur (*Georgius Rex Bohemorum*) ditionem Liticensem, in montanis Silesiae vicinis: quo mox Pragenses illi Cives, Baccalaurei, Magistri, sese contulerunt. Alij vero aliunde, Plebeij & Nobiles, docti et indocti, non exiguo numero confluxerunt (maxime in pagum Kunwald dictum) Anno 1459. Scripturarum lectioni, precibus, et operibus pietatis, intenti. Pastores habebant e Calixtinis, qui superstitionibus relictis, ad Apostolicae simplicitatis formam sese componebant: quorum praecipuus fuit Michael Zambergius, pius ac devotus Senex. Illi omnes in universum, sese mutuo Christianis communi, pijs amabili, nomine, FRATRES & SORORES compellare caeperunt; quod et obtinuit, ut illis Fratrum Bohemicorum, $\kappa\alpha\tau'\grave{\epsilon}\xi o\chi\acute{\eta}\nu$, titulus esset attributus, et huc usque."

As to the above-mentioned *Calixtini* your Lordship will be pleased to receive this following short account, from the 51st page of the same History. "Vulgus enim plebis & cleri, in solum Calicem (i.e. the Cup in the Sacrament, which the Roman Church had long denied to the

---

[3] Johann Heinrich Maius (or May) (1653–1719), German Lutheran divine, Professor of Theology at Giessen 1688. Bray was prime mover in the founding of the SPCK and the SPG. A copy (four and a half pages) by Wanley of May's paper to Bray is attached.
[4] J. A. Comenius, *Historia Persecutionum Ecclesiae Bohemicae* (1648).

Laity) intenti, inde Calixtini dicti; reliqua Magist. Hussi dogmata secure negligere. Taboritae vero, —— cum alijs paucis, puritatem ac simplicitatem in omnibus Articulis & Ceremonijs urgere, caeperunt. Clamabant Illi, ab Ecclesiae ritibus, in omnibus, secundum non esse: clamabant Hi, nullas Superstitiones tolerandas esse." So that the Calixtini, if they might be indulged with the Blessed Cup in the Eucharist, could agree with the Roman Church, in other matters, well enough.

With all our most humble Duty to your most Noble Consort, our very good Lady; I crave leave to be particularly looked upon as,

May it please your Lordship,

Your Lordships most obedient, most faithful,

& most thankful servant

Humfrey Wanley.

MS: Welbeck Wanleyana = British Library, Loan 29/258. *Date*: 'Tuesday, 24 January 1715/6. From your house in St James's Square.'

164. *To* Thomas Tudway *24 January 1716*

Worthy Doctor,

I received your dateless Letter[1] the last Saturday, safely; as also another from the Master of Christs College, wherein he seem's to vindicate his Estimate of his Manuscripts too far, in mine opinion.

He call's his Apostolarion[2] (a little book in 24to containing not half the New Testament) an invaluable Jewel, &c. and ask's Fifty Golden Guineas for it. Alass! the book is Common in all Libraries; hath been Printed I believe, an hundred times over; and his individual book hath been examined & collated by Dr Mill, & all the Variantes Lectiones therein, also Printed. Who can come to a Treaty upon such unreasonable Terms, as were never heard of before, in any Age, or in any Countrey. Be pleased, therefore, to advise him, if he at the bottom intend's to do any thing, to bring down his total Sum to £400; to ask me that Sum for his whole Collection of MSS; and then see if I shall not

[1] BL Harley MS 3782, fo. 37, endorsed by Wanley 'Dr Tudway, 20 January 1715/6'.
[2] BL Harley MS 5537. Despite Wanley's tactical denigration it is an important copy—see *Scrivener's Introduction to the Criticism of the New Testament*, 4th edn., ed. E. Miller (1894), i, p. 286, no. 25. Mill had collated it and printed variants in his edn. of the NT (1707).

bid him as a Candid & Fair Chapman in the Market.[3] My Lord putt's me in hopes of seeing you soon in Town, which will be a most acceptable thing to

Worthy Sir,

Your most faithful servant

Humfrey Wanley.

MS: British Library, Harley 3782, fo. 171. *Date*: 'From my Lords House in St James's Square, 24 January 1715/6.' *Address*: 'To The Reverend Doctor Tudway, at his House against Pembroke-hall in Cambridge.'

165. *To* Edward Harley *26 January 1716*

May it please your Lordship,

In Obedience to your Noble Commands of the 22d Instant,[1] I went yesterday morning to Mr Noel's, and declared your Pleasure unto him; which I found him very ready to comply withal. That this might have the better Effect, I thought it would be fitting for me to sett forth a good Pattern. I therefore filled up the Box I, with mine own hands; consisting chiefly of Septentrional and other outer-course Books, and I placed at the Top, the loose-leaves of Catalogue before transmitted unto You. I helped also to Nail most of the Boxes, &c. and tarried untill Six Boxes were filled. This Morning I went again betimes, and Order'd the remaining Books to be putt into their Boxes; and likewise began, to look over once more such of Dr Hickes's Books as were left behind. For your Lordship may remember that I have before advertised you of some crafty play, there. When I had revised half the Folio's, and laid some of them by for you, Mr Noel come's back from the Dean of Peterborough,[2] without having been able to do any thing to day. But he must go again on Monday, and is promised that he shall speed. In the mean time, the greatest part of Basil Kennets books lie at

---

[3] Tudway reported (25 Jan. 1716, BL Harley MS 3782, fo. 39) that Covell 'will not refuse' 330 guineas.

---

[1] Welbeck Wanleyana = BL Loan MS 29/248. On Wanley's advice Harley bought heavily from Hickes's library (he had died 15 Dec. 1715), chiefly 'Septentrional' books in which Harley's collection was deficient.

[2] White Kennett (1660–1728), antiquary and historian, Dean of Peterborough 1708. His brother Basil Kennett (1674–1715), President of Corpus Christi College, Oxford 1714, had accumulated a miscellaneous collection of books and antiquities during the period of his chaplaincy to the British factory at Leghorn, 1706–13.

Oxford, charged with His Legacies, whereas the Assits will not discharge the Bond-Creditors. The Dean therefore saith that Noel must fetch them up from Oxford. Then the Dean promised to assist him in buying the late Arch Bishop of Canterburies Library,[3] in which the Byzantine Historians, the Councils, Bibliotecha Maxima Patrum, Tractatus Tractatuum, &c. are said to be compleat: together with a vast number of other Books in the Best Binding & Covers, being Presents. But Mr Dean (Noel saie's) tacked this Condition to his favor, that He should lett the Dukes of Devon & Buckinghamshire, & the Earl of Sunderland,[4] or any of them, have what they shall like out of Dr Hickes's & His Brothers Books forthwith. At the same time Mr Dean said he himself would not take any Lords Note in England. Hereupon, I was obliged to change my measures. The Box VII, being last to be filled, had not books enow in it, I therefore clapped a dosen of Dr Hickes's other folios therein; among which are a Somner noted by his Hand,[5] the completest Jacobus Laurus I ever saw,[6] & other uncommon books; together with 28 Dutch Quarto's & Octavo's about the Laws & History of their Countrey, which may be returned, if disliked. And I staid so long at Noel's, untill I saw all your 8 Boxes Nailed down & Loaded, & Drove out of the Lane towards your Carriers Inne, Mr Noel's Man going along with the Cart, in order to see the said Boxes Safely delivered unto your Carrier.[7]

The Contents of the Boxes thus sent towards you, are as followeth,

Box	Folios	Quartos	8vos. &c.	
I containeth	21	28		76
II				306
III				340
IV			102	
V	38			10
VI	30			20
VII	40	(besides Dutch 4tos & 8vos 28) &		39
VIII			142	28

[3] Tenison's library remained intact at St Martin-in-the-Fields for nearly a hundred and fifty years: it was sold by Sotheby and Wilkinson on 3 June, 1 July 1861, 23 Jan. 1862.

[4] William Cavendish (*c.*1673–1729), 2nd Duke of Devonshire, White Kennett's patron; John Sheffield (1647–1721), 1st Duke of Buckingham; Charles Spencer (*c.*1674–1722) 3rd Earl of Sunderland. The famous 'Sunderland Library', long kept at Blenheim after being pledged to his father-in-law, the 1st Duke of Marlborough, was sold 1882–3.

[5] Probably William Somner, *Dictionarium Saxonico-Latino-Anglicum* (Oxford, 1659).

[6] Probably Giacomo Lauro, *Antiquae Urbis Splendor*, a series of engravings of Roman antiquities with descriptions at the foot (1st edn. pubd. Rome, 1612–14, and several in the seventeenth century thereafter).

[7] Cox, the Royston carrier, left from the Vine in Bishopsgate Street.

I have been often searching Noel about the Prices you give; that I might know whether I could serve you that way. He always said, that for Dr Fowkes's Books,[8] You gave (one book with another) a Guinea per Folio; 12s. for better Quarto's; & Six Shillings apiece for the other Quartos, & all other Lesser Books. I would not come in to this way of Reckoning: for I said a Quarto is a Quarto, & would not allow of any distinction among them. Then, I would have a difference between 4tos & 8vos &c. as You see them ranged above. If your Lordship will write to me that you think 6s. apiece enough for 4tos & 3s. apiece for 8vos & other Lesser books, I hope to Make Noel take it, & be contented. This very Article will save you many a pound: and as to the late A.Bishop's books I will still endeavor to gett them cheaper for you; & yet you shall have the choise of the whole.

In Order to prevent all after claps, with regard to those of Mr Kennets Books, that are now bought, (for the Lords say, if Noel will not come to them, they will come to him) I have taken upon me to look upon the Collection, & lay by for you, such of them as I best like my self. I have made good progress this day, and (God willing) shall finish to morrow. Boxes are bespoke, and as soon as I have done, I will see them putt therein, & nailed up; and then I shall brush E.H. upon them, that they may be safe untill the next Return of your Royston Carrier; whom your Lordship may empower to receive them for you, and also be pleased to advertise me thereof. The Price of these Books will be the same as those of Dr Hickes's; only Noel desire's your Lordship to send up speedily such as you will not keep, that they may be inserted into the Catalogue he will make to please the Town withall, and also to throw off so much dead weight. And I perceive, that he would be glad to receive his money, as soon as Bas. Kennets books are at an End, that he may be the Better able to buy the late Arch.-Bishops. As to the Prints & Drawings,[9] I am utterly against his being assisted therein by any person; and therefore have agreed with him, that he shall discover truely what they cost, and you shall have them, allowing him reasonable profit. This I thought the best way of proceeding for you, on many accounts. Since my Coming hither, I have found two most kind Letters from your Noble Lordship,[10] the

---

[8] Perhaps Phineas Fowke (1638–1710), physician and theologian of Little Wyrley Hall, Staffordshire. Harley was interested in his *papers* in 1724: see Wanley, *Diary*, p. 279(6).

[9] See further no. 177.

[10] 24, 25 Jan. 1716, Welbeck Wanleyana = BL Loan 29/248. Harley wished to have

one came from Bath Court, the other was brought by Mr Cuttle, to whom I will deliver the books according to your Order, knowing them all very well. I will, God Willing be at Wymple on the 11th. proximo unless your Business, or my Noble Lords Your Fathers happen to require mine attendance here. But, as to these, & other Matters I hope to say more by the next Post; for indeed I am very weary in my body; but in my Soul shall never be weary of praying for the prosperity of my noble Lady your Consort & Sweet Miss Peggy,[11] because I am, with as much truth as ever man was capable of

May it please your Lordship,

Your most faithful, most obedient, & thankful servant

H. Wanley.

MS: Welbeck Wanleyana = British Library, Loan 29/258. *Date*: 'From your Lordships House at St James's Square, 26 January 1715/6, 7 aclock.' *Address*: 'To The Right Honorable Edward Lord Harley, at Wymple in Cambridgeshire.'

166. *To* John Covell [*1*] *7 February 1716*

Reverend Sir,

Had not another Gentlemans necessary business called him away from hence my noble Lord would not have parted with honest Dr Tudway so soon. I lay hold of the Opportunity which his Departure giveth me, of letting you know that I have truly represented the State of the Matter relating to your Collection of Manuscripts, to his Lordship. He is, indeed a Lover of Curiosities of many kinds; and God Almighty hath been pleased to bless him with a Fortune so plentiful, as that he is able to purchase any thing that he liketh. But then, I must tell you again, he is a wise man, and knoweth the Value of his Ready Money, especially of Ready Money at this time, as well as any body. He is throughly sensible that your parcel of MSS. is but small, and that the sum demanded is great. However, I have prevailed so far with

Cavendish's *Life of Wolsey*, a transcript of Leland's *Itinerary*, and a volume of 'modern' manuscript poems sent via Cuttle, a servant from Wimpole.

[11] Lady Margaret Cavendish Holles Harley, later Duchess of Portland, only daughter and heir of Edward Harley, born 11 Feb. 1715. She was regularly addressed as 'sweet Peggy' by her grandfather Robert Harley and cf. Matthew Prior's lines to 'noble, lovely, little Peggy', *Literary Works*, ed. H. B. Wright and M. K. Spears, 2nd edn. (Oxford, 1971), i, p. 527. Wanley refers to her as 'sweet pretty Miss' or some such endearment.

him, as that he will not shame me, by refusing to ratifie what I said; but will give you Three Hundred Pounds for your Collection of MSS. with the Little Clog Almanac[1] that is among them, and all your Collection of Papers & Letters relating to the Greeks, to Learning, & Learned men.[2] That is, in short, all Papers or Letters Written, which do not relate to your private affairs. For this Sum, he expecteth to have the whole Cargo delivered up unto me, with a Receipt under your Hand, for the same. And upon my further importunate Instances, I have obtained of His Lordship, that He will make Doctor Covel, a Learned Gentleman whom he much esteemeth, a present fit for Him to receive, as a token of His Lordships Respect & Value for Him; but He will give no more for the things, than as I have said.

My Lords Money, the principal Verb, is Ready; and I think the Sum more than the Things are worth. If you will Trade on that Condition, and Stand to my Noble Lords Kind Liberality, Send me Word, & I will soon attend You. If not, you will have no further Trouble on this account, from

Reverend Sir,

Your most obliged, humble servant

H. Wanley.

MS: British Library, Add. 22911, fo. 188. Copy in Cambridge University Library MS Mm.vi.50, fo. 298. *Date*: 'Wymple [1]7th February 1715/6.' *Address*: 'To The Reverend Doctor Covel, Master of Christs College in Cambridge.'

[1] 'A kind of calendar notched upon a square block of wood or other material' (*OED*). There are two in the Harleian collection, BL Harley MSS 197, 198, placed among the D'Ewes books but not apparently belonging there. But they were catalogued by Wanley in vol. i. of the *Catalogus Brevior* (now BL Add. MS 45701), which he compiled between 24 Apr. 1708 and 18 Feb. 1709. Covell's attestation at the sale of his manuscripts to Harley, d. 27 Feb. 1716 (BL Add. MS 22911, fo. 201), states that he sold to Harley 'All my written Books, Papers, & Parchments whatsoever; together wth my wooden Clog Almanac'. An engraving of a Clog almanack appears as the frontispiece to William Hone, *The Every-day Book; or, Everlasting Calendar of Popular Amusements*, ii (1827), and an account of it is given in the Preface.

[2] Except for BL Harley MS 6943, a volume of letters to Covell, 1670–1710, these eluded Wanley. Now BL Add. MSS 22910–14, acquired at the Dawson Turner sale in 1859.

167. *To* John Covell *20 February 1716*

Reverend Sir,

The Kind Letter which you was pleased to send unto me today, came safe;[1] and I heartily thank you for it. Mr Garwood my Noble Lords Chaplain[2] hath occasion to go to Cambridge to morrow, upon some of his own Affairs, and my Lord hath been pleased to lend him his Coach. I shall take the Opportunity of this Coach to wait on you to morrow-morning, in order to put a good End to our tedious Affair; and shall produce proper & Satisfactory Credentials. Our good Lord & Lady drank to your Health this day, as they have done many times before; and evidently shew that they have the worthy Master of Christs College in much Estimation. Be pleased to get a Box ready for me, strong & capacious enough; with a good Cord. My Visit will be but short; but it wil be fully to the purpose. I shal be glad to meet my good friend Dr Tudway at your house; and am with perfect Respect,

   Reverend Sir,

      Your most faithful, & most humble servant,

                                        Humfrey Wanley.

MS: British Library, Add. 22911, fo. 190. Copy in Cambridge University Library MS Mm.vi.50, fo. 300. *Date*: 'Wymple, 20th Febr. 1715/6.' *Address*: To The Reverend Dr Covel, Master of Christs-College in Cambridge.'

168. *To* [John Anstis] *23 February 1716*

Worthy Sir,

I lay hold of this Sudden Opportunity of returning my hearty Thanks to you & Mr Mickleton,[1] for your twin Letter, which want of time will not now permit me to answer Singly.

Mr Hearne's Rous[2] is not yet come hither; but my noble Lord

---

[1] Covell to Wanley d. 20 Feb. 1716 (BL Harley MS 3778, fo. 119), accepting Wanley's offer of £300 for the collection.

[2] Robert Garwood (1690–1765), of Pentlow, Essex; Pembroke College, Cambridge 1707.

---

[1] James Mickleton (1688–1719), antiquary, owner of the Mickleton collection of manuscripts relating to the antiquities of the County Palatine of Durham, now in Durham University Library. See *Durham Philobiblon*, i (1950), pp. 40–4.

[2] J. Rossi [i.e. John Rows], *Historia Regum Angliae*, ed. T. Hearne (Oxford, 1716).

think's himself much obliged to you for the kind notice that you have given him touching Mr Lhwyds MSS. the Refusal whereof was absolutly promised by Mr Vice-chancellor to my Lord Oxford.[3] I therefore intreat you, to call on Dr Lancaster[4] forthwith, and induce him to write to Oxford in my Lords behalf, that the disposal of these things to Sir Thomas Seabright may be stopped. I shall write to both by the Post, but that will come in later.

As to the Seals & Catalogues, my Lord can say nothing, until my return to Town; in the mean time, you may enquire after the Character of Mr John Sturt, who (in my poor opinion) will be found the best Engraver for your purpose.

The Bishop of Elies Books are as yet all in Bags & Cases; & are likely long to continue thus.[5] So that it is impossible to come at Paris de Grassis. In the mean time, you may please to know that my Lord hath a book here, which is likely enough to be a Copie of it.[6] The Title followeth,

Rituum Ecclesiasticorum, sive Sacrarum Cerimoniarum SS. Romanae Ecclesiae, Libri Tres, non ante in Germania impressi. Quorum argumenta versa pagella indicabit. Cum Indice copiosa. Coloniae Agrippinae, apud haeredes Arnoldi Birkmanni, anno 1557 (*12 mo*).

The next Page, is thus; AD LECTOREM. Habes, optime Lector, Rituum Ecclesiasticorum sive Sacrarum Cerimoniarum sacro-sanctae Romanae Ecclesiae Libros tres; Opus argumento suo & jucundum tibi, & utile. Nam quae ratio Creandi Pontificis, quae reliquorum Antistitum, qui modus admittendi Imperatoris cum urbem invisit, quae Divorum nostrorum Apotheoses, exin qui pietatis ordo, dum Divinis Pontifex operatur, a Calendis Ianuariis ad anni finem; postremo veluti Coronis ac fastigium operis, Summa quaedem ad institutam rem pertinens, explicatio personarum ac officiorum, quae operanti Pontifici adsunt,

---

[3] See no. 140.

[4] William Lancaster (1650–1717), Provost of The Queen's College, Oxford 1704, Archdeacon of Middlesex 1705. He negotiated the purchase in 1715 of Robert Burscough's manuscripts.

[5] See no. 145.

[6] Augustinus Patritius, surnamed Piccolomineus, Bishop of Piacenza 1483–96, was the author of *Caeremoniale Romanum*, dedicated to Innocent VIII. Not originally planned for publication it was ptd. with pontifical permission in 1516 by Christopherus Marcellus under the title *Rituum Ecclesiasticorum* quoted by Wanley here. The then pontifical Master of Ceremonies, Paris de Grassis, was incensed at its publication, afraid that it would lower papal dignity, and asked Leo X to destroy all copies of it. Anstis and Wanley may have confused the author with his opponent.

his libris continentur. Est et in fronte Operis, Reverendissimi & Doctissimi Corcyrensis Archiepiscopi Christophori Marcelli ad sanctissimum Pontificem Leonem Decimum Epistola. If this be your book, at your first Command, I will transcribe the third Chapter of the third book for you, being intituled DE SERVIENTIBVS ARMORVM; whom I take not for Heralds, but rather Halberdiers. My Lord hath also the following Book, Origine de Cavalieri, di Francesco Sansovino; nella quale si tratta l'Inventione, l'Ordine, & la Dichiaratione della Cavalaria di Collana, di Croce, & di Sprone. Con gli Statuti in particolare della Gartiera, di Savoia, del Tosone, & di San Michele, &c. In Venetia, 1566. 12mo.[7] 'Tis a curious book.

Pray give my humble service to Your good Lady, Mr Dale, Mr Chetwood, & Mr Mickleton, & thank the last for his kind remembrance of my poor Spouse, & Me. My good Lord say's he shall be very glad to see him here; and so also will be sincerely

Dear Sir,

Your most obedient, humble servant

Humfrey Wanley.

My Lord much approve's Mr Mickleton's design about your Picture.

MS: British Library, Stowe 749, fo. 18. *Date*: 'Wymple, 23 Febr. 1715.'

169. *To* Thomas Tudway *23 February 1716*

Worthy Doctor,

Upon my return hither from Cambridge I made a faithful Report to my Lord of my last Reception by the Master, and restored his Money accordingly. I also delivered the Masters Letter to his Lordship; wherein He was pleased to value the four contested books at a very moderate & small Sum; namely Two Hundred Pounds. Hereupon, my Lord began to think that the Business began to be impracticable; and, consequently, to look about him for a better method of laying out his Money.

To day your Letters came, wherein you signifie many Complements on the Masters behalf; which, not being attested by his hand, my Lord doth not build much upon. However, supposing Him to be in the

---

[7] Francesco Sansovino, *Origine de Cavalieri* (Venice, 1566).

mind that you mention; my Lords pleasure is that I should acquaint
you, that He is unwilling to send me again to Cambridge, unless
things are perfectly adjusted between us beforehand; that [we m]ay
have no more Mistakes. In Order to this, I am to acquaint you from
his Lordship that He will give no more Than Three Hundred
Pounds for the WHOLE & INTIRE Collection of the Masters Manuscripts. That what further Gratuity He may think fit to allow, must
be left to His own Breast. That, in the Collection, he expecteth to
find all Books, Parchments, & Papers whatsoever, not being written
by the Masters own Hand; particularly, all those not mentioned in
the Doctors Catalogue; and among them more particularly, the book
of Oriental Songs, the Horologium in Arabic, the Poran, & Clavicula
Salomonis.[1] My Lord also claimeth, in particular, the four Patriarchal Letters to the Master;[2] as also the Nectarius in folio;[3] but he
will Lend them back to the Master, whensoever they shall be
desired; and also shew him further Tokens of Respect upon proper
Occasions. If the Master, or You, shall Signifie unto me that all these
Points are Agreed upon & Adjusted between You, so that there shall
be no more Qubling; I will soon come back again, with his Lordships Commands; but without this previous & necessary Notice, it
will not be permitted.

Worthy Doctor, my good Lord thinketh himself much obliged unto
you for the pains that you have taken in this Affair, wherewith he is
very well satisfied, let it turn which way it will: and He doth hereby
give you his very hearty Thanks for the same. As for me, You know I
am always with Sincerity,

Your most faithful, & most humble Servant

Humfrey Wanley.

---

[1] See no. 162.

[2] No doubt these were part of Covell's 'whole Collection of Original Letters from
learned Men, Greeks, & others' which at the time of the sale were 'now either Mislaid,
or not ready to come at' (BL Add. MS 22911, fo. 201). For Wanley's attempts to 'come at'
them, see his letter to Covell of 25 Mar. 1716 (no. 172) referred to below, and nos. 173,
174, 185. Although promised, only one vol. (BL Harley MS 6943) seems to have come to
the library: this may be the 'good parcel' requested by Wanley (in his letter to Covell)
25 Mar. 1716 (no. 172) and perhaps referred to in Wanley to Edward Harley, 1 Nov. 1716
(no. 182). The rest were acquired by the British Museum at Dawson Turner's sale in
1859 and are now BL Add. MS 22910–14. The only 'Patriarchal' letter seems to be that
from Parthenius, Patriarch of Constantinople, d. 1676. BL Add. MS 22910, fo. 106. See
further no. 185, Wanley, *Diary*, pp. 210–11(5) and n. 1.

[3] BL Harley MS 5633, a tract of Nectarius, a seventeenth-century Patriarch of
Jerusalem.

MS: British Library, Add. 22911, fo. 193. Copy in Cambridge University Library MS Mm.vi.50, fo. 300. *Date*: 'Wymple 23 Febr. 1715/6.' *Address*: 'To Doctor Tudway at Cambridge.'

170. *To* John Covell *24 February 1716*

Reverend Sir,

Your honest Servant brought your Letter to my Lord, and another to me from Doctor Tudway,[1] this Afternoon. My Noble Lord hath been busied with a Gentleman who came unto him upon special Affairs; and they are now, in Company together, so as not to be soon ready to take Leave. However, his Lordship (although he hath not the present opportunity of writing unto you with his own hand) desire's that you will accept of his very kind Respects. He is very thankful for the two Letters that you have been pleased to write unto him; he seemeth inclined to send me again to you, the next Monday morning; and I know his Noble Nature to be such, as wil make you easy in all particulars. I forbear to multiply words, at present, because the Sun begin's to decline, & I would not have your Servant benighted. But I crave leave to congratulate you upon our long-desired amicable agreement, & am with all possible respect,

Reverend Sir,

Your most humble, & obedient Servant

H. Wanley.

MS: British Library, Add. 22911, fo. 196. Copy in Cambridge University Library MS Mm.vi.50, fo. 307. *Date*: 'Wymple 24 February. 1715/6.' *Address*: 'To The Reverend Doctor Covel Master of Christs-College in Cambridge.'

171. *To* [Arthur Charlett] *11 March 1716*

Reverend Sir,

You may please to remember the Conversation I had the honor to have with you in Town, touching Mr Edward Lhwyd's MSS: and how I shewed that my noble Lord had the promise of the preference in buying them, exclusive of all others; and also, how you your self was pleased to write unto me, much to the same purpose. But it seem's that

[1] BL Harley MS 3782, fo. 45.

after we have been beating the bush, another is about to run away with the Hare; and that there is some motion made toward selling this Parcel to Sir Thomas Seabright. I should be heartily sorry if this should be done to my Lord, who hath all along thought himself the buyer; and will be willing to give more for the Things than Sir Thomas hath offered, let that offer amount to what it will. And I doubt not, but when Sir Thomas shall b[e] apprised of the long time my Lord hath been about them, but that he will shew himself so much a Gentleman, and so much my Lords friend, as to surcease, and yield up his Claim to my Lord.[1]

I would desire you, Sir, to use your good Offices for my Lord in this matter, by speaking to all parties Concerned, and acting as you shall think most conducive to his Lordships Service. I am sure he will take your good endeavors in most thankful part, as will plainly appear hereafter. I shall easily know your Success, if you please to direct for me at my Lord Harleys, Wimple in Cambridgeshire, by Royston-bag, & way of London: and do remain always,

Reverend Sir,

Your most obliged, humble servant

Humfrey Wanley.

MS: Bodleian, Ballard 13, fo. 135. *Date*: 'Cambridge, 11 March 1715/6.'

172. *To* John Covell *25 March 1716*

Reverend Sir,

Upon my return hither I presented the Commendations you charged me with to my noble Lord & Lady, who were pleased to enquire[1] after your health with much kindness. My Lord hath looked over the Catalogue of your Books[2] which I have taken, & like's the Collection, in the Bulk, very well: even so far, as to be a further Customer either for such books only as he shall particularly like, or

---

[1] See no. 140 n. 4.

---

[1] enqure MS.

[2] i.e. printed books. This (entitled 'Bibliothecae Covellianae Catalogus breviculus'), d. 5 Mar. 1716, runs to forty-four closely written leaves plus index. Now in Welbeck Wanleyana = BL Loan MS 29/259 misc. 16. Wanley's offer was unsuccessful, and after Covell's death they were sold at auction by Christopher Cock, 9 Mar. 1724.

else for the whole, as you your self shall think best. He liketh well also of
your Old Cameos & Intaglias; and hath observed so much of what I have
said unto him touching your other Antiquities, Coins, Medals, & other
Curiosities Natural & Artificiall; as to be not unwilling to purchase the
Whole, at once.[3] But, in Order to this, he would be before hand apprised
of what he may expect to find for his Money; and expecteth likewise that
your Price be reasonable, and fit for him to comply with. I look upon this
Ouverture to be the most considerable, in this kind, that was ever yet
made unto you; because it give's you an Opportunity of turning your
whole Collection into Money, now, at this latter Stage of your Life, after
so long an enjoyment of them; and this money will be much more
acceptable & advantagious to your Relations & Executors, than your
Things, can ever be. If you are willing that I should come again & take a
short List of your other Things; let me know it, and I believe my Lord
will soon send over, him that is with true respect,

 Reverend Sir,

  Your most faithful, & very humble servant

           H. Wanley.

My Lord was much surprised & concerned when he found that I
returned from you empty-handed. For, he said he thought you would
have sent him all the Letters & Papers that belong to him: or at least
the best part of them. Pray therefore lett your Messenger bring a good
parcel, at the least, along with him.[4]

MS: British Library, Add. 22911, fo. 207. Copy in Cambridge University Library MS
Mm.vi.50, fo. 309. *Date*: 'Wymple 25th March 1716.' *Address*: 'To The Reverend Dr
Covel Master of Christs College, in Cambridge.'

173. *To* John Covell *3 April 1716*

Reverend Sir,

 Yesterday Doctor-Tudway delivered your kind Letter[1] to me; & I
had the Honor of Communicating the Contents thereof to my Lord,

---

[3] See no. 173: these were also included in the sale of Covell's library in 1724 (see n. 2
above). Wanley's catalogue of the coins and medals is in BL Add. MS 22911, fos. 265–80.

[4] See no. 169 n. 2.

[1] d. 1 Apr. 1716, BL Harley MS 3778, fo. 121. For the proposals advanced here, see
no. 169 n. 2 and no. 172 nn. 2, 3.

soon after. His Lordship & my Noble Lady shewed themselves much rejoyced to hear that you are in a perfect State of Health; and finding that it was your Birth-day, they drank to the Continuance of it, for many years to come. As for answer to your Letter, my Lords Sentiments are, as followeth.

He will be willing to purchase your whole Library together, at a price reasonable between Man & Man. And, He will also, whensoever you shall desire it, Lend you from hence any reasonable Number of those books, for any reasonable term of Time. But this Favor He will grant to no other person whatsoever.

With your Library (or without it) He is not unwilling to purchase your Coins, Medals, Antiquities, & other Curiosities, Natural & Artificial; after having perused a List of the same, to be made by me. This List need not take up any part of your Time, either by keeping you in your Lodge, or in your Chamber; any more than my taking the Catalogue of your Books did, or ought to have done. For, in the First place, I am not void of the Experience requisite for taking such a List. Secondly, I can well enough spare you & Dr Tudway the labor of taking off Impressions from the Intaglias, and yet give them their due. And, Thirdly, I can dispatch the whole without giving you any other Interruption, than only laying the things before me: for, I can come into the Room & go out of it, & Dine elsewhere, without your Molestation or Charge.

As for your making Notes about every particular thing; my Lord judgeth it intirely needless to him. For, what he shall Buy, will be done by his own Views, & in his own Way: so that Time need not be spent in what will not NOW conduce to His satisfaction, or to Your advantage. When he shall have Bought them, he saith, you may make what Remarks & Observations you please; and he will Thankfully receive the same from you.

As for the finishing the Treatise you are now upon; and likewise the account of your Travails; He think's they ought to yield to this Business now before you, which is of far greater Importance to You & Yours, by reason of the Great Sum of Money which He may NOW be induced to part with. A List of your Things, His Lordship saith may be Begun now, & Dispatched out of Hand: and, after your Audit, you may Agree & Trade together, to your own great Profit & Emolument: But if you putt him off until this Book, & t'other Book be Finished, and until the Lord know's how many Notes are made: I foresee, that you will

find the Edge of my Lords Curiosity so far abated, through the tediousness of the Delay (or more probably by his having Furnished himself in the mean time) that then, He will, by no means, part with his
Money, or take your Things off your Hands.

My Lord saith, He doth not know what you mean by affirming
that it *is a very hard request*, to send Him the Letters & Papers of
Greeks & other Learned Men written to You. He saith, They are
His; because He Bought them; and honestly paid for them; and
therefore He hath a just Right to Expect them. I am very sensible
that the Labor of Selecting them from those of your own Hand-
writing will be but little. And therefore, since you say you are likely
to be busied about your College-matters for some time: if you please
to give me leave, I will come over & do that Service for you. And
herein, you may confide intirely in me; that I will neither imper-
tinently pry into, or discover any Secret of Yours; nor do you the
least Wrong, in any other respect whatsoever.

As to the Time you spent in Sitting to Mr Guinier,[2] my Lord
return's you his hearty Thanks, and hath now shewn that respect to
your Effigies, as to Set it up in His own Dressing Room; and putt's an
high Value upon it, merely for Your Sake. He is affectionately
disposed in his Mind towards You: and, I think, it is greatly your
Interest to keep him in this good Disposition; which will be, by
complying with what He offer's, without throwing in unnecessary
Delays, that will turn only to your own Hindrance.

In expectation of a fresh Line or two from You, I remain, with all
due respect

Reverend Sir,

Your most faithful, & obliged humble servant

Humfrey Wanley.

MS: British Library, Add. 22911, fo. 208; fair copy in Harley MS 3778, fo. 123. Copy in
Cambridge University Library MS Mm.vi.50, fo. 310. *Date*: 'Wimple, 3 April 1716.'
Address: 'To The Reverend Doctor Covel, at Cumbertone.'

[2] Claud Guineer. His portrait of Covell has not been identified; he is known only
from his portrait of Harley's daughter Henrietta (Charles H. C. Baker, *Lely & the Stuart
Portrait Painters* (1912), ii, p. 199). See also Covell to Wanley d. 1 Apr. 1716, BL Harley
MS 3778, fo. 121ᵛ.

174. *To* John Covell *10 April 1716*

Reverend Sir,

I have had the Honor to Communicate to our Noble Lord the Contents of yours of the 7th Instant.[1] And I find that His Lordship hath, in his heart, that Value & Consideration for you, and the pressure of your College-Affairs upon You, as to Yield in the matter by You proposed: so that He will not Send me again until the 7th of May next.

As to what remain's of your Covenant with my Lord, not yet fulfilled; it relateth particularly to the Letters & Papers written by the Hands of Greeks & other Persons of Letters, exclusive of what is written by your own Hand.[2] And although these things have not as yet been delivered up unto Him, according to agreement; & His Lordships Curiosity in this respect, & His Desire to peruse them, have been very great: nevertheless, as I said before, he will endeavor qualifie the same, and not Send me to Cambridge, in order to make the Lists of the other Things he desireth to have of you, untill the first Week in May shall be over.

In the mean time, and indeed as long as I live, I shall be with all due Respect,

Reverend Sir,

Your most humble servant

Humfrey Wanley.

MS: British Library, Add. 22911, fo. 212. Copy in Cambridge University Library MS Mm.vi.50, fo. 314. *Date*: 'Wymple 10 April 1716.' *Address*: 'To The Reverend Dr Covel Master of Christs College Cambridge.'

175. *To* [Arthur Charlett] *15 April 1716*

Reverend Sir,

Particular business hath kept me from returning you my Noble Lords Thanks, attended by mine own, for the favor of your last kind Letter dated the 26th ultimo.[1] His Lordship taketh your Good will &

[1] BL Harley MS 3778, fo. 124.
[2] See no. 169 n. 2.

---

[1] BL Harley MS 3778, fo. 35.

Wishes, in most kind & thankful part; still desiring your farther Endeavors & Good Offices, in procuring him Mr Lhwyds MSS. He will give more for them than Sir Thomas Seabright, or any other person; and therefore thinks it but reasonable that they should come unto him, as the highest & best bidder; especially considering his former pretensions, which he never designed to lay-aside, or yield-up. Nor doth he now think the matter so far gone against him; but that if You & His other Friends do vigorously interpose, the things may come to him for his Money; as being more proper for him than for any other Library in Oxford, by reason of the great Collection that he hath already made of British & Irish Writings.[2]

His Lordship observed, with much pleasure, the good account you was pleased to give of the vigorous applications of your Minds in promoting Knowledge & good Literature; & of the continuance among you of that Laudable Spirit of Industry, which hath distinguished Oxford from all other Universities. The New Catalogue; the fine Bible;[3] The New Buildings at University & Queens Colleges; with the Codringtonian Library,[4] &c. declare this great Genius I have been speaking of, not to be yet decaied, or grown old. I am, Sir, with all Sincerity & Respect,

> Your most obliged & humble servant
>
> H. Wanley.

MS: Bodleian, Ballard 13, fo. 136. *Date*: 'Wimple 15 April 1716.'

[2] See no. 140 n. 4.

[3] For the new Bodleian catalogue of printed books, see no. 107 and n. 2; for the new Oxford Bible of 1717, see no. 140 n. 5.

[4] 'The Trustees of Dr Radcliff have pulled down all the Houses contiguous to the Masters Lodgins in Univ. Coll, as also all the little Tenements in Logic Lane, designing the Next Yeare to do the same by all the Lodgins, the Intent being to erect two Sides of a New Quadrangle on the East and North, exactly answerable to those already built, agreable to the Intrest & Will of Dr Radcliffe, the 4th Side will be only a Fair Garden wall on the South in the Room, where the Masters Stables &c stand at present: Col. Codrintons noble Library was also began the same Day' (Charlett to Wanley d. 26 Mar. 1716, BL Harley MS 3778, fo. 35ᵛ).

John Radcliffe (1650–1714), Fellow of Lincoln College, Oxford 1669, fashionable physician and benefactor of University College (to which he had already given an east window for the chapel in 1687 and large sums of money in 1692–4) and the University— the Radcliffe Camera and Observatory were erected from funds bequeathed to the University by him. At Queen's the rebuilding of the college, which began with the new library in 1692–4, was far advanced: the hall was completed in May 1715 and the chapel was nearing completion (J. R. Magrath, *The Queen's College* (Oxford, 1921), ii, p. 66 f.). Christopher Codrington (1668–1710), Fellow of All Souls College, Oxford 1690, left £10,000 (and £6,000 worth of books) to All Souls, which sufficed to erect, furnish, and endow the magnificent library named after him.

176. *To* Edward Harley *26 May 1716*

May it please your noble Lordship,

Yesterday-morning betime, I went to Noel's, where Charles told me that his Master would be at home soon after 11 a clock, as afterwards happened. I found but very few more of Setties books brought thither; but that divers Gentlemen lay in Ambush for them, whom I was resolved to disappoint, if I possibly could: so that I resolved to Lounge there all day, or at least untill Noel should come. The time I spent in the Ware-house laying aside more books for you. There Noel found me, & I sent him to Settie forthwith, where he found some more things, but not the Whole Cargo, the remains of which Noel said he had sent for. In the Evening, perceiving the Siege laid after these things, I would fain have persuaded Noel to have carried me unto him; but all in Vain. However, I prevailed so far, as that he should go himself & bring me what lay at Sittie's. This was done; then, at the Genoa-Armes (where he expect's to be always treated by me)[1] I persuaded him to promise to send me what lay in his House of Sitties, this morning, & I would cause a Case to be made for them. This is done; & the Catalogue of the glorious Parcel will be herein enclosed; excepting only what I know you have already. These I have in salva Custodia, secure from any bodies Garbling. I expect the rest on Monday; and if there be time sufficient will send them down this week. I do not doubt but to bring down Noel to a price moderate enough for them: as perhaps may be found in my next Letter. I persuaded him to Visit Mr Dean K——[2] to day, & shall know soon how affairs go, on that side. I am sorry that Mr Thompson's Physic should hinder his coming to Wymple; however, he might have sent the Things. But I hope your Lordship will have them before He find's any more. Your Lordships forbearing to Visit the Old Gentleman at Cambridge,[3] will be one mean to bring him to a true knowledge of his trifling behavior towards You. Noel sent to the wrong place for the Duplicates; but I have sett him right.[4] Your Lordships great hast,

---

[1] Cf. Wanley's remark: 'I seldom or never am at the Genoa-Armes, but some part or other of my Lords business is in agitation. And it seems but reasonable that his Lordship should defray me' (Welbeck Wanleyana = BL Loan 29/259 misc. 48).

[2] Presumably White Kennett, Dean of Peterborough.

[3] Covell. Harley was visiting his old Oxford tutor William Stratford (1672–1729) at Cambridge, and decided to avoid Covell.

[4] Harley had returned to Noel two cases of duplicates and books he did not want from Hickes's library and from other purchases made earlier in the year.

hindred you from sending me up some Bill or other; but I beg it may
be done by the next post, I being now put to my shifts for want.[5] For I
can neither menage your Lordships business, nor maintain my poor
Family without present Money. I think there remain's no more for me
to write about now, but to intreat Your Lordship & my Noble Lady
always to believe me to be, Her noble Ladyships, &

 May it please your Lordship,
  Your most faithful, & most obliged servant
               Humfrey Wanley.

MS: Welbeck Wanleyana = British Library, Loan 29/258. *Date*: 'Katherine-street, 26
May 1716.' *Address*: 'To The Right Honorable Edward Lord Harley at Wymple in Cambridgeshire.'

177. *To* Edward Harley *14 June 1716*

May it please your Lordship,

 Mr Noel came hither about half an hour before, & hath just now
Eaten his Pie with me. He seemeth a little Crest-fallen; so that I know
not how to understand him aright. As to the D. K——'s[1] things, he saith
he met him accidentally the last Night; & that Mr Dean utterly
refuse's to let him have them, unless the Prints formerly mentioned, be
delivered up. And that the Deane owneth that they are not marked on
the out[2] side, according to his Wife's Assertion. I did therefore advise
him to procure another Set; if he can. A.D. Baynard,[3] Noel saith, is
Superannuated; but, I believe he hath not seen him, since I was with
him. Noel saith he hath bidden 105£ for Mr Southouse's[4] books
(among which is the Rafaels Bible) upon Sight of the same. His
Money will be taken, unless the Seller can get more elsewhere. Mr
Noel (I find) doth not make so much hast to get in Johnson's Heraldical MSS. as I could wish.[5] In Short, after all the great Brags, I believe

[5] A bill for 10 guineas was sent, 27 May 1716 (Welbeck Wanleyana = BL Loan MS 29/248).

[1] White Kennett. The prints are presumably those mentioned in no. 165.
[2] *back* interlined above *out*, presumably as a gloss.   [3] Not identified.
[4] Perhaps Thomas Southouse (1665–*c*.1703), or Filmer Southouse (1676–1706), who planned, but did not write, a history of Faversham; both were sons of Thomas Southouse (1641–76), of Gray's Inn, Kentish antiquary. 'Rafaels Bible' is presumably *Imagines Veteris ac Novi Testamenti* (Rome, 1674): see no. 10.
[5] John Johnson, 'the late Armes-Painter', of Little Britain. See Wanley, *Diary*,

he hath lately pretty well Cleared his Pocket by buying. He pretend's he hath been often after the Parcel of Oriental MSS. & Printed books which I mentioned in mine by the last Post;[6] but cannot find the Seller, who keepeth a Ware-house. The Duke hath not returned him any Answer, he saith, as yet; So that I know not what to say to Mr Granger about the book with the Red Cover.[7] Mr Noel hath not sent beyond sea for the Parcel consigned unto him; but pretend's that he will do so to morrow. As to Settie; another Gentleman, I find, must find the Money, but Noel pretend's all the purchase must come unto him without Exception. I do not find when Mr Cock's will come to Town; and therefore, if I can do your Lordship no better Service here,[8] I had rather come down to Wymple where I may Serve you more effectually. Your Lordship said nothing to me concerning the Small Parcel of Books I selected for You at Mr Bateman's; with regard to which, I desire to know your Noble Pleasure.[9] And further, I desire that in the Bill which I intreat may be sent by the next Post, you will also Provide for the Spanish History of Herrera in 5 Vollumes, lying at Mr Smith's Shop for you;[10] about which, I formerly wrote.

I would not open my other Letter, for this new Matter; but thought it better to charge your Noble Lordship with the Postage of this fresh one; at the same time taking such Precaution, as that no othere Eie but mine own seeth me Subscribe with all Duty

Your good Lordships most faithful, &
most humbly devoted servant

Humfrey Wanley.

MS: Welbeck Wanleyana = British Library, Loan 29/258. *Date*: 'Genoa-Armes 14 June 1716. 9 o'Clock.' *Address*: 'To The Right Honorable Edward Lord Harley at Wymple in Cambridgeshire.'

pp. 5(6), 7(5), 12(3). The heraldical manuscripts referred to were apparently bought before the end of June 1716: see Edward Harley to Wanley d. 4 July 1716, Welbeck Wanleyana = BL Loan MS 29/248, and further Wanley, *Diary*, pp. xxxviii–xxxix.

[6] Wanley's letter not traced.

[7] The Duke I cannot identify. 'Mr Granger' is perhaps Thomas Granger († 1732); see no. 151 n. 2.

[8] Probably Charles Cocks; the 'Service' presumably related to the acquisition of manuscripts from Lord Somers's library: see no. 178 n. 3.

[9] Christopher Bateman; Wanley's catalogues of Bateman's books were returned by Harley on 20 June 1716 (Welbeck Wanleyana = BL Loan 29/248).

[10] A bill for £15 was sent by Harley, 15 June 1716 (Welbeck Wanleyana = BL Loan 29/248). The 'Spanish History' is presumably one of the historical works of Antonio de Herrera y Tordesillas. For various Smiths engaged in bookselling in London about this time, see Plomer, *Dictionary*.

178. *To* Edward Harley   *11 October 1716*

May it please your Lordship,

   While we were Eating here of the plentiful Dinner that was provided; come's in one Mr Cromwell[1] from Huntingdon, only to pay his Respects to my Lady & to your Lordship, as he said. I will not say that the Gentleman is an Enemy to Nature, because I saw he participated of both Eatables & Potables, with much Humanity & Frankness.

   Mr Cosin's[2] hath whispered unto me, that he may know somewhat relating unto your business, if it might be well got out from him. I said that I being an utter Stranger to him, could pretend to no interest there: but, however, desired him to come & take part of a Bottle with us, & see if it will produce any good Effect for you. They are now both in the Room with me; but others by.

   Mr Cromwel, of his own accord, made mention unto me of Lord Somers's Library, which, he saith is Carryed to Sir Joseph Jeckyll's Chambers, or House.[3] He saith he is exceedingly well known unto Sir Joseph. I have therefore pretended to take this Opportunity about that Collection, of delivering him up into your own Hands. If he see's you, or my Lady, & can tell you any thing worth hearing, he will do it. I think we ought not to make Enquiries here; & therefore will take care that he shall find but little Impertinence, in my Noble Ladies
   & Your good Lordships
         most obedient & humble servant

                                             H. Wanley.

I hope this will find her Noble Ladiship & Your Lordship safely gotten up.

---

[1] Not his real name, according to no. 179, and 'a very false Loon' to boot.

[2] John Cosins or Cossen, gentleman waiter to Edward Harley at Wimpole.

[3] Somers, Whig lawyer and statesman (Lord Chancellor 1697–1700), died on 26 Apr. 1716. His estate was divided between his two sisters; the elder married Charles Cocks of Worcester; the younger married Sir Joseph Jekyll (1663–1738), made Master of the Rolls in 1717 for managing the impeachment of Robert Harley in June of that year. Somers's library passed to Jekyll, but in 1729 it was divided between Jekyll and Charles Yorke, the younger son of Philip Yorke, 1st Earl of Hardwicke, Lord Chancellor 1737. Philip Yorke had married Somers's granddaughter on the Cocks side. The papers and letters, which passed to Charles Yorke, were destroyed by fire at his chambers in Lincoln's Inn, 27 June 1752. Jekyll's library was sold 26 Feb. 1739. Wanley was especially interested in Somers's Anglo-Saxon charters—see Wanley, *Catalogus*, pp. 301–3—and made frequent attempts to acquire them, but without success; they cannot now be traced. See no. 181 and further Wanley, *Diary*, pp. xxxvii–xxxviii.

MS: Welbeck Wanleyana = British Library, Loan 29/258. *Date*: 'Wymple 11th October, 1716.' *Address*: 'To The Right Honorable Edward Lord Harley at Bath Court, by the Royal Palace, near St James's.'

179. *To* Edward Harley *14 October 1716*

May it please Your Lordship,

I heartily thank God for My Ladies & Your safe arrival in Town; & for that I can truely inform you that Sweet pretty Miss continueth merry & in perfect Health. Your business here is well-minded, so far as I can see. Mr Wotton's pieces will be good, when finished.[1] He is now gone to dine with the Lord Thomond,[2] with design to return to morrow morning. Yesterday his Whip was taken away out of the Hall, by John Nobody; who perhaps may play more such Pranks, if not discovered & Chastised. I intend to send Mr Jefferies & Mr Garwood to Morrow to Mr Hooker, because I would fain have his little Collection ready for your Lordship, at your Return.[3] I know not where I was, in this short Catalogue[4] at your Departure; but I did yesterday finish page 43: which ended with book 1313. IV. K. 9. with which Performance, I doubt not but your Lordship will be well enough satisfied. We Live in Plenty here, wanting nothing; nor wasting anything. I have had a Letter from Signior Alberto concerning the Brandy which he forgot to charge, amounting to £1.16.[5] Upon Mr Cuthill's return, I had a Mind to tast it. I judge it to be New, and not to be of the best French Brandy. It may be the best he had; & may also be worth the Money he values it at; but I think I usually meet with much better. The parcel is but small, & it will do well enough in Punch: and therefore One would

---

[1] John Wotton (1678–1765), animal and landscape painter. See no. 180.

[2] Henry O'Brien (1688–1741), 8th Earl of Thomond.

[3] Of Harley's staff at Wimpole mentioned here, Jefferies appears from this letter to have been steward; Cuthill and Crownfield were members of the household; Robert Garwood was Harley's private chaplain. Jonathan Hooker (b. 1656), Fellow of Exeter College, Oxford 1682, was Rector of Sandy, Bedfordshire. On his collection see further nos. 180, 181, 182, 183, 184, 185, 188.

[4] The catalogue of Harley's ptd. books (now BL Lansdowne MS 816); the books bear running numbers 1–7040 and are press-marked I.A.1 to XXVII.O.32. The catalogue was begun 5 Sept. 1716 and finished 14 June 1717.

[5] Signor Alberto Croce of the Genoa Arms was Wanley's wine merchant. See Alexander Pope's letter to Wanley asking him to buy for him 'a Douzaine of quartes of goode & wholesome Port Wine, such as yee drinke at the Genoa Armes' (*The Correspondence of Alexander Pope*, ed. G. Sherburn (Oxford, 1956), ii. p. 304).

take no notice of it. Yesternight Mr Garwood & I had a mighty mind to a Sneaker, & therein to remember all your Noble Family: but we drop'd the Matter, lest we might be thought extravagant & sawcy; although, in mine own house I would most certainly have had one, finding my self a little pained by Gravel, as Mr Garwood also complained. To day we hear that there are Lemons in the House already pared, which may rot for want of using; which Excuse or Pretence being plausible, we shall lay hold on the same to night, & Mr Jefferies will participate.

Mr Crownfield hath sent the Jad Chazaka, fol. IV Vollumes, & J. Huss fol. II Vollumes, all decently bound at £6.5.0. which I have laid up. The rest will come as soon as Dawson shall have bound them.[6]

Mr Baker hath sent the Bible & Picture; but reserveth the latter part of my last to him, to be discoursed on, when we shall meet next. I believe he will comply, in all things.[7]

I sent your Lordship a Letter by one whose Name is not Cromwell, as I thought he said; but who I hear is a very false Loon, & marked accordingly. Here is a small parcel from the Higler for your Lordship. This is all that I can now Write, who am as in all Duty & Gratitude obliged,

Your Lordships most faithful, & most humbly devoted servant

Humfrey Wanley.

The Setts of Graevius & Gronovius will be useful here; as also some of the Unmarked books.

Mr Garwood had a pair of Gloves, which are gone after Mr Wotton's Whip.

Mr Jeffreys's Accompts are to be got ready forthwith, & to be Audited on Tuesday: so that he cannot go to Sandy until Wednesday next. Perhaps Mr Hooker may call here to morrow; I wish he may.

MS: Welbeck Wanleyana = British Library, Loan 29/258. *Date*: 'Wymple 14 October 1716.' *Address*: 'To The Right Honorable Edward Lord Harley at Bath Court near the Royal Palace at St James's Westminster.'

[6] For Dawson see no. 183 n. 2. The 'Jad Chazaka' is presumably as Mr J. S. G. Simmons suggests to me, the *Mishneh Torah*, subtitled *Yad Hachazakah*, of Moses ben Maimon (Maimonides, 1135–1204), ed. Joseph Athias, 2 vols. (Amsterdam, 1702), The Huss is presumably *Historia et Monumenta*, 2 vols. ([Nuremberg?], 1715). They cost £4 and £2.5.0 respectively to bind (BL Harley MS 3778, fo. 150).
[7] Thomas Baker (1656–1740), antiquary and historian of Cambridge, Fellow of St John's College, Cambridge 1680–1717, when he was deprived as a nonjuror, although he continued to reside. Manuscripts to the value of £40 were bought from him by Harley in 1715 (Wanley, *Diary*, pp. 4(5), 8(1)(= 8 April 1715), 13(5)). See also no. 186.

180. *To* Edward Harley *18 October 1716*

May it please your Lordship,

After the due tender of my bounden Duty to my good Lady & your Noble self, I presume to advertise you that pretty sweet Miss was merry & in perfect health this Morning, I thank God for it. Mr Wotton returned hither on Sonday-Evening; but talk's of a journey he must soon make into Norfolk, in Order to make Pictures for a whole Pack of Hounds there. Mr Garwood & Mr Jeffreys returned hither from Sandy yesterday in the Evening, having brought with them an absolute Promise about the Antiquities, vizt that Mr Hooker will either bring them within a very few days, or else send them by his Servant. The Journey to him was become necessary; and the things would have tarried there much longer than they are now likely to do. The Lady hap'ned to be there yesterday; and being asked about her Collection, she answered that she was robbed of it all, & of many other things besides. I humbly thank your Lordship for the honor of your kind Letter,[1] & am much rejoiced to hear that my Noble Lord your Father is grown better. I perceive that you have not yet Visited Mr Anstis, from whom I had a Letter yesterday, shewing that there have been many Roman Antiquities found in Kent & secured by the Gentleman his Friend; & intimate's a probability of the discovery of many more: Your Lordship may very easily have them all. He saith also, that he hath lately found the fine MS. Psalter that hath been so long mislaid. I wish your Lordship would secure the same & also the old Saxon MS. in his Custody; because two such books are not now to be had in all England, for Money.[2] He also maketh me an Overture for some of the Duplicates of your Heraldical MSS. for which he will give you all his old MSS, which now appear to be more in Number than he himself

---

[1] 16 Oct. 1716, Welbeck Wanleyana = BL Loan MS 29/248. Robert Harley was imprisoned in the Tower.

[2] Described by Wanley eighteen months earlier: (1) 'an antient & valuable Copie of Ælfricks Grammar, with some Saxon Homilies at the end'; (2) 'the Psalterium Gallicanum of St. Hierom . . . written about the time of the last King Æthe[l]dred, with the Litany & some prayers, being one of the most beautiful books that can be seen' (Wanley, *Diary*, p. 7(9)). Wanley adds that Anstis declares they are not his (though Wanley saw them in his study with 'his own Numbers & Marks upon them'), and Wright (*Diary*,p. 7 n. 6) does not find them in the Anstis sale catalogue of 12 Dec. 1768. It may be that (1) is BL Harley MS 3271, an early eleventh-century copy of Ælfric's grammar with about 40 fos. of miscellaneous OE and some Latin pieces following it (Ker no. 239, not listed by Wanley). See also nos. 182, 184.

thought of. I wish your Lordship would close with him in this Article, for I know divers of them to be valuable; & besides, thereby you will bind him the more strongly to serve you in other Matters. I shall presently write to him, & desire him to attend your Lordship. He saith also that the late Colonell Colchester had a very large Collection of MSS. which formerly belonged to Sir John Maynard his Grand-father;[3] and that Mr Stephens your Relation may, possibly, be service-able in procuring them. As to your Business here, I have finished Class IV, & wholly Figured the same; I have also just Catalogued the Shelf D. in Class V. (in the Catalogue marked thus, 1479. V.D. 26.) at the top of Page 48. and might have gotten somewhat further, but that I have been the two last days disorder'd in my Head & Stomac; but now, it is some what easier, with

Your Lordships most true & faithful servant

Humfrey Wanley.

MS: Welbeck Wanleyana = British Library, Loan 29/258. *Date*: 'Wymple 18 October, 1716.' *Address*: 'To The Right Honorable Lord Harley at Bath-Court near the Royal Court of St James's Westminster.'

181. *To* Edward Harley *25 October 1716*

I hope your Lordship hath seen Mr Anstis.

May it please your Lordship,

I did forbear writing by the last Posts, because we here surely believed that you would have returned, before this time. But now we have laid aside all expectation, as believing that your return will not be suddenly. Pretty, sweet Miss, I hear, is at least as well as ever she was in her Life: and I hope in God my Noble Lady, & Your Good Lord-ship & my Noble Lord Your Father, are so also.

Mr Noel sent by the Royston Carrier certain Cases, & other parcels of Books, of which he makes great Account, in his late Letter to me, which I shall answer presently: With them, came hither yesterday in your Cart from Royston, some other Cases & one large Chest, so very heavy that Six Men had much ado (in my sight) to carry it into the

[3] Sir John Maynard (1602–90), King's Serjeant 1660, Lord Commissioner of the Great Seal 1689. His manuscripts (87 vols.), commonplace books, legal transcripts, records, etc. were purchased by Lincoln's Inn, 1818.

servants Hall. The least of the parcels are brought up into your Library; but I open none, because I would not make any confusion; having opened the Parcel that came by the last Higler.

Herein, your Lordship will find two Letters inclosed, which came yesterday.

I have been somewhat out of Order, since my last, & was apprehensive of an Ague: but I thank God I am grown very well, & am upon your business as usuall. I have finished with Class V. but before I went upon pasting-on the several Numbers, I had a Mind to inspect, a little, the running Number from the beginning, which I added to this short Catalogue, as your Lordship knoweth. Therein, to my great grief, I found a brace of Blunders, which have given me the lord know's how much Trouble since; in altering & amending, for above a thousand Numbers successively. Error (as Spencer describe's it) hath a very, very, long train. Certainly I am now grown as fearful of a Mistake, as a Dog is of a Whip; & therefore shall adjust matters Shelf by Shelf, which will prevent all repetition of the Laboris improbi. I am now gotten into 1581. VI. B. 7. being the third Volume of Athan Kircher's Oedipus Aegyptiacus (your first Volume whereof wants a Sheet in a material place) & in the Midle of page 52.[1] I wish your Lordship would bend your Thoughts to secure the late Lord Somers's Saxon Charters in the first Place. They were 24 in Number, & all kept together in a very little Oval Deal Box; to the best of my Remembrance.[2] The Society of Pembroke Hall have agreed to lett your Lordship have their Old Tho. Aquinas for the Money you offered.[3] Mr Hooker hath not yet been here, nor sent the things. Mr Jeffrey's hath business which will call him there the next week. Good Mr Garwood hath been constantly earnest with me to present his most humble duty to my Lady & Your Lordship; but [in]deed it went out of my mind before. I hope you both will receive the same now, & also that of Her Noble Ladiships, &

---

[1] i.e. *Universalis Hieroglyphicae veterum Doctrinae temporum injuria abolitae instauratio* (Rome, 1652–4). Harley promptly bought another (perfect) set (Edward Harley to Wanley d. 27 Oct. 1716; Welbeck Wanleyana = BL Loan MS 29/248).

[2] See no. 178 n. 3.

[3] Not identified. In his letter to E. Harley, 23 Dec. 1716 (no. 189), Wanley promises to provide the 'date' of the Aquinas at the end of the letter, but most of the page is torn off and nothing remains of his transcript. I can find no Aquinas listed in BL Lansdowne MS 816, Wanley's short catalogue of the ptd. books at Wimpole, begun 5 Sept. 1716, finished 14 June 1717. There is no record of the sale at Pembroke College, Cambridge.

My Lord,
    Your Lordships most humble most obedient, & most faithful
    servant

                                                Humfrey Wanley.

MS: Welbeck Wanleyana = British Library, Loan 29/258. *Date*: 'Wymple 25 October, 1716.' *Address*: 'To The Right Honorable Edward Lord Harley at Bath-Court near the Royal Palace at St James's Westminster. *Printed*: A. S. Turberville, *A History of Welbeck Abbey and its Owners* (1938), i, p. 372 (extract).

182. *To* Edward Harley *1 November 1716*

May it please your Lordship,
    I return my most humble Thanks for the great honor & favor of your
last kind Letter of the 27th ultimo,[1] which would have been answered
by the same Post, but that Dr Tudway came purposely to dine with us,
with intention to return to Cambridge the same Evening with Mr
Jeffreys; but yet he tarried all Night. In the belief of his going away
presently, I omitted writing having gained a good Opportunity of discoursing with him, alone, touching your business with Dr Covel. He
think's the Letters will not be Imbezeled if they tarry in his Custody
some time longer; but that I may demand them in Your Lordships
Name, the next time I come to Cambridge.[2] That as to the Doctor's
Circumstances, he Live's well, is very Bountiful to his Relations, &
Charitable to the Poor; so that he doth not lay up any Money. That He
is Sensible, that His Relations Worship him only for what they can
Wring out of Him; & when they hear he hath received a Sum, there
come's a Posse to whine it out of his Pocket forthwith; as was done for
the sum he received of your Lordship. That the Sorel's (the nearest
Relations)[3] do not love that their Unkle should be infested with
Troops of Sturdy Beggars; and see no Reason why the Old Gentleman
should be Stripped before he be Dead; they themselves being in a
Condition to tarry until he be Dead before they Stripp him any
further, having had very good Plunder already. On the other Side, the
Old Man finding that all their Eies are fixed on his Books, & that if

---

[1] Welbeck Wanleyana = BL Loan 29/248.
[2] See no. 169 n. 2.
[3] Probably the family of Dr Henry Sorrell (b. 1690), Christ's College, Cambridge
1706, MD 1717. See Wanley, *Diary*, pp. 210(5)–11.

they had got the Money they would produce, among themselves, he
might e'en hang himself: is resolved to keep them while he live's, &
consequently, the Vulturs in some sort of Decency, if not Subjection.
That as to the remaining part of the Drs Collection, You may have it
for your Money, after the Dr ha's Whoffled & Plaid his part about the
price as accustomed, which must be after his College-Accompts shall
be audited. I have desired him to watch over the Dr Duly.

That Night we all went to Bed in good time, & I in perfect Health;
but the next Morning I was awaken'd by a strong fit of an Ague &
Fever; pain & Swelling of the Glands about the Throat, Head-ach,
Tooth-ake, pain in my Back, & violently in both Thigh-Bones. I know
not what I had done to deserve this, but I found I must, as the old
Saying is, e'en Grin & Abide it. Dr Heathcot[4] came hither accidentally, & told me I should be soon better, & so, I thank God,[5] through the
kind Diligence & Attendance of Mrs Browne, & all your other
Servants, I am. I am come down into your Library where I write this;
yet I am but weak; my head heavy; my Stomack hot; & I much ado to
hold my pen in my Hand. If I am better this afternoon, I will try to do
you some business: if I shall not be able, I hope your good Lordship
will be pleased to excuse me.

None of your Boxes or Cases will be Open'd. The smallest are
brought up hither being the safest Place. I doubt not but the Books
will prove very fine: Noel ha's sent me a list of some of them, which
are truly Rarities, especially the Durandus of 1459, the Captain of the
Band.[6] He say's he shall soon have the Catalogue of the Library by
the Doctors means, whom Your Lordship saw at his House. That he
will refer the Price of the MSS. to me, that I may Moderate the
Matter between Your Lordship & Him; in Order to which he thinks I
must come up to London. I think when he has the MSS. he may send
them down hither, & that I may make a Valuation of them here: not
that I grutch the going to London, or any where else, in your Lordships Service. My Intention was good when I desired Mr Anstis to
attend your Lordship; I hope you have seen him elsewhere; especially now that he may procure you the old Library at Wyrksop by his

[4] Perhaps Gilbert Heathcot (?1664–?1719), Christ's College, Cambridge 1681, and
Leyden ('the physic line') 1686, MD Padua 1688, Licentiate of the Royal College of
Physicians 1719.
[5] Good MS.
[6] i.e. Guillaume Durand, *Rationale diuinorum officiorum* ([Mainz:] J. Fust and
P. [Schöffer], 1459) (*GW* 9101, Hain 6471, Proctor 66). See further no. 189.

Friendship.[7] Signior Alberto hath written that he hath a fine little Monkey, which he would present to my Lady, if worthy Her Ladyships acceptance. I think it may serve pretty sweet Miss to play with, especially if her health continue's as good as it is now; as I hope in God, it will, ever. As to the Box from Coventre, I wrote to Mr John Basset to call for it. The Bridles are all warranted to be of the best Goods, & but 2s. 8d. per Bridle; which is very cheap. I wish your Lordship could send down a Bottle of good Ink. I heartily thank God for the Continuance of my Ladies Health & Yours, & also of my Lady & Lord Oxford: to all whom, I could wish my humble duty were presented: as Mr Garwood also desire's that his may be acceptable to my Lady & your Self. My Lord, I am almost tired; & must write presently to Noel & Alberto, be pleased therefore to forgive,

> Your Lordships most faithful & humble servant

> > > > H. Wanley.

Noel write's as if he is likely to agree with Dean Kennet for the remainder of Basil's Books, &c.

Mr Hooker not yet having sent the Antiquities according to his Promise: Mr Jeffreys is gone to day, to know where the thing stop's.

MS: Welbeck Wanleyana = British Library, Loan *29/258. Date*: 'Wymple, 1 November 1716.' *Address*: 'To The Right Honorable Edward Lord Harley at Bath-Court, near the Royal Palace of St James's Westminster.'

183. *To* Edward Harley *18 November 1716*

May it please your Lordship,

I hope in God that this will find My Noble Lady, Sweet Pretty Miss, & your good Lordship, all in perfect Health; and my Lady Duchess so well recovered as to make a new Will (revoking all former Wills) in Order to Your being well rid of that Legion of Devils, Franklin.[1]

---

[7] Worksop was the Nottinghamshire seat of the Duke of Norfolk. Its fine library was lost in a fire which destroyed the house, according to various accounts, in 1759, 1761, or 1762. Anstis's help was presumably exercised by virtue of his position as Norfolk Herald; the Dukes of Norfolk had been from 1672 hereditary Earls Marshal and hence head of the College of Heralds.

---

[1] Lady Harley's mother bequeathed the bulk of her estate, about £8,000 a year, to her niece, Lady Frances Spencer, daughter of the Earl of Sunderland. But in spite of her

Yesterday, Evening, Dawson came hither, having sent the books remaining with him, by the Waggon.[2] The Man hath had a fit of Sickness lately, otherwise had sent them before. He came on foot, and as I found, only for payment of his Bill. It came to £1.6.2. He had also 3 books, & some pieces of Old Glass, both which I bought for you at 2s. 6d. so in the Whole I paid him £1.8.8. and took his Receipt in full. Dawson told me that Mr Baker often talk's of your Lordship with Wonderful Affection & Respect; and intimating that he will Leave You his Manuscript Collections.[3] There must be something in this; for I never made the least mention of any such matter to any third Person whatsoever: and am of Opinion that the sooner your Present come's to his Hands, it will be the better. I take more pains in your business here, than if You were present. I am in page 82 of the Catalogue, having done with book 2205. VIII. G. 14. My Eyes grow moist, & I believe a little Rest may do them some good. I write this the rather, because my poor Wife grow's very disconsolate at Cambridge, because she cannot see me; and I have certain account that her Spirits droop so much, that she will fall into Sickness (as She once before did) unless I see her soon. I would therefore beg leave of Your Lordship to ride to Cambridge on Saturday next, upon Scrub; & that I may return again on Monday or Tuesday after, as you shall think best. If your Lordship shall please, I can demand your Papers of Dr Covel; I may deliver your Present to Mr Baker; if it be sent to me at Alderman Chambers's. I would also pay the Ten Guineas to Pembroke Hall, they having consented to Your keeping their book.[4] This may be done,

will the estate passed to her daughter (GEC, *Complete Peerage*, iii (1913), p. 251 n(a)). Wanley would have been especially incensed that the beneficiary was the daughter of Harley's chief rival in the book market. The accursed Franklin I cannot identify.

[2] Plomer, *Dictionary*, pp. 101–2, distinguishes Thomas Dawson the elder, bookbinder at Cambridge, 1675–95(?), mentioned in a will of 1675 as living in his freehold tenement, the 'Nag's Head', and Thomas Dawson the younger, bookseller in High Street, Cambridge. His name appears on five works ptd. for him at the University Press 1695–1706. He died in 1708. Elizabeth Dawson his widow succeeded to his business and carried on to her death in 1728. G. D. Hobson, *Bindings in Cambridge Libraries* (Cambridge, 1929) illustrates (pl. LXX) a binding (of the MS Book of Benefactors of St. John's College, Cambridge) which he ascribes to the younger Dawson. But from the college accounts this can be dated 1712 and is presumably the work of the father rather than the son. The present reference and that in Wanley to Edward Harley, 14 Oct. 1716, is presumably also to the elder Dawson. It is interesting in this connection that Hobson says there is little in this binding to remind one of Cambridge work of the previous century; it is much more like London work of the Harleian type.   [3] See no. 179 n. 7.

[4] See no. 181. Paid 29 Nov. 1716 (Welbeck Wanleyana = BL Loan MS 29/248). The banking firm of Sir Robert Child and Partners, of Temple Bar, acted for Harley.

by Your Lordships sending me a Note on Sir Robert Child. And if your Lordship would vouchsafe to Honor Honest Dr Tudway with another, I know it will be of great Use & Service unto him. And at the same time, a small Note for my self will not only recruit me, but keep me in Heart. Mr Hooker hath broken his last promise by not sending, but I believe, will bring the things when he comes with Mr Harvey. I hear Nothing at all from Noel about Lord Somers's books. I could wish your Lordship would see Mr Bressan's Pictures, & buy the Boy painted by Hanibal Caraccio.[5] He lives in the Yard of Somerset House, near the Stables, at the Green Flower-pots, near the Water-Stairs. That done, Your Lordship may easily (in a fine day) take Oars to Cupids Garden, & get the Master of the House shew you all the Antiquities there (after you have called for a Betty of Claret) and perhaps, you may buy what of them are his, at a cheap rate.[6] The rest, I believe the Duke of Norfolk will give you. Mr Cuttle desires your Lordship to send some Tobacco; Six Gross of good Corks for Quart Bottles, & four Gross for Pints; & some Mountain Wine in Bottles, half an Hogshead, at the least. Mr Garwood joyn's with me in his humble Duty; and I am, for ever, Your good Lordships most faithful servant

H. Wanley.

MS: Welbeck Wanleyana = British Library, Loan 29/258. *Date*: 'Wymple, 18th November 1716.' *Address*: 'To The Right Honorable Edward Lord Harley at Bath Court in the Royal Palace at St James's Westminster.' *Printed*: P. L. Heyworth, 'A Betty of Claret', *Notes and Queries*, 216 (1971), p. 52 (extract).

[5] Bressan I cannot identify. Annibale Carracci (1560–1609), Bolognese painter.

[6] Cuper's Gardens, Lambeth was in the seventeenth century the garden of Thomas Howard, 2nd Earl of Arundel, ancestor of the Dukes of Norfolk. It was rented by one Cuper who had been the Earl's gardener, hence its name. In Cuper's Gardens there were formerly some mutilated statues, the 'refuse' of the collection brought by the Earl of Arundel from Italy (a large part of which was given to the University of Oxford by his grandson in 1667). Most of the 'refuse' was removed in 1717, having been purchased by a Mr Willer of Beaconsfield and a Mr Freeman of Fawley Court. Those statues which remained were covered with rubbish. They were dug out by a subsequent proprietor (Theobald) and most were given by him to Richard Boyle, 3rd Earl of Burlington, who removed them to his house at Chiswick. Before dispersal the fragments were described and engraved for John Aubrey's *Natural History and Antiquities of the County of Surrey*, v (1719)—the description, p. 282 f., the engravings (eight plates), after p. 414. See D. Lysons, *The Environs of London*, i (1742), pp. 319–20. The Gardens were still used as a tavern in the mid-eighteenth century. See further no. 184.

184. *To* Edward Harley *30 November 1716*

May it please your Lordship

I return your Lordship my most hearty Thanks for your most kind & dear Letters written unto me; & above all for the tender Expressions therein contained, relating to my Health.[1] Indeed I look upon Health as the chiefest Blessing in this World, next to that of a Contented Mind. The Latter, I thank God, I possess: for the business I do here, being Your Business; I am therein heartily Contented, Easy, & Merry. I stick closer to it, indeed, than either You or my Noble Lady desired; but I take Comfort & Delight in it, and wish, that (were it consistent with Human Nature) I might finish the whole at one Sitting. But, since this is impossible, I take the boldness to acquaint your Lordship, that, this afternoon, I have quite finished with that part of a Class, being over the door going into the Lesser Room. The last book of it, is marked IX.E.29 (the running Number being 2571) & is described in the 96th page of this Short Catalogue. The Green Strings your Lordship sent down, are putt up, & the Room look's with an uncommon & grand Air; the rest are put up in the lesser Room, where Five more are still Wanted. For, One came without a Tassel. One Skrew broke in Trial; for I bad the Workman try each, whether it would bear any weight, after it was put up; as thinking it better that he should break a Skrew or two, than I (or any other) break our Necks: as to the rest, the Number sent down was deficient. Five will do as well as Six, to the full; because one of them being to hang in the Corner of the little Room, at the lower End, will serve two Classes as well as one. Of these Five Green Strings, Three must be of the same Length with the others: the other two Strings must be but 23 Inches long, or $23\frac{1}{2}$ including their respective Tassels: for, as your Lordship very well remember's, the Joyners work there, comes down as low, almost as the Window. The sooner they are sent down, the better; that the Room may look Uniform. Here is a Parcel of Skrews & Rings come, but, not being used, they ought to be returned back.[2]

[1] 'I wish you would not tamper with any of the phisitians of cambridge, if you will send up your case I will carry it either to Dr Mead or Dr Sloan wch you like best, and will send you down the Directions, I belive if you used moderate exercise you would be better, you may have Scrub when ever you please' (Edward Harley to Wanley d. 27 Nov. 1716; Welbeck Wanleyana = BL Loan MS 29/248).
[2] This is presumably a description of what was three years later, when the new

As to my Health, my good Lord, I thank God I am grown easy again. I have had many touches of the Ague, Fever, Cold, Gravel, Cholic, Gout, Rheumatism, Sore Throat, Tooth-ach, &c. &c. and after all, am recovered Easy, & Merry. Some of these I brought here with me; the rest have attacked me a Stranger; but (I thank God) have been bravely repulsed. It hath not been my Case alone; for some in the House, & others without, have been afflicted, as bad as my Self, and with the same Symptoms. I did think, indeed, of giving Dr Green of Cambridge[3] a Fee, in Order to know the Original Cause of my Maladies; but not then hearing from your Lordship, I could not go. I therefore took Cognisance of my Self, & came to two Resolutions, i. to get and keep my Stomach in Order; & 2. to keep-off Colds. As to the First, I am grown much better; even grown so well as to eat of Your Lordships Beef, both Boyled & Roasted, which I had not done in 6 weeks before: & Mr Cuttle (who now hath the Tooth-Ach) said my Stomach (or Appetite to Food) is as good as he ever knew it. Moreover, I walk a little, after Prayers, before Meals; which encourage's the Stomach. As to Colds, I keep my Self warm, (not too Hot) & go little in the open Air; & shall be sure to obey the salutiferous Precepts Your Lordship was pleased to send me, in Your Last.

I hear my poor Spouse hath been ill, (but the most being owing to her anxiety, in not being able to see me in 13 weeks, excepting only one quarter of an hour). She is now much easier upon the Message I sent, that I would see her as to morrow: Yet, they say, she hath a Cold upon her. My desire is, to return hither the next Tuesday; but if either her Importunity, or any thing else material, which I cannot now foresee should fall out so as to keep me untill Wednesday, I hope Your Lordship will be pleased to excuse me. Both Mr Garwood & Mr Wenman[4] will go along with me, & return with me. They have been ill, too; & in my Way: & the latter is hardly Currant now.

In my next, from Cambridge, I hope to have the Honor to lett your Lordship know that Mr Hooker will send the Antiquities; & why they

Library was built, to become the Ante-library (now called the Book Room). On 4 July 1716 Edward Harley wrote to Wanley, 'you will be wanted at Wimple, now the room for my books is finisht' (Welbeck Wanleyana = BL Loan 29/248). See Royal Commission on Historical Monuments, *Cambridgeshire*, i (1968), p. 215 for a plan of Wimpole; a photograph of the Library and Book Room appears as pl. 140.

[3] Probably Christopher Green (1652–1741), Fellow of Caius College, Cambridge 1674, MD 1685, Regius Professor of Physic 1700.

[4] Formerly Secretary to the Duke of Newcastle, Lady Harley's father.

stay so long. At Cambridge I shall talk with Dr Tudway; & if there-upon we shall find it best for me to Visit Dr Covel, or Mr Thompson, I will do so; otherwise not: for Your Lordships Silence thereupon, leaveth me at Liberty to Act as I shall think will conduce best to Your Noble Service. I will wait on Mr Baker, & say unto him all that is Proper. And also pay the Ten Guineas to Pembroke hall placing the Remainder to mine Accompt with your Lordship. I am glad your Lordship hath seen some of Mr Anstis's books; and believe that now you will exchange some of your Heraldical MSS. with Him. Those two old MSS. are very fine ones indeed; but he would never lett me have them cheaper than for what he ask's your Lordship.[5] The fine Heraldical MS. he shewed you, is that (I suppose) which belonged to Tho. Wriothesley, Garter.[6] He hath another, formerly owned by Mr Attorney General Noy; a Singular Book: I wish your Lordship had them both. I suppose the two Voll's of Inscriptions lent You, were of Mr Lhwyds, bought by Sir Thomas Seabright; & that the *Sigilla Comitum Flandriae*, is that by *Vredus*, which is a very good & choice Book.[7] I wish your Lordship will find some fine Day, to go to Cupids Garden in, & see the Antiquities there. The great & fine Joint of the Column there, I believe belong's to the D. of N. and if he give's it your Lordship, with what other Antiquities he hath there, with the Library at W. (all by means of Mr Anstis)[8] your Charge with the Gardiner &c. will be but small. As to Mr Mickleton's 4 Old Vollumes of Church Musick of temp. Hen. VIII. when I shall receive them, they shall be your Lordships, to be sure, as every thing else is, that I have.[9] I hear

---

[5] See no. 180.

[6] Sir Thomas Wriothesly († 1534), Garter King of Arms 1505; William Noy (1577–1634), Attorney General 1631. I cannot identify the manuscripts.

[7] For Lhwyd and Sebright see no. 140 and n. 4. Oliver Vredius, *Sigilla Comitum Flandriae* (Bruges, 1639).

[8] See no. 182 n. 7, no. 183.

[9] Harley wrote that Anstis 'read me part of a letter from mr Mickleton in wch he says he has four vol. of Ch: Musick in H:8ths time wch he designs for you' (Edward Harley to Wanley d. 29 Nov. 1716; Welbeck Wanleyana = BL Loan MS 29/248). Bodl. MSS Mus. Sch. e. 420–3 (*SC* 26555–7) are three volumes (of four, the tenor book is missing) containing English church music of the mid-sixteenth century, probably in the autograph of John Taverner (see *Music and Letters*, v (1924), p. 335). These once belonged to Wanley, but are ruled out by the inscriptions in the first and second vols.: 'Liber Humfredi Wanley 18 Nov. 1715'. But they are so satisfactory in other respects that it is tempting to assume that Wanley made a mistake in the date—as he did, for example, on letters written on consecutive days to his wife 13, 14 March 1716. Early in 1718 Mickleton presented Wanley with a collection of Durham songs: they are in BL Harley MS 7578 fos. 84–117, with a note (on fo. 117ᵛ) by Wanley, d. 17 Feb. 1717/18, recording the gift.

Sweet pretty Miss, hath not been very well of late, & hath cutt another
great Tooth. I pray God send her, & my most Noble Lady your Illustrious Consort perfect Health, & Happiness. The same I sincerely
wish your Good Lordship, & a Total Victory over all your base &
undermining Enemies: [I am] for ever, with the greatest Respect,
   Your noble Lordship's most faithful, most humble, &
      most obedient Servant

                                                    Humfrey Wanley.

MS: Welbeck Wanleyana = British Library, Loan 29/258. *Date*: 'Wymple 30 Novr
1716.' *Address*: 'To The Right Honorable Edward Lord Harley.'

185. *To* Edward Harley *4 December 1716*

May it please your Lordship,
   Notwithstanding the promise I made in my last Letter, I did forbear
to trouble your Lordship with a Letter by the last Post, because the
Matter I had to write, was but this. Viz. that some time ago, Mr
Hawkins the President of Pembroke-Hall[1] called at Wymple on Mr
Garwood, & Dined with us: and before he went invited Mr Garwood
and me to Dine with him on the Monday-last. Mr Garwood went, &
there met with Mr Hooker, who made the first Mention of His things;
mr Garwood being all along, either Silent; or at least, upon the
Defensive. The Reason of the Delay Mr Hooker said was double: 1.
He had promised a Gentleman a Friend, who courts a Gentlewoman
in his Neighbourhood, that He should certainly see those Things
before they go out of his Hands: & 2ly because he think's he can
procure some other Antiquities, found in the same place with his, to
add unto them. In Conclusion, he invited Mr President & Mr
Garwood to come & see him, & Mr Garwood to bring a Servant with
him, & that Servant Shall carry away the Cargo to Wymple, without
further Delay. Mr President is in Cambridge, but the Service will be
done before Christmass.
   We had but indifferent Weather hither, the Snow beating hard in
our Faces about half the Way. I finding the necessity of Speed & Hast,
proved a better Horseman than Mr Garwood expected. At my Coming

---

[1] The Master of Pembroke (1707–28) was Edward Laney. Reginald Hawkins was a
Fellow (1691). The office of President at Pembroke = Vice-Master, presiding in the
absence of the Master.

to Alderman Chambers's I found my poor Spouse much altered for the worse, since I left Her; and she was bad enough then. In short the Grief she ha's taken for this our Separation is Such, as She is grown almost Blind with Crying, and could neither Write nor Read any more. I have had much adoe to Pacify Her. The two first Nights were almost wholly spent in Crying; & it come's on Her, before Company. Her Spirits are so low, that although the poor Woman Hath striven against Melancholy, She nevertheless is overcome with Vapors; Her Face is grown less, & Mind totally Oppressed. I have hereupon promised to bring her nearer to me; that is, to Mr Williams of Kingston,[2] if he will board her & her Maid. She like's a Glass of Your Wymple Beer, now & then; & if your Lordship will be pleased to give me some few Bottles for her; it will be a great Kindness to me. I staid with her till Yesterday-morning, when I went to Mr Baker, with whom I had much Conversation. The Result of which is, that He Hath a good Study of Printed Books by Him, divers of which he useth continually, & cannot now spare; & these over & above those which he hath actually given-in to the College Library. He hath also a few old MSS. about 8 in Number, but not worth much. He hath also about 40 Volumes in fol. all of His Hand-Writing, & chiefly relating to Cambridge; which he cannot part with now, nor while he lives; but is willing that they may be assured unto Your Lordship now, in any way or manner that I will propose. But this to be known only between us. Hereupon I advised with a Lawyer of the proper Way of transacting such an affair as this, but concealing the name of the Business, & all proper Names. I proposed a Deed of Gift; a Bond; a Will; but He liked none but a Bargain & Sale, with Delivery of the Goods; & then Borrowing them again; giving a Note under his Hand, to redeliver the same upon Demand. This Evening we are to meet about it, & if he shall approve this Method, I will dispatch the Business & Prevent Afterclaps.

The Master of Pembroke could not see me Yesterday, but will do so this Night, when I shall (God willing) Pay him the Ten Guineas, & take a proper Receipt.

If Mr Baker & I agree, (as we certainly shall, unless he change his Mind) I will try to carry-off the 8 Old MSS.[3] and engage him into a

---

[2] A village about two miles from Wimpole.
[3] There is nothing to suggest that Wanley managed to persuade Baker to part with the '8 Old MSS.'. For the forty folio vols. see no. 186.

Promise of not parting with any more Books & Papers, either to the College, or any Person, untill Your Lordship shall have had from him, what You shall want from his Collection. He is much more lean, than he was two Months ago, which make's this menagement necessary,although I tarry here until Saturday; for I know not how soon he may drop-off. Dr Tudway hath been hearty in extolling your Lordship both with Mr Baker, & at the Master of Christs, who hath served me another pretty Trick. He had promised Dr Tudway to come-to at last, & before he should be compelled to be honest: & particularly that I should have a Sight of the Letters; & (as the Dr thought) that I should take them away with me. I was, therefore, to render my self thither by ten o'Clock; all to be well, all feuds & Dissensions to be forgotten; & our Spouses to dine with Him & Us at Christs. In Order to this, at Eight o'clock, his Man came with a Solemn Invitation for Us & Mrs Beaver: & Went to the Dr for them & Mr Garwood. I had not been in his Lodge, one quarter of an hour, but I would have given a Guinea that I had not come. He ripped up the Story of his Dealing with me, in such a Manner, & fortified it with such Circumstances, that had I been a Stranger, I should have thought him very hardly dealt withall. But, as it was, I knew, & could call God to witness that his recital was partly false, & partly prevaricating & partly biassed to his own Side. Thus, he said, that by Letters or Papers relating to Learning or Literature, he meant those Fragments I took away, & what others of the like kind he should happen to find; & nothing else. That he believed Your Lordship had sent him a better Present than the 30 Guineas I delivered to him, to be sure 50 at the Least: and that I was the Occasion of his being no better paid for the Sea-Chart.[4] I answerd I gave him all your Present, which Your Lordship (and others too) thought Sufficiently ample. That as to the Chart, I was obliged to drag up-hill, to get him 12 Guineas for that which he sent up at Ten. He intimated then a Mistrust, as if I had kept all but 12 Guineas from him; or kept the money long. I desired how this could be, when my Noble Lord told him, in my hearing, that he should be paid the next day; and that when he came the next day, he found the Money in a Paper Sealed up with my Lords Seal; Superscribed to Him; Dated; & the Value Specified; by my said Lords own Hand? I thought my Self not rightly Used; but in Order to prevent an Utter Breach, I bore it; especially considering that Patience & Time might bring forth something to your

[4] See nos. 122, 125.

advantage. At length he told me I might see some of the Letters, which I was glad to do. But he only let me see the Shapes of them, & read some of the Titles he putt on them; as from Draco the 3d Greek Interpreter, from his Wife Smaragda, & Daughter Theodora. From Joannes Thalassinos the Logotheles of Constantinople; Dositheus Patriarch of Jerusalem, Neophylus Metropolite of Philippopoli, Mellitus a Bishop; other Greek Bishops, &c. & others of divers of our Learned Men. These Parcels I saw not before: but, alass, according to him they relate not to Learning, but to Business. The Answers, you own are mine, quoth he; you would have me give you the Original Letters, (many of which I have quoted in my writings) & only retain my draughts of Answers, Would you? I thank you heartily. At last he said you should have them all: When, Master, said I? after I am dead, said He. I thank you, replied I; better late than never. He is in many Minds, but in proper time, may be quickened.[5] In the meanwhile, he is really Cataloguing his Things, in Order to reduce the Appraisement of each particular into one Sum Total. I believe your Lordship will never be able to Agree with him about them; but when they come into other Hands, his Opinions & Stories will not keep them up at his Price; and his Notes of them will be Valuable, because Instructive.

When I found I could not do with him what I came about; I was resolved however, to do some thing. So I put him in Mind of Procopius's Arcana Historia, & how Alemannus had purposely omitted somethings in the MS. which related to the Wicked Life of Theodora the Empress: and that he had gotten, from Vossius (who had perused Alemannus his MS.) the Words (although erroneously written) which filled up the Lacunae.[6] I desired therefore, that I might translate the same for your Lordship, (they not being elsewhere in England, as I know of); I have done so; but was forbidden to meddele with his Translation or Notions. Dr Tudway was at me Yesterday & to Day, about the 30 Guineas.[7] He represented in very modest Manner the great Obligations he already stand's in to your good Lordship, and

---

[5] On Covell's 'Letters' see no. 169 n. 2.

[6] Procopius's *Historia Arcana* (so called because it was pbd. after the death of the author) purports to be a supplement to his *Histories*, containing material omitted from them, in particular scandalous tales about the Emperor Justinian's wife Theodora, previously a courtesan. Nicolaus Alemannus (1583–1626) pbd. his edn. at Lyons (1623), but omitted some details found in his manuscript version, obtained by Covell from Vossius, who had read the manuscript.

[7] Presumably for work done in compiling BL Harley MSS 7337–42: see no. 153 n. 2.

how unfortunately it happens for him that Your Lordship should continue so long at London. That he had Order'd his Payments, for the time when he thought to Deliver his Second Volume; which being Elapsed, he was forced to take up Money elsewhere. That this is now Demanded, and he know's not well what to do. He therefore desired me to represent this his Case to Your Noble Lordship with all humility, by this Post: in hopes, that it may be crowned with the same Good Success, as bef[ore]. And indeed, that his Affairs are more doubtful than as set forth by him, I can easily believe. He say's by means of his Correspondents, he hath gotten together the greatest Collection that ever was made; but he reject's above half, as not being choise enough for Your Lordship; only Mr Dean Aldriches Pieces he insert's wholly.[8] I could wish your Lordship would be pleased to take the honest Doctors reduced Circumstances farther into your Noble Consideration, as soon as may conveniently be. I hope pretty sweet Miss is in perfect Health; which I do from the bottom of my heart, pray may ever attend my Lady Your most Virtuous & Excellent Consort, and your Noble Lordship, with Her.

The Post is almost going out; & I must see Mr Baker & the Master of Pembroke this Evening, who am

Your Lordships,

most faithful, most humble, & most obedient Servant

Humfrey Wanley.

MS: Welbeck Wanleyana = British Library, Loan 29/258. *Date*: 'Cambridge, Coffee-house, 4 Decr 1716.' *Address*: 'To The Right Honorable Edward Lord Harley at Bath-Court in the Royal Palace, at St James's Westminster.'

186. *To* Edward Harley *6 December 1716*

May it please your Lordship,

Yesterday the Waggoner brought hither Three Hampers of Beer or Ale (as we suppose) directed to my poor Spouse; for which we both return our most humble & hearty Thanks. It will do her much good, in my Absence when I cannot be present to Comfort Her. She look's brighter than She did when I came hither. In my last I was bold to request your Lordship to give her a few Bottles, and at the same time

[8] Aldrich composed or adapted from the Italian about thirty anthems.

You have been pleased to send many, far beyond my Expectation. Yesterday Mr Baker & I did Agree upon the Form of the Bargain & Sale of his MS. Collections unto your Lordship;[1] but with an Amendment from what I had drawn up. For he said He knew Your Lordship very well & could therefore trust You; but who would be your Executors he knew not, nor could trust. That it being a Possible Case that Your Lordship may Decease before Him; he was Unwilling to Deliver his Collections to Your Executors upon their Demand, or Stand to their Courtesie.[2] I Amended it as well as I could according to His Mind; and Shewed him the same, wherewith he was Content. In the Evening I went again to Pembroke Hall, & Paid the Master the Ten Guineas for the Book, & took His Receipt.[3] This Morning I went again to Mr B. with the Bargain & Sale written upon Stamp'd Paper, And the Inventory of the Books aforesaid, which I took Yesterday; and He hath Executed the Same to Your Lordships Use, in the presence of Mr Billers a Grave Gentleman of the same College, in whom only he would Confide.[4] A Guinea being Mentioned as one Inducement, I paid the same to him, in Mr Billers's presence. Moreover, fearing that I may have been out in some point of Form or other, I will take Care to send up the said Deed & Schedule; and if it be not regular, Mr B. will

---

[1] Baker accumulated material over many years for an Athenae Cantabrigienses and his collections are in forty-two volumes—vols. 1–23 now BL Harley MSS 7028–50, vols. 24–42 now Cambridge University Library MSS Mm.1.35–53. CUL MSS Mm.2.22–5 also contain transcripts of material from the Harleian volumes. The deed of 'Bargain & Sale' to Harley of twenty-one vols., together with an inventory, and a memorandum (d. 24 Dec. 1719) assigning a further two vols. (for an extra guinea), are in BL Harley MS 7028 (fos. 1–3); a copy of the deed of sale and the memorandum of 24 Dec. 1719 is in Society of Antiquaries MS 264, fos. 51ᵛ–2ᵛ. The receipt d. 31 Dec. 1716 is with Baker's letter to Wanley d. 28 Dec. 1716 in Welbeck Wanleyana = BL Loan MS 29/251). A brief description of the whole collection is in an Appendix to Robert Masters, *Memoirs of the Life and Writings of the late Rev. Thomas Baker* (Cambridge, 1784); a very full catalogue by J. E. B. Mayor of the volumes at Cambridge is in *Catalogue of the Manuscripts Preserved in the Library of the University of Cambridge*, v (Cambridge, 1867), pp. 193–567. See also Wanley, *Diary*, p. xxxvii. Earlier (14 Mar. 1715) Baker had sold Harley a collection of letters of various writers for £40 (see Wanley, *Diary*, p. 13(5)), now scattered in BL Harley MSS 6988–7018. For a full list see Wright, *Fontes*, under Baker. For an index to all the Baker manuscripts see [J. J. Smith *et al.*], *Index to the Baker Manuscripts* (Cambridge, 1848).

[2] A condition of the sale was that Baker should retain his manuscripts until his death, and the sale is confirmed in his will (ptd. Masters, *Life*, p. 134). Baker did, in fact, predecease Harley. For the promptness with which Harley was informed of the onset of the illness (a stroke) from which Baker died, see *HMC Portland Papers*, vi, pp. 72–3.

[3] See no. 181 n. 3. Receipt for £10.15.0, d. 5 Dec. 1716, attached.

[4] John Billers (*c.*1649–1721), Fellow of St John's College, Cambridge 1671–1717, when he was ejected as a nonjuror.

do it again, in any other Form that Your Lordship shall better approve of. He had left the Things to the College, & must alter his Will accordingly. He saith whenever he shall find himself very ill, he will send them up to Mr Billers, & send for me from Wymple forthwith; but would have all kept secret, because talk about it will Hound the College upon him.

I could not forbear Eying his Books, according to Custom; and have had much talk with him about them. Yesterday & to day we have gott out all his MSS. and a Select parcel of Printed books, which I have bought of him for You at 20 Guineas. They are worth more by far; yet I begged his K. Henry VIIths Picture for you into the Bargain. His MSS Collections (sold unto Your Lordship as aforesaid) are worth above 100 Guineas; and I desire that Your Lordship would be pleas'd to Order these 20 Guineas to him as soon as may conveniently be. I have got the Cargo here at my Lodging, & will see't safe at Wymple on Saturday: by which Post, your Lordship will receive a Short Catalogue of the same. He hath some other Things of Value which he cannot spare now; but in time you will have them. Such are,

Mr Rich. Smith's Catalogue of his Historical Books, in 4 or 5 Quartos, MSS.[5] The Printed Catalogue is very Erroneous & defective.

Mansel's Catalogue interleaved, with Vast Additions.[6]

Matth. Parkeri Antiquitates: *Lond.*[7] Interleaved, with vast Additions by Mr. B——r. He hath two; but the books differing much from one another; Your Lordship must have them both.

[5] Now Bodl. MS Rawl. D.1377 (*SC* 15562) in five parts. According to an inscription by Baker, he had it from Bagford, and a further inscription in Hearne's hand records it as a gift to him from Baker in March 1727. It is curious that Baker says in his inscription that he sends it 'to help to compleat your collection of Mr Bagford's Papers'—when Bagford's papers had for long been in the Harleian Library. Another part of the catalogue (originally in the possession of William Fleetwood, Bishop of Ely 1714) was bought by the BM at the Heber sale (pt. xi, lot 77) and is now BL Add. MS 21096. Phillipps MS 8439 = Heber sale, pt. xi, lot 1128 contains the title-page and Preface only of the catalogue. Wright, *Fontes*, under Smith, records part of a catalogue of his books d. 1664 in BL Harley MS 4706 fos. 98–117ᵛ, the rest in BL Sloane MSS 771, 1071.

Richard Smith (1590–1675) of Little Moorfields, was Secondary of the Poultry Accompter 1644–55; his library was especially rich in early English ptd. books, works on English liturgy and history; it was sold at auction in 1682. The printed catalogue, *Florum Historiae Ecclesiasticae gentis Anglorum libri septem... Collectare R. Smitheo*, was pbd. at Paris, 1654.

[6] Andrew Maunsell's *Catalogue of English Printed Bookes* (1595), *STC* 17669, now Cambridge University Library MS Mm.i.50, left by Baker to his friend Conyers Middleton in trust for the University Library.   [7] *De Antiquitate Britannicae Ecclesiae* (1572).

He hath also the *Parliaments* Ten Shilling Piece of Gold, being the last that it ever Coined, the Year is 1660, and the Mark Ɪ. He saith it is a mighty Rarity; but yet, that You may have it.

I have agreed that whensoever in this parcel of the Printed books, you shall find any Duplicate, that you care not for; it may be returned, & you receive another book in lieu thereof. Here are Duplicates, but I believe your Lordship will not part with them. My poor Spouse & I unfeignedly offer up our Prayers to God Almighty for the Health & Prosperity of our Most Noble Lady, Pretty, Sweet Miss, & Your Noble Lordship: I being, as in greater Duty bound,

Your Lordships most faithful, & most obedient servant,

Humfrey Wanley.

MS: Welbeck Wanleyana = British Library, Loan 29/258. *Date*: 'Cambridge, 6 December 1716.' *Address*: 'To The Right Honorable Edward Lord Harley at Bath-Court in the Royal Palace at St James's, Westminster.'

187. *To* Edward Harley *6 December 1716*

May it please your Lordship,

This afternoon I wrote unto your Noble Lordship a full Account of my Transactions with Mr Baker, which will turn much to your Advantage, although my stay here hath & will prove 3 days longer than I intended. After that Letter was written, Sealed, & Sent to the Post-house I had a mind to beginn upon the Catalogue I promised therein; but Your Lordships Commands came to me by Your Servant John the Under-Cook, sent by Mr Twy-bill. The Post is now going out, so that I am almost affraid that this will come too late. I can therefore only say, what your Lordship was pleas'd to say in one of Yours unto me; viz. that Jones is a great Rogue. Before I came away I did bid him £200 for the Parcel of MSS. which I laid by: and they are worth the money. His Play is by Lies, & false Suggestions.[1]

The Clock hath Struck Six.

My Lord, be pleased to See the Things, but bid no more Money. He will yield in Time. He is a Sort of Covellius Heros; and you should carry the matter with State & Rigor. Nothing less will go down with

[1] Richard Jones († 1722), bookseller of Little Britain. Wanley's catalogue (d. 16 May 1716) of the books referred to here is in Welbeck Wanleyana = BL Loan MS 29/260 misc. 85.

him. I dare not write more now, the time being elapsed: but the next
Post I shall approve my self in more ample Manner

Your Good Lordships dutiful servant

H. Wanley.

MS: Welbeck Wanleyana = British Library, Loan 29/258. *Date*: 'Rose, in Cambridge 6.
Decr 1716.' *Address*: 'To The Right Honorable Edward Lord Harley at Bath-Court in
St James's Palace Westminster.'

188. *To* Edward Harley *16 December 1716*

May it please your Lordship,

Not having the Honor to recieve any Commands from you the last
Week, I know not whether that which I have done with Mr Baker be
acceptable, or not; nor whether You have received the Bargain & Sale,
which Dr Tudway promised to send up by the Letter-Carrier; I being
loth to trust it by the Post. Nor do I know your Lordships Pleasure,
whether you will Communicate any part of the Catalogue, I am now
compiling, unto Him at Cambridge, or not.

As to this Catalogue, I have sett upon it heartily since my return
hither; so, that the last night I finished page 107 of the same, whose last
book is no. 2763. X. A. 16. the two Shelves over the Window in the
lesser Room being all included & marked.

Mr Anstis saith he hath gotten some Roman Antiquities (lately dug
up in Kent) for your Lordship. I think it would be well to call on him
for them; and also to allow him the liberty of Borrowing what other
Seals he shall want for his Book,[1] even in your Absence, upon his
restoring those now in his hands, which he saith he ha's done with.
His Friendship may & will stand your Lordship in great stead.

Noel write's me word that Dr Mead putt's him in great hopes of his
buying Lord Somers's Library;[2] as he shall do that of Dr South by
means of my recommending him to Mr Church.[3] He further saith that

[1] Probably his 'Aspilogia', a treatise on the seals of England; left in manuscript, now
BL Stowe MSS 665–6.

[2] Richard Mead (1673–1754), physician and collector. For Somers's library see
no. 178.

[3] Presumably Robert South (1634–1716), Public Orator at Oxford 1660, Prebendary
of Westminster 1678, and John Church (1675?–1741), lay vicar of Westminster Abbey
c.1700.

he shall soon receive from beyond-sea, one of the finest Parcels of Books that ever came to England.[4]

I have received another Letter from Mr Warburton of Hexham,[5] (whose former Letter I did not answer) touching his Roman Inscriptions: but shall write to him Mr Noel, &c. presently.

Mr Hawkins the President of Pembroke-hall is not well; so that the visit is not yet paid to Mr Hooker. Thus with Mr Garwoods most humble Duty & Mine, to Our most Noble Lady, pretty Miss, & your good Lordship; I do particularly remain

Your Lordships most faithful, & most humble servant

H. Wanley.

MS: Welbeck Wanleyana = British Library, Loan 29/258. *Date*: 'Wimple, 16 December 1716.' *Address*: 'To The Right Honorable Edward Lord Harley at Bath-Court in St James's Palace Westminster.'

189. *To* [Edward Harley] *23 December 1716*

May it please your Lordship,

Yesterday a little before Noon, your Noble Commands[1] found me in my Station; which I no sooner Read, but thought with my self which might be the best way of fulfilling the same: and soon came to a resolution of not looking into your Things alone. I therefore called Mr Cuttle your Lordships truly-faithful & willing Servant, and so we fetched in so many of the Cases, & searched them untill we found the *Rationale*, & *Justinian*, with Teniers book, in the Belly of one of them. We brought in four Lesser Cases more, & at the last found the *Tullies Offices* in the least of them.[2] All these Cases we have left in the Room:

---

[4] Wright (*Diary*, p. xxxix) suggests that this may refer to a consignment which came from the Continent (presumably from Noel's agent Suttie) and included many from the Hospital of St Nicholas at Cues on the Mosel.
[5] John Warburton (1682–1759), antiquary, Somerset Herald 1720. He had no formal education but was an avid collector; in his early life and still at this time, an exciseman.

---

[1] Letter of 21 Dec. 1716, Welbeck Wanleyana = BL Loan 29/248.
[2] Guillaume Durand, *Rationale diuinorum officiorum* ([Mainz:] J. Fust and P. [Schöffer], 1459) (*GW* 9101, Hain 6471, Proctor 66). The Justinian is perhaps *Institutiones* (Mainz: P. Schöffer, 1468) (Hain 9489, Proctor 85); BL Harley MS 7526, fos. 152–3 contains Wanley's transcript of 'Notes at the End of my Lord's two Books', one of which is this edn. of the *Institutiones*. The 'Tullies Offices' may be *De Officiis* (Mainz: J. Fust and P. Schöffer, 1466) (*GW* 6922, Hain 5239, Proctor 82), and 'Teniers book' *Le Theatre des peintures de David Teniers* (Brussels and Antwerp, 1660). The 1459 Durandus and the

each Case containing it own books, excepting only the Three books abovementioned. These I Carried up, together with Thomas Aquinas; but somewhat heavily, for I thought Your Intention might be to Present them to somebody or other, in as much as Your Lordship had Order'd me to send you the Date of *Thomas*, which perhaps might also accompany them.[3] Lord! thought I, this is very grievous, to part with a Durandus of 1459, one of the most beautiful of Books, & of so great & extreme Rarity, as that it will easily produce 30 Guineas or more, in the Market! But the Lords will be done! After the books found, I went to the Wainscoat Cabinet, Mr Cuttle being imployed in putting the books into the Cases in the same Room, and found its Key in the Lock; whereby I came, at length to the Writings, being 3 in Number; which I have not, nor will not look into; for by the Seals & Hands, I believe them to be what your Lordship meant.[4] Lower, I found the other Books mentioned by Your Lordship, which are all Old, excepting one big Folio, MS. looking modern, & like Poetry. This I left behind, as thinking it not meant by Your Lordship. For all the rest but one, being old, & without Covers; I presently fancied that You send for them, and the other Three, only to be well Bound, as they richly Deserve.[5] Among them is The Tullies Offices of 1466 in Paper, which I shall send up, with the others, it being included within Your Lordships Command. The Plan &c. of Your House in Bath-Court was not in that Cabinet, but in the other mentioned by your Lordship: which being found: Mr Cuttle & I agreed to Shut up the Room. But since I perceived that the Key was in your least Cabinet, & many things lying about: as I would not by any Means stay alone in the Room, so I would not Deliver the Key thereof to any Person without your Express Order; nor even keep it my Self, without due Precaution. I therefore in Mr Cuttles Presence, folded it up in Paper, & Sealed it up firmly, twice, with His Seal; which is now become my Voucher. Hereby we are capable of obeying Your Commands, if hereafter you shall Command us any Service in the same Room: or else I can send up the

---

1468 Justinian are both listed in Wanley's 'Catalogus Veterum Editionum' in Harley's library (BL Harley MS 3886, begun on 26 Apr. and finished on 6 June 1722). The 1466 edn. of 'Tullies Offices' appears in two copies—one vellum, the other paper—but also in five later edns., all ptd. before 1474.

[3] Torn off. See no. 181 n. 3.

[4] Legal and estate documents, listed by Harley.

[5] Wanley was right: see Edward Harley to Wanley d. 29 Dec. 1716, Welbeck Wanleyana = BL Loan MS 29/248.

same, upon the first Notice, according to any your least Direction. I received two Padlock-Keys, belonging to the great Case, which needed not to have been sent down; because, in the Carriage, both the Padlocks were broken off (the staple only of one of them remaining, but the Ends so turned together close, as to be some security) and the Cords burst: such was the great Weight thereof. But in order to some further Security, I have caused another heavy Case to be laid upon it, until your further Pleasure may be known. All the things abovementioned, Mr Cuttle & I will put up to Morrow (God willing) into a Box, in careful Manner; & send the same up, by the next Higler. The Box wherein your Present to Mr Baker was; was in Mr Cuttle's Custody.[6] The Waggon will not go to Cambridge until Saturday; and I think it very expedient that he should have it by Christmass; & therefore will send it to morrow, with a Letter, & signifie unto him your Lordships Pleasure touching the 20 Guineas.

I am very glad to hear that Your Lordship hath gotten yet more fine books; & with them safe here; & the *Rationale* &c. well down again. The Date of the Tho. Aquinas, will be on the next Page; to which I shall add that of Your Old Latin Bible. I am glad also, that you have lett Noel have so much Money more.[7] He is a Strange Fellow indeed; but still Jones is worse. Your Lordship may now pretty well gess at the Teazing I have endured by them. Mr Garwood, as well as my self, present's his most humble Duty to our Most Noble Lady & to your very good Lordship. We hear that sweet pretty Miss ha's been Ill of late, in cutting more Teeth; but hope that all will go off, with & for the best.

My Lord, Christmass is now upon us in a Manner. I must in the first Place return your good Lordship Thanks for the fine Collar of Brawn, which you was pleased to Order for me, by Mr Twybill. I have given it to my poor Spouse; and as I understand, it will be delivered unto Her, to Morrow. It will last long, and never be touched but to my Noble Ladies Honor & Yours. Dr Tudway & his Fireside will participate thereof more than others; which will not be ungratefull unto him, in this Time of His Necessity. My Lord, I must also return you my most humble & hearty Thanks, for the Confidence you have been pleased to place in me, in seeking after the Things you have sent for. Indeed, I behaved my self, just in the same manner as I should have done, had

---

[6] A piece of plate.

[7] Harley wrote (21 Dec.) that he had paid Noel £700 since coming to town.

you been present. But the thing look's so kindly to me, that I esteem it above all the great Favors that You ever conferred upon me. Yet, my Lord, I must again say, tis almost Christmass, & we are grown out of Money. Out of the last Bill, Pembroke-hall had 15s & Mr Baker a Guinea, besides incidental Charges during my stay in Cambridge. I must therefore earnestly intreat your Lordship to lett me have £30 for we want many things Necessary; and are to pay one 5£ of Course. I shall therefore humbly desire your Lordship to Lett me have two Notes, one of 5£ and the other of £25 and to give me leave upon receipt of the Bills to go to Cambridge for two or three days; in Order to putt my poor Affairs there, into proper Order. The Accompt between your Lordship & Me, is now grown long, not having been adjusted since the last April: but I have all particulars down in Black & White, & keep all my Vouchers. If it would suit with Your Lordships Conveniency I shall rejoice to receive the Notes I desire by the first Post; who am, as eternally bound in Gratitude,

　　My Noble Lord,
　　　　Your most faithful, & most obliged, humble servant
　　　　　　　　　　　　　　　　　　　　Humfrey Wanley.

I am got up somewhat above half-way up Class X.

MS: Welbeck Wanleyana = British Library, Loan 29/258. *Date*: 'Wymple 23 December 1716.'

190. *To* Edward Harley *3 January 1717*

May it please your Lordship,

　My Coming hither was to kill two Birds with one Stone; to See my Poor Spouse, & to Buy the Mourning you was pleased to Give me. I began the last first, by fixing upon a Cloth at My honest friend Mr Mortlocks, before I saw her, although I did afterward consult her touching the Trimming. The Taylor had the Cloth that same Hour, & all things got Ready as soon as might be; and still I am here. The boy brought Scrub this morning as I bad him, but I could not go, the Taylor having disappointed me, & broken his promise. The Wascoat, indeed was ready for me, but I look'd I know not how in it. It is very short (although he hath had Cloth sufficient) and the Ends of the Sleeves hold not out to their proper Place, by 3 Inches, at least. I could not but look on my self as a sort of Punchanello, or an Overgrown Boy in it. The Taylor is as Vain & Proud, & Conceited, as the most fantastical Man of the business; he ha's, however, promised to alter; but I perceive, is very angry. This Ridiculous man's Caprice keep's me here till Saturday, although I have done my business.

On Tuesday I attended at Pembroke-hall, after many Invitations, the last being made in form, by the Master and Society. There, among others, I met Sir Clement Cotterel, Mr Slater, & Dr Paske.[1] Your Lordships Health was drank very affectionatly; and afterwards, in the Common-Room, repeated with the Noble Additions of my Lady, pretty Sweet Miss, my Lady & Lord your Father, & of all your Noble Family.

Yesterday, I went to Mr Baker, who is most wonderfully pleased with your present, which I found standing on his Cabinet. I believe he design's an Inscription, & to leave it to his Family, as a perpetual Monument of Your Noble Friendship for Him. I paid him the 20 Guineas, & took his Receipt for the same; and I have gotten another small Parcel of him consisting of 5 folios; 13 4tos & 55 lesser books. They came to me late this day, so that Time will not serve for my taking a List of them now, by this Post; because most of them consist of divers Tracts bound up together. They are curious & valuable. I have promised that Your Lordship shall return him the same Number of other Books (among your Duplicates) of the same Sizes; to his Contentation, & Satisfaction. We are agreed; & by degrees, I will hope to get you every valuable book he ha's that You Want, or Like. May God Grant an Happy New Year, & many unto Your Lordship & all above-mentioned, in answer to the many zealous prayers of

Your Lordships most humble, faithful, & thankful servant

H. Wanley.

MS: Welbeck Wanleyana = British Library, Loan 29/204, fo. 529. *Date*: 'Cambridge, 3 January 1716.' *Address*: 'To The Right Honorable Edward Harley at Bath-Court, in the Royal Palace at St James's, Westminster.' *Printed*: *HMC Portland Papers*, v, pp. 523–4 (extracts).

[1] Sir Clement Cotterel (1685–1758), Fellow of Trinity Hall, Cambridge 1709, Master of the Ceremonies 1710; Thomas Slater (*c.*1665–1736), MP for Cambridge 1715, 1722–36; Thomas Paske († 1720), Fellow of Clare College, Cambridge 1698, MP for Cambridge University 1710–20.

191. *To* Edward Harley *10 February 1717*

May it please your Lordship,

Your Lordships kind letter came to me safe this afternoon; and to morrow, I will let Mr Baker know, that my Lady cannot spare the Ass for Dr Ferrari,[1] as desired; because She shall have occasion to use it, Her Self. I will do it as handsomly, as I can; because I fear that Mr Baker (notwithstanding what he hath written) will think that the Ass might have been lent, untill Her Noble Ladiships Return.

The last time I went to Cambridge, upon Second Thoughts, I took with me the Greatest part of the Catalogue I have now made, & shewed it to Mr Baker, with desire that he would help me with his Notes, where I have been at a loss: but to lett me have the same back again with me, without suffering any person to see those Papers. I had his Promise; and before I returned hither, did receive the said Papers from Him. His Judgement on them is, that it is a Good Catalogue; that although it be the first Draught, it is fit to serve instead of one fairly written. He hath given me (according to my earnest desire) a paper wherein I find the Authors of some Anonymous Tracts: and saith, that he hath found Help equivalent, from what I have specified in the same Catalogue, of which he was not before apprised. He desired also, to borrow of your Lordship, for some short time *Peter Wentworth's book, I.L.27. Gabr. Harveij Smithus, &c. IV.H.19. Histoire de l'Imprimerie & dela Librarie, &c. X.D.2.*[2] I should have mentioned these in my last; but though they were in my head when I began to write, I forgot the Article before I had done; for which I beg his & your Noble Lordships pardon. But I desire your Leave to send them unto him, as soon as may be.

When I saw him last, I had a desire to look upon the MSS. in that College Library; I saw some of them, and among others, took Notice

---

[1] Dominick Ferrari († 1744), incorporated LL D from Naples 1710. Tutor and Library Keeper to Thomas Coke of Norfolk, afterwards Earl of Leicester.

[2] According to Wanley's catalogue of ptd. books at Wimpole (BL Lansdowne MS 816): Peter Wentworth, *Exhortation to Her Majestie for Establishing Her Successor to the Crowne* (1598), *STC* 25245; Gabriel Harvey, *Smithus, vel Musarum Lachrymae pro obitu D. Thomae Smithi* (1578), *STC* 12905; [Jean de la Caille], *Histoire de l'Imprimerie et de la Librairie jusque'en 1689* (Paris, 1689). While Wanley's catalogue was in his possession, Baker seems to have taken from it a list of Harley's most valuable bibles: see CUL MS Mm.i.50, Baker's interleaved copy of Maunsell's *Catalogue of English Printed Bookes* (1595), pp. 399–408.

of a Deed, which being given to Mr Baker by his Bookseller, he gave to the Place. It is an Original, Dated A.D. 1075 containing the Acts of the Council Holden at London in that Year, & Signed by those who were Assessors therein. It is Printed in the Second Vol. of Sir Henry Spelman's Councils, but not correctly; nor from any Original.[3] To your Lordship it is very Valuable, as giving you the Acts of a great Synod, Authentically; a Date of an Hand of that Antiquity; & the Hands or Signs of our most Eminent Church-men of that time. I desire to know Your Lordships Noble pleasure; whether I may not write to Dr Jenkin the Master, to procure an Exchange between You & the College for this Old Parchment, for some Duplicate Book, or a small matter (suppose a Guinea) in money. In Order to this I have already Mr Baker's Consent; who will declare himself willing that Your Lordship should have it.

My Lord, in your Catalogue I am gotten into page 161, and have dispatched the Shelf XV.C. whose last running Number is 4452. When this Class shall be finished, I must begin the Next, where your Collection of English Bibles will be the First Books that occurre. I have already altered the Course of your Books, almost all along, I hope for the better; they having not been putt up (as they say) for good & all. In that, I thought I had no need of fresh Directions, because I made the same Number of Books serve for the same Shelf, unless the Shelf was over-crammed, or not full. But here the Matter is otherwise; your Collection of English Bibles, is dispersed about two Classes; and perhaps, in other Rooms of the House: and it may be, some may lie in Cases yet either unopened, or unobserved by me. My Mind is not to give my self unnecessary trouble in this particular; and yet, I would willingly that your Bibles should stand with as much regularity (both as to Date & Assise) as they will well admit of. In Order to this, I desire your Lordship to apprise me of your Pleasure as soon as may be; that being my Rule.

I have a great Mind that you should have the fine Bible you saw at St John's College, among their MSS., and have spoken to Mr B. about it, who will willingly serve you therein. It is by much the finest Book of

---

[3] St John's College, Cambridge MS L.9 = M. R. James, *A Descriptive Catalogue of the Manuscripts of St John's College, Cambridge* (Cambridge, 1913), no. 236. An eleventh-century charter, contemporary with the Council according to James, who thinks the signatures of the subscribers may be autograph. Ptd. H. Spelman, *Concilia*, ii (1664), p. 7, D. Wilkins, *Concilia* (1737), i, pp. 363–4.

the English Nation of its kind; and but one more that dare in the least to enter into competition with it; & that, not to be had for any Money whatsoever. The College know not when, nor of whom, nor how, they came by it; which will make for you. Your Lordship heard that they have been bidden a good Sum for it, but refused the same. I would willingly have this in your Collection (now while I have friends there) and am of Opinion, with Mr B. that for a Duplicate of the same Impression, your Lordship making up an Equivalent to them in Money, for their Library, you may Compass it; if you lay hold on the present Opportunity.[4] Upon your good Lordships Intimation, I will send for some Lemons from Cambridge to morrow, and (in your own other materials) communicate the same to your Principal Servants here, of both Sexes, in Honor of our most Noble Lady, pretty sweet Miss, & Your Noble Lordship, & of all Your Illustrious Family: This shall be done according to the Duty of Mr Garwood, and

Your Lordships most humble & most faithful servant

Humfrey Wanley.

MS: Welbeck Wanleyana = British Library, Loan 29/204, fo. 532. *Date*: 'Wympole, 10 Febr. 1716/7.' *Address*: 'To The Right Honorable Edward Lord Harley, at Bath-Court in the Royal Palace at St James's Westminster.' *Printed*: HMC *Portland Papers*, v, pp. 524–5 (extracts).

192. *To* Edward Harley *16 June 1717*

May it please your Lordship,

On Friday-afternoon last I concluded & shut up the First Volume of your Shorter Catalogue; and yesterday I sent the whole to Mr Baker; that I may have his help against the Anonymous or Pseudonymous Authors, especially those of Cambridge. I could have wished that You had followed my Advice with relation to Bishop Barlow's Books in the

---

[4] Wanley seems to have been rebuffed. Harley wrote: 'I am sorry you had no better success about the Bible, I do not doubt your endeavors were to the utmost, and deserved to have been better answered. I desire for the future that you will never have anything to do with any colledge or Hall in that university, or Oxford, upon account of getting any books printed or mss from them, by any way either by Gift, exchange or sale, they shall never come among my Books, nor will I have anything to do with them.' (Edward Harley to Wanley d. 19 Mar. 1717; Welbeck Wanleyana = BL Loan MS 29/249). I cannot identify the bible: the library possesses a number of possible candidates.

Bodleyan, & Queen's College Libraries at Oxford.[1] I attribute the no Regard had unto it, to be the natural Consequence of my Obscurity in Writing: for I believe you apprehended my request was, to send your whole Catalogue to Oxford, when finished, and at the same time, my mind was only to gain the Titles of their Anonymous & Pseudonymous Books, without letting them see a line of the same. Mr Baker ha's received it, and sent me the enclosed.[2] He does not know that I know Mr Dean Kennet, who ha's been my acquaintance above these twenty Years. I shall finish the Alphabet to your Catalogue as soon as I can; and soon after, I will enter upon an Index to the same; which I promise you, before-hand, shall be a good one: and this I say, as having little assistance from either University, but standing upon my own Bottom.

As to Mr Baker, I think soon to send him a letter, and one of your Duplicate Bibles of A.D. 1537[3] not by way of Gift, in your Name; but by way of Loan & Friendship, & then I will answer the inclosed, & desire him to save himself trouble. In the mean time, I again offer to your Lordships Consideration your business with Mr Anstis, Mr Mickleton, & Mr Warburton of Hexham, or else your Affairs will fall to the ground.[4] I know you are busy now; but if you invite Mr Mickleton to dine with you some day: it will quit cost. He lodge's at his Chambers in Coney-Court, in Gray's Inne, no. 14. Why may not you make this man your Friend, and take His Things? He Love's You & Your Family, and at this present time ha's a great Cargo by Him. I forbear the Detail of his Things at this time; because I would have him surprise you (as I was surprised this day was a Seven-night) with a Free-Offering. It grow's late; all the servants are gone abroad to take the Air, except one whome I have retained at 1s. price to carry this to the Tiger immediatly. So that I have no more time, than to add, that I (and Mr Garwood) am always, our most noble Ladies, pretty Misses, &

Your dear Lordships most humble, faithful, & obedient servant

Humfrey Wanley.

---

[1] Thomas Barlow (1607–91), Bodley's Librarian 1652–60, Provost of The Queen's College, Oxford 1658–77, Bishop of Lincoln 1675. Such of his books as were not in the Bodleian he bequeathed to the Univesity, the rest went to Queen's, where a new library was built to receive them. BL Harley MS 6466, a volume of miscellaneous Wanley material, contains (fo. 94ʳ) the beginning of an undated draft memorandum on the disposition of Barlow's books: fos. 80ᵛ–81ʳ may be a continuation of this.   [2] Not found.

[3] 'Matthew's version', the folio bible of 1537 (Darlow and Moule no. 34).

[4] For Anstis see no. 180 and n. 2; for Mickleton, no. 208 and n. 1; it is not clear what business with Warburton is referred to.

MS: Welbeck Wanleyana = British Library, Loan 29/204, fo. 546. *Date*: 'Wympole, 16 June 1717.' *Address*: 'To The Right Honorable Edward Lord Harley at Bath-Court, within the Royal Palace of St James, Westminster.' *Printed*: HMC *Portland Papers*, v, pp. 527–8 (extract).

193. *To* George Holmes *11 September 1717*

Dear Sir,

By drinking bad wine, after I went from the Genoa-Armes the last night, I have found my self much disorder'd in my Head this day. But that is not the principal Cause of my Absence from your good Society[1] this Evening. I am now with my son & Daughter in Law, who invited my Spouse & me to come to them this Day. Here are also five more of our Common Friends; and I not being very well, all are unwilling that I should go abroad any where but home. However, I send you the old book (now my Lords) which I desire may be returned by the Bearer, whom I will order to tarry for it (an hour or two) untill Mr Talman[2] and all the other Gentlemen there present shall have sufficiently viewed it. It is a Lectionary of an old Benedictine Monastery in Germany.[3] The Arch Bishop at the End may represent St Hanno for ought I now know. As for him at the beginning I know him not, unless he be a person mentioned in an Evangelical Parable; which I the rather suspect by reason of the Inscription in his Book VOCA OPERARIOS ET REDDE ILLIS MERCEDEM. I am to send it, with many other Books into the Countrey to morrow; in the mean time, & always, I am with sincere Respect, all the Worthy Gentlemens of your Company, &

Good Sir,

Your own most faithful & humble Servant

Humfrey Wanley.

---

[1] The revived Society of Antiquaries. Wanley, together with John Talman and Bagford, was an original founding member of the Society of Antiquaries, which first met 5 Dec. 1707 but lapsed after 20 Feb. 1708. A (presumably later) draft of proposals for the constitution of a Society of Antiquaries ('an Antiquity Society') in Wanley's hand is in BL Harley MS 7055, fo. 3 f.; it appears to be directed to Edward Harley—at any rate Wanley clearly intended a close connection between the Society and the Harleian Library. Wanley's grandiose scheme (it is ptd. by Joan Evans, *A History of the Society of Antiquaries* (Oxford, 1956), pp. 40–4) came to nothing; but the Society was revived at a meeting at the Mitre Tavern, Fleet Street, in July 1717, when Wanley was one of twenty-three present. For the early history of the Society, see Evans, chs. iii, iv.

[2] John Talman († 1726), amateur artist, first Director of the Society of Antiquaries.

[3] Not identified.

MS: British Library, Add. 28167, fo. 42. *Date*: '11 Septr 1717.' *Address*: 'To Mr George Holmes, at the Mitre-Tavern in Fleetstreet, with a parcel.'

194. *To* [Arthur Charlett] *12 April 1718*

Reverend Sir,

    I earnestly beseech you to Pardon & Forget my so long Silence: Indeed I have been, & still am so busy, that (I believe) I have written no Letter, since my last to your Self, except one lately to my Lord of Chester,[1] by my Lord Harleys particular Command. Indeed I should not have Trespassed so long upon your Patience, but that I had before fully apprised Mr Isted of your Business; who is altogether of my Opinion, That it will be best to receive Pecuniary Satisfaction from Kemp, according as upon my Evidence, it shall be agreed between Him & Kemps Council.[2]

    Mr Will Thomas[3] is extremely Thankful for the many & great Favors you was pleased to shew him at Oxford: and will for ever be ready to shew his Gratitude for the same.

    My Lord Harley will soon be in Oxford; it will much rejoice me to hear that you have seen Him.[4]

    I return thanks for the inclosed specimen of Trivet.[5] I know Dacier's Spicilegium, & Trivet therein.[6] We have two MSS. of Trivet in the Library; but the best, I have heard, is that in the Library of

---

[1] Francis Gastrell (1662–1725), Canon of Christ Church, Oxford 1703, Bishop of Chester 1714. He had been chaplain to Robert Harley in 1700, when Harley was Speaker of the House of Commons.

[2] Kemp had died 19 Sept. 1717 and difficulty had arisen over Charlett's interest in the Roman coins which Kemp had been collecting on his behalf for some years: see Charlett to Wanley d. 5 Dec. 1717 (BL Harley MS 3778, fo. 37), 10 Feb. 1718 (BL Harley MS 3778, fo. 41), no. 200 n. 2, and no. 217. Isted seems to have been acting as counsel for Charlett (BL Harley MS 3778, fo. 39).

[3] William Thomas (1676–*c*.1765), secretary to Robert Harley; revised John Dart's biography of Chaucer for Urry's edn. of Chaucer's works (1721), completed by Thomas's brother Timothy after Urry's death.

[4] BL Harley MS 7055 contains (fo. 48) a memorandum drawn up by Wanley, d. 11 Apr. 1718, of books etc. to be seen, apparently by Edward Harley, on a journey to Salisbury, Bath, Wells, Oxford, and elsewhere, and suggestions for books he is to attempt to procure from Longleat, the Bishop of Bath and Wells etc. At fo. 45 is a list of books to be seen at Oxford, and probably part of the same memorandum.

[5] The 'specimen' contains proposals for a new edn. by Anthony Hall (1679–1723), Fellow of The Queen's College, Oxford 1706, who pbd. *Annales sex Regum Angliae* (Oxford, 1719), and a continuation in 1722.

[*See p. 384 for n. 6*]

Merton College.⁷ In my poor Opinion, there are divers Tracts un-
published, which deserve to see the Light sooner than a Second
Edition of Trivet.

I am not unapprised of Mr Hearne's Affair.⁸ If he hath, by much
unnecessary Painstaking, pulled down the Resentments of His
Friends & Superiors; He must Thank Himself. Indeed somewhat was
necessary to be done, even in Defence of Your Selves; and this on
several Respects. As for Will. of Newbury; there is about as much need
of Reprinting him now, as of Trivet. I am always,

    Reverend Sir,

      Your very much obliged, & humble servant

                        Humfrey Wanley.

MS: Bodleian, Ballard 13, fo. 137. *Date*: 'West-Minster, 12 April, 1718.'

195. *To* Samuel Palmer¹ *22 June 1718*

Sir,

Upon your very kind offer of Serving my Noble Lord Harley, in the
East, with Relation to old Manuscripts, I cannot but lett you hereby
know, that I am sure your Good Will & Endeavors in this Behalf, will
be accepted in the Kindest & most Thankful Manner. And that
although his Lordship be now absent, I know his Mind so well, as to
say that the following things will be acceptable unto Him.

⁶ Luc d'Achery, *Veterum aliquot scriptorum spicelegium*, 13 vols. (Paris, 1657–77); Trivet
in vol 8 (1668), p. 411 f.

⁷ The Trivets in the Harleian Library are BL Harley MS 29 and perhaps Harley
4322, a seventeenth-century transcript. The Merton Trivet is presumably Merton
College MS 256 (F. M. Powicke, *The Medieval Books of Merton College* (Oxford, 1931),
no. 1248).

⁸ Apparently Hearne's pricing of his edn. of Camden's *Annales rerum Anglicarum et
Hibernicarum Regnante Elizabetha* (Oxford, 1717), at 40s. had scandalized Oxford to such
an extent that the Vice-Chancellor forbade his printing his next work (William of New-
burgh's *Historia Sive Chronica Rerum Anglicarum*) at the Theatre (BL Harley MS 3778,
fo. 41ᵛ). But it appears that his preface to Camden also caused offence (Harley 3778, fo.
43). *Historia Sive Chronica Rerum Anglicarum* was nevertheless pbd. (Oxford, 1719). See
Macray, pp. 186–9.

¹ Samuel Palmer, merchant in Cyprus. He appears in Wanley's 'Notes of Things
proper for the Library in the Hands of Particular Persons': 'Mʳ Sam. Palmer in Cyprus,
ha's Collected some Greek MSS. for my Lord; & did promise to give him two
ἀλάβαστρα.' (Wanley's Memorandum Book, 1721, BL Lansdowne MS 677, fo. 3; ptd.
Wanley, *Diary*, p. 427.)

I. The Antient Greek Bible at Teflis.[2] Which he would have by all means. Such a book being what his Lordship principally Wants. Here you may be pleased to observe, that His Lordship is willing to buy all the Greek Manuscripts that can be gotten, let their Subjects be what they will, both Antient and Modern, upon Paper or Parchment, provided they come cheap. Herein you must be the Judge, how far to go, upon the Appearance that the Things make. If you think the Prices exorbitant, at any time, the Things may be lett alone.

II. In Case of Duplicates, they may be still bought notwithstanding; because one Book may help out another, and in this Case, Store is no sore. My Lord know's that Psalters, Gospels, & all books relating to the Greek Ecclesiastical Service, are extremely Common, and consequently will come for Little.

III. His Lordship would buy as many MSS. of the Gr. Heathen Writers, as can be gotten though they should happen to be Dear.

IIII. His Lordship would have a good old Synodicon, or two, or more. That is a Large Volume or more of the Greek Councils.

V. The Works of the Greek Fathers you will find plentiful & Cheap.

VI. The Greek Historians & Lawyers, my Lord would have, as many as can be gotten.

VII. Get as many Copies of the Old Testament, & of St Pauls Epistles, & of the other Epistles & of the Apocalypse, in Greek as may be.

VIII. If a Greek book is torn, or other wise in bad condition, do not reject it. Even Fragments may be welcome, to us, who know how to render them useful.

IX. Be pleased to insert a paper into each Book, specifying the Place, where, & time when bought, & of whom; and all remarkable Traditions especially concerning the Bible abovementioned, & other Valuable books.

X. My Lord would have as many Greek Charters or Old Deeds, with (or without) their Seals, and Greek original Letters, as may be Had. Such things are to be found in Monasteries, Cathedral Churches, and in Private Families.

XI. By way of Cairo, & Alexandria, you may meet with more Greek MSS. and also others in Coptic; & a Samaritan Pentateuch or two: A Book with the Hieroglyphics of the old Ægyptians, would be received as a great Rarity.

---

[2] See again Wanley, *Diary*, p. 77(7). This manuscript cannot be identified with any manuscript now extant: see *Diary*, p. 77 n. 4.

XII. Get as many Coptic & Syriac MSS. as may be: especially Histories and Books of the Scripture.

XII. My Lord would be glad of a Georgian Bible in MS. upon Velum, as old as may be: and of an old one in Armenian upon Velum. If these can't be had: those upon Paper must serve: with others of their Historical books, and a good Copie of the Georgian Bible in Print, Bound after their best manner.

XIII. A book or two in the Mendaean Language; and in any of the Tartar-Languages will be wellcome.

XIV. Good Histories, and Original Letters in any language will be welcome; and any piece of Antiquity of Marble, Brass, &c. The Price of any Parcel shall be paid to Mr Granger upon arrival of the Things.

MS: Welbeck Wanleyana = British Library, Loan 29/260 misc. 71; draft, unsigned. *Date*: '22 June 1718.' *Address*: 'Instructions for Mr. [Samuel] Palmer, about to sett forward to Persia.' *Endorsed*: 'The fair Draught (being much-what in the same words with this, was delivered to Mr Samuel Palmer, 22 June 1718. Who hath promised to Execute every Article thereof faithfully, to the best of his Power.'

196. *To* Nathaniel Noel[1] *18 October 1718*

You have now reviewed this Numerous & Fine Collection of Books; which, as you know, belonged to a very Noble Family.[2] 'Tis easy to see that the Names & Armes of so many Noble Personages as remain in, or upon them, will render them, by far, more Vendible than other Copies. And if you shall take the late Dukes Armes from the lesser & inferior Books, & clap them upon others: you will find those others also to go off at a Price much more advanced.

Here are (according to my Computation) Folios, 1004; Quartos, 689; Octavos, &c. 1414, besides Imperfect Volumes or single Books damaged, which run in without any price. My Lord saith, that of these

[1] *Fl.* 1681–c.1753. He was the bookseller chiefly employed by Harley, both for purchases in the English market and, through his agent George Suttie, on the Continent. See Wanley's *Diary*, *passim*, for Wanley's transactions with him. For an account of the MSS acquired by him for Harley through his foreign agent George Suttie, see C. E. Wright in *Cultural Aspects of the Italian Renaissance*, ed. Cecil H. Clough, pp. 473–5.

[2] The Duchess of Newcastle, Lady Henrietta Harley's mother, had died on 24 Dec. 1716, and this led to the removal of the Holles library from the family seat, Welbeck Abbey, Nottinghamshire. Harley kept all the manuscripts and such printed books as he wanted. Wanley's computation (d. 7 Oct. 1718) of the balance of saleable books is found with this *aide-mémoire* (misc. 72(a)). See Wright's account of the business, Wanley, *Diary*, pp. xl–xlii.

Folios, many are worth several Pounds apiece; and that among the others, divers there are worth 20 shillings a book & more: and others of great & good Value, according to their respective Contents, Editions, & Conditions. And his Lordships Opinion is, that considering the Great Number of Historical & other most Valuable books in this Collection, which seldom or never do appear, in public Sales, that his 689 Quartos, with the 1414 Octovos & lesser books, will easily make good his 1004 Folios, to the Value of £1000 at least; and he doe's not doubt, but that you know how to vend them at a much greater Sum. Nevertheless, since He promised you the pre-emption, before all others; He is pleased to ask no more than £800 for them; which Price is much lower than that which he thought to have insisted upon.

If He bidd's too unreasonably low; Say, My Report of Offers so unequal & so little expected, after my Lords great Condescension, would look like a Consent to it: and as if, indeed, I had taken private Money of Him. Look you Mr you know the Whole Family have their Eies upon You. If you do not behave your self so as to prevent their Clamors, they will undoubtedly exclaim upon as an unworthy Man, & not fit to be dealt with hereafter. They have not hindred Lord Duplin from Trading with you;[3] and I know my Lord ha's promoted your Interest when he could have hurt it. This Noble Family can help you as to Lord Somers's Books;[4] and as to the Cambridge Duplicates you cannot have them without my Lord.[5] You ought therefore, upon this great Occasion, bid so handsomly as that they may not believe the Reports that go of you, to be true.

If he continue still resty & stubborn; Say, Why, you know that twas my Lord who first brought you into a Name & Repute. You know He gave you too much for Fowkes's Books.[6] He ha's bought of you many Books of Hickes,[7] Payne,[8] Dorrington,[9] &c. which would have been

---

[3] George Hay, 7th Earl of Kinnoull († 1758), styled Viscount Dupplin 1709–19, when he succeeded to the title; MP for Fowey 1710; he married Abigail, younger daughter of Robert Harley by his first wife, in 1709.

[4] John Somers (1651–1716), Lord Chancellor 1697. His library stayed in his family. See no. 178 n. 3.

[5] Perhaps duplicates from Harley's library of ptd. books at his Cambridgeshire seat, Wimpole Hall.

[6] Phineas Fowke or Fowkes (1638–1710), physician and theologian, Fellow of Queen's College, Cambridge 1658, MD 1668. He practised in London for some years and died at Little Wyrley Hall, Staffordshire.

[7] Hickes had died 15 Dec. 1715. Noel bought his library 17 Dec. 1715 (see his Memorandum Book, BL Egerton MS 3777, under that date) and offered Harley first refusal of individual items. Harley purchased chiefly 'Septentrional' books.

[*See p. 388 for nn. 8 and 9*]

Shop-keepers. By His Influence, you bought Lanes,[10] Huttons,[11] Souths,[12] &c. from which he immediatly took great quantities off your Hands. He ha's been & yet continues the best of all your Customers; & you have gotten clearly by him as much Money as he asks for this Collection; and yet he Desire's none of your Ready Money, only that this Sum may be placed to Accompt, and He will soon clear off the rest.

You see how Noble my Lord ha's been to you. He ha's left you Extraordinary books; He lett's you have a Cavendish;[13] He will send up a Baronage:[14] He will try to get you a Rushworth (for he ha's not one complete, as yet, himself).[15] What would you further Desire? Pray, what do you do?

After the Bargain, oblige him to keep the Price secret from all persons whatever: or else not to own that he gave less than £1000 for them.[16]

As to the Dukes Name in his Catalogue; say, I suppose you'l use it if you be not forbidden.

MS: Welbeck Wanleyana = BL Loan MS 29/260 misc. 72(b). *Endorsed*: 'Heads to be insisted upon with Mr Noel upon the Sale of my Lords Welbeck-books, 18 October 1718.'

---

[8] Possibly William Payne (1650–97), Fellow of Magdalene College, Cambridge.

[9] Theophilus Dorrington (1654–1715), religious controversialist. See Hearne, *Collections*, iii, p. 127.

[10] Not identified.

[11] Noel's Memorandum Book, under 10 Aug. 1716, records his purchase of Hutton's ptd. books. See also Wanley, *Diary*, p. xxxix.

[12] Presumably Robert South (1634–1716), religious controversialist; Student of Christ Church, Oxford 1651, Rector of Islip, Oxford 1678.

[13] Perhaps George Cavendish, *Life of Cardinal Wolsey* (1641), on which see nos. 115, 214.

[14] Presumably Sir William Dugdale's *Baronage of England* (1675, 1676).

[15] John Rushworth, *Historical Collections of Private Passages of State, &c. 1618–48*, 7 vols. (1659–1701).

[16] Harley originally proposed a price of £600 (E. Harley to Wanley d. 9 Oct. 1718, Welbeck Wanleyana = BL Loan MS 29/249) and set £500 as his lowest price (Harley to Wanley d. 12 Oct. 1718, Welbeck Wanleyana = Loan 29/249). Despite Wanley's blandishments Noel seems not to have agreed to give more than £450 for the books (Harley to Wanley, 19 Oct. 1718, Welbeck Wanleyana = Loan 29/249). Yet in his Memorandum Book under 22 Oct. 1718 Noel records that he paid Harley £500 for 'a parcel of book wch came from Welbeck' (BL Egerton MS 3777, p. 42).

197. *To* [William Holman]¹ *27 January 1719*

Worthy Sir,

After my very hearty Thanks for the favor of your last kind Letter, I take this Opportunity of Mr Morleys Journey into your Parts, to lett you know that I have, according to your Desire, looked into the Chartulary of Dunmow, at the Beginning whereof there now remain's only One Entry concerning the Bacon, (or Pork) and that is in the Words next following,

Anno D*omi*ni m*il*l*esi*mo *quingentesi*mo *decim*o Thomas Ley, Fuller de Coggyshale in Com*itatu* Essex', venit *et* petit una*m* p*er*na*m* baconis de Dunmowe, videl*icet* octav*o* die Mens*is* Septenbr*is* in d*omi*nica anno R*egni* R*egi*s Henrici Octavi post *Con*questu*m* secu*n*do. Et jura*tus* fuit s*ecun*dum forma*m* donac*io*nis *et* cora*m* Ioh*ann*e Tyler, ad tunc pr*ioris* Loci predicti et eiusd*em* Loci *con*ventu*s*, et multor*um* alior*um* Vicinorum. Et lib*er*at*a* fuit eid*em* Thome vna*m* p*er*na*m* Baconis.

The Book in my Noble Lords Library is Marked thus, 42.C.12.² and I considering from what is above-written that the Custom was founded upon a particular Donation, was willing to search the Book for it, but hitherto in vain; after about five hours labor. But now, being gotten to the last Leaf save one or two, I find this other Entry.

M*emoran*d*um* qu*o*d quidam Ric*ard*us Wright de Badeburgh juxta Norwycu*m* in Com*itatu* Norf*olcie*, yoman, venit huc *et* petit le Bacon de Dunmowe, videl*icet* 17 die April*is* Anno R*egni* R*egi*s H*en*rici *Sex*ti post conq*uestu*m *vicesimo terti*o. Et juratus fuit s*ecun*dum formam Donac*io*nis p*re*dic*t*i, *et*c., coram Ioh*ann*e Canon, ad tunc Prioris loci p*re*dic*t*i et ejusdem loci Conve*n*tu *et* multorum alior*um* vicinor*um*. Et lib*er*at*um* fuit eidem Ric*ard*o vnu*m* Fleke de Bacon, *et*c.

By this inaccurate Entry it may seem that the Forma Donationis, was the Tenor of the Oath to be taken before the Bacon could be claimed: which Bacon nevertheless I conceive not to have been given

¹ William Holman (1670?–1730), Nonconformist minister of Halstead, Essex, antiquary and historian of Essex.
² BL Harley MS 662; Davis no. 318. Wanley marks the scribe's inaccuracies ('Septenbris', 'prioris', 'multorum', 'aliorum', 'Vicinorum', 'vnam', 'pernam') with a marginal *sic*.

by the Prior & Canons out of their own Singular Wantoness; but that what they did in this kind, was by Virtue of some agreement, and upon some Benefaction received. I find no other Entries to this your Purpose; but shall be glad to see you here in Town, that I may not only Shew you the book it Self, with others in your Way, as relating to Essex: but further, that upon your other Occasions, (as far as I am able) I shall act as will become Sir,

    your very humble & faithful Servant

                                 Humfrey Wanley.

MS: Essex Record Office, D/Y 1/1. *Date*: 'From my Lord Harleys house in Dover-street Westmr 27. January 1718/19.'

198. *To* William Holman *30 March 1719*

Worthy Sir,

    It is some time since Mr Morley delivered unto me your elaborate Collections relating to Pandfield[1] which hitherto I have not had leasure to peruse: but now, being about to Visit my poor old Mother in the Countrey, for about a Month or Six Weeks, my Noble Lord is pleased to allow me Time just to run it over; in doing which, as your honest true Friend, I take the Liberty of Suggesting the inconsiderable particulars following, to be received or thrown aside, according to your own good Pleasure.

Pag. 1.   In the Welsh Tongue *Pant* signifie's a Valley, and *Pen* a Head, or Top of a Hill. You will please to consider the Scituation of this Place whether it be Low or High, or upon an Hill. I believe that divers other Rivers in England & Wales are called *Pant*: as several Villages have the Name of *Panton*, which hath also been assumed by divers Families.

                       Puntfend; I quaere whether this should not be written Puntfeud? certainly, about the time of our K. Henry III, the Names of Persons or Places ending with *feld* were written with *feud*, of which usage, very many instances may be easily shewn.

[1] Panfield, near Braintree, Essex, Benedictine alien priory.

Pag. 2. line 9. *quod*. Should not this be *quam?* Yet, I own, it may be so written in Domesdei.

12. *modo*, doth not *modo* here & in the subsequent lines, signifie *Now?* that is, the Time when the Survey was made.

12, 13. *Semper 5 Carucatae Hominum*; I do not see that you have Translated these Words.

14. *Bordarij*, is this word commonly Englished *Borderers* as in pag. 3. lin. 3?

16. *restaurari*; doth not this signifie to be re-stocked?

pag. 3. lin. 18.*Hempsted*; should not this be *Hemsted?* and so elsewhere.

pag. 6. lin. 7. *Esq*: do you find him so stiled in his Life-time, or in his last Will?

pag. 7. lin. 7. *Pictur'd*; is not Cutt, Carved, or Engraven? (Figured)

pag. 6, & 7. The account of these Cottons is somewhat confused. Alice Langham was the Wife of John Cotton & Mother to Nicholas Cotton, her Eldest Son, who died A.D. 1500. She her self dies anno 17 Hen. VIII, leaving her Son Sigismund upwards of 4 years old. But if he was then not above 5 years old, how could he die anno 33 Hen. VIII, and leave William his Son then 33 years of Age?

pag. 11. lin. 12. is *Beak'd & Legg'd* the proper Heraldical Term?

pag. 14. lin. 12. *Chevernels* or Chevronelles?

pag. 15, & 16. *Willielmo*, &c. is it so written at length? I believe not. If it be contracted, it should be written Willelmo, &c.

pag. 18. lin. 7. *Hominum*; did not Homines signify a sort of feudatory Tenants?

8. *recepit*, doth not this verb refer to Libera femina?

10. *Servi*, Bond-men?

pag. 19. lin. 17. the *Hand* & Seal; I doubt whether Waleran's Hand was Set to his Deed.

3. *Essexa*; in my Lords Copie of the Cartae Antiquae in the Tower (marked in this Library 34.C.2 & 34.C.3.) it is Essessa at fol. 221,b. which may be the truer Reading.

5. *in* omnibus; my Lords copie saith *ab* omnibus.

6. *Walerandus*; in this book it is Walerannus, truer.

7. cum tota decima *sua* alterius Terrae; in this book it is sue alterius terre

8. Woddestrata; in the said Book Wodestrata; better.

pag. 22, lin. 4,5. Puntfend; I believe it should be Written in both places Puntfeud; the Marginal Citation is not clear to me.

24. lin. 12. *the Great Roll*; suppose it were expressed thus, *from a Roll written anno 11 Edw. III.* This distinguisheth it from the Great Roll of the same year & King, which is a Record in Westminster.

pag. 25. lin. 17. For what were. *Gold-Weights appointed*?

pag. 28. line 21. *Requie*; it should be Requiem: from the Verse, Requiem aeternam dona eis Domine, used in the Service of the Dead.

pag. 33. lin. 13. Saxon Characters; It is hardly probable that these Characters were Saxon, that is, what our Ancestors used before the Conquest, since you own the Language was French. I believe they might be English, but that is not now Material, and the Expression would be better left out.

pag. 34. lin. 1, 2. Gothic Characters; I do not believe them to be such as were used by the Goths, but a sort of English Hand which is well known, & properly called *Church-Text*. The same I mean also, against that Term, toward the bottom of the same Page.

Thus, in Obedience to your Command, I convince you that I have looked over your Treatise, which (as I can easily perceive) hath cost you very much Time & Pains; and thereby can gess what great Trouble you must needs be put to, in describing the several Manors, &c. of your whole County, as you have done these. But in Order to do so, I believe, you will find it absolutely necessary to come up to Town and Consult the Offices of Records & the several Libraries both in London & Westminster, where I can assure you many very valuable Materials for your good purpose do lie & remain, which will be best Seen by your own exacter Eies, & weighed by your own mature & solid Judgement. To give you one instance whereof, I can (from my Lords

Library) assure you that Pannfeld-Manor called the Priory, was granted (inter alia) to John Devereux for his Life. The Record of this, is in the Tower, 3 part. Pat. anno.22.R.2.m.18. There is also another, relating to the Church of Gerton, which was obtained by Pannsfeld & Wells, anno.48.E.3. besides multitudes of others which, in all probability, may be found there. And here, principally, (I mean, in Town) you will meet with Helps for Compiling a Series of the Priors of Pandfeld, & of other Religious Houses in your County, and for enlarging your Relations of Your several principal Families or Persons, & noted Places, with the most remarkable matters that have happen'd to them, or of Facts done there. And, in the mean time, you will have Time to polish & adorn the Style of your Work, to examin your Orthography or way of Spelling, and to add the wanted Points, &c. all along. Pray, Sir, take not these Hints unkindly from me who mean you very heartily well; and expose not to others Sight, what I so freely have written in Confidence of Secresy, & in private Friendship.

Since my last Letter, I have met with a Copie of the Third Entry about your Dunmow-Bacon, which was communicated by Mr John Stow A.D. 1604, to Mr Wever as I believe; and is not now to be found in my Lords Register of that Priory.[2] It is in the following Words, "Memorandum, quod quidam Stephanus Samuel de Ayston-parva in Com*itatu* Essex' Husband-man, venit ad Prioratum de Dunmowe die Nativitatis beate Marie, anno Regni Regis Edwardi quarti post Conquestum Septimo; et petijt Pernam Baconis: et jurat coram Rogero Bulcott tunc Priore, & Conventu istius Loci, et multitudine aliorum Vicinorum, liberata fuit eidem Stephano una Perna Baconis, &c." This Note is in one of my Lords MSS. inscribed 41.A.17, at fol.9.[3]

Upon occasion of your mentioning Thomas Bourgchier Archbishop of Canterbury, and his Gift of Pantfeld, I thought it not improper to inspect the Obituary of Christ-church of Canterbury (a very curious Manuscript in the Library of the Royal Society at Crane-Court, in Fleet-street)[4] and find that the Entrance made by that House upon his Obit, is only thus, "III Kal*endas* Aprilis.—Item obijt Reverendissimus in chr*ist*o pater & d*omi*nu*s*, d*omi*nu*s* Thomas Bowrschyre Tituli S*anc*ti Ciriaci in Termis, Sacro-sancte Romane Ecclesie Presbiter Cardinalis, et hujus Sancte Cantuariensis Ecclesie Archiepiscopus, qui contulit huic Ecclesie xxvii Capas de rubro Tessuto, (*Copes of*

[2] BL Harley MS 662; Davis no. 318.
[3] BL Harley MS 604.   [4] Now BL Arundel MS 68.

red Tissue?) cum toto apparatu pro Sacerdote, Diacono, & Subdiacono ejusdem Secte. (*of the same Suit, or Livery, or Fashion*) Item contulit Ecclesie quandam Ymaginem pulcherrimam de *Sancta* Trinitate, de Auro, cum Gemmis ornatam."

I forbear to be further troublesome unto you at this time; but with sincere & cordial Wishes for the continuance of your good Health, & that of your very worthy Friend the Generous Mr Morley, I remain
Sir,

Your most faithful, & very humble servant

Humfrey Wanley.

MS: Essex Record Office, D/Y 1/1. *Date*: 'From my Lord Harleys in Dover-street, Westminster, 30 March 1719.' *Address*: 'To Mr William Holman at Halstead in Essex.' *Endorsed*: 'Send to Mr Tindale.'

199. *To* Edward Harley *16 May 1719*

May it please your Lordship,

This Morning I had the Honor & Happiness of your Lordships very kind Letter,[1] which hath much revived my poor Spouses Spirits & mine, who were affraid that Letters might have miscarried. Yesterday in the Afternoon, Mr Edward Owen deliver'd unto me a Transcript of the Order which the City made in my Favor, this day was a Sennight; whereby they signified their Approbation of what hath been transacted between Mr Pickerne & me, after my own way, & without new Covenants.[2] This day I have seen a pretty parcel of old MSS, formerly belonging to the Monastery of Llanthony near Gloucester; which, if they will be sold, I hope will come to your Lordship.[3] My Wife dares not go to Oxford; and therefore, God willing, on Monday we shall sett

[1] 14 May 1719, Welbeck Wanleyana = BL Loan MS 29/249.
[2] This refers to a Coventry Council order d. 5 Mar. 1719, assigning the lease of a house, occupied by William Pickern, from Pickern and John Gifferd to Humfrey Wanley (Council Minute Book 1702–22, ref. A14(e) Jeaffreson). Edward Owen was town Clerk of Coventry for the first two decades of the eighteenth century. I am indebted for this information to Mr Anthony Davis.
[3] The only manuscripts in the Harleian collection from Llanthony (secunda), the Augustinian Priory of the BVM and St John the Baptist in Gloucestershire, or from the earlier foundation of Llanthony (prima), are BL Harley MSS 459–63, bought (together with others) from Peter Le Neve. But from a list in Wanley's hand d. 2 Feb. 1707 (Bodl. MS Rawl. D.888, fo. 45ᵛ) of books sold to Robert Harley, Wright (*Fontes*, under Peter le Neve) identifies only Harley 460, 461, and queries 463. All of 459–63 were bound in one vol. in the sixteenth century.

out for London; and I hope I shall on Thursday Morning attend your Lordship with my Wives Duty to our most Noble Lady & the dear Sweet one, & to your Lordship, & Service to Mr Prior[4] & the Honest Major, attended by my own in the same respectful & submissive manner: I being for ever, Your Lordships most Obliged servant

H. Wanley.[5]

MS: Welbeck Wanleyana = British Library, Loan 29/205, fo. 78ᵛ. *Date*: 'Coventre, 16 May 1719.' *Address*: 'To The Right Honorable Edward Lord Harley in Dover-street near Pickadilly, Westminster.' *Printed*: HMC *Portland Papers*, v, pp. 582–3 (summary).

200. *To* [Arthur Charlett] *14 June 1719*

[Rev]erend Sir,

Although I have been but seldome at the Genoa-Armes since my return from Coventre, yet I had the good Fortune to be there present, when the Post brought your very kind Letter of the 8th Instant.

I am very glad that my poor old Coins came safe; indeed my Nephew told me he hoped to have an Opportunity of sending them by the President of Magdalen College.[1] They are but few, and some of them in bad Condition; but I hope to send better in their stead; and in a little Time to augment the others with an Accession of fresh Heads, which I shall find out in Town if I can; or else beg of my Lord for you, when at Wympole, where he hath good store of Medals, as well Antient as Modern. And I doubt not of prevailing with His Lordship in this Matter; not only because I found him inclined to make John Kemp's Bargain good to you, in Case he had bought that Collection;[2]

---

[4] Matthew Prior (1664–1721), poet and diplomat. Harley was his patron and sponsored the sumptuous edn. of his collected poems (1719), said to have brought him 4,000 guineas—to which Harley added £4,000 of his own for the purchase of Down Hall, near Harlow, Essex. Prior was often resident at Wimpole and died there.

[5] On the reverse, apparently part of the letter, a long and detailed description of St Mary's Hall, Coventry, ptd. below, Appendix VIII.

---

[1] Joseph Harwar (1654–1722), President of Magdalen College, Oxford 1706.

[2] In his will Kemp directed that his collections should be offered to Robert Harley or to his son for £2,000. The offer was declined: Edward Harley wrote to Wanley, 15 Dec. 1717, 'I have enclosed our letter to mr Kempe wch I desire you will send him. We have set him at Liberty about his Brothers things' (Welbeck Wanleyana = BL Loan 29/249). The collection was sold at auction 23–7 Mar. 1721 in 293 lots for £1,093. 8s. 6d. Despite his first refusal, Harley had intended to purchase the whole collection at a later date, and did buy some items at the auction: see Wanley, *Diary*, p. 24(9) and n. 8.

but because I have often heard Him speak of you, both before
J. Kemps Decease, & Since, even lately, with much Decency,
Kindness & Respect.

Within a few Weeks I hope to be at Wympole, where his Lordship
hath lately built Five large Rooms for a Library, which I hope to fill
this Somer, with as Choice a parcel of Books as any in England.[3] Com-
parisons, I know, are Odious; and Two private Persons I know, who at
this present, can out-Number His Lordship;[4] but then in Value, they
are said to be much inferior. I speak abstractedly from my Lord
Oxfords Books, which if added to the others, would make such a
Collection, as perhaps England never yet knew. As my Lord Harleys
books are, they are the finest & most useful Collection mine Eies ever
yet beheld; and if all Library-Histories & Relations were to be
searched into; I believe it will not appear, that so valuable & numerous a Collection, amassed together within so small a s[p]ace of Time;
was ever, in any place, putt in Order at once. And what I here say, I am
persuaded will be allowed by such of the Litterati as shall come and
see them, when the Library shall be Open'd.

As for my poor Mother, I left her Well & seemingly hearty on the
18th ultimo on the 20th she was taken Sick, and on the 28th quietly
resigned up Her Soul to God who gave it, in the 88th year of Her Age,
her poor Lamp of Life being quite exhausted.[5]

Had I come to Oxford as I intended, I should have seen Mr
Bowles,[6] whom I have heard of from divers; and paid my Respects

[3] The Library at Wimpole was built to the designs of James Gibbs. For a description
of the Library and the Ante-library, see Royal Commission on Historical Monuments,
Cambridgeshire, i (1968), p. 221; a plan of the house faces p. 215; the Library and the Book
Room (= Ante-library) are illustrated, pl. 140. In the general account of the house
(p. 215), the RCHM dates the Library 1719–20, but on the evidence of this letter (and of
Wanley to Edward Harley, 20 June 1719) it should perhaps be 1718–19; the Book Room
appears to have been completed in 1716: see no. 184.

[4] Certainly Thomas Rawlinson (1681–1725), elder brother of Richard Rawlinson
(1690–1755) benefactor of the Bodleian; it is estimated that he owned about 200,000
vols., dispersed in sixteen sales between 1721 and 1734. The other, perhaps Charles
Spencer (1674–1722), 3rd Earl of Sunderland, Lord Privy Seal 1715, First Lord of the
Treasury 1718, who at his death had amassed at Althorp a magnificent library of 20,000
(chiefly printed) books.

[5] Wanley's bible (Welbeck Wanleyana = BL Loan MS 29/272), containing notices
in his hand about his family, records that his mother died 28 June 1719, not on 28 May as
the date of this letter implies. Charlett's letter of 'the 8th Instant', which would settle the
matter, does not appear to be extant. But Wanley left his mother well on 'the 18th
ultimo', which suits his remarks about departure from Coventry in his letter to Edward
Harley, 16 May 1719. It seems likely that the bible entry is in error rather than the date
of this letter.

[*See opposite page for n. 6*]

unto you, Sir, in the First Place, in Case of your being Resident in the College.

Some Time since, after Dinner, in discoursing about Books, His Lordship mentioned Domenico Fontana's Treatise about the Erecting the great Guglia near St Peters Church in Rome; and as if an Exemplar of it which he had lately seen, was in too bad a Condition for him to Buy. Hereupon, I said I knew a Gentleman who had one of Them, which I believed might be at His Lordships Service. I meant You, Sir, to whom I had the Honor to present it when at Oxford. And I do say, that if you would be pleased to pleasure my Lord with it, & the other Tracts bound up in that Volume; his Lordship will receive it as a particular Mark of your Esteem for Him. And I dare add further, that You shall not meet Kemps usage from my Lord; but you may name your Price in Money; or otherwise put me in a Way how you may be gratified otherwise, and it shall be done faithfully & readily. I crave your Answer hereupon soon; and that if you are willing to pleasure my Lord in this affair, that you would take the first Opportunity of the Carrier, and put the Book, well wrapp'd up in Paper, into a Convenient Box, for fear of its taking Wet.[7]

I was not privy to Mr Greenway's Business with the College; & saw him but once, while I was in the Countrey.

As to the New Edition of Dugdales Warwickshire, Mr Hurt told me it should contain about 30 Sheets of fresh Matter; and the Typographical Errata of the present Book be carefully Corrected. Hereupon, my Lord will Subscribe for one Copie of the Largest Paper.[8]

My Wife, I thank God, is in pretty good Health, and desire's you to accept of Her respectful Service; and so doe's He who shall always sincerely remain

Reverend Sir,

Your most faithful, & obliged humble Servant

Humfrey Wanley.

---

[6] Joseph Bowles (1694–1730), Fellow of Oriel College, Oxford 1719, Bodley's Librarian 1719–29.

[7] Domenico Fontana, *Della transportatione dell'Obelisco Vaticano, e delle fabriche di Nostro Signore Papa Sisto V* (Rome, 1590). Duly despatched to Wanley: see Charlett to Wanley d. 16 June 1719 (Welbeck Wanleyana = BL Loan MS 29/253).

[8] This 'new' edn. of Dugdale's *Warwickshire* (1st edn., 1656), apparently originating in Oxford, was not published.

For the future, you may please to direct for me at my Lord Harley's House in Dover-street near Pickadilly; & then, all Letters & Parcels will find me, wheresoever I shall be.

MS: Bodleian, Ballard 13, fo. 138. *Date*: '14 June 1719.'

201. *To* [Arthur Charlett] *20 June 1719*

Reverend Sir,

The other day, as I was sitting with my Noble Lord after Dinner, both your Letters of the 16th and 17th instant, were brought in.[1] And my Lord again renew'd those kind Expressions, which I have heard him use, in respect of you, multitudes of Times. He was exceedingly pleas'd to hear that You comply'd so readily with my proposal of obliging him with that Book;[2] with that readiness I say; for since my last, we have found another fine Copie of it out; in the hands of a friend of Yours & Mine, who hath nothing but what is at my Lords Command. Yesterday morning early, my Noble Lady & my Lord sett out for Wympole, (as 'tis said) to see how their Workmen in or about the Chapel, Library, Stair-case, Garden, &c. go on; and are expected up soon. As to the Library there, the books are all in heaps upon the Ground, & some Waggons Loads are here to be sent down & added to them, so that the great Work of putting all in Order, will not begin suddenly; nor when it is begun, can I now (the Summer being so far advanced) tell when the Library will be open'd. But notice you shall have of it from me, God willing. I shall take care to look after the Box, if it be not sent to Dover-street; and, as I assured you in my former, you shall not find your self trifled with by my noble Lord, although (to my great grief) John Kemp trifled both with you & me. I desire to know what will be acceptable unto you, and in what manner? a fine book, a piece of Plate, or what, or how? For I observe, that although you esteemed the book, as very well understanding its worth, yet, like a Gentleman, being informed that it would do my Lord a pleasure; you kindly sent it up immediatly, & without bargaining. I am therefore, and ever was, and always shall be of Opinion, that such generous Proceedings, should meet with the most handsome Returns.

I have not yet seen mine old Friend Mr Denison since he came to

---

[1] Welbeck Wanleyana = BL Loan MS 29/253.　　　[2] See no. 200 n. 7.

Town; nor Mr Isted of late: but I remain always, as my poor Spouse does,

Reverend Sir,

Your most humble, & most obliged servant

Humfrey Wanley.

I unfeignedly wish you a good journey to, benefit by, & a safe return from, the Bath; & shall, God willing, be sure to answer your first Letter; tho' I've little time.

MS: Bodleian, Ballard 13, fo. 139. *Date*: '20 June 1719.'

202. *To* [John Gibson?][1] *7 July 1719*

Good Sir,

I have looked upon the little parcel of MSS & Printed books, which you so punctually sent to my Lord's yesterday, according to your Promise; and like the greatest part of them, well enough. Since I saw you, I have reflected a little about what you related to me concerning Mr Smith, of Venice.[2] Namely, that he value's his Collection of Books

---

[1] John Gibson, a Scottish book dealer with agents in Italy, who for the next several years supplied Harley with manuscripts and early ptd. books acquired there. See Wanley, *Diary*, Biographical Index under Gibson, and n. 2 below; for an account of purchases made by Gibson for Harley, 1720–6, see C. E. Wright in *Cultural Aspects of the Italian Renaissance*, ed. Cecil H. Clough, pp. 463–8.

[2] Joseph Smith (?1674/6–1770), lived in Venice for nearly 70 years, from 1744–60 as British Consul. See Wanley, *Diary*, Biographical Index under Smith. During that time he accumulated and offered for sale at least three libraries rich in manuscripts—a fourth was sold in 1773 at Sotheby's after his death. Gibson acted as intermediary in negotiations between Smith and Harley for two collections of manuscripts: (1) 121 MSS, offered to Harley in a letter from Smith to Gibson d. 11 Oct. 1720 (BL Lansdowne MS 841, fo. 98), for £1,500. Wanley thought the price 'horribly extravagant' (*Diary*, p. 74(7)) and seems to have responded with a lower bid, which Smith refused (*Diary*, p. 85(1)). Wanley had already heard a month before (17 Dec. 1720) that the collection had been bought by Charles Spencer, 3rd Earl of Sunderland, for £1,500 (*Diary*, p. 78(5)), at whose house Wanley viewed them 6 Feb. 1723 (*Diary*, p. 187(7)). (2) 101 MSS examined by Wanley, 5 Oct. 1722 (*Diary*, p. 163(6)). Negotiations about these went on intermittently for nearly four years (see *Diary*, p. 161 n. 1) before they were returned to Italy (*Diary*, p. 403(3)).
It may be that the collection of 'Classical Authors' referred to in this letter substantially comprises the 121 MSS in (1) above. If so, the discrepancy between the £600 of this letter and the £1,500 asked fifteen months later is hard to explain. In a letter to Wanley (d. 14 Nov. 1720; Welbeck Wanleyana = BL Loan MS 29/250) about the 121 MSS for £1,500, Harley comments: 'I think they dont come up to what my expectations was raised to. The number of Greek is not great, nor is the whole number so great as might

at about £2400; it being particularly curious, and the Books chosen with admirable Judgement. That among them, the Manuscripts are very considerable, not only for their Beauty, but for their Number & Value. That, in this Parcel of MSS. all the Classical Authors, both Greek & Latin, are to be found, both those in Greek, as well as those in Latin. That particularly the Homer, & the Dante, are very finely written and Illuminated; as many others which you did not then numerically Mention. That Mr Smith was willing to deliver up this Parcel of Manuscripts Classical, consisting of above One Hundred distinct books, or Volumes; besides certain other MSS. containing many pieces of the works of the Fathers, both in Greek & Latin, at the Price of Six Hundred Pounds.

As to this, my Lord is pleased hereby, to give you thanks for remembring him at so great a Distance; and further, to buy such of the books you have now sent in, as he shall find most in his way, at honest & reasonable price. As to Mr Smith's MSS. your Proposal (being made in his Name) doth somewhat embarass him. Not the Sum of £600: which (though always a great Sum of Money to You or Me) his Lordship, nevertheless, can easily spare, at this, or at any other time. But the difficulty lies here: How can his Lordship be assured that this Parcel can prove to be worth so great a Sum, and Order them to be sent forthwith, upon this only Report that you have made? His Lordship cannot yet be induced to believe that all the Works of the Classical Authors, both Greeks & Latins, are to be seen in Mr Smiths Collection: because almost all Libraries help one another; and in that Respect, he know's of no one Library in the World, compleat; nor doe's believe that his own (although now, very considerable) is, or ever can be absolutely compleated; so as to want no one Classical piece, at this time, actually in being, in one place or other. Yet he would be willing to commend Mr Smith's Industry, if he adds to his yet growing Collection, as many MSS. really antique, curious, & valuable because useful, as soon as he conveniently can; not doubting, but that if he well look's about him, the number even of his Classical MSS. will be thereby augmented. The Price, being such a Sum, his Lordship (as I hinted before) cannot absolutely agree to, just ἐν τῷ νῷ, untill he

be expected. 121 MSS is not so great considering the number of years it is said they were collecting . . . I should be glad to give £500 for them but no more.' More than two dozen manuscripts once owned by Smith are now in the King's collection in the British Library.

shall be apprised by Mr Smith, what he may fairly expect to meet with, in the Bargain, for his Money. Mr Smith therefore would do well (as all others do in this Case) to send over His Lordship a Catalogue of his MSS. of all kinds;[3] and therein, begin with Running Numbers, as 1, 2, 3, &c. answering to the same Sett in or upon the Books. In this Catalogue also (which need not be Spun out into a great length) he may specify the Authors Name, or Names, the several Tracts contained; the Antiquity of the Book, according to its Date, or his own best Information & Judgement. A short Specimen (in 3 or 4 Lines each) of such of the Hands as He shall judge to be most antient & singular. A short Account of the book, as whether of Parchment or Paper; of what Size, as in greater, midling, or small Folio, &c. whether if written with many Abbreviations; or in fine, plain & loose Hand. How Illuminated, or otherwise adorned; or otherwise what its condition may be, with respect to Worms & Water. What Number of Leaves is comprehended in each Book; and such like Notices, as may convey proper Ideas to his Lordship, of these Things, although he be at so great a Distance. Without such Notices no Man will part with the Price demanded; and if the Things by such a Catalogue can be made reasonably appear to be worth it, between Man & Man, I believe my Lord will accept of them & Pay the Money.

MS: Welbeck Wanleyana = British Library, Loan 29/258; fair copy, unfinished. *Date*: '7 July 1719.'

203. *To* [Arthur Charlett] *29 September 1719*

Reverend Sir,

The first certain News I had of your Return to Oxford, was from your own Letter dated the 23 Instant.[1] I had a mind, indeed, to have return'd you thanks, at the Bath, for sending the books to my Lord, according to my Desire: but was hindred by some Misinformation which came to my Lord, that You was gone from thence. And this Misinformation I impute to your keeping up your self so close, by reason of your late Indisposition; your freedom from which no Man

[3] No catalogue of Smith's manuscripts earlier than *c.*1735 has been traced. See S. De Ricci, *English Collectors of Books and Manuscripts, 1530–1930* (Cambridge, 1930), p. 55 n. 1.

[1] Welbeck Wanleyana = BL Loan MS 29/253.

whatsoever can more cordially Congratulate, than I do. My Noble
Lord think's himself very much obliged by your Sending up that Book.
Your Copie of Demenico Fontana exceeded his Lordships, as much
as His Alessandro Francini[2] exceed's Yours. His Lordship was always
your Friend before, but that good Opinion is thereupon encreased;
not so much upon the Value of the Thing Sent, according to Desire, as
considering the Readiness & Good Will, you was pleas'd to shew on
that Occasion. Upon this Account I dare pronounce that you shall not
find Kemps Play at His Lordships Hands, but when I get next to
Wymple, I hope soon to send you some more Roman Coins of different Persons, to add to those few I sent you before. Besides this I hope
His Lordship, with your Assistance, will find out some acceptable
Present for You.

As to Mr Hammond of Bath, and the Oxford-Bookseller mentioned
in one of your former Letters, I have heard of them both: but (begging
Pardon) do not think the latter has the very best Stock of any Bookseller in England.[3]

At this present, I want to peruse *Antonij Reiserj Index Librorum MSS.
Bibliothechae Augustanae, Augustae*, 1674, 4to.[4] I read it over carefully in
the Bodleian Library; but much want to look into it again. I cannot
suddenly find it out in Town: but if you could please to send me one
from Oxford (where I suppose there are many) the favor will be
heartily acknowledged, and the book in ten days time, after Receipt
returned, by

    Reverend Sir
        Your most humble and obliged Servant
                                    Humfrey Wanley.

Be pleased always to direct to me in Dover-street.

MS: Bodleian, Ballard 13, fo. 140. *Date*: 'Genoa-Armes, 29 September 1719.'

[2] Alessandro Francini, *A New Book of Architecture. Set forth by Robert Pricke* (1669).
[3] Described by Charlett (6 July 1719; Welbeck Wanleyana = BL Loan MS 29/253) as
'famous for the best and largest Collection of Books, that any Shop can boast of, in great
Britain, and his Prices beare proportion, to other Vendibles and Rentables, of this City'.
Hammond lent books on payment of a 5*s*. entrance fee (Charlett to Wanley d. 23 Sept.
1719; Welbeck Wanleyana = BL Loan MS 29/253). Plomer, *Dictionary*, lists Henry and
John Hammond, booksellers of Bath and Devizes *c*.1695–*c*.1721, apparently in partnership together. The Oxford bookseller referred to I cannot identify.
[4] Anton Reiser, *Index Manuscriptorum Bibliothecae Augustanae* (Augsburg, 1675).

204. *To* William Sherard *5 October 1719*

Worthy Doctor,

By the last Post, I acquainted my Noble Lord of the fresh Mark you have given Him of your good Will, in the several Matters relating to the Reverend & Learned Mr L'Isle.[1] And I judge my self so well apprised of His Lordships good Mind and Pleasure relating to Antiquities in General, & Books in Particular; that, I dare avouch, he will be pleas'd, to understand that I give the following Instructions, without any Loss of Time (which Mr Lisle & You can putt in effectual Execution, in my Absence) in the manner, as if I had done so by his own positive Order.

First then, as to Mr Lisles two Greek Manuscripts,[2] my desire is that they be sent down to me at Wymple (by the Royston Carrier, who Inne's at the Vine near Bishop-gate, & goe's out every Friday-morning:) with a Letter, directing me what Price is expected for them, & I will take Care that the Money be returned up, without Delay.

Secondly, I know my Lord will be glad of the Old Roll of the Hebrew Bible at Aleppo, now Bound up into 12 Books. Mr L'Isle is therefore desired to Get it at Reasonable Price (Mr Sam. Palmer said it was Valued at about £20, 25, or 30:) and brought hither as soon as may be. If there be any old Tradition relating to it, or the Writer of it, or the former Owners of it, or any Place where it was Preserved: let it be sent in Writing, attested by the Hand of the old Priest in whose Hands it now is.[3]

Thirdly, as to the Monastery of Νουμηνία in Scio,[4] my Lord will not only be well pleased to have *All* the Manuscripts in that Room you spake of to me, and particularly the Τετραβαγγέλιον in old Capital Letters you so often mentioned: but He would have a through

---

[1] Samuel Lisle (1683–1749), Wadham College, Oxford 1706; Chaplain to the Levant Company at Aleppo 1710–19; Archdeacon of Canterbury 1724; Bishop of St Asaph 1744, of Norwich 1748.

[2] BL Harley MSS 5619, 5689. They were delivered by Lisle 18 Jan. 1720: see Wanley, *Diary*, under that date, p. 20(5).

[3] Lisle reported that the book was not ancient and that it was priced at £60 (Wanley, *Diary*, 18 Jan. 1720, p. 20(5)), at which Wanley appears to have lost interest in it.

[4] i.e. the monastery of Nea Moni on Chios. Lisle reported the MS to be 'a very fine and very antient Book in small folio, written all in Capitals, and (as he Remember's) without Accents.—And that it is an Ἐυαγγέλιον, beginning with St John's Gospel on Easter-day' (Wanley, *Diary*, 18 Jan. 1720, p. 20(5)), but despite Sherard's efforts on Wanley's behalf it did not come to the Library: see *Diary*, 17 Apr. 1721, p. 99(8).

search made at the same time, in other Parts thereof, and as much
brought away, at once, as may be handsomly gotten together. As for
Example, in the Chapel or Church, you will find some old Biblical &
Liturgical Books that may be spared. In their Archives (if they have
any) you may expect the Original Deeds of their Founders & Benefactors, Registers, Τυπικά, Χρυσόβουλλα, Letters, and other such
Matters, which are curious amongst Us, although not of the least Use
to them. Indeed, my Lord is always for *all*, even to the least Fragment
of Paper or Parchment, or broken Seal. And it may not be amiss to putt
you in Mind, that most of the Monks thereof, will be found to have
some Books or Written Papers in their own Possession, which they
may be easily induced to part with.

Now, Sir, as to Smyrna and the Metropolite thereof; I cannot
think that His Greek Catena Patrum goes over the whole Scripture,
or even over the Septuagint; because such a Work would be too big
for any Single Book.[5] As to the Price of 1000 Crowns, I think it horribly exorbitant for any book; but perhaps you might mistake it for
100 Crowns, which seem's to be much more reasonable. However, I
would desire you, Sir, to write to Him for a more particular account
of the Book; its Bulk; number of Leaves; Age; How much of the
Scripture is explain'd; who are the Principal Authors of the Catena;
& what is the lowest Price of it. You may also desire him to Send you
a Copy of the Old Testament in Greek of the Version of the
Septuagint, in one ore more Volumes, which he can easily get from
the Greek Monasteries or Churches; and my Lord will be sure to
pay any reasonable Price for it. He may also, at such Places find
Greek διπλώματα or Instruments, which will be welcome to my
Lord, either with, or without the Seals. I am,

Worthy Sir, Your most obliged, & very humble Servant

Humfrey Wanley.

MS: London, Royal Society Sh. 648. *Date*: 'Dover-street, 5 October 1719.' *Address*: 'To
The Worthy Doctor William Sherard.'

---

[5] Sherard reported (*Diary*, 18 Jan. 1720, p. 19(4)) that the Metropolite had died, but
that Edmund Chishull (1671–1733), Vicar of Walthamstow, Chaplain at Smyrna 1698–
1702, had an 'antient' Catena Patrum. Though not, in fact, ancient it was later bought,
now BL Harley MS 5791 (*Diary*, p. 19 n. 4).

205. *To* Arthur Charlett *17 November 1719*

Reverend Sir,

By the last Post I received your kind Letter Dated the 13th instant;[1] and have recollected my poor Thoughts about the Parcel of Pamphlets you mention;[2] I find I have now no more to say, than that the same were amassed together, in pursuance of a Verbal Command of K. Charles I, by a Person who was Book-binder to Him, or to K. Charles II, or to both. The honest Man was almost Ruined by his long Service: and therefore (after many Years of fruitless Patience & Waiting in Vain were elapsed) he conveyed away the Pamphlets, averring them to have been bought with His own Money, and Seized on a large Parcel of the Kings Books, which were in his Custody for Binding, untill his Bills should be paid off. In this Condition the Things remained untill the Man died; since when, they have been *Moved up & down* many times by the Relations of the Deceased; and *privatly* Offer'd to Sale; the Price being Variable, according to the Circumstances of the Times & Persons. What the *lowest* Price was, I never heard. I have known some, indeed, who have shewn a Disposition of Buying; but inquiring into the Title of the then Possessors; for want of due Satisfaction, flew off; being loth to venture their or their Families entring the Lists against Powers too Mighty for Them.

I return you Thanks, Sir, for the Information you are pleased to give me about my worthy friend Mr Ellison, deceased;[3] whose good Company I used frequently to enjoy, with Mr Elstob, Mr March,[4] &c.

My Noble Lord hath often made mention of you in Terms of much Civility & Respect; and, I am sure, would be heartily glad to gratifie you for Your Book, in such manner as would be most agreable to You,

---

[1] BL Harley MS 3778, fo. 51.

[2] The Thomason Tracts: see no. 115 n. 4.

[3] Cuthbert Ellison (*c.*1678–1719), Fellow of Corpus Christi College, Oxford 1702. He left money for an annual commemoration speech on Charles I, and another on Laud: 'Two Subjects very unfashionable for Panegyric, yet I may venture to conjecture, they will never want, in that learned College, either Orators or Auditors' (Charlett to Wanley d. 13 Nov. 1719, BL Harley MS 3778, fo. 51).

[4] Probably Humphrey March, a contemporary of Wanley's at St Edmund Hall, Oxford 1695.

if he knew how. I therefore desire your Instructions herein, as being
with all Sincerity,

Reverend Sir,

Your most humble, & obliged Servant

Humfrey Wanley.

MS: Bodleian, Ballard 13, fo. 143. *Date*: 'Wympole, 17 November 1719.' *Address*: 'To
The Reverend Dr Charlett Master of University College in Oxford.' *Printed*: S. G.
Gillam, 'The Thomason Tracts', *Bodleian Library Record*, ii (1941–9), pp. 223–4 (extract).

206. *To* Ann Wanley *22 November 1719*

My dearest Love,

It is with great Comfort & Pleasure that I now take pen in Hand to
acquaint you, that I am (praised be Almighty God for it) as well in
Health, as I have been at any time for divers Years past. My Stomach
digests Three Meals every Day; I drink enough to suffice my Nature;
and I go on with my Lords business; doing every day somewhat,
although it be in the darkest time of the year, & the business its self
both difficult & tedious. I am glad Mr Christian hath been with you,
and that my poor loving token to you is delivered. I desire you to go to
Him, immediatly upon the Receipt of this, and lett him know (with my
Service) that my Lady was pleas'd yesterday to make mention of Her
Triangular Seal still remaining in his Hands, with Intimation that I
should write to Him, that He should finish the same in the best
Manner he possibly can, and soon. And pray tell him, that I desire
him, for his own Sake & Interest, to gratifie our Noble Lady, who hath
already had so much Patience with him, in the first Place, postponing
all other Business whatsoever. Her Noble Ladyship order'd me to lett
you know that She kindly remember's you; & I sent You my true Love
by Mr Prior.

I pray go, on Tuesday next, & thank Mr Noel for his Letter; but lett
him know, that He omitted two Articles of Business Material, vizt The
Earl of D——'s Books & Mr Stebbings Manuscripts, about both
which Parcels I would fain hear from him by the first Opportunity.[1]

[1] Perhaps Basil Feilding, 4th Earl of Denbigh, who had died in March 1717. For
Wanley's earlier interest in his books see his letter to him, 28 Nov. 1713 (no. 134).
Samuel Stebbing or Stebbings († 21 Aug. 1719), Rose Rouge Pursuivant 1698, Somerset
Herald 1700; member of the 1707 Society of Antiquaries. Wanley failed to acquire either

The Key & two Books came both safe the last Night, and please my Lord. I shall write more about them in my Next. I have had some Talk with Mr Morley about our small Affairs. His Advice is, to sell that parcel at Glenfield for Four Hundred Pounds, and not Under. This I will do as soon as we can; and also sell the other Parcel in Leicester, that we may not be plagued with Driblocks of Rents, & large Payments out of it. Pray lett me know if you would have me make my Will here, or stay till you see in Town.[2]

Your truly loving Husband

Humfrey Wanley.

My Service to Mr Beaver, Mr Noel, Mr Hawkins & all their Families; Mrs Mitchel, Mrs Steffkin, &c.

MS: Welbeck Wanleyana = British Library, Loan 29/258. *Date*: 'Wimple, 22 November, 1719.' *Address*: 'To Mrs Wanley at the Corner of Bedford and Shandois Streets near Covent Garden Westminster.'

207. *To* Arthur Charlett *24 November 1719*

Reverend Sir,

In answer to this your last Letter dated the 20th Instant,[1] I can only say that I am sorry it lieth not in my Power to be Serviceable to the University in the Affair you mention about the Collection of Pamphlets. If it did, I assure you Sir, I should willingly do my best, without expecting or Receiving any Gratuity whatsoever. But, really I know not where, or in whose Hands they are, nor at what Price they are now Sett. The last Time I saw them, is now many Years since. They were then in the Custody of one Mr Sissen a Druggist at the Red Cross in Ludgate-street, who hath been long Deceased. I believe my Noble Lord here may have entertained some Thoughts of purchasing them; but I dare say, if the University will have them, He will shew that Regard to Her, as to make no Opposition; in a Case wherein He might

collection, but some of Stebbing's papers are in BL Harley MS 6944, and one manuscript (Harley 3869) formerly owned by the Feildings, found its way into the library. See Wanley, *Diary*, 18 Jan. 1720, p. 18(2), and Wright, *Fontes*, under ffyldying.

[2] Wanley died intestate. Letters of administration granted to his widow are in PRO Prob. 6/102/X/J 3171.

[1] Welbeck Wanleyana = BL Loan 29/253.

not think Himself obliged to Have so much Complaisance for any Single Person, whose Collections are not intended for Perpetuity. If the University have come to a Resolution of Buying them, as You seem to intimate; Without doubt, it is grounded upon prudential Considerations; as that the Thi[n]gs will for the most part prove Fresh, & not Duplicates to what They have already: That the Bodleyan Library is a proper Repository for English Pamphlets: and that the Universities Money had better be laid out in Them, than in Books of Learning: and that this will be the Opinion of Posterity, as well as of the present Generation. Sir, I find no Fault, I utter my Mind at your Request, and with the Privacy you require; desiring to be understood in this manner only, that is, with Candor.[2]

As for Mr Clarke,[3] although he hath been pleased, more than once, to use me with much Humanity & Kindness; and I consequently find my self under Obligations unto Him, I can not how ever be at any Certainty when I can wait upon Him. My Time is all my Lords and I go no where but as I am lead by His Business; nor make any Visit upon mine own Fancy. As to the Value of your Fontana particularly, I know not well what to say. The whole Book cost me about 56 Shillings prime; and in all, stood me in about 3 pounds. Fontana's Treatise is grown very scarce; and yet it hath went cheap even of late years, at several open Sales; namely, at 10 or 12 Shillings. The dearest rate I have heard it ever went at, was at the old Earl of Anglesey's Sale of Books, when it produced £3:10:00.[4] I remain with all true Respect,

[2] The University's interest in the Thomason Tracts lapsed for another year. On 7 Dec. 1720 (BL Harley MS 3778, fo. 63) Charlett wrote to Wanley at the request of the Vice-Chancellor to ask Wanley to visit George Clarke, MP for the University, to discuss the best means of procuring the collection for the University, if Harley had no thought of buying them (see also Wanley, *Diary*, p. 78(2)). That Wanley reserved Harley's interest appears from Charlett to Wanley d. 17 Dec. 1720 (BL Harley MS 3778, fo. 15), but Harley wrote to Wanley (18 Dec. 1720, Welbeck Wanleyana = BL Loan MS 29/250) 'I have no thoughts about ye collect: of pamflets so you may use your own Discretion in yt affair.' Harley's lack of interest was not communicated to Charlett by Wanley until 28 Mar. 1721 (no. 217). But three years later Harley's interest revived and he asked to examine, and was brought, the twelve vol. catalogue of the collection: see *Diary*, p. 268(10) (2), and n. 3.

[3] George Clarke (1661–1736), politician and architect. Fellow of All Souls College, Oxford 1680, MP for Oxford University 1685, 1717–36. He filled a number of government posts between 1684 and 1714.

[4] Arthur Annesley (1614–86), 3rd Earl of Anglesey 1661. His splendid Library was sold at auction in London 25 Oct. 1686.

Reverend Sir,
    Your most obedient humble servant

Humfrey Wanley.

MS: Bodleian, Ballard 13, fo. 144. Copy in Welbeck Wanleyana = British Library, Loan 29/258. *Date*: 'Wymple 24 November 1719.' *Address*: 'To The Reverend Dr Charlett Master of University-College in Oxford.' *Printed*: S. G. Gillam, 'The Thomason Tracts', *Bodleian Library Record*, ii (1941–9), p. 224 (extract).

208. *To* Richard Sare *29 November 1719*

Worthy Friend,

    I was first advertised by my Son in Law Mr Beaver, and since by the Publick Prints, of the unfortunate Death of Mr Mickleton of Grayes Inn which was very Surprizing to me, who expected not his fall so soon. He did indeed make, at different Times many Solemn promises to me, of bequeathing all his manuscripts, being Bookes, deed's, Rolls Letters and other Papers to the Noble Lord here, whome I serve; in case He should decease without Issue; but whither He died Testate, or if he did, whither he Performed the numerouse promises He made me, I know not. Being therefore at this distance, and knowing none other so near Neighbour to the deceased; I intreate you to enquire, soon, how his Affairs are left: and more particularly if he was Married, if he left a Will; if so, if he was as Good as his word. He has I believe a Sister in Town who keeps a Shop in the new Exchange; my Wife knows her. If Mr Spearman of Durham be in Town He can and will, I beleive, give You good Information. Pray my humble Servis to a good and Worthy Gentleman. In short, if nothing be done, my Noble Lord Harley will be willing to buy all the MSS. and such other things as he shall like, with his ready mony, at reasonable and Moderate Price. I commit and entrust this Affair to Your Friendship & Prudence of both which I have a great opinion. I will reimburse Your incidental Charges, and in expectation of some Line or two by way of Answer; remain as sincerely as any Friend You have.[1]

---

[1] Mickleton had chambers at 14 Coney Court, Gray's Inn; Sare's shop was at Gray's Inn Gate. Sare replied (3 Dec. 1719, BL Harley MS 3781, fo. 25) that Mickleton died very greatly indebted; it was thought that the repulse he had met with in his courtship led him to drink and extravagance, the mortgage of his Durham estate, and to his death by drowning in the Thames on 25 Nov. 1719. At his death his landlord and the authorities at Gray's Inn took the precaution of putting a padlock on his rooms. Wanley did enter

MS: Welbeck Wanleyana = British Library, Loan 29/258; copy in another hand. *Date*: 'Wympole near Royston, in Cambridgeshire 29 November 1719.' *Endorsed*: 'Copie of a Letter sent to Mr Richard Sare Bookseller in Holbourne. 29 Novr 1719' by Wanley.

209. *To* William Sherard[1] *30 November 1719*

Worthy Sir

I had much sooner given you an account of my safe arrival here, had not I expected to have seen you in Town some weeks ago; or had I not been hindred by business, Company or other Incidents. However, I hope you will please to excuse my long silence, and give me leave to acquaint you, that the Marbles and other antiquities first sent came safe; that is, not much[2] damnified: and my Lord will pay the money we agreed upon, at the Time, I have since delivered unto His Lordship the Leaden Seales, &c. which you presented unto Him, and for which He kindly thanks you; together with the Large parcel of Seals & Hones &c. the price of which you left wholly to His Lordship. For these I find his Lordship willing to allow Twenty Guineas; and I doubt not but he will Crown the whole with a regal of your Liking. His Lordship speakes frequently of you with Respect & kindness; and (I do assure you) esteem's your gentleman like usage of Him, at an higher rate than he does all that he hath received of you. He hath looked in your book of inscriptions, and wishes it was copied with more accuracy; as also that it contained copies of *all* that you have taken with your own hands; among those he apprehends to be want-ing, is a very obscure inscription of Ten lines (beginning with *ΔΕΙΝΗ*) under the Figure of a Woman standing between two Children, as in a sort of Nich. If you have the Inscription copied His Lordship would gladly receive a Transcript thereof; if not he desires your advice how he may safely get the stone to be so well cleaned, as that the Letters may appear with some tolerable plainess. I think

into negotiations to purchase the collection and made a list of the manuscripts in it (Welbeck Wanleyana = BL Loan MS 29/259 misc. 23). See Wanley, *Diary*, pp. 55(5), 56(9, 10, 2, 4, 7). But the collection went to Gilbert Spearman (1675–1738) of the Middle Temple, Mickleton's intimate friend and relation by marriage, and finally to Durham University. For Wanley's earlier interest see no. 192.

---

[1] Sherard, Consul to the Turkey Company at Smyrna 1703–17, was an intermediary in acquiring books and antiquities from the East for Harley.

[2] such MS.

I apprised you, in London, that His Lordship is willing to receive those other Inscriptions you left in Turkey near the Sea Coast, to be brought as ballast, and at the prime Cost, according to your kind Proposal; and therefore, I suppose you wrote for them, when you wrot for the Glass Urne instead of that so unfortunately broke. Now the Parliament is mett,[3] in Case that Noble Personage (You know whom I mean)[4] becom up to Town, I should be glad if you would sett about getting the old Manuscript Benedictional I so often mention unto you. Herein I can give no Direction how to proceed but this I say, & promise, that if you procure the Book You shall be no Loser by it. Thus with my Respects to the Doctor, Your good Brother,

I remain.

MS: Welbeck Wanleyana = British Library, Loan 29/258; copy in another hand. *Date*: 'Wymple near Roystone in Cambridge Shire 30th Nov: 1719.' *Endorsed*: 'Copie of a Letter sent to Dr Will. Sherard late Consul at Smyrna. 30 November 1719' by Wanley.

210. *To* Ann Wanley *6 December 1719*

My Dearest

I write this now, only to lett you know, that I came from Cambridge yesterday-afternoon in good Health. I find my self in good Favor with our Noble Lord & Lady. Dr Tudway, Mrs Tudway, Miss Webby, & Mrs Scarfe, as also honest Mr Mortlock & his Spouse, send their Service to You & to Mrs Beaver. My Lady ha's been pleas'd to remember you with much kindness many times. And my Lord once, the last week, talked to me about the Snuff-box. I answer'd as you bad me, saying you desired only a plain Silver Snuff-box, gilt within; of about 27 shillings Value. My Lord said that would not do; that my Lady design'd you a piece of Plate of some Value; that I knowing what you want better than They, He would have me speak out freely, and say what would be acceptable. I then Named a Tea-Kettle; and do believe that Orders are already given to make one for you.

Pray lett Mr Noel know (with my Service to his Spouse & Aunt, as

---

[3] The new session had begun 23 Nov.

[4] William Cavendish (*c*.1673–1729), 2nd Duke of Devonshire. The Benedictional of St Ethelwold is the manuscript referred to. For Wanley's attempts to procure it through Sherard's offices, see Wanley, *Diary*, pp. 19(4), and n. 7. It finally came to the British Museum in 1957, now BL Add. MS 49598.

well as to Him Self) that I much wonder why I dont hear from him, all this while, when there are so many Articles for him to Write to me about, Namely, the Books abroad; and, at home, those of Sir Thomas Sebright, Mr Wase, Dr Wyncupp, & Mr Stebbing.[1]

I think to write to my Sister by the Next Post; and doubt not but to find Sir Thomas Gery more kind to me than Mr Wright.[2] I wish that Mr Noels books were come, that I might return and assure you, in person, that I am with all Truth

My dearest,

Your most faithful & intirely loving Husband

H. Wanley.

Pray desire Mr Noel to write to me by the next Post.

MS: Welbeck Wanleyana = British Library, Loan 29/258. *Date*: 'Wympole, 6 December, 1719.'

211. *To* Arthur Charlett *9 December 1719*

Reverend Sir

Yours of the 5th Instant dated from Bath,[1] came hither this After-noon. I was before apprised both by the Prints, and by private Letters, of Dr Hudsons Decease, and of Mr Bowles's Succeeding Him in the Bodlyan Library.[2] But I heard nothing before of his Bequest to our Colledge Library: nor of my Honest Worthy Friend Mr Kecks Legacies[3] (which I much approve of) until this Information from Your Self; for which Sir, I most hartily thank You; Since what you wrot

[1] Duplicates from the library of Sebright, books belonging to Christopher Wase (1662–1711, Magdalen College, Oxford 1677, coin collector) and Thomas Wyncupp (or Whincop, † 1713, Fellow of Corpus Christi College, Cambridge 1670–82, Rector of St Benet's, Cambridge 1676–83 and of St Mary Abchurch and St Lawrence Pountney, London 1681–1713) were reported ready for Harley's inspection 11 Jan. 1720 (*Diary*, p. 16(6)) and inspected by him 13 Jan. 1720 (*Diary*, p. 17(5)). See further Wanley, *Diary*, p. 16 n. 3. For Stebbing see no. 206 n. 1.
[2] Wright is presumably the husband of Wanley's sister Ellen.

[1] BL Harley MS 3778, fo. 55.
[2] Hudson, Bodley's Librarian, died 27 Nov. of a dropsy; he left first choice of all the books in his study to University College. Bowles was elected the next day.
[3] Robert Keck (1686–1719), University College, Oxford 1702, Inner Temple 1713. Not, according to J. Foster, *Alumni Oxonienses: 1500–1714*, ii (Oxford, 1891), a Fellow, but Charlett says he was. He left five hundred guineas to the Royal Society, the same amount to University College, and a hundred guineas to Denison his tutor.

touching the Collection of Pamphlets,[4] I have not heard my Noble Lord here, make any mention of them: and if the University are minded that He Should Secure them, I beleive it would be well for some one, or other, to Lett him know it.

I observe what you are pleased to write (upon occation of Fountana's Book) with regard to Mr Hammond's Shop, in Bath, the Authors you mention are well known here; but you specify not any particular Edition of Shakespeare; or Pope, if you mean his Homer: nor do we here know what workes of Mr Addison are now printing.[5] If you please to lett me know certainly what will be acceptable unto you, and what will be the price, my Lord will order the Money to be paid in London to whomesoever You or Mr Hammond shall appoint.

I saw Dr Ratcliffe's Statue at Mr Birds, as also that of K:H:6th[6] before I came hither;[7] where I am no more Straitly attached than in proceeding years. Thus in expectation of your further Commands I remain with all due Respect Reverend Sir

Your most obliged and most humble Servant

MS: Welbeck Wanleyana = British Library, Loan 29/258; copy in another hand. *Date*: 'Wimple, near Royston, in Cambridge Shire 9 Decembr 1719.' *Address*: 'To The Reverend Dr Charlett at the Bath.'

212. *To* [John Anstis] *20 March 1720*

Sir,

I am agreably surprised at the Sight of this book,[1] which may be (perchance) the very book I mentioned to you; but I will not be

---

[4] i.e. the Thomason Tracts. Charlett implied (Charlett to Wanley d. 5 Dec. 1719, BL Harley MS 3778, fo. 55) that the University was willing to resign them to Harley if he was interested: 'and so preserve them entire, for the Use of Curious & Honest Consulters, our principal design being, to prevent the Dissipation, or Destruction, or mis Employment of them, in bad or Fanatic Hands.'

[5] Joseph Addison, *Works*, ed. Thomas Tickell (1721).   [6] K:6th MS.

[7] Francis Bird (1667–1731), sculptor. He did much work in the course of the rebuilding of St Paul's and was responsible for many tombs and memorial statues, including the Grabe monument (executed at Robert Harley's expense) in Westminster Abbey, 1711. The statue of Dr John Radcliffe, benefactor of University College, Oxford, as well as of the University and City, was erected in his New Quadrangle at University College, 28 Nov. 1719. That of Henry VI was executed for Eton College in 1719 (Rupert Gunnis, *Dictionary of British Sculptors 1660–1851* (1953), under Bird). Bird's workshop was in Lincoln's Inn Fields.

---

[1] Sent to Anstis by Morgan Graves, antiquary, son of Richard Graves of Mickleton,

positive, because that which I saw was larger than this, and in worse clothing; nay more, (to the best of my remembrance) the Pictures followed the Calender, which is not so antient as the rest of the book. All these Objections may be easily answered, I know, by owning that the book has been beaten, circumcised, & dislocated by the tools of a Bookbinder. If this be so, it will not be worth while for me to stand out. It may be the same book for ought I can now remember to the Contrary; but if it be, it is much Disguised since I saw it. I believe I have seen instances of Earl Edmund & Thomas his Son bearing the Armes of England, under a Label of 5 points.

As to the Deeds in my Lords Library, there never was any Index, Repertory, or Catalogue of them taken as yet; but you, who have been at several times a generous Benefactor to it, will be sure to find both my Lords willing to do you any sort of pleasure that you can desire, with relation to them.[2] They will always have a particular Regard to any Student who intend's to Print for the public Information: and if so, a fortiori, you that are an old Friend & Benefactor, will be sure to be Welcome.

As to the Catalogue you lately returned, you forgot what I told you: vizt that, at one time, I did forbear to putt down a mark at those books I might think my Lord had not: and at another, I might so mark more than enough. I am pretty sure that my Lord will buy very few books, if any, at that Sale. You are therefore free, as to him. And if either of you two have a book you both like, I look upon it as much the same thing. You therefore will do well to call on Mr Moetjens a Bookseller in the Strand (between Katherine Street & Doileys) and he will shew you the same Catalogue, which you may mark at your Pleasure; and he will execute your Commission faithfully at the Sale, in person, at the Cheapest Rate.[3]

Gloucestershire (Anstis to Wanley d. 20 Mar. 1720; Welbeck Wanleyana = BL Loan MS 29/251). The only manuscript in the Harleian collection to have been owned by Graves is Harley 3650, the twelfth-/thirteenth-century Register of the Augustinian Priory of Kenilworth (Davis no. 501). This passed to James West († 1772) of the Inner Temple in 1731 and on 28 Jan. 1737 to Harley by gift—the only book of West's, according to Harley's inscription on fo. 1 (see *The Book Collector*, xi (1962), pp. 158–74, plate B[a]), which survived the disastrous fire in his chambers three weeks earlier.

[2] Wanley did later compile an index to the Harleian Charters, now BL Add. MS 45711. See *Fontes* under Anstis for a full account of his gifts to the Harleys.

[3] The catalogue is probably that of the library of Jean-Jacques Charron, Marquis de Ménars († 1718); the sale at The Hague was announced for 10 June 1720, but was held at least a week earlier. James Moetjens (who is not listed by Plomer, *Dictionary*) offered to

My very humble service, with my sick Spouses, to Madam Anstis, & your Fireside, concludes me Sir,
  Your most obedient humble servant

Humfrey Wanley.

MS: British Library, Stowe 749, fo. 93. *Date*: '20 March 1719/20.'

213. *To* Arthur Charlett *24 March 1720*

Reverend Sir,

Yesterday in the afternoon (& not before) I received yours of the 14 Instant, by the penny-post.[1] In Answer to which, I can only say that I know of no better Manuscripts of Asser than those already published. As to what Mr Wise would have about the Age of the MS. he calls Marianus, I can give him but little help, not having seen the book these 20 years; and learning not much from his Specimen of its Character. It is not improbable but that it may have been written in or near the Reign of our King Henry the Second: but if I were on the Spot, I believe I might ascertain its Age to a Year or Two.[2] Dr Fiddes ha's, some time since, apprised me of his Design; which I dare venture to say, will make him Sweat many a time, before he will be able to usher his Collections, of that kind, into the world in Perfection.[3]

I have been in Town about 2 Months, but have been almost all the time ill of a very violent Cold. I am not well recover'd from it, as yet:

---

serve Harley at the sale (see Wanley, *Diary*, p. 34(12)), but Paul Vaillant was used and bought there the Codex Aureus (BL Harley MS 2788). See Wanley, *Diary*, p. 38 n. 5.

---

[1] Charlett's letter (Welbeck Wanleyana = BL Loan MS 29/253) is d. 12/13 Mar., on the verso of a letter from Francis Wise d. 12 Mar.

[2] Francis Wise (1695–1767), Fellow of Trinity College, Oxford 1719–46, Under-Keeper of the Bodleian 1719, Keeper of the Archives 1726, Radcliffe Librarian at Oxford 1748–67. The Bodleian 'Marianus' is Bodl. MS Bodley 297 (*SC* 2468), a twelfth-century copy of a composite chronicle based on Florence of Worcester; as far as 1082 it is based on the work of Marianus Scotus, and was formerly known as 'Mariani Scoti Chronicon'; a crude facsimile of seven lines is attached to Wise's letter. Wise's edn. was pbd. at Oxford, 1722.

[3] Richard Fiddes (1670–1725), chaplain to Robert Harley 1713–14. His life of Cardinal Wolsey (pbd. 1724) was undertaken at the suggestion of Francis Atterbury, Bishop of Rochester, formerly Dean of Christ Church, Oxford, Wolsey's foundation. Fiddes had announced his intention to Wanley the previous January and asked his help (see Wanley, *Diary*, p. 18). He frequently visited the Harleian Library to collect material (*Diary*, pp. 45(20), 64(4), 81(1)). See further no. 214 and n. 4.

and my poor Spouse is at this time so bad of a Worse Cold, as to be
thought in Danger; I pray God preserve Her. My Lord is at Wimple,
and expected up again shortly. Before He went, I putt his Lordship in
mind of You, and he desire's that you will please to Name *not this or that
Book*, but *to fix upon any one Book*, and it shall be soon sent You, with
Thanks.[4] I remain most respectfully,

    Reverend Sir,
        Your most obliged servant to command

                                       Humfrey Wanley.

MS: Bodleian, Ballard 13, fo. 146. *Date*: 'Covent-garden, 24 March 1719/20.' *Address*:
'To The Reverend Doctor Charlett, Master [of] University-College in Oxford.'

214. *To* [Arthur Charlett] *9 April 1720*

Reverend Sir,

    I return you most hearty Thanks for the Favor of your last Letter
Dated the 4th Instant.[1] In Answer to which, I must acquaint you that
my poor Wife sends her true Respects to you, with Thanks for the
Regard you are pleas'd to shew for Her Health. Indeed She Recover's
but slowly; and I who have been long ill, am grown better than Her.

    I am obliged to both my Brethren of the Bodleian Library for their
good Wishes to me. And as my Lords Library grow's apace, it will be
in my power also to do them Friendly Offices. For, if my Noble Lords
live some years longer, and go on with Usual Success, Their Library
will be as valuable as any in England, and yield to but two or three in
the World.[2]

    Sir, I return you Thanks for your intended Present of the Equi-
valent to your Fontana; but I desire to be excused from accepting of it.
I presented it to you as a small token of my Gratitude, having received
multifarious Benefits from You. You was pleased to specifie many
Books, any one of which you seemed willing to accept in Exchange for
it; but here, in your Absence, my Lord did not know which of them you

---

  [4] In exchange for Charlett's copy of a work by Domenico Fontana: see no. 200
and n. 7.

   [1] Welbeck Wanleyana = BL Loan MS 29/253.
   [2] It is interesting that Wanley still associates Robert Harley with the Library,
although the evidence makes it clear that it was in effect controlled by his son Edward—
and had been for some years.

like best; and therefore desired that you would declare your good Liking more particularly. But now, with my Lords privity, (who often mention's you with great Respect) I say, that the most valuable Book you have mentioned, is Bayles Dictionary. Be pleased therefore, Sir, to let me know soon, whether you like best Bayles French-Original, or the English Translation, and my Lord will order it to be sent down to you, as soon as his Bookseller can get it; and a Print or Two of my Head (if I can now get them) shall go along with Bayle. I speak with some Diffidence about the Print, because they have been Sold off, long ago. In Answer to your Quaere, I take Leave to tell you, that Mr Smith the best Mezzo-Tinto-man in Town, had his own Price for Working the Plate, and promised me to do his Best upon it. But, indeed, the Print prove's very bad & heavy, and that (as I have been told) out of narrow & party-Reasons.[3]

I never had any Thought of republishing any thing of Asser Menevensis.

I believe my Lord Oxford ha's nothing to do with Dr Fiddes's Life of Cardinal Wolsey,[4] the necessary Materials toward which (supposing it designed for a Standard-Book, to be published for the Honor of the Nation, & benefit of the Student, & not to get a present Penny by) will not be collected & Transcribed in Seven Years. And if Any man will have them, He must not only look through England, but into the Archives of all those Powers of Europe with whom our Kings had any Concern, during the Time of His Employment; or else His Book will not afford us all that Information, which might have been had. I find I grow too tedious, and therefore, for the present will take my Leave with sincere Respect, being always

Reverend Sir,

Your most Obliged & very humble Servant

Humfrey Wanley.

[3] John Smith (1652?–1742), of Covent Garden. Cf. Hearne to Richard Rawlinson, 11 May 1718: 'As for Humph. Wanley, whom you mention, I know very well the Vanity of the poor Man, which he hath sufficiently shew'd, as in other Things, so particularly in the Picture of himself you speak of, which, it seems, he causes to be sold publickly about, not before any Work of Learning (which he wants as much as any Pretender whatsoever), but purely to be hung up in the Closets & Repositories of great Men, amongst which he thinks that himself ought to be reckoned most deservedly' (*Collections*, vi, p. 174), and for a more colourful anecdote see Hearne, *Collections*, vi, p. 225.

[4] Charlett had suggested that Harley (a Christ Church man) was Fiddes's patron in the enterprise. For Wanley's own plans (which came to nothing) for a life of Wolsey based on that of Cavendish, see no. 115 and J. A. W. Bennett, 'Wanley's *Life of Wolsey*', *Bodleian Library Record*, vii (1962–7), pp. 50–2.

I have lately made my Will; and therein put down a small token of my Gratitude to you.[5]

MS: Bodleian, Ballard 13, fo. 147. *Date*: 'From my Lodgings, 9 April 1720. *Printed*: J. A. W. Bennett, 'Wanley's *Life of Wolsey*', *Bodleian Library Record*, vii (1962–7), p. 52 (extract).

215. *To* Andrew Hay[1] *26 April 1720*

Mr. Andrew Hay,

You being upon your Departure towards France and Italy, by my noble Lord's Order, I give you this Commission; not now expecting that you can execute every Part of it in this Journey, but yet hoping that you will dispatch those Articles which are of the greatest Importance, and put the others into a proper Posture, against the Time of your next Return thither.[2]

In Paris, Father Bernard Montfaucon has some Coptic, Syriac, and other Manuscripts, worth the buying. Among them is an old Leaf of the Greek Septuagint, written in Uncial or Capital Letters. Buy these, and the leaden Book he gave to Cardinal Bouillon, if he can procure it for you, or direct you to it.[3]

In the Archives of the Cistertian Monastery of Clervaulx (or Claravalle) I am told there are some original Letters, or Epistles, written by

---

[5] Wanley died intestate.

---

[1] Andrew Hay (*fl.* 1716–45), studied painting under Sir John Baptist Medina in Scotland, later a dealer in pictures, sculpture, bronzes, etc., with extensive connections in France and Italy. For an account of purchases made by Hay for Harley, 1720–4, including the present Commission, see C. E. Wright in *Cultural Aspects of the Italian Renaissance*, ed. Cecil H. Clough, pp. 468–70.

[2] Wanley delivered the Commission to Hay on 3 May 1720 (*Diary*, p. 42(17)). Hay was successful in acquiring in Paris an important parcel of manuscripts from the library of the French collector Pierre Séguier († 1672) (*Diary*, p. 50(5)), but thereafter appears not to have prosecuted his Commission very actively; Wanley wrote to him 28 Apr. 1721 (*Diary*, p. 101(9)) by way of a reminder, and on 17 Apr. 1722 wrote demanding the Commission's return (*Diary*, p. 138(6)); Hay complied 20 Apr. 1722 (*Diary*, p. 139(6)).

Wanley's Commission derives largely from the accounts of J. Mabillon and M. Germain, *Museum Italicum* (Paris, 1687) and B. de Montfaucon, *Diarium Italicum* (Paris, 1702). The identifications of particular manuscripts which follow are tentative.

[3] Hay had inspected and reported on Montfaucon's antiquities four months earlier, but did not view the manuscripts (Wanley, *Diary*, 12 Jan. 1719/20, p. 17(1)). See also no. 219 n. 1.

the Hand of St. Hierome upon Phylira, or Bark. One or more of these
will be acceptable, if not too outrageously valued.

The Duke of Savoy has many Greek MSS. as also the Egyptian
Board, or Table of Isis, adorned with Hieroglyphics; being that which
hath been explained by Pignorius, Kircherus, &c. — Let me have
some Account of these.[4]

At Venice, buy a Sett of the Greek Liturgical Books printed there; I
mean a Sett all of the First Edition, if they may be had: if not, let us
have the other.[5] Buy also Thomassini Bibliothecae Venetae, in
Quarto.[6] Get a Catalogue of Mr. Smith's MSS. there, and enquire how
Matters go about Giustiniani's Greek MSS.[7] — In the Booksellers
Shops, &c. you may frequently pick up Greek MSS. which the Greeks
bring from the Morea, and other Parts of the Levant.

Remember to get the Fragments of Greek MSS. you left with the
Bookseller, who bought Maffeo's Library.

The Family of Moscardi at Verona, have many valuable Antiquities;
and among the rest, four Instruments of the Emperor Theodosius,
junior, (now imperfect) written upon Phylira. These must be bought,
and especial Care taken of them. The First begins, —*dem relectis*—
The Second —*ius vir in Ast*— The Third *ius vir in*— The Fourth *ni
Siciliensis.*[8]

At Florence, the Dominicans, or Franciscans, have a large Collection of Greek MSS. — You may see them, and get a Catalogue of
them, if you can.[9] Buy Ernstius, or some other Catalogue of the Grand
Duke's MSS.[10]

At Milan, in the Ambrosian Library, is a very ancient Catullus; Part
of Josephus in Latin, written upon Bark. A Samaritan Pentateuch in
Octavo, Part of the Syriac Bible, in the Ancient, or Estrangele Characters; divers Greek MSS. in Capital Letters, being Parts of the Bible;

[4] The library of the House of Savoy was made over to the University of Turin by
Vittorio Amedeo II in 1720. A disastrous fire in Jan. 1904 destroyed about 24,000
volumes, including most of the manuscripts in the Savoy donation.

[5] See Wanley, *Diary*, p. 24(4) and n. 2.

[6] Giacomo Filippo Tomasini, *Bibliothecae Venetae Manuscriptae* (Udine, 1650).

[7] See no. 202 and n. 2. Smith had written to William Sherard early in the year to say
that the Venetian family of Giustiniani were not prepared to part with their collection of
Greek manuscripts (Wanley, *Diary*, 18 Jan. 1719/20, p. 19(4)), but they were later sold to
Thomas Coke (1697–1759), Earl of Leicester 1744 (Wanley, *Diary*, 18 May 1721,
p. 107(12)).

[8] See Mabillon and Germain, *Museum Italicum* (Paris, 1724), i, pp. 23–4.

[9] See Mabillon and Germain, *Museum Italicum* (1724), i, pp. 160–3.

[10] Heinrich Ernst, *Catalogus librorum Bibliothecae Mediceae* (Amsterdam, 1641).

with other Books of great Antiquity, both Greek and Latin.[11] You may look upon them, and send me some Account.

At Monza, (about ten Miles from Milan) is an imperfect Antiphonarium Gregorii I. Papae—It is all written upon purple coloured Parchment, with Capital Letters of Gold.[12]—Buy this if you can.

The Family of Septata, at Milan, have a Latin Writing upon Bark.—Buy this, if it will be parted with.

In the Archives of the Church of Ravenna, are divers Instruments written upon Bark.[13]—You may see them.

At Rome, the Greek Monks of St. Basil have very many old Greek MSS. written in Capitals, particularly a Book of the IV Gospels, and some Pieces of St. Gregory Nazianzen upon St. Paul's Epistles. Buy as many as you can, for I hear they are poor, and therefore they may sell the cheaper. They have likewise a Greek Charter of Roger King of Sicily, in five Pieces, together with some other Instruments in Greek, written upon Bark, or Vellum. Buy these also, if you can.

The Fathers of the Oratory at Rome (Monasterium Vallicellanum) have many very ancient MSS. both Greek and Latin.[14] See them at least, even supposing that they will not sell.

In the Cathedral Library at Pisa, are many ancient MSS.[15] Let me have some Account of these also.

The Monks of Bovio (in Monasterio Bobiensi, near, if not in Pavia) have many very ancient MSS, and among the rest a Book of the Gospels in Latin, wherein St. Luke is written LUCANUS.—They have many old Deeds in their Archives.[16]—Buy what you can.

---

[11] The 'very ancient Catullus' in the Ambrosian Library is a persistent and erroneous belief of Wanley: see his Commission to an unidentified correspondent, 15 Oct. 1698 (no. 53). The library possesses five manuscripts of Catullus, none earlier than the fifteenth century. Josephus is Biblioteca Ambrosiana, Cimelio MS 1 of the sixth-/seventh-century, *CLA* iii, no. 304. The Samaritan Pentateuch is perhaps Codex Ambrosianus, a fifth-century Greek version (Gen.–Josh.), Codex F of the OT. The Syriac bible is perhaps the Ambrosian manuscript of the translation into Syriac of the Greek text of the Septuagint contained in Origen's *Hexapla*, made 616–17 by Paul, Bishop of Tella in Mesopotamia, from the Nitrian Convent of St Maria Deipara.

[12] 'Verum his omissis, exstat in eodem Modoëtiae [Monza] sacrario codex ex membranis purpureus, Gregorii Antiphonarium, sed mutilum, quadratis litteris aureis exaratus' (Mabillon and Germain, *Museum Italicum*, i, p. 211).

[13] Referred to by Mabillon and Germain in their account of the Ambrosian Library (*Museum Italicum*, i, p. 12).

[14] Mabillon and Germain, *Museum Italicum*, i, p. 65 f.

[15] Ibid., p. 186 f.

[16] Wanley seems not at all clear about the location of the Irish monastic foundation of Bobbio, which is better described as lying between Genoa and Piacenza; but five years

At Cava (about a Days Journey from Naples) is a Benedictine Monastery. In the Archives, or Treasury, is a Greek Deed of Roger, King of Sicily, with his Golden Seal appendant.[17] Buy this, if you can. In the Library are some old MSS. See them at least, if you cannot buy.

At Naples, in the Library of the Augustin Friars of St. John de Carbonara, is a Greek MS. of the Gospels (or of Homilies upon the Gospels) all written in Capitals with Letters of Gold, upon purple Parchment.[18] This must be bought. There is also a Dioscorides in Greek Capitals; being a large Book with Figures of the Plants, &c.[19] This must also be bought. There is also a good Number of other ancient MSS. both Greek and Latin: among the latter is an Hieronimus de Scriptoribus Ecclesiasticis in Saxon Letters;[20] and the Gospels in Latin, where St. Luke is called LUCANUS.[21] Buy of these what you can.

If the Greek Manuscripts of the Monastery of St. Savior, near Messina in Sicily, or any of them, do remain there yet, or in that Neighbourhood, as it is probable they may, notwithstanding the late Wars, they will doubtless come exceeding cheap. You will enquire however how this Matter stands.[22]

Pray Sir, all along in your Journey, endeavour to secure what Greek MSS. and Latin Classical MSS. you can, provided they come at reasonable Prices: and let me be favoured with an Account of your proceedings as often as may be convenient.

---

later he apparently believed it to be near Naples—see *Diary*, pp. 372(3) and n. 1, 410(8). On the 'Book of the Gospels in Latin, wherein St. Luke is written LUCANUS', see n. 21 below. Mabillon and Germain, *Museum Italicum*, i, p. 213 f.

[17] The library of the Benedictine Abbey of the Holy Trinity, near La Cava in the province of Salerno, founded in 1011, is particularly rich in charters. See *Codex Diplomaticus Cavensis* (Naples, 1873–93), Mabillon and Germain, *Museum Italicum*, i, p. 114 f.

[18] MS Naples Greek 2*, formerly Vienna supp. gr. 12.

[19] Codex Neapolitanus (formerly Vindob. Gr. 1: Suppl. Graec. 28) of the late sixth century, a large folio of 170 pp. with illustrations of medical plants in colour.

[20] 'Codex antiquissimus litteris Saxonicis . . . Hieronymus de Scriptoribus ecclesiasticis cum Gennadio' (Mabillon and Germain, *Museum Italicum*, p. 108). Presumably Naples, Bibl. Naz. Lat. 2 (formerly Vienna 16), Hieronymus-Gennadius de viris illustribus, an eighth-century palimpsest in Irish minuscule from Bobbio, *CLA* iii, no. 391. For the presence of Bobbio manuscripts in the Library of St John de Carbonara in Naples, see Wanley's Commission of 15th Oct. 1698 n. 11 (no. 53).

[21] 'In alio veterrimo codice Evangeliorum, litteris quadratis exarato, Evangelium secundum Lucanum adscribitur, quod in alio item Bobiensi legere meminimus' (Mabillon and Germain, *Museum Italicum*, i, p. 109).

[22] These manuscripts are still to be found in Messina; they now belong to the University Library.

Mr. Hay,

In executing this Commission, my noble Lord cannot give you positive Direction how to bid upon every Occasion, by Reason of this his great Distance from those Parts; and must therefore rely upon your Fidelity; your Prudence, your usual Dexterity in Business, and your personal Affection to him. You will be sure always to buy as cheap as you can, for I foresee that some of the Things his Lordship chiefly wants, or is desirous of, will not come for a small Matter. In most of the Monasteries you will be able to buy for ready Money; but it may be at a cheaper Rate with the Greek Monks of St. Basil's Monastery at Rome, whose MSS. are good, and themselves in want.

I beseech God to bless and prosper you all along in this so long a Journey, and to bring you back again with Safety and good Success; and you may be sure that you will be more welcome to but very few, than to

Good Sir,
> Your very hearty Well-wisher,
> And most Humble Servant,

> HUMPHREY WANLEY.

MS: Not traced. Draft d. 26 Apr. 1720 (endorsed in James West's hand, 'given me by Mr. Noel June 12 1744'), preserved in the West papers at Alscot Park, Stratford-upon-Avon, was sold at Sotheby's, 29 Oct. 1962, as part of lot 185, not traced. *Date*: '26th April 1720.' *Printed*: *Catalogue of the Harleian Manuscripts* (1759), i, p. 5 n. 1, rptd. *Harleian Catalogue*, i (1808), p. 6 n. 1.

216. *To* William Sherard *8 November 1720*

Worthy Doctor,

I have sent to my Lord the Titles of such of your Books, as I thought he might want. They are these,[1]

> The 3 Greek books.
> Vaillantij Coloniae. chart mag.

[1] Of which the following can be identified: Jean Foy Vaillant, *Numismata aerea imperatorum Augustarum et Caesarum in coloniis, municipiis et urbibus jure Latio donatis* (Paris, 1688); Francesco Allaei, *Arabis Christiani Astrologiae nova methodus* (Rennes, 1655) = Osborne, *Catalogus Bibliothecae Harleianae*, ii, no. 13939; Balthasar de Monconys, *Journal des Voyages de Monsieur de Monconys* (Lyons, 1665–6); Scipione Ammirato, *Delle Famiglie Nobili Fiorentine* (Florence, 1615) = Osborne, *Catalogus*, i, no. 6685.

Wanley's 'Register of Knights Fees' is BL Harley MS 6700, although not listed in Wright, *Fontes*, as having belonged to Sherard.

Allaei Astrologia fol.
Bibliotheca Lombardiae.
Moncony's Travels. chart. mag.
Dante. MS.
Register of Knights Fees in Com Leicest. A.D. 1347. MS.
Nascita di frà Paolo. MS.
Letter by the Publisher of Macchiavel.
Armes of the Florentine Nobility.

I having asured his Lordship that your Price will be according to reason; he sends his Service to You, and desires you to send them down to him by Mr Beale the Orrewell Higler, who set's out every Friday-morning, for Wimple, from the Swan without Bishopgate. Pray, Sir, be pleased to send them accordingly this next Journey, because my Lord will expect them; and to keep this Direction by you, because it may be useful another time. I shall be extremely glad to see you, at any time & place you shall nominate to
    Worthy Sir,
      Your most humble Servant
                      Humfrey Wanley.

MS: London, Royal Society Sh. 649. *Date*: '8 November 1720.' *Address*: 'To Doctor William Sherard, at Dr Sherard's house in Mark-lane.'

217. *To* [Arthur Charlett] *28 March 1721*

Reverend Sir,
    I return you hearty Thanks for your late kind Remembrances of me,[1] and particularly for my Lord of Chesters book; which, I think, doe's very well deserve the Thanks wherewith your learned Body ha's particularly honor'd Him.[2]

[1] 24 Mar. 1721; Welbeck Wanleyana = BL Loan 29/253.
[2] In defence of the privilege of the universities in 1719, Gastrell challenged George I's presentation of Samuel Peploe to the Wardenship of Manchester College, on the grounds that Peploe obtained the necessary qualification of BD from Archbishop Wake rather than from Oxford. The Court of King's Bench, when appealed to, found in favour of Peploe. Gastrell vindicated himself in a work which was ptd. in folio edns. at both universities: *The Bishop of Chester's Case, with relation to the Wardenship of Manchester. In which it is shewn that no other degrees but such as are taken in the University can be deemed legal qualifications for any ecclesiastical Preferment in England* (1721). In gratitude, Oxford in full Convocation passed a vote of thanks to him.

As to Mr Wise's Queries, I will give him some Answer, as soon as I can gett a little time, and am a little better recover'd from a great Cold which I lately got. My Lord has a recent Transcript of Asserij Annales said to have been taken ex antiquissimo Codice. It begin's thus, *Igitur Britannia Romanis* —— and ends with these Words, — *et Rollonem Ducem Normannorum.*[3] Mr Wise will easily find whether it be that published by Dr Gale in his Quindecim Scriptores,[4] or not; for I have not the book at Hand, & have no leisure to consult it, if I had. Nor have I yet had time to wait on Dr Clarke with my Lords Answer to your Question; which is, that he will by no Means oppose the University touching the great Parcel of Tracts; and therefore will entertain no Thoughts of buying them.[5] My Lord has a MS. of Asser's Life of K. Ælfred, as translated into English by Mr Hollinshead, & transcribed by Mr John Stow, who hath also added a Continuation to it.[6] If you think this Proper to be printed with the Black English Letter, I believe my Lord will (upon his return up) be easily intreated to lend it to you.

As to the beginning our Date from the 25 of March, I take it to have been introduced among us by our Divines & Canonists: but why we did not comply with our Neighbours, by taking up the New Style at a proper Time; I believe, Sir, you can remember, as well as any Gentleman now living.

I am Sorry you went so soon out of Town, having had a desire of shewing you some few of my Lords fine Books, which are not yet sent down to Wympole; but there, I believe you may find them in the Somer, with the free Consent of my Lord, who will be glad to see you at all times.

Kemps Things are all Sold by Auction, and You sadly cheated; as I have been grossly imposed upon & affronted by this sorry fellow, who is about going to answer for his Villany in the other World.[7]

I am, with sincerest Respect,
    Sir,
        your most obliged humble Servant
                                        Humfrey Wanley.

[3] BL Harley MS 685, fos. 1–45.
[4] *Historia Britannicae, Saxonicae, Anglo-Danicae, Scriptores XV*, ed. Thomas Gale (Oxford, 1691).
[5] See no. 207 and n. 2.
[6] BL Harley MS 563.
[7] See no. 200 n. 2, no. 194 n. 2.

MS: Bodleian, Ballard 13, fo. 151. *Date*: 'Bedford-street, Covent-Garden, 28 March, 1721.' *Printed*: S. G. Gillam, 'The Thomason Tracts', *Bodleian Library Record*, ii (1941–9), p. 225 (extract).

218. *To* Bernard de Montfaucon[1] *12 May 1721*

Etsi Importunitas eorum qui Otio abundantes, Epistolis crebris ijsque inanissimis, vel Occupatissimos interpellent, Reprehensione digna semper existimaverim: haud tamen duxi committendum, quin Tibi salutem (Vir doctissime) plurimam ex animo impertirem. Id enim diutinus amor erga Te meus, nostrumque quale quale venerandae Antiquitatis studium, quodam modo postulare videbatur. Nam cum plures et politioris Literaturae, et reconditioris Doctrinae libros a te in lucem productos, (ut tuos in adornanda sanctorum Patrum opera, labores exantlatos taceam) vidisse mihi saltem, si non perlustrare contigerit: cur non Amorem meum atque Benevolentiam, Viro per totum orbem celeberrimo, testatum reddam; ea scilicet tempestate, cum incisas aeri vetustissimi Lampadis delineationes mittit tibi Dominus meus illustrissimus; et eximius Vir Dominus Wilhelmus Sherardus tuus literulas nostras tibi in manus tradere, in se recepit?[2] Si dixeris, Quisnam est iste qui varijs districto Curis molestiam creet? Me semel tibi inservijsse scito, cum annis abhinc circiter quinque supra viginti, amico tuo D. Joanne Millio suadente, Homiliam quandam S. Athanasio tributam, e Graeco bibliothecae Bodleianae Codice Manuscripto, in tuum usum descripserim, Millioque cum epistolio ad Te nostro tradiderim; a quo tamen postea, nihil de Te, nec de rebus tuis audivi.

Circa id tempus, recordor me ab illo mutuo accepisse librum quendam Gallicum Parisijs impressum, in 8vo ut aiunt, auctore quodam e

---

[1] Bernard de Montfaucon (1655–1741), Benedictine of the Congregation of St Maur at Paris, one of the greatest of Maurist patristic scholars. He produced editions of Athanasius (1698), Origen (1713), and Chrysostom (1718–38). His *Palaeographia Graeca* (1708) virtually originated the science of Greek palaeography. An English draft of Wanley's letter is in Welbeck Wanleyana(= BL Loan MS 29/259 misc. 6). Montfaucon's reply d. 7 July 1721 is in BL Harley MS 3780, fo. 167.

[2] On 18 May 1721 Wanley handed over to William Sherard for delivery to Montfaucon 'a Sett of My [M^r *MS*] Lords prints of his Lamp, M^r. Priors Letter, & My own for Bernard Montfaucon' (*Diary*, p. 106(11)). The 'prints'—engravings by Vertue—were, in Montfaucon's view, of an 'Urn' (*L'Antiquité expliquée et représentée en figures*, *Supplément*, 2nd edn. i (1724), pp. 139–41 and pls. 50–52). It had been in Colbert's collection and was given to Harley by Prior. See further, *Diary*, p. 106 n. 7.

Com-monachis tuis, de cujus Nomine & Cognomine jam penitus sum oblitus.[3] Is vir perdoctus, cum in Codicem quendam bibliothecae Monasterij S. Victoris antiquissimum incidisset, ratusque esset in illo contineri Testamentum Novum unius ex ijs Versionibus quae in Ecclesia Latina ante S. Hieronymi obtinebant tempus: ejusdem Specimen quoddam (Divi scil. Matthaei Evangelium) litterato orbi communicavit; Sententias rogans simul et Consilia doctorum de eadem Versione, deque illius Editione, in communem Christianorum utilitatem publicanda. Cum autem Millius noster ad te rescripsisset eam non esse pervetustam illam Italicam Versionem, quam saepissime commemorat, praesertim in Prologis S. Hieronymus: amicus tuus, hoc scripto libello, nomen suum contra doctissimum Millium vindicavit, citatisque quam-multis ex Ambrosio, Augustino, alijsque Sanctis Ecclesiae Patribus testimonijs, de Codice suo, deque versione Italica, et ipsi Millio, et pluribus alijs in ea re versatissimis, abunde satisfecit. Hujus Nomina ideo scire cupio, ut praelibatum libellum una cum Specimine, in meum Usum comparem. Nam ejusmodi Codicum aliquos in Angliae bibliothecis etiam num delitescere, praeter illum Theodori Bezae codicem Cantabrigiensem, et Oxoniae codicem Actuum Apostolorum Laudinum, satis est credibile.[4]

Inter alia Vigiliarum tuarum δείγματα, vidi Typicon Irenes Imperatricis, in Analectis Graecis per Te A.D. 1688, cum Versione tua Latina divulgatum;[5] laboribusque tuis me multum profuisse, lubens agnosco. Verum, cum Τυπικόν Theodorae filiae Constantini Palaeologi, fratris Imperatoris CP, nec non Sebasto-cratoris; Uxoris Ioannis Comneni, Stratopedarchae; Matris Theodori Comneni, Proto-stratoris; Euphrosynes nuptae Constantino Comneno Proto-sebasto, et aliarum quatuor filiarum: quod compilari fecit, veluti in

---

[3] Wanley refers to Jean Martianay's edn. (1695) of the Old Latin text of St Matthew from Codex Corbeiensis I. An uncial of the eighth century and probably English, it was at Corbey in Picardy, then at St-Germain-des-Prés (not St Victor) in Paris until the French Revolution. Only five leaves survive, three at Avranches in the Bibliothèque Municipale, two in the Public Library of Leningrad: see *CLA* vi, no. 730. Martianay's was the first ptd. edn. of an Old Latin biblical manuscript.

[4] Codex Bezae, also known as Codex Cantabrigiensis (Cambridge University Library MS Nn.ii.41; *CLA* ii, no. 140), a NT bilingual Greek and Latin manuscript of the fifth century, presented to Cambridge by Theodore Beza in 1581. The Laudian Acts, Greek and Latin of the sixth or early seventh century (Bodleian MS Laud Gr. 35, *SC* 1119; *CLA* ii, no. 251), was presented to the Bodleian Library by Archbishop Laud in 1639.

[5] See *Analecta Graeca…Latine verterunt et notis illustrarunt Monachi Benedictini Congregationis Sancti Mauri* (Paris, 1688).

perpetuam Regulam Monasterij pro quinquaginta Sancti-monialibus a se fundati pariter atque dotati, nuncupatique *Μονὴ τῆς ὑπεραγίας θεοτόκου τῆς βεβαίας ἐλπίδος τῶν χριστιανῶν* (forsan e 2 Epist. ad Corinth.I.7) manu mea descripserim: aveo a te edoceri ubinam loci Monasterium illud situm fuerit? nam de eo certi nihil ultra adhuc investigare potui, licet quamplurimos cum libros, tum Mercatores atque alios Viatores, Anglos, Graecos, Armenos, &c. diu frustra consuluerim.

Me tanquam tui aemulatorem, mi Bernarde, con-fratrisque Ioannis Mabillonij, in pervestigandis manuque mea delineandis vetustioris aevi Characteribus, ad Inscriptiones Graecas & Latinas, Numismata, Codicesque, varijs Seculis, varijs Regionibus, calamo scriptos, amici fere praedicant: qua de re, excellentissimi Domini mei jussu, post longissimam desuetudinem, constitutum est, me (cum per Otium licuerit) Palaeographiae tuae, ope Graecorum Codicum, Marmorum, Nummorum, &c. qui nostram exornant Britanniam, Additiones quasdam subnectere, in proprium & privatum Domini mei usum, haud eo consilio, ut Ineptiae meae, ullo temporis progressu, typis mandarentur.

Non est absimile vero, Famam aliquam te dudum adsequi Bibliothecae Harleianae; sed incertam, sed forte mendacem: de qua igitur, si quidpiam explorati volueris, certo scias in illa, tam Manuscriptorum quam Impressorum librorum Multitudinem non contemnendam contineri. Codices omne genus MSS. undique conquirere incepit, annis abhinc minus sexdecim, praenobilis Vir Robertus de Harley Comes Oxoniensis, ac haud ita pridem Magnus Magnae Britanniae Thesaurarius; cujus vestigijs inhaerens Amplissimus vir Edwardus Dominus Harley, &c. ejusdem nobilissimi Comitis filius unicus, adeo Collectionem jamdudum praeclaram, novis continuisque Accessionibus locupletavit, ut nunc constet manuscriptis codicibus Graecis, Latinis, Hebraicis, Arabicis, &c. Theologicis, Iuridicis, Medicis, Historicis, Heraldicis, Mathematicis, &c. circiter sexies mille; ut de Cartis Originalibus numero circiter 14000; et de Rotulis seu Voluminibus supra quingentis, simulet de altera Avorum Bibliotheca, hic omnino sileam. Impressi Libri, summa cura selecti, numerantur fere ad viginti millia: inter quos, de Raritate plurimi vel rarioribus Codicibus MSS. certant: puta ij qui Maguntiae per Ioannem Fust & Petrum Schoiffer, in ipsis pene artis Typographicae incunabilis, impressi sunt; Durandi, v.g. Rationale, A.D. 1459; Clementinae cum Apparatu, A.D. 1460; Ioannis Ianuensis Catholicon, ejusdem Anni, si non potius sit Ioanni

Guttembergio adjudicandum; SS. Biblia A.D. 1462; ut recentiores reliquos faciam missos. Tu tecum cogita de ingenti Manu aliarum Editionum primitivarum, per Italiam, Germaniam, Galliam, Angliam, &c. impressarum, quas oculis lustrare, manibus adtrectare, homini hujus rei curioso, fere stupori foret. Praeterea, ut alia quoque studiosis Subsidia pariter atque Oblectamenta presto adessent: crede mihi, neque vetustiora Graeca aut Latina Marmora; Gemmae antiquae; Nummorum maxima vis, Graecorum scil. Romanorum, recentiorum, praesertim ad Britanniam nostram spectantium, aliatenus desiderantur: quibus licet addere Doctorum Effigies, magno numero ab inclytissimis Artificibus graphice depictas.

Si nimia tibi nostra videatur Loquacitas, eam Amori in te meo acceptam refer; veniamque des illi prima vice peccanti, qui in posterum fuerit

Tibi officiosissimus

Humfredus Wanley.

MS: Paris, Bibliothèque Nationale, fonds français 17711, fo. 144. *Date*: 'E Bibliotheca Harleiana, 4 Idus Maij A.D. 1721.' *Address*: 'Venerabili viro Domno Bernardo de Montfaucon Monacho Benedictino, e Congregatione S. Mauri.'

219. *To* William Sherard *18 May 1721*

[*opening lines lost*] Bouillon; and to buy them of him, if you can. If this cannot be, to use his Advice in buying what Greek, Coptic [*five words lost*] Latin MSS. you can. By his means, you may likewise procure the Book written against Dr Mill of Oxford, with the Specimen of the old Italic Version; being both mentioned in my Letter to him.[1]

By his means likewise, and from the Booksellers in Paris, you may procure for my Lord, Thomassini Bibliothecae Venetae, 4to. Henrici Ernstij Index Codicum MSS. Latinorum Bibliothecae Mediceae,

[1] Montfaucon, to whom Wanley had written a week earlier: see no. 218. The *Diary*, 18 May 1721, p. 18(11), makes it clear that Sherard was to deliver the letter. Cf. Wanley's commission to Andrew Hay, 26 Apr. 1720 (no. 215): 'In Paris, Father Bernard Montfaucon has some Coptic, Syriac, and other Manuscripts, worth the buying. Among them is an old Leaf of the Greek Septuagint, written in Uncial or Capital Letters. Buy these, and the leaden Book he gave to Cardinal Bouillon, if he can procure it for you, or direct you to it.'

Sherard wrote from Paris, 11 July 1721 (BL Harley MS 3781, fo. 58), and reported Montfaucon as having said he knew of no Greek, Coptic, or Syriac manuscripts for sale there.

12mo. S. Cyrillus in Jeremiam, Gr. Lat. 8vo, published by Balth. Corderius; wherein is a Catalogue of the un-published Greek MSS. remaining in the Escurial; as remember'd by Alex. Barvoetius. The Volume of Index to Harduin's Councils. The severall Volumes of Analecta Graeca, published in Greek & Latin by F. Mount-faucon & others, in 4to A.D. 1688. A Book in fol. printed at Tregire, A.D. 149.. intituled Catholicon Aremorico–Francico–Latinum, by one John Legaduc, as is said. The old Bishop of Auvrenches, & Father Pezron, had it in Paris; and a Lawyer at Brest or St Malo's had another of them. Two Copies of Young Thevenots Travels, of the French Edition in 4to. And Vita della Contessa Matilda di Canosa, per Ambrogio di Morales.[2]

When you shall be arrived in Holland, my Lord desire's you to call at Voorbourg within half an hour of the Hague; & to see what Greek & other MSS. & Letters of learned Men, &c. do remain in the Possession of old Mr Vossius; & to gett a Catalogue & a Valuation of them if it may be had.[3] At the Hague to call upon Mr Aymon, who formerly sold some MSS. & Papers to my Lord Oxford, and in whose hands there yet remain some others which my Lord desires to have. viz. the Original Letters of Cardinal Visconti about the Council of Trent, which he hath lately published in Print: two Volumes of the Works of Confucius, in folio, translated: the Maps of China, in 8vo. The Letters & Memoirs of Don Heretada de Mendoza. A fine Arabian MS. in 4to containing the Prayers & Rites of the Turks in their Mosques; and 4 quiers (or books) in large Octavo, printed in the Chinese language, &

[2] The following can be identified: G. F. Tomasini, *Bibliothecae Venetae Manuscriptae* (Udine, 1650); Heinrich Ernst, *Catalogus librorum . . . Bibliothecae Mediceae* (Amsterdam, 1641); Balthasar Corderius, *S.P.N. Cyrilli . . . Homiliae xix in Ieremiam . . . ex antiquissimo codice M.S. Regiae Bibliothecae Scorialensis descriptae* [with 'Catalogus praecipuorum auctorum ineditorum graece MSS qui in Bibliotheca Scorialensi asservantur: opera A. Barvoetii'] (Antwerp, 1648); Jean Hardouin, *Conciliorum Collectio Regia maxima* (Paris, 1715); *Analecta Graeca . . . Latine verterunt et notis illustrarunt Monachi Benedictini Congregationis Sancti Mauri* (Paris, 1688); Jean de Thévenot, *Relation d'un voyage fait au Levant* (Paris, 1664–84).
[3] According to Wanley (*Diary*, 2 Mar. 1715, p. 2(5)), the nephew of Isaak Vossius (1618–89), the Dutch classical scholar, still had in his possession 'The Vossian Study', including Greek and Latin manuscripts and letters of learned men to Isaak Vossius and his father Gerhard Jan Vossius (1577–1649). A collection of the correspondence of the father was acquired by Harley, 15 Aug. 1715 (*Diary*, p. 14(1)), but most of the rest found its way into the hands of Richard Rawlinson and is now in the Bodleian Library—Bodl. MSS Rawl. letters 79–84g (*SC* 14962–73). A year after this letter, by which time 'old Mr Vossius' was dead, Sherard showed Wanley a list of manuscripts left by him (32 in number), but Wanley chose not to pursue the matter further (*Diary*, p. 142(5)).

containing their Mathematicks; which two last, he gives instead of a MS. explaining the Theologie of the Mahometans, which is now out of his Power: and for the said Books, &c. you are desired to pay him 250 Florins or Dutch Guilders, i.e. £25 Sterling.[4] He ha's, or had a pretty little MSS. Latin Bible, and may perhaps have some other things in my Lords way, which he leave's to your own good Judgement & Discretion to procure for him. Mr Johnston the Bookseller at the Hague is his intimate friend, & was pr[ivy] to Mr A.D. Stubs's Agreements with him. And as to all Moneys which you shall lay out in my Lords Affairs, you may Draw upon him at your Pleasure, with Assurance that your Bills will be honor'd. Perhaps, in Holland, you may meet with an Opportunity of procuring the old Syriac MS. from Mr Lent, who live's near Herborn in Hessen;[5] who may also have some good Greek MSS. in his Possession. In Amsterdam live's Azariah a Jew, who print's & sells Bibles in all Languages. There, or elsewhere, you may please to buy for my Lord the following Bibles, in the largest Volumes & the best Binding you can; viz. the Malayan, Armenian, Russian, Polish, Danish, Wennish, Finlandish if different from the Lappian; Biscayan, if there be such a book; and that of the Grisons. My Lord is likewise very desirous of having that Greek Bible printed (of late years) at Leipsic in 4to[6] and the Grammar & Lexicon to the Vulgar Greek, lately printed at Hall in Saxony.[7] Thus with my sincere Wishes for your good Journey, Success in all your Undertakings, & Your Return in Health & Safety, I remain,

Worthy Sir,

Your much obliged & very humble Servant,

Humfrey Wanley.

[4] For Wanley's earlier dealings with Aymon, see no. 123 n. 2. The list of desiderata is entered by Wanley in his *Diary*, 18 May 1721 (p. 107(4)), and some of the works mentioned here also appear in the postscript to Wanley's 'Brief Account' of the Aymon material in BL Loan MS 29/259 misc. 37. The Visconti letters alone from this list were secured for Harley—sent by Sherard, 29 Nov. 1721 (*Diary*, p. 124(12)), now BL Harley MS 3479. Aymon's edition of the Visconti material is *Lettres, anecdotes et mémoires historiques du Nonce Visconti* (1719).

[5] See no. 143 for Wanley's first mention of this manuscript, and *Diary*, 20 April 1722 (p. 139(7)) and 19 Nov. 1722 (p. 174(8) and n. 6), for his continuing interest. The MS has not been identified.

[6] Probably Ludolph Kuster's revision (1710) of John Mill's Oxford edn. of the Greek NT (1707), Darlow and Moule no. 4735.

[7] Perhaps the polyglot NT first ptd. in Leipzig in 1713 (Darlow and Moule no. 1451), in which the modern Greek version was taken from A. H. Francke's diglot edn. pbd. in Halle, 1710 (Darlow and Moule no. 4961).

MS: London, Royal Society Sh. 650; draft, incomplete. *Endorsed*: 'My Lord's Commission which He desires Mr Sherard to Execute in France & Holland. 18 May 1721.'

220. *To* Arthur Charlett *2 June 1721*

Reverend Sir,

I doubt not but you have long Expected some further Answer to your last kind Letter of the 24th of March last.[1] But I hope you will please to excuse me, when you Consider that I am not Master of my Time, and that my Lords Business (when I am well) keep's me fully Employ'd. And although, since my last, I have been in the Cottonian Library, and have carried the Paper upon which I now write, about me for several Weeks past: yet this is the first Opportunity I have gain'd of writing unto you at my Leasure, without breaking into others Time, or trespassing upon other Persons.

I hear that the Bursar you was pleas'd to mention, is my worthy old Friend Mr Denison, whom I should have been heartily glad to have embraced. I know he was long in Town, but I could not wait on him for the reason abovementioned; nor have I been able to attend Mr George Clarke; yet I hope to do so, before he leave's the Town.

As to Mr Wise's other Quaeres, he may please to know that his Cottonian Asser,[2] is not written by one Hand, but by several, and much about the same time, according to the Custom of writing Books, of old. The Beginning is of the best and stanchest hand, and seem's to have been written about A.D. 1000, in the English Hand of that Time, and not all in Saxon Letters as misrepresented by A.Bp Parker, who printed from this very Book;[3] yet Proper Names (according to Custom then very Common) are written with Saxon Letters when required, as with ð, þ, p, &c. My Authority for adjusting the Age of that Exemplar, is an Original Charter of King Æthelred Dated A.D. 1001,[4] which, as to the Hand, agreeth very well with the first part of the Asser, OTHO.

[1] Welbeck Wanleyana = BL Loan MS 29/253. For Wanley's original reply see no. 217.

[2] Cotton Otho A.xii.

[3] In his *Ælfredi regis res gestae, lingua Latina sed literis Saxonicis* [1574], STC 863. Despite Wanley's correction here, Wise (p. 137) assumes that Parker means that the manuscript was written in Anglo-Saxon characters and uses this as an argument for declaring that Parker did *not* therefore print from Otho B.xii (*Asser's Life of King Alfred*, ed. W. H. Stevenson (rptd. Oxford, 1959), pp. xv–xvi).

[4] In Cotton Augustus ii.22, Sawyer no. 898.

A. 12. I do not remember any MS. in Oxford exactly of that Hand; yet, I fancy some Notion may be had of it, if Mr W[is]e pleases to look upon those Canons in Bibl. Bodl. ma[r]ked Supra M. 4. Art. 138.[5]

As to the Catalogue of English Bishops there, in CLAVDIVS B. 7.[6] I lookd upon it, and found it to be a Fragment cutt out of some other Book, & clap'd in there. Upon considering the Hand, I thought it might be of about A.D. 1230, and examining the last Bishops written by that Hand (for there are some Continuations) I am so Confirmed as to let that my Opinion stand. That Catalogue is not fit to be printed as it is; because much better (I believe better than any yet printed) may be made up from the Cotton—and other Libraries.

I am in some hope that my noble Lord will send me to Oxford some time this Somer. In which Case he will send the MS. of John Stow's Writing by me, if you desire it.[7] He is now out of Town, otherwise I could scarcely have written this Evening. Mr James Hill, Mr Dobyns,[8] and some other Friends are come in; so I must conclude, being with the greatest Respect

Reverend Sir,

Your most obliged & very humble servant

Humfrey Wanley.

Mr Hill sends his Respectful Service to your Self, & Love to Mr Wise: whom with Mr Bowlde[9] I have a great Regard for.

MS: Bodleian, Ballard 13, fo. 152. *Date*: 'Covent-Garden, 2 June 1721.' *Address*: 'To The Reverend Dr Charlet Master of University-College, in Oxford.' *Printed*: K. Sisam, *Review of English Studies*, vii (1931), p. 8 n. (extract), rptd. *Studies in the History of Old English Literature* (Oxford, 1953), p. 148 n.

[5] Bodl. MS Bodley 865 (*SC* 2737), three manuscripts bound together. Wanley refers only to the third, an early eleventh-century English manuscript of Capitula of Theodulf, Bishop of Orleans.

[6] Cotton Claudius B.vii, art. 9.

[7] BL Harley MS 563, a translation by Stowe of the works of Asser, Florence of Worcester, Aelred of Rievaulx, and Trivet.

[8] Probably Robert Dobyns (b. 1665), of Evesbatch Court, Herefordshire, father-in-law of James Hill, barrister-at-law of Middle Temple 1690. He exhibited large numbers of Herefordshire deeds to the Society of Antiquaries, 27 Apr. 1720 (Wanley, *Diary*, Biographical Index under Dobbins, citing Minutes of the Society of Antiquaries). He and James Hill visited the Harleian Library together, 9 May 1721 (*Diary*, p. 44(9)).

[9] Presumably Joseph Bowles, Bodley's Librarian (Wise was Under-Keeper); Wanley may have had a cold.

221. *To* The Curators of the Bodleian Library
20 October 1721

Whereas about twenty years ago, being then in London, at the instance of Dr Charlet, and with the Consent of Dr Hans Sloane, I compared many Thousands of his Books with Dr Hyde's Catalogue, and after long Labor during several Weeks, found out a great Number of Books which were Duplicates in Dr Sloanes Library, and yet wanting in the Bodleyan; of which Books I also took a List, and was assisting at their putting up, when Dr Sloane gave them to the University;[1] which Services I then valued at Seven Pounds & Ten Shillings, which Money remaineth still due to me, notwithstanding a demand I made of it to Dr Mander when he was Vice-chancellor:[2] If the now Reverend & Learned the Vicechancellor, the Kings Professors, & the Procurators, being the Curators of the Bodleyan Library, after so many years elapsed, shall judge it meet to gratifie me for my Labor & my Good Will also, at the Rate that then I valued my time at; it is my Desire that the said Seven Pounds & Ten Shillings be imployed in the procuring of some one or more good & useful Book or Books to be put into the said Library, wherein I have Served to my great Benefit (both of Information & Maintainance) without the trouble of any Entrance into the Benefaction-book.[3]

Witness my Hand,

Humfrey Wanley.

MS: Bodleian, Add. C. 78, fo. 21. *Date*: '20 October 1721.' *Printed*: Macray, p. 164 n. 1.

[1] Charlett acknowledged both Sloane's gift and Wanley's 'fair Catalogue' in a letter d. 8 Oct. 1700 (Welbeck Wanleyana = BL Loan MS 29/253); the books so given were 'placed according to Your Marks in the Bodleian Library' and received by the University 'with great esteem and Respect'. But the donation proved disappointing and indeed something of an embarrassment: see Hudson to Wanley d. 29 Apr. 1701, ptd. Ellis, *Original Letters*, pp. 302–3. According to Macray (p. 169), Sloane's benefactions were generally of poor quality: between 1701 and 1738 he gave more than 1,400 vols. to the Bodleian, but only 415 are specified in the Benefactors' Register.

[2] Roger Mander (1649–1704), Master of Balliol College, Oxford 1687, Vice-Chancellor 1700-2.

[3] The Library purchased Paolo Alessandro Maffei, *Raccolta di Statue antiche e moderne data in luce da D. de Rossi* (Rome, 1704), now Arch. A.157. It is recorded in the Benefactors' Register, ii, p. 128. Wanley gave an early fourteenth-century MS Latin bible at the same time (now MS Auct. D.5.18, *SC* 27664), a book owned by him since 1690. Wanley is thanked by Bowles on behalf of the Curators in a letter d. 9 Dec. 1721, Welbeck Wanleyana = BL Loan MS 29/251).

222. *To* Joseph Bowles *21 November 1721*

Good Sir,

By my Lord's Order,[1] I apprise you of his desire to know what was
done at the Library-Visitation, on the 8th Instant, with relation to the
Duplicates which he was willing to take-off from the Library, at
reasonable price.[2]

I also desire to be informed whether the Reverend & Learned the
Curators, were pleased to accept of my poor present, at their said
Visitation.[3]

If You have not already performed your promise in presenting my
most hearty Respects & Thanks to Dr Delaune,[4] Dr Charlett, my good
Lord of Chester,[5] Dr Stratford, Dr Terry,[6] the Provost of Queens,[7] Dr
Clarke, Mr Wyat,[8] Mr Wise, and the rest of my Patrons & Friends in
Oxford I desire that you will please to do it speedily; lest they should
find me guilty of Forgetfulness, or ill Manners, or (what is worst of all)
Ingratitude.

Be pleased to lett Mr President of St Johns know, that upon my
arrival here, my friend the Bookseller, was gone a long Journey, & his
Ware-house locked up. Very lately, upon his Return, he told me that
He ha's but the first part of Doletus;[9] having, before it came into his
Hands, parted with a Second part of that Book to one Mr Richardson
a London-Apothecary. The price of the Book ha's, by this mine
honest & most reasonable Friend, been hoisted up to 12 pounds, upon

---

[1] 16 Nov. 1721, Welbeck Wanleyana = BL Loan MS 29/250.

[2] For the Curators' authorization of the sale of duplicates to Harley, see Bowles to
Wanley d. 9 Dec. 1721, Welbeck Wanleyana = BL Loan MS 29/251. The first purchase
appears to have been the Complutensian Polyglot, the first Polyglot bible, ptd. in 6 vols.
at Alcalá de Henares by Arnaldo Guillen de Brocar between 1514 and 1517: see Wanley,
Diary, p. 126(1) and n. 4, and Bowles to Wanley d. 17 Dec. 1721, BL Harley MS 3777,
fo. 226.

[3] See no. 221 and n. 3.

[4] William Delaune (1669–1728), President of St John's College, Oxford 1698.

[5] Francis Gastrell.

[6] Thomas Terry (1678–1735), Sub-Dean of Christ Church, Oxford, Regius Professor
of Greek 1712.

[7] John Gibson (1678–1730), Provost of The Queen's College, Oxford 1716.

[8] Perhaps William Wyatt, Schoolmaster of Christ Church, Oxford, son of William
Wyatt, Principal of St Mary Hall, Oxford, and Orator of the University († 1712).
According to Hearne (*Collections*, viii, p. 365), he was nominated head of Felstead
School, Essex, in 1725.

[9] Probably the *Commentariorum Linguae Latinae* of Étienne Dolet, 2 vols., 1st edn.
(Lyons, 1536–8), or 2nd edn. (Basle, 1537–9).

the Character given of it by Mr Mattaire;[10] and that this Mr Richardson gave Six Guineas for his Book, or Second part of it.

Be pleased to lett Dr Clarke know that I am not yet got down to Wympole; where I shal not forget the matter relating to Durandus.[11] Also, please to acquaint Mr Provost of Queens, that I expect the most proper Opportunity of writing to my noble Lord the Earl of Oxford, in Obedience to his Commands.

Pray, Sir, be pleased to favor me with your Information touching the Premisses, and you will add to the heap of Obligations you have already laid upon

Your most faithful friend, & very humble Servant

Humfrey Wanley.

P.S. Mrs M——s who came in the Coach up with us, is a very merry, good-humor'd Gentlewoma[n]. She often spake of You, and bad me (as my Spouse ha's also done) to send her Service.

MS: Bodleian, Add. C. 78, fo. 22. *Date*: 'Bedford-street, Covent-garden, 21 Novr 1721.' *Address*: 'To Mr Bowles, Head Library keeper to the University of Oxford.'

223. *To* John Anstis *25 January 1722*

Honorable Sir,

I open'd not your Letter[1] until this Morning, and thank you heartily for it. My Lord would gladly conferre with you upon the Affair mentioned in the Note therein closed;[2] and to this End, desire's your good Company at Dinner some day, and the sooner the better.

As to the Statutes of the Garter by K. Edward VI, the Date is 17 March 1552, anno 7 of his Reign. The Book is fairly Written &

---

[10] Michael Maittaire (1670–1747), bibliographer, historian of printing. References to the Doletus are in his *Annales Typographici*, II. ii (1722), pp. 564, 846, presumably pbd. late in 1721 and (as so often) post-dated. A very long and laudatory account of the book occurs in vol. III. i (1725), pp. 54–61.

[11] See no. 224.

---

[1] 24 Jan. 1722, BL Harley MS 3777, fo. 25.

[2] Information from John Warburton, Somerset Herald, about 'the present Proprietors of the Bookes in Yorkshire'. For these see Wanley's Memorandum Book, BL Lansdowne MS 677, fo. 36ᵛ, ptd. Wanley, *Diary*, p. 429.

Illuminated, upon Velum; and may chance to please you when you see it.[3]

I am, with true Respect, Sir,
  Your most humble Servant

Humfrey Wanley.

MS: British Library, Stowe 749, fo. 182. *Date*: 'Dover-street, 25 January 1721/2.' *Address*: '[To the Honor]able John Anstis Esqr Garter, at [the Colleg]e of Armes, in Great Carter-lane.'

224. *To* [George Clarke] *23 March 1722*

Honorable Sir,

I have not been unmindful of the promise I made unto you in Oxford, of sending you some account of my Lords Durandus, when I should be arrived here;[1] which happen'd not untill the day before yesterday. I have now His Lordships Book before me, and do make the following Observations upon it.

It is Printed *all* upon very good Velum; & yet remain's intire, & clean.

The Printers used here no Signatures, nor Catch-words; which are omitted likewise in other old Printed books.

Notwithstanding the earliness of its Date, the Stock of Printing Letter then prepared by Fust & Schoiffer was very large: for (to omitt the great Number of Jugations & Abbreviations, which run through the book & must have been a very troublesom & costly Work to make & bring to this Perfection) they had two Alphabets of Minuscules, and two more (if not three) of Majuscules. Of these, the smallest Letter make's the Text of the Book; & the larger is used in the Date only, because otherwise, the Work would have Swelled out into too great a Bulk: whereas the Clementine Constitutions which came out the next year, 1460,[2] (which book I have here also by me) being a much lesser Work, is printed with the above-mentioned bigger sort of Minuscule

---

[3] BL Harley MS 394.

[1] Promised in Wanley to Bowles, 21 Nov. 1721 (no. 222). The 'Durandus' is *Rationale diuinorum officiorum* (Mainz: J. Fust and P. [Schöffer], 1459), of Guillaume Durand (*GW* 9101, Hain 6471, Proctor 66).

[2] Clement V, *Constitutiones* (Mainz: J. Fust and P. Schöffer, 1460) (*GW* 7077, Hain-Copinger 5410, Proctor 67).

Letter; and the Apparatus or Gloss of Johannes Andreas upon them is of this small Letter which makes the Text of Durandus. I think it needless to putt down the first & last Words of every Column throughout the Book, because yours in All Souls Library wants many Leaves; and shall content my self with presenting to you those only of the first page of every Ten Leaves, not doubting but that some of them will agree with that of your College.[3]

Then follows (in the last Column) the Date printed as is aforesaid, with larger Letter, & with red Ink, in the following Words,

Presens racōnalis diuino2̸ codex officō2̸ venustate capitaliū decoratus rubricationibusꝗ distinctus. Artificiosa adinuētione imprimendi ac caracteri3andi: absꝗ calami exaratioñ sic effigiatus. Et ad eusebiam dei industrie est ɔsūmatus Per Johannē fust ciuē Magūtinu3. Et petrū Gerns3heym Clericum dioceβ eiusdem Anno dñi Millesimo quadringentesimo quīquagesimonono. Seх̄ die Octobris.

I have before mention'd the Funt of Capitals used in printing this Book; which are of three sorts, like those used by the same Fust & Schoiffer (of Gernszheym) in their other Labors. One is of the smallest sort, used in the body of the Text upon all Occasions. Another, much larger, is used only at the Beginning of Sections or Paragraphs; of which kind, I doubt not, but that they had a full Alphabet, although I find not the G & the four last Letters of it in this Work: and these are almost always printed with the rest. The largest Sort, or Principal Letters are adorned with Flourishes of different Colors, and were most certainly Stamped at the same time with the others, as will easily appear to an attentive Eie. The Rubrics are also of Red Letters (not of Black, as in our Common Prayers) keeping their true & proper distances (without offence to a skilful beholder) being done at once with the Rest; & the whole performed in much better manner, than my Informants say can now be done in Oxford, or in London. In some of the Places where these Rubrics, or the Midling sort of Capitals are wanting (perhaps, through the Defect of the MS. original they followed) somebody or other (it may be the Illuminator) ha's filled up the Vacancies with his Pen. I understand the preceding Words in the date, *venustate capitalium decoratus rubricationibusque distinctus*, to

---

[3] Press-mark L.R.5.l.1, the oldest ptd. book in the Library, wanting thirty-six leaves at the end. Wanley's list of 'first & last Words' is omitted here.

Signifie or import that they were so actually printed, & come forth
from the Press, without any Recourse to, or Assistance from the
Illuminators Hand. And so I believe the Psalter before printed by
these two Artists, A.D. 1457,[4] will prove, when it shall be brought to
England: for Lambecius says in his 2d. Vol. of the Imperial Catalogue,[5] pag. 989. that the same Psalter which he found in the Archi-
Ducal Library at Inspruck, and transported into the Imperial one of
Vienna, was likewise *venustate Capitalium decoratus, Rubricationibusque
sufficienter distinctus*: and so was my Lords Clementines (*suis Rubrica-
tionibus sufficienter distinctus*) abovementioned, printed by the same
persons A.D. 1460, upon Velum: although the Illuminator ha's gone
over almost every midling Capital with his fresh Writing Ink. And the
same person I suppose, or one of the same Occupation, ha's been
busie with my Lords Durandus. I am not yet able to satisfie my self as
to the matters of Fact so long since, & so far off transacted; but it
seem's probable that the Illuminators of Books might have made some
Complaints upon the decay of their Trade, when the Printers could
Print-off decorated & flourished Letters: and therefore were by
Authority (whether Imperial, or Papal, I yet know not) empower'd to
Adorn all Books that should be Printed for the future, as they had
done the Manuscripts in times passed, according to the Rates wherein
their Customers & they could agree.

I observe, that the Catholicon of Joannes Januensis printed this
year, 1460, at Mentz[6] (of which my noble Lord here hath the finest
Exemplars, both upon Velum & paper) doth constantly leave spaces
for the Capitals to be filled up by the Illuminators, as is done accordingly. I know not what to say to this, unless it be that the book
(although it be a great Work) yet is not of the Letter used by Fust &
Schoiffer; who, it may be, might have obtained some Privilege in that
behalf; and if it was begun by John Guttenbergh, who was sometime
Partner with them; they are said to have parted asunder & each to have
sett-up on their own stock, & to have printed. Yet, I could never yet see
any book printed by Guttenbergh to this day: perhaps, this might have
been begun by him, & in prosecuting the great Work he might yield to

---

[4] *Psalterium cum canticis, hymnis* (Mainz: J. Fust and P. Schöffer, 1457) (Hain 13479,
Proctor 64).

[5] P. Lambeck, *Commentariorum de Augustissima Bibliotheca Caesarea Vindobonensi*
(Vienna, 1669).

[6] i.e. the *Catholicon* of Joannes Balbus (Mainz: [J. Gutenberg?], 1460) (*GW* 3182,
Hain-Copinger 2254, Proctor 146).

his Fate, and so his Name be passed over by those, who nevertheless omitted their own; for here, no Workmans name is mentioned.

In my Lords Bible printed by the said Fust & Schoiffer upon Velum A.D. 1462,[7] I find Rubrics & Capitals as before in the Durandus all printed by the Press, & yet so much scope left for the Illuminator, as to find him (or Her) a good job of Work. I put in HER, because in those days, and for many Ages before, Maidens & Women practised the Illuminating of Books as a Trade; nay, more, the transcribing many in Learned Languages; I forbear to say Composing such; and even that is true.

My Lord hath a Tract bearing Date A.D. 1464; but it being printed with Writing Ink on only one Side of the Paper, it belong's rather to another Tribe, and is not to your present purpose & mine.[8]

In my Lords Sextus Liber Decretalium, printed by Fust & Schoiffer A.D. 1465, upon Velum;[9] Spaces are every where left for the Illuminator; who having thereby more Employment, took the less pains with the smallest Capitals at the beginning of a Sentence, &c.

MS: Welbeck Wanleyana = British Library,Loan 29/258; fair copy, unfinished? *Date*: 'Wympole, 23 March, 1721/22.'

225. *To* Johann Daniel Schumacher[1] *1 May 1722*

Worthy Mr John-Daniel Schumacker,

Upon the Notice you are pleased to give me of your approaching Departure, I crave Leave to desire you to buy in Holland for my Lord,

---

[7] *Biblia* (Mainz: J. Fust and P. Schöffer, 1462) (*GW* 4204, Hain-Copinger 3050, Proctor 79).

[8] The xylographic 'Grotesque Alphabet' of 1464 (now press-mark A. 131 in the Print Collection of the British Museum), as is clear from a note of Wanley's d. 5 Feb. 1722 preserved in a copy by Thomas Baker in Cambridge University Library MS Mm.i.43, p. 520. For a full discussion of this problematical piece, see Campbell Dodgson, *Catalogue of Early German and Flemish Woodcuts Preserved in the Department of Prints and Drawings in the British Museum*, i (1903), pp. 124–31. It is ptd. with a collotype facsimile of the entire alphabet as *Grotesque Alphabet of 1464*, ed. C. Dodgson (1899).

[9] Boniface VIII, *Liber sextus decretalium* (Mainz: J. Fust and P. Schöffer, 1465) (*GW* 4848, Hain-Copinger 3586, Proctor 81, *BMC* i, p. 23).

[1] Johann Daniel Schumacher (1690–1761), a native of Alsace, Librarian to Peter the Great; he visited England in 1722 and visited Wimpole in March, accompanied by Wanley. For his departure and Wanley's concern to engage him on Harley's behalf, see Wanley, *Diary*, pp. 140(13), 141(4), 142(14), (2).

a Bible in each of the Languages Following, in case you can easily meet with them: vizt Armenian; Cosack, if there be any such; Finnish; Gjorgian; Grison or Rhetish; Helvetian, or Switz; Laplandish; Lithuanian; Malayan, if there be an whole Bible; Norwegian; Tartarian, if there [be]² a Bible, or any Biblical book in any Tartar-Language; and Slavonian, both in the Hieronymian or Glagolitical, & in the Wallachian Letter. I omitt the Russian, because you have been pleased already to promise that you will take Care about it.

You will please to take Care to procure from Mr Professor Wolfius at Hamburg his two τετραναγγέλια or books of the Four Gospels, written in Greek Capital Letters,³ in case they will come for about 30 Guineas (or as much under as you can:) and to send them safely packed up, to London, with all the convenient Speed you may. And if he hath any more Greek MSS. to buy them also, as cheap as you can, according to your own good Discretian & Judgement, and send them hither, with the others.

I desire you will please to use proper Means for my Lords obtaining from Mr Zacharias Uffenbach of Franckfort, his Prayer-book in German, printed at Mentz A.D. 1457;⁴ such of his Books as are printed on the one Side of the Leaf only; and some few others of his old printed Books & MSS, such as may be to my Lords good liking.

For these, or any of these acceptable Services, my Lord will indemnifie you with great Thanks & by paying the Moneys punctually, according to your Orders. I beseech God Almighty to bless & prosper you all along in this Voyage, & in his own due time, to bring you hither again in safety to him who is, in all Sincerity

Worthy Sir,

Your most faithful, obedient, & obliged Servant

Humfrey Wanley.

Be pleased to direct your Letters for me at the Right Honorable Edward Lord Harleys, in Dover-street, Westminster.

---

² MS omits 'be'.

³ Schumacher was unsuccessful in his attempt to purchase the Greek Gospels owned by Johann Christoph Wolf (1683–1739), Professor of Hebrew at Hamburg, but one of the manuscripts (BL Harley MS 5684) found its way into Harley's possession in 1731. See Wanley, *Diary*, pp. 140 n. 5, 148(5) and n. 3, 154(11).

⁴ Zacharias Conrad von Uffenbach (1683–1734), German scholar and collector. Wright (*Diary*, p. 140 n. 4) points out that the only known book ptd. by Fust and Schoeffer in 1457 is a Psalter in *Latin*: see Irvine Masson, *The Mainz Psalters and Canon Missae, 1457–59* (1954). Uffenbach's library was purchased after his death by J. C. Wolf, who pbd. a catalogue of it at Hamburg in 1736.

MS: Leningrad, Archive of the Academy of Sciences, Fond 121. *Date*: 'From my Lord Harleys Library, 1 May 1722.' *Printed*: Ruth C. Wright, 'Letters from Humfrey Wanley to Eric Benzelius and Peter the Great's Librarian', *Durham University Journal*, NS i (1940), pp. 194–5.

226. *To* Edward Harley *8 May 1722*

May it please your Lordship,

I return most hearty Thanks for your being pleas'd to take me into your Remembrance, and should have paid my Duty to you in a Letter before now, had I certainly known the place of your Residence; but not being apprised of that, I thought that your Lordship expected no Letters from me.

I obeyed your Commands with relation to Mr Vaillant; who will be sure to keep his promise.

The Duplicates which your Lordship is to furnish Mr Noel with, according to Agreement, are

Plinij Historia Naturalis. *Venet.* 1469. fol. mag. Conclusio fol. penult. atris.[1]

Les Vies de Plutarque. à Paris chez Michel de Vascosan, 1565. fol. crass.[2]

Cicero de Finibus. Venet. 1471. per Ioannem de Colonia Agrippinensi 4to ampl.[3]

Iohannis de Sacrobusto Spera Mundi. 4to ten.[4]

Mr Noel is in Tribulation for the £200 that he remitted last; because G.S.[5] write's that the Man who recieved will answer no Letters, yet G.S. ha's bought more old Books & MSS. & Noel say's he must immediatly remitt the same Money over again. He is also purchasing the Library of Mr Williams late his Majesties Printer. It consists of above 3000 Books, all in fine Condition; and is said to be a very valuable Collection. He promise's to lett your Lordship have of them what you shall want at the price he give's; the rest he will keep up until Winter,

---

[1] Hain 13087, Proctor 4018.
[2] The 2nd edn. of the translation by J. Amyot, Bishop of Auxerre.
[3] *GW* 6885, Hain 5328, Proctor 4036.
[4] Not identified.
[5] George Suttie.

when he will make a public Sale.[6] But, I find, he intend's to have recourse to your Lordship for Assistance, soon.

Dr Sherard is going to Paris to buy a Collection of Natural Curiosities, which will cost him 1000 Pistoles besides all his Charges; so I find his £30 will now be welcome.[7]

Mr Strype ha's sent one of his Papers, which make's two in his Life of Grindal. I keep it safely for you.[8]

Mr Schumacker desired heartily to be recommended to your Favor before his Departure. I gave him an Order to buy the two old Greek MSS. of the Gospels, & some few other Things; and am now made known to Mr Stirling the Merchant, his Correspondent here.[9]

Mr Gibson having gotten a small but curious parcel of Books & MSS. I have gotten hither all those which I thought your Lordship would like. Among them is a Homers Odysseis in Greek, upon Paper; a very fine Aulus Gellius, Terence, & Æneas Sylvius his first Book of Cosmography with his Effigies in the Principal Letter, it having been that Popes own book.[10] Mr Gibson say's that this present parcel is the dearest that he ever had, but he will make you as easy as he can. He expects soon another much finer, & which came at much cheaper Rates:[11] in it are said to be the Comment of Proclus Diadochus upon Platos Parmenides, Greek, in the *Six* Books. Many are of Opinion that this Work hath not been as yet Printed. There is likewise Homers Ilias & Odysseis written in Greek upon the finest Velum A.D. 1465, by Ioannes Rossus the Cretan (who wrote your Lordships fine book of

---

[6] John Williams († c.1722), printer, manager of the King's Printing House in Blackfriars from 1691. His library was bought by Noel and picked over by Wanley (see E. Harley to Wanley d. 15 July 1722, Welbeck Wanleyana = BL Loan MS 29/250). Those books set aside were viewed by Harley 11 Sept. 1722, and those bought were finally sent 27 Dec. 1722. For a list see Wanley, *Diary*, pp. 180–2. Noel does not seem to have made 'public sale' of the books as is suggested here.

[7] See Wanley, *Diary*, p. 142(5).

[8] See Wanley, *Diary*, pp. 140(11), (15), 141(7), 142(6), 143(9), 152(3). For Harley's interest in Strype's papers see *Diary*, p. 36(6) and n. 5.

[9] For the Greek Gospels see n. 225 n. 3. Schumacher had introduced Wanley to Stirling on 1 May 1722 (*Diary*, p. 142(2)).

[10] John Gibson (*fl.* 1720–6), a Scot who from about 1720 dealt in manuscripts and early ptd. books acquired in Italy from agents apparently operating from Florence. For a full list of the parcel see Wanley, *Diary*, p. 143(1); those mentioned here are BL Harley MSS 5673 (Homer), 2768 (Aulus Gellius), 2721 (Terence), 3976 (Aeneas Sylvius).

[11] For the 'present parcel' Gibson agreed on a price of £350: see Wanley, *Diary*, p. 162(2); for the 'much finer' parcel see *Diary*, p. 145(7), and for a list p. 159(1). Those mentioned here are BL Harley MSS 5671 (Proclus, see *Diary*, p. 159 n. 4), 5600 (Homer, see also *Diary*, p. 110(3)).

the four Gospels) with such Illuminations, that the Italian that bought it, affirm's it to be *una Raccolta veramente Reale*, and further, that the old Readings sometimes cited by Eustathius are to be found herein.[12] He will be able to do your Lordship further Service in procuring you valuable Books from abroad; and hath been honest to you.

From my own Lodging.

My Lord, upon occasion of my writing by this Post, I have now been at Luffingham's to know if any Message would be given me by the Christian, but he had none besides his Duty in General.

Mr Hill will make a fine Picture of Mr Schumacker, who paid him his whole Price upon his Second Sitting;[13] and mine will be soon finished, so as to furnish-out a good Performance upon a very mean Subject.[14]

Mr Chapman brought back the Parcel last deliver'd to him, at his day; all well done, except some unevenesses in Lettering, which a good Workman is yet frequently guilty of. Mr Elliot has brought in likewise his last parcel, yet with some of the Titles curtaild. I gave Mr Chapman a parcel of the MSS. last bought, but want more of your Morocco Skins for him. I gave Mr Elliot a choaking parcel all for Calf-skin; and made him promise to be punctual with me.[15]

Young Mr Varenne ha's been with me, but I keep two of his Books untill your Lordships return up.[16]

I had the Honor of drinking to the present good Healths of my most noble Lady, the sweet young Lady, and your good Lordship with Mr Granger, from whom I have gotten a Pot full of a sort of Sweetmeat made in China, which I doubt not but will prove to my Ladies & your Palat.

I have also gotten some of the very best Spanish Snuff for my Lady, lately come to Mr Beaver.

---

[12] Harley's 'fine book of the four Gospels' is BL Harley MS 5790 (d. 1478), written for Francis Gonzaga, Cardinal of St Maria Nuova (F. H. A. Scrivener, *Introduction to the Criticism of the New Testament*, 4th rev. edn. (1894), Evann. no. 448).

[13] Not identified, but see Wanley, *Diary*, p. 322(14).

[14] Hill's 1722 portrait of Wanley is in the Students' Room of the Department of Manuscripts at the British Library, described by Wanley in his letter to Schumacher, 26 May 1722 (no. 227), as Hill's 'Master-piece', and apparently intended for Schumacher: see no. 228.

[15] Christopher Chapman (*fl.* 1704–56) and Thomas Elliott († 1763), the two book-binders chiefly employed by Harley.

[16] Matthew de Varenne, bookseller: see Wanley, *Diary*, Biographical Index under Varenne. Not listed by Plomer, *Dictionary*.

Mr Rogers the Clergy-man,[17] Mr Hill & Mr Reason[18] are[19] just come in to me. I therefore conclude wishing your Lordship all Health & Prosperity, as being with the truest Respect

       Your Lordships most dutiful & most obedient & faithful Servant

                                      Humfrey Wanley.

MS: Welbeck Wanleyana = British Library, Loan 29/258. *Date*: 'From the Library, 8 May 1722.' *Address*: 'To The Right Honorable Edward Lord Harley at Wympole near Royston, in Cambridgeshire.'

227. *To* Johann Daniel Schumacher   *26 May 1722*[1]

Dear Sir,

     Mr Stirling ha's been so kind as to send me your very kind Letter,[2] for which I return you most hearty Thanks. I shall be glad to receive the 2 Greek MSS. & the German book, as soon as may be.[3] As to my little account of my noble Lords Library, it ha's been drawn up soon after your departure;[4] but I can not send it until I have my Lords Leave; and he is now in Herefordshire with my Lord Oxford, who was taken dangerously ill, on a sudden. His Lordship is expected here in Town soon, his Father being much better. When my Lord ha's seen what I have written, it will be transcribed; & I will send it to Mr Stirling out of Hand.

     The inclosed Letter came to my hands by mere Chance: I paid 2s 6d for the Postage, for which I shall reckon with Mr Stirling.

     I am sorry you can find no more of the Bibles we want, than those in the Armenian & Suiss, Languages; yet those shall be welcome, & thankfully paid for.

     Mr Hill & Mr Christian are at your Service; & I drank your Health with them the last Night. Mr Hill has made your Picture very well, & very like you. Mine goe's on bravely, and will be his Master-piece.[5] I am represented therein, as holding a fine Brass-Head of the Emperor

---

[17] Not identified.

[18] Probably John Reissen or Reyssen, brother of Charles Christian (Reissen), a painter. See Wanley, *Diary*, Biographical Index under Reissen.

[19] & MS.

[1] Not, as *Durham University Journal*, NS i (1940), p. 195, 'undated'.

[2] Not found.   [3] See no. 225 nn. 3, 4.

[4] Not found.   [5] See no. 226 n. 14.

Hadrian, bigger than the Life, and of Grecian Workmanship; which
with other Antiquities, MSS. & rare Printed Books, have come in,
since you went from hence. I hope to hear from you again quickly; and
in the mean time do remain sincerely,

Worthy Sir,

Your most faithful friend, & most humble Servant

Humfrey Wanley.

MS: Leningrad, Archive of the Academy of Sciences, Fond 121. *Date*: 'Dover-street, in
Westminster, 26 May 1722.' *Address*: 'To Mr John-Daniel Schumacker, at Mr Nayelins
@ Berlin.' *Printed*: Ruth C. Wright, 'Letters from Humfrey Wanley to Eric Benzelius
and Peter the Great's Librarian', *Durham University Journal*, NS i (1940), pp. 195–6.

228. *To* Johann Daniel Schumacher *31 May 1722*

Dear Sir

Your second kind Letter of the 5th of June N.S. with that [of]
Monsieur Bene inclosed,[1] came safe to my Hands, who return you
most hearty thanks for the same. I percieve that Monsieur Wolfius
esteem's his two MSS. and consequently ha's no Thoughts of parting
with them; but when you talk with him vivâ voce, I doubt not but you
will be able to induce him to take Money for them. I must [th]erefore
desire you to buy them as cheap as you can, but yet to Buy them
although [th]ey should cost more than what I last mentioned to you;
and also to buy what o[th]er Greek MSS. are in his Possession.

I hope you will have a more favorable Answer from Mr Uffenbach;
some [o]f whose most antient Printed Books will serve to adorn my
Noble Lords Library, to my great Pleasure & Satisfaction.

My Lord Harley is not yet returned from Herefordshire; but, in his
Name, [I] return you thanks for your Care in these his Affairs.

My Picture goe's on well, and will be finished about a fourtnight
hence; [it] then will soon be deliver'd to Mr Stirling for your Use.[2] In
the mean while, I remain,

Worthy Sir,

Your most faithful & obliged Servant

Humfrey Wanley.

[1] Welbeck Wanleyana = BL Loan MS 29/257; Daniel Bene was Schumacher's
correspondent in Hamburg: see Wanley, *Diary*, p. 148(5). For Wolf and Uffenbach see
no. 225.   [2] See no. 226 and n. 14.

[I] often drink to your own good health, [and] to that of Madam Anouski.

MS: Leningrad, Archive of the Academy of Sciences, Fond 121. *Date*: 'Westminster, 31 May, 1722.' *Address*: 'A Monsieur Monsieur Jean Daniel Schumacker, a Amsterdam.' *Printed*: Ruth C. Wright, 'Letters from Humfrey Wanley to Eric Benzelius and Peter the Great's Librarian', *Durham University Journal*, NS i (1940), pp. 196–7.

229. *To* [William Holman] *11 June 1722*

Reverend Sir,

Yours of the 5th Instant[1] came to my Hands on Friday-morning last, upon Reading of which I laid aside my other Business, and have turned over not only the Registre of Waltham in this Library,[2] but have likewise consulted many other Books, in Hopes of finding some-what to your purpose: but my Success hath not been answerable to my Labor. My Lord hath another Registre of Waltham fairly Written by the Hand of Fuller the last Abbat there;[3] but this being now at Wym-pole, I cannot presently look into it for you. The words you cite from Domes-dei, I find to be so in the Record, because they are so written in Sir Simonds D'ewes's Abridgement thereof.[4] Yet the writing of **Walefaram** instead of **Walcfaram** therein, was a Blunder easily made by the Norman Clerks who wrote those two Volumes of Domes-dei which now remain in the Exchequer; in like manner as (in Warwick-shire) they have written **Cliptune** for **Cliftune** thro' Ignorance of the Language & Hand-writings used by our Saxon Ancestors; to omitt the mention of Hundreds more of their Errors in this kind. So in Fullers History mentioned by you,[5] his **Walthfare**, might better have been **Walcfare** or **Walhfare**, but Mr Newcourts writing it **Wallifare** after the Monasticon, when *Written* Help might have been had, shew's him not to have been very Curious, or not very well vers'd in our Antient Language.[6] Every body almost knows that the Monasticon, as it is a

[1] BL Harley MS 3779, fo. 279; for Wanley's reply see Wanley, *Diary*, pp. 149(10), 150(12).
[2] BL Harley MS 391, Davis no. 989.
[3] BL Harley MS 3739, Davis no. 992. Robert Fuller was Abbot 1526–40.
[4] BL Harley MS 623.
[5] Thomas Fuller, *The history of Waltham-abby in Essex* (1655).
[6] Richard Newcourt the younger († 1716), in his *Repertorium Ecclesiasticum Parochiale Londinense*, ii (1710), p. 627. Cf. William Dugdale, *Monasticon Anglicanum*, ii (1661), p. 11, for the form Wallifare.

most imperfect performance; so it is most unaccuratly printed, especially in words which require the greatest Care & Accuracy; I mean the
Proper Names of Places & Persons. I my self having formerly compared some of the very Originals expresly cited by the undertakers
Dodsworth & Dugdale: have had thereby reason enough to be aston-
ished at their Negligence. But lett this pass.[7]

In the Confessor's Charter of A.D. 1062, both in the Latin part of the
Instrument, and in the Boundaries of the Lands, it is written according to the most antient manner **walhfare** where the **h** denote's a
guttural pronunciation (in like manner as **axsian** or **acsian** *to ask* or
demand, were more antiently written **ahsian**; *&c*) and discover's an
Etymology. Here, as in Domesdei, according to your Observation, it
follow's Upminster. But in some other places, it follow's *Walde* &
precede's *Upminster*. Thus in the Charter of Refoundation (if I may so
call it) by K. Henry II, I find,—*Waldam & ejus ville Ecclesiam cum suis
pertinentijs: duas Solandas de* WALCFARE *cum suis pertinentijs: Upministre cum
suis pertinentijs*. In the Confirmatory Charter of K. Henry III (i.e. the
young King, Son to K. Henry II) the same Words come, & in the same
Order; but the *Solandas* is here written *Sholandas*. In the Charter of
K. Richard I, made before he was King, the whole Passage is, as in the
last. But in another made after his Coronation, it is expressed thus,
*Waldam & ejusdem ville Ecclesiam cum omnibus pertinentijs suis: Duas Scolan-
das de Wacafare cum suis pertinentijs: Upministre cum suis pertinentijs*. Here,
Wacafare is mollified (it being a rough Word) according to the
smoother pronunciation of the French; as *Upministre* for *Upminstre*.
This is dated at *Nunancurt, per manum Willelmi de Longo-campo Elyensis
Episcopi Cancellarij nostri, quarto-decimo die Marcij*. But in a former
Charter of this King (dated *apud Westmonasterium, primo anno regni
nostri, Nono die Octobris, per manum Willelmi de Longo-campo Elyensis Electi,
Cancellarij nostri*) it is more truely written *Walcfare*. In, or among the
Chartae Antiquae in the Tower (of which here is a corrected Copie in
two Folio-Volumes)[8] in the Latin-part of the Confessor's Charter, it is

---

[7] The unattributed charters which follow are cited from BL Harley MS 391; they are
listed in the elaborate nineteenth-century edition of Dugdale's *Monasticon* (eds.
J. Coley, H. Ellis, and B. Bandinel), vi (i) (1830), p. 58 n. i.

[8] The Chartae Antiquae are 41 rolls consisting of twelfth- and thirteenth-century
transcripts of royal and other charters from Ethelbert to Henry III; calendared by
Joseph Ayloffe, *Calendars of the Ancient Charters . . . in the Tower of London* (1774). Only
one volume of Harley's 'corrected Copie' seems to have survived—now BL Harley MS
6748.

written *Walcfare*, but in the Boundaries, **walhfare**, as in my Lords Chartulary. In those of the Kings Henry II, & III, they agree likewise with the said Book. Among these same Records, I find two more Charters of K. Richard I, which are not in this Registre;[9] the first (RR. no. 7) is Given *per manum Eustachij Elyensis Episcopi Cancellarij nostri, apud Rupem Audel', 18 die Septembris, anno decimo Regni nostri*; here we find the whole passage as before, only your place is written thus *Walefar'*, how truly I know not. The other (RR. no. 9. which yet seem's to be the older) is imperfect, but yet afford's, to you, this remarkable passage *et de 40 Acris apud Walde; Et de 104 Acris apud Upministre*: Here Walcfare is omitted, perhaps as having been possibly, included in *Walde*; which perhaps you may find out by enquiring of the owners of Land there, or of other Countrey-men Inhabitants thereabout. This Patent hath a *Teste*, namely, *H. Dunelmensis Episcopo, 7 die Novembris apud Westmonasterium*; and Hugh Bishop of Durham was made a Justiciar of England, by this King, in the first year of his Reign; as Sir Will. Dugdale shew's in his *Orig. Iurid.*[10] For want of Abbat Fullers Registre above-mentioned, I cannot trace this Place further down, in the Charters or Royal Patents of our Kings; but in the Popes Confirmatory Bulls, I meet with the following Passages, in this antient Registre,[11] viz. In those of

Lucius III, 12 kal. Iunij, 1182.　　*Walldam et ejusdem ville Ecclesiam, cum pertinentijs suis: Duas Solandas de Walcfare cum pertinentijs suis. Upministre cum suis pertinentijs.*

　　　　　kal. Octobris, 1184.　　*Waldam, &c.* as before.

Urbanus III, 10 kal. Iunij,1187.　　—— *Dias Solendas de Walkefare, &c*—as before.

Clemens III, 4 Non. Iulij, 1188.　　—as the last—

Celestinus III, 4 Non. Ianuar. 1191.　　—as before, save—*Duas Solandas de Walcfare*—*Upministre cum pertinentijs suis*.

Innocent. III, 10 Kal. Aug. 1199.　　*Et in Berkesire Westwaltham cum omnibus suis pertinencijs: Duas Solandas de Walcfare cum pertinentijs suis. Upminstre cum pertinentijs suis.* Here *Walda* is much disjointed

---

[9] See Ayloffe, p. 42.　　[10] Dugdale, *Origines Juridiciales* (1666).
[11] i.e. Harley 391.

(perhaps by mistake) from *Walc-fare* & *Upminstre*; and they so sett down, as if they lay in *Berkshire*; whereas in the Charter of Earl Richard above-mentioned, *Walda*, *Walcfare*, & *Upministre*, together with many other places, are particularly said to be in Essex; (*Hec in Exexia, fol. 39,b. lin. ultimo*).

Innocent. IV, 17 Kal. Iul.1250.

De Nasinges, de Eppinges, de Wermele, de Nethleswelle, de Alricheseia, et de Walda, Villas & ipsarum Ecclesias, cum terris, boscho, pratis, pasturis, aquis, pischarijs, molendinis, & omnibus pertinentijs suis, Decimas & Redditus quos habetis ibidem. And a great way lower, *Villas que vulgariter nominantur Brikendona, Stanstede, Passefeld, Upministre, Thorendone, Melnho, Westwaltham, Resseworthe, Tippedene, cum omnibus pertinentijs; Decimas & Reditus quos in eisdem Villis habetis.* Here poor *Walcfare* it utterly omitted, as being perhaps included in *Walda*, as I hinted before. It seem's that the Abbey had but a small portion of Land, namely two *Solands* in *Walkfare*, and the very Terms of the Boundaries abovementioned shew that the Circuit could not be great: but to say certainly what quantity of ground a *So-land* contained, without the assistance of Glossaries, is more than I can pretend to; unless it were the same as a Plough-land. So much for Walkfare.

As to your History of Waltham-Abbey,[12] as large as it is, it may be
further enlarged by the help of many things which are to be met with in
Town, or in my Lords Library. My Lord ha's a Manuscript History of
K. Harold the Founder of the Place, written by a Chanon of Waltham,
whose hand-writing is elsewhere seen in this Library, although his
Name do not appear. This Writer recover's K. Harold from the
grievous Wounds he recieved at *Battel*; send's him on Pilgrimage to
the Holy Land; Maintain's him privatly after his Return, as an Hermit,
for many Years; and Saint's him after his Decease.[13] As to the great
charge & Pains you are at, and the small Encouragement you have
hitherto met with: I do not wonder at it: yet I would advise you to go
on; and am of Opinion that you will find the End of your Labors to be
Crown'd with Success; without the Loss of your Time to your Family,
and to your own Content & Satisfaction.[14] I beg your Pardon for the
Trouble I give you, who am, without Complement,

    Reverend Sir,

      Your most faithful, humble Servant

                        Humfrey Wanley.

MS: Essex Record Office, D/Y 1/1. Copy in British Library, Lansdowne 814, fo. 62.
Date: 'Dover-street, 11 June 1722.'

230. *To* [Edward Harley] *12 June 1722*

May it please your Lordship,

    Although I am very loth to disturb you in any of your Retirements,
Privacies, or other Occasions; Yet I hope you will pardon my Bold-
ness, when you will please to call to mind that I have not had the
Honor of any Letter from you, since you sett out for Downe[1] & Wym-

---

[12] Never completed by Holman, but the later Essex histories of Tindal, Salmon, and
Morant were based on his collections, which filled more than 400 vols. Nearly 250 of
these survive, now in the Essex Record Office, except for those on the Hundred of Panfield, now Bodl. MSS Rawl. Essex 8 and 15.

[13] 'Vita et Miracula Haroldi quondam Regis Angliae' in BL Harley MS 3776.

[14] 'Tis almost an endlesse worke to write the Antiquities of so large a County and if I
had foreseen the Difficulties attending it I should never have attempted it' (Holman to
Wanley d. 5 June 1722, BL Harley MS 3779, fo. 278).

---

[1] Down Hall, near Harlow, Essex, the home of Matthew Prior. Prior purchased it in
1719 with the help of £4,000 from Harley, to whom the house reverted at Prior's death at
Wimpole in Sept. 1721.

pole. It is now some time since I sent my Duty to your Lordship, directed to you at Aywood;[2] but perhaps, that Direction was imperfect, or irregular; & so my short Epistle might miscarry. Yet, some time afterwards, I heard that your Lordship would please to write to me by the next Post: but no such Letters have yet come to my hands.

I have many Articles of your Business to apprise your Lordship of; but I shall hold-in my Hand untill your Return hither; or, at least, untill I have your Direction at a greater Certainty, than I now have. Nevertheless, some Matters I will now venture to committ to this Paper, whether it shall reach you, or not: v.g.

My Lord Bishop of Peterburgh[3] ha's deliver'd to me a Catalogue of his out-of-course Books printed from 1480 to 1600, exclusive; mostly, in English. Many of them your Lordship hath; & many others need not now be bought; of the Rest I make an Extract; and from it your Lordship will soon see which You most Want & Like. At Mr Schumackers Request, I have drawn up a sort of Synopsis, or short Account of your Noble Library:[4] but I did not transcribe it for him, because it hath not had your Lordship's *fiat*. I am affraid that he is gone from Holland for Hamburgh, &c. before this time, and knowing not of my Self what to do in this Matter, I desire to receive your Orders forthwith. For if it come's too late, it will not do him the Service he Expected. I just begun a Book upon your going to Downe; it is Finished, & actually Bound. It is so contrived and ha's so many Additions & Observations touching Printers & Printing (the whole, & every particular, relating only to Your own Library) that I know your Lordship will approve of it, & turn it over with Satisfaction; & cause me to make it at Wympole still more complete.[5] By reason of this your Lordships long absence, I am obliged to desire your Lordship to send me a Note for 20 Guineas by the Next Post; the far greatest part of which Sum I must pay away, upon the very day that I receive it.

Mr Ch. Christian & I often drink to your Lordships good Health & Prosperity together; & so we did this afternoon, that he dined with me. Your Lordship may be assured that none here forgets that of our

[2] Eywood, Herefordshire, the principal residence of the Harleys from the seventeenth century.

[3] White Kennet. See Wanley, *Diary*, p. 149(1).

[4] Not traced. Schumacher had visited Wimpole in March 1722: see BL Harley MS 3781, fo. 30ʳ.

[5] BL Harley MS 3886, an alphabetical index of Harley's early ptd. books, begun 26 Apr., finished 6 June 1722. See Wanley, *Diary*, p. 149(8).

Noble Lord Oxford; & we all hope that You will both come up together in that most perfect State of health, which is so ardently pray'd for, by his Lordships, and
> Your Lordships most faithful & dutiful Servant
>> Humfrey Wanley.

MS: Welbeck Wanleyana = British Library, Loan 29/258. *Date*: 'Covent-garden, 12 June 1722.'

231. *To* [Edward Harley] *9 August 1722*

May it please your Lordship,

Yesterday-afternoon, the Post-man brought me hither your very kind Letter of the Third Instant;[1] for which new favor, and the kind Expressions therin contained, especially those relating to my noble Lord your Father, & your truly-honorable Cousin, I can never be sufficiently thankful. Indeed the Kindness, or rather Affection, wherewith not only They, but Your noble Lordship, and indeed Your whole Family have always treated me, ha's been not only a great Encouragement to me in my faithful, though poor Service all along, but is now the greatest Comfort I take in this Life; as finding that notwithstanding my Years begin to decline, I am rather better accepted than ever, by those whom I am chiefly desirous of pleasing. And this Benevolence of you all toward me, I protest sincerely, I had rather preserve as it is, without further Advantage; than be Master or Possessor of the best Preferments in Great Britain.

I have just now written to Mr Crynes, according to your Lordships order.[2]

[1] Welbeck Wanleyana (= BL Loan MS 29/250).
[2] Nathaniel Crynes (1686–1745) of Coventry, Fellow of St John's College, Oxford 1707. On 23 July Wanley had commissioned him to buy from the Library of Coventry 'the Avicenna; & the Mamotrectus, wth the Grammatical Treatise prefixed, whose Title is Macte . . . at 10 Guineas' (Wanley's Memorandum Book 1721, BL Lansdowne MS 677, fo. 43ᵛ, ptd. *Diary*, p. 433). Harley (letter d. 3 Aug. 1722, Welbeck Wanleyana = BL Loan MS 29/250) instructed Wanley to draw a bill for 10 guineas payable to Crynes.
But the purchase was not carried through: all the books appear in a collection from Coventry Free School auctioned by Hodgson & Co., 11 Nov. 1908, from the catalogue of which they can be identified as follows: Avicenna, *Canon Lib. 1–5* [Strassburg: Adolf Rusch, before 1473] (*GW* 3114, Hain 2197, Proctor 245), lot 298. J. Marchesinus, *Mamotrectus* (Mainz: P. Schöffer, 1470) (Hain 10554, Proctor 94), lot 294. Johann Brunner, *Grammatica rhythmica* (Mainz: [Peter Schöffer, 1468]) (*GW* 5592, Copinger 2766, Proctor 86), lot 294: bound with the *Mamotrectus*.

Since my last, I have inspected another parcel lately bought by Noel; & laid aside a few things for your Lordships View.[3]

I have little Library-news; all things of that kind being almost at a Stop, by reason of your long Absence.

I have recieved from Woodman the Bookseller two Clan-ricards Memoirs in Sheets; & one well Bound for my self as a Present. At first I would not take it, being from him; but he saying it was for kindness done in looking over the Preface, I recieved it as a present from Mr O'Sullevane, & thanked him for it this Morning. And it was his Gift.[4]

The other day Mr Downes[5] brought hither a pocket-book consisting of two Almanacs for 1645, one by a Cavalier, the other by a Parliamenteer, in the Spare Leaves whereof the Honorable & Learned antiquary Mr Gervas Holles ha's Entred with his own fair Hand the Marriages, Births, Christenings, Deaths & Funerals of some Scores of His & my most noble Ladies near Relations.[6] The book Dr Ferrari found lying upon a Stall, & bought it for two pence; then, thinking my Lady had most right to it, he chose to make an humble Present of it to her Ladiship, by the mean of Mr Downes & Me.[7] I sent it up to my Lady yesterday, by Mr Morley; who told me to day that her Ladiship ha's accepted thereof, from the worthy Doctor, very thankfully.

I have not been out in my Conjecture, when I gessed that there would be a vast Concourse of People to see the Spectacle of this day;[8] and therefore would by no means make any Addition to the Croud. Since the Shew passed by, here have come back again passing by this house, many Myriads of People, on foot, in Chairs, or in Coaches; but were chiefly Women. It seems that the bad weather ha's kept them from gadding abroad for a considerable time: so that, upon this Occasion (and the weather not being foul) they took a resolution, with one accord, to desert their several Houses & Affairs, in order to fill-up the

[3] Wanley, *Diary*, p. 155(8).

[4] James Woodman († 1728), bookseller of Russell St., Covent Garden; Thomas O'Sullivan of West Tipperary, Irish scholar and antiquary, was the author of the anonymous dissertation affixed to the *Memoirs of the Marquis of Clanricarde* [= Ulick Bourke] (1722). See Wanley, *Diary*, p. 55(10).

[5] Not identified: see Wanley, *Diary*, Biographical Index under Downes.

[6] Not traced. Gervase Holles (1606–75), antiquary of Lincolnshire, MP for Grimsby 1640–1, 1661. See *Diary*, p. 156(14) and n. 2.

[7] i.e. Harley's wife, Lady Henrietta Cavendish Holles Harley. She was a Holles on her father's side, John Holles, 1st Duke of Newcastle (of the creation of 1694).

[8] The burial of John Churchill, Duke of Marlborough, who died 16 June 1722, and was buried at Westminster Abbey. The body was later removed to the chapel at Blenheim.

Streets & Scaffolds, to exercise their Tongues, & by Falls, or Fallings out, to make work for the Chirurgeons.

Mr Du Hamels Spouse was yesterday brought to bed of a chopping Boy, to whom I must be Godfather.[9] Upon this occasion, and otherwise, I must intreat your Lordship to send me an Order for Ten Guineas, by the next Post;[10] which will keep me in Breath for a good while. That God Almighty will preserve You all in Health, Peace & Prosperity, is the un-feigned Petition of him who is, for ever,

Your Lordships most faithful, & most dutiful Servant

Humfrey Wanley.

MS: Welbeck Wanleyana = British Library, Loan 29/258. *Date*: 'Bedford street, Covent-garden, 9 August, 1722.'

232. *To* Peter Le Neve *4 April 1723*

Sir

Yesternight, and not before, I had some Opportunity of letting my Lord know that you had returned the Registre of Castell-Acre,[1] in Safety; and spake likewise concerning the MS. you left here with me:[2] touching which, he Order'd me to send you his Service & Thanks for your Favor. That having already some Books of the same King, upon like Subjects,[3] he would willingly buy this also, at a fair & reasonable [rate], but that forasmuch as the book is abused and imperfect in several places, and seem's to him at presen[t to] contain but little matter worthy of remark; he think's half the Sum demanded, is enough to the full. If [that] may be accepted, it shall be speedily paid; if not, he desire's only to run it over in a little Time, as he can g[et] Leasure, and it shall be return'd to you faithfully. I desire your Answer by the bearer, who am

[9] Jacob Duhamel, jeweller of Duke St., York Buildings, 1715–37.
[10] Sent 14 Aug. 1722 (Welbeck Wanleyana = BL Loan MS 29/250).

[1] BL Harley MS 2110 = Davis no. 215.
[2] According to the *Diary*, p. 215(6), 'an Original book of Payments from K. Henry Eighth's Privy Purse, Signed by that Kings hand at the End of each Months Accompt. it begin's at 17 November ann Regni 20; and proceed's to 31 December anno 24to.' Cf. *Diary*, pp. 218(5) (= 10 Apr. 1723), 230(14).
[3] Harley possessed a number of manuscripts dealing with the domestic and household affairs of Henry VIII; only BL Harley MS 6807 is very like the manuscript described here.

Sir,

    Your most obliged, humble Servant

                  Humfrey Wanley.

MS: British Library, Harley 4713, fo. 248. *Date*: 'Dover-street, 4 April, 1723.' *Address*: 'To Peter le Neve Esqr Norroy, at the College of Armes, in Great Carter-Lane.'

233. *To* Edward Harley *29 October 1723*

May it please your Lordship,

    I have now been 3 days at Mr Noels, in Peace & Quietness. I have garbled the three Cases & the Trunk, and from them have sett down every thing that I suppose to be in your Lordships way of Collecting; and even among them, I believe that some among them may prove to be Duplicates.[1] My Opinion was, that Mr Sutties Catalogue did specifie more things than are now come; but Mr Noel say's that here is all that he ha's sent any account of.[2] I have an Account of the MSS. sent by Mr Suttie, and will begin to compare it with the Things to-morrow: and now Mr Noel desire's that he may view his Things in my Custody, at his Leisure, against your coming up to Town, in Order to some Agreement, that no further Time may be lost. This Request seem's to be but reasonable. My Notion, indeed, was that there were more Greek MSS. behind, and here appear but two: I may have been mistaken; but by my Papers, I shall find out the Truth, especially after your Lordships Return, who ha's many of them in your own hands. But, however, Mr Noel makes no Difficulty of coming into any sort of Examination.

    I hope my last Letter came safe into your Lordships Hands; and that you will please to Order me some Note accordingly.[3] I hope that my most Noble & Illustrious Lady, and the dearest Young Lady will please to number me among those who bear them the highest Respect.

    With these things, above-mentioned, are two parcels of Medals, one antient, the other modern. Both reserved for your Sight, & yet neither worth it. Some others not yet come.

[1] The consignment, of which the books referred to here are a part, is first reported in the *Diary*, 11 Feb. 1723, p. 189(6). They arrived piecemeal in the course of the summer and autumn, but were not actually bought until 18 Jan. 1724 (*Diary*, p. 269(6)), under which date the list of books sent with this letter (but omitted here) is printed. See Wanley, *Diary*, p. 250 and n. 4.

[2] See Wanley's remarks in *Diary*, p. 228(2). The catalogue cannot now be traced.

[3] A note for £10 sent 30 Oct. 1723, Welbeck Wanleyana = BL Loan MS 29/250.

I am, may it please your Lordship,
    Your ever-dutiful & most obedient Servant
                                        Humfrey Wanley.

I wish an hundred hearty good Wishes to Mr Tim. Thomas.[4]

MS: Welbeck Wanleyana = British Library, Loan 29/258. *Date*: 'From my Lodging 29 October, 1723. past nine.' *Address*: 'To The Right Honorable Edward Lord Harley at Wimpole near Royston in Cambridgeshire.'

234. *To* Hans Sloane *10 March 1724*

Honorable Sir,

By my noble Lords Order, this morning I went to Mr Brown's the Bookseller,[1] to bespeak such Books as his Lordship had marked in his Catalogue in Order to buy; but was soon inform'd that You had marked several of the same Books. Hereupon, I said, that I knew my Lord to be so honorable in his Nature, as willingly to yield-up unto you his pretensions to many Books; because you had done so to him, when he came first to a former Parcel, as you, Sir, do now to this.

Sir, in the nature of my Lords Printed Library, Biblical & Liturgical Books make-up one main Article; and Grammars & Lexicons, another. I know (notwithstanding my Lords Absence) that he will & does readily yield up divers things to you, which he intended to have had: so that now you interfere only as to these following,

			l	s	d
pag. 22. no.	223.	Biblia Rumanscha – – – price	2.	10.	o.x
	224.	Biblia Finlandica	1.	15.	– x
	237.	Russian Prayer-book	–	15.	– x
	238.	Slavonian Psalter	–	10.	6.
	154.	Bohemian Bible	1.	10.	–
	164.	Lithuanian Testament	–	10.	6.x
23.	176.	Slavonian Prayers	, –	12.	–

---

[4] Timothy Thomas (1694–1751),chaplain to Robert Harley, Rector of Presteigne, Radnor 1727, in the gift of Edward Harley.

---

[1] Daniel Browne, bookseller and auctioneer of Temple Bar 1672–1729. The catalogue was of the libraries of Edward and John Chamberlayne; the sale took place 11 Mar. 1724. See Wanley, *Diary*, pp. 271(21) and 272 n. 1 for details, and for Sloane's resigning his claims in favour of Harley, *Diary*, pp. 280(17), 281(6).

			l	s	d
	560.	Danish Bible	–	6.	–
	561.	Polish Bible	–	7.	6.
	563.	Bohemian Bible	–	5.	–
	578.	Hungarian Testament	–	2.	6.
	579.	Bohemian Testament	–	4.	–
24.	600.	Slavonian Liturgy	–	3.	6.x
	605.	Muscovite-prayers	–	3.	–
	609.	Quebec-Rituel	–	5.	– x
50.	1307.	Dictionar. Lat. Suecicum	–	1.	6.
	1326.	Gram. Slavonica	–	2.	6.
	1331.	Gram. Suecana	–	2.	6.
	1338.	Polish & Dutch Grammar	–	2.	6.
51.	1340.	Principia Ling. Bohem	–	–	6.

These are for all; for I know my Lord yield's up the others, as I have already said. And, as to these, I verily believe that He will willingly compound with you, as to the books in the List above specified, if you will please to lett him have those six marked with **x**, although you shall take all the others. He ha's a true veneration for your Person & truly Honorable Character, and will always shew it by convincing Proofs: and I hope you will second your former instance of good will to him (who collect's these things ex professo) by allowing him to be the Purchaser, which will yet much more oblige him. I am, always
  Honorable Sir,
    Your most obliged & most humble Servant
                          Humfrey Wanley.

MS: British Library, Sloane 4047, fo. 145. *Date*: '10 March 1723/4.' *Address*: 'To The Honorable Sir Hans Sloane, Bart.'

235. *To* John Gagnier[1] *27 August 1724*

Reverend Sir,
  By the allowance of my noble Lord here, I take this opportunity of acquainting you, that He hath some Hebrew & other Oriental Manuscripts, in number about 23; whose complete Titles & Dates (so far as they are discoverable) he would have translated into Latin; each upon

---

[1] See no. 132 n. 1.

a single Paper, & putt into the Book it refer's to; according as heretofore you did by some others for me:[2] any your pains shall be gratified
to content. If you are willing to serve my Lord on this occasion, I
desire you will please to certifie me thereof by the next Post; directing
me when, where, & to whom, I shall deliver the Box for you; and
withal promising to apprise me of its safe coming to your Hands, and
that you will shew the said MSS. to no man whatsoever; but send them
up to me with the said Titles & Dates, within 8 or so days after your
Receipt of them.[3] If you see Mr Bowles or Mr Wise, you may acquaint
them that my Lords Library goes-on as usually, & very noble things
are lately come in. Thus, with my hearty service to your good Fire-
side, I remain

 Sir,
  Your most humble Servant

            Humfrey Wanley.

When one Book contain's divers Tracts, you will please to take due
care.

MS: Welbeck Wanleyana = British Library, Loan 29/260 misc. 88. *Date*: 'From the Earl
of Oxfords in Dover-street, Westminster, 27 August, 1724.' *Address*: 'To The Reverend
Mr Gagnier, at his House in Halliwell, Oxford.'

236. *To* John Gagnier *15 October 1724*

Reverend Sir,

 I heartily thank you for the Pains you have taken with, & the Information you have given us of, my Lords MSS. They came safe, and
you would have had a *quantum meruit* for your Labor, had the Service
been at an End. But you dealt not with one of the Hebrew MSS.
according to its demerits; I mean that of which divers Leaves are
inverted, & others transposed.[1] You should have taken that Book to
pieces, & have sett all to Rights; that so it might have been delivered to
the Binder, & have received a new Livery against Winter. Here, I
know no Hebrician able enough to do it; so that I am compelled to

 [2] See Wanley, *Diary*, p. 228(2).
 [3] See *Diary*, pp. 312(14), 315(19).

 [1] According to Gagnier (letter d. 18 Oct. 1724, Welbeck Wanleyana = BL Loan MS
29/260 misc. 88), this was a copy of the Talmud.

send it down again, desiring you to do it for my Lord. In the same Box
I have also putt up about 25 other Oriental MSS. of which we here
desire better Information than what we have hitherto had. There are
likewise some loose Papers, if any of them belong to any of the Books
be pleased to restore them to their Places; if any be Letters, lett us
know so; as also if the Calligraphy in Hebrew, &c. be of the Hand of R.
Isaac Abendana.[2] Upon a Stick is a Parchment which came with a Roll
of *Esther*; we want a Translation of it.[3] In a lesser Box (both will be
Carriage paid) you will find a Pot, with an Hebrew Inscription around
it. My Lord desires a Translation of it. I must again desire you to send
me word of the Time that I may send them to your Carrier; & that you
will please to promise me (as you did before) that no man shall see
them, or any of them; & that you will please to dispatch them with all
the speed you can. This done, you shall receive my noble Lords
Thanks, to your Satisfaction. Thus, with my kind Respects to your
good Fire-side, I remain,

   Sir,

     Your most humble Servant,

                           Humfrey Wanley.

MS: Welbeck Wanleyana = British Library, Loan 29/260 misc. 88. *Date*: 'From the Earl
of Oxford's house in Dover-street, near Piccadilly, Westminster, 15 October, 1724.'
Address: 'To The Reverend Mr Gagnier, at his House in Haliwell, Oxford.'

237. *To* Giovanni Zamboni[1] *13 October 1725*

Honorable Sir,

   If my Lords multifarious business will permitt, he will come-down
into the Library this Day, and look-upon your Manuscripts. When he

---

[2] (*c*.1650–1710), Jewish theologian, he taught Hebrew at Cambridge and later at
Oxford. He annotated BL Harley MSS 3947, 3948.

[3] Not identified. See Wanley, *Diary*, p. 318(6).

---

[1] Giovanni Giacomo Zamboni († 1753), Resident in England for the Duke of
Modena, the Landgrave of Hesse Darmstadt, and the King of Poland (Elector of
Saxony) 1707–51. These manuscripts, like others sold by Zamboni to Harley (see Wanley, *Diary*, pp. 302(16), 312(1) (2)), came from Johann Büchels (1659–1738), Librarian to
the Elector Palatine of Düsseldorf, and ultimately from the Electoral Library: see *Diary*,
p. 312 n. 7. Most were from the library of Johann Georg Graevius (Graef) (1632–1703),
the Dutch classical scholar whose library had been acquired by the Elector Palatine in
1703. For identifications of these Zamboni/Graevius MSS see *Diary*, p. 385

hath so done, you shall have speedy Information, from him who is with a most sincere Respect,

Honorable Sir,

Your most faithful & obliged Servant

Humfrey Wanley.

MS: Bodleian, Rawl. lett. 124, fo. 130. *Date*: 'Dover-street, 13 October 1725.' *Address*: 'To The Honble Signior Zamboni, at his House in Conduit-street.'

238. *To* Giovanni Zamboni *15 October 1725*

Honorable Sir,

Yesterday my Lord came hither, & looked into many of your Things. Among them, I could not find a Greek book in 4to written upon Paper, wherein were contained Hesiods Ἔργα καὶ Ἡμέραι, his Θεογονία & Ἀσπίς, which I saw among them the 25th of January last, at Mr Mattaires.[1] This Gentleman upon my asking him, the last night, concerning it; answered, that he remembered no such book. I acquainted my Lord with the several Circumstances relating to your Parcel; and he said, that he willingly forbear's the 2 Volumes of Letters, the Saxon Spiegel, & Suleimân's Prayers; if held-up too dear.[2] As to the rest, he desire's to know your lowest Price; which if it prove moderate & reasonable, will soon bring this Business to an End. I am, with the most Sincere Respect,

Honorable Sir,

Your most obliged, humble Servant

Humfrey Wanley.

n. 6. See also Wright, *Fontes*, under Zamboni and Graevius. Zamboni's papers, including correspondence with Büchels relating to Graevius MSS and lists of the latter, are Bodl. MSS Rawl. letters 116–38 (*SC* 15004–26); they were purchased after his death from a creditor by Richard Rawlinson and went, with the mass of Rawlinson's collections, in 1756 to the Bodleian, where they remained unopened until 1878.

---

[1] A. C. Clark, 'The Library of J. G. Graevius', *Classical Review*, v (1891), pp. 365–72, notes (p. 372) that the Hesiod is the only valuable Greek MS missing (it is no. 56 in the catalogue of Graevius's MSS, pbd. after his death in 1703) and suggests that Maittaire, a great collector of Greek MSS, may have kept it.

[2] Not bought: see Wanley, *Diary*, p. 385(4). But the two volumes of letters of learned men assembled by J. G. Graevius (examined by Wanley 30 Mar. 1725, returned to Zamboni 9 Apr. 1725 as too dear) came into the Harleian Collection later and are now BL Harley MSS 4933–6 (*Diary*, p. 378(6) (9) and n. 5).

MS: Bodleian, Rawl. lett. 124, fo. 134. *Date*: '15 October 1725.' *Address*: 'To The Honble Sigr Zamboni, at his House in Conduit-Street.'

239. *To* John Anstis *20 October 1725*

Sir,

I have not been unmindful of you or your Commands since I waited upon you; but first my Lords absence, & then your own Journey to Oxford, caused me to deferre writing. As to the book of Sir Edward Cokes Pedegree,[1] my Lord (with his kind service unto you) said that you had been a Benefactor to the Library, & therefore may command any thing that he hath: and I will at any time deliver it at any time to your messenger that shall come hither for it in Library hours. The Book of the Laws & Customs of the Kingdoms of Jerusalem & Cyprus,[2] is at Wimpole, but when my Lord goe's thither, will be sent up for. The other book you enquired after, his Lordship hath not. He desire's to know whether you have retrieved the two Books Mr Baker of St Johns in Cambridge lent to Dr Fiddis, and where they are.[3]

The Tract which I mentioned to be copied from a printed book, is in French Verse, & bears this Title, "Cronique abresiet par Nicase Ladan dit Songeur, demourant a Bappatines, Chevautcheur ordinaire de tesaure de Treshault, tres-puissant, et redoubte Prince Charles par la grace de Dieu Prince des Espaignes, Archi-duc d'Austrice, &c. et Serviteur a Messire Ferry de Croy Seigneur du Reur, Conseillier & Grant Maistre d'Hostel du dit Prince; commenchant l'an Mil, quatre Cens, Quater vingz et douze; et finant en la fin du mois Doctobre Mil,

---

[1] BL Harley MS 6687 A–D, originally a very thick 8° of Littleton's *Tenures* (1572) interleaved, now bound in 4 vols; Coke's 'pedigree' is on fos. 10–16. They were given to the Library on 6 Aug. 1715 by 'Madam Thynne': see Wanley, *Diary*, p. 13(7), and Biographical Index under Thynne.

[2] Not identified. But it was certainly in the Library—it was used by John Beaver, Wanley's son-in-law, on at least two occasions: see *Diary*, pp. 142(7), 145(4).

[3] Fiddes had died at Anstis's house at Putney. Anstis replied: 'I have in my custody mr Bakers two Volumes, as I acquainted him, and since we cannot find any thing compiled by Doctor ffiddis relating to the lives of More & ffisher, though he often said, he had finished the former, and since I beleive no one will undertake the writing these Lives, I shall return these Volumes, as mr Baker shall direct, who consented that they might continue in my hands, till we had found what proceedings Dr ffiddes had made on these Subjects' (21 Oct. 1725, BL Harley MS 3777, fo. 29). Fiddes issued a prospectus for a volume containing the lives of More and Fisher. According to *DNB*, he 'had written a good deal of the work when his health broke down', but the MS of his life of More was lost.

Cinq cens, et quinze." The Date at the End is thus, "Imprime en
Anvers, par Michel Hoochstrate demorant au dit lieu, chez le cimen-
tere noster Dame, l'an Mil, cinq cens, et saize; par congie & previlege
de nostre Prince."[4]

There was another Note about *Chinese paper*, the intent of which
hath slipped out of my Memory;[5] which if you please to refresh, you
may command in any thing relating thereunto, the Service of
  Sir,
      Your most faithful & obedient Servant
                                        Humfrey Wanley.

MS: British Library, Stowe 749, fo. 256. *Date*: 'Dover-street, 20 October 1725.' *Address*:
'To John Anstis Esqr Garter King of Armes, at his House in Putteney.'

240. *To* John Anstis *22 October 1725*

Sir,

Mr Josephus Simpson[1] is now with me, and by him I send unto you
Sir Edward Coke's Book, which contain's a good part of his Pedigree,
with other notes relating to himself, &c. besides the Law-matters: as
also your Author, in My Lords MS. of Nicase l'Adam; this last without
my Lords particular Order (whom I have not seen since the receipt of
your Letter) as thinking that his general one, relating to you, sufficient.
Nevertheless, a Note should have been sent for these books, for
mortalities Sake, as in the unexpected Case of Dr Fiddis.[2] I unhappily
forgot the Memorandum of King Richard the Seconds Knighting the
young Lord (afterward K. Henry V, in Ireland). It is in my Lords MS.
inscribed 68. C. 3. at fol. 4. in that Poetical Narration about the latter
End of that unfortunate Kings Reign, commonly ascribed to one of the

---

[4] BL Harley 1131. Nicaise Ladam (1465–1547), Grenade Herald to Charles V. Cf.
Anstis to Wanley d. 25 Oct. 1725: 'In yr Catalogue you will be pleased to put Adam
instead of Adan, for so the contraction Adā is to be read'; he also corrects Wanley's
tesaure to *l'escuire*, 'for the Chevauchers & all Officers of Arms were in that Country
under the Escuier' (BL Harley MS 3777, fo. 31). No copy of the printed book seems to
have survived.

[5] 'I do not remember any thing about Chinese paper' (Anstis to Wanley d. 21 Oct.
1725).

---

[1] Probably Joseph Simpson, the younger († 1736), the engraver. See no. 239 and
Diary, p. 389(3).

[2] See no. 239 n. 3. Anstis returned the manuscripts 25 Oct. 1925.

Duke de Maines Gentlemen called Ianico (the same Name, I suppose, with Inigo) and this Manuscript of my Lords was that Princes Book, ha's his name Written at the End, and is adorned with Paintings (and particularly of this Knighthood) suitably to the dignity of a Prince of the Blood of France, and to the manner of the then present time.[3] I am heartily glad that you have retrieved Mr Bakers Books; and do easily believe, that Dr Fiddis made no use of them. I am, Sir, with true respect,

    Your most humble Servant

H. Wanley.

MS: British Library, Stowe 749, fo. 258. *Date*: '22 October 1725.' *Address*: 'To John Anstis Esqr at his House in Putteney.'

241. *To* Giovanni Zamboni *16 November 1725*

Honorable Sir,

    This come's desiring you to favor me, by the bearer, with your Cata-logue of Graevius's MSS. which may perhaps be useful to me in find-ing the Names of some whose anonymous Papers are among them.[1]

    I return you thanks, Sir, for your last kind invitation of me to Dinner; but the great Cold I have lately gotten; the Day, being Sun-day; and your Hour of Dining, which is in the time of our Church-Service, do absolutely prohibit my attendance, untill a more convenient Opportunity. In the mean time, I shall remain, with the most sincere Respect,

    Honorable Sir,

        Your most faithful & obedient Servant

Humfrey Wanley.

MS: Bodleian, Rawl. lett. 124, fo. 136. *Date*: '16 November 1725.' *Address*: 'To The Honble Signior Zamboni.'

---

[3] BL Harley MS 1319 (Wanley writes '68.c.3' in error for '68.c.23'), requested by Anstis 15, 21 Oct. 1725 (BL Harley MS 3777, fos. 27, 29). The manuscript contains sixteen illustrations.

---

[1] See no. 237 and no. 238 n. 1, and *Diary*, p. 393(7).

242. *To* [Edward Harley] *28 January 1726*

May it please your Lordship,

I doubt not but that the Letter I had the Honor of writing to You the last Night,[1] ha's safely reach'd You before now. I send herewith Rob. Vilvain's book, which I intreat your Lordship to accept kindly from me, although my bodily Indisposition occasioned me not to present it sooner. The Author seem's a Trifler to me; yet his performance, for the Sake of some Lines, should be preserved some where or other.[2]

I have now gone through the Bridgesian Catalogue,[3] which I send likewise. Without doubt there are many excellent Historical & other Books of Use which you have not: but I advise not your Lordship to lay out any great Sum upon them. If you buy the 3 last,[4] and 2 or 3 more, it will be a good accession to the Library, in my Opinion. I have here & there marked some; rather to be marks of my Diligence, than for any other Reason. When your Lordship shall send it back to me, with your positive Orders how to proceed; they shall be punctually obeyed by him whose Pride is, in being

> Your Lordships
>   most dutiful, & obliged Servant
>
>   Humfrey Wanley.

MS: Welbeck Wanleyana = British Library, Loan 29/258. *Date*: 'From my Lodging, 28 of January 1725/6.'

[1] Not found.

[2] Robert Vilvain (1575?–1663), physician and benefactor of his native city of Exeter. Wanley's opinion chimes with that of Wood, who declared that his writings were 'nothing but scraps, whimseys and dotages of old age' (*Athenae Oxonienses*, ed. P. Bliss, iii (1817), p. 632). It is not clear which book Wanley presented.

[3] John Bridges (1666–1724), antiquary. He compiled manuscript collections for a history of Northamptonshire (now Bodl. MSS Top. Northants c. 1–f. 5, *SC* 16618–69), from which a *History of Northamptonshire* was pbd. 1762–91. His library was auctioned over a period of twenty-seven days between 7 Feb. and 21 Mar. 1726. Wanley used both Noel and Thomas Bacon († 1736, MP for Cambridgeshire 1722–36) to bid at the sale: see *Diary*, pp. 405(5) and n. 2, 406(2), 407(1).

[4] For Wanley's concern to secure these three manuscripts, see *Diary*, pp. 406(2), 408(12), 409(5), 410(8) (9) and n. 1. Only one, a Lucian, now BL Harley MS 5694, came into the collection.

243. *To* Giovanni Zamboni *9 March 1726*

Honorable Sir,

I have lately taken a new Lodging in Clarges-street, Piccadilly;[1] where I shall be proud of the Honor of seeing you, after I am settled. In the mean time, I send this to acquaint you that I have Occasion to use that book of P. Bertius[2] which I lent you; and desire that you will please to return the same by the Bearer hereof, together with the Padlock & Key which belong to the little Chest bought by my Lord, together with the MSS.[3] Hereby you will add to the Obligations you have already conferred upon,

    Honorable Sir,

        Your most obedient, & humble Servant

                               Humfrey Wanley.

MS: Bodleian, Rawl. lett. 124, fo. 138. *Date*: '9 March, 1725/6.' *Address*: 'To The honorable Signor Zamboni, at his house in Conduit-street.'

    [1] Where he died, 6 July 1726.
    [2] Petrus Bertius (1565–1629), of Leiden.
    [3] Graevius's.

APPENDIX
OF
DOCUMENTS

I. PALAEOGRAPHICAL SURVEY OF ENGLISH HANDS FROM THE EARLIEST TIMES

BL Sloane MS 4061 fo. 268; fair copy.[1] [*c*.1702][2]

The great Advantages that Mankind in general, have in all Ages, reap'd from that Measure of Learning which was to be found among them; have constantly induced those Princes & States (not to mention private persons) who cordially endeavor'd to promote the Welfare of their several Countries, to encourage all such as were enclin'd to bend their Thoughts This way, in Order to discover those things that might tend to the public Good. And 'tis to this Original that we must ascribe the great Improvements that have been lately made in the Several Arts & Sciences Mathematical & Mechanical, as also those new Inventions of all sorts that the World is grown so very fond of.

In this Kingdom we have Universities wherein the Learned Languages, the Liberal Sciences, and the several Faculties are publicly taught & Profess'd: In Town there are Colleges & Inns for Physicians & Lawyers of all Sorts: but no public Encouragement, that I know of, for the Study of our English History and Antiquities, unless the *College of Arms* be excepted, where, yet, 'tis said, that the greatest part of their Learned Labors is spent in Genealogies & Tricking out Coats of Arms for *New*, as well as for *Old* Families.

Beyond the Seas, many Soveraign Princes have their *Antiquaries*, whose peculiar Business it is, to study & cultivate the Antient & Modern Antiquities, especially those relating to their own Countrey. Particularly at Upsal in Sueden, there is a College of Antiquaries established for this purpose. And these men who have so enjoyed the Public Favor & Encouragement, have from time to time, brought those things to light, as have been very acceptable & usefull to the rest of the Learned World.

Twas this Consideration that induc'd our most Learned men in the beginning of the last Age, to endeavor to erect a Society or College of Antiquaries in London; & likewise to retrieve all those scatter'd Books

---

[1] Printed (in part) by Nichols, *Literary Anecdotes*, i (1812), pp. 103–4.
[2] See nos. 84, 37 and n. 1.

& Writings which they thought might be useful to themselves, or to Posterity, in their Disquisitions upon this noble Subject.

Had this Society been settled upon a sure Foundation; without doubt, we should have been furnish'd with many Excellent Works that we now want: and consequently, this Generation might have been saved the Labor of informing Posterity touching divers matters necessary for them to know. And amongst their other Labors, the world might justly have expected a large Volume *De re Anglorum Litteraria et Libraria*.

A Work of this Nature grows dayly more necessary, as the Wor[ld gr]ow's older. For since the Improvement, & Common Use of *Printing*; the Writing of *Manuscripts* is quite grown out of Use in these parts of Europe: nor can it be suppos'd ever to come in Fashion again, because Printing multiplies the Copy of a Book infinitely quicker. And Considering the frequent Revolutions in Kingdoms & States, besides the Accidents, which in particular Places, are suppos'd to destroy, in times of Peace, some one Library of MSS or other, once in ten years: we may rationally conclude, that as the number of MSS is prodigiously lessned in these two last Centuries: so, in 500 years to come, there may be but a very few, if any, of those Manuscripts remaining, that are now preserv'd in our Public or Private Libraries.

Since then, Posterity is likely to be depriv'd of those Manuscripts that are now in being; unless due care be taken, they will give but small Credit to our Editions of antient Writings of all kinds; nor will they comprehend the meaning of the *Terms* now commonly in Use. Or if here & there, a MS should chance to escape, at that time; for want of greater Numbers, such a Book or Writing would hardly be Read, or the Abbreviations be Decipherable: which, even now, do perplex most Learned Men in the present Generation, & have occasion'd infinite Errors in the Printed Copies for want of true Reading. As to *Charters* & *Records*, Posterity will suffer yet more: for the Series of *Hands* being once broken, they can never know what they want; nor consequently, discover when they are impos'd upon by *False Writings*.

One Objection lies against what ha's been said about a *future destruction* of Manuscripts. How can it be suppos'd that 500 years hence our MSS should be almost all destroyed, when we have now in being vast Numbers of Books & Writings 500 years old, & others older, till we go beyond a Thousand? If these have endured for so many Ages, why may they not as many More? To this, might be Answer'd that in 500 years time, the Antient Books & Writings of *England* may as well be destroyed, as all the numerous Libraries of *Italy*, *Greece*, *Asia*, *Egypt*, &c. And, as to any of our Books & Writings that are older than the *Conquest*, I believe, that 'twill be found that they all belonged to One Monastery or other. But if we consider the Number of Monasteries Founded before the Conquest; their large *Libraries*, & the great Quantities of Writings kept in their Treasuries at the time of the *Dissolution*: we shall easily find, that we have not now remaining (so far as can be found after sufficient Enquiry) on[e] *Original Writing* of a hundred, nor one *Book* of Fourty. And if these have perish'd in less than 20[0] years, what will remain after 500 years more? As to the *Public Records* of the Nation, they have not had a much better fate: since those of the *Saxon Kings* are all utterly destroyed; and those of [se]veral Kings next *after the Conquest* (except *Domesday book*) are also lost, as may easily appea[r] upon enquiry at any of the *Offices*.

It is therefore most humbly proposed, that for the Use & Benefit of the present & succeeding Generations, a compleat Volume or Volumes should be Collected from all such Books, Charters, Records, Coins, Seals, Inscriptions upon Stones, upon Bells, upon Glass-windows, &c. and from such other pieces of Antiquity as are now remaining in this Kingdom & Elsewhere; beside's later Writings: And therein might be exhibited

I. The State of the *Runic* & *Roman* Hands, as they were at the time when our Saxon Ancestors are supposed to have taken their Letters from them.

II. All the *Anglo-Saxon* Hands, as well in the *Latin* as in the *Saxon* Tongues; from the oldest Monuments now extant, down to the Conquest: together with all the Alphabets, Cubital & Great Uncial Letters, Ligatures, Abbreviations, & Occult ways of Writing used in those Ages.

III. All the same variety of the *Normanno-Saxon* Hands, from the Conquest, to the Reign of K. Edward III.

IV. All the *English* Hands, from that time to the year 1700. particularly the Pipe, Exchequer, Chancery, Court, Text, Secretary & other Set Hands: with due Remarks & Observations throughout the Whole, concerning the Alterations in the Forms of the Letters; Disuse of old Letters, &c. and the Bringing in of New Ones.

V. Of Counterfeits & Copies of Original Writings, which might be compared with & examined by Genuin Ones, and the Differences Noted.

VI. Specimens of the Original Hand-Writing of eminent English Men & Women in all Ages.

VII. Specimens of some Italian, French, Flemish, German, Spanish, Langobardic, Irish, Welsh, and other Hands; shewing the Resemblance & Differences between them & the English Hands of the same Age.

VIII. A Chapter concerning Points, Accents, [N]otes or Figures for Numbers, Weights, Measures, Music, &c.

At the Beginning might be a large Preface treating of the Original & Progress of Wri[ting] and Illuminating Books; the different Ways & Materials used by most Nations: together w[ith S]culptures of the different Postures of Writing, Shapes & Forms of Volumes, Books, Instrument[s o]f Writing, & other Matters proper to be taken notice of in a Discourse of this Nature.

If such a Work should be found useful to the Public; there might afterwards be added to it some other Tomes, exhibiting the Series of the *Greek* & *Latin* Hands: as also the Alph[ab]ets or Specimens of the Letters of such other Nations as have Writing amongst them.

II. VISITING FOREIGN LIBRARIES

BL Harley MS 5911, fo. 2; draft. [1700?][1]

Books of Travels and Relations of Journey and Voiages are almost infinite. Nor do we want Authors who have accuratly treated of every Countrey of Europe, both in it's Ecclesiastical, Civil, Natural and Political capacitie. We have their Men, Manners, Religion, Laws, Force, Cities, Churches, Pictures, and other Rarities described to us at length: but yet, we have no one book (that ever I heard of) that give's us a tolerable view of their Libraries. The very best performance's of that kind being vastly imperfect, by reason of the want of Diligence or Judgement in those who undertook to describe them. And we find that Travellors have made their descriptions of Libraries, and of the chief books contain'd in them, not according to their good or bad State and Appearance; but either as they happen'd to be informed by their Keepers, or as they found them described, tho' injudiciously, in other Writers: so that the Accounts we have of them, are still extreamly lame and defective.

It can't be denied, but that there are many excellent books in Libraries beyond the seas, which would prove of vast use to us, did we but know where they are kept: and others that we do know of, if we had but Copies of them.

We are almost positive that the old Italic Version of the Bible, which the Latin Church used before St Hierome's Translation; as also that a good part of Origen's Hexapla & Octapla; in short, that many noble Authors are still extant in Foreign Libraries, that are by us supposed to be utterly lost; and perhaps, may soon be so, thro' the ignorance or carelessness of their present possessors.

On the other hand, we know in what particular Libraries some most valuable books are now to be found, which were never printed, nor are known to be extant any where else. And of this, abundance of instances might soon be made; but one or two may serve, *v. gratia*, Eusebius his *Eclogae Propheticae de Christo*, in Greek, in the Emperors Library, which give's us a very great part of the true Septuagint, as it

---

[1] See Pepys's memorandum d. 18 June 1700 approving the proposal (Tanner, *Private Correspondence*, i, pp. 366–7), and Sloane's offer, transmitted via Hickes, to raise £100 a year to support him (Hickes to Wanley, 23 May 1700, BL Harley MS 3779, fo. 132).

was left corrected by Origen. *The Acts of the Apostles & Epistles of St James, St Peter, St John, St Jude, & St Paul*, in Greek, in the great Duke of Tuscanie's Library at Florence, which were written 1300 years since, and have very considerable Commentaries upon them, which were never yet printed. The Roman Kalendar in the Emperors Library, written in the time of Constantius son to Constantine the Great, at the end whereof, are divers noble Tracts never printed.

Besides, they have great numbers of valuable books, which tho' printed, yet either their Copies have not been collated, as the French Kings Livie, which was within a few years, brought to him from mount Athos. Others they have, which are known not to have been faithfully or carefully collated, as the Pandects at Florence. And many more whi[ch] are suspected by us to be untruly represented in Print, by corrupting, interpolating an[d] suppressing divers material passages; as many foreign Editions of the Fathers, not to mention other Antient or Modern Authors.

It is humbly conceived therefore, that it will conduce very much to the benefit of Learning in this Kingdom, if some fit person or persons were sent abroad, who might make it his or their business

1. To view the Libraries of France, Italy & Germany; and to give us a good accou[nt] of their present State, and of the most valuable MSS. therein.

2. To collate with printed Editions, the most remarkable and pretious Copies of the works of the Antients, now remaining amongst them written in Capital Letters. Where[by] we may reasonably hope to have a true Text restored to many places now unintelligible.

3. To transcribe some particular books in Greek or Latin, which we have no Copies of in England, and have not been yet printed. By which means, there will be an accession of more Learning to the Kingdom than it ha's at this present. And the Papists are communicative enough, for Love or Money, of any book that does not immediatly concern their Controversies with Protestants.

4. To enquire carefully, all along, what books they have illustrating or appertaining to our English History. And particularly, to get an accurate account of the English Records and Register books formerly belonging to Monasteries in this Kingdom, which being carried away to Rome, at the Dissolution of Abbies, are (as it is said) still preserved there, in the Archives of the Vatican Church.

5. To take off Copies of the most rare Coins, Medals, Intaglias, & other curious pieces of Antiquity, different from what we have in our English Cabinets, and not described in books printed upon that subject.

6. To buy up books of value, especially Manuscripts, as occasion shall serve.

Which design ha's been highly approved of (as appear's by particular Testimonies under their own hands) by

The Reverend Dr Paynter Rector of Exeter College, & Vice-chancellor of the University of Oxford.

The Reverend Dr Wallis Geometry-Professor in the same University.

The Reverend Dr Mill Principal of Edmund Hall in the same University.

The Reverend Dr Hyde Head Library-Keeper & Professor of Hebrew & Arabic in the same University.

Mr Henry Dodwell late History-Professor in the same University.

The Reverend Dr Charlett Master of University College in the same University.

The Honorable Mr Pepys late Secretary to the Admiralty, and Fellow of the Royal Societie.

Hans Sloane M.D. and Secretary to the Royal Societie.

The Reverend Dr Aldrich Dean of Christ-church in the University of Oxford.

The Reverend Dr Delaune President of St Johns College in Oxford.

Wm Sherard M.D. Fellow of St Johns College in Oxford.

III. 'DRAUGHT OF A WARANT TO BE SIGNED
BY HER MAJESTY, COMMANDING ALL
KEEPERS OF HER MAJESTIES RECORDS &
LIBRARIES, TO SUFFER MR WANLEY TO
PERUSE & TRANSCRIBE WHAT HE SHALL
THINK FIT WITHOUT PAYING FEES.'
BL Harley MS 7055, fo. 11; draft.[1] 1713.

Whereas We are Informed that our Trusty & Wel-beloved Humfrey
Wanley at the Instance and Advise of divers of our faithful & Loving
Subjects, hath Undertaken to Collect & Publish One or More
Volumes of such Antient [E]nglish Historians as have not been
hitherto Printed; together with additional Notes & Remarks Illus-
trating the same:

We being willing (besides what We have already done & still do, for
the Publication of the Leagues & Treaties) that the History of this
Nation should be farther Cultivated, to the End that the Princely &
Heroic Actions of Our Royal Progenitors may be more especially Sett
forth & declared to late Posterity; & that many Observable Transactions & Occurrences may be Rescued & Secured from Oblivion &
Utter Destruction:

Do hereby Declare our Royal Will & Pleasure, unto All our Officers
& Keepers of Our Records in Our Tower of London, Chapell of the
Rolls, Paper-Office, Signet-Office, Augmentation-Office, Exchequer,
Parliament-Office, the late Court of Wards & Liveries, and All other
Repositories of Records in Westminster; the Records appertaining to
Our Principality of Wales, Duchies of Lancaster & Cornwall &
County-Palatine of Chester; the Cottonian Library, Our Library at
Cotton-house, the Library at our College of Arms, the Prerogative-
Office; and All other Our Offices of Records whatsoever; That They
do at all times, when so required by the said Humfrey Wanley, give
Him free & full Liberty, Admittance & Access to the Sight & quiet
Perusal of all Tables, Indexes, Kalendars, & Repertories to their
Respective Offices belonging. And that they do also allow the like
Liberty to the said Humfrey Wanley (or whomsoever he shall appoint)

---

[1] An earlier draft follows, Harley 7055, fo. 12.

to Transcribe or Copie from such Rolls, Books, Parchments, Papers, Seals, or other Pieces of Antiquity in their Custody, whatsoever He shall judge necessary for the Carrying on this his Undertaking; without Asking or Receiving any Fee or Reward for the same, or for such their extraordinary Attendance on him.

Moreover, out of Our Royal Disposition to the furtherance of a Work which Lends so much to the Honor of this our Kingdom, & the public Benefit of Learning (which We are at all times ready to Countenance & Encourage): We do hereby Order & Command the Keeper of Our Libraries to Lend gratis, unto the said Humfrey Wanley such of our Books Printed or Written, as he shall find useful to him in Carrying on this Work; He the said Humfrey Wanley promising, under his Hand, safely to restore the same within convenient time.

And to the End, that all & every of our Officers abovementioned may readily conform themselves to Our Will & Pleasure in the Premisses and yield their due Obedience thereunto, We have Authorized these Presents under our Royal Signet & Sign-Manual, commanding Our said Officers to acknowledge a Sight hereof as their Sufficient Warant & to Act accordingly.

Given at our Court at   the   day of   1713, in the twelfth Year of Our Reign.

IV. PUBLICATION OF THE ACTS OF THE PRIVY COUNCIL

BL Harley MS 7055, fo. 13; draft. [1713?]

Since Her Majesty ha's been pleas'd to encourage Mr Rymer in Searching out, & Publishing the several Leagues, Treaties, &c between England & other States, many have received Benefit from those discoveries, and it has highly advanced Her Majesties Honor in that She ha's vouchsafed to promote so useful an Undertaking in this Time of War.

From hence, some people are of Opinion, that it would be yet more Glorious for her Majesty (because it may be more Instructive & Useful to the World) if Her Majesty would be pleas'd to encourage some Fit Person in the Publication of The Antient Acts of the Privy Council, down to such Time when it shall be thought fitt to leave off. Together with such Original Instructions, Letters, &c. as shall now be found, and are mentioned in those Acts of Council.

Tis easy to observe that by this Work, we shall have the most Valuable & Authentic History of our Nation, for some Centuries of years, that has yet appear'd in the World. Here we shall find the secret Springs discover'd & laid open, which hitherto have been concealed from the World, since most of our Historians relate Matters of Fact, only as they have been told. Here we may find Accounts of things which may not only correct our other Historians, but Supply their Defects; for many Matters of Moment have been debated in the Privy Council, which have never been touch'd at by our Historians, because they could never attain to the Knowledge of them. And here we may find many Thousands of Noble Memoirs relating to[1] those Heroes our antient English Nobility, which have hitherto escap'd the Diligence of our Printed Authors, and yet would have best contributed to the Honor of their several Families, & to the Preservation of their Memories down to late Posterity.

[1] 'relating to' interlined, original 'of' not cancelled.

V. COLLECTING PASTEDOWNS FROM BODLEIAN BOOKS

Welbeck Wanleyana = BL Loan MS 29/259 misc. 29; fair copy.[1] [1698?][2]

Whereas, in former Ages, it ha's been customary, in Binding of books, to affix a Leaf or Leaves of some other old books, at the beginning and end of them; as also sometimes to Past a Leaf upon the inside of the Cover of a book newly bound up; as appears by many such books remaining to this day in the Bodleian Library, and other places. Which Fragments having no Relation to the Subject or Matter of the books they belong to; nor contributing in the least to their Value; nor having ever been thought worth the taking notice of in any Catalogue whatsoever; nor being of any manner of use in the Library to any man, as they now lie, hid, dispersed and unknown.

And forasmuch as Humfrey Wanley of University College, ha's for some years past endeavored to acquaint himself with the several ways of *Writing* heretofore used, in England and other Countries; and ha's also entertained thoughts of gathering into one or more Volumes, a Specimen of the *Writing* of every *Countrey* & *Age*, digested Regularly according to their respective Antiquities; In order to which, he ha's already, from like antient books, collected many hundreds of such Fragments in Paper & Parchment, some of which, are those that he now produces: He makes it his humble Request to Mr Vice-Chancellor & the Curators, that they would be pleas'd to permitt him to take off, from the books in the Bodleian Library, such useless Fragments of Parchment & Paper as he shall find necessary to his purpose, if it may be done without damage to the books. Each fragment being capable of becoming, in some sort, useful to him in a Collection, tho' it be worthless when single.

Which Collection, when compleated by the large additions he expects to meet with in London, and ha's promises of, from beyond the Seas, may prove of great use, not only in exhibiting at once, the several *Hands* of *England, Ireland, France, Italy, Holland, Germany, Spain,*

---

[1] Copy in BL Harley MS 5911, fo. 10. Printed: Milton C. McGatch, 'Humphrey Wanley's Proposal to the Curators of the Bodleian Library on the Usefulness of Manuscript Fragments from Bindings', *Bodleian Library Record*, xi (1982–5), pp. 94–8.

[2] See no. 43.

Greece, &c, for many Ages together, and those in such Variety, as will exceed what may be found in any one Library; but will (as he humbly conceives) give a man great Light into the *Nature of Letters* in General, and the particular way of fashioning them in such an *Age* and *Countrey*: so as by them a man may know *when* & *where* such a book was written: or whether the Characters of such a Book, Deed or Charter will comport with those used in Such a Countrey at such a Time. It will also furnish him wth other Observations, of the *different kinds of Parchment, Paper & Ink, different manners of Colouring & Illumination, Different ways of spelling, writing or abbreviating such words* and the Reasons of them, &c. Moreover, it will insensibly draw on & as it were persuade any body that peruses it, into a facility & Readiness in *Reading the Antient* Hands, which often perplex those who are not much conversant with Manuscripts, when they come to make use of them.

And the same Humfrey Wanley does hereby oblige himself to Mr Vice-Chancellor and the Curators, if they will in their great Wisdom think it fit to grant his said humble Request: that, after he ha's made such use of these things as he intends, he will repose his whole Collection in the Bodleian Library. Whereby, the Library will again have (but put into Order & rendred useful) the very same Fragments, which are now desired to be taken (or rather borrowed) out of it. And (as was before suggested) That Collection may furnish a Student in these Matters, with the Notice of more things in a very short Time; than he can otherwise gain by many years Travel & Pains.

Endorsed: The proposal seems to me very reasonable, and may be of very good use.

John Wallis.

I am of the same opinon, since Mr Wanley undertakes that the very individual Original papers & parchments shall be put into the books he designs.

H Aldrich.

VI. BODLEIAN MS BALLARD 48, FOS. 160–1[1]

June 26, 1699.

Strabo is certainly a very noble Authour, and so far out of print, that (when he can be met with) he's not to be purchased, but at a great rate. And tho' Several industrious & able Scholars have already taken a deal of pains in polishing him, & Setting him forth accurately; yet ye learned Say, that many things are Still wanting, and of necessity must be done, before we can pretend to Say we have Strabo correct and Set in his true light.

In order to this, there is an absolute necessity of consulting the MSS. and ye more copies (especially those of ye best note) are consulted, upon this occasion, the more honorable, exact and usefull is ye Edition likely to prove. Not that the Editor is bound to Stop at every little point, accent or article, whether it is expressed or not, whether it be plac'd before or after Such a word &c. when such a trifle makes no alteration in ye Sence: But to be nice so far, as to let nothing of wieght & moment escape him; & where there is great dissonancy between ye Several copies, in such a place &c. not to be too hasty in giving judgment; & when occasion requires, to take the opinions of judicious persons along with him. And indeed, the Gentlemens very desire of knowing what MSS we have of this Author, gives me great hopes, that they will oblige us with the best Edition of him.

I am Sorry to find that the Manuscript copies are so extreamly Scarce in England, that recourse must (of necessity) be had to those beyond ye Seas: and where all or ye best copies of him lie, I wish I was able to tell.

There are very many libraries abroad, both Publick & Private, which are well replenish'd with Greek Manuscripts & other valuable books, ye Owners or Keepers of which have never yet acquitted themselves of that Duty which they owe to ye Commonwealth of Letters, in publishing their respective Catalogues. And of those Catalogues that have been printed, tis a Shame to See how erroneous & imperfect most of 'em are: (Though I Still know how to be thankfull for what we have). And of these printed ones, my particular ill luck has been & is Such, that (notwithstanding my best diligence) I could never meet

---

[1] See no. 63 n. 29.

with Some of 'em to this day. Thomassins Bibliothecae Venetae for one; wch yet I know to be extant more than once in England. These are ye reasons why I cannot inform the Cambridge Gentlemen of more MSS of Strabo, than these which presently follow: Tho' I hope they are enow to furnish them with a Stock of Readings, Sufficient to clear all ye dubious or corrupted places in the whole work.

In Oxford we have ye greatest part of him in Lincoln-College Library; but in Latin: as I Suppose that MS is also, wch is in the Publick Library at Cambridge. Nor do I hear that there is any Greek Copy of Strabo in England, besides that at Eaton-College, wch is reported to contain only ten Books.

Georgius Gemistius Pletho made large Excerpta out of Strabo, de Terrarum orbij figura &c. wch is extant in many Libraries, as in ye Elector of Bavaria's at Munichen. The Medicean at Florence; amongst Cardinal Bessarion's books at Venice. Many copies of it in the French Kings Library at Paris. 'Tis likely too to be at Leyden amongst the MSS of Isaac Vossius; for So I understand ye title Strabonij fragmentum. It was moreover in ye Elector Palatins Library at Heidelberg, wch was afterwards carry'd away, ye greatest part of it to the Vatican; another part to ye Electoral Library aforesaid at Munich, & the rest torn in pieces. And lastly, I don't know, whether a Geographical Tract of this Pletho, in the Bodleian Library, may not be these Excerpta ex Strabone, till they are compar'd together.

Guarinus Veronensis translated Strabo into Latin, and his Translation is extant in the French King's Library, and our Lincoln-College MS. I Suppose to be turn out of Greek by ye Same hand.

The Greek Copies of Strabo, I have notice of (besides Pletho's excerpta) bear these titles

Strabonis Geograph.   libri 9.
Strabonis Geographiae   libri 17.
Strabonis Geograph.   libri 17.
Strabonis Geograph.   libri 17.
Strabonis Geographia.

These were all in ye King's Library at Paris, an. 1636 as appears by the MS Catalogue made of it that year. And considering ye vast additions that have been made to it Since; one may reasonably expect to find more Copies there, wch have come in Since ye reign of Lewis ye 14th.

In ye Vatican Library, as appears by an old MS Catalogue, is a Greek Copie of Strabo, containing 16. books.

Among Cardinal Bessarion's MSS at Venice, as appears by a MS Catalogue, are Strabonis Geographj librj, a decimo usque ad 17um in pap. Strabonis Geographj duodecim primj libri. pap. and afterwards— Strabonis Geographia in pergameno invenitr in bibliotheca, & tamen non est descripta in Indice Cardinalij Bessarionij.

In ye Great Duke of Tuscanie's Library at ye Monastery of St Laurence in Florence, as appears by a MS Catalogue taken by Mr Langius a Dane an 1652 are

> Strabonis Geograph. l.10.fol.Plut.28.no.5.
> Strabonis Geographica fol. Plut. 28 no.15.
> Strabonis Geogr. librj aliquot. Plut.28.no.19.
> Strabonis Geogr. l.10.priores. Plut.28. no.40.

These are all I have as yet met with; but if these will not Suffice, enquiries may be made at Colberts & other Libraries in Paris. at ye Vatican, Queen Christina's, ye Cardinals Barbarinj, Altierj &c. in Rome. The Ambrosian at Millain. the Dominican's in Florence: St Savior's at Messana in Sicily. the Duke of Brunswicks at Wolfenbattel in Germany. &c.

VII. 'PROPOSAL FOR PRINTING A VOLUME OF OLD ENGLISH HISTORIANS, FROM MY LORDS LIBRARY.'

Welbeck Wanleyana = BL Loan MS 29/259 misc. 28; fair copy. [1713?][1]

My Lords Library, at present, can furnish Materials for

One Volume, or more, of Epistles & Letters, all worthy to see the light:

And for,

One or more additional Volumes to the Monasticon Anglicanum; replete with matter not inferior to any of the former; but in Accuracy, Notes, and other Ornaments of Seals, &c. much excelling them.

As to His Lordships Manuscripts relating to the History of Great Britain; they are what I beg Leave to call Copies, or Originals.

Copies or recent Transcripts, (such as those on the Shelf 59.B.) I think cannot be so reputably Printed, without consulting their Respective Originals, while they are still in being, although in other Places.

By Originals, I mean Antient Exemplars written on Parchment or Paper: and these may be distinguished, as Shorter Annals, or Greater Histories.

By Short Annals I understand such as those of Bury St Edmund 66.A. 16; and at the End of 39.C.10. Those of Burmundesey 36.C.14; and divers others of good Use, in this Library.

By Larger Histories or Chronicles, I mean continued Discourses by Persons of eminent veracity & merit; such as Robert of Gloucester, 36.B.3: John Hardyng, 42.C.11, and others, in English: The Chronicle of the Dukes of Normandy, 92.D.6: Petrus de Langetoft, 35.A.15, & 36.B.4: Polyhistoire, 42.A.12: Le Prinse du Roy Richart II, 68.C.23, &c.

But setting aside those Histories in English, when others appear to be more considerable; & these in French as wanting a Translation, which will be difficult to make: there still remain the Chronicles of

1. John Bever Monk of Westminster, from Aeneas to A.D. 1307 (42.B.4: 107 leaves in folio).

---

[1] See no. 136 and n. 2.

2. Roger of Chesters Polycratica temporum, of which my Lord hath two Copies: One older, bought of Mr Noble (about 210 leaves in 4to) the other later, but somewhat larger, given by Coll. Worseley (about 213 leaves in small fol.). The former endeth about A.D. 1313, the latter about 1326, but may be brought down to the year 1377, by the help of another Copie, which I very lately discovered.

3. Robert of Avesbury de Gestis Mirabilibus R. Edwardi III, (36.B.2: 61 leaves in 4to). My Lords Copie is imperfect, & cometh down no lower than the year 1357. But, I believe, the Defect may be supplied by the help of another Copie yet extant.

These three Men were Writers of Note during the Times wherein they Lived; their Works have been often cited by our later Historians; and still remain unprinted to this day.

If His Lordship shall be rather willing to lay an Obligation on the North-Britans; it may be done by Publishing his MS. of Fordun with the Additions, just as it now is (59.C.18: 276 leaves in large fol.) whereof no more hath ever been Published, than barely Fordun's First Five Books, without any of the Additions: which is but a very small Portion, in respect to the Whole.

VIII. DESCRIPTION OF ST MARY'S HALL, COVENTRY

Welbeck Wanleyana = B.L. Loan MS 29/205, fo. 77. 16 May 1719.[1]

In St Maries Hall in Coventre, instead of the midle part of a Screen at the Bottom, is a piece of Stone-work, in the midst whereof a large Plate of Brass is fixed, which under these Armes, give's the following Inscription, in Square Text Letters.

Rob. Dudley Earl of Leicester adorned with Ragged Staves	Queen Elizabeth 1568	City of Coventre

Memorandum that the ryght highe & mightie Prince Iohn late Duke of Northumberlande Deceassed, for the right honorable Seale which he bare to the Citie of Coventre, & to the pore inhabitauntes of the same, by his dede indented dated the xiith of August in the thirde yere of the raygne of our late soveigne lord kynge Edwarde the sixte Dimysed graunted & to ferme lett vnto the Maior Bayliffes & Commynaltye of the said Cytie all his Manovr of Chellesmore with the parke & all ryghts Members and appurtenances of the same for the terme of iiijxx and xix yeres, for the Vses Intente & purposes following, that is that they & theyr successours for the relief of the pore of the said Cytie should yerely take to pasture in the said parke the number of iiijxx kyen or heyefors & xxtie geldynge of soche pore Inhabitaunce of the said Cytie & subburbe as shall not haue ells where nighe the said Citie sufficiente pasture painge wekely for every Cowe or heifor id and for every Geldynge iid

---

Memorandum also that the right honorable Robert Earle of Leycestr sone to the said late Duke of Northumberland for the lyke right honorable & earnest Zeale that he had to the aduavncement & settyng forwarde of the said godly intente of his said Father vppon his greate sute & request made to the Queenes Maiestie our souereign lady

[1] It fills three (fos. 77ʳ–78ʳ) of the four pages of Wanley's letter to Edward Harley, 16 May 1719 (no. 199); the letter proper and the address occupy fo. 78ᵛ. See *VCH Warwickshire*, viii (1969), pp. 141–3, and for a full account Joan C. Lancaster, *Official Guide to St. Mary's Hall* (Coventry, 1948).

queen Elizabeth hath obtayned her Maiesties letters patentes vnder
her greate seale of Engelande: whereby she gravnted to the said Maior
bayliffes & Commynaltie and their Successoures for ever, the sayde
Manor and parke of Chellesmore and other the premisses to Fee
ferme for the ententes and vses aforsayde.

Memorandum also that the said Maior Baylyffes and Comynaltye haue
covenanted and gravnted to & with the saide Earle his executoures &
administratours truly to obserue and performe the intentes vses and
purposes before mencioned, & also that the said premisses nor any
parte therof shall not be ouer charged but allwayes kepte in suche
plyght as the saide nomber of catell Maye be at all tymes for the saide
moneye well & sufficiently kept according to the season of the yeare for
ever, as by the saide Indenture wherof the one partie remaynethe with
the sayde Mayor Baylyffes and Commynaltie, and the other parte withe
the saide Earle bearinge Date the fourth daye of Aprell in the Tenth
yere of the saide Queene Elizabeth appeareth which was in the yere of
grace, 1568.

Under the said Screen of Stone, stand's a very large Oaken Chair,
formerly used (as 'tis thought) by the Master of the Gilds who built
this magnificent Hall. There is much Carving about it, in the Nature
of Church-work. On the Right side of it out-wards, is a Madonna with
her little Jesus in her Lap, & an Angel above. The pummel for support
of the right arm, is now broken, but seem's to have been in the shape of
a Dog worrying a Sheep. The Top of this Side is remarkable for Two
Lions standing on their hind-feet, with their Tales between their
Legs, supporting a Crown, wch is now broken at the Top. The
Pummel for the left Elbow is cutt like a Frier oppressing an innocent
Lamb or Sheep. At the Top above the left shoulder is the *Elephant &
Castle*, being the Armes of this City. The Seat of this Chair is above a
yard wide within; being curiously adorned with Church work, as is
above said both within & without on the back, with different Samples
or Patterns of Stone-work for Windows; as is also the Stone-mantle-
tree of the Chimney in the Mayores's Parlor here, being a large Room
within this, wherein Her Worship & the better Sort of Women Dine,
at the Public Feasts.

Going up the Hall, on the Left Hand are these Inscriptions,
&c.

When florishing state gan once to fade, and
    common wealth decay
No wonder that, in cities great, (for what
    endureth ay?)
Iohn, late Duk of Northumberland, a prince
    of high degree
Did graunt fair landes for commons weale,
    as here in brasse yow see.
And Leicestre, mid thos great affaires,
    wherto high place doth call,
His fathers worthy steppes hath trac'd, to
    prop that els might fall.
On forth, in prince & countries cause, hold
    on this course your dayes:
Such deedes do noble bloud commend,
    such win immortal praise.

in English square Letters, all the English Verses. Words underlined, are painted of a Red color.

Next, were the Armes of some Knight of the Garter, with Supporters, now quite rubbed out.

On the Windows above, were the figures of four Men, in their Habits, at full length, with their Armes. But they are now so defaced & broken, as that I cannot say who they were, although all their Heads yet remain.

[The first of the lowest Row might have been of Edward the Black Prince: part of whose Motto yet remain's there.]

Edward, the floure of chevalre,
    whilom the Blacke Prynce hyght:
Who prisoner tooke the French Kyng
    Iohn, in claime of grandames ryght
And slew the kyng of Beame in fielde,
    wherby the ostrych penn
He wan, and ware on crest here first,
    which poesie bare Ich Dein
Amid thes martial feates of armes,
    wherein he had no peere,
His bountie eke to shew, this seate he
    chose, And lov'd ful deere.
The former state hee gat confirm'd,
    and freedome did encreace:
A president of knyghhood rare, as
    well for warre as peace.

The Armes of the City in Colors. On the Windows were the figures of four other Men in their Habits; the two upper-most were of the Earl of Stafford, & John Moubray Duke of Norfolk, whose pourtraitures & Armes are still pretty well preserved. [*Margin*: There are Inscriptions above them but out of the Reach of my Spectacles.] The two others beneath them, are almost totally [*Margin*: under the last figure

remains] gone, & the place supplied (as in this &

other Coventre-buildings) with broken shreads of other Painted Glass, serving only to make a shew, & signifying nothing. On the Wall, between this & the next Window, hang the Pictures of . . . . Davenport an Alderman here, and good Benefactor. Likewise, of . . . Wheatley another Alderman & worthy Benefactor part of whose Land given by him to the City, is what hath given me the Trouble of this Journey hither.

Since time that first this auncient towne, earle Leofrike feoffed
    free:
At Godines suite, and merite straunge, or els it would not be,
In princes grace, by long descent, as old recordes do date;
It stood maintein'd, until at length, it grew to citties state,
Quene Isabell, sole heire of Fraunce, great favour hither cast,
And did procure large fraunchises, by charter ay to last,
We ow therefore in loialtee, our selves and all wee haue
To Elizabeth our lady liege, whom god in mercy saue.

In this Window were also four figures at full length; the two upper-most, as I gess by the Armes under them, are of Humfrey Duke of Gloucester, & John Duke of Bedford his elder brother. In the lower part, at the top (as in other Windows here) each of the four Corners hath an Angel as Protector; not to insist upon two smaller just over their heads, whereof one only is now missing. They both seem to have been Learned Men, or of the Long Robe, but neither Title nor Armes to distinguish the first by. The last i.e. the chief Figure hath the Coif on his Head, and underneath part of his Armes, that is only, on a Chief Or, a label of 3 points Azure, between 4 Torteauxes. At the bottom yet remains part of a Name (perhaps his) seeming to be of William Preston.

On the next Side or Jamb of the Wall, hangs an old Picture of K. Charles I.

Among the Patches about this picture, is the Sinister half of an Escocheon now lying on its side shewing the Armes of some woman empaled by her Husband, thus
In the great Place for the Side-
Board, & in the Warden's
Buttery no Glass remarkably
fine, doe's now remain.

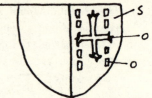

Toward the upper End, is the Armes of Qu. Elizabeth, & here the Cap of Maintenance, Sword, & Mace, &c. used to be hung. Next above

AVXILIIS OLIM STETIT ALMA COVENTRIA REGVM:

DVM FORTVNA FVIT. MAGNOS COLIT HINC EDOVARDOS

HENRICOSQVE SVOS, VRBS NON INGRATA, PATRONOS:

IAMQVE ADEO AFFLICTVS CRESCIT SPES ALTERA REBVS:

ELISABETHA, TVIS, PRINCEPS MITISSIMA, SCEPTRIS.

LÆTIOR ILLVXIT NVLLO PAX REGE BRITANNIS

ERGO AGE DIVA, TVIS SIS FOELIX CIVIBUS VSQVE,

EXVPERANS PATRIAS ET AVITAS ÆMVLA LAVDES.

The Window above, had four other Figures, now almost ruined; the Chiefest of them is of one of our Kings. Above them, are the Armes of this Citie, & of divers particular persons. [*Margin*: Here hang the Pictures of K. Charles II. and of K. James II. both at the whole length.] The Upper end of the Hall is adorned by a very large & fine piece of Arras, wherein are the Effigies of K. Henry VI, his Unkle the Cardinal of England, & the Chiefest of his Nobility are represented. Above, are Many of the Apostles, & He Saints, as St George, &c. Against this King is his Queen Margaret, attended by her Ladies, & protected by She Saints. Between them is the B.V.M. attended by many Saints & Angels and *Justitia* above her. In the Great Window remain the Figures and Armes described by Sir Will. Dugdale, which I therefore omitt here. Note each King hath a Close Crown, & Sur-coat of his Armes; usages which prevailed indeed in the time of K. Hen. VI. when this hall was built, but not much before.

Coming down the Hall, on the other Side, are two Damaged whole-length Pictures of K. Will. & Q. Mary. Underneath,

PRINCEPS ILLE NIGER, (NIVEIS CVI VERTICE PENNIS

CRISTA MINAX, VICTI REGIS CÆSIQVE BOHEMI

EXVVIIS,) HEROS EDOVARDVS MAGNVS IN ARMIS,

HIC SEDEM POSVIT. SIC DICTA EST PRINCIPIS AVLA.

HOC AVTHORE, FVIT LIBERTAS CIVIBVS AVCTA:

MVNERIBVSQVE ORNATA SVIS RESPVBLICA CREVIT.

HINC DEPICTA, VIDES? PASSIM SVA PENNA PER VRBEM,

TESTATVR MAGNI MONIMENTVM ET PIGNVS AMORIS.

Over the Door entring into the Mayoresses Parlor, are two old Pictures of Q. Elizabeth & K. James I. Lower in the Hall,

LABENTES FATIS (QVID ENIM PERDVRAT IN ÆVVM?)

FORTVNAS VRBIS TANDEM MISERATVS AGRORVM

EXTENDIT FINES, NORTHVMBRIVS ILLE IOHANNES.

CVMQVE FVIT BELLO DVX INVICTISSIMVS, ARMIS

IN MEDIIS, COLVIT PACIS, VIR PROVIDVS, ARTES.

EXEMPLOQVE SVVM VOCAT AD PIA FACTA ROBERTVM.

In the Window above, are four Figures entire in their Habits; viz. Thomas Arundell Archbp of Canterbury, & Roger Walden Bp of London, above: and Will. Beauchamp Lord of Abergavenny & Johan his Lady, with their Armes, below.

On the Next Jamb or Buttress of the wall, hang the Pictures of Sir Thomas White, & of Mr Will Jesson (my Mothers Great-Unkle) both Great Benefactors to this Corporation. Then The Atchievement of Rob. Dudley Earl of Leicester; then

NON TANTVM MERVIT LEOFRICVS CESTRIVS OLIM:

NEC CONIVX GODINA, PII DVX FŒMINA FACTI?

GODINA, AH, TVRPI QVÆ LEGE COACTA MARITI,

FERTVR EQVO, DIFFVSA COMAS, NVDATA PER VRBEM,

ASSERVITQVE SVOS: CVLPENT VTCVNQVE MINORES,

VICIT AMOR PATRIÆ LIBERTATISQVE CVPIDO.

Over this is an old decaied Picture of the ridiculous Legend of the Lady Godeva's riding Naked through this City; which is here represented as having more Churches, than we see now. In this window, are also Four Figures. Those above are of Richard Beauchamp Earl of Warwick & Isabel his Wife: the lower two are of William Whytchirche, & another, being (probably) two principal men of these Gilds. They bare no Armes.

Below, is the White Bear & Ragged Staffe, within a Wreath, used by

Earl Rob. Dudley as his Badge; & then lower yet in the Hall, these
Verses,

QVANTVM HODIE PATREM REFERENS LEICESTRIVS HEROS

RETRO SVBLAPSAM QVI NOSTRAM RESTITVIT REM:

SVSTINET IN PEIVS RVITVRAM VRBISQVE SALVTEM.

IMODO, QVO VIRTVS TE FERT: SIC ITVR AD ASTRA.

ET QVIBVS INSISTIS, FŒLIX PROCEDE PATERNIS

AVSPICIIS, MANEATQVE TVOS HÆC CVRA NEPOTES.

The four Figures of this Window are almost entire. The two
upper-most are of Bishops, but their Names out of the reach of my
Eies. Dn̄s Iohannes . . .   . . . Ricardu . cro
     Paly of 10 A. & S. in a Bend S. a Spread Eagle O.
     G. a *Garb* ?O

The two lower figures have no Armes, but Devices, as of Citizens.
The Roof of this Structure is of fine Workmanship, & is adorned with
the Armes of this City, the Figures of Saints, Angels, &c. In some
Rooms beyond the Mayoresses Parlor, the Windows were Painted
very finely; but now all almost gone, exepting some few Saints wanting half their Bodies, &c. The most entire are the Figures of St John
Baptist & St Catherine, having below these words, *Orate pro an* . . .
Henrici Peyto & . . . . the next figures were of the B.V.M. & the little
Jesus; next to it might have been the Trinity, now consisting of fragments of other Glass ill patched together. Here seem's to remain part
of the Figure of Thomas a Becket, &c.

I have been at *Jesus-hall*, my Grandfather Burton's late Dwelling
house,[2] which was built (although not mentioned by Sir William
Dugdale) for the Habitation of Twelve Priests. Here hath been horrid
destruction of the fine Painted Glass since I was there. Two Rooms
taken out of the Dining-room, & the other turn'd into a Bedchamber,
where the Tapistry cover's one of the Window's intirely; perhaps to
the preservation of the Glass. Yet here remain some Habits, Armes,
Rebuses, and other fancies worth delineating; and a few more in the
house adjoyning, called the *Vicaridge-house*, wherein I was born.[3]

-----

[2] Humfrey Burton († 1685), Wanley's maternal grandfather, was Clerk to Coventry
Council 1636–85.

[3] Nathaniel Wanley (1634–1680), Wanley's father, was Vicar of Holy Trinity,
Coventry, from 1662.

INDEX

The index does not distinguish between text and footnotes; a page reference may refer to either or both. Endnotes and lists are not indexed. Commissions, dissertations, and other scholarly ana are indexed only selectively.